Valuing Labour in Greco-Roman Antiquity

Mnemosyne Supplements

MONOGRAPHS ON GREEK AND
LATIN LANGUAGE AND LITERATURE

VOLUME 481

The titles published in this series are listed at *brill.com/mns*

Valuing Labour in Greco-Roman Antiquity

Edited by

Miko Flohr
Kim Bowes

BRILL

LEIDEN | BOSTON

Library of Congress Cataloging-in-Publication Data

Names: Penn-Leiden Colloquium on Ancient Values (11th : 2021 : Leiden, Netherlands), creator. | Bowes, Kimberly Diane, 1970- editor. | Flohr, Miko, editor.
Title: Valuing labour in Greco-Roman antiquity / edited by Kim Bowes, Miko Flohr.
Other titles: Mnemosyne, bibliotheca classica Batava. Supplementum ; 481.
Description: Leiden ; Boston : Brill, 2024. | Series: Mnemosyne supplements, 0169-8958 ; volume 481 Monographs on Greek and Latin language and literature | Includes bibliographical references and index.
Identifiers: LCCN 2024001751 (print) | LCCN 2024001752 (ebook) | ISBN 9789004694835 (hardback) | ISBN 9789004694965 (ebook)
Subjects: LCSH: Labor–Greece–Congresses. | Labor–Rome–Congresses. | Work–History–To 1500–Congresses. | Social values–Greece–Congresses. | Social values–Rome–Congresses. | Civilization, Classical–Congresses. | LCGFT: Conference papers and proceedings.
Classification: LCC HD4844 .P466 2021 (print) | LCC HD4844 (ebook) | DDC 331.0938–dc23/eng/20240214
LC record available at https://lccn.loc.gov/2024001751
LC ebook record available at https://lccn.loc.gov/2024001752

Typeface for the Latin, Greek, and Cyrillic scripts: "Brill". See and download: brill.com/brill-typeface.

ISSN 0169-8958
ISBN 978-90-04-69483-5 (hardback)
ISBN 978-90-04-69496-5 (e-book)
DOI 10.1163/9789004694965

This book is printed on acid-free paper and produced in a sustainable manner.

To Ralph Rosen and Ineke Sluiter
The kindest and best of colleagues

Contents

List of Figures and Tables XI
Contributors XIV

1 Introduction: Value at Work 1
Miko Flohr and Kim Bowes

SECTION 1
Revisiting the Canon

2 Plato's Exemplary Craftsman 23
Ineke Sluiter

3 Πόνος and πονέω in Aristotle 41
J.J. Mulhern

4 Galen on Hands and the Teleology of Work 62
Ralph M. Rosen

5 On Valuing Roman Art and the Labour of Art Making 83
Lauren Hackworth Petersen

SECTION 2
Pushing the Boundaries of Labour

6 Emotional Labour in Antiquity: The Case of Roman Prostitution 109
Sarah Levin-Richardson

7 Meaning in the Making: Representing Glass Production in Imperial Rome 131
Bettina Reitz-Joosse

8 Who's Afraid of Wage Labour? Analysing Some Texts of the Second Sophistic 150
Christel Freu

9 The Value of Work: Work and Labour within the Roman Upper-class Household 169
Miriam J. Groen-Vallinga

SECTION 3
Labour and the Countryside

10 The Labour of Listening: Internal Audiences in Theocritus 193
Amelia Bensch-Schaus

11 *Labor* in the *locus amoenus*: Agricultural Industry as Premise of Pastoral Leisure 214
Riemer A. Faber

12 Work Underfoot: The Rustic 'Calendar' Mosaic of Saint-Romain-en-Gal 234
Nicole G. Brown

13 Rural Labour and Identity at Vagnari in Southern Italy 264
Liana Brent and Tracy Prowse

SECTION 4
Labour and Civic Values

14 Foreign Labour, Common Ground: The Value of Craftspeople in Early Democratic Athens 289
Helle Hochscheid

15 The Craftsman's View: Labour and (Self-)Appreciation as Reflected in Signatures 311
Natacha Massar

16 Professionals as *paradeigmata* of *aretê* in Hellenistic Honorific Decrees 339
Antiopi Argyriou-Casmeridis

17 Images of Craft: Activity and Presentation of Work on Gallo-Roman Tombstones 368
Fanny Opdenhoff

Index Locorum 397
General Index 410

Figures and Tables

Figures

5.1 Doryphoros (Spear-bearer), Roman marble copy of Greek bronze statue, Pompeii (Samnite Palestra), late republican era (MANN inv. 6011). Photo: © Vanni Archive / Art Resource, NY (ART383671) 95

5.2 Bronze herm of the Doryphoros by Apollonios, Villa of Papyri (Herculaneum), first century BCE (MANN inv. 4885). Photo: Scala/Ministero per i Beni e le Attività culturali /Art Resource, NY (ART362732) 96

5.3 Fresco of a potter at the wheel and Vulcan, Pompeii (II 3, 8), first century CE (SAP inv. 21631). Photo: Scala/Art Resource, NY (ART501072) 99

5.4 Fresco of a female painter, Pompeii (VI 1, 10), first century CE (MANN inv. 9018). Photo: © DeA Picture Library/Art Resource, NY (ART421611) 100

5.5 Marble grave relief of a silversmith, first century CE, 79.9 × 58.5 × 31.7 cm (The J. Paul Getty Museum, Villa Collection, Malibu, California, 96.AA.40). Photo: Bruce White Photography 102

7.1 Glass droplet. Photo: author 132

7.2 Roman oil lamp from Asseria showing a glassblower's workshop. Photo: Archaeological Museum in Split, Croatia (inv. no AMS-Fc-1094) 143

12.1 Mosaic from Saint-Romain-en-Gal, 200–225 CE, surviving portion 4.34 × 5.66 m. Musée d'archéologie nationale, Saint-Germain-en-Laye. Winter, panels 1–7; Spring, panels 8–14; Summer, panels 15–21; Autumn, panels 22–28. Photo: © Art Resource, NY, Photographer Michel Urtado 235

12.2 Mosaic from the House of the Months at El Jem (ancient Thysdrus), 200–235 CE, 1.86 × 2.73 m. Musée Archéologique, Sousse. Photo: Gilles Mermet (© Art Resource, NY) 243

12.3 Mosaic from Saint-Romain-en-Gal, oblique view from entry. Photo: CC BY-SA 2.0, Photographer Carole Raddato 248

12.4 Mosaic depicting the Labours of Hercules, Saint-Paul-lès-Romans, Villa des Mingauds, Drôme, 170–180 CE, 4.91 × 7.37 m. Musée de Valence. Photo: © Musée de Valence, Photographer Serge Van Poucke 254

12.5 Circus Mosaic, second century CE, 4.97 × 3.2 m. Musée de la Civilisation Gallo-Romaine, Lyon. Photo: © Art Resource, NY, Photographer Eric Lessing 257

12.6a–b Mosaic from Saint-Romain-en-Gal, a. Sowing of beans (December); b. Personification of Autumn. Photo: © RMN-Grand Palais / Art Resource, NY, Photographer Michel Urtado 259

13.1 Map of southern Italy showing the location of Vagnari. Photo: M. Carroll / I. De Luis 266

13.2 Plan of the site showing the location of the Vagnari Vicus and Cemetery. Photo: C. Small 267
13.3 Plan of the Vagnari Cemetery (2002–2019). Photo: F. Taccogna 269
13.4a Metal objects from the Vagnari burials: Iron 'punch' (P6829) from F309. Photo: J. Weiland 272
13.4b Metal objects from the Vagnari burials: Iron 'brackets' (harvesting tools?) (P5132 from F213 and P5178 from F218). Photo: A. Small 272
13.5 Large iron pruning tool P6642 from F288. Photo: Authors 274
15.1 Signature of Eucheiros on a Little Master cup. Photo: © Trustees of the British Museum 318
15.2 Signature of Ergotimos on a stand. Photo: © Metropolitan Museum of Art, inv. 31.11.4 319
15.3 Signature of Lysiades, on an exaleiptron, Lyon, Musée des Beaux-Arts, inv. E 387. Photo: © Lyon MBA 327
15.4 Signature of Nikosthenes on a Nikosthenic amphora. Photo: © Royal Museums of Art and History 332
15.5 Signature of Hephaistion on a mosaic from Pergamon. Photo: © Antikensammlung der Staatlichen Museen zu Berlin – Preußischer Kulturbesitz. Photographer Johannes Laurentius 333
16.1 Map of the findspots of the inscriptions discussed in this chapter. Photo: M. Flohr 340
17.1 Funerary stele of Amabilis, Bordeaux, Musée d'Aquitaine inv. 60.1.82. Photo: © Mairie de Bordeaux, Musée d'Aquitaine. Photographer L. Gauthier 371
17.2 Detail of the lower part of the inscription, funerary stele of Amabilis, Bordeaux, Musée d'Aquitaine, inv. 60.1.82. Photo: © Mairie de Bordeaux, Musée d'Aquitaine. Photographer L. Gauthier 373
17.3 Detail of the left foot, funerary stele of Amabilis, Bordeaux, Musée d'Aquitaine, inv. 60.1.82. Photo: © Mairie de Bordeaux, Musée d'Aquitaine. Photographer L. Gauthier 373
17.4 Detail of the right hand, funerary stele of Amabilis, Bordeaux, Musée d'Aquitaine, inv. 60.1.82. Photo: © Mairie de Bordeaux, Musée d'Aquitaine. Photographer L. Gauthier 374
17.5 Detail of the left hand, funerary stele of Amabilis, Bordeaux, Musée d'Aquitaine, inv. 60.1.82. Photo: © Mairie de Bordeaux, Musée d'Aquitaine. Photographer L. Gauthier 375
17.6 Funerary monument of Reginus, Metz, Musée de la Cour d'Or, inv. 75.38.66. Photo: licensed under Creative commons: BY-NC-ND 3.0, IDAI Objects, Photographer Till Schläger https://arachne.dainst.org/entity/6485767/image/6485767 378
17.7 Depiction of tools on the left side of the monument from Metz. Drawing: Pannoux 1983, fig. 8. © S. Pannoux 379

17.8 Stele of Sabinianus, Autun, Musée Rolin, inv. M L 143. Photo: © Autun – Musée Rolin, F. and O. Harl. http://lupa.at/25165. Photographer Ortolf Harl 2015 380
17.9 Stele of a potter, Bourges, Musée du Berry, inv. 1857.1.3. Photo: © Collection Musées et Patrimoine Historique de la Ville de Bourges, F. and O. Harl. http://lupa.at/32726. Photographer Michel Reddé 1970–1975 382
17.10 Stele of Belliccus from Sens, Sens, Musées de Sens, inv. J 79. Photo: © Sens – Musées de Sens, F. and O. Harl. http://lupa.at/25966. Photographer Ortolf Harl 2015 383
17.11 Stele of Maternianos from Bourges, Bourges, Musée du Berry, inv. 1961.51.1. Photo: © Collection Musées et Patrimoine Historique de la Ville de Bourges, F. and O. Harl. http://lupa.at/32717. Photographer Michel Reddé 1970–1975 385
17.12 Stele of an unknown male from Sens, Sens, Museés de Sens, inv. J 133. Photo: © Sens – Musées de Sens, F. and O. Harl. http://lupa.at/25980. Photographer Ortolf Harl 2015 386
17.13 Two joining fragments of a funerary monument from Sens, Sens, Museés de Sens, inv. J 128 and J 129. Photo: © Sens – Musées de Sens, F. and O. Harl. http://lupa.at/25970. Photographer Ortolf Harl 2015 387

Tables

12.1 Proportion of labour to non-labour scenes, Mosaic from Saint-Romain-en-Gal 237
13.1 Vagnari burials with metal tools and implements 271
13.2 Grave goods in Vagnari burials with metal items 273
13.3 Grave goods by age category 277
16.1 Types of benefactions of professionals in the fields of Arts & Education 341

Contributors

Antiopi Argyriou-Casmeridis
Postdoctoral Researcher, National and Kapodistrian University of Athens

Amelia Bensch-Schaus
Lecturer, Temple University and the University of Pennsylvania

Kim Bowes
Professor of Classical Studies, University of Pennsylvania

Liana Brent
Assistant Professor of Classical and Medieval Studies, Bates College

Nicole Brown
Associate Professor of Classics, Williams College

Riemer A. Faber
Professor of Classical Studies, University of Waterloo

Miko Flohr
Lecturer in Ancient History, Leiden University

Christel Freu
Professor of Roman History, Université d'Evry-Paris Saclay

Miriam Groen-Vallinga
Assistant Professor, Department of History, Art History and Classics, Radboud Universeit

Helle Hochscheid
Assistant Professor, University College Roosevelt, Utrecht University

Sarah Levin-Richardson
Associate Professor of Classics, University of Washington

Natacha Massar
Curator of Greek Antiquities, Royal Museums of Arts and History, Brussels

John J. Mulhern
Lecturer in Classical Studies, University of Pennsylvania

Fanny Opdenhoff
Junior Professor of Archaeology and Cultural History of the Mediterranean, Universität Hamburg

Lauren Hackworth Petersen
Professor of Art History, University of Delaware

Tracy Prowse
Associate Professor of Anthropology, McMaster University

Bettina Reitz-Joosse
Associate Professor of Latin Language and Literature, University of Groningen

Ralph M. Rosen
Vartan Gregorian Professor of the Humanities and Professor of Classical Studies, University of Pennsylvania.

Ineke Sluiter
Professor of Greek Language and Literature, University of Leiden.

CHAPTER 1

Introduction: Value at Work

Miko Flohr and Kim Bowes

The COVID-19 pandemic revealed itself to the world in full force a couple of months before the colloquium from which this volume results was originally scheduled to take place. As an unprecedented, systemic and worldwide crisis, the pandemic produced an enormous upsurge in value discourse as societal and cultural principles and practices were suddenly turned upside-down: what is the desired ratio between safety and risk in the public sphere? Who has the authority to infringe upon fundamental liberties, and to what extent? What is the value of (scientific) expertise and knowledge, and what is the value of lived expertise and intuition? Suddenly, it seemed, everything was up for revaluation. In Europe and North America, the pandemic particularly exposed labour and its value. On both sides of the Atlantic, intense debates were held about what constituted 'essential work', and how it should be facilitated—and what it meant that so many people whose work was deemed essential had incomes far below their national average. At the same time as the pandemic hit, the meaning of work changed for everyone: suddenly, office-workers (and academics) had to do their professional work from a place that they normally associated mostly with their private lives and with leisure. People working in shops and factories suddenly found themselves at home, either with their days empty, or their workload doubled. For many people, the sudden disruption of their working lives led to a rethink of what they valued (and did not value) in their work. It was particularly prescient, then, that the papers in this volume were written and the conference itself took place at a moment when not only human values in general, but particularly the value of work, became a focus of such particular and urgent attention.

1 The Penn-Leiden Project

This volume results from the eleventh Penn-Leiden Colloquium on Ancient Values. In their programmatic introduction to their 2003 volume on manliness and courage in classical antiquity, the very first volume resulting from the Penn-Leiden project, Sluiter and Rosen sketched how the study of value discourse touches upon 'core issues of cultural identity and construction of self and soci-

 | DOI:10.1163/9789004694965_002

ety, including the behavioural norms by which one judges the social value of others and is in turn judged oneself'.[1] They also stressed the way in which value discourse can be transhistorical: the study of value discourse in antiquity can be used to contextualize (and better understand) value discourse in our contemporary world—both in the immediate aftermath of the 9/11 attacks, when the first volume of this project was produced, and during and after the COVID-19 pandemic, when this volume took shape. Thinking about value discourse connects worlds far apart.

The intellectual agenda of the Penn-Leiden project started from the ancient lexicon, and was both philological and conceptual: Sluiter and Rosen write how 'a sound philological exploration of the ancient conceptual framework … supplemented by the study of actual behaviour' would 'form the basis for extrapolation and further theorizing'.[2] In introducing the volume on manliness, Sluiter and Rosen highlighted their interest in both concept formation and the rhetorical and performative character of the use of concepts in discourse. Subsequent volumes developed this approach by focusing on value discourse from different perspectives. We refer the reader to the introductory chapters in the volumes resulting from the ten preceding Penn-Leiden Colloquia to develop a sense of the way in which the Penn-Leiden project has studied value discourse from a broad range of conceptual vantage points: manliness, free speech, city and countryside, badness, others, aesthetics, the past, landscape, competition and nighttime.[3] We note that each of these vantage points not only came with a unique perspective on ancient value discourse—each volume covers a different place in the cultural landscape of the Greco-Roman world—but often also added a new element to the conceptual anatomy of valuing practices. For example, as Sluiter and Rosen have highlighted in several introductions, the individualistic focus of the volume on ἀνδρεία and *virtus* was followed by a more community-oriented focus in the volume on free speech, and by a spatially focused approach in the third volume of the series, on city and countryside.[4] As argued by Ker and Pieper, the volume on valuing the past added in the factor of (historical) time.[5]

1 Sluiter and Rosen 2003, 3.
2 Sluiter and Rosen 2003, 4.
3 Free speech: Sluiter and Rosen 2004; city and countryside: Rosen and Sluiter 2006; badness: Sluiter and Rosen 2008; others: Rosen and Sluiter 2010; aesthetics: Sluiter and Rosen 2012; the past: Pieper and Ker 2014; landscape: McInerney and Sluiter 2016 competition: Damon and Pieper 2018; nighttime: Ker and Wessels 2020.
4 Sluiter and Rosen 2006, 2.
5 Ker and Pieper 2014, 1.

By exploring ancient value discourse around 'labour' and 'work', this volume broadens the Penn-Leiden project towards the study of everyday human practices—things that humans do (routinely) on an everyday basis, like eating, sleeping and moving around. It is self-evident that there is a value discourse around such activities, and that such activities can play a fundamental role in discourse about values: if person X does activity Y under circumstances Z ('Fullers stand with their feet in rotten urine while they work'), this can, in itself, be judged as more or less desirable, normal or acceptable ('It is dirty, and I do not want to have to do anything with it!'); on top of that, however, such a situation can also in itself come to play an illuminating role in discussing what is desirable, normal or acceptable, and under which circumstances ('You know what is dirty? Fullers standing with their feet in rotten urine!').[6] It is this discursive power of everyday practices like labour and work that makes them an indispensable part of the Penn-Leiden project on the 'language, discourse and conceptualization of values in classical antiquity'.[7]

2 Definitions of Labour and Work

It is worth pausing here to consider what has been meant by words like 'labour' and 'work', and how they will be used in this volume. This is particularly important as the following chapters will interrogate the aspects of work and labour to which value is attached. That is, asking how work is valued—morally, economically, socially—involves asking what work *is*.

Modern dictionary definitions of labour emphasize exertion, and to a lesser extent, obligation: 'an instance of physical or mental exertion, a piece of work that has been or is to be performed; a task'; definitions of work are far more general—'to act, do, function, operate'.[8] Modern sociological theories about 'labour' and 'work' have generally insisted on their distinct qualities: labour encompasses mostly remunerative activities while work includes all kinds of efforts 'that add value to goods and services', many of which are not remunerated and thus are often marginalized, like household work.[9] Such theories also draw an important defining line between work or labour on the one hand,

6 On the actual (limited!) use of urine by fullers see Flohr and Wilson 2011, 150–151; Flohr 2013, 103–104.

7 Sluiter and Rosen 2012, 6.

8 'Labour/labour, n.' OED online. 2022; 'work, v.' OED online. 2022.

9 Tilly and Tilly 1998, 22.

and leisure on the other, which serves as a notional if not actual antonym.[10] This volume will largely (although not completely) ignore these modern distinctions, and start from the idea that the concepts encompassed by 'work' and 'labour' in practice are overlapping and circumscribe an important sphere of human activity. We further argue that the English lexical distinctions and definitions are largely unhelpful in ancient contexts: the following chapters cumulatively suggest that Greeks and Romans had different sets of definitions for work/labour, in which the work versus labour and work versus leisure distinctions evident in English, and in capitalist societies more generally, are hard to apply consistently.

Thus, in what follows, labour and work will be used interchangeably to refer to something broader than profession or occupation or remunerated activities, although profession and remuneration are everywhere present here. That is, the volume speaks consistently beyond the OED definition of 'labour'. At the same time, it addresses something narrower than simply the effort to survive, and defines labour/work as those activities directed to particular ends and/or desires. That is, the volume employs a somewhat narrower usage than the OED definition of 'work'. Thus, farming and attentive listening, sculpting and philosophical thinking, emotional support and manual labour all fall under the rubric of work/labour considered here. A worker or labourer is simply anyone who does these things. This is not to argue that all these kinds of labour were called by the equivalent terms in Greek and Latin—although the range of activities and value attachments described by words like πόνος, *labor* and *opera* were, this volume argues, surprisingly wide and nuanced—but we do believe that they all fall within one sphere of human activity, and that people could think of them, debate or compare them in similar or comparable terms.

In starting from a broad working definition of work/labour we hope to both draw attention to a broader range of activities than those addressed in traditional studies of Greek and Roman professions, and in doing so become alert to a more diverse valuation of work which, in ancient philosophical texts, is particularly dependent on context—how work is done, who does it, and to what ends. As the essays in this volume show, ancient Greeks and Romans valued work not only by virtue of activity types—as often defined by profession—but as much or more so as a consequence of those activities' framing attributes—skill, status of the doer, ends to which the work was carried out, the nature of the thing produced, or the character of the consumer. As argued below, these qualifying attributes were often missed in earlier, more negative evaluations of

10 Anderson 1961. See more recently on the subject Lucassen 2021.

work in antiquity: returning them to the discussion requires a broader definition of our terms, a breadth which, as the first chapters of this volume will suggest, are already present in the nuanced meaning of πόνος, *labor*, *opera* and other ancient terms for work.

One of the qualifiers that is not highlighted in the modern definitions of work/labour but lurks behind many of the ancient discussions of work is repetition. The notion that an activity which is repeated over and over is thus improved by doing and earns its practitioner a set of skills is one of the places where ancient thinking on work lingers. In a non-mechanized society, repetition was not only socially ubiquitous but thus also ontologically interesting in a way that is not captured by modern definitions and their post-industrial connotations. In this way, knowledge creation, poetic performance, glassmaking and sculpting all share something in ancient discourses of work that is missing in a heuristic based on modern conceptualizations of work and labour.

Also missing from modern categories, but a constant theme in this volume, are the ambiguous relationships between activity, agent, object and consumer. In modern labour theory, activity sits at the fore. Even in Marxist paradigms where the agent and object are ontologically linked to activity, the consumer of the final product is left to a different sphere. It is the potential ontological integration of all four of these elements in ancient thought—from the work to the end use of its product with all the various actors in between—which makes the valuation of work so complex and nuanced. It was not simply the fact that an activity was 'good' or 'bad': the character of the person doing it, the character of the entity who would consume the final product, the physical properties of the activity or the final product—all these contributed to the valuation of ancient labour. Indeed, all labour need not be valued in the same way: the skill required might be valued, yet the activity denigrated for its unpleasantness or form of remuneration; the final product might be praised for its beauty, or excoriated for its end use. Silk-working is one such contradictory category. Fulling is another: the fuller's skill in transforming garments from old to new-looking was the object of much praise, while their handling of other people's valued possessions could be an object of derision.[11] The product here is also distinct from the dependency status of the labouring agent—a nuance that was often missed in earlier approaches to work in antiquity.

11 Flohr 2013, 324–328.

3 Ancient Work and Classical Scholarship

Work/labour has a long and charged intellectual history in the study of Greek and Roman antiquity; the terms of modern academic discourse were essentially defined in the later nineteenth century, in debates that explored the position of the ancient Mediterranean *vis-à-vis* modernity.[12] While scholars differed in their assessment of the position of work and labour in Greek and Roman society, the cultural evaluation of labour was a key element in this scholarship, and over the mid-twentieth century the field became increasingly dominated by a school of thought in which, based on particularly literary and philosophical texts, work and labour were often (though not universally) evaluated negatively.

M.I. Finley's *The Ancient Economy* perhaps can be seen as the most elaborate and mature expression of this perspective. Finley argued that Greek and Roman elites kept their distance—practically and culturally—from physical labour, and instead glorified landed property, leisure and political business. Hence, Finley believed, they had a positive view of wealth: 'among the necessary conditions of freedom were personal independence and leisure'. Not having to work was, according to Finley, a good thing; conversely, the key characteristic of poverty (*penia*) was 'the harsh compulsion to toil'.[13] While admitting that there were clear signs to the contrary in some of the evidence, Finley argued that, in the end, the overall judgment was not very positive:

> Skill was honoured and admired to be sure, but pride in craftsmanship is a psychological phenomenon that is not to be confused with a positive evaluation of work as such. Even Plato was a great admirer of workmanship and made innumerable positive analogies to the skilled craftsman, while ranking that skill very low in his hierarchy of values.[14]

While in later scholarship Finley became the figurehead of the negative approach to work and labour by classical scholars, his ideas were deeply rooted in twentieth-century classical studies, and could be connected to a range of statements by Greek and Roman authors at the heart of the classical canon.[15] Here, we want to particularly highlight two: Aristotle's *Politics* and Cicero's *On Duties*.

---

12 For a more comprehensive historiographical overview of this issue see Flohr and Wilson 2016. Some earlier discussions include Veyne 1987, 117–137; Mrozek 1989, 46–53, 125–132.

13 Finley 1973, 40–41.

14 Finley 1973, 82; Characteristically, Finley gave no references.

15 See on this earlier scholarship Flohr and Wilson 2016.

Aristotle, at various points in his *Politics*, suggests that τὸ βάναυσον ('the artisanate') has an uneasy relationship with citizenship. In Book 3, he argues that either artisans should not be made citizens *or* that the virtue (ἀρετή) associated with citizenship should not extend to all citizens (Arist. *Pol.* 1278a7–11. Trans. Rackham 1944, 197):

> In ancient times in fact the artisan class in some states consisted of slaves or aliens, owing to which the great mass of artisans are so even now; and the best-ordered state will not make an artisan a citizen. While if even the artisan is a citizen, then what we said to be the citizen's virtue must not be said to belong to every citizen, nor merely be defined as the virtue of a free man, but will only belong to those who are released from menial occupations (ἔργα ἀναγκαῖα).
>
> ἐν μὲν οὖν τοῖς ἀρχαίοις χρόνοις παρ' ἐνίοις ἦν δοῦλον τὸ βάναυσον ἢ ξενικόν, διόπερ οἱ πολλοὶ τοιοῦτοι καὶ νῦν· ἡ δὲ βελτίστη πόλις οὐ ποιήσει βάναυσον πολίτην. εἰ δὲ καὶ οὗτος πολίτης, ἀλλὰ πολίτου ἀρετὴν ἣν εἴπομεν λεκτέον οὐ παντός, οὐδ' ἐλευθέρου μόνον, ἀλλ' ὅσοι τῶν ἔργων εἰσὶν ἀφειμένοι τῶν ἀναγκαίων.

Those involved in ἔργα ἀναγκαῖα, Aristotle specifies, include δοῦλοι ('slaves'), βάναυσοι ('handworkers') and θῆτες ('hired labourers'). Later, in Book 7, when discussing the εὐδαιμονία ('happiness') of *poleis*, Aristotle makes the point that no *polis* can be happy unless it is governed by virtuous people. This means that (Arist. *Pol.* 1328b38–1329a2. Trans. Rackham, LCL 264, 575):

> … in the most nobly constituted state, and the one that possesses men that are absolutely just, not merely just relatively to the principle that is the basis of the constitution, the citizens must not live a mechanic or a mercantile life (for such a life is ignoble and inimical to virtue), nor yet must those who are to be citizens in the best state be tillers of the soil (for leisure is needed both for the development of virtue and for active participation in politics).
>
> … ἐν τῇ κάλλιστα πολιτευομένῃ πόλει, καὶ τῇ κεκτημένῃ δικαίους ἄνδρας ἁπλῶς ἀλλὰ μὴ πρὸς τὴν ὑπόθεσιν, οὔτε βάναυσον βίον οὔτ' ἀγοραῖον δεῖ ζῆν τοὺς πολίτας (ἀγεννὴς γὰρ ὁ τοιοῦτος βίος καὶ πρὸς ἀρετὴν ὑπεναντίος), οὐδὲ δὴ γεωργοὺς εἶναι τοὺς μέλλοντας ἔσεσθαι (δεῖ γὰρ σχολῆς καὶ πρὸς τὴν γένεσιν τῆς ἀρετῆς καὶ πρὸς τὰς πράξεις τὰς πολιτικάς).

There can be no virtue (ἀρετή) without leisure (σχολή), and if citizens are not virtuous, a city cannot be εὐδαίμων. Labour occurs at the expense of leisure, so it is at odds with virtue and therefore with true citizenship.

Cicero's famous passage close to the end of the first book of *On Duties* to some extent echoes Aristotle's image of those involved in labour as unfit for true citizenship, though he uses freedom rather than citizenship as his marker of status, and contrasts labour that is *liberalis* (or *ingenuus*) with labour that is *illiberalis* (or *sordidus*). *Sordidus* is labour that annoys other people by touching upon their financial independence, such as tax-farming and moneylending, and labour that is done for money, and does not involve any skill: 'for in their case the very wage they receive is a pledge of their slavery'. All *opifices* ('workers') remain on the illiberal side of the divide: *nec enim quicquam ingenuum habere potest officina* ('for no workshop can have anything liberal about it').[16] Particularly *illiberalis* are people who earn money by catering for the pleasures of other people (one could perhaps see this as tacitly including 'emotional labour', see below). Conversely, on the liberal side of the divide are forms of labour that involve intelligence or serve the common good. Trade on a larger scale, particularly when serving the community, can even be lauded—and, as is well known, agriculture tops Cicero's moral hierarchy of labour: 'But of all the occupations by which gain is secured, none is better than agriculture, none more profitable, none more delightful, none more becoming to a freeman.'[17]

Alongside several other texts, these passages in Cicero and Aristotle were fundamental in shaping the mid-twentieth-century idea that labour, and particularly professional labour, was judged negatively by Greeks and Romans. However, it is important to read these passages carefully, both for what they say and do not say about labour, and for the ideological and rhetorical agenda that they serve. In the first place, it is important to note that it is generally not the activities themselves that are being evaluated, but their socio-economic context—thus, it is not the effort of *opifices* that is illiberal, but the fact that they do it at the service of others; it is not the ἔργα of Aristotle's βάναυσοι that set them at odds with citizenship, but the fact that they were ἀναγκαῖα. Secondly, both Aristotle and Cicero have a clear ideological agenda: Aristotle is trying to define what the ideal *polis* looks like, and the political division of labour. He argues that politics is a skill that requires time and practice: involvement in ἔργα ἀναγκαῖα reduces the time and autonomy required to develop political skills.

16 Cic. *Off.* 1.150. Trans. Miller 1913, 153.

17 Cic. *Off.* 1.151: *Nihil est agri cultura melius, nihil uberius, nihil dulcius, nihil homine libero dignius*. Trans. Miller 1913, 155.

Cicero, in turn, is defining the orderly behaviour of the *homo liber*, the (male) Roman elite citizen—people essentially like himself; what he calls *illiberalis* or *sordidus* are practices that he felt did not fit this in-group of citizen-politicians but rather were the domain of a (negatively defined) out-group.

4 Recent Approaches

While Finley's reductionist view on ancient work was provocative from the start, it is only since the turn of the millennium that scholarship has definitively shifted away from his ideas. *The Ancient Economy* has been set aside in favour of a more positive and detailed examination of work in ancient life. This shift has largely taken two forms. The first has been a reassessment of the role of labour in ancient economic systems. The impact of New Institutional Economics on ancient economic studies has drawn scholars to examine questions of labour markets, labour efficiency, the factors driving specialization, the question of wages and 'real' wages, and labour hierarchies.[18] Examination of labour and contract law has also helped define and nuance what labour meant in legal contexts, particularly the complex distinctions between enslaved and free labour.[19] The second part of this shift has been work on specific types of occupations. Where Finley could speak generically of workers and craftsmen, now there are whole volumes dedicated to the specialized work of different kinds of crafts: fulling, baking, woodworking, potting, textile manufacturing—with the list expanding each year.[20] This work has drawn attention to the highly specialized nature of many types of work, particularly during the Roman empire—and the specialized knowledge and division of labour involved in everything from baking a loaf of bread to polishing cloth. This work thus draws into sharper relief the ancients' own preoccupation with skill—particularly specialized skill, the repetitive work needed to attain such skill—but also what they perceived as the more negative aspects of specialization.[21] This work, too, has shifted scholarship away from a dependence on the elite literary sources, as typified by Finley's work, towards other evidence—epigraphy, papyrology and archaeological sources, many of which, while not unknown before, have become increasingly

18 E.g. Ruffing 2008; Scheidel 2010; Tran 2013; Verboven and Laes 2016; Hawkins 2016; Wilson and Flohr 2016.

19 E.g. Cohen 1998; Thomas 2004; Silver 2006; Freu 2022.

20 E.g. Flohr 2013; Ulrich 2007; Monteix 2016, Van Oyen 2016; Hasaki 2021; Gallnö 2013; Larsson Lovén 2013; Harris, Lewis and Stewart 2020.

21 E.g. Bond 2016; Hochscheid and Russell 2021.

available in large databases. As a result, recent scholarship has begun to include something of non-elite perspectives on labour, although the New Institutional framework in which much of this work has been carried out has, perhaps, perpetuated a new top-down kind of analysis, now with the market taking the place of the elite male author.

As already noted by Ian Morris in his still-seminal 1999 introduction to the third edition of Finley's *The Ancient Economy*, the post-Finleyan literature on the ancient economy has disagreed with most with Finley's conceptions of ancient economic performance.[22] Much less discussed have been Finley's notions about ancient economic thinking.[23] As described above, the negative valuation of labour was central to Finley's characterization of a world which assigned no value to work, valued only status, and thus condemned itself to an economy without any particular economic thinking, an overgrown household operating at the level of large elite families and the state. While most of the work of the past fifteen years has rejected the rest of Finley's tenets, the question of what constituted ancient economic thinking, and its attendant and all-important system of values, has not received the same degree of attention.

The present volume addresses this issue at two levels. The chapters immediately following this introduction revisit many of the canonical texts upon which the twentieth century scholars constructed their largely negative view of labour, culminating in Finley's *The Ancient Economy*. They return to them with various apparatus of literary and cultural criticism to understand the political and rhetorical place within which these texts valued work, and unpack what are almost always revealed to be far more nuanced views. In part, that nuance is to be found in the composite definitions of work—of agent, tasks, objects and consumers—which characterize ancient definitions, and thus the contextual framework within which work is valued. It is not enough, these chapters cumulatively argue, to claim that manual labour was bad or that artists were mere craftsmen: more is almost always at stake, and more is almost always being said. Secondly, many other chapters in this volume draw on evidence produced by working people themselves and thus reflect their communities' own value discourse about labour: artists signatures, honorific inscriptions, funerary epitaphs, even grave goods all allow us some insight into how ancient workers valued their own labour, and, like the philosophical and literary sources, provide a composite view of that value via the other value systems operating in their particular cultural contexts—civic, family and philanthropic values.

22 Morris 1999.

23 An important exception are the articles collected in Andreau, France and Pittia 2004 on Roman economic thinking.

This volume, then, contributes to a missing discussion on a subject which has deep implications for ancient economic thought, even though its approach or subject are not necessarily economic. Conversely, it introduces an element of the economic into other ancient values which seem to lack it—human cosmologies and relationship with the gods; the role of the individual in the city or state; debates about how to live the morally good life. Indeed, one of its cumulative findings is that the concept of 'the good' is rarely totally divorced from labour: as Ineke Sluiter shows, the very idea of knowledge as 'good' presupposes labour as a kind of prototype of knowledge—the know-how of the τεχνικός is the prototype of knowledge itself, a know-how which is embedded in repetition and accumulated work. This notion—that things valued as good by ancient thinkers require work to exist—is central to the first chapters of this volume.

At the same time, our volume does not posit a simplistic positive view in place of a historiography of negative views. Many of its contributions address the particular context in which labour is denigrated, unpacking its composite elements—agent, activity, remuneration, object and consumer—and interrogating them for their different valuations. Wages are one such aspect: as Freu shows here, the expansion of wage labour under the Roman empire presented a dilemma for Stoic traditions, with some like Cicero viewing the commodification of work as an unmitigated evil, reserving a positive space nonetheless for those engaged in the remunerated work of the mind. At the same time, as Argyriou-Casmeridis shows, the willingness to forgo wages or offer their work at lower prices is a recurring *exemplum* of virtue in Hellenistic inscriptions honouring doctors, philosophers and musicians. In short, this volume collectively describes the many nuances of labour value discourse and proposes a set of methods for unpacking and revealing them.

5 Key Themes

The volume is organized into four major sections, based on some key methodological and thematic issues, on which more below. Throughout these sections, however, runs a set of themes that appear in multiple contributions, and which in themselves deserve some mention, as they represent the major outcomes of the volume. Each theme, in its own way, offers a novel perspective on valuing labour, and labour discourse, in the ancient world.

The first and perhaps most important thematic thread is the non-discrete valuation of labour and its embeddedness in other systems of value, many of which have been taken up in this Penn-Leiden series. Skill, application, expertise and other attributes of labour are valued—or not—in the context of civic belonging, philanthropy, excellence, social status, family, autonomy and other ideals, rather than simply on their own merits. Thus, Argyriou-Casmeridis finds poets and musicians praised for their skill as part of their euergetism to their own or visited cities; Massar finds potters and painters in Athens signing themselves with their demotic or citizenship appellation as a means of 'branding' their wares; Brown notes that the display of working rural bodies relies on images of urban spectacle; Freu's observations about wage labour are embedded in a discourse about autonomy. Even Hochscheid's Athenian metics seem to benefit from a kind of informal adoption by their host city, combined with a valuation of their particular skills as craftsmen. This intersection of labour-value with other kinds of values should again warn us against modern views of labour whose value is abstract and singular, like 'work ethic'. More positively, it should also alert us to the importance of work and labour in the constitution of things like civic belonging, self-sufficiency, religious observance, the rural life and so on. Modern scholars have not always recognized the role of labour—or at least categories of labour discourse—in the social construction of these values; integrating 'labour' into our approaches to ideas about, for instance, citizenship, or piety, allows us to find places for working people in status categories where we have, either tacitly or explicitly, omitted them.

Another important theme concerns the issue of positionality—the overlap and difference in how labourers valued themselves, and how others, particularly elite intellectuals, assigned value to labourers, their work or their products. In this volume, the elite perspective is addressed most pointedly in the first section, which takes up some of the paradigmatic philosophical and literary texts that were used to construct the Finleyan paradigm. These top-down assessments of labour's value stress ontologies and dissect most plainly the composite nature of labour's value. However, thanks to the extension of our sources outside this corpus, we can also now get a sense of how labourers thought about themselves—through graffiti, signatures, art-historical analysis and archaeological data. These not only provide a bottom-up perspective but, in part due to the nature of the sources, the language and nature of labour-value in these sources are different. More truncated signatures and graffiti rely on appellatives (like origin) and adjectives (e.g. positive or negative descriptions of products or customers) to gesture to value. In Brent and Prowse's study of grave goods, these values are conveyed through a symbolic language—tools symbolize the labour they were used for and thus the deceased's economic–social role or lifetime of effort. This bottom-up evidence is distinct in important ways from the literary and philosophical corpus and should be recognized as such: that is, it constitutes a distinct vernacular which is not simply a shorthand version of the intellectual perspective. As part of this series on ancient values, the recognition of this vernacular marks an important step forward. There is more to values than elite literature.

The present volume also distinguishes itself from earlier scholarship on work and labour because it includes chapters on both (agricultural) work in the countryside and on the occupations taking place in urban contexts, thus obliterating the traditional, almost disciplinary divide between city- and country-oriented scholarship. This is a direct consequence of the fact that our focus is on value discourse, in which both the countryside *and* the city are inescapable—and directly comparable: rural and urban labour were part of the same value discourse. Thus, the mosaic with rural scenes discussed by Nicole Brown was found in an *urban* context, on the outskirts of the Roman city of Vienna in Southern Gaul. In some texts, rural and urban labour also were weighed directly against one another—as happens in Horace's second epode on the landowning moneylender Alfius discussed in the chapter by Faber—or described in similar terms—as the chapter by Mulhern suggests, a word like πονέω can be used for all categories of effort, independent of their aim or location. For Aristotle, as quoted above, it also did not matter whether the work that kept people from leisure was urban or rural: in both cases, the result was that people had no opportunity to develop the necessary political experience. While earlier scholarship has often emphasized the difference in valuation between rural and urban work, the chapters of this volume suggest that this distinction should not be overemphasized: other distinctions mattered more, particularly the distinction between dependent and independent work, and between skilled and unskilled work.

A fourth recurring theme concerns the circumstances under which both effort and skill—in many respects the key components of work/labour—could be positively evaluated, highlighting that there was no intrinsic bias against work/labour. Thus, Socrates uses analogies derived from the everyday practices of craftsmen in building up moral or philosophical arguments. As Sluiter argues, the fact that craft knowledge could be used as 'prototypical knowledge' suggests that it was evaluated positively. Rosen's chapter highlights how Galen's foregrounding of the hand as the body part that is most emblematic of human nature and purpose also implicitly identifies (hand)work as not only something quintessentially human, but also as *good*. The literary images of glassmaking discussed by Reitz-Joosse equally show how the skill and effort of a craftsman could become part of a poetics of marvel. Mulhern's analysis of πόνος in Aristotle reveals that in the Aristotelian worldview, good things like ἀρετή, τὸ δίκαιον and εὐδαιμονία can only be achieved through sustained labour. Faber highlights how the omnipresence of work in the countryside was fundamentally important to the literary construction of *loci amoeni*. This does not mean that work/labour was *always* evaluated positively, but rather that its moral evaluation was context-dependent, not intrinsic. In the right contexts, skill and work could be very much appreciated—and the case studies brought together in this volume suggest that, actually, many contexts could be 'right'. One could also add the signatures discussed by Massar, and the funerary reliefs analysed by Opdenhoff: these genres of expression were even directly rooted in a positive evaluation of skills and labour.

A final thread addresses the question of gendered labour and its value. Women remain underrepresented in all of the source corpora on labour in the ancient world. These lacunae have meant that the elite source corpus and its few canonical discussions have particularly shaped our interpretations of the place and value of women's work. The weaving Lucretia waiting at home becomes thus not just a particular image, but stands for a whole set of values presumed, in the absence of other evidence, to be relatively all-encompassing.[24] Thus, women's labour has traditionally been presumed to have been domestic: remunerative activities were limited to weaving and wet nursing, and the value of these activities lies particularly in their home-based, family associations.[25] While recent scholarship has already begun to move away from this traditional idea, this volume opens up a whole new set of approaches to gendered labour and its valuation.[26] On the one hand, although they often remain a minority in the professions they occupy, this volume highlights women doing things that fall outside the domestic value paradigms: the poetess praised for her *eusebeia* and devotion to Apollo; the occasional women buried with tools and bearing the arm fractures of manual labour; the female devotees of poetry whose careful listening is embedded in Theocritus' *Idylls*. These women and their work fail to conform to the model of domestically centred female labour. Neither, though, do they completely stand outside that model, and, as with the intersection of value systems described above, gendered values centred on domestic life remained important: Levin-Richardson's sex workers, male and female, deliberately cultivate the appearance of supporting and caring for their clients, while Groen-Vallinga reveals the positions held by women and children in the labour-systems of the great elite households.

24 On weaving Lucretia see Caldwell 2021, 55. On wet nursing, Manca Masciardi and Montevecchi 1982.

25 E.g. Groen-Vallinga 2013, 295; Larsson-Lovén 2016, 218.

26 See also Holleran 2013, Swetnam-Burland 2021.

6 In This Volume

The chapters following this introduction are organized into four major sections, corresponding to major methodological interventions, as well as particular kinds of labour. The first section, 'Revisiting the Canon', addresses the major literary and philosophical texts which underlie the older paradigms on ancient labour. Ineke Sluiter addresses Plato's consideration of *technê* in the *Dialogues*. She interprets the use of *technê*-knowledge as proto-knowledge_a kind of intuitive archetype for what knowledge is. Socrates' constant use of 'shoemakers, fullers, cooks and doctors' to make his points thus not only depends on craft as an archetype of knowing, but as such, *technê* further takes on the implicit attributes of a virtue. John Mulhern, in turn, takes up Aristotle's many uses of πόνος. He observes that Aristotle consistently frames the concept of labour with one or more of six qualifiers—the agent, the object or beneficiary, the instrument used, its purpose and how the work is performed. Aristotle uses these contextual frames to determine the value of labour in a particular circumstance. Depending on the context, Aristotle regards both physical and intellectual labour as capable of being excellent. Ralph Rosen pays close attention to Galen's foregrounding of the hand at the beginning of his monumental *The Function of the Parts of the Body*. Hands for Galen, Rosen argues, are the instrument of human reason, and what makes humans uniquely human is their capacity to work with their hands. Bipedalism, another human quality, is linked to hands, and likewise enables this human activity of work. Finally, Lauren Petersen addresses the valuation of Roman artists—not only in their own time, but by the history of art as a discipline. She observes that since Roman historians like Pliny dismissed Roman artists as mere copyists of things Greek, modern art historians since Vasari tended to follow suit. More contemporary considerations, uncomfortable with the Roman artist as mere copyist, have substituted an attention to subject—particularly biographical assessments of imperial subjects—in place of the working artist as the fulcrum around which the discipline has turned. Absent artist biographies, artists and their labour are thus continually elided and erased.

The second section, 'Pushing the Boundaries of Labour', groups papers which, in various ways, ask us to reconsider the nature of labour and thus how it is valued both by workers and literary elites. These papers, too, offer new methodological and theoretical approaches, as well as new sources. Sarah Levin-Richardson's analysis of the graffiti from the purpose-built brothel in Pompeii reveals the other work that sex-workers engaged in—emotional labour. Praise, mourning, and other kinds of emotional support can be seen in these graffiti as an adjacent type of labour alongside sex itself. Levin-Richardson uses feminist economic theory to unpack why emotional labour might have been used by sex workers to better their situation. Bettina Reitz-Joosse introduces the concept of 'madeness' in her analysis of glassmaking and how it was perceived in Roman antiquity. The particular nature of glass as a substance, together with the particular actions required to craft it—from melting to blowing—merged into an activity-substance in Roman thought, a composite idea in which the object and the work to produce it became one. Christel Freu unpacks one of the most complex and fraught categories of ancient labour—wage labour. Following Marx' observation on the relationship between wage labour and specialization, she argues that an increasing division and specialization of labour during the late Republic and early Roman empire produced a concomitant increase in interchangeable labour in support of these new specialized crafts, a group paid largely in wages. Stoic thinkers were divided in their valuation of this development. Cicero's famous condemnation of the wage labourer as a slave in *On Duties* (mentioned above) marks the beginning of the concretization of this group as an almost wholly negative one, while other Stoics dwelled less on wage labourers' lack of autonomy and more on their penury and the aim of their labour, namely to support luxurious excess. Finally, Miriam Groen-Vallinga draws our attention to the neglected networks of women and children who staffed the great elite *domus*. Using both columbarium inscriptions of the first century CE and some sixteenth-century English household accounts as a comparative case, she underlines the invisibility of such labour in both life and death.

The third section reconsiders one aspect of ancient labour which has almost always been positively valued—agricultural labour—providing greater nuance to what has often been a somewhat flat 'farming is good' assessment. Rural work is most radically rethought by Amelia Bensch-Schaus, who posits listening as a kind of work in Theocritus' rustic *Idylls*. Active and attentive listening is combined with non-elite labour as Theocritus' shepherds, herdsmen and housewives are asked to set aside other work to 'listen' to in-text performances. The metapoetical demands on the internal audience, together with the identity of the protagonists, not only emphasize listening as labour but cast that labour in an insistently rural, non-elite labouring guise. Riemer Faber revisits another set of fundamental 'positive' texts, the bucolic construction of rural pleasure, or the *locus amoenus*. Using Theocritus, Vergil and Horace together with aspects of eco-critical theory, he notes how each poet diminishes the nature/culture binary by describing the mutual entanglement of labour and leisure, work and rest. Liana Brent and Tracy Prowse's contribution takes us back to rural workers themselves, their communities, and how the archaeology of the grave might shed some light on how these workers regarded their own labour. Examining the grave goods and human remains from the imperial estate at Vagnari in southern Italy, they find a particular use of tools—sickles, hooks, punches and blades—left in or next to graves, seemingly as a symbolic indicator of work done by the deceased. The particular gender and age patterning of these finds—mostly but not consistently found with adult men, and often found together with more plentiful grave assemblages—point to the symbolic status of labour and its changing valuation over the life course. Finally, Nicole Brown's analysis of the so-called Rustic Calendar mosaic from Saint-Romain-en-Gal reveals a subtle tension between seasonal time and the cycle of human work which harnesses it, pressing the latter into a kind of spectacle of labour. The control over the body of workers is glorified, not only through repetition and form, but also by the very fact that the elite owner treads those bodies underfoot.

The fourth and final section contains papers which, in different ways, find labour at the heart of different kinds of civic values. Citizenship, euergetism, attentiveness to the gods and attachment to one's birthplace—these chapters find each of these values mutually implicated in labour of different kinds. Helle Hochscheid suggests how this might have been true even of those set, by definition, outside citizenship status—the metics of Athens. In examining the long history of large construction projects, culminating under Pericles, and foreign workers' important role in them, she suggests that the city came to assign metics a value by virtue of both their craft and their contributions to *polis* life. Metics not only were prominent in large building projects but also had also fought in the Persian Wars and had a place in religious festivals, their skill in labour thus contributing to their positive integration in urban hierarchies more generally. Turning to Greek artists, Natacha Massar uses craftsmen's signatures on objects from pots to sculptures to understand the particular values with which these craftsmen identified. The addition of ethnic, demotic or other information to their names emphasized craftspeople's particular relationship with the deity in question, their citizenship when working abroad, or their excellence as being from a place famous for that craft. Geographic, civic and religious identity are thus entangled with craft to produce a particular kind of valued labour. Antiopi Argyriou-Casmeridis examines inscriptions from Hellenistic cities that honour individuals explicitly named as having a profession. Looking particularly at artists and educators, she notes that these people—men and women alike—are praised for their *aretê* which amounts to a kind of civic benefaction. She also notes the other virtues—generosity, good conduct, promotion of civic history—associated with these kinds of labour, while being attentive, too, to the discrepancies in what professions attracted the most honours. Finally, returning to craftspeople's vision of themselves, Fanny Opdenhoff looks at how Gallic craftsmen commemorated themselves or their family members in funerary sculpture. Departing from a careful study of the Bordeaux monument of the sculptor Amabilis, who is shown sculpting his own funerary niche, she sets this monument in the context of Gallic craftsmen's funerary commemoration more generally, finding Amabilis both adopting a shared language of civic status and also bending it to emphasize sculpture as a particular labour.

Acknowledgements

We would like to thank Cornelis van Tilburg for his help indexing this volume, and Ineke Sluiter and Ralph Rosen for their help and mentorship.

Bibliography

Andersen, N. (1961). *Work and Leisure*. New York.

Andreau, J., France, J. and Pittia, S., eds. (2004). *Mentalités et choix économiques des Romains*. Bordeaux.

Bond, S. (2016). *Trade and Taboo. Disreputable Professions in the Roman Mediterranean*. Ann Arbor.

Caldwell, L. (2021). From Household to Workshop: Women, Weaving, and the Peculium. In: B. Longfellow and M. Swetnam-Burland, eds., *Women's Lives, Women's Voices. Roman Material Culture and Female Agency in the Bay of Naples*. Austin, pp. 51–66.

Cohen, E. (1998). The Wealthy Slaves of Athens: Legal Rights, Economic Obligations. In: H. Jones, ed., *Le monde antique et les droits de l'homme*. Brussels, pp. 105–123.

Damon, C. and Pieper, C., eds. (2018). *Eris vs. Aemulatio. Valuing Competition in Classical Antiquity*. Leiden.

Finley, M. (1973). *The Ancient Economy*. London.

Flohr, M. (2013). *The World of the Fullo: Work, Economy and Society in Roman Italy*. Oxford.

Flohr, M. and Wilson, A. (2011). The Economy of Ordure. In: G. Jansen, A.-O. Koloski-Ostrow and E. Moormann, eds., *Roman Toilets. Their Archaeology and Cultural History*. Leuven, pp. 127–136.

Flohr, M. and Wilson, A. (2016). Roman Craftsmen and Traders: Towards an Intellectual History. In: A. Wilson and M. Flohr, eds., *Urban Craftsmen and Traders in the Roman World*. Oxford, pp. 23–46.

Freu, C. (2022) *Les salariés de l'Égypte romano-Byzantine*. Paris.

Groen-Vallinga, M. (2013). Desperate Housewives? The Adaptive Family Economy and

Female Participation in the Roman Urban Labour Market. In: E.M. Hemelrijk and G. Woolf, eds, *Women and the Roman City in the Latin West*. Leiden, pp. 295–312.

Gällnö, S. (2013). (In)visible Spinners in the Documentary Papyri from Roman Egypt. In: M. Gleba and J. Pástókai-Szeőke, eds., *Making Textiles in Pre-Roman and Roman Times. People, Places, Identities*. Oxford, pp. 161–170.

Harris, E., Lewis, D. and Stewart, E., eds. (2020). *Skilled Labour and Professionalism in Ancient Greece and Rome*. Cambridge.

Hasaki, E. (2021). *Potters at Work in Ancient Corinth. Industry, Religion, and the Penteskouphia Pinakes*. Princeton.

Hawkins, C. (2016). *Roman Artisans and the Urban Economy*. Cambridge.

Hochscheid, H. and Russell, B., eds. (2021). *The Value of Making. Theory and Practice in Ancient Craft Production*. Turnhout.

Holleran, C. (2013). Women and Retail in Roman Italy. In: E.M. Hemelrijk and G. Woolf, eds., *Women and the Roman City in the Latin West*. Leiden, pp. 313–330.

Ker, J. and Pieper, C. (2014). General Introduction: Valuing Antiquity in Antiquity. In: C. Pieper and J. Ker, eds., *Valuing the Past in the Greco-Roman World*. Leiden, pp. 1–22

Ker, J. and Wessels, A. eds. (2020). *The Values of Nighttime in Classical Antiquity. Between Dusk and Dawn*. Leiden.

Larsson Lovén, L. (2013). Female Work and Identity in Roman Textile Production and Trade: A Methodological Discussion. In: M. Gleba and J. Pástókai-Szeőke, eds., *Making Textiles in Pre-Roman and Roman Times. People, Places, Identities*. Oxford, pp. 109–125.

Larsson Lovén, L. (2016). Women, Trade and Production in the Urban Centres of Roman Italy. In: A. Wilson and M. Flohr, eds., *Urban Craftsmen and Traders in the Roman World*. Oxford, pp. 200–221.

Lucassen, J. (2021). *The Story of Work. A New History of Humankind*. New Haven.

Manca Masciadri, M.A. and Montevecchi, O. (1982). Contratti di baliatico e vendite fiduciarie a Tebtynis. *Aegyptus*, 62(1/2), pp. 148–161.

McInerney, J. and Sluiter, I. (2016). *Valuing Landscape in Classical Antiquity. Natural Environment and Cultural Imagination*. Leiden.

Miller, W. (1913). *Cicero. On Duties*. Cambridge, MA.

Monteix, N. (2016). Contextualizing the Operational Sequence: Pompeian Bakeries as a Case Study. In: A. Wilson and M. Flohr, eds., *Urban Craftsmen and Traders in the Ancient World*. Oxford, pp. 153–182.

Morris, I. (1999). Foreword. In: M. Finley, *The Ancient Economy*, 3rd edition. Berkeley, pp. ix–xxxvi.

Mrozek, S. (1989) *Löhnarbeit im klassischen Altertum*. Bonn.

Pieper, C. and Ker, J., eds. (2014). *Valuing the Past in the Greco-Roman World*. Leiden.

Rackham, H. (1944). *Aristotle. On Politics*. Cambridge, MA.

Rosen, R. and Sluiter, I., eds. (2003). *Andreia. Studies in Manliness and Courage in Classical Antiquity*. Leiden.

Rosen, R. and Sluiter, I., eds. (2006). *City, Countryside, and the Spatial Organization of Value in Classical Antiquity*. Leiden.

Rosen, R. and Sluiter, I., eds. (2010). *Valuing Others in Classical Antiquity*. Leiden.

Ruffing, K. (2008). *Die berufliche Spezialisierung in Handel und Handwerk. Untersuchungen zu ihrer Entwicklung und zu ihren Bedingungen in der römischen Kaiserzeit im östlichen Mittelmeerraum auf der Grundlage griechischer Inschriften und Papyri*. Rahden.

Scheidel, W. (2010). Real Wages in Early Economies: Evidence for Living Standards from 1800 BCE to 1300 CE. *Journal of the Economic and Social History of the Orient*, 53, pp. 425–462.

Silver, M. (2006). Slaves versus Free Hired Workers in Ancient Greece. *Historia: Zeitschrift für Alte Geschichte*, 55(3), pp. 257–263.

Sluiter, I. and Rosen, R., eds. (2004). *Free Speech in Classical Antiquity*. Leiden.

Sluiter, I. and Rosen, R. (2006). General introduction. In: R. Rosen and I. Sluiter, eds., *City, Countryside, and the Spatial Organization of Value in Classical Antiquity*. Leiden, pp. 1–12.

Sluiter, I. and Rosen, R., eds. (2008). KAKOS. *Badness and Anti-Value in Classical Antiquity*. Leiden.

Sluiter, I. and Rosen, R., eds. (2012). *Aesthetic Value in Classical Antiquity*. Leiden.

Swetnam-Burland, M. (2021). Women's Work? Investors, Money-Handlers, and Dealers. In: B. Longfellow and M. Swetnam-Burland, eds, *Women's Lives, Women's Voices. Roman Material Culture and Female Agency in the Bay of Naples*. Austin, pp. 29–50.

Tilly, C. and Tilly, C. (1998). *Work Under Capitalism*. Oxford.

Thomas, Y. (2004) Travail incorporé dans une matière première, travail d'usage et travail comme marchandise: Le droit comme matrice des catégories économiques à Rome. In: J. Andreau, J. France and S. Pittia, eds., *Mentalités et choix économiques des Romains*. Bordeaux, pp. 201–226.

Tran, N. (2013). *Dominus tabernae. Le statut de travail des artisans et des commerçants de l'Occident romain (Ier siècle av. J.-C. – IIIe siècle ap. J.-C.)*. Rome.

Ulrich, R. (2007). *Roman Woodworking*, New Haven.

Van Oyen, A. (2016). *How Things Make History. The Roman Empire and its Terra Sigillata Pottery*. Amsterdam.

Verboven, K. and Laes, C., eds. (2016). *Work, Labour and Professions in the Roman World*. Leiden.

Veyne, P., ed. (1987) *Histoire de la vie privée, vol. I. De L'Empire romain à l'an mil*. Paris.

Wilson, A. and Flohr, M., eds. (2016). *Urban Craftsmen and Traders in the Roman World*. Oxford.

SECTION 1

Revisiting the Canon

CHAPTER 2

Plato's Exemplary Craftsman

Ineke Sluiter

1 Introduction

In this chapter, we demonstrate that even an elite author like Plato betrays the contemporary cultural presence of a generally positive attitude to work and workers; this is *presupposed* in the communicative situation of the dialogues and thus offers a counterweight to the well-known explicitly negative passages. Our argument takes its place in the revision in the last decades of the traditional view on the low status of work, labour and crafts in premodern societies. That revision is part of a larger movement, in which debates on premodern economy, technology and money-making have been redirected by attempts to shed the evaluative biases of studying the ancient world from a modern perspective, with modern concepts, norms and values in mind. Similar academic developments concern issues such as globalization or connectivity.[1]

In thinking about work, the 2012 book by Catharina Lis and Hugo Soly, for instance, emphasizes the importance of the 'polyphony' of ancient sources. In their study of attitudes towards work and workers in pre-industrial Europe they may even have erred a bit on the positive side, in their—in itself fully justified—attempt to tease out all the available evidence for the appreciation of crafts, labour and workers.[2] They are right, for example, in pointing out a generally positive evaluation of the Herculean model of *ponos*, 'toil, labour,' but they omit the fact that terms like *ponos* and *mochthos*, 'toil, trouble,' also

1 See the Introduction by the editors to this volume. For the debate on the economy and technological innovation, see e.g. Greene 2000. Specifically on technology and the debate on an alleged ancient 'blocage', see Bur 2016, chapter 1, and the forthcoming volume edited by Flohr, Mols and Tieleman. On money-making, see now Leese 2021. For globalization and connectivity, see e.g. Pitts and Versluys 2015; Hodos et al. 2017.

2 For a judicious evaluation of Lis and Soly 2012, see Verboven 2014. Neesen 1989 had already anticipated this positive reassessment; on Athens, see in particular Neesen 1989, 58 ff., pointing out, e.g., that in 580/79 BCE demiurges had been elected archons (Arist. *Ath. Pol.* 13.2) (1989, 63 with n. 77), and that there is widespread evidence of the professional pride of workers (1989, 97–100). Similarly, Van den Hoven 1996 investigates more positive assessments, which, for *ponos*, she finds in particular with some groups of philosophers (Stoa, Cynics) (1996, 21–30). See below, n. 5 on *ponos*.

 | DOI:10.1163/9789004694965_003

automatically carry within themselves a more ominous association, in which 'toil' is connected with 'moral badness', 'poverty,' and 'low status.' Those are the overtones of the related adjectives *ponêros* and *mochthêros*, often simply translated as 'bad', and the nouns *ponêria* and *mochthêria* 'badness'. Moreover, the verb *poneô* is the intensive form of *penomai*, 'to work > to be poor'. *Ponos* 'toil' shares its root with *penia* 'poverty'. The whole nexus, then, of toil, moral badness, poverty and low social status is undeniably embedded in the language itself.[3] In addition, the example of Hercules himself is more likely to apply to the 'toil' or 'effort' of athletics, and by extension, intellectual labour,[4] than to manual labour, although even this does not make Lis and Soly any less correct in pointing out that there are many contexts in which work and workers are evaluated positively:[5] this back-and-forth only reinforces the notion of polyphony. Their work has since been corroborated by many other studies.[6]

Similarly, the magisterial *Story of Work* by Jan Lucassen takes a much wider view on work than simply the notion that it is what makes a living. The book demonstrates consistently that work is a value that is essential for the meaning-making efforts of human beings and their sense of identity. Also from a global comparative perspective, then, it seems to make sense to take a new look at ancient labour in terms of 'value', and there is no *prima facie* reason why the value approach could not also be relevant for an author like Plato. The question is, how and where?[7]

Many of the studies aiming at a reassessment of what was going on in antiquity (with work, progress, or technology) do so through one or both of two (relatively) new approaches. The first one is to counter the previous emphasis on elite written sources, notably by philosophers, by taking into account dif-

---

3 Sluiter 2008, 10, n. 26 'badness, poverty, and low status have the same package-deal relationship in the lexeme KAKOS as in the *ponêria* group'. On *ponos*, see Loraux 1982.

4 See, e.g., the use of Heracles made by Pindar, both in the context of the athletic achievements he celebrates, and as a model for the poet himself (Nieto Hernandez 1993). As Vernant puts it (1985, 275): 'Héraclès n'est pas un travailleur' (and cf. 1985, 367 n. 33, pointing out that there is no structure of cohesion in Heracles' labours, as there would have been had it been his 'work'). For Plato on *ponos*, see below.

5 They could also have chosen to refer to the large list of heroes with specialized tasks ('Helden als Sondergötter') as (to name but a few) doctors, doormen, cooks, chaser-away of flies, key-bearer, mixer of water and wine etc.: Usener 1896, 247–273.

6 I'm singling out here the study by Massar 2020, who concludes that '[*t*]*echnitai* were appreciated, employed, and encouraged because of the *technê* in which they had trained' (2020, 87), while also acknowledging that not all professions 'enjoyed the same cultural and social recognition' (2020, 89). In actual life, there were hierarchies of professions.

7 Vernant 1985, 270 explicitly denies this connection between work and value in Plato: 'On peut dire que pour Platon le travail reste étranger à toute valeur humaine.'

ferent bodies of evidence: literary texts (for ancient Greece: Homer, Hesiod, the lyric poets, comedy), but also inscriptions, and in particular other forms of material culture and information on how work was organized in antiquity. The second approach complements this extension of the range of evidence by reverting to those traditional and authoritative texts of the philosophers with a new and less trusting focus: this time, the rhetorical, political and ideological purposes of these sources take centre stage, e.g. their antidemocratic tendencies. While such political *parti-pris* has been acknowledged before, now it is being connected to the philosophers' representation and evaluation of work and workers, and thus becomes part of socio-economic history. Philosophers, like everyone else, tend to frame their texts in certain ways, and their biases can be analysed.[8]

The first approach, adding different voices and sources, not only helps to put on display the polyphony represented by different types of sources or genres of literature, but also calls attention to variations in assessments of different kinds of work. Farming, for instance, is always seen positively, no matter how elitist the source.[9] The second approach tempers the influence of the elite sources by pointing out their ideological preoccupations and prejudices.

In this chapter we will use the case of Plato to add a new angle to the second approach. Undoubtedly, some of the negativity about labourers that we can find in his work can be defused by an analysis of his ideological biases. However, we can go further than that: in a cognitively inflected reading of the (psychologically plausible) communicative behaviour of Socrates and his interlocutors, we can reveal shared cultural beliefs about work that are positive. This positive attitude is un-reflected and not connected with explicit views on work elsewhere in the dialogues.

The argument proceeds in several steps. First, we discuss the overt and explicitly negative statements on work and workers in Plato. Next, we explain the concept of 'common ground.' We then present the two elements in the Socratic dialogues that together make up the argument for a positive under-

---

8 Such a double approach, the inclusion of less studied evidence and the rhetorical evaluation of authoritative texts, has also been used, for example, in the reevaluation of the so-called 'bad emperors', such as Nero, who clearly enjoyed a much different reputation among the ordinary people in Rome than among the senators who wrote his history in a clearly biased way. See Hekster 2009 (senatorial history); 2011 (using other types of evidence).

9 See Murnaghan 2006 on farming as one of the arenas in which aristocrats could compete for honour, standing and authority. Knowledge of farming could also take the form of mastery of the *discourse* of farming, which could allow rich people to connect to the authentic credibility of the poor, honest farmer, while it could also qualify people for 'a central role in communal life' (Murnaghan 2006, 93), as a speaker.

lying view of work in that common ground: first, the fact that *technai* represent the most readily available and recognizable examples of a body of knowledge; and second, the fact that *technê*-knowledge is seen as something morally good. This last point turns out to have antecedents in the earlier poetic tradition.

The thesis we will defend, then, is this: in spite of the generally negative assessment of work in Plato, Socratic discursive strategies betray an underlying positive cultural evaluation of τέχνη-work in the common ground between Socrates and his interlocutors (even the higher-class ones).

2 Plato on Work and Craftsmen: The Negative Part of Polyphony

The familiar negative sentiments in Plato we will report only briefly, as a foil to what will follow.[10] In the sixth book of the *Republic*, Socrates points out the social influences that will keep the most gifted people from pursuing philosophy, thus leaving the field wide open to what he contemptuously calls *anthrôpiskoi*, 'manikins' (495c), who come from the *technai* ('arts, crafts, techniques, disciplines') and are attracted by the prestige of philosophy. These eager takers, who are giving philosophy a bad name, are 'immature people, who have been physically deformed by their jobs and work, and are mentally just as warped and stunted by their handicrafts' (ἀτελεῖς μὲν τὰς φύσεις, ὑπὸ δὲ τῶν τεχνῶν τε καὶ δημιουργιῶν ὥσπερ τὰ σώματα λελώβηνται οὕτω καὶ τὰς ψυχὰς συγκεκλασμένοι τε καὶ ἀποτεθρυμμένοι διὰ τὰς βαναυσίας τυγχάνουσιν, 495d).[11]

This passage emphasizes the negative effect of handwork on body and soul and it is followed (495e) by the (to us) highly offensive image of 'a small, bald metalworker (*chalkeus*), who has come into some money. Fresh out of debtors' prison, 'he's had a bath and is wearing brand-new clothes and a bridegroom's outfit, and he's about to marry his master's daughter because she's hard up and has no one to look after her'.[12] This is what is happening to philosophy, the daughter, who is being wooed by unworthy working-class people, rather than by someone of the level of the metalworker's master. The result of such a union will be inferior offspring (i.e. bad ideas, 496a). There is no doubt about the elitist

10 For denigration of artisans by ancient writers, see e.g. Hackworth Petersen 2010.

11 Trans. Waterfield 1993, slightly adapted; the Greek construction is anacoluthic and mirrors the brokenness of the people described.

12 Based on Waterfield's 1993 translation. Technically, the 'master' is also a *technikos*, but this part of the simile is dropped without any comment or elaboration.

negative image projected here. As always, the physical imperfections (baldness, short stature) suggest moral and social inferiority.[13]

Like other elite authors, Plato evaluates *ponos* positively, but that should not be taken as a positive comment on work and workers. His Socrates recognizes (*Resp.* 535d) that *philoponia*, the willingness to undertake toil and exertion, is necessary for an education in the ideal state. However, such *philoponia* cannot be lopsided, only aimed at the physical exertions of the gymnasium and the hunt, while there is *misoponia*, an 'aversion to exertion', where intellectual efforts are required. Plato, then, fully subscribes to an elite version of *ponos*, a valuable exertion of body and mind.[14] In that sense, it is fitting that in the *Apology* Socrates evokes his own Herculean efforts to investigate the truthfulness of the oracle that had claimed that 'no one is wiser than Socrates'. 'I must give you an account of my wanderings (πλάνην) as if I was performing labours (ὥσπερ πόνους τινὰς πονοῦντος) to prove the oracle to be irrefutable' (*Ap.* 22a). No Greek audience will have missed the implicit reference to Heracles.[15] But in this combination of physically walking around and intellectual research it is not 'work' in the Lis and Soly sense that Socrates is talking about.

Plato's overt statements about work, then, especially in terms of *banausia, cheirotechnia, cheirourgia*, 'handiwork', are negative in tone.[16] *Ponos* does not mean 'work'. Its application to elite pastimes requiring effort (the gymnasium, philosophy) cannot be used as the basis for an argument about the positive assessment of work *tout court.*

---

13 Cf. Lis and Soly 2012, 27; for other examples of negative statements about work or labourers in Plato's dialogues, see *Resp.* 590c, βαναυσία δὲ καὶ χειροτεχνία διὰ τί ὄνειδος φέρει; 'why does low handiwork bring reproach?'; *Alc. I* 131b, opposing what a 'good man' knows to *technai* that are *banausoi* (handiwork, but here clearly meant as 'vulgar'); *Symp.* 203a7 also creates a hierarchy in which only one type of *sophia* (the communication between gods and men) makes its possessor *daimonios* ('inspired'), while cleverness in a *technê* or handicraft (*cheirourgia*) makes one (only a) *banausos*, 'handworker', but again clearly with overtones of 'vulgarity', given the opposition; and *Leg.* 644 states that training aimed at moneymaking or other forms of cleverness without mind or justice is *banausos* ('vulgar') and unbefitting of a free citizen, and not worthy of being called *paideia* in the first place. For such denigration of artisans and the insulting use of *banausos*, cf. Hackworth Petersen 2010. For the package deal of moral, social and physical inferiority in classical Athens, see Sluiter 2008.

14 See above, n. 4. There is no Greek equivalent for our 'work' (Vernant 1985, 274; Loraux 1982, 172). *Ponos* always needs to be interpreted in context, especially for its evaluative overtones. In the *Republic, ponos* mostly refers to agriculture (e.g. *Resp.* 369e), always valued positively (see Murnaghan 2006) or the gymnasium (e.g. *Resp.* 410b). *Mochthos* and *mochtheô* are not attested in Plato.

15 De Strycker and Slings 1994, 279–280 ad loc.

16 See n. 13 for *banousos*.

3 Assessing 'Common Ground'

How, then, can we prove our claim that there is a more positive underlying view of work, or at least of the *technai*? The theoretical insight we will use in the remainder of this chapter derives from cognitive linguistics and the basic principles of human interaction and communication. When two (or more) people are in conversation, different things happen at the same time. They are monitoring their interactions in different ways, for instance, from a point of view of politeness and social appropriateness. But they are also developing their conversation and the exchange of information by 'moves' that will need to make sense to their partner. One condition for this to happen is that a move cannot lack all connection to the situation, the relationship between the partners, or previous exchanges. Moves should be 'anchored' in what is called 'common ground'. In a technical sense, common ground refers to 'the sum of [two people's] mutual, common, or joint knowledge, beliefs and suppositions'.[17] Items in the common ground do not need to be made explicit, because all the interlocutors know them, they are aware that the others know them, and they are aware that this awareness, too, is shared and mutual. 'Anchoring' in the common ground guarantees that whatever is added as new by a communicative move is connected to something familiar and cognitively available.

Common ground can be manipulated in various ways, but that will not concern us here. For our purpose, what is important is that the Socratic dialogues can be analysed in a way that brings to light and makes explicit (for us) what is presupposed by all speakers and thus cognitively available and (presumed to be) acceptable to all of them. Some elements of the common ground will be shared culturally (e.g. that there is an oracle in Delphi and that the officiating priestess is called the Pythia);[18] other elements may be part of the specific interpersonal context (e.g. information about characteristics of one of the interlocutors).[19] Our focus will be on the former: the cultural common ground

17 For this definition, see Clark 1996, 93. 'Anchoring' is a concept describing how what is perceived as new is connected to what is considered familiar, see Sluiter 2017 and https://anchoringinnovation.nl. For the linguistics of anchoring, see Sluiter 2021; anchoring in common ground: Allan and Van Gils 2015; Kroon 2015, 2021.

18 Shared cultural common ground explains, e.g., why in *Ap.* 21a, having mentioned Delphi and oracle-consultation, Socrates can say 'well, the Pythia answered …' using the definite article (ἀνεῖλεν οὖν ἡ Πυθία). The Pythia needs no further introduction, belongs in the Delphic setting, and can be referred to as a known entity.

19 Situated cognition: Cave 2017; Corthals and Sluiter 2023.

of Socrates and his interlocutors and of Plato and his audience. And we will show that positive ideas about work, specifically about *technai*, are part of that common ground.

4 Technai

Our argument to discover the positive underlying assumptions about *technê* proceeds in two steps. First, we will show that whenever Socrates and his interlocutors are talking about *knowledge*, it is *technê*-knowledge that is in the common ground as the culturally most readily available example (i.e., the prototype) of knowledge. It is part of the shared cultural information that *technai* have specific bodies of knowledge associated with them. A second common-ground assumption we will point out is that *technai* are generally associated with a *positive morality*.

4.1 Technê-*Knowledge is Prototypical Knowledge*

Plato's representation of the progression of thought in the early Socratic dialogues is psychologically and cognitively credible. This goes for the behaviour of Socrates' interlocutors, but also for that of Socrates himself. In both cases, we can detect so-called 'prototype effects.' When people work with categories ('furniture', 'birds', but this can also be extended to abstract concepts, such as 'knowledge' or 'virtue') they do not simply count items 'in' or 'out', as either members of the category or not. They are also capable of ranking examples as better (more central) or worse (more peripheral) ones. A chair is a better example of furniture than an ashtray, and in the US, a robin is the best example of a bird. The best example of a category is called the prototype. People can produce and recognize such an example most quickly.[20] Prototypes are typically in the common ground, since they are a culturally shared phenomenon.

In the early Socratic dialogues, Socrates and his interlocutors usually try to pin down the essence of a virtue (the 'what is x'-question).[21] Typically, the interlocutors start from the most readily available example from their direct personal experience. 'What is courage?' 'Well', says Laches, who is a general, 'that is staying in line at one's assigned post'.[22] In this case, the military associ-

20 Prototype theory goes back to Eleanor Rosch 1973, 1975. For a good account in connection with classical Greek texts, see Rademaker 2005, 19–26.

21 Smith 1998 points out that it is possible that Socrates himself is not in principle searching for definitions. However, since his interlocutors frequently claim some form of expertise, they should be able to explain 'what x is'.

22 Pl. *La.* 190c4.

ations of *andreia*, 'manly courage', are widely shared in Greek society. This, then, is a prototype effect and courage in war is part of the cultural common ground. This first attempt at definition, here and in other dialogues, never stands up to scrutiny, but the important thing is that this representation of thinking through readily available examples is a recognizable part of human cognition.[23]

Socrates' behaviour is also psychologically plausible and it will lead to another prototype effect. The context in which the dialogues take place is often an educational and investigative one: either Socrates is coaching young men (or, as for instance in the case of *Laches* again, the actual question is about how to educate young men, in this case in 'manliness and courage', combined in the Greek term *andreia*); or he is talking to sophists, who claim expertise as educators in moral excellence or virtue, *aretê*. This educational context can be seen as a psychological prompt, a form of (semantic) priming,[24] for Socrates' most characteristic intuition: that *virtue is a kind of knowledge*. It should be, if it can be taught. This is actually quite a daring and new intuition, one to which the Socratic dialogues revert time and again. It is something that needs clarification for Socrates' interlocutors. It is always helpful to base explanations on examples, rather than on abstract principles, and it is of course important to select examples that would be readily recognizable to one's addressee. It is here that we see another prototype effect. The best and most readily available example of knowledge, its prototype, is *technê*-knowledge. The new and unusual idea of virtue as knowledge is being anchored in the common ground by the analogy of the *technai*, which all represent a recognized body of knowledge, of which the practitioners can give an account, and which is transmitted in teaching. Socrates can count on the recognition value of the *technai*.[25] They are a helpful cognitive model for Socrates' interlocutors to think about the virtues.[26]

---

23 The best general description of the dialectical progression in the Socratic dialogues is still Goldschmidt 1947. For the cognitive plausibility of the thought-process of Socrates' interlocutors and discussion of the *Laches* example, see Sluiter and Rosen 2003, 5–8, where it is argued that the military context for 'courage' is not just a personal thing for Laches but is culturally shared: mental categories are built from the ground up, starting from 'best examples.'

24 See Chivers 2019 for a critical assessment of priming theories in social psychology. Semantic priming has not been called into question. In this context it would refer to the fact that the concept of 'knowledge' should come up faster in a context of education or investigation than in a neutral context.

25 Smith 1998, 133; Parry 2020 [2003] section 2 offers a long list of all the *technai* to which Socrates has recourse.

26 Parry 2020 [2003], section 2 discusses Plato's use of *technai* to illustrate important philosophical points, in particular to explain virtue, ruling and the creation of the cosmos. He

As an example of how easily the *technai* may be adduced in the search for an understanding of a virtue, here is an exchange from Plato's *Republic*, where Polemarchus has just taken recourse to the authority of the poet Simonides to provide a definition of justice: 'giving what is owed to each person is just'.[27] When Socrates suggests that Simonides' phrase 'what is owed' may actually mean 'what is appropriate', Polemarchus regards this as a platitude: 'well, of course' (332c). And then Socrates (the 'I') brings in the *technai* quite abruptly as a way to focus the discussion (with Polemarchus still as the mouthpiece of Simonides)(332c):

> 'But listen', I said, 'suppose [Simonides] were asked: "So, Simonides, take the art (*technê*) that we know as medicine. What is it? What does it give that is owed and appropriate, and to what does it give it?" What do you suppose his reply would be?'
>
> 'Obviously', he answered, 'he'd reply that it is the art of giving drugs, food, and drink to bodies.'
>
> 'What about cookery? What art do we say it is? What does it give that is owed and appropriate, and to what does it give it?'
>
> 'It gives taste to cooked food.'
>
> 'All right. So which art (*technê*)—the art of giving what to what—might we call justice?'[28]

Notice the casual way in which the notion of *technai* is introduced, as an example that needs no further introduction itself. Socrates never motivates it, and Polemarchus goes along with it.

In this instance, there is not so much emphasis on the knowledge aspect of the *technai*, but elsewhere there is.[29] In the *Charmides*, Critias at some point comes up with a definition of *sôphronein* as 'knowing oneself' (τὸ γιγνώσκειν ἑαυτόν, 164d), and he is asking Socrates to agree with him. Socrates, of course, wants to investigate first: 'if *sôphrosunê* is knowing (*gignôskein*) something, then clearly it would be a form of knowledge (*epistêmê*) and knowledge of

---

singles out two aspects, the role of reflexive knowledge (i.e. the capacity to give a reasoned account of what one is doing), and the fact that *technai* are oriented towards the welfare of their object (see section 4.2 below). Balansard 2001 argues that the Socratic use of *technai*-arguments derives from the sophists and is meant ironically, as a rebuttal. This does not affect my own argument on the role of *technai* in the common ground.

27 Pl. *Resp.* 331e: τὸ τὰ ὀφειλόμενα ἑκάστῳ ἀποδιδόναι δίκαιόν ἐστι.

28 Trans. Waterfield 1993, slightly adapted; see Hemmenway 1999 on this *Republic* passage and its use of *technê*-analogies.

29 See Annas 1981, 24–26 on this passage.

something'. Yes, says Critias, it is knowledge of oneself. And Socrates instantly brings in medicine, as another (clearly well-known) form of knowledge, of health, and this analogy is followed by that of housebuilding and other *technai*: all of them considered under the rubric of *epistêmê* (Pl. *Chrm.* 165c–166b).

Most of Socrates' interlocutors, particularly the younger ones, willingly go along with the analogy and never question or protest against the use of the *technai* as a tool for thinking, but the hostile sophist Callicles does (Pl. *Grg.* 491a):

> By the gods, … you simply never stop your perpetual talk about shoemakers, fullers, cooks, and doctors, as if that's what we are talking about.
>
> Νὴ τοὺς θεούς, ἀτεχνῶς γε ἀεὶ σκυτέας τε καὶ κναφέας καὶ μαγείρους λέγων καὶ ἰατροὺς οὐδὲν παύῃ, ὡς περὶ τούτων ἡμῖν ὄντα τὸν λόγον.

And some of Socrates' none-too-clever political opponents have a vague inkling that this *technê*-discourse is all by itself a dangerous aspect of Socratic rhetoric: in the attempt by the Thirty to contain Socrates' activities, Critias demands that he abstain from future reference to 'shoemakers, builders, and bronze workers.'[30] These passages mostly show the extent to which the *technê*-analogies were recognized as a fixed part of Socratic discourse, however much his opponents may have been unwilling or incapable to grasp their actual role.

That role is the stability provided by the *technai*: their possessors really know something,[31] and everyone knows this. The information is in the common ground. So when Socrates in the *Apology* recounts his attempts to disprove the claim of the oracle that nobody is wiser than him, he is initially looking for someone with expert moral knowledge.[32] He goes to a politician with a reputation for wisdom (*sophia*), but discovers that there is no real wisdom there (*Ap.* 21b–c). Then he embarks on the Herculean wanderings mentioned above (section 3), which bring him to anyone with a reputation for wisdom, the poets for instance, but all in vain. As a last resort, he turns to the *cheirotechnai* (Pl. *Ap.* 22c–d):

30 Xen. *Mem.* 1.2.37: ὁ δὲ Κριτίας, Ἀλλὰ τῶνδέ τοί σε ἀπέχεσθαι, ἔφη, δεήσει, ὦ Σώκρατες, τῶν σκυτέων καὶ τῶν τεκτόνων καὶ τῶν χαλκέων· καὶ γὰρ οἶμαι αὐτοὺς ἤδη κατατετρῖφθαι διαθρυλουμένους ὑπὸ σοῦ ('but Critias said: "Well, you will have to stay away, Socrates, from these, the shoemakers and the builders and the bronze workers. In fact, I think they have been worn away completely by being constantly talked about by you"').

31 Goldschmidt 1947, 102.

32 Smith 1998, 131 n. 5 points out that *technê* and *epistêmê* can be used interchangeably in the early dialogues for such moral knowledge.

> Finally, then, I went to the handworkers. For I was aware that I did not know a thing, so to speak, but I knew about them at least (γ') that I would find they knew many beautiful things. And I was not disappointed in this: indeed, they knew things I did not know, and in that respect they were wiser than me.
>
> τελευτῶν οὖν ἐπὶ τοὺς χειροτέχνας ᾖα· ἐμαυτῷ γὰρ συνῄδη οὐδὲν ἐπισταμένῳ ὡς ἔπος εἰπεῖν, τούτους δέ γ' ᾔδη ὅτι εὑρήσοιμι πολλὰ καὶ καλὰ ἐπισταμένους. καὶ τούτου μὲν οὐκ ἐψεύσθην, ἀλλ' ἠπίσταντο ἃ ἐγὼ οὐκ ἠπιστάμην καί μου ταύτῃ σοφώτεροι ἦσαν.

The handworkers have *epistêmê* ('knowledge'), a bottom-line aspect of wisdom. Unfortunately, they, too, do not have enough self-knowledge to understand the limits of their knowledge, so there is no real wisdom here either. But Socrates' intuition that here at least he would be certain to find knowledge was correct. What is more, his use of the Greek particle γε ('at least', 22d1) shows that he reasonably assumed that *at least* this expectation would be fulfilled.[33] He could probably count on this being an expectation shared by his listeners. Once again then, a positive statement about handworkers is presented as something obvious, and thus as part of the common ground.

What the Platonic representation of Socratic discourse shows, then, is that there is a widely recognized positive association between the *technai* and a body of knowledge, which can be transmitted between teachers and students. The know-how of the *technikos* is the prototype of the category of knowledge. Since *technai* spring to mind as the most readily available, *positive* examples of a form of knowledge, the *technê*-analogy cements and anchors the knowledge component of virtue, which is the Socratic intuition that may have prompted the analogy in the first place. Most importantly for our purposes, in spite of overtly negative statements about workers elsewhere in Plato, this analysis shows that Socrates and his partners, and Plato and his audience, share in a readily available positive cultural association of the *technai*.

4.2 Technê *is Inherently Moral*

Technê-knowledge is the best example of knowledge. So, if moral excellence (virtue) is also a knowledge-based practice, however unfamiliar that claim may be, then virtue does indeed share characteristics with a *technê*. This more familiar example may, then, serve as a cognitive and rhetorical frame, a form of

33 For the scope particle γε, see the *Cambridge Grammar of Classical Greek* 2019, 692.

scaffolding for thinking and speaking about virtue. But there is also a corollary to this argument: the frame works both ways. It also means that *technê* becomes tinged with the characteristics of a virtue: *technai* are taken to be inherently moral. If *technê* is a frame for thinking about virtue, virtue is also a way to think about *technê*: they become *mutual* frames.[34]

This idea is not just a construction of the Platonic dialogues, it is actually a widely held view, not only in antiquity, but also today. In his famous book about the Craftsman, Richard Sennett claims that craftsmanship is about 'the right way' (to make something), it is 'the skill of making things well' and entails 'the desire to do a job well for its own sake'.[35] He also takes the step from qualitatively good work to morally good work, by emphasizing the dignity of the craftsman, and the authority that is based on quality of skill plus ethics.[36]

In Plato, too, the two steps can be discerned: the (market-driven) need to do good work is familiar to Socrates and his interlocutors as well as to Plato and his audience, as is made clear from a passage in the *Meno* (91c–e). Socrates is speaking with Anytus (one of his future prosecutors), who is railing against sophistic education and the dangerous damage done by it. Socrates replies that he finds it hard to believe that someone like Protagoras should have been making a lot of money as an educator for over 40 years and never been found out to have made his students worse by their association with him. Whereas any shoemaker mending old shoes or any tailor stitching up torn clothes would be found out within a month if they made things worse rather than better. There is an assumption here that people will deliver good-quality work. In this case, we can still distinguish technically skilled work (shoemaker, tailor) and the moral effects of a bad educator. However, the step to the moral qualities of the *technikos* is also made explicitly.

One might think that *technê*-knowledge in itself is ethically neutral: you can use it for good or bad purposes.[37] In fact, in the Socratic dialogues (here the first book of the *Republic*), this thought is explored. The knowledge of a doctor would also make him a good poisoner. The knowledge of a guard would also enable him to become a good thief.[38] And yet, this is theoretical only, and

34 For 'framing', see Coulson 2001, Tolmach Lakoff 2000, Coulson 2001.

35 Sennett 2008, 8–9; 11.

36 Sennett 2008, 54, (dignity); 61–62, (authority); see further 2008, 294–295 for the ethics of craftsmanship. Lis and Soly 2012, 46–47; 53 also emphasize this.

37 See e.g. Sennett 2008, 22–23 ('craftsmanship is certainly, from an ethical point of view, ambiguous'), but Sennett here still believes that classical Greece despised craftsmen. Nevertheless, he sees a tendency to do the right thing.

38 Pl. *Resp.* 334a. See Hemmenway 1999.

denied vigorously: a craftsman, a practitioner of a certain art, is always said to be someone who makes a moral and responsible use of his knowledge. If the doctor turns into a poisoner, he is no longer acting as a doctor when he is doing so. The questions whether this goodness of the *technikos* is due to an additional master-*technê* of morality, or whether a doctor needs to stay away from the dangerous additional *technê* of money-making (both points of contention among philosophers) need not concern us here:[39] the intuition that *technê* is inherently aimed at the good is there, as part of the common ground. The idea of 'the benefit of *technê*' and the association of work and virtue were conventional.[40]

5 *Aretê* and Work in the Earlier Poetic Tradition

Talking about the 'conventional nature' of the association between work and knowledge, and in particular work and virtue, is simply a different way of stating that it belongs to the cultural common ground of the communicative situation in the Platonic dialogues. In order to illustrate this conventional nature, we could just refer to Lis and Soly again, but instead we will briefly point to some concrete examples from the poetic tradition.

In the Odyssey, Odysseus builds his marriage bed and the bedroom it occupies with his own hands. A tree stump forms one of the bed's legs and anchors it to the ground. Odysseus describes the expert and knowledgeable workmanship he put into it in great technical detail, as an indignant response to the remark by Penelope suggesting that the bed had been moved—this reaction proves his identity to Penelope (*Od.* 23.181–204).[41] It is clear that the unmovable nature of

39 Cf. Barney 2007.

40 So Wolfsdorf 2008, 106; cf. Roochnik 1986; Balme 1984, 150: 'The conclusion is that the vast majority of Athenians supported themselves by the labour of their own hands, that work was considered both virtuous and necessary, and that the attitude of contempt for banausic crafts and manual labour was limited in Athens to a few intellectuals who are prominent in our tradition'. On the passage from *Republic* 1, see in particular Hemmenway 1999. For the connection between hard work and virtue, see Lis and Soly 2012, 16–26. Incidentally, the nervousness of the abuse of technical knowledge is very persistent in classical antiquity: it also leads to the prophylactic addition to the definition of the orator: *vir* ***bonus*** *dicendi peritus* (Cato the Censor *apud* Quint. *Inst. Or.* 12.1.1, and widespread in the later tradition).

41 Note the emphasis on hard work (κάμον, 23.189), quality of work (εὖ, 23.193, 197) and knowledge (ἐπισταμένως, 23.197). Also, the mention of technical tools (e.g., carpenter's rule, drill, 23.197, 198). Lis and Soly 2012, 18 give more examples of Odysseus' technical abilities, but the marriage bed is the one with the clearest moral overtones, although this is not made explicit.

the bed is also symbolic for the permanence of the marriage and the loyalty of husband and wife, although this moral aspect remains implicit.

Explicit connections between work, its material effects (riches), and moral excellence are also part of the epic tradition. In Hesiod's *Works and Days* this is expressed, for example in the lines, εἰ δέ κεν ἐργάζῃ, τάχα σε ζηλώσει ἀεργὸς πλουτεῦντα· πλούτῳ δ' ἀρετὴ καὶ κῦδος ὀπηδεῖ ('and if you work, the idle man will soon envy you as you grow rich. Excellence and fame follow riches', 312–313).[42] The Homeric Hymns to Heracles and Hephaestus each end with the conventional prayer δίδου δ' ἀρετήν τε καὶ ὄλβον ('give us excellence and wealth').[43] The phrase is applicable to any deity, but is especially apt in the context of these two short hymns, each devoted to a deity with a special connection to work and the arts.[44] The hymn to Hephaestus enjoins us to sing of Hephaestus, who taught men work (*aglaa erga*). Earlier they lived in the mountains like wild animals, but now they have learned to work (*erga daentes*) because of Hephaestus, famous for his technical skill (*kluto-technês*), and they live comfortably. The prayer for 'excellence and wealth' caps the hymn. *Aretê* '(moral) excellence', is connected with work.[45]

6 Conclusion

In this chapter we have used some psychological and cognitive tools and concepts to demonstrate that the overtly negative statements about work in Plato should be relativized, not only through the now well-known exposure of ideological (elite) bias, but also by the presence of more positive associations in the cultural common ground of the communication. We used (semantic) priming as a possible explanation for Socrates' tendency to think about virtue as a kind of knowledge—given that the context of the dialogue is educational. We used information about mental categorization and prototype theory to argue for an underlying positive association for *technê*-work, in that, culturally,

42 See West 1978 ad loc., with more examples of the conjunction of riches and moral excellence or prestige.

43 *HH Heracles* (15.9): χαῖρε ἄναξ Διὸς υἱέ· δίδου δ' ἀρετήν τε καὶ ὄλβον; *HH Heph.* (20.5–8): νῦν δὲ δι' Ἥφαιστον κλυτοτέχνην ἔργα δαέντες | ῥηιδίως αἰῶνα … | εὔκηλοι διάγουσιν ἐνὶ σφετέροισι δόμοισιν. | ἀλλ' ἵληθ', Ἥφαιστε· δίδου δ' ἀρετήν τε καὶ ὄλβον.

44 Allen et al. 1936 ad loc.

45 The translations of the Homeric Hymns by Hugh Evelyn White and (in the Loeb series) Martin West translate *aretê* as 'success' and 'status,' respectively. Both correctly identify associations of the term, but the fact remains that its primary meaning is excellence, including moral excellence.

technê-knowledge is the best example (prototype) of the category of knowledge *tout court*. We used the notion of common ground as the common and shared basis for communication, into which new information can be 'anchored'. The idea that virtue is a kind of knowledge is new; but this idea can be explained and explored by having recourse to the best-known example of knowledge. And finally, we adduced framing theory for the mutual framing of virtue as (*technê*-)knowledge and *technai* as something inherently virtuous, the second culturally shared positive element underlying Socratic conversations.

In a way, then, we were analysing what Plato's texts betray almost in spite of himself. Where discussion of work and handwork are 'in focus', the statements he ascribes to his mouthpieces are negative. When the conversation is not primarily about work, but about the ethical and philosophical notions central to his interests, his language reveals commonly held, and thus culturally shared presuppositions. In that common ground, there is also room for the polyphony pointed out so well by Lis and Soly, for instance, in the tradition of mockery of doctors and other professionals.[46] A trace of this can be found, for instance, in the gentle mockery of the doctor Eryximachus in the *Symposium*.[47] However, if we want to discover the positive parts of this polyphony, there is no need to leave Plato behind entirely. Hidden in the dialogues are at least two widely shared cultural views of the *technai*: they represent the best example of a body of knowledge, and they come with the *a priori* assumption that such knowledge will be used for something good; and that there is a moral aspect to honest workmanship.

Acknowledgements

Research for this paper was supported by the Anchoring Innovation Gravitation Grant (NWO 024.003.012). I would like to thank audiences at the Penn-Leiden Colloquium, and the OIKOS study group of cognitive approaches to ancient literature for their helpful remarks, and the editors of this volume for their generous support. The earliest version of this argument was presented to a conference on rethinking Indian industrialization of crafts ('Anchoring innovation in handloom weaving in India', Chirala 2018). I am grateful to the participants of that conference as well. Finally, I'd like to thank Bob Corthals for his careful reading of the text.

46 Brecht 1930.

47 See Hunter 2004, 54.

Bibliography

Allan, R. and van Gils, L. (2015). Anchoring New Ideas in Common Ground: A Linguistic Approach. Retrieved from http://www.academia.edu/24015356/Anchoring_new_ideas_in_common_ground_A_linguistic_approach.

Allen, T.W., Halliday, W.R., and Sikes, E.E., eds. (1936²). *The Homeric Hymns*. Oxford.

Annas, J. (1981). *An Introduction to Plato's* Republic. Oxford.

Balansard, A. (2001). *Technè dans les dialogues de Platon. L'empreinte de la sophistique.* Sankt Augustin.

Balme, M. (1984). Attitudes to Work and Leisure in Ancient Greece. *Greece and Rome* 31, pp. 140–152.

Barney, R. (2007). The Carpenter and the Good. In: D. Cairns, F.-G. Herrmann and T. Penner, eds., *Pursuing the Good, Ethics and Metaphysics in Plato's* Republic. Edinburgh, pp. 293–319.

Brecht, F.J. (1930). *Motiv- und Typengeschichte des griechischen Spottepigramms*. Leipzig.

Bur, T. (2016). *Mechanical Miracles. Automata in Ancient Greek Religion*. Diss. Sydney.

Cave, T. (2017). Situated Cognition: The Literary Archive. *Poetics Today* 38.2, pp. 235–253.

Chivers, T. (2019). What's Next for Psychology's Embattled Field of Social Priming. *Nature* 576, pp. 200–202.

Clark, H. (1996). *Using Language*. Cambridge.

Corthals, B. and Sluiter, I. (2023). Situated Cognition. Sophocles, Milgram, and the Disobedient Hero. In: F. Budelmann and I. Sluiter, eds., with the assistance of B. Corthals, Minds on Stage. *Greek Tragedy and Cognition*. Oxford, pp. 211–228.

Coulson, S. (2001). *Semantic Leaps. Frame-Shifting and Conceptual Blending in Meaning Construction*. Cambridge.

Emde Boas, E. van, Rijksbaron, A., Huitink, L., and Bakker, M. de (2019). *The Cambridge Grammar of Classical Greek*. Cambridge.

Finley, M.I. (1965). Technical Innovation and Economic Progress in the Ancient World. *The Economic History Review* 18, 29–45.

Flohr, M., Mols, S., and Tieleman, T., eds. (f.c.) *Anchoring Science and Technology in Greco-Roman Antiquity*. Leiden.

Goldschmidt, V. (1947). *Les dialogues de Platon. Structure et méthode dialectique*. Paris.

Greene, K. (2000). Technological Innovation and Economic Progress in the Ancient World: M.I. Finley Reconsidered. *The Economic History Review* 53, pp. 29–59.

Hackworth Petersen, L. (2010). Crafts and Artisans. In: M. Gagarin, ed., *The Oxford Encyclopedia of Ancient Greece and Rome*. Oxford [consulted online 9 Jan. 2020].

Hekster, O. (2011). Imagining Power: Reality Gaps in the Roman Empire. *BABESCH* 86, pp. 111–124.

Hekster, O. (2009). *Romeinse keizers. De macht van het imago*. Amsterdam.

Hemmenway, S. (1999). The *Techne*-analogy in Socrates' Healthy City: Justice and the Craftsman in the *Republic*. *Ancient Philosophy* 19, pp. 267–284.

Hodos, T., ed. (2017). *The Routledge Handbook of Archaeology and Globalization*. New York.

Hoven, B. van den (1996). *Work in Ancient and Medieval Thought. Ancient Philosophers, Medieval Monks and Theologians and their Concept of Work, Occupations and Technology*. Leiden.

Hunter, R. (2004). *Plato's* Symposium. Oxford.

Kroon, C. (2015). 'Anchoring' as a Communicative Device in Roman Historiography: A Discourse Linguistic Perspective. Retrieved from http://www.academia.edu/24059119/Anchoring_as_a_communicative_device_in_Roman_historiography_a_discourse_linguistic_perspective.

Kroon, C. (2021). Communicative Anchoring in Latin: Devices and Strategies for Common Ground Management. In: A.M. Martín Rodríguez, ed., *Linguisticae Dissertationes. Current Perspectives on Latin Grammar, Lexicon and Pragmatics: Selected Papers from the 20th International Colloquium on Latin Linguistics* (Las Palmas de Gran Canaria, Spain, June 17–21, 2019), pp. 641–660. (Bibliotheca Linguae Latinae; Vol. 9). Ediciones Clásicas.

Leese, M. (2021). *Making Money in Ancient Athens*. Ann Arbor.

Lis, C. and Soly, H. (2012). *Worthy Efforts. Attitudes To Work and Workers in Pre-industrial Europe*. Leiden–Boston.

Loraux, N. (1982). Ponos. Sur quelques difficultés de la peine comme nom du travail. *Annali del Seminario di studi del mondo classico. Sezione di archeologia e storia antica* 4, pp. 171–192.

Lucassen, J. (2021). *The Story of Work. A New History of Humankind*. New Haven–London.

Massar, N. (2020). Skilled Workers in the Ancient Greek City: Public Employment, Selection Methods, and Evaluation. In: E. Stewart, E. Harris and D. Lewis, eds., *Skilled Labour and Professionalism in Ancient Greece and Rome*. Cambridge, pp. 68–93.

Murnaghan, S. (2006). Farming, Authority, and Truth-Telling in the Greek Tradition. In: R. Rosen and I. Sluiter, eds., *City, Countryside, and the Spatial Organization of Value in Classical Antiquity*. Leiden, pp. 93–118.

Neesen, L. (1989). *Demiurgoi und Artifices. Studien zur Stellung freier Handwerker in antiken Städten*. Bochum.

Nieto Hernández, M.P. (1993). Heracles and Pindar. *Mètis. Anthropologie des mondes grecs anciens* 8, pp. 75–102.

Parry, R. (2020 [2003]). Episteme and Techne. In: E.N. Zalta, ed., *The Stanford Encyclopedia of Philosophy* (Winter 2021 Edition), https://plato.stanford.edu/archives/win2021/entries/episteme-techne. (Consulted 28 August 2022).

Pitts, M., and Versluys, M.-J., eds. (2015). *Globalisation and the Roman World. World History, Connectivity, and Material Culture*. Cambridge.

Rademaker, A. (2005). Sophrosyne *and the Rhetoric of Self-Restraint. Polysemy and Persuasive Use of an Ancient Greek Value Term*. Leiden.

Roochnik, D. (1986). Socrates's Use of the Techne-Analogy. *Journal of the History of Philosophy* 24, pp. 295–310.

Rosch, E. (1973). On the Internal Structure of Perceptual and Semantic Categories. In: T.E. Moore, ed., *Cognitive Development and the Acquisition of Language*. New York, pp. 111–144.

Rosch, E. (1975). Cognitive Representations of Semantic Categories. *Journal of Experimental Psychology: General*, 104, pp. 199–233.

Sennett, R. (2008). *The Craftsman*. New Haven.

Sluiter, I. (2008). General Introduction. In: I. Sluiter and R. Rosen, eds., KAKOS. *Badness and Anti-Value in Classical Antiquity*. Leiden, pp. 1–27.

Sluiter, I. (2017). Anchoring Innovation: A Classical Research Agenda. *European Review* 25, pp. 20–38.

Sluiter, I. (2021). Old is the New New: The Rhetoric of Anchoring Innovation. In: R. Boogaart, H. Jansen and M. van Leeuwen, eds., *The Language of Argumentation*. Cham, pp. 243–260.

Sluiter, I., and Rosen, R.M. (2003). General Introduction. In: Rosen, R. and Sluiter, I. eds. *Andreia. Studies in Manliness and Courage in Classical Antiquity*. Leiden, pp. 1–24.

Smith, A.M. (1998). Knowledge and Expertise in the Early Platonic Dialogues. *Archiv für Geschichte der Philosophie* 80, pp. 129–161.

Strycker, E. de, and Slings, S. (1994). *Plato's* Apology of Socrates. *A Literary and Philosophical Study with a Running Commentary*. Leiden.

Tolmach Lakoff, R. (2000). *The Language War*. Berkeley-Los Angeles.

Usener, H. (1896). *Götternamen. Versuch einer Lehre von der religiösen Begriffsbildung*. Bonn.

Verboven, K. (2014). Reflections on Catharina Lis and Hugo Soly, Worthy Efforts: Attitudes towards Work and Workers in Pre-Industrial Europe (Leiden and Boston: Brill), 2012, 664 p. *Tijdschrift voor Sociale en Economische Geschiedenis* 11, pp. 67–87.

Vernant, J.-P. (1985 [1965]). *Mythe et pensée chez les Grecs. Études de psychologie historique*. Paris.

Waterfield, R. (1993). *Plato's* Republic. Oxford.

West, M.L., ed. (1978). *Hesiod* Works and Days. Oxford.

Wolfsdorf, D. (2008). *Trials of Reason. Plato and the Crafting of Philosophy*. Oxford.

CHAPTER 3

Πόνος and πονέω in Aristotle

J.J. Mulhern

1 Introduction

This chapter addresses Aristotle's use of πόνος and πονέω, which are the words he uses most frequently for labour, in value contexts. Although some influential writers have asserted 'the disdain of Greek and Roman elites for work in general and for manual work in particular',[1] Aristotle's treatment of labour was reminiscent of earlier Greek traditions, in which, as Loraux has pointed out, πόνος might indicate an activity painful, or at least costly, but also worthy of praise—the labours of a hero (Heracles) or the endurance of a warrior (Leonidas, Hdt. 7.224), or something less, but often something ambivalent in this way.[2] Because πόνος was ambivalent, Aristotle's challenge was to explain how to evaluate instances and patterns of it. What would make it appropriate for the citizen, or someone else, to engage in πόνος?

There is a hint of the direction he would take in *Politics* 1277a38–b6; Aristotle is discussing the goodness of a citizen, though using ἐργασία instead of πόνος, where his focus is on an occupation or pattern of work rather than on a single instance. Here he says:

> One kind of work (ἐργασία) is that of the manual labourers. These are, as the very name itself implies, those who live by their hands. … The functions (ἔργα) of subjects of this sort are not to be learned by the good politician or by the good citizen, except that he himself may perform them on occasion to benefit himself (εἰ μή ποτε χρείας χάριν αὐτῷ πρὸς αὐτόν).[3]

Χρείας χάριν, with the sense of χρείας ἕνεκα, and αὐτῷ recall Aristotle's list of circumstances in the *Nicomachean Ethics* (*NE*) 1111a3–5, especially ἕνεκα τίνος and ἐν τίνι; ποτε would recall πότε if πότε were there in the *NE*, which it is not.[4]

1 Lis 2012, 4. See also the introduction to this volume.
2 Loraux 1982, 175. Now also Lis 2012, 17.
3 Trans. Robinson 1962, 12–13. Except as noted, translations are taken from Barnes 1984.
4 Sloan 2010, assuming that the conventionalized *septem circumstantiae* of a much later period must match point for point the list in *NE* 1111a3–8 and that this list, which addresses a failure of

 | DOI:10.1163/9789004694965_004

These circumstances are among the ἐν οἷς καὶ περὶ ἃ ἡ πρᾶξις ('circumstances of the action and the objects with which it is concerned') mentioned in 1110b33–1111a1. Evaluating an instance or pattern of πόνος requires knowing more than what the act is (τί); who is performing it (τίς) also must be known, as well as who is its object or beneficiary or target (ἐν τίνι), the instrument used (τίνι), its purpose (ἕνεκα τίνος), and how it is performed (πῶς)—six in all; Aristotle elsewhere recognizes other circumstances, as will appear below. These circumstances come into play, though not all in every case, in Aristotle's evaluations of instances and patterns of πόνος. Thus, for him, deciding what labour might be appropriate is not able to be reduced to a single consideration such as utility or duty or to a simple rule.

Although πόνος (110 occurrences) and πονέω (139 occurrences) occur widely in the Corpus Aristotelicum, most frequently in the *Problems* (48 occurrences and 57 occurrences respectively), the examples in this chapter will be drawn mainly from among the works in which Aristotle is giving guidance to his intended audience—*Nicomachean Ethics* (12 occurrences), *Magna Moralia* (7 occurrences), *Eudemian Ethics* (7 occurrences), *On Virtues and Vices* (1 occurrence), *Politics* (21 occurrences) and *Oeconomica* (3 occurrences).[5] Some of these occurrences are associated with his circumstantial analysis, indicating that πόνος or πονεῖν is appropriate or inappropriate, some are not. The focus will be mainly on nine passages of guidance in which there are 26 occurrences

knowledge of the καθ' ἕκαστον, must be complete and exhaustive for Aristotle, which, though suggested in line 3, does not reflect his practice elsewhere, has read the equivalent of πότε back into the *NE*: 'Regardless of the ambiguity of Aristotle's Greek, five of the seven circumstances are easily identifiable, ... The other two circumstances, "where" and "when", may be found in the phrase περὶ τί ἢ ἐν τίνι πράττει. ... The second half of the phrase, ἢ ἐν τίνι, refers to the temporal realm within which an act may happen (239).' Sloan offers no argument for this last assertion and is unable to find a supporting parallel in Aristotle, as indicated by his note 10. Had Aristotle wanted to indicate when here, he certainly could have used πότε, which occurs in *NE* 1137a16, where it is contrasted with τίνι, and elsewhere—84 occurrences in the corpus overall. That Aristotle uses the when circumstance even though it may not be in his *NE* list will be clear from passages cited below. Aristotle, just as every other capable writer, has different ways of making the same point. He sometimes uses the genitive without ἕνεκα, for example, to indicate motive, as at *NE* 1137a1—ἢ χάριτος ἢ τιμωρίας—the so-called genitive of purpose, where the purpose may be to give either advantage or disadvantage. See Smyth 1984, 331, § 1408.

5 Word counts and texts have been retrieved from the *Thesaurus Linguae Graecae Digital Library*, ed. Maria C. Pantelia. University of California, Irvine. http://www.tlg.uci.edu. On Aristotle's intended audience see Mulhern 2007. While the cited article addresses only the intended audience of the *Politics*, Mulhern 2008 provides grounds for supposing that the same audience was intended in these other works.

and three passages with one occurrence each. These 29 occurrences overall represent about one fifth of those outside the *Problemata*.

What do πόνος and πονέω mean? The question arises not only because of their ambivalence elsewhere in Greek literature but also because Aristotle used them in quite different contexts. It is inviting to suppose that there may have been a core meaning to which all the others were related; but short of an explicit statement on the author's part which tells us so, that supposition would be difficult to support. An alternative is to suppose that Aristotle used the words with different meanings where the context required him to. So, for example, the sense might be identified as pain where it is being contrasted with pleasure; or it might be identified as exertion where it is being contrasted with rest; or as exercise in the sense of not just any exertion but of purposive exertion when he is discussing the athlete's preparation for competition, in one occurrence linked with mention of the training diet (ἀναγκοφαγία, 1339a6). Another option is that Aristotle sometimes may have had more than one sense in mind at any given time because of the conceptual connections in his own analysis or in that of some physician or anatomist or psychologist whose work he knew. So, for example, if exertion was thought to cause strain which causes pain, perhaps he sometimes had all three in mind. It is clear, though, that Aristotle used these expressions for both work with the mind, as English-speaking academics do when they say, 'I'm working on a paper' or 'I'm working on the virtues', and work with the body.

A credible answer to the question of meaning requires a thorough survey of the corpus and an interpretation of what Aristotle seems to intend with each occurrence, recognizing that in some cases there may not be enough evidence to decide. Then, as will appear in what follows, where these words are connected with central concepts in his practical writing, εὐδαιμονία, τὸ δίκαιον, ἀρετή and τὰ πολιτικά,[6] the translation must be made to fit the context. Extensions

6 The first three of these were discussed extensively in the still broadly influential older literature, especially in editions of the *Nicomachean Ethics* and in lectures on that work, such as those of H.H. Joachim, which were delivered from 1902 to 1917 and edited and published posthumously in the middle of the century (Joachim 1951). Εὐδαιμονία, traditionally rendered into English by 'happiness', is presented by Aristotle as the highest good attainable by action, with people agreeing on its name but disagreeing over what it is. Some recent controversy on it is summarized and discussed in Walker 2011, who argues that Aristotle's point depends on his use of κατά. A book of the *Ethics* is devoted to τὸ δίκαιον and the associated excellence of character; an important paper on its place in Aristotle's thought, which distinguishes it from the notion of a right as it has developed from late Roman times, is Schofield 1995–1996. Recent research on ἀρετή presents it as excellence wherever found, even in competitive athletics, though Aristotle often has excellence of intellect or of character in mind. The meaning

of the effort undertaken in this chapter should be similarly complete in their examinations of, for example, ἐργασία and ἐργάζομαι, which occur 79 times and 107 times respectively in the corpus.

2 Πόνος and εὐδαιμονία

In the *NE*, two passages addressing εὐδαιμονία stand out—one in Book 1 and one in Book 10. Aristotle tells us expressly in Book 1 that it is for the sake of this (ταύτης γὰρ χάριν), i.e., εὐδαιμονία, that we do everything else. Thus the 'why' circumstance is in play here, as is the 'who' circumstance (1101b31–1102a10, with occurrences boldfaced at 1101b35 and 1102a8, trans. Ross):

> Praise is appropriate to excellence; for as a result of excellence men tend to do noble deeds (*encomia* are bestowed on acts, whether of the body or of the soul—but perhaps nicety in these matters is more proper to **those who have made a study** of *encomia*);[7] but to us it is clear from what has been said that happiness is among the things that are prized and complete. It seems to be so also from the fact that it is a first principle; for it is for the sake of this that we all do everything else, and the first principle and cause of good is, we claim, something prized and divine.
>
> Since happiness is an activity of soul in accordance with complete excellence, we must consider the nature of excellence; for perhaps we shall thus see better the nature of happiness. The true student of politics, too, is thought **to have studied** this above all things; for he wishes to make his fellow citizens good and obedient to the laws.
>
> ὁ μὲν γὰρ ἔπαινος τῆς ἀρετῆς· πρακτικοὶ γὰρ τῶν καλῶν ἀπὸ ταύτης· τὰ δ' ἐγκώμια τῶν ἔργων ὁμοίως καὶ τῶν σωματικῶν καὶ τῶν ψυχικῶν. ἀλλὰ ταῦτα μὲν

---

of τὰ πολιτικά, which is an old title, according to Diogenes Laertius, seems to have received less attention than the other three, even in Newman's edition of the *Politics*. LSJ and Montanari both make clear, however, that πολιτικός indicates relation to a citizen or citizens, as one would expect from the word formation; and so, used as a substantive in the neuter plural, it should indicate the things related to the citizen. As a title, τὰ πολιτικά breaks with the titling tradition of Critias, Xenophon, and Plato, though it fits the contents of the *Politics* quite well, where Aristotle builds up to the definition of the citizen simply speaking in 1275a19, having defined the city as a certain multitude of citizens in 1274b41, and goes on to discuss other things related to the citizen, as will be seen below.

7 Perhaps including himself. See *Rhetorica* 1367b26–36.

> ἴσως οἰκειότερον ἐξακριβοῦν τοῖς περὶ τὰ ἐγκώμια πεπονημένοις· ἡμῖν δὲ δῆλον ἐκ τῶν εἰρημένων ὅτι ἐστὶν ἡ εὐδαιμονία τῶν τιμίων καὶ τελείων. ἔοικε δ' οὕτως ἔχειν καὶ διὰ τὸ εἶναι ἀρχή· ταύτης γὰρ χάριν τὰ λοιπὰ πάντα πάντες πράττομεν, τὴν ἀρχὴν δὲ καὶ τὸ αἴτιον τῶν ἀγαθῶν τίμιόν τι καὶ θεῖον τίθεμεν.
>
> Ἐπεὶ δ' ἐστὶν ἡ εὐδαιμονία ψυχῆς ἐνέργειά τις κατ' ἀρετὴν τελείαν, περὶ ἀρετῆς ἐπισκεπτέον ἂν εἴη· τάχα γὰρ οὕτως ἂν βέλτιον καὶ περὶ τῆς εὐδαιμονίας θεωρήσαιμεν. δοκεῖ δὲ καὶ ὁ κατ' ἀλήθειαν πολιτικὸς περὶ ταύτην μάλιστα πεπονῆσθαι· βούλεται γὰρ τοὺς πολίτας ἀγαθοὺς ποιεῖν καὶ τῶν νόμων ὑπηκόους.

Here Aristotle's language means that the one who genuinely is concerned with making the citizens good and obedient to the laws has worked at this, that is, εὐδαιμονία, which includes ἀρετή, above all. In the second occurrence, Ross's rendering 'study' probably has the broader sense of making an effort rather than the narrower one of thinking on or pondering something. Certainly the examples which Aristotle goes on immediately to give, the lawgivers of the Cretans and of the Lacedaemonians, did more than just ponder, though we may presume that their working at εὐδαιμονία included study in this sense also, since their aim was to fashion behaviour of a certain kind—to make the citizens good and obedient to the laws. For the κατ' ἀλήθειαν πολιτικός (the who circumstance) Aristotle is recommending a clear purpose (the why circumstance). As he says, it is clear to us—ἡμῖν δὲ δῆλον—why the πολιτικός should work on εὐδαιμονία. Thus, this passage illustrates the who and why circumstances.

It is arguable that Aristotle keeps εὐδαιμονία in view throughout the *NE* as the purpose of the πολιτικός whom he is addressing, even though he must devote much of his time to notions that are not quite so fundamental. And so it is not surprising that he comes back to treat it at length in Book 10, wrapping up loose ends or answering questions or addressing objections. He restates, if with somewhat different language, the point he has made in Book 1: it is for the sake of this that we all do everything else (ταύτης γὰρ χάριν τὰ λοιπὰ πάντα πάντες πράττομεν). But here his intent seems a bit different. While speaking to the same audience, he wants to contrast the purpose of the κατ' ἀλήθειαν πολιτικός with that of the tyrant who seeks εὐδαιμονία in amusement. Amusement ought to be pursued not for its own sake but because it is necessary for relaxation; and relaxation, Aristotle says, is necessary so that one may return to work. His point is that the purpose of work is important; and this circumstance, the purpose, helps one evaluate whether working is appropriate or not. He explains further that amusement seems to be for the sake of rest, and that those who are unable to work continuously need rest so that they can work more. As he says (1176b27–1177a1, occurrences marked in 1176b32 and 35, trans. Ross),

> Happiness, therefore, does not lie in amusement; it would, indeed, be strange if the end were amusement, and one were to take trouble and suffer hardship all one's life in order to amuse oneself. For, in a word, everything that we choose we choose for the sake of something else—except happiness, which is an end. Now to exert oneself and **work** for the sake of amusement seems silly and utterly childish. But to amuse oneself in order that one may exert oneself, as Anacharsis puts it, seems right; for amusement is a sort of relaxation, and we need relaxation because we cannot **work** continuously. Relaxation, then, is not an end; for it is taken for the sake of activity.
>
> οὐκ ἐν παιδιᾷ ἄρα ἡ εὐδαιμονία· καὶ γὰρ ἄτοπον τὸ τέλος εἶναι παιδιάν, καὶ πραγματεύεσθαι καὶ κακοπαθεῖν τὸν βίον ἅπαντα τοῦ παίζειν χάριν. ἅπαντα γὰρ ὡς εἰπεῖν ἑτέρου ἕνεκα αἱρούμεθα πλὴν τῆς εὐδαιμονίας· τέλος γὰρ αὕτη. σπουδάζειν δὲ καὶ πονεῖν παιδιᾶς χάριν ἠλίθιον φαίνεται καὶ λίαν παιδικόν. παίζειν δ' ὅπως σπουδάζῃ, κατ' Ἀνάχαρσιν, ὀρθῶς ἔχειν δοκεῖ· ἀναπαύσει γὰρ ἔοικεν ἡ παιδιά, ἀδυνατοῦντες δὲ συνεχῶς πονεῖν ἀναπαύσεως δέονται. οὐ δὴ τέλος ἡ ἀνάπαυσις· γίνεται γὰρ ἕνεκα τῆς ἐνεργείας.

One is not advised to work for the sake of amusement, but one might be advised to take amusement by way of rest for the sake of further work, here described as activity (ἕνεκα τῆς ἐνεργείας). The why and when circumstances especially are in play here.

3 Πόνος and τὸ δίκαιον

Six of the seven occurrences in the *Magna Moralia* are found in one connected passage on justice as involving proportional equality (equality of ratios), and they all are perfect active participles. Aristotle has given the pertinent circumstance for this discussion of πόνος just above in 1193b32–36 (trans. Stock):

> Since, then, justice consists in just and equal dealing and in a mean, we must notice that the just is said to be just as between certain persons, and the equal is a relation between certain persons, and the mean is a mean for certain persons; so that justice and the just will have relation to certain persons and be between certain persons.
>
> Ἐπεὶ οὖν ἡ δικαιοσύνη ἐν δικαίῳ καὶ ἐν ἴσῳ καὶ ἐν μεσότητι, ⟨καὶ⟩ τὸ μὲν δίκαιόν [ἐν] τισι λέγεται δίκαιον, τὸ δὲ ἴσον ἔν τισιν ἴσον, τὸ δὲ μέσον τισὶ μέσον· ὥστε ἡ δικαιοσύνη καὶ τὸ δίκαιον ἔσται καὶ πρός τινας καὶ ἐν τισίν.

Here ἐν with the indefinite in the dative plural corresponds to the interrogative ἐν τίνι at *NE* 1111a4 in Aristotle's list of circumstances, rendered by Burnet as 'the object'—that is, the object of the just act, as opposed to the subject; and, as in 1277b6, two expressions are used—not only the dative but also πρός with the accusative.[8] Aristotle is pointing out that what is just in relation to one individual, say a creditor, might not be just in relation to another individual, say a debtor, as well as that more than one individual will be in question in matters of justice. One might call this the whom circumstance.[9] Aristotle apparently is advising his audience on justice in distribution. The passage under consideration follows immediately at 1193b36–1194a6, with occurrences marked in 1194a2, twice in 3, 4, and twice in 5 (trans. Stock):

> Since, then, the just is equal, the proportionally equal will be just. Now proportion implies four terms at least; for as *A* is to *B*, *C* is to *D*. For instance, it is proportional that he who has much should contribute much, and that he who has little should contribute little; again, in the same way, that **he who has worked** much should receive much, and that **he who has worked** little should receive little. But as **the man who has worked** is to **the man who has not worked**, so is the much to the little; and as **the man who has worked** is to the much, so is **the man who has not worked** to the little.

> Ἐπεὶ οὖν ἐστι τὸ δίκαιον ἴσον, καὶ τὸ τῷ ἀνάλογον ἴσον δίκαιον ἂν εἴη. τὸ δ' ἀνάλογον ἐν τέτταρσι γίνεται ἐλαχίστοις· ὡς γὰρ τὸ Α πρὸς τὸ Β, τὸ Γ πρὸς τὸ Δ. οἷον ἀνάλογόν ἐστιν τὸν τὰ πολλὰ κεκτημένον πολλὰ εἰσφέρειν, τὸν δὲ τὰ ὀλίγα κεκτημένον ὀλίγα· πάλιν ὁμοίως **τὸν** μὲν πολλὰ **πεπονηκότα** πολλὰ λαμβάνειν, **τὸν** δὲ ὀλίγα **πεπονηκότα** ὀλίγα λαμβάνειν. ὡς δὲ ἔχει **ὁ πεπονηκὼς** πρὸς **τὸν μὴ πεπονηκότα**, οὕτω τὰ πολλὰ πρὸς τὰ ὀλίγα. ὡς δὲ **ὁ πεπονηκὼς** πρὸς τὰ πολλά, οὕτως **ὁ μὴ πεπονηκὼς** πρὸς τὰ ὀλίγα.[10]

This notion of proportion is used elsewhere by Aristotle in addressing justice, perhaps most fully in *NE* 5 (see, for example, 1134b4, where Aristotle uses πρός

8 Burnet 1900, 118.

9 Johnson 2005, 67 suggests that the dative in this kind of context should be treated as the *dativus commodi* or dative of advantage to indicate the 'beneficiary' of an action. The whom circumstance can include as well the *dativus incommodi* or dative of disadvantage, indicating not the beneficiary but the victim, as it were, as in *NE* 1132a12—ἡ ζημία τῷ παθόντι.

10 The *TLG* text reproduced here follows Susemihl and Armstrong.

with the accusative rather than ἐν with the dative). Someone who has worked much and has had a successful year may be called upon to contribute much in the way of service to the city and will receive much in the way of honour, whereas someone who has worked little and has not had a successful year will be called upon to contribute little in the way of service to the city and will receive little in the way of honour (see *Ath.* 7.3–4). This arrangement preserves proportional justice. It would be up to the πολιτικός to get things to turn out this way because it would be just (the why circumstance). Here work appears to be the basis of the merit which will govern distribution. The circumstances most obviously in play are the why and the whom. Aristotle is advising the official in charge of distribution to distribute not the same to all, without regard to circumstances, but to each according to merit for the sake of making a just distribution.

4 Πόνος and ἀρετή

The *Eudemian Ethics* contains two passages on ἀρετή which stand out, both with multiple occurrences. In 1220a13–15, which precedes the first of these passages by just a few lines, Aristotle introduces a new division of his discussion—what excellence of character is, how many parts it has, and through what it comes to be. After a few preliminary remarks, he begins with the last of these three, where it is taken for granted that the why for the κατ' ἀλήθειαν πολιτικός (the why and who circumstances) is to produce excellence of character in the citizens, as in *NE* 1102a8 above (1220a22–28), observing that the best disposition comes to be through the best (causes). He explains that the best things are done through the excellence of each thing, as the best exercises (πόνοι) and nourishment are those through which a good condition of the body comes to be, and that through a good condition of the body people exert themselves (πονοῦσιν) best.

Aristotle goes on to observe that excellence comes to be in one way and passes away in another by these same things—that is, apparently, that the excellence of health will come to be if food is taken and exercises (the what circumstance) performed and weather enjoyed in one way, but will be destroyed if they are taken or performed or enjoyed in another way (πῶς μὲν γίνεται, πῶς δὲ φθείρεται, 1220a32). This clearly is the how circumstance, and it presupposes the why circumstance—that the purpose is to attain health. Aristotle here apparently is advising his audience about the behaviour to be encouraged, presumably among citizens (the who circumstance). Solomon gives 'weather' apparently in the sense of 'season', but 'time' might be more to the point (the when circumstance). Health is an analogue here; and as is clear from a38–39, Aristotle is making his argument about excellence of character. The circumstances envisaged here include the who, what, why, how and when.

When Aristotle comes to the parts of excellence (the second item in his new division), in this case the part which is courage, he has it in mind that the πολιτικός will be seeking to have courage come to be in the citizens. Before Aristotle can get very far with this project, however, he has to make clear what he is talking about, which would not always be clear from common usage, as in the cases of those who are disposed to die but from an ignoble purpose (1229b34–1230a2, occurrences marked at 1229b39, 1230a1, trans. Solomon):

> For if dying were pleasant, the profligate would have often died because of his incontinence, just as now—since what causes death is pleasant though not death itself—many knowingly incur death through their incontinence, but none of them would be thought brave even if they do it with perfect readiness to die. Nor is a man brave if he seeks death to avoid **trouble**, as many do; to use Agathon's words: 'Bad men too weak for **toil** are in love with death.'

> εἰ γὰρ ἦν ἡδὺ τὸ ἀποθνήσκειν, πολλάκις ἂν δι' ἀκρασίαν ἀπέθνησκον οἱ ἀκόλαστοι, ὥσπερ καὶ νῦν αὐτοῦ μὲν τοῦ ἀποθνήσκειν οὐκ ὄντος ἡδέος, τῶν ποιητικῶν δ' αὐτοῦ, πολλοὶ δι' ἀκρασίαν περιπίπτουσιν εἰδότες, ὧν οὐθεὶς ⟨ἂν⟩ ἀνδρεῖος εἶναι δόξειεν, εἰ καὶ πάνυ ἑτοίμως ἀποθνήσκειν. οὔτ' εἰ φεύγοντες **τὸ πονεῖν**, ὅπερ πολλοὶ ποιοῦσιν, οὐδὲ τῶν τοιούτων οὐδεὶς ἀνδρεῖος, καθάπερ καὶ Ἀγάθων φησὶ "φαῦλοι βροτῶν γὰρ **τοῦ πονεῖν** ἡσσώμενοι, θανεῖν ἐρῶσιν."

Here there are examples of having purposes other than the noble, and so not courageous, which lead to death even though they are within one's own power. In this discussion of courage, the ἕνεκα τίνος is the circumstance mainly in question. Why should fatal work be done if it is to count as courageous? Not because it is pleasant, not because one is too weak for other work, but because it is noble, as Aristotle will point out elsewhere, as in the *Eudemian Ethics* 1229a4. The appropriate purpose is required for the instance of work or pattern of work to be appropriate. The infinitive is used in both occurrences here as a noun, with the article, as sometimes elsewhere, as at *Problemata* 868b12.[11] Since the quotation from Agathon is meant to clarify what precedes, both occurrences of

11 There are 35 other occurrences of the infinitive in the corpus besides these two.

πονεῖν probably should be translated in the same way. The circumstance mainly in view here is the why.

Aristotle associates these concepts of fear and confidence, pleasure and pain with one another elsewhere as well. In *NE* 1117b5, for example, he is discussing courage in connection with fear and confidence, pleasure and pain. Courage, he notes, is associated with pain.[12] The end corresponding to courage seems sweet, but the end is obscured by the things around it, as in athletic contests. The things around it, signified by ἐν τούτοις (1117a31), apparently are among the circumstances as the Greeks would speak of them—the pain of being struck and the labour of training for boxers, in this case. Aristotle's example of the ἕνεκα τίνος here is the reward of victory—the wreath and the honours.

5 Πόνος and τὰ πολιτικά

The *Politics* contains more passages with multiple occurrences than any of the other works of guidance, and treating these occurrences will require additional space. The work of the citizen is one of the things related to the citizen—τὰ πολιτικά—and so it is addressed here. Aristotle will distinguish it from, for example, the work of the competitive athlete, who requires a kind of body and a kind of regimen different from those of the citizen.[13]

In Book 2, Aristotle is criticizing Socrates on the sharing of possessions in the *Republic*. He will go on to point out that on the whole it is hard to live together and to share all human things. This situation he considers elsewhere also (see *MM* 1193b36–1194a6 above) in discussing proportional justice. As he says here (1263a11–15), among those who are not equal but unequal in rewards and tasks, there must be claims against those who enjoy or get much while working (πονοῦντας) little by those who get less and work (πονοῦσιν) more.

Although Jowett renders ἐγκλήματα γίνεσθαι by 'complains', the sense seems to be that claims will be made, as in claims at law. It appears that the claims might be just for at least some of those who are making them, given who they are—those who work more and get less. This is the who circumstance. The who circumstance is important in this passage, as is the why: the aim of the πολιτικός will be to see that justice is restored to the parties and that claims are minimized.

12 D. Charles 1995, 144–147.

13 On citizens and athletes: Smith 2018, 217, offers a table of possible cases of athletes' change of citizenship or double citizenship and observes that some colonial cities of Sicily and Southern Italy may have recruited successful athletes from older cities (224).

In Book 7, Aristotle concerns himself with the making of the citizens, giving his own view of a topic treated in Plato's *Statesman* 310b10–311c6. Although some of the occurrences of πόνος here are found in passages with only one occurrence and do not fall into one continuous discussion, they develop different sides of the same subject and gain from being arranged according to the setting of the household, the preparation of the parents, and the stages in the development of the citizen child in the household, as the *Oeconomica* suggests (1343b15–23, occurrence marked in 1343b22, trans. Forster):

> In the civilized and more intelligent animals the bond of unity is more complex (for in them we see more mutual help and goodwill and co-operation), above all in the case of man, because the female and the male co-operate to ensure not merely existence but a good life. And the production of children is not only a way of serving nature but also of seeking advantage; for the **trouble** which parents bestow upon their helpless children when they are themselves vigorous is repaid to them in old age when they are helpless [unable to work] by their children, who are then in their full vigour.
>
> ἐν δὲ τοῖς ἡμέροις αἱ φρονιμωτέροις διήρθρωται μᾶλλον (φαίνονται γὰρ μᾶλλον βοήθειαι γινόμεναι καὶ εὔνοιαι καὶ συνεργίαι ἀλλήλοις)· ἐν ἀνθρώπῳ δὲ μάλιστα, ὅτι οὐ μόνον τοῦ εἶναι, ἀλλὰ καὶ τοῦ εὖ εἶναι συνεργὰ ἀλλήλοις τὸ θῆλυ καὶ τὸ ἄρρεν ἐστί. Καὶ ἡ τῶν τέκνων κτῆσις οὐ λειτουργίας ἕνεκεν τῇ φύσει μόνον οὖσα τυγχάνει, ἀλλὰ καὶ ὠφελείας· ἃ γὰρ ἂν δυνάμενοι εἰς ἀδυνάτους πονήσωσι, πάλιν κομίζονται παρὰ δυναμένων ἀδυνατοῦντες ἐν τῷ γήρᾳ.

This is a case in which πόνος is appropriate for those in the household (the who circumstance) at different times because of their different ages (the when circumstance).

In the last chapters—16 and 17—of Book 7, Aristotle appears to be working from a sort of outline, reflecting his concern for the when circumstance, which outline he then fills in with details (1334b29–1336a26, occurrence marked in 1336a25, trans. Jowett):

> Since the legislator should begin by considering how the bodies of the children whom he is rearing may be as good as possible, his first care will be about marriage—at what age should his citizens marry, and who are fit to marry? … What constitution in the parent is most advantageous to the offspring is a subject which we will consider more carefully when we speak of the education of children, and we will only make a

> few general remarks at present. … After the children have been born, the manner of rearing them may be supposed to have a great effect on their bodily strength. … The next period lasts to the age of five; during this no demand should be made upon the child for study or **labour**, lest its growth be impeded; …
>
> Εἴπερ οὖν ἀπ' ἀρχῆς τὸν νομοθέτην ὁρᾶν δεῖ ὅπως βέλτιστα τὰ σώματα γένηται τῶν τρεφομένων, πρῶτον μὲν ἐπιμελητέον περὶ τὴν σύζευξιν, πότε καὶ ποίους τινὰς ὄντας χρὴ ποιεῖσθαι πρὸς ἀλλήλους τὴν γαμικὴν ὁμιλίαν. … ποίων δέ τινων τῶν σωμάτων ὑπαρχόντων μάλιστ' ἂν ὄφελος εἴη τοῖς γεννωμένοις, ἐπιστήσασι μὲν μᾶλλον λεκτέον ἐν τοῖς περὶ τῆς παιδονομίας, τύπῳ δὲ ἱκανὸν εἰπεῖν καὶ νῦν. … Γενομένων δὲ τῶν τέκνων οἴεσθαι δεῖ μεγάλην εἶναι διαφορὰν πρὸς τὴν τῶν σωμάτων δύναμιν τὴν τροφήν, ὁποία τις ἂν ᾖ. … τὴν δ' ἐχομένην ταύτης ἡλικίαν μέχρι πέντε ἐτῶν, ἣν οὔτε πω πρὸς μάθησιν καλῶς ἔχει προσάγειν οὐδεμίαν οὔτε πρὸς ἀναγκαίους **πόνους**, ὅπως μὴ τὴν αὔξησιν ἐμποδίζωσιν, …

The purpose of having intercourse (the why circumstance) is to produce the best bodies for citizens (the whom circumstance), which Aristotle connects with the age of childbearing (the when circumstance). He sees that in cities where the citizens marry too young, the young women labour more and more of them perish. Here is a case in which the labour should be avoided for the sake of the young women as well as for that of the children. He fills in the details this way (1335a11–22, marked at 18, trans. Jowett):

> The union of male and female when too young is bad for the procreation of children; in all other animals the offspring of the young are small and ill-developed, and with a tendency to produce female children, and therefore also in man, as is proved by the fact that in those cities in which men and women are accustomed to marry young, the people are small and weak; in childbirth also younger women **suffer** more, and more of them die; some persons say that this was the meaning of the response once given to the Troezenians—the oracle really meant that many died because they married too young; it had nothing to do with the gathering of the harvest.
>
> ἔστι δ' ὁ τῶν νέων συνδυασμὸς φαῦλος πρὸς τὴν τεκνοποιίαν· ἐν γὰρ πᾶσι ζῴοις ἀτελῆ τὰ τῶν νέων ἔκγονα, καὶ θηλυτόκα μᾶλλον καὶ μικρὰ τὴν μορφήν, ὥστ' ἀναγκαῖον ταὐτὸ τοῦτο συμβαίνειν καὶ ἐπὶ τῶν ἀνθρώπων. τεκμήριον δέ· ἐν ὅσαις γὰρ τῶν πόλεων ἐπιχωριάζει τὸ νέους συζευγνύναι καὶ νέας, ἀτελεῖς καὶ μικροὶ τὰ σώματά εἰσιν. ἔτι δὲ ἐν τοῖς τόκοις αἱ νέαι **πονοῦσί** τε μᾶλλον καὶ δια-

> φθείρονται πλείους· διὸ καὶ τὸν χρησμὸν γενέσθαι τινές φασι διὰ τοιαύτην αἰτίαν τοῖς Τροιζηνίοις, ὡς πολλῶν διαφθειρομένων διὰ τὸ γαμίσκεσθαι τὰς νεωτέρας, ἀλλ' οὐ πρὸς τὴν τῶν καρπῶν κομιδήν.

When he comes to the details of the constitution of the parents, he has this to say (1335b5–12, marked at 1335b8 and twice at 9, trans. Jowett):

> The constitution of an athlete is not suited to the life of a citizen, or to health, or to the procreation of children, any more than the valetudinarian or exhausted constitution, but one which is in a mean between them. A man's constitution should be **inured to labour**, but not [**inured**] **to labour** which is excessive or of one sort only, such as is practised by athletes; he should be capable of all the actions of a freeman. These remarks apply equally to both parents.

> οὔτε γὰρ ἡ τῶν ἀθλητῶν χρήσιμος ἕξις πρὸς πολιτικὴν εὐεξίαν οὐδὲ πρὸς ὑγίειαν καὶ τεκνοποιίαν, οὔτε ἡ θεραπευτικὴ καὶ κακοπονητικὴ λίαν, ἀλλ' ἡ μέση τούτων. **πεπονημένην** μὲν οὖν ἔχειν δεῖ τὴν ἕξιν, **πεπονημένην** δὲ **πόνοις** μὴ βιαίοις, μηδὲ πρὸς ἓν μόνον, ὥσπερ ἡ τῶν ἀθλητῶν ἕξις, ἀλλὰ πρὸς τὰς τῶν ἐλευθερίων πράξεις. ὁμοίως δὲ δεῖ ταῦτα ὑπάρχειν ἀνδράσι καὶ γυναιξίν.

Here the who, what and why circumstances all come into play. The who is the citizen rather than the athlete; what is advised would be different if the who were the athlete. The citizen, whether male or female, must pay attention to what will be beneficial for citizen children. The what is the exercise—purposive exercise but not violent exercise nor exercise which would develop only one part of the body, since it has the health of the citizen child in mind (the why circumstance).[14] In place of 'inured to labour' one might use 'trained by labour' for the participle, as suggested by LSJ. This passage illustrates Aristotle's use of an infrequent compound—κακοπονητική.

He is concerned also with what happens after the citizen children are born. As he says at 1336a3–5 (trans. Jowett), quoted above,

> After the children have been born, the manner of rearing them may be supposed to have a great effect on their bodily strength.

14 Newman observes *ad.* 5: 'What Plato objects to in athletes, however, is their sleepiness and inability to stand the rapid changes of diet which are inseparable from a soldier's life, whereas Aristotle rather objects to the tendencies impressed on their constitution by severe toil of one monotonous kind.' Newman 1887–1902, 3, 470.

With respect to the period of infancy, he says at 1336a26–39 (one occurrence marked at 38, trans. Jowett):

> there should be sufficient motion to prevent the limbs from being inactive. This can be secured, among other ways, by play, but the play should not be vulgar or tiring or effeminate. The Directors of Education, as they are termed, should be careful what tales or stories the children hear, for all such things are designed to prepare the way for the business of later life, and should be for the most part imitations of the occupations which they will hereafter pursue in earnest. Those are wrong who in their *Laws* attempt to check the loud crying and screaming of children, for these contribute towards their growth, and, in a manner, exercise their bodies. Straining the voice has a strengthening effect similar to that produced by the retention of the breath in violent **exertions.**
>
> δεῖ τοσαύτης τυγχάνειν κινήσεως ὥστε διαφεύγειν τὴν ἀργίαν τῶν σωμάτων· ἣν χρὴ παρασκευάζειν καὶ δι' ἄλλων πράξεων καὶ διὰ τῆς παιδιᾶς. δεῖ δὲ καὶ τὰς παιδιὰς εἶναι μήτε ἀνελευθέρους μήτε ἐπιπόνους μήτε ἀνειμένας. καὶ περὶ λόγων δὲ καὶ μύθων, ποίους τινὰς ἀκούειν δεῖ τοὺς τηλικούτους, ἐπιμελὲς ἔστω τοῖς ἄρχουσιν οὓς καλοῦσι παιδονόμους. πάντα γὰρ δεῖ τὰ τοιαῦτα προοδοποιεῖν πρὸς τὰς ὕστερον διατριβάς· διὸ τὰς παιδιὰς εἶναι δεῖ τὰς πολλὰς μιμήσεις τῶν ὕστερον σπουδαζομένων. τὰς δὲ διατάσεις τῶν παίδων καὶ τοὺς κλαυθμοὺς οὐκ ὀρθῶς ἀπαγορεύουσιν οἱ κωλύοντες ἐν τοῖς νόμοις· συμφέρουσι γὰρ πρὸς αὔξησιν· γίγνεται γὰρ τρόπον τινὰ γυμνασία τοῖς σώμασιν· ἡ γὰρ τοῦ πνεύματος κάθεξις ποιεῖ τὴν ἰσχὺν τοῖς **πονοῦσιν**, ὃ συμβαίνει καὶ τοῖς παιδίοις διατεινομένοις.

Here there is another compound—ἐπιπόνους, and the who and the when are both in play, since crying is appropriate for children of a certain age.

Aristotle expatiates on the αὔξησις or growth of the citizen at various stages in a way that illustrates well the when circumstance along with the who, what, and how (1338b38–1339a10, occurrences marked at 1338b41, 1339a6, 9, 10, trans. Jowett):

> It is an admitted principle that gymnastic exercises should be employed in education, and that for children they should be of a lighter kind, avoiding severe diet or painful **toil**, lest the growth of the body be impaired. The evil of excessive training in early years is strikingly proved by the example of the Olympic victors, for not more than two or three of them have gained a prize both as boys and as men; their early training and severe

> gymnastic exercises exhausted their constitutions. When boyhood is over, three years should be spent in other studies; the period of life which follows may then be devoted to **hard exercise** and strict diet. Men ought not to **labour** at the same time with their minds and with their bodies; for the two kinds of **labour** are opposed to one another; the **labour** of the body impedes the mind, and the **labour** of the mind the body.
>
> ὅτι μὲν οὖν χρηστέον τῇ γυμναστικῇ, καὶ πῶς χρηστέον, ὁμολογούμενόν ἐστιν (μέχρι μὲν γὰρ ἥβης κουφότερα γυμνάσια προσοιστέον, τὴν βίαιον τροφὴν καὶ **τοὺς** πρὸς ἀνάγκην **πόνους** ἀπείργοντας, ἵνα μηθὲν ἐμπόδιον ᾖ πρὸς τὴν αὔξησιν· σημεῖον γὰρ οὐ μικρὸν ὅτι δύνανται τοῦτο παρασκευάζειν, ἐν γὰρ τοῖς ὀλυμπιονίκαις δύο τις ἂν ἢ τρεῖς εὕροι τοὺς αὐτοὺς νενικηκότας ἄνδρας τε καὶ παῖδας, διὰ τὸ νέους ἀσκοῦντας ἀφαιρεῖσθαι τὴν δύναμιν ὑπὸ τῶν ἀναγκαίων γυμνασίων· ὅταν δ' ἀφ' ἥβης ἔτη τρία πρὸς τοῖς ἄλλοις μαθήμασι γένωνται, τότε ἁρμόττει καὶ **τοῖς πόνοις** καὶ ταῖς ἀναγκοφαγίαις καταλαμβάνειν τὴν ἐχομένην ἡλικίαν· ἅμα γὰρ τῇ τε διανοίᾳ καὶ τῷ σώματι διαπονεῖν οὐ δεῖ, τοὐναντίον γὰρ ἑκάτερος ἀπεργάζεσθαι πέφυκε **τῶν πόνων**, ἐμποδίζων ὁ μὲν τοῦ σώματος **πόνος** τὴν διάνοιαν ὁ δὲ ταύτης τὸ σῶμα).

Although the phrase πῶς χρηστέον of line 38 does not appear clearly in Jowett's translation, it is Aristotle's signal that he will be considering how exercise is to be used as part of a good upbringing (the how circumstance), and his account is that it has to be used differently at different stages of development (the when circumstance—μέχρι μὲν γὰρ ἥβης, ὅταν δ' ἀφ' ἥβης ἔτη τρία).

Aristotle counsels moderation in both diet and exercise in youth so that nothing will be a hindrance in the way of growth. In this discussion, the who is involved—the citizen—along with the what, which is the intensity of exercise, and the when, since timing is crucial in the development of the citizen's body. Continuing this discussion, Aristotle recommends that, three years after puberty, it is appropriate to occupy the next period of life with exercises and a training diet. He goes on to reinforce his position by pointing out that it is necessary not to exercise with the mind and the body completely at the same time, 'for the two kinds of labour are opposed to one another, the labour of the body impedes the mind, and the labour of the mind the body.' Here the who, what, and when seem to answer the question how. Notable here is the use of another compound—διαπονεῖν. Gomperz used this text in revising 1252a33 (see below).

Since the use of leisure is an important part of the life of the citizen, Aristotle must address it, as he does (1337b34–1338a1, occurrences marked at 1337b38 and 40, trans. Jowett):

> And therefore the question must be asked, what ought we to do when at leisure? Clearly we ought not to be playing, for then play would be the end of life. But if this is inconceivable, and play is needed more amid serious occupations (ἐν ταῖς ἀσχολίαις) than at other times (for **he who is hard at work** has need of relaxation, and play gives relaxation, whereas occupation is always accompanied with **exertion** and effort), we should introduce amusements only at suitable times, and they should be our medicines, for the emotion which they create in the soul is a relaxation, and from the pleasure we obtain rest.
>
> ζητητέον ὅ τι δεῖ ποιοῦντας σχολάζειν. οὐ γὰρ δὴ παίζοντας· τέλος γὰρ ἀναγκαῖον εἶναι τοῦ βίου τὴν παιδιὰν ἡμῖν. εἰ δὲ τοῦτο ἀδύνατον, καὶ μᾶλλον ἐν ταῖς ἀσχολίαις χρηστέον ταῖς παιδιαῖς (ὁ γὰρ **πονῶν** δεῖται τῆς ἀναπαύσεως, ἡ δὲ παιδιὰ χάριν ἀναπαύσεώς ἐστιν· τὸ δ' ἀσχολεῖν συμβαίνει μετὰ **πόνου** καὶ συντονίας), διὰ τοῦτο δεῖ παιδιὰς εἰσάγεσθαι καιροφυλακοῦντας τὴν χρῆσιν, ὡς προσάγοντας φαρμακείας χάριν. ἄνεσις γὰρ ἡ τοιαύτη κίνησις τῆς ψυχῆς, καὶ διὰ τὴν ἡδονὴν ἀνάπαυσις.

In this passage, which addresses the why and the when, Aristotle is talking about what is appropriate for the working man (πονῶν) who might not be a citizen. This point may be obscured by Jowett's 'serious occupations', which might lead one to think of either philosophical or political work that would be appropriate to the citizens. Instead of merely effort here, συντονία suggests stretching or straining—effort, yes, but more than just a little effort.[15] Jowett conveys the sense of more than a little effort by rendering ὁ πονῶν by 'he who is hard at work'. Aristotle introduces the when circumstance here with διὰ τοῦτο δεῖ παιδιὰς εἰσάγεσθαι καιροφυλακοῦντας τὴν χρῆσιν, ὡς προσάγοντας φαρμακείας χάριν, which Simpson has rendered lucidly by 'we must, for this reason, introduce play [amusement] keeping a watchful eye on the opportune moment for using it, as if applying it for medicinal purposes'.[16] Aristotle's point is that

15 Aristotle appears to be contrasting ἄνεσις with συντονία. These words appear in both musical and anatomical contexts (the string of a lyre might be relaxed or stretched as might a tendon, where relaxing and stretching would be opposed movements) as well as in other contexts. Thus 'emotion' instead of 'motion' for κίνησις in 1337b42 appears to be a typographical error. As far back as Moerbeke, the rendering is *motus* or an equivalent. Newman 1887–1902, 3, 513 dealt with the text this way: '"for the movement of the soul to which we have referred" (that involved in play) "is [remedial in character, for it is] a relaxation of strain and a remission because of the pleasure which accompanies it [and only in place at times when there is strain]."'

16 Simpson 1997, 156.

παιδιά is not appropriate for a steady diet but for relief of a temporary condition. This passage will recall 1176b27–1177a1 (see above).

6 Discussion: Πόνος and φύσις

The foregoing are mainly the instances of guidance in the ethical and political works in which one finds multiple occurrences of πόνος and πονεῖν, along with a few others which are related closely to them. By way of summary, Aristotle gives a range of circumstances here, but he does not mention all the circumstances all the time, only those that are required to make his point. He does use the when circumstance where it is to the point. He shows little if any concern for the where circumstance, perhaps because, if citizens are in question, the likelihood is that the citizens will be operating in their own cities or with other citizens of their own cities; and so the where question is less likely to come up in considering whether an action is appropriate.

There remain passages which are notable for some other reason. One group of these consists of discussions of work in the development of the citizen. In considering the φύσις of the citizen by way of explaining the development of excellence of character, he notes that φύσις does not work the same way all the time. He is at pains to point out that, with respect to some things that develop φύσει, we carry away the abilities beforehand—that is, we acquire the actuality afterward. This is true of sight and hearing, as he says; the ability to hear or see does not require repeated listening or watching in order to develop (1103a26–31)—only, presumably, the growth and differentiation of sense organs in the embryo.[17] But with the excellences of character it is different; we acquire them by practising them beforehand, as strength comes to be by taking a great deal of food and submitting to many exercises. These of course are bodily exercises, and one can see here the connection of deliberate exercise with the training diet. Aristotle uses the comparison of virtues of character with bodily strength in explaining how these virtues are acquired. The pertinent text has an occurrence of πόνος in the sense of bodily exercise at 1104a32. The growth that matters occurs at different stages of development—embryonic for the sensory organs, in the early years of independent life for the virtues of character. Once the child is born, the kind of work or labour of mind or body which is appropriate depends very much on age; Aristotle is concerned that, while the child should not be given an opportunity to become lazy, the wrong regimen in child-

17 Oppenheimer 1975.

hood can obstruct the proper growth of the body and damage it even as, in the Spartan case, it can make behaviour bestial (see the passage in which πόνος occurs at 1338b13). The mixture of mental and bodily work needs to be superintended closely to fit the age of the child (see above on 1337b34–1338a1). His discussion here shows a strong interest in excellence of the body because of its importance to the citizen; he is aware that some work may damage the body and make someone unfit to do what citizens would be expected to do. This seems to be the issue, for example, in *Oeconomica* 1343b3–4, where Aristotle observes that the banausic arts make the bodies of those who practice them useless, which explains why he advises that the *banausoi* should not be citizens—a point made also in *Ecclesiasticus* 38.[18] This text also shows Aristotle's regard for excellence of the body, as in the case of the φύσει δοῦλος text at 1252a33—another single occurrence, though there has been some difference of opinion about whether there is an occurrence of πονέω here at all. The OCT prints πονεῖν, with which Ross gives '*scripsi*: ποιεῖν codd. *Γ*: διαπονεῖν Gomperz'. Dreizehnter follows the codices. In the note in which he suggested reading διαπονεῖν, Gomperz was using a comparison with 1339a7–8, where the language is similar and one finds διαπονεῖν though the point is different (see above).[19] It is worth noting that, in defining the φύσει δοῦλος as able to work with the body, Aristotle is defining him by an ability rather than by a disability. Working with the body in situations which do not require foresight may be good for those who are mature chronologically but lack foresight—better perhaps than not working at all—and may actually achieve a kind of excellence. The circumstance principally in question here would be the who circumstance.

7 Epilogue

In this chapter I have offered a fresh account of Aristotle's approach to evaluating instances and patterns of labour based on the occurrences of πόνος and πονέω in connection with some of his main practical concepts in the Corpus Aristotelicum. Although in his physical works these expressions have a range of meanings, as others have seen, in the works in which he is advising the κατ' ἀλήθειαν πολιτικός they typically indicate work of some kind, either bodily or intellectual, both of which he regards as able to be excellent. Aristotle recognizes two main excellences of intellect which he and we might be inclined to

18 See Newman 1887–1902, 1, 104.
19 Gomperz 1912, I, 276–277.

associate with labour. The most obvious is τέχνη—the excellence concerned with making things, which for him covers a wider range of things than 'making' does in English idiom. He would be more likely to say, for example, that someone makes a house or a poem than we would. The other is φρόνησις, which is an excellence associated with doing things—a kind of activity which does not produce anything outside itself, such as conducting a campaign, which, as we might say, is over when one side wins. These excellences require a command of circumstances. My main finding is that his method of evaluating instances and patterns of labour depends upon circumstances, of which his most complete list is given in the *NE* 1111a3–5, though that list seems not to exhaust his inventory of circumstances, leaving out the when circumstance, which appears elsewhere, as well as the where circumstance. His reliance on the analytic framework of circumstances is as remarkable as his reliance on the more widely recognized analytic frameworks of predictables and predicaments elsewhere, since it suggests that, for him, knowing what work to perform requires more than can be captured by any single criterion or rule of action that might be prescribed no matter what the circumstances; in this respect, it is more nuanced, and perhaps more intellectually demanding, than the single-criterion approach familiar from some modern discussions of value.

Acknowledgements

My thanks are due to Rita Copeland for conversations on the history of the notion of circumstances, to Silvia Castelli for communications on organization of the chapter, and to the editors of this volume for their suggestions. I am responsible for any remaining shortcomings.

Bibliography

Applebaum, H. (1992). *The Concept of Work. Ancient, Medieval, and Modern.* Albany.

Barnes, J., ed. (1984). *The Complete Works of Aristotle*, 2 vols. Princeton.

Bodnár, I., ed. (2015). *The Aristotelian Problemata Physica.* Leiden.

Burnet, J. (1900). *The Ethics of Aristotle.* London.

Chantraine, P. (2009). *Dictionnaire étymologique de la langue grecque.* Paris.

Charles, D. (1995). Aristotle and Modern Realism. In: R.A. Heinaman, ed., *Aristotle and Moral Realism.* New York, pp. 135–172.

Dreizehnter, A. (1970). *Aristoteles' Politik.* Munich.

Finley, M. (1999). *The Ancient Economy.* Third Edition. Berkeley.

Garnsey, P., ed. (1980). *Non-Slave Labour in the Greco-Roman World*. Cambridge.

Gomperz, T. (1912). *Hellenika. eine auswahl philologischer und philosophiegeschichtlicher kleiner Schriften*, 2 vols. Leipzig.

Greenwood, L.H.G. (1909). *Aristotle Nicomachean Ethics. Book Six*. Cambridge.

Joachim, H.H. (1951). *Aristotle. The Nicomachean Ethics*. Ed. D.A. Rees. Oxford.

Johnson, M.R. (2005). *Aristotle on Teleology*. Oxford.

Jowett, B. (1885). *The Politics of Aristotle*, 2 vols. Oxford.

Lis, C. (2012). *Worthy Efforts. Attitudes to Work and Workers in Pre-Industrial Europe*. Boston.

Loraux, N. (1982). Sur quelques difficultés de la peine comme nom du travail. *Annali de Seminario di studi del mondo classico* 4(4), pp. 171–192.

Mayhew, R. (2011). *Aristotle. Problemata Physica*. Cambridge, MA.

Mayhew, R. (2015). *The Aristotelian Problemata physica. Philosophical and Scientific Investigations*. Leiden–Boston.

Mulhern, J.J. (2007). The *Aristē Politeia* and Aristotle's Intended Audience in the *Politica*. *Polis* 24, pp. 284–297.

Mulhern, J.J. (2008). Ethics, Morals, and the State: Rereading the Classical View. In: J.V. Ciprut, ed., *Ethics, Politics, and Democracy. From Primitive Principles to Prospective Practices*. Cambridge, MA, pp. 181–199.

Nederman, C.J. (2008). Men at Work: Poesis, Politics and Labour in Aristotle and Some Aristotelians. *Analyse & Kritik* 30, pp. 17–31.

Newman, W.L. (1887–1902). *The Politics of Aristotle*, 4 vols. Oxford.

Oppenheimer, J.M. (1975). When Sense and Life Begin: Background for a Remark in Aristotle's Politics. Population Policy in Plato and Aristotle. *Arethusa*, 8(2), pp. 331–343.

Owens, J. (1981). Aristotle on Leisure. *Canadian Journal of Philosophy*, 11(4), pp. 713–723.

Pellegrin, P. (2017). *L'Excellence menacée. Sur la philosophie politique d'Aristote*. Paris.

Robinson, R. (1962). *Aristotle's Politics. Books III and IV*. Oxford.

Ross, W.D. (1957). *Aristotelis Politica*. Oxford.

Schofield, M. (1995–1996). Sharing in the Constitution. *Review of Metaphysics* 49(4), pp. 831–858.

Simpson, P.L.P. (1997). *The Politics of Aristotle*. Chapel Hill–London.

Sloan, M.C. (2010). Aristotle's *Nicomachean Ethics* as the Original *Locus* for the *Septem Circumstantiae*. *CP*, 105(3), pp. 236–251.

Smith, N. (2018). Athletics and Citizenship. In: A. Duplouy and R. Brock, eds., *Defining Citizenship in Archaic Greece*. Oxford, pp. 189–225.

Smyth, H.W. (1984). *Greek Grammar*. Cambridge, MA.

Spiazzi, R.M. (1966). *S. Thomae Aquinatis in Octo Libros Politicorum Aristotelis Expositio*. Turin and Rome.

Van den Hoven, B. (1996). *Work in Ancient and Medieval Thought. Ancient Philosophers, Medieval Monks and Theologians and Their Concept of Work, Occupations and Technology*. Amsterdam.

Verboven, K. (2014). Attitudes to Work and Workers in Classical Greece and Rome. *Tijdschrift voor Sociale en Economische Geschiedenis*, 11(1), pp. 67–87.

Walker, M. (2011). Aristotle on Activity 'According to the Best and Most Final' Virtue. *Apeiron* 44(1), pp. 91–109

CHAPTER 4

Galen on Hands and the Teleology of Work

Ralph M. Rosen

1 Bodies Fitted Out for Work

It would be hard to find any humans who have not at some point in their lives stopped to ask why they have to work. The range of possible answers is broad: 'I need to work so I can earn money to survive', 'I work to keep busy', 'I work because it gives me pleasure', 'I work to help others', to name only a few. But other, more abstract antecedent questions might soon follow: is it a cosmic necessity that humans have to fill up their time on earth *doing something*, in an intentional way, in order to survive, to thrive, to be happy? Today we might ask, 'does our evolved primate sociality require some form of self-conscious, routinized exertion—something we call work—for survival?' Others, including many ancient Greeks, might simply ask, 'Were we put on this planet to work?' Is that what we are 'supposed' to do? Hesiod famously answered this question in *Works and Days* with a post-lapsarian moral imperative—humans were originally created in a mythical golden age to live at leisure, free of the necessity to work, but that age has passed and in the current iron age, as Hesiod notes, it is 'a reproach not to work' (ἀεργίη δέ τ'ὄνειδος, *WD* 311).[1]

Hesiod's account of the history of work implies that without divine intervention, humans are not in fact self-sustaining, either as isolated individuals or

---

1 Contrast another strand of Greek thought that offered a narrative of progress rather than Hesiodic decline. These anthropological (rather than mythical) accounts speculated about the conditions of human life in a primeval state which were imagined to offer a life governed largely by animal instinct and free from systematized and intentional 'work'. But unlike the easy-living of Hesiod's long-lost golden age, such a life offered suffering and misery, since humans, unlike (non-human) animals, were ill-suited to thrive in the world as they were physically and physiologically constituted. Only by exercising their rational capacities could they gradually discover *technai* which improved the quality of life. The trajectory was positive, but progress required constant work. Versions of such speculation about primitive humans can be found, e.g., in the Hippocratic *Ancient Medicine*, ch. 3; Plato, *Protagoras* 320c–323a, and Diod. Sic. *Hist.* 1.8.9. In Diodorus' account (first century BCE) of human development from a state of largely solitary misery to one of collective betterment, he notes the importance of discoveries made possible by the deployment specifically of speech, rationality and hands, a passage well aligned with Galen's anthropology in *UP*. See Rosen 2016, with further bibliography at 248, n. 11.

 | DOI:10.1163/9789004694965_005

in their attempt to live in groups. Hesiod's cosmic narrative, however, raises a more fundamental question that was also not lost on Greek thinkers: what is it about the biology of humans that makes them so ill-equipped to survive on instinct and physical makeup alone—*why* do they have such a physiology in the first place?

These are teleological questions that try to address why our bodies appear and behave as they do, and whether we can infer from them any predetermined guiding purpose. If, as it seems, humans cannot live without working, or we might say, working at living, does that mean that we should consider this 'deficiency' to be part of our nature? Are our bodies *designed* specifically to do the work we do, or do we do the work we do only as a function of what our bodies are capable of? The teleology of the human body interested Greek philosophers across the entire tradition, producing a range of theories along the way, but we find perhaps the most sustained and vivid treatment in Galen's large work in seventeen books, *The Function of the Parts of the Body* (often translated as *Usefulness of Parts* (here abbreviated *UP*), after the conventional Latin title, *De Usu Partium*), written in the late second century CE in several instalments.[2] There is no doubt about Galen's teleological foundation, since he is explicit about it repeatedly throughout the work—today we would categorize him as a proponent of 'intelligent design', intent on showing that 'nature' (φύσις) and the 'demiurge' (δημιουργός; Galen uses the two almost interchangeably) do nothing without skill and purpose, as can be inferred, he felt, from the study of the natural world in all its manifestations.[3]

In *UP*, Galen works through all the major parts of the body and their interactions, combining empirical observation with inferences about the underlying

---

2 Galen offers helpful detail in *On My Own Books* about the composition of *UP*. He composed the first book (our focus in this chapter) separately from the rest in ca. 165 CE, at the request of his friend and patron, the consul Boethus, during his first visit to Rome. The remaining sixteen books were completed in the early years after his return to Rome in 169. See *On My Own Books*, 16 K. (140 B-M) and 20 K. (143 B-M), and Boudon-Millot 2007, 190–191, 198–199. I have followed the Greek text of *UP* in Helmreich 1907, and English translations by May 1968, with occasional modifications.

3 On the Platonic background of Galen's Demiurge, see Rocca 2018, who discusses how Galen transformed Plato's Demiurge from a being whose primary function was limited to the creation of the rational (and immortal) part of human souls, into a more active, personalized being that approaches the kind of creative God associated with monotheistic religions (although cf. Moraux 1984, 762, n. 329). Galen's demiurge, i.e., 'offered the best way of showing that the organisation of the matter of living things is a deliberative and purposeful construct by a supremely rational entity', who was 'directly involved in the fabric of somatic creation' (Rocca 2018, 222). See further on Galen's demiurge and the teleology of *UP*: Moraux 1984, 762–767, Hankinson 2008, 225–229; also Schiefsky 2007, 371 and *passim*.

divine purpose of each, and following a consistent teleological principle, as he states at the opening of the work, that 'the body is the instrument of the soul', and the parts of one animal differ from those of another because nature has endowed each with a particular soul.[4] An animal's parts, in other words, exist as they are to serve the purpose that their nature requires. A horse, for example, is naturally fast, brave and proud, he says, and so it is 'provided [by Nature] with strong hoofs and adorned with a mane'. Galen's teleology amalgamates Platonic and Aristotelian strains—Aristotelian in its emphasis on the functionality and utility of the parts of the body, and Platonic in its insistence that, as products of a divine intelligence effectuated by a demiurge, they could be no better designed.[5]

Galen's combination of the two allows him to blend a naturalistic and phenomenological account of the human body's *capacity* to do the work it does (i.e., through the *functioning* of its parts to do the things necessary for the species to live) with a theological explanation for its perfection. But Galen is less clear about grander questions of cosmic purpose—final causes, in Aristotelian terms—such as *why* or 'for the sake of what' the Demiurge designed humans such that they have to work in the first place.[6] In this, Galen implicitly raises, but never quite poses, the question of why a Demiurge would design a human body that needs to work so hard, and indeed to suffer, just to survive in the world. In fact, it is never quite clear from *UP* what Galen would say is the *purpose* of human life that would account for the 'perfect' design of the human body; his discussion in *UP* is chiefly concerned with arguing for the perfect

4 On this 'teleological instrumentalism' in *UP* and its relation to the more materialistic determinism reflected in Galen's treatise *That the Capacities of the Soul Follow the Mixtures of the Body* (= *QAM*) see van der Eijk 2020. *QAM* appears, at any rate, to argue that human behaviour (as a function of a person's psychological state) is largely a function of the material conditions of the body. *UP* claims that the soul controls the body and uses it as an instrument (ὄργανον). Van de Eijk argues that *QAM* is less deterministic than might at first appear, in that individuals can always choose to alter their physiology (specifically the mixtures of their humoral qualities) in order to improve their health and happiness. This is consistent with the view in *UP* that the body is the 'instrument of the soul'. See also Hankinson 2016, 253–254 on the Aristotelianism behind Galen's speculation about the nature of the soul.

5 Plato's demiurge is an important force in his *Timaeus*, first mentioned in that work at 28a–b. On Galen's debt to Aristotelian functionalism, see Schiefsky 2007; Hankinson 2008, 225–229. On Galen's complicated relationship with Aristotle, see van der Eijk 2009 and Hankinson 2016.

6 There is a massive bibliography on Aristotelian teleology: particularly helpful are Cooper 1982; Balme 1987; Kosman 1987, 376–377; Hankinson 1989 (specifically in relation to Galen's teleology); Hankinson 1995, 127–135; Hankinson 1997, Hankinson 1998, 140–153; Johnson 2005; and Leunissen 2010, esp. 10–48.

functionality of body parts for performing what we infer they are supposed to do from our own observation and experience, not why it might be good, in a more cosmic sense, for humans to have that functionality in the first place.[7] Whether function is equivalent to 'purpose' is an ongoing matter of scholarly controversy,[8] but I would like to argue that Galen in fact comes close to conceptualizing, if only implicitly, the ultimate *purpose* of a human body's design as something we might call 'work'.

2 Galen on the Teleology of the Hand

My argument stems from a reading of the opening chapters of *UP* Book 1, which concerns the hand. Galen's decision to open the work with this particular body part is programmatic and reflects the special significance he places on this body part as the most emblematic of human nature and purpose. As he says in 1.2, echoing a variety of his philosophical predecessors,[9] 'the body is the instrument of the soul, and consequently animals differ greatly in respect to their parts because their souls also differ' (τὸ γὰρ σῶμα ταύτης ὄργανον καὶ διὰ τοῦτο

7 See Leunissen's formulation (2010, 211) of Aristotle's final cause as a 'good' that 'contributes to the existence, essence, or well-being of the whole of which it is part'. Why it might be good for that organism to exist in the first place is not especially clear either in Aristotle's or Galen's teleology. On the problems of Aristotle's use of axiological terminology ('the good', 'the best') in his teleological discussions, see Johnson 2005, 90–93.

8 Galen opens ch. 2 of *UP* Book 1 (1.1, 13 H.) saying that the 'usefulness' (χρεία) of the body parts 'is related to the soul': χρεία δ' αὐτῶν ἁπάντων (= all the body parts). He continues, 'for the body is the instrument of the soul ...': ἐστὶ τῇ ψυχῇ. τὸ γὰρ σῶμα ταύτης ὄργανον. On Galen's use of χρεία here, which May translates as 'usefulness', see May, 1968, 9: 'it does not mean function, as one might naturally suppose. Function is more nearly ἐνέργεια or "action" in Galen's terms ... The nearest Galen comes to an actual definition is in Book XVII [= 16.437,11. H.; IV. 346–347 K.], where he says that usefulness is the same as what is called utility (εὐχρηστίᾳ, serviceableness). Thus it is closely related to the final cause of Aristotle.' See now Rocca (forthcoming, with further bibliography): 'If *chreia* is difficult to render precisely into English, then it is because it is a placeholder for a number of coordinated, naturally occurring tasks (or fitting actions) that the body ... must perform to fulfil the requirement of a physiological organism.' Which is to say that sometimes 'function' is an appropriate translation for Galen's χρεία, sometimes 'usefulness', sometimes 'use'. See also Hankinson 1989, 217 n. 32: 'perhaps "function" is the least misleading general translation [of χρεία] in Galenic contexts.' On Aristotle's notion of functionality/utility, see, e.g., Korsgaard 2008, 129–150, esp. 130–134; Leunissen 2010; and Sharples 2017.

9 See e.g., Plato *Alc.* 130, a discussion in which Socrates tries to show that the soul is the body's 'user' (τὸ τῷ σώματι χρώμενον) and indeed that the soul 'is' a human (130c6). Rocca (forthcoming ad loc.) suggests that Aristotle's notion of the soul as the 'actuality' (ἐντελέχεια) of a body (*de An.* 412a22) lies behind Galen's formulation here.

πολὺ διενήνοχεν ἀλλήλων τὰ μόρια τῶν ζῴων, ὅτι καὶ αἱ ψυχαί, 1,13–16 H.), a general principle that prepares us for the long head-to-toe analysis that follows in *UP*. In beginning his discussion with the hand in particular, however, Galen stirs up some serious teleological trouble, especially in light of his attempt to draw analogies with the animal world. He continues at 1.2, 'For some animals are brave and others timid; some are wild and others tame … In every case the body is adapted to the character and faculties of the soul.' (τὰ μὲν γάρ ἐστιν ἄλκιμα, τὰ δὲ δειλά, τὰ δ' ἄγρια, τὰ δ'ἥμερα … πᾶσι δ' οὖν ἐπιτήδειον τὸ σῶμα τοῖς τῆς ψυχῆς ἤθεσί τε καὶ δυνάμεσιν, 1,16–18–12, 1–2 H.). This works well enough for Galen's assessment of animal natures: the horse is naturally swift and proud, he says, so it is provided with hoofs and a mane. Lions are brave and fierce, so they are given teeth and claws, and so on. He is leading up with these examples to the human hand, but the analogy with animals is awkward. We can observe, for example, that lions are fierce, then look at their claws, see how they work, and infer that claws exist so lions can perform their fierceness. Similarly, the horse, Galen notes, is 'equipped with[10] strong hoofs and a mane for truly it is a swift, proud animal and not faint-hearted' (ἵππῳ μὲν ἰσχυραῖς ὁπλαῖς καὶ χαίτῃ κεκοσμημένον, καὶ γὰρ ὠκὺ καὶ γαῦρον καὶ οὐκ ἄθυμον τὸ ζῷον, 2,2–4 H.). But saying that humans are 'equipped with' hands because they are rational creatures skips a step in the analogy. Horses cannot be swift without strong hoofs, but humans can be rational without having hands. With the horse, in other words, Galen arrives at the nature of the animal by observing the function of the hoof. In the case of humans, however, the observable function of the hand may *sometimes* be to serve as an *instrument* of rationality, but there is nothing about the hand's functionality as such that necessarily implies rationality.[11] While the horse's hoof directly accounts for its swiftness, hands do not directly account

10 Note the passive participle here: 'equipped with' seems a better translation than May's 'provided with' and 'adorned with' both of which she uses for κεκοσμημένον (i.e. 'The horse is provided with strong hoofs and adorned with a mane …'). While Galen does believe that the Demiurge is ultimately responsible for the form bodies take, the participle κεκοσμημένον takes no stand on how these animal bodies acquired these accoutrements.

11 Scientists still debate the evolutionary history of the hand's functionality across animal species, but of course in the non-teleological realm of modern evolutionary theory (in contrast to Galen's teleology), functionality emerges as part of a dynamic process independent of an animal's volition rather than as a static quality. The factors that influence the hand's evolutionary development are manifold and often symbiotically related, from an animal's need for basic prehension, its ability to feed itself, to work with tools, to throw objects or 'club' other animals. See, e.g., Young, 2003, Whishaw and Karl 2019 (with further bibliography). The question of the evolution of rationality remains a large and controversial topic among philosophers and historians of science; see, e.g. Sober 1981, Danielson 2004.

for human rationality; hands only help humans carry out the decisions their rational faculty may make. Here is how Galen puts the matter (2,11–15 H.):

> Now to man—for he is an intelligent animal and, alone of all creatures on earth, godlike—in place of any and every defensive weapon, she gave hands, instruments necessary for every art and useful in peace no less than in war.
>
> ἀνθρώπῳ δέ, σοφὸν γὰρ τοῦτο τὸ ζῷον καὶ μόνον τῶν ἐπὶ γῆς θεῖον, ἀντὶ πάντων ὁμοῦ τῶν ἀμυντηρίων ὅπλων χεῖρας ἔδωκεν, ὄργανον εἰς ἁπάσας μὲν τὰς τέχνας ἀναγκαῖον, εἰρηνικὸν δ' οὐδὲν ἧττον ἢ πολεμικόν.

Already Galen is signalling an important difference between humans and animals—humans seem to be endowed with no body part one can actually point to as indicative of a singular nature. All creatures need to be physically equipped for survival, and in the case of animals, nature has provided the appropriate body parts whose function is unmediated and instinctual; humans, by contrast, are born essentially defenceless, as Galen explicitly states, and left basically to figure things out by using their intelligence.

Galen presents this state of affairs as a triumph of human-ness, but it does suggest a rather garbled teleology and at least some degree of defensiveness about the general helplessness humans often feel in the face of an animal world that seems better equipped physically to survive and thrive. Humans do not really *need* horns or hoofs 'as a natural endowment' (ξύμφυτον) because they can make weapons with their hands, which in turn can make hands superior to all other animals' natural endowments designed for defence (3,1–3 H.):[12]

> Surely he is not naked, easily wounded, defenceless, or unshod but, whenever he wishes, may have a corslet of iron (an instrument harder to damage than any kind of skin), and sandals, weapons, and vestments of all sorts are at his disposal. In fact, the corslet is not his only protection, since he also has houses, towers, and city walls.
>
> οὔκουν γυμνὸς οὐδ' εὔτρωτος οὐδ' ἄοπλος οὐδ' ἀνυπόδετος ἄνθρωπος, ἀλλ' ἔστι μὲν αὐτῷ θώραξ σιδηροῦς, ὁπότε βούλοιτο, πάντων δερμάτων δυστρωτότερον

12 Rocca (forthcoming, ad loc.) notes the Stoic roots of the idea that humans dominate the animal world. See, e.g., Cicero, *Nat. D.* 2.150–152, in a discussion, put in the mouth of the Stoic Balbus, about the wonders of the human hand similar to—though more abbreviated than—Galen's topic of *UP* 1.

> ὄργανον, ἔστι δ' ὑποδημάτων παντοῖον εἶδος, ἔστι δ' ὅπλων, ἔστι δὲ καὶ σκεπασμάτων. οὐ γὰρ θώραξ μόνον, ἀλλὰ καὶ οἰκία καὶ τεῖχος καὶ πύργος ἀνθρώπου σκεπάσματα.

This may sound like a welcome advantage, but tell that to the person alone in the woods facing an angry bear, who forgot to bring along any of those clever defensive contrivances Galen is thinking of! While the bear is *never* without its defensive claws, humans can only protect themselves with a spear or flee on a horse if they *happen* to have these things with them—and nature, at least, offers no guarantee that they will.

For Galen, then, hands are most impressive for their potential to do all the things that distinguish humans from animals. In an almost rhapsodic passage towards the end of 1.2, Galen continues to muse on the wonders of the human hand, where he notes (perhaps with a touch of humour) that if humans had horns growing from their hands they would be unable to execute the many τέχναι that make them rulers over all other animals (*UP* 1.2, 3, 7–24 H., III, 4–5 K.):

> If he were born with a horn or some other defensive weapon of the kind growing upon his hands, he could not use them at all to build a house or tower, or to make a spear or corslet or other similar things. With these hands of his, a man weaves himself a cloak and fashions hunting-nets, fish-nets and traps, and fine-meshed bird-nets, so that he rules not only over animals upon the earth, but of those in the sea and the air also. **Such is the hand of man as an instrument of defense. But, being also a peaceful and social animal**, with his hands he writes laws for himself, raises altars and statues to the gods, **builds ships, makes flutes, lyres, knives, fire-tongs, and all the other instruments of the arts, and in his writings leaves behind him commentaries on the theories of them.** Even now, thanks to writings set down by the hand, it is yet possible for you to hold converse with Plato, Aristotle, Hippocrates, and the other Ancients.

> ξύμφυτον δ' εἴπερ ἦν αὐτῷ κέρας ἐπὶ τοῖν χεροῖν ἤ τι τοιοῦτον ἕτερον ἀμυντήριον ὅπλον, οὐδὲν ἂν εἶχεν ὅ τι χρήσαιτο ταῖς χερσὶν οὔτ' εἰς οἰκίας ἢ τείχους κατασκευὴν οὔτ' εἰς δόρατος ἢ θώρακος ἤ τινος ἄλλου παραπλησίου. ταύταις ταῖς χερσὶν ἄνθρωπος καὶ ἱμάτιον ὑφήνατο καὶ δίκτυον ἐπλέξατο καὶ πόρκον καὶ γρῖφον καὶ νεφέλην, ὥστ' οὐ μόνον τῶν ἐπὶ γῆς ζῴων, ἀλλὰ καὶ τῶν ἐν θαλάττῃ τε καὶ ἀέρι κρατεῖ. **τοιοῦτον μὲν αὐτῷ πρὸς ἀλκὴν ὅπλον ἡ χείρ. εἰρηνικὸν δ' ὅμως καὶ πολιτικὸν** ⟨ζῷον⟩ ἄνθρωπος χερσὶ καὶ νόμους ἐγράψατο καὶ βωμοὺς καὶ ἀγάλματα θεοῖς ἱδρύσατο **καὶ ναῦν κατεσκευάσατο καὶ αὐλὸν καὶ λύραν καὶ**

> σμίλην καὶ πυράγραν καὶ τἄλλα πάντα τῶν τεχνῶν ὄργανα καὶ ὑπομνήματα δ' αὐτῶν τῆς θεωρίας ἐν γράμμασιν ὑπελίπετο. καί σοι διά τε γράμματα καὶ χεῖρας ἔτι καὶ νῦν ὑπάρχει ὁμιλεῖν Πλάτωνί τε καὶ Ἀριστοτέλει καὶ Ἱπποκράτει καὶ τοῖς ἄλλοις παλαιοῖς.

We come close to a different teleology of human τέχναι, and the hand that executes them, than the one Galen began with, for here the hand exists in order to serve aspects of human nature beyond their capacity for reason. For one thing, Galen notes that humans are peaceful and social (εἰρηνικός, πολιτικός) so they need hands to transmit their values and culture through writing, and to make objects that bring pleasure to their lives in the form of commerce and entertainment. Where, we might ask, does intelligence (Galen is thinking here in terms of σοφία, cf. 11–12 H. in ch. 2, and the opening of ch. 3, quoted below)[13] fit in to this scheme, teleologically? Humans need to do things and make objects involving the hand, it seems, to fulfil their natures, but Galen does not seem to consider intelligence here as the *reason* or *purpose* behind these activities.

3 The Hand as 'Instrument of Instruments'

Galen wrestles with this issue at the opening of ch. 3, where he takes Anaxagoras to task for his own teleological account of the hand (*UP* 1.3, 4, 1–6 H., III, 5 K.):

> Thus man is the most intelligent of the animals and so, also, hands are the instruments most suitable for an intelligent animal. For **it is not because he has hands that he is most intelligent, as Anaxagoras says, but because he is the most intelligent that he has hands**, as Aristotle says,[14] judging most correctly. Indeed, not by his hands, but by his reason has man been instructed in the arts. Hands are an instrument, as the lyre is the instrument of the musician, and tongs of the smith.

13 See Rocca (forthcoming, ad loc., with further bibliography): 'For Galen, *sophôtaton* picks up the Platonic sense of wisdom operating not only in the rational part of the soul (*Resp.* 430e–431d) but as a virtue in itself (*Resp.* 428a, *Prt.* 329c, *Leg.* 631c–d). It also reflects the wisdom-power-goodness triad of the Demiurge (cf. Whittaker, 1992, 179–182; Runia, 2003, 104–105). And, more prosaically, *sophos* also connotes technical skill, precisely the action the hand performs under learned guidance.'

14 Aristotle, *Parts of Animals* 687a7.

> οὕτω μὲν σοφώτατον τῶν ζῴων ἄνθρωπος, οὕτω δὲ καὶ χεῖρες ὄργανα πρέποντα ζῴῳ σοφῷ. οὐ γὰρ ὅτι χεῖρας ἔσχε, διὰ τοῦτο σοφώτατον, ὡς Ἀναξαγόρας ἔλεγενἀλλ' ὅτι σοφώτατον ἦν, διὰ τοῦτο χεῖρας ἔσχεν, ὡς Ἀριστοτέλης φησὶν ὀρθότατα γιγνώσκων. οὐ γὰρ αἱ χεῖρες ἄνθρωπον ἐδίδαξαν τὰς τέχνας, ἀλλ' ὁ λόγος·

There is little question that Galen remained committed to the Aristotelian view of hands as existing *because* of human intelligence, but there is also enough detail in Galen's discussion to suggest that the teleological explanation of hands was not entirely settled in his mind. As he moves away from the philosophical considerations in the opening chapters of Book 1, as we will see, his emphasis shifts more towards how the hand actually works, anatomically, and what it can accomplish, and hints, at least, that its complex functionality was granted to the human body because its actual nature and purpose is to 'make', 'do' and 'work'.

In fleshing out his argument that hands are the instrument of rationality in 1.3, Galen raises yet more questions about what humans are supposed to do with them 'by nature' (*UP* 1.3, 4, 6–13 H., III, 5 K.):

> Hands are an instrument, as the lyre is the instrument of the musician, and tongs of the smith. Hence just as the lyre does not teach the musician or tongs the smith but each of them is a craftsman **by virtue of the reason there is in him** although he is unable to **work at his trade without the aid of his instruments**, so every soul has through **its very essence** certain faculties, but without the aid of instruments is helpless to accomplish **what it is by Nature disposed to accomplish.**

> αἱ χεῖρες δ' ὄργανον, ὡς λύρα μουσικοῦ καὶ πυράγρα χαλκέως. ὥσπερ οὖν ἡ λύρα τὸν μουσικὸν οὐκ ἐδίδαξεν οὐδ' ἡ πυράγρα τὸν χαλκέα, ἀλλ' ἔστι μὲν ἑκάτερος αὐτῶν τεχνίτης **διὰ τὸν ἐν αὐτῷ λόγον**, **ἐνεργεῖν δ' οὐ δύναται κατὰ τὴν τέχνην χωρὶς ὀργάνων**, οὕτω καὶ ψυχὴ πᾶσα **διὰ μὲν τὴν ἑαυτῆς οὐσίαν** ἔχει τινὰς δυνάμεις, **δρᾶν δ' ἃ πέφυκε δρᾶν** ἀμήχανον αὐτῇ χωρὶς ὀργάνων.

On the face of it, the analogy between the hand and the lyre is not logically satisfying: the lyre performs a specific task (making music) which only someone defined as a musician would undertake. The hand, by contrast, as an 'instrument of instruments' for humans, executes decisions made by *logos* in order to make other instruments for a human life, but *logos* describes a technical capacity and offers no 'content' of its own. The hand can do many other things besides make instruments and still be considered a hand; the lyre, qua lyre, exists only to make music. So, we may say that humans are by nature 'rational' in the sense that they are endowed with a capacity for reason (the δυνάμεις or faculties that form part of human οὐσία, 'essential being') but *why* (if we follow a Galenic/Aristotelian teleology that our bodily parts come into being to fulfil an antecedent end) have they been given that capacity by Nature in the first place? What antecedent cause becomes their final cause—for the sake of *what* do we really have hands?[15] What actually drives the musician or blacksmith to their particular professions, and what makes humans, more generally, use their hands the way they do?

This is a particularly fraught question for Galen in this context, which is not easy for him to answer, as becomes clear from the long digression about animal instincts that immediately follows his comment about human οὐσία in 1.3 (*UP* 1.3, 4, 13–15, 5 H., III, 6–7 K.):

> In observing newborn animals striving to exert themselves before their parts are perfected, we can see clearly that it is not the bodily parts that lead the soul to be timid or brave or wise.[16] Now I have often seen a young calf butting before its horns have sprouted, a colt kicking with hoofs still soft, a piglet, quite small, trying to defend itself with jaws innocent of tusks, and a newborn puppy attempting to bite with its teeth still tender. **For every animal has, untaught, a perception of the faculties of its own soul and the virtues resident in its parts.** Or why else, when it is possible for the small boar to bite with his little teeth, does he not use them for battle instead of longing to use those which he does not yet have? How,

15 For Galen's interest in 'antecedent, preceding and containing causes', concepts with Stoic origin, see Hankinson 1994, 1764–1767. Note Hankinson 1994, 1769 on Aristotelian final causes in Galen: 'Considered one way, one thing ... can be a final cause; considered relative to something else, it may merely be an instrument, a means to a further end ... And for Galen at least that regress of Final Causes must come to an end: and the final Final Cause ... will be simply "because it is for the best". That type of overarching teleology has Platonic and Stoic as well as Peripatetic overtones.' In the case of hands in Galen's treatment, he might be willing to say that they exist in the end 'because it is for the best', but the details of his description, as we will see, seem to acknowledge an antecedent state of deficiency that the creation of a hand was intended to compensate for. That is, the hand becomes the best hope for a creature who otherwise has no defences in the natural world.

16 On the Stoic background to Galen's discussion of animal instinct Sorabji, 1993, 87, and Inwood 1984, 184, who discusses the second-century CE Stoic Hierocles, who argued that animals were born with a degree of self-perception (Stoic *oikeiôsis*) along with their natural instincts. On other Stoic theories of animal psychology, see also Dierauer 1977, 211–219. On Galen's Stoicizing more generally, see Manuli 1993; Tieleman 1996; 2009; Gill, 2007; 2010.

then, is it possible to say that animals learn the usefulness of their parts from the parts themselves, when they obviously know their usefulness even before they have them?

ἔνεστι δ' ἐναργῶς ἰδεῖν, ὅτι μὴ τὰ μόρια τοῦ σώματος ἀναπείθει τὴν ψυχὴν ἢ δειλὴν ἢ ἄλκιμον ἢ σοφὴν γίγνεσθαι, τὰ νεογενῆ ζῷα θεασάμενον ἐνεργεῖν ἐπιχειροῦντα πρὶν τελεωθῆναι τοῖς μορίοις. ἐγὼ γοῦν καὶ βοὸς μόσχον πολλάκις εἶδον κυρίττοντα πρὶν φῦσαι τὰ κέρατα καὶ πῶλον ἵππου λακτίζοντα μαλακαῖς ἔτι ταῖς ὁπλαῖς καί τινα κομιδῇ σμικρὸν χοῖρον ἀμύνεσθαι ταῖς γένυσιν ἐπιχειροῦντα γυμναῖς τῶν μεγάλων ὀδόντων καὶ σκύλακα νεογενῆ δάκνειν ὀριγνώμενον ἁπαλοῖς ἔτι τοῖς ὀδοῦσιν. **αἴσθησιν γὰρ πᾶν ζῷονἀδίδακτον ἔχει τῶν τε τῆς ἑαυτοῦ ψυχῆς δυνάμεων καὶ τῶν ἐν τοῖς μορίοις ὑπεροχῶν·** ἢ διὰ τί παρὸν ἐνδάκνειν τῷ σμικρῷ χοίρῳ τοῖς μικροῖς ὀδοῦσιν ὁ δὲ τούτους μὲν ἀργοὺς ἔχει πρὸς τὴν μάχην, οἷς δ' οὐκ ἔχει πω, χρῆσθαι ποθεῖ; πῶς οὖν ἐστι δυνατὸν φάναι τὰ ζῷα πρὸς τῶν μορίων διδαχθῆναι τὰς χρήσεις αὐτῶν, ὅταν καὶ πρὶν ἐκεῖνα σχεῖν, φαίνηται γιγνώσκοντα;

The point of this digression is to show how in animals their 'natures' (although 'instincts' seems more appropriate here) are 'untaught' (ἀδίδακτοι)—they are just born knowing what they need to do (flying, fighting, hunting, swimming, etc.).[17] Humans, by contrast, as Galen proceeds to take up at the opening of the next chapter (4), are not only 'bare of weapons' (ὥσπερ τὸ σῶμα γυμνὸς ὅπλων) in body but also 'destitute of skills in their souls' (τεχνῶν τὴν ψυχὴν ἔρημος). Nature, he says, gave hands to humans to offset their nakedness and λόγος to compensate for their ἀτεχνία: διὰ τοῦτ' ἀντὶ μὲν τῆς τοῦ σώματος γυμνότητος **τὰς χεῖρας** ἔλαβεν, ἀντὶ δὲ τῆς κατὰ τὴν ψυχὴν ἀτεχνίας **τὸν λόγον**.

We may note here Galen's subtle shift in conception—hands are not here provided *because* humans have λόγος (or *because* they are σωφώτατοι—cf. 1.3), but because humans need them for survival, and they can only be effectively used if reason directs them appropriately. But this position implies a set of antecedent teleological assumptions which lie just below the surface of Galen's

17 A little later in this passage Galen quotes Hippocrates, *Vict.* 39 (145 Joly) as authoritative background to the idea of 'untaught natures' in animals: φύσιες πάντων ἀδίδακτοι. See further May 1968, 70–71, n. 10, who also cites Hipp. *Epid.* 6, 5.1, 'Nature finds ways for itself, though not from thought/understanding …' (ἀνευρίσκει ἡ φύσις αὐτὴ ἑωυτῇ τὰς ἐφόδους, οὐκ ἐκ διανοίης), and *Nat. Fac.* II, 38 K. and *Foet. Form.* 6, 25–30 Nickel (IV, 692–693 K.). Rocca (forthcoming, ad loc.) adds *De semine* 198, 6–8 De Lacy (IV, 643 K.): 'For all the organs of the body nature gave inborn powers (συμφύτους δυνάμεις) to animals, so that they can use them to perform the activities proper to them without having to be taught (ἀδιδάκτως).'

discussion of why humans, unlike animals, are naturally defenceless straight out of the box. Why should they be defenceless at birth, one might ask? Galen says in 1.4 that 'if he had been born with a natural weapon, he would have that one alone for all time, and just so, if he had one natural skill, he would lack the others. But since it was better for him to make use of all weapons and all the arts, he was endowed with no one of them at birth'.[18] No argument is offered for why being endowed with one natural weapon or skill would preclude having any others, but the statement in the second sentence is revealing. Here Galen says simply that '*because* it was *better* for him to use all the weapons and all the arts …' (ἐπεὶ δ' ἄμεινον ἦν ἅπασι μὲν ὅπλοις, ἁπάσαις δὲ χρῆσθαι τέχναις), nature did not provide him with any single weapon or art. We may question the logic of such a statement, but it reveals, I think, a key assumption about Galen's teleology of the hand: they were provided because it is a human *good* (ἐπεὶ δ' ἄμεινον) to use *many* τέχναι, not just one, reflecting the best ordering of things, and explaining why humans have hands in particular, and not, say, horns or claws. If they *had* such other accoutrements, they would not have hands (or at least not with same functionality as the human hand), which would mean they would not be able to fulfil their best nature, namely, to *do* things with those hands. Galen calls the hand, explicitly invoking Aristotle (6.7 H.),[19] the 'instrument on behalf of all instruments' (ὄργανόν τι πρὸ ὀργάνων) and Galen adds here that humans require such a versatile instrument in order to do what they are *supposed* to do as humans.

What Galen most marvels at about the hand is the versatility that arises from its particular anatomy, a theme that runs through the rest of Book 1 and continues into Book 2, which moves from the hand down the arm. As he repeatedly states, not only is the hand constructed so as to be useful for an 'intelligent animal' but its design cannot be improved upon. Indeed, one of Galen's motivations in writing *UP* is to demonstrate this general principle for all parts of the body, attributing such perfection to Nature and the Demiurge with a kind of theological zeal,[20] but Galen has a particular interest in the hand because it seems for him to define what it means to be human more than any of the other

---

18 ὥσπερ γάρ, εἴ τι ξύμφυτον ὅπλον ἐκέκτητο, μόνον ἂν ἦν ἐκεῖνο διὰ παντὸς αὐτῷ, οὕτως, εἴ τιν' εἶχε τέχνην φύσει, τὰς ἄλλας οὐκ ἂν ἔσχεν. (6, 1–4 H.).

19 Aristotle, *Part. an.* 687a20–21, and above n. 9.

20 'Theological zeal' is no overstatement. See, e.g., two passages celebrated in *UP* (and informally named) for their impassioned rhetoric on this theme, the 'Hymn to Nature' (*UP* 1, 173–179 H.; 3.237–242 K.) and *UP* 17, the 'Epode', (a name Galen himself gives to his final book in its last paragraph, 17, 451 H., IV, 366 K.) in praise of the Demiurge—an epode of the sort 'which they used to chant standing before the altars and, as they say, singing hymns of praise to the gods'. See also Jouanna 2012, 303.

parts. When he finally does get into the details of the hand's anatomy, beginning in 1.5, the theoretical framework with which he had opened the book has been established—humans have hands constructed the way they are because that is the best way for them to perform what they were put on earth to do:[21] 'Come now, let us investigate this very important part of man's body, examining it to determine not simply whether it is useful or whether it is suitable for an intelligent animal, but whether it is in every respect so constituted that it would not have been better had it been made differently'.[22] Just what it is that humans are supposed to do in their lives, as it turns out, is not a singular thing, which is why they need a body part that has seemingly limitless inventive possibilities. And the hand is ideally suited for this task, as Galen states in ch. 5, because of its complex prehensibility, its 'ability to grasp readily anything of whatever size or shape that man would naturally want to move' (*UP* 1.4, 6, 22–25 H., III, 9 K).

After a lengthy discussion of the wondrous and varied ways in which the hand can grasp things, large and small, he concludes by noting how a different design would have prevented such grasping abilities (e.g., he asks, 'what if there had been no finger opposing the four, as there is now, but all five of them had been produced side by side in one straight line?' 1.5, 8, 21–23 H., III, 10 K.). In accounting for the hand's grasping abilities at the end of ch. 5, Galen once again uses teleological language: 'Hence it was better (ἄμεινον) for the hands to act (ἐνεργεῖν) as they do now (ὡς νῦν ἐνεργοῦσι), and Nature therefore gave them a structure suited to such activities (ἐνεργείαις τοιαύταις)'. Ἐνέργεια is an Aristotelian term (e.g., *NE* 7–8) best translated as 'activity' in a more abstract sense than the more specific term πρᾶξις, an action with a moral layering (e.g., a courageous or just deed).[23] The activity (ἐνέργεια) of the hand lies in its grasp-

21 See Schiefsky 2007, 377, in a discussion of Galen's hands: 'the underlying idea, as in Aristotle, is the explanatory priority of the whole organism to its parts. The organism's activities are not explained by reference to its parts; rather, the parts are explained by reference to the *total pattern of the organism's activities, as expressed in the character and faculties of soul.*' Speaking of a city as whole conceptually prior to its constituent parts at *Pol.* 1.2.1253a20–26, Aristotle draws an analogy with body parts: 'for the whole is necessarily prior to the part; for when the whole is destroyed there will no longer be a foot or a hand except in name, just as one might call a stone hand a hand' (τὸ γὰρ ὅλον πρότερον ἀναγκαῖον εἶναι τοῦ μέρους· ἀναιρουμένου γὰρ τοῦ ὅλου οὐκ ἔσται ποὺς οὐδὲ χεὶρ εἰ μὴ ὁμωνύμως, ὥσπερ εἴ τις λέγει τὴν λιθίνην·). See Leunissen 2017, 111, on Aristotle's biological thinking about the teleology of cities.

22 φέρε οὖν τοῦτο πρῶτον αὐτοῦ βασανίσωμεν τὸ μόριον, οὐκ εἰ χρήσιμον ἁπλῶς οὐδ' εἰ σοφῷ ζῴῳ πρέπον ἐπισκοποῦντες, ἀλλ' εἰ παντοίως οὕτως ἔχει κατασκευῆς, ὡς οὐκ ἄν, εἴπερ ἑτέρως ἐγεγόνει, διέκειτ' ἂν ἄμεινον, *UP* 1.4, 6, 18–22 H.; IV, 9 K.

23 See Angier 2016, 435–436. On Aristotle's complex usage of ἐνέργεια see Chen 1956; Menn 1994; and Leunissen 2010, 51, n. 10. It is interesting that the noun πρᾶξις is found only once

ing capabilities (ἀντίληψις, *UP* 1.9, 17, 16–17 H., 24 K.) which will allow it both to perform all manner of actions and to practise innumerable τέχναι for making things, both material (like shoes and houses) and immaterial (like music, writing, and indirectly, culture). This is the *activity* (ἐνέργεια) that, Galen says, Nature felt was appropriate and best for humans, and is, therefore, the reason why humans have hands—humans are supposed to do and make things, and the ἐνέργεια assigned to the hand makes action and τέχνη (in the sense of skill or craft) possible.

Galen does not particularly set out in his discussion of hands to argue that humans are somehow defined by a desire or compulsion to work, but it is never very far from his mind that hands were given to human bodies because not much else about their bodies could ensure their survival. Hands, therefore, as we have seen, are (literally) instrumental for the work that needs to be done not only for protection but also for other activities that are (as Galen would say), 'appropriate for an intelligent animal' (*UP* 3.1). Galen even links human bipedalism to the necessity and appropriateness of 'humans as workers' in a discussion in Book 3, devoted to the feet and legs. Continuing his theme from Book 1 that humans are better off contriving *ways* to be swift through *logos* rather than being endowed with limiting body parts that could actually *make* them swift, he opens Book 3 by noting (in almost Darwinian fashion) that 'the forelimbs [found on quadruped animals] became hands; for one who was to tame the horse with his skilful hands had no need to be swift himself, and in place of speed it was far better for him to be provided with instruments necessary for all the arts'.

Once again, we see that animals can be left on their own in the world with their particular bodies and have no need to work to survive in the intentional and calculating ways that humans must, using their rational faculties. But work for humans becomes more than a mere survival mechanism for Galen, as he makes clear in an extended passage about centaurs. While he is well aware that centaurs are creatures of fantasy, he finds in them a useful heuristic for affirming why bipedalism is essential for hands to do what they are designed to do. The centaur is in essence a quadruped with two hands, and one might ima-

in *UP*, at *UP* 1.22, 23–25 H., III, 80 K., in a passage alluding to a monkey that tries to imitate 'human actions' (ἁπάσας μὲν γὰρ τὰς ἀνθρωπείους πράξεις ἐπιχειρεῖ μιμεῖσθαι), which include things like flute-playing, dancing and writing. A body part such as a hand can perform such 'actions', but these are more specified than an 'activity' (ἐνέργεια). At *UP* 1.8, 14, 23–24 H., III, 20 K. Galen makes a distinction between a body part's ἐνέργεια and its 'usefulness' (or 'function', χρεία). One can, e.g., know what a body part 'does' without understanding its function.

gine that if humans had been designed like a centaur they would be even *better* equipped than they currently are—the four legs of the horse part would make them fast, while the two hands of the upper humanoid part of the body would *in addition* give them access to that 'instrument of instruments'. This is a striking, highly suggestive passage, worth quoting in full (*UP* 3.1, 125,16–127, 4 H., III, 171–172 K.):

> Even if we should be willing to pass over all these absurdities, however, and grant that this man with the legs of a horse could be engendered and support life, he would gain nothing from such a structure except swiftness, and this would not be advantageous at all times and places, but only on smooth, level plains. **I should like to see a centaur build a house or ship, scramble up the mast to the yardarm, or perform any of a sailor's tasks. How terribly awkward he would be at all of them, and how perfectly impossible many of them would be for him! If he was building a house, how would he climb long, slender ladders to the tops of high walls? Or how would he climb to the yardarm of a ship? Would he be able to row when he could not possibly sit down properly?** And even if he could, the presence of his front legs would hinder the action of his hands. But though he was of no use as a **sailor**, perhaps he would make a good **farmer**. Here too, however, he would be even more useless, especially if his task was **climbing trees and picking fruit**. Do not think that these are the only situations where he would be absurd, but review **all the other arts and imagine him working as a blacksmith, or cobbling, weaving, mending, or writing books. How would he seat himself?** What **sort of a lap would he have on which to rest his book, and how would he handle all the other tools?** For in addition to all the other special advantages man enjoys, he is the only one of all the animals who can conveniently **sit** down on his hip bones. This fact has indeed escaped most people; they believe that man alone stands erect but do not perceive that he is also the only animal that can sit.
>
> ἀλλ' εἰ καὶ ταῦτά τις ὑπερβαίνοι πάντα τὰ ἄτοπα καὶ συγχωρήσειε καὶ γεννᾶσθαι δύνασθαι καὶ διαζῆν τὸν ἱπποσκελῆ τοῦτον ἄνθρωπον, οὐδὲν αὐτῷ πλέον ἐκ τῆς τοιαύτης κατασκευῆς ὅτι μὴ τὸ τάχος· οὐδὲ τοῦτ' αὐτὸ ἁπλῶς οὐδ' ἐν ἅπασι χωρίοις, ἀλλ' ἐν τοῖς ὁμαλέσι τε καὶ λείοις πεδίοις μόνοις. εἰ δέ που δέοι πρὸς ὄρθιον δραμεῖν ἢ κάταντες ἢ λοξὸν ἢ ἀνώμαλον, ἡ νῦν οὖσα κατασκευὴ τῶν ἀνθρωπείων σκελῶν ἀμείνων μακρῷ. οὕτω δὲ καὶ ὑπερπηδῆσαι καὶ πέτρας ὀξείας τε καὶ ὀρθίους ὑπερβῆναι καὶ ὅλως ἁπάσας τὰς δυσχωρίας διελθεῖν ἀμείνων ἄνθρωπος τοῦ τερατώδους ἐκείνου Κενταύρου. ἐβουλόμην δ' ἂν αὐτὸν ἰδεῖν

> ἢ οἰκοδομούμενον ἢ ναυπηγούμενον ἢ διὰ τῶν ἱστῶν ἐπὶ τὰς κεραίας τῶν πλοίων ἀναρριχώμενον ἢ ὅλως τῶν ναυτικῶν ἔργων τι μεταχειριζόμενον, ὡς ἄτοπός τε δεινῶς ἐν ἅπασιν ἦν ἂν καὶ πολλαχῇ τελέως ἀδύνατος. πῶς γὰρ ἂν ἐν ταῖς οἰκοδομήσεσι διὰ μακρῶν καὶ λεπτῶν κλιμάκων ἐπὶ τοίχους ὑψηλοτάτους ἀνῄει; πῶς δ' ἂν ἐπὶ τὰς κεραίας τῶν νεῶν; οἷος δ' ἂν ἐρέσσων ἦν, ᾧ γε μηδὲ καθῆσθαι καλῶς ἐνεχώρει; κἂν εἰ τοῦτό γε αὐτῷ ὑπῆρχε, τὰ πρόσθια σκέλη τὰς τῶν χειρῶν ἐνεργείας ἐκώλυεν ἄν. ἀλλ' ἴσως μὲν ἂν ναύτης ἄχρηστος, γεωργὸς δ' ἂν ἦν χρήσιμος. ἀλλ' ἐνταῦθα καὶ πλέον ἀχρηστότερος, καὶ μάλιστ' εἰ πρᾶξαί τι δέοι τοῖς δένδροις ἐπαναβαίνοντα καί τινας τῶν καρπῶν δρέπεσθαι. μὴ τοίνυν ταύτην μόνην αὐτοῦ θεώρειτὴν ἀτοπίαν, ἀλλ' ἐπὶ τὰς τέχνας ἁπάσας ἴθι καὶ σκόπει χαλκεύοντα καὶ σκυτοτομοῦντα καὶ ὑφαίνοντα καὶ ἠπώμενον αὐτὸν καὶ γράμματα γράφοντα, πῶς μὲν καθιεῖται, ποίοις δὲ μηροῖς ἐπιθήσει τὸ βιβλίον, ἢ τῶν ἄλλων ὀργάνων ἕκαστον ὅπως μεταχειριεῖται. πρὸς γὰρ αὖ τοῖς ἄλλοις ἅπασιν οἷς ἄνθρωπος ἐξαιρέτως ἔχει, καὶ τὸ καθέζεσθαι χρησίμως ἐπὶ τῶν ἰσχίων τούτῳ μόνῳ πάντων ζῴων ὑπάρχει. λέληθε δὲ καὶ τοῦτο τοὺς πολλοὺς καὶ νομίζουσιν ὀρθὸν μόνον ἑστάναι τὸν ἄνθρωπον, οὐκ εἰδότες, ὅτι καὶ τὸ καθέζεσθαι μόνος ἔχει.

Galen's practical objection to the idea of humans having four legs plus two arms is that, although they would be able to run faster than they would with two legs (but this, he says, only if the ground is smooth!), all other activities we associate with being human would be impeded if not prevented. The activities that Galen lists here as emblematic of human life—activities that would be impeded or impossible if humans were not bipeds with humanoid hands—are particularly interesting. All of these are professions of one kind or another—housebuilding, shipbuilding, sailing, even farming (where bipedalism would be necessary for picking and climbing). As if that is not enough, he moves on to the many professions that require the ability to 'sit on his hip bones'—a uniquely human trait according to Galen—blacksmiths, cobblers, weavers … and, as he ends with a flourish, writing books. We can see that for Galen the hand's mechanical capabilities are not limited to practical affairs but are also essential even for what we would call cultural achievement (and he might well say, for *paideia* itself). Books are tools too, as Galen observes, and can only exist as a function of hands (and hips). Implicit in this entire passage, then, is the assumption that work in the form of the various τέχναι is definitional for human life, and that it is *because* of this that humans have been given hands—definitional in that τέχνη is required for humans to live a life appropriate to an 'intelligent' animal, and the τέχναι require labour broadly conceived. If it were not, after all, cosmically *necessary* for humans to undertake all the τέχναι he mentions here, why would it be such a bad thing for humans to be designed like a centaur? Such a creature might be perfectly content to run fast while making limited use of its hands.

4 Conclusion

If humans are 'social' creatures (πολιτικοί), as Galen says (1.2., 3,16 H., channelling Aristotle, who adds 'by nature', φύσει [*Pol.* 1253a1–2])—they need to be endowed with the physiological means to effectuate their sociality.[24] Hands provide such an instrument, and their particular form and functionality in Galen's view enable humans to do the things they have been teleologically designed for as social creatures. Galen's Aristotelian view of human sociality as 'natural' implies some measure of instinctiveness—humans will be born predisposed to do things appropriate to social animals without having to be taught—but their physiology, as his discussion implicitly acknowledges, is quite limited in comparison to other animals, and it is only through another natural endowment, the capacity for reason, *logos*, that they are able to direct their body parts to carry out the functions that allow them to live as nature has intended. For Galen, the hand, that wondrous 'instrument of instruments', was designed for the primary purpose of allowing humans to do the things that they were *not* born instinctively knowing how to do. Galen often alludes to this basic physical defencelessness and intellectual cluelessness at birth, and the hard work it takes throughout one's life to pursue personal happiness and social good.[25] Much of that work is emotional and intellectual, as Galen discusses at length in such works as *Affections and Errors* and *Character Traits*, but there is also much physical, bodily work that an individual must take on if they want to live the best possible human life. In Galen's teleology, after all, beyond the basic non-rational appetites and impulses that humans share with animals, there is very little that comes to them naturally and without intentional (which is to say, guided by *logos*) exertion, labour or other kinds of action that constitute 'work'. We may note, for example, an emblematic passage in *Affections and Errors* (from Book 2 on 'errors'), which stresses the inherent animality of humans, and the amount of intentionality and hard work (education, self-discipline, cultivation of reason, *et sim.*) necessary to achieve some measure of virtue and happiness.[26] Of all the body parts, hands are the most important

24 See above, where the passage is quoted in full. See also Galen's remarks about the function of fingernails at *UP* 1.22: 'Human fingernails are such parts and for this reason they were made much softer and more delicate than the claws of wolves, lions, or leopards. For they are not the defensive weapons of a wild beast, but parts belonging to a civilized, social animal and adapted for grasping objects accurately.'

25 Such themes are particularly pervasive throughout *Affections and Errors*, *Character Traits* and *Avoiding Distress*. See next note.

26 In speaking of the cultivation of the rational capacity, he writes that 'when this [λογική] is well schooled and attains its own [state of] good condition, the subject is far happier than

means by which humans can carry out their work. Indeed, Galen regards the hands are the primary 'do-ers' of the body in all realms of life, from making things individually and collectively, to ensuring social and political collaboration through the technologies of writing and other arts.

To some degree, Galen's interest in the work that the hand performs in human life, both physical and social, may well have been an inescapable consequence of the moral layering of work that permeated Greek intellectual culture since Hesiod, namely, that work is always a virtue, and idleness a vice. But it is clear from *UP* as well that he inferred his teleology of work from his observation that, just as the individual parts of the body must act together to achieve a unified end, so at the macro-level human communities only flourish when their constituent bodies take on the kinds of intentional activity we have come to call work. In any case, Galen certainly held that we are all 'born to work' and believed that he had the anatomical and philosophical arguments to demonstrate that work was a positive, enriching enterprise for them, and part, at least, of what teleologically defines being human.

Acknowledgements

I am deeply grateful to Julius Rocca for allowing me to consult a draft of his commentary on Galen's *The Function of the Parts of the Body* (= *UP*), forthcoming with Cambridge University Press, and for his own very helpful comments on an early draft of this chapter. Many thanks also to P.N. Singer for offering his characteristically incisive comments on an early draft.

Bibliography

Angier, T. (2016). Aristotle on Work. *Revue Internationale de Philosophie* 278, pp. 435–449.

Balme, D. (1987). Teleology and Necessity. In: A. Gotthelf and J.G. Lennox, eds., *Philosophical Issues in Aristotle's Biology*. Cambridge, pp. 275–286.

those who are slaves to bodily pleasures. For indeed, we do not differ in any other capacity from goats and dogs, or pigs, sheep or donkeys (οὐδὲ γάρ τοι διαφέρομεν ἄλλῃ τινὶ δυνάμει τράγων καὶ σκυλάκων ὑῶν τε καὶ προβάτων καὶ ὄνων). And there is no other study that can delight the soul of a man with good natural endowments more than that of analysis—once, that is, he makes some progress in it. It is very hard work to begin with, as is almost every true study (κατ' ἀρχὰς μὲν γὰρ ἐπίπονός ἐστιν, ὥσπερ καὶ αἱ ἄλλαι σχεδὸν ἅπασαι)'. (*Affections and Errors* 59 De Boer, v, 87–88 K., tr. Singer 2013).

Chen, C.-H. (1956). Different Meanings of the Term *Energeia* of Aristotle. *Philosophy and Phenomenological Research* 17.1, pp. 56–65.

Cooper, J.M. (1982). Aristotle on Natural Teleology. In: M. Schofield and M. Nussbaum, eds., *Language and Logos*. Cambridge, pp. 197–222.

Danielson, P. (2004). Rationality and Evolution. In: A.R. Mele and P. Rawling, eds., *The Oxford Handbook of Rationality*. Oxford, pp. 417–436

Dierauer, U. (1977). *Tier und Mensch im Denken der Antike. Studien zur Tierpsychologie, Anthropologie und Ethik. Studien zur antiken Philosophie* 6. Amsterdam.

Eijk, P. van der (2009). 'Aristotle! What a Thing for You to Say!' Galen's Engagement with Aristotle and Aristotelians. In: C. Gill, T. Whitmarsh and J. Wilkins, eds., *Galen and the World of Knowledge*, pp. 261–281.

Eijk, P. van der (2014). Galen on the Nature of Human Beings. In: P. Adamson, R. Hansberger and J. Wilberding, eds., *Philosophical Themes in Galen*. London, pp. 89–134.

Eijk, P. van der (2017). The Place of Disease in a Teleological World-Wiew: Plato, Aristotle, Galen. In: J. Rocca, ed., *Teleology in the Ancient World. Philosophical and Medical Approaches*. Cambridge, pp. 217–241.

Eijk, P. van der (2020). Galen on Soul, Mixture and Pneuma. In: B. Inwood and J. Warren. *Body and Soul in Hellenistic Philosophy*. Cambridge, pp. 62–88.

Gill, C. (2007). Galen and the Stoics: Mortal Enemies or Blood Brothers? *Phronesis* 52, pp. 88–120.

Gill, C. (2010). *Naturalistic Psychology in Galen and Stoicism*. Oxford.

Gottschalk, H.B. (1987). Aristotelian Philosophy in the Roman World from the Time of Cicero to the End of the Second Century AD. *ANRW* II. 36.2, pp. 1079–1174.

Gottschalk, H.B. (1997). Continuity and Change in Aristotelianism. In: R. Sorabji, ed., *Aristotle and After*, *BICS* suppl. 68. London, pp. 109–115.

Hankinson, R.J. (1989). Galen and the Best of all Possible Worlds. *Classical Quarterly* 39, pp. 206–227.

Hankinson, R.J. (1994). Galen's Theory of Causation. *ANRW* II 37.2, pp. 1757–1774.

Hankinson, R.J. (1995). *Philosophy of Science*. In: J. Barnes, ed., *The Cambridge Companion to Aristotle*. Cambridge, pp. 109–139.

Hankinson, R.J. (1998). *Cause and Explanation in Ancient Greek Thought*. Oxford.

Hankinson, R.J. (2016). Galen's Reception of Aristotle. In: A. Falcon, ed., *Brill's Companion to the Reception of Aristotle in Antiquity*. Leiden, pp. 238–257.

Helmreich, G. (1907, v. 1) (1909, v. 2). *Galeni de usu partium libri xvii*. Leipzig.

Inwood, B. (1984). Hierocles: Theory and Argument in the Second Century AD. In: *Oxford Studies in Ancient Philosophy* 2, pp. 151–183.

Johnson, M.R. (2005). *Aristotle on Teleology*. Oxford.

Jouanna, J. (2012). Galen's Concept of Nature. In: J. Jouanna, *Greek Medicine from Hippocrates to Galen*. Leiden, pp. 287–311.

Korsgaard, C.M. (2008). *The Constitution of Agency: Essays on Practical Reason and Moral Psychology*. Oxford.

Kosman, L.A. (1987). Animals and Other Beings in Aristotle. In: A. Gotthelf and J.G. Lennox, eds., *Philosophical Issues in Aristotle's Biology*, Cambridge, pp. 360–391.

Leunissen, M. (2010). *Explanation and Teleology in Aristotle's Science of Nature*. Cambridge.

Leunissen, M. (2017). Biology and Teleology in Aristotle's Account of the City. In: J. Rocca, ed., *Teleology in the Ancient World. Philosophical and Medical Approaches*. Cambridge, pp. 107–124.

Manuli, P. (1993). Galen and Stoicism. In: J. Kollesch and D. Nickel, eds., *Galen und das hellenistische Erbe*. Stuttgart, pp. 53–61.

May, M.T. (1968) *Galen. On the Usefulness of the Parts of the Body*. Ithaca.

Menn, S. (1994). The Origins of Aristotle's Concept of Ἐνέργεια and Δύναμις. *Ancient Philosophy* 14, pp. 73–114.

Moraux, P. (1984). *Der Aristotelismus bei den Greichen. Von Andronikos bis Alexander von Aphrodisias, II*. Berlin.

Rocca, J. (2018). Galen and Middle Platonism: The Case of the Demiurge. In: H. Tarrant, D. Layne, D. Baltzly and F. Renaud, eds., *Brill's Companion to the Reception of Plato in Antiquity*. Leiden, pp. 206–222.

Rocca, J., ed. (2017). *Teleology in the Ancient World. Philosophical and Medical Approaches*. Cambridge.

Rosen, R.M. (2016). Towards a Hippocratic Anthropology: On Ancient Medicine and the Origins of Humans. In: L. Dean-Jones and R.M. Rosen, eds., *Ancient Concepts of the Hippocratic*. Leiden, pp. 242–257.

Schiefsky, M. (2007). Galen's Teleology and Functional Explanation. In: D. Sedley, ed., *Oxford Studies in Ancient Philosophy* 33. Oxford, pp. 369–400.

Sedley, D.N. (1991). Is Aristotle's Teleology Anthropocentric? *Phronesis* 36, pp. 179–196.

Sedley, D.N. (2007). *Creationism and Its Critics in Antiquity*. Berkeley–Los Angeles.

Sharples, R.W. (2017). The Purpose of the Natural World: Aristotle's Followers and Interpreters. In: J. Rocca, ed. *Teleology in the Ancient World. Philosophical and Medical Approaches*. Cambridge, pp. 151–168.

Sober, E. (1981). The Evolution of Rationality. *Synthese* 46.1, pp. 95–120.

Sorabji, R. (1993). *Animal Minds and Human Morals. The Origins of the Western Debate*. Ithaca.

Tieleman, T. (1996). *Galen and Chrysippus on the Soul. Argument and Refutation in the* De Placitis, *Books II–III*. Leiden.

Tieleman, T. (2009). Galen and the Stoics, or: the Art of Not Naming. In: C. Gill, T. Whitmarsh and J. Wilkins, eds., *Galen and the World of Knowledge*. Cambridge, pp. 282–299.

Young, R.W. (2003). Evolution of the Human Hand: The Role of Throwing and Clubbing. *Journal of Anatomy* 202, pp. 165–174.

Whishaw, I.Q. and Karl, J.M. (2019). The Evolution of the Hand as a Tool in Feeding Behavior: The Multiple Motor Channel Theory of Hand Use. In: V. Bels and I. Whishaw, eds., *Feeding in Vertebrates. Evolution, Morphology, Behavior, Biomechanics*. Springer, pp. 159–186.

CHAPTER 5

On Valuing Roman Art and the Labour of Art Making

Lauren Hackworth Petersen

Teoricamente il mondo romano non ha considerato l'artista un uomo eccezionale, nè ha dato una considerazione speciale all'attività artistica.

Theoretically, the Roman world did not consider the artist an exceptional person, nor did it give special consideration to artistic activity.[1]

•••

I(ulius) MVS//TICVS SCVL

I(ulius) Musticus sculpted it.[2]

∴

1 Introduction

The writing of Roman art history has perpetuated a number of entrenched narratives that have effectively rendered invisible the makers of Roman art. This chapter tackles this issue by focusing on the discourse of art making in an ancient Roman context and in subsequent, critical eras. In doing so, it confronts art-historical meta-narratives and the discipline's paradigms in the making of history, which is to say that this chapter is mostly historical, but also historiographical. Further, it attempts to expose how and where silences in

1 Calabi Limentani 1958, 7. Trans. author.

2 *CIL* 12, 2319. See Allmer 1875, 471–472 (no. 787). The inscription is from a signed funerary bust of Julia. See also Calabi Limentani 1958, 163 (no. 91).

 | DOI:10.1163/9789004694965_006

art-historical texts facilitate the privileging of the dominant, elite-centred narratives around art making despite the material evidence we have at hand that speaks to other possible narratives.

Let me begin by delving into a bit of historiography by offering a couple of general and sweeping observations, with full admission that many readers will take issue with aspects of them. The observations concern conventional art-historical methods and narrative framing structures. Surveys of art, particularly from the early modern era onward, have depended on and placed great value on concepts such as artistic genius—intellectual and creative labour, if you will—and on concepts such as artistic or stylistic development in forming the so-called canon, the archive that scholars have traditionally tapped for the subjects of inquiry. This is due, in part, to the legacy of Giorgio Vasari's 1550 *Le vite de' più eccellenti pittori, scultori, e architettori*, a foundational text authored by an individual who was often identified as the 'first' art historian. Vasari structures his meta-narrative chronologically: he opens the treatise with a discussion of the early-Renaissance artist Cimabue and concludes with Michelangelo and Titian, who, for Vasari, represent the pinnacle of achievement in the arts. This narrative structure is also intimately tied to concepts of biological determinism. Specifically, Vasari writes in the preface that '… the nature of this art resembles that of the others, which, like human bodies, are born, grow up, become old, and die' only to be reborn to a state of perfection in the Renaissance period.[3] And, within the treatise itself, each chapter charts the career of the artist, from birth to death, to a type of rebirth with the writing of the treatise. In many respects, Vasari created a paradigm that has long seemed intractable as a method in art history, giving primacy as it does to individual artists, and thereby valuing artist biography and development.

This paradigm is oftentimes unforgiving, especially unforgiving when narrating a pre-1400 history of European art (not to mention arts outside the European tradition). We see this especially in the case of Roman art, where, retrospectively, scholars have mined ancient texts, such as Pliny the Elder's *Natural History*, for names of Roman artists, a method much indebted to the priorities of individual 'greatness' created by Vasari; however, such searches render little, with some notable exceptions.[4] The study of Roman art thus sits uneas-

3 Trans. Bondanella 1991, 5–6.

4 Books 34–36 of Pliny the Elder's first-century *Natural History* focus on the visual arts (namely painting and sculpture). No Roman bronze sculptor is cited in the text, but a few names of Roman marble sculptors (36.33–43) appear, as well as some Roman painters. Plenty of Greek artists or artists with Greek names are cited throughout. For a robust discussion, including bibliography, see De Angelis 2008, esp. 84–87.

ily within that larger art-historical paradigm. In fact, I would suggest that the study of Roman art *resists* standard biographical narratives and their attendant concepts of 'artistic genius' and originality familiar to the western art-historical tradition. Further, I, as an art historian, am painfully aware of the paradox that the makers of the tremendous artistic record that is 'Roman art' are frustratingly unknown to us as individuals, despite the fact that we may possess hundreds of names from a variety of ancient sources.[5] This chapter explores what this supposed lacuna has meant to the study of Roman art and plays a bit with the title of Linda Nochlin's groundbreaking article, 'Why Have There Been No Great Women Artists?' by asking, 'Why have there been no great Roman artists?' as a starting point for thinking about the makers of art in Roman society. To be clear, I do not claim that Roman artists were necessarily prevented from achieving greatness, as Nochlin does with women artists on account of institutional structures and societal constraints placed on female practising artists.[6] Rather, this chapter briefly surveys what we know (and don't know) about Roman artists and demonstrates that the history of Roman art has felt acutely this absence of names and lives of 'great' artists, by which I mean famous or even generally well-known artists, namely painters and sculptors. This, in turn, has given shape to the ways we have traditionally narrated the history of Roman art, which, I suggest, risks devaluing the labour of art making.[7] I would add that while much of what is presented here may at first seem commonplace, the sum of the parts reveals, I think, a rather unsettling story of Roman art and its makers.

2 The Literary Record

As a student of the classical tradition, I begin by inviting us to confront what we inherit from the ancient literary record in the writing of art history. With few exceptions, ancient writers, both Greek and Roman, tend to denigrate artists/craftsmen.[8] In ancient Rome, artists were usually described as sordid

5 We possess about 400 names of artists from a variety of sources, usually inscriptions or a passing reference in ancient texts; Blagg 1987, 730.

6 Nochlin 1971.

7 For recent methodological approaches to valuing craftmaking in the ancient world, broadly defined, see Hochscheid and Russell 2021. Unfortunately, this book was not yet available to me at the time of writing this chapter.

8 Parenthetically, I should add that the terms artist and craftsman seem to have been interchangeable in an ancient context. *Faber* and *artifex* could describe makers of objects—both arts and crafts, as *ars* refers to both art and craft interchangeably (Burford 1972, 14).

and lowly, often coming from servile stock especially during the time of military expansion; that is, artists were often the subjects of Roman conquest, alongside plundered objects themselves, and were responsible for the making of Roman luxury and the arts that were deeply valued and prized. One oft-cited passage, among the many that survive on this topic, serves to illuminate just how ignoble artisans were perceived to be by those in elite circles. Cicero, in his discussion of occupations suitable for aristocrats, makes clear that no Roman of any standing would engage in the manual arts. He writes, 'All craftsmen, too, are engaged in vulgar activities, for a workshop or factory can have nothing noble about it'.[9] The only craft or art form that he isolates as having possible merit is architecture, which required intelligence over manual skill or labour and therefore would have been an appropriate profession for someone of middle rank, but not of the aristocracy.

One could also turn to the second-century CE Syrian author Lucian of Samosata, who presents a satirical account of his upbringing, having to choose between two diametrically opposed professional paths—education or an apprenticeship with his uncle as a sculptor. In his dream one position is presented as follows (Lucian, *Sat.* 5–9. Trans. Harmon 1921, 223):

> What it shall profit you to become a sculptor this woman has told you; you will be nothing but a labourer, toiling with your body and putting in it your entire hope of a livelihood, personally inconspicuous, getting meagre and illiberal returns, humble-witted, an insignificant figure in public, neither sought by your friends nor feared by your enemies nor envied by your fellow-citizens—nothing but just a labourer, one of the swarming rabble. … Even if you should become a Phidias or a Polycleitus and should create many marvellous works, everyone would praise your craftsmanship, to be sure, but none of those who saw you, if he were sensible, would pray to be like you; for no matter what you might be, you would be considered a mechanic, a man who has naught but his hands, a man who lives by his hands.

ἡλίκα μὲν οὖν τὰ ἀγαθὰποριῇ λιθοξόος γενόμενος, αὕτη προείρηκεν· οὐδὲν γὰρ ὅτι μὴ ἐργάτης ἔσῃ τῷ σώματι πονῶν κἀν τούτῳ τὴν ἅπασαν ἐλπίδα τοῦ βίου τεθειμένος, ἀφανὴς μὲν αὐτὸς ὤν, ὀλίγα καὶ ἀγεννῆ λαμβάνων, ταπεινὸς τὴν γνώμην, εὐτελὴς δὲ τὴν πρόοδον, οὔτε φίλοις ἐπιδικάσιμος οὔτε ἐχθροῖς φοβερὸς οὔτε τοῖς πολίταις ζηλωτός, ἀλλ' αὐτὸ μόνον ἐργάτης καὶ τῶν ἐκ τοῦ πολλοῦ

9 Cic. *Off.* 1.150–151. See on this text also the introduction to this volume.

> δήμου εἷς, ἀεὶ τὸν προὔχοντα ὑποπτήσσων καὶ τὸν λέγειν δυνάμενον θεραπεύων, λαγὼ βίον ζῶν καὶ τοῦ κρείττονος ἕρμαιον ὤν· εἰ δὲ καὶ Φειδίας ἢ Πολύκλειτος γένοιο καὶ πολλὰ θαυμαστὰ ἐξεργάσαιο, τὴν μὲν τέχνην ἅπαντες ἐπαινέσονται, οὐκ ἔστι δὲ ὅστις τῶν ἰδόντων, εἰ νοῦν ἔχοι, εὔξαιτ' ἂν σοὶ ὅμοιος γενέσθαι· οἷος γὰρ ἂν ῇς, βάναυσος καὶ χειρῶναξ καὶ ἀποχειροβίωτος νομισθήσῃ.

It is again the manual or physical labour of art making that is of pointed concern in this passage, which in turns renders invisible any intellectual or creative capacity in the making of art objects. Being a great artist in antiquity might have brought some fame and recognition, but the life of that artist was not necessarily one to be valued and emulated, according to the elite, who distanced themselves from such work in no uncertain terms.[10] Perhaps these attitudes, especially around the art of sculpting, may explain why we can point to a 'great' Roman architect, or two, and maybe even a couple of painters, yet we seem particularly hard pressed to identify a great Roman sculptor, whose messy work was perceived to have been grounded in manual labour over intellectual labour.[11] Nonetheless, ancient writers do praise and value good craftsmanship and their own ability to recognize it, much like an art connoisseur in our modern use of the word.[12] For far too long, these attitudes, along with those from other elite-authored sources, in which art objects themselves may be valued but not the makers of those objects or the labour involved, have been taken at face value in modern scholarship, internalized, and treated as normative.

Peter Stewart's discussion of who made Roman art (in *The Social History of Roman Art*) makes clear how problematic the study of Roman artists can be. While we can list on one hand the names of what we might call great or famous artists of the Roman world, even these individuals' lives remain largely unknown. This is in part due, I think, to the narrative that Pliny constructs for us. For example, he specifically identifies early 'great' painters (fourth and second centuries BCE) as coming from the upper ranks of society: Fabius Pictor

10 And, as is well cited, Plutarch remarked, 'It does not necessarily follow that if a work is delightful because of its gracefulness, the man who made it is worthy of our serious regard. … No one, no gifted young man, upon seeing the Zeus of Pheidias at Olympia or the Hera of Polykleitos at Argos ever actually wanted to be Pheidias or Polykleitos' (Plut. *Per.* 2.1, trans. Burford 1972, 12).

11 Of course, there is the story of the sculptor Pygmalion, made famous by Ovid in *Metamorphoses* (10.243–297). The work, in its entirety, is arguably about art, artists and artistic form even if from the realm of myth. See Barolsky 2010, 35–44. Also see Feldherr 2010, 257–276, for a discussion of Pygmalion, art making, viewing and cult experience.

12 Also see Burford 1972, 14–15.

was from a distinguished family in Rome and achieved fame by painting the walls of the Temple of Salus in Rome; and the poet Pacuvius won celebrity for his painting in the Temple of Hercules in Rome.[13] After that, according to Pliny, the art of painting was 'no longer practiced by men of rank' (*NH* 35.7), and artists seem to be of relatively little interest to him, with one notable exception—Studius, the Augustan-era painter whom Pliny credits with a critical role in the history of Roman landscape painting, but whose biography is frustratingly unknown to us (including agreement on his very name).[14] Thus, while Pliny credits Studius with artistic innovation, we know very little of the artist himself.[15] He writes that Studius must not be cheated of his due, for he (Plin. *NH* 35.116–117. Trans. Rackham 1952, 347–348):

> … first introduced the most attractive fashion of painting walls with pictures of country houses and porticoes and landscape gardens, groves, woods, hills, fish-ponds, canals, rivers, coasts, and whatever anybody could desire, together with various sketches of people going for a stroll or sailing in a boat or on land going to country houses riding on asses or in carriages, and also people fishing and fowling or hunting or even gathering the vintage. His works include splendid villas approached by roads across marshes, men tottering and staggering along carrying women on their shoulders for a bargain, and a number of humorous drawings of that sort besides, extremely wittily designed. He also introduced using pictures of seaside cities to decorate uncovered terraces, giving a most pleasing effect and at a very small expense.

> … primus instituit amoenissimam parietum picturam, villas et porticus ac topiaria opera, lucos, nemora, colles, piscinas, euripos, amnes, litora, qualia quis optaret, varias ibi obambulantium species aut navigantium terraque villas adeuntium asellis aut vehiculis, iam piscantes, aucupantes aut venantes aut etiam vindemiantes. Sunt in eius exemplaribus nobiles palustri accessu villae, succollatis sponsione mulieribus labantes, trepidis quae feruntur, plurimae praeterea tales argutiae facetissimi salis. Idem subdialibus maritimas urbes pingere instituit, blandissimo aspectu minimoque inpendio.

---

13 Ling 1991, 212.

14 For a good discussion of the problems in linking the painter named Studius with any biographical details, see Ling 1977, esp. 1–3.

15 On the Roman painter Studius, see Ling 1977.

It would seem that Pliny places great value on Studius' innovation in painting, his creativity or intellectual labour—his genius in ushering in a new painting style. There are, of course, additional Roman artists to be found in Pliny's texts, but the bulk of his discussion on ancient painting focuses on Greek artists rather than Roman (more on the topic of the alleged primacy of Greek art over Roman to follow). For example, there is Famulus, the famed painter of Nero's Golden House. And what do we know of the biography of Famulus? Very little, beyond Pliny's brief discussion of him in the very same section on painting and painters in Greece and Rome (Plin. *NH* 35.120. Trans. Rackham 1952, 349):

> Another recent painter was Famulus, a dignified and severe but also very florid artist; to him belonged a Minerva who faced the spectator at whatever angle she was looked at. Famulus used to spend only a few hours a day in painting, and also took his work very seriously, as he always wore the toga, even when in the midst of his scaffolding [easels]. The Golden House was the prison that contained his productions, and this is why other examples of his work are not extant to any considerable extent.

> Fuit et nuper gravis ac severus idemque floridis tumidus pictor Famulus. Huius erat Minerva spectantem spectans, quacumque aspiceretur. Paucis diei horis pingebat, id quoque cum gravitate, quod semper togatus, quamquam in machinis. Carcer eius artis domus aurea fuit, et ideo non extant exempla alia magnopere.

What Pliny presents here is less a biography than a praise of the artist's skill on one hand, and what we have come to interpret as some quirky personality traits and work habits on the other.[16] Meanwhile, the architects of the very same building, Severus and Celer, are elevated as possessing qualities of genius and courage (*ingenium et audacia*) in the writings of Tacitus.[17] In other words, scholars have not interpreted Pliny's anecdote to mean that Famulus was necessarily an intellectual artist worthy of emulation, whereas architects were valued for genius and courage, as portrayed by Tacitus.[18] Further, when it comes to sculp-

16 On Famulus and painting workshops (and attendant issues around artist anonymity), see Allison 1995; Meyboom 1995.

17 'The architects and engineers were Severus and Celer, who had the ingenuity and the courage to try the force of art even against the veto of nature and to fritter away the resources of a Caesar' (Tac. *Ann.* 15.42. Trans. Jackson 1937, 279).

18 Furthermore, Vitruvius, the architect, wrote the highly influential treatise on architecture. Of Vitruvius, we can presume a relatively high social status and education given

ture, the names and lives of 'great' Roman sculptors, whose art form is widely attested from the period, elude us for the most part in the literary tradition but not from the material remains themselves.

3 Writing Roman Art History without Artist Biographies

As historians of Roman art, participating in the discipline's methods and entrenched traditions, we have unwittingly fallen victim to the silences in our ancient sources and to their assumptions and priorities. And, without artist biographies—and with relatively few works that survive that are securely attributed to named artists—to help define and shape narratives of Roman art, one could argue that we have made a rather simple, yet no less problematic, substitution; the history of Roman art has largely been a history of the emperors, their families, and artistic commissions.[19] We think we know a great deal about the lives of emperors drawn from ancient sources such as Suetonius' *The Twelve Caesars* (and the *Historia Augusta* for the later emperors, questionable as that source may be). With these biographies at hand, it is the personalities of the emperors, their political agendas, and patronage that have traditionally framed the history of Roman art. For instance, we tell the story of imperial art as one that is driven by political agendas, from Augustus, with his interest in reviving the religious and social *mores* of the Romans—a new Golden Age—and his concomitant embrace of classical Greek artistic styles, to Vespasian, with his alleged return to the values of the Republic, as telegraphed through the revival of a portrait style that is at once distinguished from the art of the Julio-Claudians and associated with a new imperial ideology, or Hadrian, who is often recognized as a philhellene in terms of his intellectual interests and pursuits; his artistic commissions, including architecture, are thus viewed primar-

---

that his writing stresses the intellectual and theoretical bases of his profession in his treatise. Vitruvius reveals that he was a military architect who served under Julius Caesar before serving Augustus (Book 1, preface, section 2). His treatise, interestingly, is the sole surviving written work by an ancient artist, though no architecture of his survives. On the sole treatise by an artist, see Pollitt 1983, 120. In an unfortunate twist of fate, Apollodorus of Damascus (of Syria), the well-known architect of the Forum of Trajan, was summarily dismissed (banished and killed) by the subsequent emperor, Hadrian, because he deigned to challenge the emperor's own architectural ambitions (Cassius Dio 69.4.1).

19 Also see Squire 2015, who arrived at a similar, independent conclusion subsequent to my 2011 work on this topic.

ily through the lens of Hellenism.[20] These familiar narratives, among others, are by and large the organizational framework of most textbooks and monographs on Roman art—a framework that makes visible and values the patrons of art, but renders invisible and devalues its makers.

In addition, scholars of Roman art have inherited a larger art-historical tradition that favours not only names of artists—and with them, notions of originality, creativity and artistic genius—but also the insidious and pervasive organic paradigm of birth–flowering–decay over time. Specifically, art historians wrestle with Rome's artistic debt to Greece, with much of Roman art being discussed as copying/imitating/emulating Greek art. With classical Greek art and its pantheon of well-known painters and sculptors representing, in the eyes of many early writers of art history, a pinnacle of artistic achievement, Roman art represents its slow decline, because it is perceived as lacking originality or intellectual labour. As a result, we have tacitly accepted the primacy of Greek art over Roman art. These notions, in fact, derive in part from the ancient world, namely from Romans' own views of their artistic legacy. Pliny's text on art is primarily, as Miranda Marvin puts it, one that identifies 'the great artists of the world as Greeks of the classical era. The history of art was to Pliny fundamentally the history of the arts in Greece, their natural home'.[21] Further, Horace's famous quip that 'captive Greece conquered her savage captor and introduced the arts to rustic Latium' (*Epist.* 2.1.156–157),[22] makes clear that the art of Greece had its grip on Rome.

Indeed, Roman practices of collecting Greek art preoccupied the fiercely competitive elite patrons of the late republican era and beyond. The market for imported art objects, in addition to imported materials, was robust, essentially feeding a seemingly insatiable appetite.[23] Scholars have noted that Romans desired to collect 'as many different types or kinds of statues as possible', what one scholar terms the acquisitive 'war-booty mentality', a mentality that reiterated the earlier, middle republican (264–133 BCE) mindset when triumphant generals 'crammed plundered statues and paintings into the hulls of ships bound for Rome'.[24] From the first century BCE onwards, however, it

20 The bibliography on Hadrian is tremendous; see especially Vout 2010.

21 Marvin 2008, 15. As Marvin observes, it is a bit of an understatement that the Romans were deeply conflicted about the arts, as both foreign to Rome and essential to Roman high culture, but also a source of perceived corruption.

22 As translated in Marvin 2008, 11.

23 Welch 2006.

24 Welch 2006, 131.

was mostly the politically active elite who bought statues from Greece for their villas to form ready-made collections, as the letters from Cicero make clear.[25] Plundered sculptures and raw materials, namely stone, and vast quantities of it, arrived by the shipload. For example, the Mahdia shipwreck (c. 100–70 BCE) contained a 300-ton cargo that included fourth-century BCE Greek artefacts, in addition to a number of newly manufactured objects in bronze and marble.[26] Further, M. Scaurus, during his aedileship in the mid-first century BCE, is reported to have had imported 360 marble columns for decoration in his *temporary* theatre.[27] The imported stone, white and coloured—yellow, pink, grey, green, black, purple, etc.—destined for architectural and sculptural use, came from mainland Greece, islands in the Aegean Sea, Turkey and Egypt, and spoke of Roman conquest.[28] Collecting statues in a domestic context quickly became a sign of wealth, luxury, good taste and erudition.[29]

But with original Greek statues in limited supply, the Romans, as is well documented, emulated revered statue types from the past to form new collections. Scholars have studied this phenomenon in great detail (in fact, it is often true that when introductory textbooks discuss Greek freestanding sculpture, it is a Roman version that survives and is illustrated).[30] Some private art collections even contained pendant pieces of nearly identical copies of Greek statues; the viewer was invited to contemplate the subtle differences between the two in terms of stylistic execution and possible significance.[31] Authenticity was thus not a primary criterion in Roman collecting practices, even among the elite; rather, it was principles of display that stimulated the contemplation of the

25 Selections of Cicero's letters are compiled in Marvin 1989, esp. 41–43. For a study of collecting from the textual sources, also see Tronchin 2012b.

26 For a quick introduction to the Mahdia shipwreck, see Mattusch 2015, 151–152. The full study of the Mahdia shipwreck is Hellenkemper Salies, von Prittwitz und Gaffron, and Bauchhenss 1994. On the Roman transport of statues and materials more generally, see Russell 2015. For a discussion of cultural appropriation, see essays in Loar, MacDonald, and Padilla Peralta 2018.

27 Plin. *NH* 36.2.5: 'In the aedileship of Marcus Scaurus there was the spectacle of 360 columns being taken to the stage of an improvised theatre that was intended to be used barely for a month.' Trans. Eichholz 1962, 5.

28 On the import of stone, see Anderson 1997, 166–179.

29 This topic has received much scholarly attention. See esp. Bartman 1991; Bergmann 2002; Gazda 2015; Mattusch 2005. Also see the essays in Tronchin 2012a.

30 This topic is vast. See esp. Bartman 1991; Beard and Henderson 2001; Friedland and Sobocinski 2015; Gazda 2002; Hallett 2005; Hölscher 2004; Marvin 1989 and 2008; Perry 2005; Varner 2006.

31 Bartman 1991, esp. 80–82.

viewer.[32] The fabulous 1954 discovery in the Bay of Naples at Baiae of some 400 fragments of plaster casts, belonging to between 24 and 36 sculptures, reveals that the Roman copy industry filled a high demand.[33] As such, scholarly focus has been placed on the value of art collecting and its patronage, not on the makers of the art objects themselves.

The early modern period contributed significantly to the paradigm that privileged Greek originals over Roman copies that made this seemingly biological determinism natural and also intimately connected to the perceived status of the artists. For example, Anton Raphael Mengs (1728–1779) especially disparaged Roman copies of great Greek works, believing that they were specifically 'made by slaves and freedmen who were the ones who practiced these arts in Rome',[34] which suggests a condemnation of Roman art and its creators on two accounts. Artists of the Roman period are denied any serious recognition partly due to the debt Roman artists pay for 'copying' Greek works of art and partly due to their perceived servile origins. We thus seem to have perpetuated a tradition and practice in which the Romans themselves and subsequent writers minimize and even de-value the contributions artists made to the vast visual legacy that does survive from the Roman world. In a loose sense, then, historians of Roman art remain a trifle haunted about Rome's place in the history of art; by and large, Rome *did* look to Greece for its artistic inspiration. As such, the scholarly tendency is to make it 'fit' into the oldest and most traditional of art-historical narratives, that of biography, but with biographies of the emperors and their political agendas and interests, along with the collecting and viewing practices of the elite and the well-to-do, supplanting the artistic creativity and skill of the Roman artists who literally made the visual world—and the luxurious arts—that we study possible.

I posit that it is important to confront both what Roman art history has taken from the past and how it has been made to conform to normative narrative structures. By way of one example that exposes just how fraught the terrain is, I take a different tack and ask that we consider the case of the Doryphoros, which is an extremely thorny subject to be sure (Fig. 5.1). This standing nude youth is a sculpture that we think we know quite well; its appearance is ubiquitous in surveys of Greek art, being identified as representative of art from the classical period, and we know the original artist and something of his philosophy of art. We also know that this Doryphoros is one of many

32 Gazda 2015, 379–380.

33 Frederiksen 2010; Landwehr 2010.

34 D'Azara and Fea 1836, 260: 'opere fatti da' servi e da' liberti, che erano quelli che si occupavano in queste arti in Roma' (as cited in Marvin 2008, 127).

'copies' to have been made by and for Romans. Yet, it rarely makes an appearance in Roman art history, and instead it stands as an example of Greek achievement in art—an irony, to be sure. Displayed in the archaeological museum at Naples (inv. 6011), this particular Doryphoros once adorned the so-called Samnite Palaestra at the Triangular Forum at Pompeii.[35] Its ancient setting was thus appropriate, as Marvin notes that the Spearbearer was 'widely recognized' as an exemplar 'of many virtues associated with athletic competition' and that replicas were quite common in gymnastic settings around the Empire.[36] We thus might pose the question, whose Doryphoros is it—does credit belong to Polykleitos or to an unnamed sculptor working in the Bay of Naples, or some combination of the two? Surely the latter two possible responses do not possess the cultural appeal that the name Polykleitos does, and the same was likely true in Roman times as well. And yet, as Marvin points out with *another* image of the Doryphoros, a bust from the luxurious setting at the Villa of the Papyri, it is signed in Greek 'Apollonios, son of Archias, the Athenian made this' (Fig. 5.2).[37] Apollonios assumes credit for the sculpture, based as it is on Polykleitos', although we know nothing else of this sculptor, except that he possibly came from Greece to Italy (Baiae) to set up a workshop to 'take advantage of the rich hellenophiles around the Bay of Naples'.[38] One thus has to imagine that the name Polykleitos must not have been far from the lips of Romans upon viewing this image and its Greek inscription, and that perhaps Apollonios is competing for some of that fame. Here, we seem to have a Greek artist migrating to the Bay of Naples to feed the appetite of villa owners for adorning their properties with sculptures drawn from the Greek world, with his signature functioning as a sign of luxury, perhaps, in a highly competitive market for both patrons and artists.[39] Meanwhile, the marble full-length statue from a palaestra defies modern values—it copies a Greek original and was crafted by an unknown artist or set of artists; it is largely invisible in discussions of Roman art and art making.

Admittedly, recent work has shifted from a focus on *Kopienkritik*, as it 'often results in the dismissal of extant objects as perfunctory replicas'.[40] By turn-

35 Plin. *NH* 34.55 identifies the statue as Doryphorus, manly-looking boy (*doryphorum viriliter puerem*), or what artists call a 'Canon' or model statue (*quem canona artifices vocant*).

36 Marvin 1997, 23.

37 Stewart 2008, 16; Marvin 2008, 224. Naples, MANN inv. 4885.

38 Apollonios of Athens does not appear in Pliny's catalogue of sculptors (nor does his father, Archias). On this artist and the sculpture shop at Baiae, see Mattusch 2005, 276–282.

39 For a thoughtful discussion on the economics of Pompeian domestic decoration and artist activity, see Flohr 2019, esp. 118–121 for an analysis of the market for sculpture at Pompeii.

40 Longfellow and Perry 2018, 1.

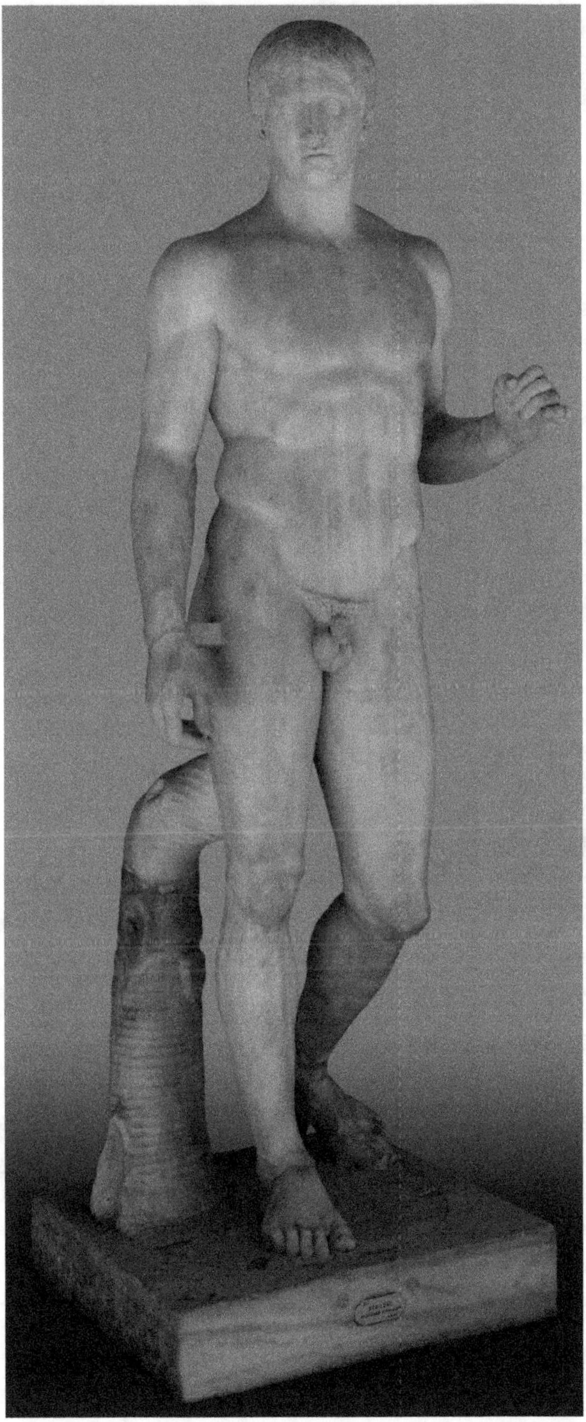

FIGURE 5.1
Doryphoros (Spear-bearer), Roman marble copy of Greek bronze statue, Pompeii (Samnite Palestra), late republican era (MANN inv. 6011)
PHOTO: © VANNI ARCHIVE / ART RESOURCE, NY (ART383671)

FIGURE 5.2 Bronze herm of the Doryphoros by Apollonios, Villa of the Papyri (Herculaneum), first century BCE (MANN inv. 4885) PHOTO: SCALA/MINISTERO PER I BENI E LE ATTIVITÀ CULTURALI /ART RESOURCE, NY (ART362732)

ing to physical and local contexts, scholars focus on the range of responses that sculpture, painting and architecture ensembles may have elicited among a variety of ancient viewers.[41] This is a valid and important approach, but it again gives primacy to the viewers and patrons of artistic commissions in everyday settings, while continuing to render the makers of art and their labour largely invisible. And it would seem that once scholars move from elite com-

41 Longfellow and Perry 2018, 1–2.

missions to those of everyday Romans, who also remain largely anonymous and who are often viewed as imitating the life of the elite, their aesthetic values and tastes come into question, alongside the technical skills of the artists they employed—essentially devaluing both the patron and the labour of the artist in the making of the vast visual culture that belongs to Roman art history.[42]

4 Roman Artists in Archaeology and Epigraphy

To make artists of Roman art and their labour more visible, we must look beyond the literary tradition and stitch together other strands of evidence. We do possess a good corpus of signed works as well as images of artists at work and, most importantly, funerary monuments in which artists seem to celebrate their profession. The bust of the Doryphoros made by Apollonios the Athenian, or the oft-cited Pompeian mosaic signed by Dioskourides the Samian, among other examples, suggest that Greek artists, or artists with the appearance of being Greek, were instrumental in producing Rome's visual culture, which is not surprising given both the Roman embrace of Greek art *and* the influx of Greeks into Roman Italy.[43] These 'signatures' written in Greek and the seemingly overt identification of these artists as coming from the Greek world perhaps lend a certain cultural cachet to the works themselves, not to mention to the patron himself. But beyond this, we know precious little about such artists and their histories, not to mention their actual ethnic backgrounds. In painting, we know even less, as Lawrence Richardson's study of figure painters working in the Bay of Naples region so aptly demonstrates. While he is able to identify an individual painter's body of works, the artists themselves remain, for the most part, anonymous—for example, The Boscotrecase Painter, The Iphigenia Painter, The Infancy of Bacchus Painter, etc.[44] The notable exception is Lucius, who seems responsible for much painted work, with a variety of subjects, throughout Pompeii.[45] He signed one house with *Lucius pinxit* (II 2, 2, known as the House of Octavius Quartio).[46] Despite the fact that he signed his

42 See, for example, Clarke 1991, esp. 193–235; Clarke 2003; Zanker 1998. For an alternative view, Petersen 2006.

43 Stewart 2008, 12. The mosaic comes from the so-called Villa of Cicero outside of Pompeii. For an image of the mosaic, see Stewart 2008, fig. 2; Ciarallo and De Carolis 1999, 266. Naples, MANN inv. 9985.

44 Richardson 2000.

45 Richardson 2000, 147–153. See Ling 1991, 213, on Lucius as possibly concealing this Greek cognomen, and thus perhaps his servile origins.

46 *CIL* 4, 7535. For a photo see Spinazzola 1953, fig. 460.

work, this artist's notoriety comes from what we have perceived as his relative ineptness as a painter. In the words of Richardson, 'he was never more than a marginally competent journeyman'.[47] Signatures seem to offer up very little, except that these individuals may have claimed some value for their labour, despite our tendency to overlook and devalue the contributions of their artistic legacies.

Throughout Pompeii, images of artists at work tend to depict these individuals accompanied by their patron deities, much like workers in other professions.[48] For example, flanking one side of a doorway to a rather large piece of property (II 3, 8), perhaps a workshop, a fresco shows a potter hard at work at the wheel, with the products of his skill beside him (Fig. 5.3).[49] Dominating the pictorial field is an image of Hephaestus/Vulcan, the god of fire whose artistic creations, as we know, are celebrated in ancient literary sources. Accompanying Vulcan and the potter were images of Minerva and Mercury, fittingly the gods of arts and crafts, and of commerce. While the artist here may be viewed as smaller in scale and of a relatively low stature, physically and socially, his work is overseen by and under the protection of the gods in a way that might be loosely analogous to later images of Vasari's divinely inspired creators.[50] Also from Pompeii comes a rather unusual fresco of a female painter (VI 1, 10, known as the House of the Surgeon; Fig. 5.4). She is shown mixing colours on her palette. Between the artist and the herm statue of Priapus is an image of Cupid holding the painting in progress. This fresco has received relatively scant scholarly attention,[51] but it is fascinating for the image of a female artist, a topic about which we know even less than artists generally beyond Pliny's mention of Iaia of Cyzikos, who worked in Rome around 100 BCE, was single, and painted mostly portraits of women.[52] Nonetheless, what these Pompeian

47 Richardson 2000, 150.

48 The linking of artists with patron deities suggests that artists were so integral to the workings of Roman society that even gods could be closely associated with art making as they were in other aspects of Roman life.

49 On this workshop image, see Fröhlich 1991, 313; Peña and McCallum 2009, 59–60. Pompeii, SAP inv. 21631.

50 Also see the Pompeian shop sign for 1.8.10 (*taberna vasaria*), which depicts at left a potter's workshop with an altar at the far left (the image of the deity does not survive). Four potters are shown working at wheels, with a woman holding two vessels toward the one at the lower right. For an image, see Ciarallo and De Carolis 1999, 164; also see Peña and McCallum 2009, 60–62; Fröhlich 1991, 307–308. Pompeii, SAP inv. 45622.

51 See Ciarallo and De Carolis 1999, 262. Naples, MANN inv. 9018.

52 'There was no painter superior to her for her expedition; while at the same time her artistic skill was such, that her works sold at much higher prices than those of the most celebrated portrait-painters of her day. …' (*NH* 35.147–148. Trans. Bostock). See also, Ling 1991, 212.

FIGURE 5.3 Fresco of a potter at the wheel and Vulcan, Pompeii (II 3, 8), first century CE (SAP inv. 21631)
PHOTO: SCALA/ART RESOURCE, NY (ART501072)

images (among others) do have in common is the relative anonymity of the artists themselves. We see artists at work, but beyond that we can recoup little of the lives of the depicted individuals. Like signatures, however, they may offer up a sense of value or pride among those who laboured in the arts.

FIGURE 5.4 Fresco of a female painter, Pompeii (VI 1, 10), first century CE (MANN inv. 9018)
PHOTO: © DEA PICTURE LIBRARY/ART RESOURCE, NY (ART421611)

In the funerary realm, we have reason to feel slightly more optimistic about what facets it might reveal about Roman artists, in part because these monuments were intended to record for perpetuity something of the lives of the deceased and how they wished to be remembered (and perhaps they suggest some modest wealth based on artistic success).[53] Here I consider a tombstone of a silversmith, although many more examples survive. The funerary stele shows a Roman dressed in citizen attire; he wears the tunic and toga and is depicted with austere facial attributes as was typical of the first decades of the first century CE (Fig. 5.5). His hands are busy working a silver vase with a mal-

53 For example, a subset of funerary reliefs as catalogued in Zimmer 1982. Also see, Calabi Limentani 1958, for inscriptional evidence.

let and an engraving tool, although he seems to gaze steadily toward viewers rather than focusing on his work. The inscription is minimal, reading, 'Publius Curtilius Agatus, freedmen of Publius, silversmith'.[54] He was once a slave but was freed, and his cognomen, Agatus, might be a Latinized version of the Greek name, Agathos.[55] Unlike the images coming from Pompeii, this funerary marker seems to emphasize the citizen status of the artist; he appears in the most traditional style of funerary portraits.[56] Beyond the identification of this artist's name, legal status and profession, we know nothing else of him. His work and labour as an artist, however, form a key component of his self-presentation as a Roman and as a maker of highly prized objects in the cult of luxury.

It is also important to bear in mind that artists could be enslaved members of a large elite *familia*, as evinced by the capacious *columbaria* at Rome, which yield some important evidence, albeit rather limited. For example, the *columbarium* of the Statilii on the Esquiline set aside for the vast staff of the family was home to 825 burials, mostly enslaved individuals and former slaves.[57] Among the job titles were personal attendants, gardeners, cooks, doctors and the like, but also artists or artisans: Licinius, a painter/colourist (*colorator*); Nicepor, a marble worker/sculptor (*marmorarius*); and Secundus, a stuccoist (*tector*).[58] Beyond name and job-title, we know little except that these were dedicated labourers pressed into the service of the Statilii in the making of the visual surroundings of the family. Where we, with their owners, read the titles as evidence of the elite's life of luxury, to the artists and labourers the titles may have signified membership in a large and extended community that perhaps valued its labour in a different way than the elite did.[59] The point is simple: there is another side to luxury and the visual arts than the consumer habits of the social elite.

---

54 Bodel and Tracy 1997, 14: *P(ublius) Curtilius P(ubli) l(ibertus) Agat[ho] | faber argentarius.*

55 Lapatin 2015, for Roman luxury arts more broadly, and pg. 326, for this funerary relief specifically.

56 One could, in fact, compare this image to other reliefs, which likely came from the funerary realm; for example, the funerary altar depicting a sculptor *at work* (Zimmer 1982, 157–158, and fig. 80; Stewart 2008, fig. 4), or the gold leaf worker, also shown *at work* (Burford 1972, 81, and fig. 41).

57 On these *columbaria* see also Groen-Vallinga, this volume.

58 Licinius: *CIL* 6, 6251; Nicepor: *CIL* 6, 6318; Secundus: *CIL* 6, 6360; Hasegawa 2005. Also see Brizio 1876, 63–64, for a brief discussion of these domestic artisans; Varro *Rust.* 3.2.9, for reference to a fresco-worker, stucco-worker and the art of a stucco-worker (*pictor, tector* and *opere tectorio*) as translated in Hooper 1967.

59 In his study of Rome's *columbaria,* Dorian Borbonus points out that niches and plaques of similar or equal size and shape, put each person commemorated 'on the same level

FIGURE 5.5 Marble grave relief of a silversmith, first century CE, 79.9 × 58.5 × 31.7 cm (The J. Paul Getty Museum, Villa Collection, Malibu, California, 96.AA.40)
PHOTO: BRUCE WHITE PHOTOGRAPHY

5 Conclusion

While it may be true that artisans tended to be enslaved workers, former slaves, or foreigners (that is, Greeks), not all of them were, and even so, status hardly matters; rather, their skills were integral—no, vital—to the shaping of the eco-

visually' (2014, 5). This 'uniformity of design' does not elevate any one person above another visually, and if death mirrors life, socially. In this context, then, occupational title marked a role in a community or a relationship to others.

nomic, political, social and visual life of ancient Rome. Society depended on artists and their technical (manual) skills to produce the highly valued objects individuals desired but could not create for themselves. In daily life and in the funerary realm, evidence does survive to suggest that despite all of the elite-authored rhetoric, artisans/artists commemorated their skill in the making of Rome's visual and material culture—whether on painted shop signs, in relief, or epigraphically. And yet, when we ask, 'who made Roman art', the relative silence is telling. The answer to this question has implicitly been the patrons of art, those who had a stake in it all. And while there may have been no great Roman artists in the Vasarian sense of the term, we know that there has been great Roman art, prized and valued by ancient and modern viewers alike. Now, I do not propose that we attempt to rewrite a history of Roman art based on its artists, but I do hope that as we ask more about the making of Roman art we expose just how entrenched elite, ancient writers and (early) modern scholars have been in denigrating and ultimately erasing Roman art's makers and their labour from narratives in Roman art history. While the literary and historical traditions have eclipsed and made invisible makers of Roman art, the individuals themselves have left a vast—and highly valued—artistic legacy. We would do well to recall that the makers themselves seem to have valued, commemorated, and maybe even celebrated their labour and contributions to this material legacy.

Acknowledgements

I wish to extend my sincere gratitude to Kim Bowes and Miko Flohr for the kind invitation to participate in the conference (2021) and contribute to this volume. The ideas for this paper were presented many, many years ago, and it has been a pleasure to revisit and revise them in the context of this conference (Petersen 2011). I should also like to note that the bibliography on this topic, and many facets within, is vast. My approach here is to take a bird's-eye view of the history of Roman art history through the lens of social history and to make visible what the art-historical tradition has largely rendered invisible.

Bibliography

Allison, P. (1995). 'Painter-Workshops' or 'Decorator Teams'? *Mededelingen van het Nederlands Instituut te Rome* 54, pp. 98–109.

Allmer, A. (1875). *Inscriptions Antiques* (Inscriptions Antiques & de Moyen Age de Vienne, vol. 3). Vienna.

Anderson, J. (1997). *Roman Architecture and Society*. Baltimore.

Barolsky, P. (2010). *A Brief History of the Artist from God to Picasso*. University Park, PA.

Bartman, E. (1991). Sculptural Collecting and Display in the Private Realm. In: E. Gazda, ed., *Roman Art in the Private Sphere. New Perspectives on the Architecture and Decor of the Domus, Villa, and Insula*. Ann Arbor, pp. 71–88.

Beard, M. and Henderson, J. (2001). *Classical Art. From Greece to Rome*. Oxford.

Bergmann, B. (2002). Art and Nature in the Villa at Oplontis. In: *Pompeian Brothels, Pompeii's Ancient History, Mirrors and Mysteries, Art and Nature at Oplontis, and the Herculaneum 'Basilica'* (Journal of Roman Archaeology, supp. 47). Portsmouth, R.I., pp. 87–120.

Blagg, T. (1987). Society and the Artist. In: J. Wacher, ed., *The Roman World*. London, pp. 717–742.

Bodel, J. and Tracy, S. (1997). *Greek and Latin Inscriptions in the USA. A Checklist*. Rome.

Bondanella, J.C. (1991). *The Lives of the Artists*. Oxford.

Borbonus, D. (2014). *Columbarium Tombs and Collective Identity in Augustan Rome*. New York.

Bostock, J. (1855). *Pliny the Elder, The Natural History* (www.perseus.tufts.edu).

Brizio, E. (1876). *Pitture e sepolcri scoperti sull'Esquilino dalla Compagnia fondiaria italiana nell'anno 1875*. Rome.

Burford, A. (1972). *Craftsmen in Greek and Roman Society*. Ithaca, NY.

Calabi Limentani, I. (1958). *Studi sulla società romana. Il lavoro artistico*. Milan.

Ciarallo, A. and De Carolis, E., eds. (1999). *Pompeii. Life in a Roman Town*. Milan.

Clarke, J. (1991). *The Houses of Roman Italy, 100 B.C. – A.D. 250. Ritual, Space, and Decoration*. Berkeley.

Clarke, J. (2003). *Art in the Lives of Ordinary Romans. Visual Representation and Non-Elite Viewers in Italy, 100 B.C. – A.D. 315*. Berkeley.

D'Azara, G. and Fea, C. (1836). *Opere di A. Rafaello Mengs sulle belle arti*, vol. 2. Milan.

De Angelis, F. (2008). Pliny the Elder and the Identity of Roman Art. *RES: Anthropology and Aesthetics* 53/54, pp. 79–92.

Eichholz, D.E. (1962). *Pliny. Natural History, Volume X: Books 36–37*. Cambridge, MA.

Feldherr, A. (2010). *Playing Gods. Ovid's* Metamorphoses *and the Politics of Fiction*. Princeton.

Flohr, M. (2019). Artisans and Markets: The Economics of Roman Domestic Decoration. *American Journal of Archaeology* 123/1, pp. 101–125.

Frederiksen, R. (2010). Plaster Casts in Antiquity. In: R. Frederisken and E. Marchand, eds., *Plaster Casts. Making, Collecting and Displaying from Classical Antiquity to the Present*. Berlin, pp. 13–33.

Friedland, E. and Sobocinski, M., eds. (2015). *The Oxford Handbook of Roman Sculpture*. New York.

Fröhlich, T. (1991). *Lararien- und Fassadenbilder in den Vesuvstädten: Untersuchungen zur 'volkstümlichen' pompejanischen Malerei.* Mainz.

Gazda, E., ed. (2002). *The Ancient Art of Emulation. Studies in Artistic Originality and Tradition from the Present to Classical Antiquity.* Ann Arbor.

Gazda, E. (2015). Domestic Displays. In: E. Friedland and M. Sobocinski, eds., *The Oxford Handbook of Roman Sculpture.* New York, pp. 374–389.

Hallett, C. (2005). Emulation versus Replication: Redefining Roman Copying. *Journal of Roman Archaeology* 18, pp. 419–435.

Harmon, A.M. (1921). *Lucian.* Volume 3. Cambridge MA.

Hasegawa, K. (2005). *The* Familia Urbana *during the Early Empire. A Study of* Columbaria *Inscriptions.* Oxford.

Hellenkemper Salies, G., Prittwitz und Gaffron, H. von and Bauchhenss, G., eds. (1994). *Das Wrack. Der antike Schiffsfund von Mahdia,* 2 vols. Cologne.

Hochscheid, H. and Russell, B., eds. (2021). *The Value of Making. Theory and Practice in Ancient Craft Production.* Turnhout.

Hölscher, T. (2004). *The Language of Images in Roman Art,* translated by A. Snodgrass and A. Künzl-Snodgrass. Cambridge.

Hooper, W.D. (1967). *Marcus Terentius Varro. On Agriculture.* Cambridge, MA.

Jackson, J. (1937). *Tacitus. Annals: Books 13–16.* Cambridge, MA.

Landwehr, C. (2010). The Baiae Casts and the Uniqueness of Roman Copies. In: R. Frederiksen and E. Marchand, eds., *Plaster Casts. Making, Collecting and Displaying from Classical Antiquity to the Present.* Berlin, pp. 35–46.

Lapatin, K. (2015). Luxury Arts. In: B. Borg, ed., *A Companion to Roman Art.* Malden, MA, pp. 321–343.

Ling, R. (1977). Studius and the Beginnings of Roman Landscape Painting. *Journal of Roman Studies* 67, pp. 1–16.

Ling, R. (1991). *Roman Painting.* Cambridge.

Loar, M., MacDonald, C. and Padilla Peralta, D., eds. (2018). *Rome, Empire of Plunder. The Dynamics of Cultural Appropriation.* Cambridge.

Longfellow, B. and Perry, E. (2018). Introduction: Roman Art Reconsidered. In: B. Longfellow and E. Perry, eds., *Roman Artists, Patrons, and Public Consumption. Familiar Works Reconsidered.* Ann Arbor, pp. 1–12.

Marvin, M. (1989). Copying Roman Sculpture: The Replica Series. In: K. Preciado, ed., *Retaining the Original. Multiple Originals, Copies, and Reproductions.* Washington, D.C., pp. 29–45.

Marvin, M. (1997). Roman Sculptural Reproductions or Polykleitos: The Sequel. In: A. Hughes and E. Ranfft, eds., *Sculpture and Its Reproductions.* London, pp. 7–28.

Marvin, M. (2008). *The Language of the Muses. The Dialogue between Roman and Greek Sculpture.* Los Angeles.

Mattusch, C. (2005). *The Villa dei Papiri at Herculaneum. Life and Afterlife of a Sculpture Collection.* Los Angeles.

Mattusch, C. (2015). Bronzes. In: E. Friedland and M. Sobocinski, eds., *The Oxford Handbook of Roman Sculpture*. New York, pp. 139–154.

Meyboom, P. (1995). Famulus and the Painters' Workshops of the Domus Aurea. *Mededelingen van het Nederlands Instituut te Rome* 54, pp. 229–245.

Nochlin, L. (1971). Why Have There Been No Great Women Artists? *ARTnews* 69/9, pp. 22–39 & 67–71.

Peña, T. and McCallum, M. (2009). The Production and Distribution of Pottery at Pompeii: A Review of the Evidence; Part 1, Production. *American Journal of Archaeology* 113/1, pp. 57–79.

Perry, E. (2005). *The Aesthetics of Emulation in the Visual Arts of Ancient Rome*. Cambridge.

Petersen, L. (2006). *The Freedman in Roman Art and Art History*. Cambridge.

Petersen, L. (2011). Why Have There Been No Great Roman Artists? Paper delivered at the College Art Association Annual Conference (New York), Session: *Artists' Biographies from Antiquity to the Present* (sponsored by the Italian Art Society).

Pollitt, J. (1983). *The Art of Rome, c. 753 B.C. – A.D. 337. Sources and Documents*. Cambridge.

Rackham, H. (1952). *Pliny. Natural History, Volume IX: Books 33–35*. Cambridge, MA.

Richardson, L. Jr. (2000). *A Catalog of Identifiable Figure Painters of Ancient Pompeii, Herculaneum, and Stabiae*. Baltimore.

Russell, B. (2015). Transport and Distribution. In: E. Friedland and M. Sobocinski, eds., *The Oxford Handbook of Roman Sculpture*. New York, pp. 189–205.

Spinazzola, V. (1953). *Pompei alla luce degli scavi nuovi di Via dell'Abbondanza*. Rome.

Squire, M. (2015). Roman Art and the Artist. In: B. Borg, ed., *A Companion to Roman Art*. Malden, MA, pp. 172–194.

Stewart, P. (2008). *The Social History of Roman Art*. Cambridge.

Tronchin, F., ed. (2012a). *Collectors and the Eclectic. New Approaches to Roman Domestic Decoration. Arethusa* 45/3.

Tronchin, F. (2012b). Roman Collecting, Decorating, and Eclectic Practice in the Textual Sources. *Arethusa* 45/3, pp. 333–345.

Varner, E. (2006). Reading Replications: Roman Rhetoric and Greek Quotations. *Art History* 29/2, pp. 280–303.

Vasari, G. (1550, trans. 1991). *The Lives of the Artists*, translated by J. Bondanella and P. Bondanella. Oxford.

Vout, C. (2010). Hadrian, Hellenism, and the Social History of Art. *Arion* 18/1, pp. 55–78.

Welch, K. (2006). *Domi Militiaeque*: Roman Domestic Aesthetics and War Booty in the Republic. In: S. Dillon and K. Welch, eds., *Representations of War in Ancient Rome*. Cambridge, pp. 91–161.

Zanker, P. (1998). *Pompeii. Public and Private Life*, trans. D. Lucas Schneider. Cambridge, MA.

Zimmer, G. (1982). *Römische Berufsdarstellungen*. Berlin.

SECTION 2

Pushing the Boundaries of Labour

CHAPTER 6

Emotional Labour in Antiquity: The Case of Roman Prostitution

Sarah Levin-Richardson

1 Introduction

Emotional labour is often described as a phenomenon of late capitalism.[1] Using archaeological, epigraphic, and literary evidence concerning sexual labour in Roman antiquity, I argue that emotional labour existed in antiquity too—if never labelled as such. If this unexplored facet of ancient economic behaviour is hard to quantify in terms of prevalence and contribution to the overall economy, it nevertheless had real value. For sexual labourers who performed emotional labour, it offered the hope of economic stability and perhaps even social mobility. For those who managed or invested in sexual labour (such as pimps), the emotional labour of their workers could boost profit through increasing the number of paying clients or encouraging repeat customers.

Feminist scholars have long encouraged more nuanced approaches to questions of economic production and value. As feminist economic geographers Katherine Gibson and Julie Graham summarize, this body of work has 'focused on the legitimate contribution to economic life made by nonmarket and alternative market transactions, unpaid labour, and noncapitalist economic sites'.[2] This chapter, by acknowledging the existence and value of emotional labour, contributes to a fuller understanding of the ancient Roman economy.

I begin in part I with a short overview of emotional and affective labour, showing how it has been a productive lens for exploring sexual labour in modern contexts. I then use Pompeii's purpose-built brothel as a case study in part II, arguing that the structure's graffiti and archaeological finds demonstrate sexual labourers proclaiming concern for their clients, boosting their egos, and drinking with them. I broaden the discussion in part III to representations of sexual labourers in Greco-Roman literature, finding the performance of emotional labour a common literary trope. We read of historical and fictional

---

1 Hardt 1999, 90, 97; Hochschild 2012, ix.
2 Gibson-Graham 2006, 75.

 | DOI:10.1163/9789004694965_007

sexual labourers performing care (sometimes authentic, sometimes not) for their clients, and of sexual labourers using this labour to mitigate economic precarity or for upward mobility. I return to the question of value in part IV, using Pompeii and its set of 45 graffiti with sexual acts and prices as a test case. It seems that sexual labourers who performed emotional labour (such as those who worked in the purpose-built brothel) did *not* charge higher fees for their services than other sexual labourers. Emotional labour was thus not directly monetized; rather, I suggest that it may have provided a competitive advantage in attracting or retaining clients in a competitive market. I end by suggesting other places to look for emotional labour in antiquity, including among individuals enslaved in domestic households, where it may have been a survival strategy.

One important note about terminology: in order to capture the fullest spectrum possible of those who sold sex, I use the generic phrase 'sexual labourer' throughout, unless the original Latin or Greek text uses a more specific term (see also the end of part III for an analysis of terminology in literary sources).[3]

2 Emotional Labour

The concept of emotional labour arose at the intersection of two mid-to-late-twentieth-century scholarly traditions.[4] As explained by Kathi Weeks, socialist feminist scholars had been taking traditional accounts of the economy to task over what counted as labour and whether gendered work such as domestic labour was 'productive'.[5] At the same time, sociologists of labour were investigating the changing dynamics of worker alienation as white-collar and service-sector jobs became more common.[6] Arlie Hochschild, a sociologist herself, bridged these trends, asserting that the manipulation of emotions in work contexts—often but not always performed by female workers—was in fact labour, and that the performance of such emotional labour had the potential to alienate workers from their very sense of self.[7]

3 Scholars have shown that the reality of sexual labour in both Greek and Roman culture was much more complex than the dichotomy of 'prostitute' versus 'courtesan'; see, e.g., Flemming 1999, 47; Kurke 1999; McClure 2003 9–26; Glazebrook and Henry 2011, 5; Levin-Richardson 2019, 143–144.

4 Weeks 2007. I owe huge thanks to Stephanie Clare for bibliographic suggestions (and related conversation) on emotional and affective labour. Any errors or lapses remain my own.

5 Weeks 2007, 234–239.

6 Weeks 2007, 239–241.

7 See especially Weeks 2007, 240–242; Hochschild 2012, 17–23, 89–91.

As defined in Hochschild's 1983 monograph *The Managed Heart: Commercialization of Human Feeling*, emotional labour 'requires one to induce or suppress feeling in order to sustain the outward countenance that produces the proper state of mind in others'.[8] A similar concept of affective labour was developed in the field of political theory by Michael Hardt and Antonio Negri in the late 1990s and early 2000s.[9] This labour, Hardt writes, 'is immaterial, even if it is corporeal and affective, in the sense that its products are intangible: a feeling of ease, well-being, satisfaction, excitement, passion—even a sense of connectedness or community'; moreover, it is characterized by 'the creation and manipulation of affects'.[10] Whereas Hochschild argued that emotional labour has deleterious effects on workers, Hardt has predicted—not without criticism—that affective labour, as part of the now 'dominant' service and informational sectors of the economy, has the potential to create networks in which workers unite for social and political change.[11]

If scholars' academic training and field of desired intervention dictate whether they use 'emotional labour' or 'affective labour', the areas of study are broadly similar.[12] The focus of Hochschild's work—and the work of many other scholars who use either emotional or affective labour as a theoretical lens—is the emotional labour required, and monetized, by employers (often in the service sector). Areas of exploration include flight attendants (as in Hochschild's original study), restaurant and hotel staff (especially in high-end establishments), those involved in the 'introduction industry' (international matchmaking), and those practising care work, among many other areas of investigation.[13]

8 Hochschild 2012, 7.

9 See, e.g., Hardt 1999; Hardt and Negri 2000; Hardt and Negri 2004. For the intellectual traditions out of which this work arose (namely, Italian *Operaismo*/Workerism), see, e.g., Dowling, Nunes and Trott 2007; Trott 2007; and Wright 2007. For feminist critique of Hardt and Negri's concept of affective labour, see, e.g., Schultz 2006; Rodríguez 2007, 74–75; and the overview in Lanoix 2013.

10 Hardt 1999, 96. See also Hardt and Negri 2000, 292–294; Hardt and Negri 2004, 108.

11 For the dominance of the service and informational sectors, see Hardt 1999, 90, 97. For emotional labour's potential, see Hardt 1999, 96–100; Hardt and Negri 2000, 285–289, 294; Hardt and Negri 2004, xiii–xviii, 108–109; for critique, see, e.g., Schultz 2006; Dowling 2007; Lanoix 2013, 91. Hardt and Negri do acknowledge the potential for alienation, as well (2004, 111).

12 Hardt and Negri suggest that the difference is that 'unlike emotions, which are mental phenomena, affects refer equally to body and mind' (2004, 108); however, it is clear in Hochschild's definition of emotional labour that embodiment is a key aspect as well (the 'outward countenance'; 2012, 7).

13 For luxury hotels, see, e.g., Otis 2016; for elite restaurants, see Dowling 2007; for the 'introduction industry', see, e.g., Meszaros 2017; for care work, see, e.g., Hochschild 2000; Ehren-

The role of management in training their employees to perform emotional labour is often a primary focus, especially in contexts of neoliberalism and capitalism.[14]

In her examination of flight attendants, for example, Hochschild argues that 'the *emotional style of offering the service is part of the service itself* …', and that 'the product is a state of mind'. The airline customer is meant to feel a 'sense of being cared for in a convivial and safe place' with the expectation that one role of flight attendants is to 'enhance the status of the customer'.[15] These expectations are conveyed through manuals as well as weeks-long training programmes (which continue as refresher courses), where the focus is 'the passenger's feeling'.[16] This is true among hotel workers examined by Eileen Otis, too, where 'trainees learned to regard customer self-esteem as a source of profit'.[17] A hotel manager was recorded asking his team, 'Why do we smile? … To give guests self-esteem. They are paying for their self-esteem and respect.'[18] Similarly, the written philosophy of a high-end restaurant examined by Emma Dowling included: 'we want our guests to feel at home and cared for. We have to make them feel that they are the only ones at the party that are important to us'.[19]

---

reich and Hochschild 2003; Rodríguez 2007; Lanoix 2013; Vora 2014. In the afterword to the twentieth-anniversary edition of her monograph, Hochschild takes stock of the studies on emotional labour: 'Scholars studied emotional labour among such employees as social workers, retail sales clerks, Disneyland ride operators, waitresses, receptionists, youth shelter workers, telemarketers, personal trainers, nursing home caregivers, professors, policemen, midwives, door-to-door insurance salesmen, police detectives, hair stylists, and sheriff's interrogators' (2012, 200). See also Wharton 2009 for an overview of scholarship on emotional labour to that date.

14 See, e.g., Hochschild 2012, 8. Hardt and Negri assert that 'the cooperative powers of labour power (particularly immaterial labour power [including affective labour]) afford labour the possibility of valorizing itself' (2000, 294); see, however, the critique at Trott 2007, 224: 'whilst a minority of "privileged" intellectual, artistic or creative workers may well be both capable of, and willing to, valorise their own labour; this is unlikely to be the case in most other sectors. How many workers in a Toyotist factory, temporary labourers entering data into a spreadsheet, or affective fast-food workers would, I wonder, maintain the productivity levels currently expected of them if the individual personifications of capital responsible for overseeing, ordering and directing their daily work were to disappear over night?'

15 Hochschild 2012, 5 (emphasis in the original), 6, 7, 16, respectively.

16 Hochschild 2012, 113. For manuals, see, e.g., Hochschild 2012, 95–97.

17 Otis 2016, 927.

18 Otis 2016, 927.

19 Dowling 2007, 120.

Workers are themselves aware of these expectations for emotional labour, which is framed both by management and by workers themselves as a form of acting. In the case of flight attendants, Hochschild notes that 'the editors of an unofficial flight attendants' newsletter, the *Pan Am Quipper*, described this stance succinctly: "We deal in the *illusion* of good service. We want to make passengers *think* they are having a good time"'.[20] Likewise, among the hotel workers studied by Otis, 'workers exercised interpretive autonomy'.[21] Specifically, workers framed this as 'giving face' or producing status: 'In giving face, workers suggest that they *produce* rather than recognize customer status.'[22] Hochschild summarizes that throughout all of this, 'impersonal relations are to be seen *as if* they were personal. Relations based on getting and giving money are to be seen *as if* they were relations free of money'.[23]

Emotional labour can also be an individual strategy, including for those performing sexual labour.[24] For example, Kimberly Kay Hoang's studies of sexual and emotional labour in contemporary Vietnam finds emotional labour to be a common strategy among a variety of sex labourers. Low-end sex labourers—women who work out of barber shops and provide a roughly 20-minute interaction for the equivalent of three US dollars—perform emotional labour in restraining their own negative feelings about clients.[25] Mid-tier sex labourers often cater to foreigners, evoking feelings of love in order to maintain a high standard of living or to emigrate out of Vietnam.[26] One woman, Tram, was 27 years old and a married mother of three when she met William, a 70-year-old American. William's interest in Tram developed quickly, and within five months Tram divorced her husband and remarried William, who was providing financially for Tram. Tram told Hoang, 'I still love my [first] husband. I have to pretend to love William and I have to take good care of him because he has done so much to help my family already. It's not that I don't love William. It is just a different kind of love; the kind of love where you grow to love the person because they have done so much for you'.[27] William, for his part, told Hoang,

20 Hochschild 2012, 134–135, emphasis added.

21 Otis 2016, 929.

22 Otis 2016, 929, emphasis added.

23 Hochschild 2012, 106; emphasis in the original. See also Dowling 2007, 120 on her experience as a waitress: 'I was supposed to understand myself as a real person interacting with other real people, not "merely" a paid worker providing a service for a paying customer.'

24 For other scholarship on sex work and emotional labour, see, e.g., Brents and Hausbeck 2010, 16.

25 Hoang 2010, 260–262.

26 The rest of the paragraph is summarized from Hoang 2010, 263–266 and Hoang 2013, 23.

27 Hoang 2010, 264.

'I fell in love with Tram from the first day that I met her in Azul ... She knows how to care for me. She is affectionate and she makes me feel loved.'[28] Among high-end sex labourers, where the interactions between women and clients are framed as dating (with the women receiving expensive gifts), emotional labour included appearing with the client in public. Hoang explains, 'high-end sex workers make *Viet Kieu* men [Vietnamese men who work overseas and return to Vietnam for vacations] feel desired and loved by a trophy woman', thus boosting the masculinity of their client vis-à-vis other men.[29]

The successes and limitations of emotional labour can be seen in the trajectories of the 71 Vietnamese sex labourers followed by Hoang.[30] Thirty women were able, like Tram, to parlay their sexual and emotional labour into marriages. However, increasingly stringent immigration policies and a global recession meant that only twelve were able to emigrate from Vietnam, and only four of those women were able to avoid working (another stated goal of the women). The other eight women found themselves as their family's primary wage earner, often through low-paid labour such as working in restaurants, nail salons, or house cleaning.

3 Emotional Labour in the Purpose-Built Brothel

Pompeii's purpose-built brothel (VII.12.18–19), with close to 150 texts and images scratched into the walls, provides unparalleled insights into how sexual labourers and clients represented themselves and their relationships with each other.[31] These graffiti moreover represent a significant outlay of time, as recent studies by Polly Lohmann have shown that even with a metal implement like a stylus or hairpin, it takes both effort and time to create legible texts on ancient plastered walls.[32]

In one graffito, the writer performs his grief at the impending death of a certain Africanus: 'Africanus is dying. The boy Rusticus writes. You will learn who mourns for Africanus' (*Africanus moritur | scribet · puer Rusticus | condisces cui dolet pro Africano*).[33] The fact that the writer refers to himself with

28 Hoang 2010, 265.

29 Hoang 2010, 266–270 (quotation on 270).

30 Hoang 2013, 23 for this paragraph.

31 For a discussion of ancient literacy in the context of Pompeii, see especially Levin-Richardson 2013, 320–327. For graffiti as a carefully constructed genre of representation, see, e.g., Williams 2010, 292–295; Williams 2014, 494–495; Levin-Richardson 2019, 56–61.

32 Lohmann 2018, 247–255.

33 *CIL* 4.2258a Add. pp. 1748–1749. For analysis of this graffito, see Levin-Richardson 2019, 62, 132–133; cf. Solin's analysis at *CIL* 4 Add. p. 1749.

the erotically charged term *puer* suggests that Rusticus was a young male sex labourer; Africanus, one would think, was a client of Rusticus. To understand the scenario leading to this public proclamation of grief, a reader must imagine something more than Africanus' one-time purchase of Rusticus' sexual labour. Rather, readers are meant to imagine a relationship between the two that extended over a longer period of time and perhaps involved an emotional dimension. This was a savvy statement on Rusticus' part: not only did it cement his connection to Africanus (who perhaps left Rusticus a small legacy or gift in his will), but it also advertised to all other clients that Rusticus was more boyfriend than boytoy.

Indeed, greetings between sex labourers and clients are common in the brothel, and suggest real, imagined, or hoped-for connections between the two groups.[34] We read of sex labourers hailing named clients or sending general greetings at least three times. Extending over nearly two-thirds of the east wall of room f, Ias inscribed an enormous greeting to a client named Magnus: 'Ias [sends] greeting to Magnus' (*Ias Magno salute*).[35] It seems likely that Ias wanted to accentuate this relationship, writing on the opposite wall, 'Ias with Magnus everywhere' (*Iias cum Ma|gno ubique*).[36] Mola, proclaimed a 'fucktress' in one graffito (Μόλα φουτοῦτρις), offers a greeting to all potential clients on the wall opposite: 'Mo[l]a [sends] gr[ee]t(ings)' (*Mo*[phallus]*a* | *s*[-]*l*), and this is not a practice restricted to female sexual labourers.[37] A certain Castrensis—whom I have argued elsewhere is a male sex labourer—follows suit: 'Beautiful Castrensis [sends] gr(eetings)' (*calos Castrensis s*(*alutem*)).[38] Clients reciprocated the greetings, too, as in 'Hey mistress Fabia!' (*va*(*le*) *issa* | *Fabia*); or 'Conqueress Victoria, hey!' (*victrix Victoria va*(*le*)), both from room f.[39]

---

34 See also Levin-Richardson 2019, 62–63.

35 *CIL* 4.2231 Add. p. 215, p. 1745. Length of the graffito is 1.9 m (according to my measurements); length of the room, according to Zajac 2008, 33, is 2.91 m. For the likelihood that Ias is a prostitute, see Levin-Richardson 2019, 62.

36 *CIL* 4.2174 Add. p. 1735.

37 *CIL* 4.2204 Add. p. 1741; *CIL* 4.2237 Add. p. 215, p. 1745. For the name as Mula rather than Mola, however, see most recently Solin at *CIL* 4 Add. p. 1741.

38 *CIL* 4.2180 Add. p. 1736; Levin-Richardson 2015. Solin believes the final *s* does not belong to this graffito (Solin at *CIL* 4 Add. p. 1736). *CIL* 4.2206 Add. p. 215, pp. 1741–1742 (*Callidrome va*(*le*); 'Callidromus, hey!') may also fall in this category, though the writer is not named, and the gender of the addressee is contested; see further Levin-Richardson 2019, 117 and Solin at *CIL* 4 Add. pp. 1741–1742.

39 *CIL* 4.2239 Add. p. 1745; *CIL* 4.2212 Add. p. 215, p. 1742. For other greetings in the brothel, see *CIL* 4.2201 Add. p. 1740 (a greeting from Marcus to a woman named Scepsis) and 2208 Add. p. 1742 (a greeting from Sabinus to Proclus, both males).

Furthermore, nine graffiti use the formula '[male name], you fuck well', as in 'Felix, you fuck well' (*Felix | bene futuis*) or a variation—which seems to have been written three times in total across two different rooms of the brothel—that includes a greeting: 'Victor, may you fare well who fucks well!' (*Victor | valea qui bene | futues*).[40] This formula is found almost exclusively in Pompeii's brothel; there is only *one* definite example of a second-person form of *futuere* written elsewhere at Pompeii.[41] For context, most graffiti at Pompeii were written in the third person, even in claims of authorship such as the death notice discussed above ('the boy Rusticus writes;' *scribet · puer Rusticus*).[42] This is true of claims of sexual activity, as well, where third-person forms are preferred, as in 'Phoebus the perfumer fucked best' (*Phoebus · unguentarius | optume futuit*) from the brothel.[43]

The reader of a second-person statement like 'Felix, you fuck well'[44] is left with two distinct impressions: 1) that the client performs the appropriately masculine (i.e., penetrative) sexual role, and 2) that the writer of the statement is *impressed* by the client's sexual performance. It is the attestation of sexual labourers—the voice in which these statements were written, if not also the actual writers—that validates the masculinity of clients.[45]

The objects found during excavation of the brothel suggest other ways in which sex labourers might have had to manage their own emotions or evoke particular emotional responses in others. Among the items recovered were two glass cups and a glass bottle, which I have suggested elsewhere were used to offer alcohol to clients.[46] More to the point, it is possible that sex labourers were expected to keep clients company as they drank—perhaps feigning interest in

40 *CIL* 4.2176 Add. p. 1735; *CIL* 4.2260 Add. p. 216, p. 1749; see also 2274 Add. p. 216, p. 1751; 2218 Add. p. 1743 (cf. Solin's reading at *CIL* 4 Add. p. 1743). The other five graffiti using this formula are: 2185 Add. p. 1737–1738; 2186 Add. p. 1738; 2187 Add. p. 1738; 2219 Add. p. 1743; 2253 Add. p. 1747.

41 According to a search of the Epigraphik-Datenbank Clauss Slaby (EDCS) for forms of *futu-* at Pompeii; definite example: *Filus salax | quia to[t] muliero|rum difutuisti* (*CIL* 4.5213 Add. pp. 1874–1875; text from Solin at *CIL* 4 Add. pp. 1874–1875). Similar in some ways to the brothel's second-person graffiti is *Eulale bene valeas | cum Vera tua coniuge | et bene futue eam* … (*CIL* 4.1574 Add. p. 208, p. 1671), but note the form *futue* (translated by Varone 2002, 164 as 'fucking'). I hesitate to add the extremely fragmentary *CIL* 4.8620, restored (tentatively) by Solin 1968, 114–115 as *Eumacia fu*[*tu*]*er*[*is*] *va*(*le*).

42 *CIL* 4.2258a Add. p. 1749.

43 *CIL* 4.2184 Add. p. 215, p. 1737.

44 *CIL* 4.2176 Add. p. 1735.

45 See also Levin-Richardson 2011, 65; Levin-Richardson 2019, 103, 115–116.

46 Levin-Richardson 2019, 36, 100–101, 116.

their clients' work or families, or stroking their egos (a situation attested in literature; see further below).

In sum, the brothel's sex labourers expressed grief at the illness of clients, inscribed greetings to clients, voiced amazement at the sexual prowess of their clients, and probably chatted with clients as they drank.

4 Emotional Labour among Greco-Roman Sexual Labourers

Greek and Roman literature also presents evocative moments of sexual labourers performing emotional labour. For example, the Greek comic playwright Ephippus draws out the emotional labour performed by courtesans (*hetairôn*): 'Then, if one of us happens to be unhappy when he goes into her house, she's sweet and flattering ... and coaxes him and makes him cheerful, and in a flash she makes whatever's upsetting him disappear, and puts him in a good mood.'[47] Even the philosopher Socrates is made to comment upon the (deceptive, according to him) emotional labour of sexual labourers, addressing a woman named Theodote (Xen. *Mem.* 3.11.10. Trans. Marchant 2013).[48]

> And inside it [your body] you have a soul that teaches you what glance will please, what words delight, and tells you that you should give a warm welcome to an eager suitor but slam the door on a roughhouser; yes, and when a friend has fallen sick, to show your anxiety by visiting him; and when he has had a stroke of good fortune, to congratulate him eagerly; and if he is eager in his suit, to put yourself at his service heart and soul.

Keeping in mind the roles of generic conventions and of authorial intent—and that sexual labourers were 'good to think with' in antiquity—fictionalized accounts offer parallels to the types of emotional labour already seen in Pompeii's purpose-built brothel and suggest further possible arenas for such labour.

Literature sometimes represents sexual labourers performing care for their clients (compare Rusticus' articulation of grief for Africanus in the brothel). This set of expectations is most clearly delineated by a client in a Roman comedy. Phaedria demands of his love interest: 'Day and night love me, miss me, dream of me, look for me, think of me, hope for me, delight in me, be entirely

47 Ath. 13.571e. All translations of Athenaeus by Olson 2010–2011. For Athenaeus, see further McClure 2003.

48 For this passage, see McClure 2003, 120.

with me. In short, be my heart as I am yours.'[49] Indeed, Amy Richlin has shown that one trope in Roman comedy is that sexual labourers crafted their sexual desire to mirror that of their clients, as when the sexual labourer Philematium says, 'What you feel like doing, that's what I feel like doing, my pleasure.'[50] We can see an expectation of concern in *Dialogues of the Courtesans* 9, in which Pannychis takes up with another man when her client Polemo goes off to war. Upon the unexpected return of Polemo, she needs him to know that she thought of him constantly. Using their respective enslaved attendants (Dorcas and Parmeno) as go-betweens, Pannychis wants her servant to relay, '"My mistress was always asking what you were doing and where you were."' Pannychis adds, as an aside to Dorcas, 'And it would have been a lot better if you'd added that [I] was always crying and talking of Polemo.'[51] Luckily Dorcas has done just this, communicating that '"when someone had returned from battle and there were said to be a lot of fatal casualties, [Pannychis would] tear her hair, beat her breast, and grieve at every message."'[52]

In Roman historiography, the performance of emotion and care on the part of sexual labourers is called out for particular praise. For example, Plutarch's description of Flora, one-time lover of Pompey, claims that when Pompey stopped seeing her, 'she herself did not take this treatment as a mere courtesan (*hetairikôs*) would, but was sick for a long time with grief and longing'.[53] This trope can be found in other genres, such as declamation. In one of Seneca's *Controversies*, on whether a man should acknowledge the child born of his good-for-nothing, ailing son and a prostitute, Porcius Latro offers the following defence of the grandfather doing just that, praising the prostitute's devotion to the son: 'What a woman I saw! She was herself attending to what had to be done; attentive at the sick man's bedside she ran to do every service, her hair

49 Ter. *Eun.* 193–196. Trans. Barsby 2001. A dark(er) side to the expectation of emotional labour can be seen in *Hecyra*, where not only is a sexual labourer required to flatter her client, but her speech is restricted to *only* such statements. This is the implication made by the character Philotis, a prostitute (*meretrix*) who left Athens to go to Corinth for two years with 'that brute of a soldier and endured two whole years of misery with him;' she recalls: 'There I wasn't allowed to say anything except what would please him, and that was strictly defined' (Ter. *Hec.* 86–87. Trans. Barsby 2001); another character observes, 'I don't imagine you enjoyed having the soldier regulate your speech' (94–96). Cf. Fitzgerald 2000, 75 on restrictions on the speech of enslaved individuals in Roman culture.

50 Plaut. *Mostell.* 296–297. Trans Richlin 2017, 235. See also Richlin 2017, 280, 430.

51 *Dial. meret.* 9.301–302. All translations of *Dialogues of the Courtesans* by Macleod 1961.

52 *Dial. meret.* 9.302; see below for the performative—and potentially inauthentic—nature of this kind of emotional labour.

53 *Pomp.* 2.3. Trans. Perrin 1917.

not merely dishevelled but torn out. "Where is the prostitute (*meretrix*)?" I said to myself.'[54] Papirius Fabianus echoes this rhetoric in his turn: 'How true it is that I saw nothing of a prostitute's (*meretriciae*) way of life in that house! At the bedside sat a woman, sad-faced, ailing, herself much like the patient, her eyes cast down.'[55] Seneca and Plutarch thus acknowledge—and yet attempt to disavow as rare—that emotional bonds could exist between sexual labourers and their clients.

In other literary representations, sexual labourers affirm a client's ego (often their masculinity). In one of Lucian's *Dialogues of the Courtesans*, the client Leontichus is telling Hymnis gruesome (but made-up) stories about war in an attempt to impress her. When Hymnis is horrified and gets ready to leave, Leontichus offers her twice the fee to stay, stating 'I thought you'd be delighted to hear my tale'.[56] The expected reaction, as Leontichus informs us, should be the performance of delight. At stake is Leontichus' sense of masculinity, which needs Hymnis as an audience to validate. In an example from Roman comedy, Erotium says of her client, 'Look, I can see him, the man who is of the greatest use and benefit to me. I reciprocate of my own accord, as he deserves, *so that he's the most important person in our house*.'[57]

In addition, some of the ways that this labour could be valued can be gleaned through these fictional accounts. For example, in *Dialogues of the Courtesans* 8, Ampelis, an older courtesan, counsels Chrysis, a younger courtesan who is currently being physically abused by her client. Ampelis tells her this is actually a *good* thing, as it suggests that Chrysis has effectively inspired love in her client: 'If a man isn't jealous or angry, Chrysis, and never hits you, cuts your hair off, or

54 Sen. *Controv.* 2.4.1. Trans. Winterbottom 1974.

55 Sen. *Controv.* 2.4.3. Trans. Winterbottom 1974. See also Strong 2016, 53. The same speakers then go on to defend the position of *not* acknowledging the child, pointing to the fact that the child, being born of a prostitute, has unknowable paternity, and that her profession brings shame not just to herself, but to anyone associated with her (her child, her husband, the grandfather if he chooses to acknowledge the grandson as his). There are also literary examples of sexual labourers soothing clients with broken hearts (*Dial. meret.* 11; the client is depicted crying and whimpering with heartbreak over another woman), and emotional labour may be hiding behind the description of sexual labourers' charm. In *Casina*, for example, Cleo notes: 'My dear, it's not the job of wives, but of prostitutes (*meretricium*), to charm other men' (Plaut. *Cas.* 585–586. Trans. De Melo 2011–2013); see also Ter. *Hec.* 858–860.

56 *Dial. meret.* 13:317.

57 Plaut. *Men.* 357–359; emphasis added. All translations of Plautus by De Melo 2011–2013 unless otherwise noted. Erotium continues, '… out of all men Venus wanted me to hold you alone in esteem, and not undeservedly so: you alone let me flourish through your generosity' (*Men.* 370–372).

tears your clothes, is he still in love with you? … And so, if Gorgias hits you, and shows jealousy, as you say, you may be hopeful, and should pray that he always continues in the same way.'[58] To show that this approach pays off monetarily, Ampelis ends by telling Chrysis that one of her own clients 'began to burn and blaze with passion … He began to weep and strike me, he threatened to kill me, he tore my dress; there was nothing he didn't do, and in the end he gave me a talent and kept me for himself alone for eight whole months.'[59]

In another of the *Dialogues of the Courtesans*, Crobyle, an impoverished widow, instructs her daughter in the proper bodily comportment, behaviour, and emotional performance of a courtesan.[60] The mother puts forward the example of a successful neighbouring courtesan: 'In the first place, she dresses attractively and looks neat; *she's happy with all the men, without being so ready to cackle as you are, but smiles in a sweet bewitching way*; later on, she's very clever when they're together, never cheats a visitor or an escort, and never throws herself at the men …'[61] After detailing in addition the proper way to eat and drink, Crobyle concludes, '… her only aim is to attract the man *and make him love her*; these are the things they all praise in her. *If you can learn all this, we'll be just as prosperous as she is.*'[62] In this account, emotional labour—specifically, the daughter managing her own emotional responses such as smiling in order to 'make [the client] love her'—is one tool along with refined behaviour that will not only raise the family out of poverty but allow them to become prosperous. The value is quantifiable to Crobyle; she entices her daughter to perform these various types of labour since 'it would be easy for you both to keep me and provide yourself with clothes, that you would be rich, and have purple dresses and maids'.[63] In another *Dialogue*, a mother chastises her daugh-

58 *Dial. meret.* 8.299.

59 *Dial. meret.* 8.300.

60 *Dial. meret.* 6:292–293.

61 *Dial. meret.* 6.294; emphasis added. Cf. the 1979–1980 *Airline Guide to Stewardess and Steward Careers*; as Hochschild summarizes, 'Under the subheading "Appearance," the manual suggests that facial expressions should be "sincere" and "unaffected." One should have a "modest but friendly smile" and be "generally alert, attentive, not overly aggressive, but not reticent either." Under "Mannerisms," subheading "Friendliness," it is suggested that a successful candidate must be "outgoing but not effusive," "enthusiastic with calm and poise," and "vivacious but not effervescent." As the manual continues: "Maintaining eye contact with the interviewer demonstrates sincerity and confidence, but don't overdo it. Avoid cold or continuous staring." Training, it seems, begins even before recruitment' (Hochschild 2012, 95–96).

62 *Dial. meret.* 6.294; emphasis added.

63 *Dial. meret.* 6.293. In other literary depictions, it is a general sense of economic security that is at stake. For example, Astaphium, an older maid enslaved to a sexual labourer in the

ter for performing emotional labour *without* recompense. The mother notes that even though her daughter Musarium is 'constant and affectionate', the client 'sits, bringing us to ruin, giving nothing himself, and forbidding you to take from those who will give.'[64]

The trope of sexual labourers performing emotional labour for remuneration was so commonplace that it could be mocked. In a snippet of Anaxilas, a comic playwright, the character Neottis compares sexual labourers to monsters, explaining, 'You could call any whore (*pornas*) a Theban Sphinx, because they never talk straight, but speak in riddles, *claiming to love you, and be sweet on you, and enjoy sleeping with you*. Then she says, "I'd like a [corrupt] or a chair with four feet!".'[65] We see the monetary benefits of this type of behaviour also in Roman comedy. The hanger-on of *Menaechmi* makes the following observation: 'A prostitute (*meretrix*) only flatters as long as she can see something she can snatch.'[66]

Many of the examples above suggest that sexual labourers carefully crafted performances of emotional labour.[67] This was a sort of open secret, offering opportunities for sex labourers to be agents and causing anxiety about the authenticity of their feelings and behaviour in Roman culture more broadly. Laura McClure observes that 'in a parody of epic invocation from the fragmentary prologue of Menander's *Thais*, a character complains of these feigned emotions: "Sing to me, Goddess, of this sort of woman, | one who is bold, voluptuous, and altogether clever (*pithanên*), | who is unjust, who shuts out her lovers, who begs excessively, | *but who loves no one and yet always pretends to* (*prospoioumenên*)."'[68] Indeed, Catharine Edwards has argued that one reason

Truculentus, observes, 'In what way are we greedy? How is it actually that we treat them [clients] badly? No lover has ever given enough security to his girlfriend' (Plaut. *Truculentus* 238–239).

64 *Dial. meret.* 7:297.

65 Ath. 13.558d–e; emphasis added.

66 Plaut. *Men.* 193. Cf. Cyamus, slave of Diniarchus: '… the prostitute (*meretrix*) here entangles my wretched master in poverty through her flattery; she'll deprive him of possessions, light, reputation, and friends' (Plaut. *Truculentus* 572–574).

67 See also McClure 2003, 107–136. Partly this is the result of generic conventions; as McClure notes, the 'collective experience of performance and public display brought a theatrical vocabulary to the narratives and dramatic texts that shaped Athenaeus' discourse on hetaeras …' (2003, 107; see also 109–110). She continues, however, 'This public presence in everyday life, combined with their literary representation, contributed to the view of courtesans as consummate performers who constructed themselves wholly through artifice' (2003, 108).

68 Men. *Thais* F163 KA. Trans. McClure 2003, 119, emphasis added.

sexual labourers and actors were categorized as *infames* ('without honour') is due to this type of performativity for money that calls into question authenticity.[69] And, as she notes, sex labourers and stage performers were routinely assumed to move freely between the two roles.[70] Even if the individuals who performed these types of labour were refused honour (with some exceptions), the value of their labour can be seen in elite boasts about sponsoring theatrical or gladiatorial spectacles, or even bringing celebrity fighters or actors to the stage.[71] In our case, sexual and emotional labour could have value even though the workers themselves were held in low esteem.

Inauthenticity and performativity abound in the literary depictions discussed above: the stage-direction-within-a-staged performance when the client Phaedria demands, 'Day and night love me, miss me, dream of me, look for me, think of me, hope for me, delight in me, be entirely with me. In short, be my heart as I am yours';[72] the scheming (and even scripting!) between Pannychis and her servant to present the impression that the former has been worrying herself with grief over her client;[73] the extensive 'stage directions' given by Crobyle to her daughter so that the latter can perform the role of courtesan properly;[74] the fear that monstrous women will eat a client out of house and home by '*claiming to love you, and be sweet on you*';[75] the expectation seen in the quip 'A prostitute only flatters as long as she can see something she can snatch' that once a sex labourer has what she wants, the performance of flattery will abruptly cease;[76] and the tirade against the 'sort of women ... *who loves no one and yet always pretends to.*'[77]

Hochschild observed the performative quality of emotional labour in her original study of flight attendants as well: 'Sometimes the recruitment literature explicitly addresses friendliness as an *act*. Allegheny Airlines, for example, says that applicants are expected to "*project a warm personality* during their interview in order to be eligible for employment". Continental Airlines, in its

69 Edwards 1993, 118–119; Edwards 1997, 79.

70 Edwards 1993, 128–131; Edwards 1997, 81. Two names of courtesans in Athenaeus evoke theatrical performance: 'Stage' (Proscenion, Ath. 587b) and 'Stage Pounder' (Theatrotoryne, Ath. 157a) (trans. McClure 2003, 71, 73; see also McClure 2003, 116, 121–122).

71 See, e.g., *CIL* 10.1074d; for the public honour given to the actor Gaius Norbanus Sorex at Pompeii, see *CIL* 10.814; see further Levin-Richardson forthcoming.

72 Ter. *Eun.* 193–196.

73 *Dial. meret.* 9:301–302.

74 *Dial. meret.* 6:292–294.

75 Ath. 13.558d–e.

76 Plaut. *Men.* 193.

77 Men. *Thais* F163 KA.

own words, is "seeking people who convey a spirit of enthusiasm"'.[78] Hochschild continues, 'The trainees, it seemed to me, were also chosen for their ability to take stage directions about how to "project" an image. They were selected for being able to act well—that is, without showing the effort involved. They had to be able to appear at home on stage'.[79]

If many of the texts above represent emotional labour as part of the multifaceted offerings of 'courtesans' specifically, Seneca reminds us that emotional labour could be identified among 'prostitutes', too. Moreover, as McClure has shown for Athenaeus and Serena Witzke for Roman comedy, the terminology used to describe individuals who perform sexual labour is determined by the writer's attitude towards the character: the same character can be described with both high- and low-register terms of prostitution depending upon the needs of the narrative.[80] Finally, if emotional labour—along with other refinements such as musical ability and intellectual capacity—was conceptualized in some of these texts as part of what differentiates a 'courtesan' from a 'prostitute', the texts also reveal that this could be a tool or tactic used by *any* individual offering sexual labour.

5 Emotional Labour and Value

I have argued so far that individuals could and did perform emotional labour as part of, or as ancillary to, their sexual labour. To what extent was that labour remunerated or valued? Were sexual labourers who provided emotional labour able to garner higher prices for their services?

Pompeii can be our test case. Pier Guzzo and Vincenzo Scarano Ussani have catalogued 47 graffiti at Pompeii that offer a named individual or sexual act for a specific price.[81] Updated readings of these graffiti provided by Heikki Solin in the most recent fascicle of *CIL* 4 (supplement 4.2), combined with my own analysis, removes a few graffiti while adding a few others, for a total of 45 examples.[82]

78 Hochschild 2012, 97; emphasis in the original.

79 Hochschild 2012, 98.

80 McClure 2003, 11, 13, 18; Witzke 2015.

81 Guzzo and Scarano Ussani 2009, 121–122 [tabellae 1 and 2]; cf. Thomas McGinn's catalogue, which includes prices in Pompeian graffiti and as represented in literature (2004, 42).

82 Levin-Richardson 2023. *CIL* 4.1307 Add. p. 1644; 1751 Add. p. 211, p. 464, p. 1686; 1784 Add. p. 1689 (note that the end of the graffito, which Guzzo and Scarano Ussani 2009, 121 interpret as a price of eleven *asses*, is not very clear, however); 1969 Add. p. 1720; 2193 Add. p. 1739; 2228 Add. p. 1744; 2279 Add. p. 216, p. 1751; 2450 Add. p. 1772; 3964 Add. p. 1795; 3999

Prices in these graffiti range from one to 27 *asses*, with two *asses* being the most common. Prices mentioned in the purpose-built brothel—where, as argued above, individuals performed emotional labour—are not very different, ranging from two to sixteen *asses*.[83] Moreover, the corpus of Pompeian graffiti with prices does not seem to call attention to or advertise emotional labour. Many of these statements include only a name and price; when additional information is given, it often specifies the type of sexual act (eleven examples; usually oral sex);[84] or identifies the individual selling sex as a *verna*, a 'home-born slave' (nine examples);[85] or describes the individual with the phrase *bellis moribus*, 'with good manners' (five examples).[86] It is possible that emotional labour underlies the advertisement of homeborn-slave status—in literature, homeborn slaves could be praised for their affection and loyalty towards their owners[87]—or that *bellis moribus*, a phrase found only at Pompeii and only in the context of prostitution, might have encompassed emotional labour.[88] But even if one or both of these scenarios holds, higher fees are not associated with those so described: *vernae* command two to eight *asses* (with two *asses* being the most common price for *vernae* as with sex labourers in general); and those described with the phrase *bellis moribus* charge from two to ten *asses*.

It seems, then, that emotional labour might not have led directly to a higher fee paid by a client (or at least not in a way that we can track through graffiti). It may, however, have attracted more customers, or more repeat customers. This is the case in Hochschild's original study of emotional labour in the air-

---

Add. pp. 1796–1797; 4023 Add. p. 1799; 4024 Add. p. 1799; 4025 Add. p. 1799; 4150 Add. p. 1808; 4259 Add. p. 705, pp. 1819–1820; 4277 Add. p. 1821; 4439 Add p. 705, p. 1832; 4441 Add. p. 1832; 4592 Add. p. 1841; 4593 Add. p. 1841; 5105 Add. p. 1871; 5127 Add. p. 1872; 5203 Add. p. 1874; 5204 Add. p. 1874; 5206 Add. p. 1874; 5338a Add. p. 1881; 5345 Add. p. 1882; 5372 Add. p. 1883 (note that the price might be one or two *asses*, depending on the reading; see further Solin at *CIL* 4 Add. p. 1883); 5408 Add. pp. 1887–1888; 7068 Add. p. 1909; 7339; 7764; 8034; 8160; 8185; 8224; 8454; 8465a; 8483; 8511; 8812; 8939; 8940; 10078; Varone 2000, no. 40.

83 Two *asses*: *CIL* 4.2279 Add. p. 216, p. 1751; five *asses*: 2228 Add. p. 1744 (listed by Guzzo and Scarano Ussani 2009, 121, among 'casi incerti'); sixteen *asses*: 2193 Add. p. 1739.

84 N = 5 for fellatio (*CIL* 4.1784, Add. p. 1689; 1969 Add. p. 1720; 5408 Add. pp. 1887–1888; 8160; 8185); n = 3 for cunnilingus (*CIL* 4.3999 Add. pp. 1796–1797; 8939; 8940); n = 3 for other (*CIL* 4.1751 Add. p. 211, p. 464, p. 1644 (*futuere*); *CIL* 4.2193 Add. p. 1739 (*futuit*); *CIL* 4.8483 (*mentula*); one might add *CIL* 4.10078 (*cinaede*)).

85 *CIL* 4.3964 Add. p. 1795; 4023 Add. p. 1799; 4025 Add. p. 1799; 4592 Add. p. 1841; 4593 Add. p. 1841; 5105 Add. p. 1871; 5203 Add. p. 1874; 5204 Add. p. 1874; 5345 Add. p. 1882; see further Levin-Richardson 2023.

86 *CIL* 4.4024 Add. p. 1799; 4025 Add. p. 1799; 4592 Add. p. 1841; 5127 Add. p. 1972; Varone 2000, no. 40.

87 See, e.g., Stat. *Silv.* 2.1 and 5.5.

88 On this phrase, see further Berg 2018, 56–57.

line industry, where emotional labour was thought to provide a competitive advantage among airlines that otherwise were offering similar services and charging the same prices (which were regulated by law in the US until 1978).[89] Hochschild's summary of this economic scenario might apply in the case of Pompeii's sexual labourers, too: 'When competition in price is out, competition in service is in'.[90]

For the owner or manager of the Pompeii's purpose-built brothel, emotional labour may have been an economic strategy to distinguish prostitution in the purpose-built brothel from street prostitution, attracting more, or better, clients.[91] Compare the marketing of the bath complex in Julia Felix's properties (II.4.3) at Pompeii as *nongentum*, 'for prestige clients' as Eve D'Ambra translates it.[92] D'Ambra further comments, '... did this play to the aspirations of potential tenants who wanted to see themselves as prosperous, or upwardly mobile strivers worthy of a "classy" establishment? Here we have the exploitation of real estate for commercial gain, as well as the developer's propensity to play up to clients' self-image and sense of worth (if we hadn't known this was a very old game, we do now)'.[93]

For the sex labourers themselves, emotional labour could be used to encourage gifts, money in addition to their fee, or the promise of manumission from clients (all of which are attested in legal and literary texts).[94] Given the precarity that characterized the lives of enslaved and poor free sex labourers—not to mention the systematic sexual and non-sexual violence they routinely encountered—even a small gift or a few coins could make a difference in their life.

---

89 Hochschild 2012, 91; see also 104–105: 'In all their courses, [flight attendants] were constantly reminded that their own job security and the company's profit rode on a smiling face. A seat in a plane, they were told, "is our most perishable product—we have to keep winning our passengers back". How you do it is as important as what you do. There were many direct appeals to smile: "Really work on your smiles." "Your smile is your biggest asset—use it"'.

90 Hochschild 2012, 92.

91 Levin-Richardson 2019, 146.

92 *CIL* 4.1136; D'Ambra 2021, 88–89. D'Ambra comments, 'According to Pliny the Elder (*NH* 33.31), the *nongentii* formed a subset of the equestrian order, that is, the nine hundred who would constitute the "best people"' (2021, 89).

93 D'Ambra 2021, 89.

94 Flemming 1999, 46, 49; Levin-Richardson 2019, 117–118. In addition to the examples discussed in the main text above, see, e.g., [Quint] *Maj. Decl.* 14–15.

6 Conclusion

Once we begin to look for emotional labour, we find it in other contexts. Literary sources represent enslaved individuals tempering their owners' moods and modelling their own affective states upon their enslavers. We see one example of this in the Roman comedy *Heauton Timorumenos*, when the father, sad because his son has gone off as a mercenary without telling him, observes, 'I sat down, and slaves ran up and took off my shoes. I saw others bustling about, setting the table, preparing the dinner, *every one of them doing his very best to soothe my grief*.'[95] In another comedy (*Amphitryon*), an enslaved attendant notes, '... it seems right for a decent slave to stick to this principle: just as his masters are, so he too should be himself: he should model his expression on theirs: he should be unhappy if his masters are unhappy and he should be cheerful if they are happy.'[96]

The performance of emotional labour by enslaved individuals was not restricted to the genre of comedy. The poet Statius praises the deceased enslaved favourites of his friends partly for their performance of emotional labour. According to Statius, Glaucias was able to mitigate his owner's moods; addressing Glaucias' grieving owner Atedius Melior, Statius rhetorically asks, 'Who shall soothe your breast with the merry talk you loved? Who relax your cares, your mind's secrets? Who shall calm you when angry bile inflames and you wax wroth with your servants, turning you from your hot choler to himself?'[97] Praising another friend's deceased favourite slave, Statius writes to the boy's owner, 'With you he was grave and happy, his mood never his own, from your face he took his countenance.'[98]

In these sources, we might see traces of anxiety on the part of both enslaved individuals and enslavers. For the former, the emotional state of their owner could have direct and dire consequences, from beatings to being put up for sale (and with that, possible separation from family members). In the *Heauton Timorumenos*, in fact, the father's grief leads him to sell off most of the enslaved

95 Ter. *Haut.* 124–127; emphasis added.

96 Plaut. *Amph.* 959–961. The bind that this put enslaved individuals in was recognized by slave owners; in the very same play, the mistress of the house comments upon how slaves will never give a truthful answer, moulding their answer to fit what they think their enslaver wants to hear. Her husband, in turn, asks a nearly impossible task: for his slave to speak the truth, even if it is not what he wants to hear (Plaut. *Amph.* 750–752).

97 *Silv.* 2.1.56–59. Translations of Statius by Shackleton Bailey rev. Parrott 2015. For *deliciae* in these poems, see Laes 2010.

98 *Silv.* 2.6.52–53, with modifications.

members of his household.[99] Emotional labour in this case may be seen as a survival strategy aimed at preventing those outcomes. For slave owners, passages like that in the *Amphitryon* might raise anxiety about a lack of authenticity among those with whom they lived (and upon whom they relied for nearly everything). If modern examples of emotional labour blur the boundaries between 'private' and 'public' (to use those terms very loosely; these spheres are not and never were truly separate),[100] it is not surprising that we see emotional labour in antiquity among individuals for whom the division between labour and leisure was effectively nil (namely, sexual labourers and enslaved household members).

Finally, the unveiling of emotional labour among a range of low-status individuals raises further questions about status and labour in Roman culture. Is the lack of direct remuneration for emotional labour partly the result of it being performed most commonly by low-status individuals? Is the performance of emotional labour partly *constitutive* of a subaltern or subordinate status?[101] I invite readers to ponder these questions and continue exploring the various incarnations and ramifications of emotional labour in antiquity.

Bibliography

Barsby, J. (2001). *Terence*, 2 vols. Cambridge/London.

Berg, R. (2018). Introduction: Unveiling Roman Courtesans. In: R. Berg and R. Neudecker, eds., *The Roman Courtesan. Archaeological Reflections of a Literary Topos*. Rome, pp. 43–63.

Brents, B. and Hausbeck, K. (2010). Sex Work Now: What the Blurring of Boundaries around the Sex Industry Means for Sex Work, Research, and Activism. In: M. Ditmore, A. Levy and A. Willman, eds., *Sex Work Matters. Exploring Money, Power, and Intimacy in the Sex Industry*. London, pp. 9–22.

D'Ambra, E. (2021). Real Estate for Profit: Julia Felix's Property and the Forum Frieze. In: B. Longfellow and M. Swetnam-Burland, eds., *Women's Lives, Women's Voices. Roman Material Culture and Female Agency in the Bay of Naples*. Austin, pp. 85–105.

De Melo, W. (2011–2013). *Plautus*, 5 vols. Cambridge–London.

Dowling, E. (2007). Producing the Dining Experience: Measure, Subjectivity and the Affective Worker. *Ephemera* 7.1, pp. 117–132.

99 Ter. *Haut.* 130, 142–144.

100 See, e.g., Schultz 2006, 81.

101 This can coexist with emotional labour being one of the mechanisms through which individuals could safeguard or elevate their status.

Dowling, E., Nunes, R., and Trott, B. (2007). Immaterial and Affective Labor: Explored. *Ephemera* 7.1, pp. 1–7.

Edwards, C. (1993). *The Politics of Immorality in Ancient Rome*. Cambridge.

Edwards, C. (1997). Unspeakable Professions: Public Performance and Prostitution in Ancient Rome. In: J.P. Hallett and M.B. Skinner, eds., *Roman Sexualities*. Princeton, pp. 66–95.

Ehrenreich, B. and Hochschild, A. (2003). *Global Woman. Nannies, Maids, and Sex Workers in the New Economy*. New York.

Fitzgerald, W. (2000). *Slavery and the Roman Literary Imagination*. Cambridge.

Flemming, R. (1999). *Quae corpore quaestum facit*: The Sexual Economy of Female Prostitution in the Roman Empire. *Journal of Roman Studies*, 89, pp. 38–61.

Gibson-Graham, J.K. (2006). Imagining and Enacting a Postcapitalist Feminist Economic Politics. *Women's Studies Quarterly*, 34:1/2, pp. 72–78.

Glazebrook, A. and Henry, M. (2011). Introduction. In: A. Glazebrook and M. Henry, eds., *Greek Prostitutes in the Ancient Mediterranean, 800 BCE–200 CE*. Madison, pp. 3–13.

Guzzo, P. and Scarano Ussani, V. (2009). *Ex corpore lucrum facere. La prostituzione nell'antica Pompei*. Rome.

Hardt, M. (1999). Affective Labor. *Boundary 2*, 26:2, pp. 89–100.

Hardt, M. and Negri, A. (2000). *Empire*. Cambridge, MA.

Hardt, M. and Negri, A. (2004) *Multitude. War and Democracy in the Age of Empire*. New York.

Hoang, K. (2010). Economies of Emotion, Familiarity, Fantasy, and Desire: Emotional Labor in Ho Chi Minh City's Sex Industry. *Sexualities*, 13, pp. 255–272.

Hoang, K. (2013). Transnational Gender Vertigo. *Contexts*, 12, pp. 22–26.

Hochschild, A. (2000). Global Care Chains and Emotional Surplus Value. In: W. Hutton and A. Giddens, eds., *Global Capitalism*. New York, pp. 130–146.

Hochschild, A. (2012). *The Managed Heart. Commercialization of Human Feeling*. 2nd edition. Berkeley.

Kurke, L. (1999). *Coins, Bodies, Games, and Gold. The Politics of Meaning in Archaic Greece*. Princeton.

Laes, C. (2010). Delicia-Children Revisited: The Evidence of Statius' *Silvae*. In: V. Dasen and T. Späth, eds., *Children, Memory, and Family Identity in Roman Culture*. Oxford, pp. 245–272.

Lanoix, M. (2013). Labor as Embodied Practice: The Lessons of Care Work. *Hypatia*, 28.1, pp. 85–100.

Levin-Richardson, S. (2011). *Facilis hic futuit*: Graffiti and Masculinity in Pompeii's 'Purpose-built' Brothel. *Helios*, 38, pp. 59–78.

Levin-Richardson, S. (2013). *Fututa sum hic*: Female Subjectivity and Agency in Pompeian Sexual Graffiti. *Classical Journal*, 108, pp. 319–345.

Levin-Richardson, S. (2015). *Calos* graffiti and *infames* at Pompeii. *Zeitschrift für Papyrologie und Epigraphik*, 195, pp. 274–282.

Levin-Richardson, S. (2019). *The Brothel of Pompeii. Sex, Class, and Gender at the Margins of Roman Society.* Cambridge.

Levin-Richardson, S. (2023). *Vernae* and Prostitution at Pompeii. *Classical Quarterly*, 73.1, pp. 250–256.

Levin-Richardson, S. (forthcoming). Identifying Gender. In: J. Berry and R. Benefiel, eds., *The Oxford Handbook of Pompeii and Environs*. Oxford.

Lohmann, P. (2018). *Graffiti als Interaktionsform. Geritzte Inschriften in den Wohnhäusern Pompejis*. Berlin.

Macleod, M.D. (1961). *Lucian*, vol. 7. Cambridge–London.

Marchant, E.C. (2013). *Xenophon* Memorabilia, Oeconomicus. Cambridge–London.

McClure, L. (2003). *Courtesans at Table. Gender and Greek Literary Culture in Athenaeus.* Oxford–New York.

McGinn, T. (2004). *The Economy of Prostitution in the Roman World. A Study of Social History and the Brothel.* Ann Arbor.

Meszaros, J. (2017). American Men and Romance Tourism: Searching for Traditional Trophy Wives as Status Symbols of Masculinity. *Women's Studies Quarterly*, 45, pp. 225–242.

Olson, S.D. (2010–2011). *Athenaeus* The Learned Banqueters, vols. 6–7. Cambridge–London.

Otis, E. (2016). Globalization, Gender, and Service Labor at a Luxury Hotel. *Gender and Society*, 30, pp. 912–934.

Perrin, B. (1917). *Plutarch's* Lives, vol. 5: *Agesilaus and Pompey, Pelopidas and Marcellus.* Cambridge–London.

Richlin, A. (2017). *Slave Theater in the Roman Republic. Plautus and Popular Comedy.* Cambridge.

Rodríguez, E.G. (2007). The 'Hidden Side' of the New Economy: On Transnational Migration, Domestic Work, and Unprecedented Intimacy. *Frontiers*, 28.3, pp. 60–83.

Shackleton Bailey, D.R. rev. Parrott, C. (2015). *Statius* Silvae. Cambridge–London.

Shultz, S. (2006). Dissolved Boundaries and 'Affective Labor': On the Disappearance of Reproductive Labor and Feminist Critique in *Empire*. Translated by F. Peters. *Capitalism Nature Socialism*, 17.1, pp. 77–82.

Solin, H. (1968). Pompeiana. *Epigraphica*, 30, pp. 105–125.

Strong, A. (2016). *Prostitutes and Matrons in the Roman World.* Cambridge.

Trott, B. (2007). Immaterial Labor and World Order: An Evaluation. *Ephemera*, 7.1, pp. 203–232.

Varone, A. (2000). Inscrizioni parietarie inedite da Pompei (*REG.* IX, *INS.* 12). In: G. Paci, ed., *ΕΠΙΓΡΑΦΑΙ: Miscellanea epigrafica in onore di Lidio Gasperini.* Rome, pp. 1071–1093.

Varone, A. (2002). Erotica Pompeiana. *Love Inscriptions on the Walls of Pompeii*, trans. R. Berg. Rome.

Vora, N. (2014). Domestic Work, Affective Labor, and Social Reproduction in South Asian America: A Tribute to Laxmi Soni. *Feminist Formations*, 26.2, pp. 162–185.

Weeks, K. (2007). Life Within and Against Work: Affective Labor, Feminist Critique, and Post-Fordist Politics. *Ephemera*, 7.1, pp. 233–249.

Wharton, A. (2009). The Sociology of Emotional Labor. *Annual Review of Sociology*, 35, pp. 147–165.

Williams, C. (2010). *Roman Homosexuality*. 2nd edition. New York–Oxford.

Williams, C. (2014). Sexual Themes in Greek and Latin Graffiti. In: T. Hubbard, ed., *A Companion to Greek and Roman Sexualities*. Malden, MA, pp. 493–507.

Winterbottom, M. (1974). *The Elder Seneca*, vol. 1: Controversiae *I–VI*. Cambridge–London.

Witzke, S. (2015). Harlots, Tarts, and Hussies? A Problem of Terminology for Sex Labor in Roman Comedy. *Helios*, 42, pp. 7–27.

Wright, S. (2007). Back to the Future: Italian Workerists Reflect Upon The *Operaista* Project. *Ephemera*, 7.1, pp. 270–281.

Zajac, M. (2008). *Lessons from the* Lupanar. *Functional Design and Economic Operation of the Pompeian Purpose-Built Brothel*. M.A. Thesis, Arizona State University.

CHAPTER 7

Meaning in the Making: Representing Glass Production in Imperial Rome

Bettina Reitz-Joosse

1 Introduction

When I was eight years old, a glassblower visited my primary school to give a live demonstration of his craft. To this day, I vividly remember my amazement when the heated glass glowed and became manipulable, expanded like a balloon and seemed to shape-shift under the glassblower's light touch. Afterwards, I used some of my pocket money to purchase from this glassblower the only thing I could afford: a small blue glass droplet, which looked just like the ones I had seen come into existence. I still own this droplet (Fig. 7.1). The reason that it was—and is—special to me is neither its beauty nor its utility. What makes it special is rather that I know, saw, and experienced how it was made. My understanding and my memory of its *making* has changed what it means to me.

As a reader of the preceding paragraph, your attitude towards this glass droplet has now also undergone a change. You did not experience its creation at first hand, but you read my description of its making. To tell a story of making, then, adds new meaning to a finished object or type of object.[1] This paper aims to throw light on this relationship between making, its depiction, and the impact of material objects on human viewers and users. More specifically, I investigate this relationship with regard to imperial Roman glass vessels: how does the making of such glass vessels relate to the meaning that their contemporary viewers, owners and users attached to them? I propose to add to our understanding of this relationship by analysing a number of Roman depictions, literary and visual, of processes of glassmaking.

Glass is already known from ancient Egypt and the Ancient Near East in the second millennium BCE, and its presence is well documented in the ancient Greek world.[2] However, the first century BCE saw a transformative technolo-

1 I explore this dynamic specifically in regard to architecture and processes of construction in Reitz-Joosse 2021.

2 On the development of glass technologies in the Greco-Roman world, see the overview of Stern 2009.

FIGURE 7.1
Glass droplet
PHOTO: AUTHOR

gical discovery: glassworkers in the Syro-Palestinian region realized that glass could be expanded and shaped by human breath. The development and refinement of glassblowing in the Roman empire in the decades that followed led to an enormous expansion of the production of glass vessels, which could now be made more quickly and with less raw material.[3] The rapid spread and transformative effect of this novel technology in the early empire has recently been much explored from a technical, logistical and economic perspective.[4] In this chapter, I hope to add a new perspective by turning to literary and visual depictions for insights into Roman ideas about the processes of glassmaking and glassblowing—and therefore, ultimately, also about its products, glass vessels.

There are several Roman imperial texts which depict the making of raw glass, of glass objects and glassblowing. I focus on three in particular: Pliny the Elder's chapters on the production of raw glass and two poems on glassworking—the first ascribed to Mesomedes of Crete, the second preserved as an anonymous fragment. I also discuss a visual depiction of glassblowing on an oil lamp from Roman Asseria. Based on these analyses, I attempt to identify several key

3 On glassblowing as an example of Roman imperial innovation see Flohr 2016. For a Roman writer's sense of the enormous importance of this discovery, see Sen. *Ep.* 90.31.

4 See, for example, Wiesenberg 2015 (experimental archaeology regarding Roman glass furnaces), Foy 2017 on circulation of raw glass and glass vessels, Rosenow et al. 2018, or the ERC GlassRoutes project.

elements of the Roman discourse surrounding the creation of glass objects, including the notion of glass as an 'imperial composite,' the agency of fire in making and shaping it, and the overwhelming sensory impact and 'magical' qualities of glassblowing.[5] The juxtaposition of the 'elite' perspective of literary texts and the depiction of glassblowing on the Asseria oil lamp also helps to bring into sharper focus what disappears from view in literary discourses: for example, the collaborative nature of glass production.

In a final section of this chapter, I introduce the notion of 'madeness' to relate this discourse of (glass-)*making* to attitudes towards the *made*—Roman glass vessels. I argue that for Roman owners, viewers and users, ideas about how glass objects were created had a significant impact on the value they attached to finished objects.

2 Pliny the Elder on Roman Glassmaking

Book 36 of Pliny the Elder's *Natural History* concludes with a section on glassmaking (189–199), which has been both an important source of information and a thorn in the flesh of scholars studying ancient glass technologies. While his explanation of the ingredients of ancient glass and of their provenance offers invaluable information, it also contains some decidedly puzzling elements.[6] In this chapter, I leave technical questions aside to focus on the ideas and values which Pliny connects with the process of glassmaking, and the ways in which these relate to the value(s) of glasswork as they were perceived by Roman users in this period. Three aspects in particular stand out in Pliny's account.

5 Schneider 2021 usefully compiles all mentions of glass in Roman imperial literature, with a view to contextualizing archaeological research about glass. His overview of literary mentions of glass is more wide ranging, since it does not focus on production specifically but also includes texts discussing the use, price, or appearance of glass objects. He briefly discusses Pliny the Elder (147–149) and cites Mesomedes without discussion (154–155), but does not mention any of the key themes surrounding glassmaking that I focus on in this chapter.

6 For example, why does Pliny at 36.194 offer such a confusing ratio for mixing quartz and soda (on which see Rottländer 2000, 27)? What does he mean when he claims that glass could be chased like silver (*argenti modo caelatur*, 36.193)? Among the many attempts to understand Pliny's challenging passage, a 20-year collaboration between classicists, archaeologists, ancient historians, mineralogists, physicists and chemists stands out as a particularly determined effort, resulting in Rottländer 2000. See also Freestone 2008, who relates Pliny's text to recent archaeological insights into Roman glass technologies.

First, Pliny presents raw glass as an 'imperial composite:' a human-made substance created by combining materials and technologies drawn from disparate regions of the world and the Roman empire.[7] Traditionally, Pliny explains, raw glass was exclusively produced with sand from a particular section of the Belus River in 'that part of Syria which is called Phoenicia', mixed with soda (*nitrum*), preferably sourced from Egypt. Now, he writes, sands from the river Volturnus in southern Italy are also in use. Pliny stresses that the technologies used to produce raw glass and to shape it were originally developed in Sidon; he also compares technologies supposedly used in India, as well as 'ready-made' glass-like obsidian, which he says occurs in Ethiopia (36.196), India, Italy (Samnium), and along the Spanish coast (36.197). He adds that raw glass is now also produced in Gaul and Spain (36.194). Pliny's interest in specific materials and their origins, qualities and human uses, is characteristic of the encyclopedic *Natural History* in its entirety.[8] Nonetheless, his text alerts us to the easily neglected fact that many Roman owners or users of glass objects would have understood that what they held in their hands was a composite substance, created by humans from materials which had been drawn from different parts of the vast Roman empire.[9]

Another focal point in Pliny's discussion is shared with all other representations in this chapter: the role of fire in the processes of making and shaping glass. Pliny moves seamlessly from his section on glassmaking and glassworking into a reflection on fire as a creative force, writing (Plin. *NH* 36.200. Trans. Author):

> … and after all things have been treated which depend on man's talent for making art reproduce nature, it occurs to me to wonder that there is almost nothing that cannot be achieved by fire.
>
> … et peractis omnibus quae constant ingenio arte naturam faciente, succurrit mirari nihil paene non igni perfici.

---

7 In this respect, Pliny goes much beyond views on glass as expressed, for example, by Greek philosophers, who classed glass with metals, without noting the fundamental difference between the refining of metals and the true transmutation of materials required to produce glass (Stern 2009, 521; Beretta 2009, esp. chs 2 and 4).

8 Pliny's views on materials have recently been the subject of important new scholarship: see especially Anguissola 2022 and Grüner and Anguissola 2021.

9 The relationship between Pliny's own encyclopedic project, which aims to organize the whole of nature and culture, and Roman imperial ideology is, for example, explored by Carey 2003, Murphy 2004, or Beagon 2013.

Having provided a series of examples for the transformative power of fire, Pliny continues: 'It (i.e. fire) is a vast, unruly element of nature, and one which causes us to doubt whether it is more a destructive or a creative force' (*inmensa, inproba rerum naturae portio et in qua dubium sit, plura absumat an pariat*).[10] Pliny stresses the centrality of fire and its agency in the process of making and shaping glass and metal and the dangers and the challenges which accompany its use under precarious human control. Anguissola stresses that the end of Book 36 of the *Natural History* marks the transition from man-made marvels to gemstones created by nature, and that fire occurs at this transition since 'fire escapes the distinction between producer and product'.[11] As we shall see, fire—its collaborative agency and its dangerous, uncontrollable properties—all feature in all the representations of glassmaking and glassworking treated in this chapter.

Only worth a brief mention to Pliny is the danger attached to working with glass. He acknowledges this in Book 36, writing (Plin. *NH* 36.193. Trans. author.):

> The sharpness of glass is everywhere so great that it cuts to the bone, faster than you can even feel it, any part of the body it has breathed upon.
>
> acies tanta est quacumque, ut citra sensum ullum ad ossa consecet quidquid adflaverit corporis.

Whether Pliny here refers to the danger involved in handling raw glass ingots or that of working with liquid glass remains unclear. In any case, his interest in this passage is focused on a noteworthy property of the material itself, in line with his scientific interests, rather than on the human cost at which this knowledge would have been acquired. The other great danger of working with glass in antiquity, namely the inhalation of poisonous fumes, remains unmentioned by Pliny or any other Roman author.[12]

3 Working with Glass in Poetry I: Mesomedes (*AG* 16.323)

I now turn from glassmaking (the production of raw glass from its base ingredients) to glassworking (the shaping of raw glass into final products). While

10 Finally, Pliny adds, citing Empedocles, Hippocrates and Varro, that fire also has a curative and medicinal force (36.202).

11 Anguissola 2022, 15.

12 On the dangerous side of the profession, see Stern 1999, 256.

glass*making* was confined to a few specialized production centres, glass*working* occurred in 'secondary' workshops in many different regions of the Roman empire. Glassworking could involve the making of beads, the creation of flat window panes, the pouring of molten glass into moulds, and also, most importantly, the technology of blowing, either within or without a mould.[13] I now turn to two poems from the Roman imperial period, both written in Greek, which feature processes of glassworking.

An early second-century CE poem by Mesomedes of Crete, a freedman of the emperor Hadrian, depicts the process of glassworking as follows (*AG* 16.323 = 2.13 Regenauer):[14]

> A workman brought this glass, having cut it off. Into the fire he placed the chunk, hard as iron. The glass ran out like wax, heated completely by the all-devouring flames. And for mortals it was a miracle to see that which had been drawn from the fire flowing [down], and the workman trembling, lest, falling down, it [the thread] might tear. On the edge of the two lips he placed the lump …
>
> Τὰν ὕελον †ἐκόμιζε
> κόψας† ἐργάτας ἀνήρ,
> ἐς δὲ πῦρ ἔθηκε βῶλον
> ὡς σίδηρον εὐσθενῆ.
> ἁ δ' ὕελος, οἷα κηρός
> ἐξεχεῖτο παμφάγοισι
> φλοξὶν ἐκπυρουμένα.
> θαῦμα δ' ἦν ἰδεῖν βροτοῖς
> ὁλκόν ἐκ πυρὸς ῥέοντα
> καὶ τὸν ἐργάταν τρέμοντα,
> μὴ πεσὼν διαρραγῇ.
> ἐς δὲ διπτύχων ἀκμὰς
> χειλέων[15] ἔθηκε βῶλον
> ⟨ ⟩

13 For an overview of the different technologies with a rich bibliography, see Stern 2009.

14 Trans. author. The most thorough analysis of this poem is Regenauer's 2016 edition, translation and commentary (426–440). See also Deroy 1989, 182 and Stern 2007, 353–354.

15 Regenauer 2016 retains the MSS's χειλέων (rather than emending to χηλέων, 'claws', as other editors have done), following the argumentation of Stern 2007, 354: 'the poet was referring to the long blades of the most important glassblower's tool, a springy iron U-shaped implement called jacks in modern parlance. Jacks resemble sheep shears; they are identical to ancient scissors …'.

This poem is transmitted in the *Anthologia Planudea* (323), where its attribution to Mesomedes is also preserved. Although the poem displays many formal characteristics of an epigram, it is written in a lyric metre (trochaic dimeters), while its diction also gestures towards epic, in particular Homeric depictions of the workshop of Hephaestus in the *Iliad*.[16]

The poem has probably suffered some corruption, as shown by the metrical impossibilities in the opening lines.[17] Furthermore, its abrupt ending has led scholars to hypothesize that we are missing a section at the end: the poem breaks off at the point when the workman apparently begins the process of shaping.[18] However, enough of the poem remains to allow us to draw some conclusions about Mesomedes' presentation of the process of working with molten glass.

The poem proceeds as follows: the workman cuts or hacks off a piece of raw glass (although the text is uncertain) (1–2), and places it into the furnace (3–4). The glass softens from the heat (5–7). The workman prevents the liquid glass from flowing down and tearing (8–11), and places it on the blades of a tool (12–13), although we do not learn to what purpose.[19]

Mesomedes deliberately takes up and then immediately subverts a well-known epigrammatic convention by opening the poem with a demonstrative pronoun (τάν).[20] In many epigrams, such a pronoun refers to a particular object, which then forms the subject of an ecphrastic poem describing the object. This poem, however, as the reader quickly comes to understand, is not an ecphrasis of a static, finished object: rather, it opens with a lump of raw glass, which will be transformed into something else in the course of a poem about the process of making.

Two elements stand out in the poet's depiction of the process of shaping glass. First, Mesomedes, like Pliny, stresses the transformative power of fire, able to change the state of the solid glass lump to liquidity. Of particular interest is his phrase παμφάγοισι / φλοξὶν ('all-devouring flames'). The latent personification of the hungry flames as a creature of insatiable hunger strengthens the sense of the fire's agency and hints at the danger and the achievement involved in bending its wild nature to human will.[21] Second, the phrase θαῦμα δ' ἦν ἰδεῖν

16 Regenauer 2016, 430 and *passim*. On the relationship with Il. 18.372–377 (the making of the tripods) esp. 347.

17 Regenauer 2016, 432.

18 Regenauer 2016, 439–440.

19 See n. 15 above.

20 Regenauer 2016, 432 *ad* 1.

21 Cf. Regenauer 2016, 436–437 *ad* 6–7.

βροτοῖς ('and for mortals it was a miracle to see') seems to imply a separation between the mortal onlookers, for whom the process is a θαῦμα, and the workman himself, who by implication is raised above the status of mere mortals through his ability to manipulate the ḥard glass into a new shape. The evocation of the Homeric depictions of Hephaestus' workshop adds to this impression of making as a divinely inspired activity.[22] These themes, and several others, reappear in the second poem under consideration.

4 Working with Glass in Poetry II: *P.Oxy.* L 3536 = *APHex* I.15

APHex I.15 (*P.Oxy.* L 3536) is a poetic fragment in Greek hexameters. The papyrus on which it is preserved dates to the third century CE, while the poem is tentatively dated to the late second or the early third century CE.[23] The author of the poem was almost certainly familiar with Mesomedes' poem, since he picks up some of the earlier text's vocabulary and expands Mesomedes' short metaphorical expressions into more elaborate comparisons.[24] While the exact interpretation of the process depicted by Mesomedes remains challenging, the anonymous author of this hexameter poem is without doubt depicting glass-blowing in action:[25]

> … building for men … He first heated the very point [of the iron], then snatched from nearby an idle lump of [glass?], [which he] expertly laid inside the hollow kiln. As it tasted the strong fire, the crystal melted like wax under the blows of Hephaestus. And as he blew in the liquid air from his mouth, the man modulated its breath, as if essaying the pleasurable art of the pipe. The glass received … arched [into a circle?] in front of him, taking the shape of a sphere. It would then receive another impulse of divine [breath?], for repeatedly he would blow air in, whirling it like a shepherd does with his crook …

. . . .

τε]ύ̣χων ἀνθ̣ρώποιcι μ[.....]η̣λ̣α̣ [
πρ]ῶτα μ[ὲ]ν̣ οὖ̣ν θέρμην̣ε̣ν ἄκρ̣ην γλω̣[χῖνα ⏑ — ⏓

22 Regenauer 2016, 438.

23 The poem has been edited in Perale 2020 as *APHex* I.15 (194–199). See Perale 2020, 194–195 for considerations regarding the dating of the poem.

24 Regenauer 2016, 429–431, Perale 2020, 195.

25 I cite the text of Perale 2020, 196. The translation is Perale's with slight adaptations.

ἥ]ρπαςε δ’ ἐγγύθι βῶλον ἀεργεννη.[⏖ — ⏓
θῆ]κε δ’ ἐπιςταμένως κοίλης ἔντοςθε κ[αμίνου.
ἡ] δ’ ἄρα γ[ε]υςαμένη θαλεροῦ πυρὸς ἠΰτ[ε] κ[η]ρό[ς
μ]αλθάχθη κρύςταλλος ὑφ’ [Ἡ]φαίςτοιο βο[λ]άων.
καὶ] ῥ’ ὅτ’ ἀπὸ ςτομάτων διερὴν ἐνέπ[νευς]εν ἀΰτμ[ήν
εἵλ]κυς’ ἀνὴρ, ὡς εἴ τέχνης πειρώ[με]ν[ο]ς αὐλ[οῦ
τ]ερπνοτάτης· ὕελος δ’ ἐπεδέξατο π[— ⏖ — ⏓
ς]φαιρηδὸν δὲ πάροιθεν ἐκυρτώθη πε[⏑ — ⏓
ὁρμὴν δ’ ἄν θείης ἑτέρην ἀνεδέξ[ατ ⏑ — ⏓
πολλάκι μὲν γὰρ ὀπ[ο]ῖα καλαύρ[ο]πα βου[κόλος — ⏓
δῑν]ῶν ἐμπνείεςκε .ι.... [.]. [...]... [
[ ].[
. . . .

The poet represents the different steps of the procedure in considerable detail: the glassblower heats the tip of his blowpipe (2), gathers a chunk of glass (pre-softened) by touching his heated blowpipe to the chunk (3), and places the blowpipe with the attached glass into the furnace (4), thereby melting the glass glob (5–6). Then the blowing begins: he inflates the glass by blowing into it (7–8), a process which is compared to aulos-playing (8–9). The glass expands and becomes spherical (line 10), and this is then followed by a comparison between the glassblower and a herdsman who swings a *kalaurops* (apparently a wooden throwing stick with weights on each end). The comparison may be with vigorous swinging or swirling of the blowpipe in order to lengthen and shape the vessel. Here the poem breaks off.

I want to draw attention to some elements of this depiction which particularly relate to the experience, perception and estimation of this particular form of making in the Roman world. It has long been recognized that makers rely on their sensory awareness—the way something looks, sounds, feels, or smells—to guide them in the process of making.[26] For observers, too, making is—and was—a multi-sensory experience: they feel the heat of a furnace, hear the noises of weaving, or smell dye or paint. Experimental archaeology has recently made strides in reconstructing the sensory surround of Roman processes of making.[27] However, human sense perception is always mediated and culturally contingent: even if it were possible to recreate the noises or smells of a Roman workshop perfectly, this would not in itself be sufficient for appreciat-

26 Ingold 2013, *passim*.

27 See, e.g., O'Sullivan/Souyoudzoglou-Haywood 2019.

ing the sense experience of a Roman maker or observer.[28] Narrative depictions offer another, complementary way of approaching the sensory side of manual creation. *P.Oxy.* L 3536 presents a narrative reimagination of the sensory experience of glassblowing. For example, the poet mentions the 'heat' (θέρμηνεν, 2) of the furnace and (like Mesomedes) describes that the glass is softened like wax (ἠΰτε κηρός, 5). While heated glass can obviously only be touched with specialist tools, the poet offers a comparison with a softened material which any reader will have had experience of touching in softened state. Further sensory clues come from the expression γευσαμένη θαλεροῦ πυρός, 'tasting the strong fire'. In this phrase, the sense experience seems to reside not with the human maker and his imagined audience but with the material itself, as the poet imagines the glass *itself* as 'tasting' the fire. The idea of tasting combines the sense of touch with that of taking something inside oneself: the heat of the fire is thought to enter the crystal, thereby rendering it soft and workable.[29]

The poet also compares blowing into the pipe to aulos-playing (8–9). On the one hand, this comparison helps to conjure up the visual experience of the onlooker, who sees someone blow into a long hollow 'pipe'. On the other hand, the remark ὡς εἴ τέχνης πειρώμενος (8) also hints at the experience of the player himself, introducing a sense of experimentation and learning-by-doing which is essential to making.[30] The comparison between glassblowing and flute-playing is also relevant for one final reason: the art of flute-playing is called 'most delightful', and it is an example of a *technê* that leads to no product other than itself.[31] The comparison thus evokes the experimental element of glassblowing for the blower himself, the performative element of glassblowing, and the pleasurable excitement of its audience—thereby expanding the purely visual θαῦμα ἰδεῖν of Mesomedes into a multi-dimensional sensual experience for different participants.

I now turn to the way in which collaboration is handled in this fragment. We know that Roman glassblowers did not work in industrial-scale workshops, but neither did they work entirely alone: the fire of the furnace required skilful stoking in order to be kept at the required temperatures, and depending on the complexity of the process, a blower also needed an assistant to hand him his

28 See especially Routledge's *Senses in Antiquity* series and Toner 2014.

29 The idea appears to reverse the metaphor of Mesomedes' 'all-consuming' fire, since here it is the glass which absorbs the fire. It is, however, as often in poetic texts, difficult to judge how vivid this metaphor would have been to a contemporary reader, since γεύομαι is also used to indicate 'to experience' in a more general sense (LSJ s.v. γεύω II.3).

30 Ingold 2013, 13; Sennett 2008, 199–213.

31 Cf. Cicero, *Fin.* 3.24.

tools.[32] In this poem, however, the glassblower is not collaborating with human colleagues, but rather with the force of fire, personified as Hephaestus (line 6), who softens the glass with his 'blows' so that the glassblower can then shape it.[33] Both Mesomedes and the author of the hexameter poem thus emphasize the agency of the fire during the process of glassworking, but while Mesomedes' all-devouring flames suggest a wild, untamed and potentially dangerous entity, the hexameter poem rather emphasizes the divine quality of the fire and its gracious collaboration with the human maker.

Hephaestus, however, is not the only divine presence in this poem. In line 11, the glass 'receives another impulse of divine …' (Perale surmises that the missing word at the end of 11 may be the Homeric ἀϋτμῆς, 'breath'). The fact that the breath of the glassblower appears to be called θεῖος, divine, creates an impression of similarity between the two collaborators (Hephaestus and the glassblower) and their respective command over the forces of fire and air. Even more explicitly than in Mesomedes' poem, the human glassblower seems temporarily to transcend his human state through the act of creation.

The vocabulary of the passage suggests that there is also a more specific sense in which a divine element is thought to be active in the process of glassblowing. The vocabulary of this passage recalls that of Stoic ontology and cosmology.[34] According to Stoic doctrine, the world consists of matter pervaded and animated by πνεῦμα, usually conceived of as a mixture of fire and air, and in any case conceptually linked to both 'breath' (its literal meaning) and heat. In this passage, glass is animated by a combination of fire and breath (cf. also ἐνέπνευσεν, 7; ἐμπνείεσκε, 13). The impulse of the blower's breath is described as a ὁρμή, 11, the technical term for the impulse of the Stoic soul (which consists of πνεῦμα) towards an object. The glassblower himself thus appears as akin to the Stoic demiurge, able to animate matter through pneuma.[35] The shape of the blown vessel (σφαιρηδόν, 10) reminds the reader of the shape of the cosmos, which, in Stoic cosmology, is conceived of as spherical.[36] In ancient philosoph-

32 On the logistics of stoking the furnaces, see Wiesenberg 2014 and Taylor and Hill 2008. On collaboration in Roman workshops more generally Kristensen and Poulsen 2012, Munro 2021.

33 The adjective θαλερός, used to qualify the fire (5), also seems to contain a latent personification, since it is predominantly used to refer to youthfulness or strength of humans or their bodies (LSJ s.v. θαλερός).

34 For an overview see Sedley 1999, White 2003.

35 Note, however, that the Stoic demiurge is not external to the cosmos he creates. Insofar as the glassblower is external to his product, he resembles the Platonic demiurge more than the Stoic one.

36 On the spherical earth and cosmos, see, e.g., Cleomedes, *Cael.* 1.5, Aetius 2.2.1 (*Stoicorum*

ical writing, the activities of a divine creator of the world are frequently elucidated by relating them to the familiar activity of a craftsman.[37] Here, the poet reverses the direction of this well-known comparison, elucidating the activity of the glassblower in terms reminiscent of the Stoic demiurge.

5 Throwing Light on the Glassblower: A Roman Oil Lamp from Asseria

While Mesomedes and the author of *P.Oxy.* L 3536 praise the technical skill of the glassworker himself, both poems ignore the contribution of other members of the workshop. Although experimental archaeology has shown that achieving the required temperature in the furnace was a particular technical and logistical challenge, both poets depict only a sole human workman who shapes the lump of glass into its new form.[38] One explanation for this may be that the poems are seeking to suggest a parallel between the creative activities of the (semi-divine) workman and their own inspired process of (poetic) creation. Such a 'metapoetical' layer can frequently be discerned in ancient poetic texts, and it may be intended here, although the fragmentary nature of both poems prevents us from drawing any more specific conclusions.[39] In any case, an analogy between the poet and a (single) artisan suggests itself more readily than an analogy between a poet and a team of workers.[40]

A visual depiction of glassblowing, roughly contemporary with Pliny's text, provides a complementary perspective on the idea of the 'lone artisan', however.[41] So far, three Roman terracotta oil lamps have come to light which depict

---

Veterum Fragmenta 2.547), Aetius 2.22.3 (*Stoicorum Veterum Fragmenta* 2.654), Diogenes Laertius 7.144 (*Stoicorum Veterum Fragmenta* 2.650).

37 The very world 'demiurge' puts the creator in relation to the craftsman. The classic ancient account is Plato's *Timaeus* (starting at 28a). A particularly interesting example from the Stoic tradition is Galen's *De Semine* 2.5.56–60.

38 See n. 32 above.

39 In my opinion, the fragmentary state of both texts renders it difficult to assess the degree to which this layer of meaning is foregrounded. Regenauer 2016, at least, is convinced that the metapoetic meaning of Mesomedes' poem is the key to its interpretation (esp. 428, 431).

40 This is certainly not to say, however, that an analogy between poetic work and 'distributed' manufacture is never suggested in ancient literature. Along with many others, I have argued that Statius' *Silvae* 4.3, a depiction of a group of workmen constructing a road in verse, should be read metapoetically: Reitz-Joosse 2021, 146–171 with bibliography.

41 Lehmann 2012 proposes a methodology for analysing images depicting making in progress, arguing that images of making are capable of communicating the 'social, material,

FIGURE 7.2
Roman oil lamp from Asseria showing a glassblower's workshop
PHOTO: ARCHAEOLOGICAL MUSEUM IN SPLIT, CROATIA (INV. NO AMS-FC-1094)

the process of glassblowing, all produced around 70 CE, presumably from the same mould.[42] I focus here on one of those lamps (Fig. 7.2), found at Podgrade near Benkovac in Croatia (Roman Asseria) and currently housed in the Archaeological Museum of Split.[43] Its disc depicts two human figures, ranged on either side of a large furnace. On the right, a blower is blowing a bottle-like vessel while sitting on a low stool. The figure on the left, slightly smaller in size, appears to be rendering him assistance, probably by working the bellows.[44]

---

technical, cultural and aesthetic dimensions of the production of artefacts' (13). She distinguishes between four functions of such images (archival, instructional, participatory and display). Of these, my analysis focuses on the third (the kinesthetic identification of the viewer with the creative process) and the fourth function (the showcasing and hiding of certain elements of the creative process).

42 One was found near Ferrara (Baldoni 1987), one recently at Spodnje Škofije near Koper in Slovenia. According to Lazar, the lamps from Asseria and Spodnje Škofije were made from the same mould (Lazar 2006); it seems likely that the Ferrara lamp also came from the same mould (Baldoni 1987, 23).

43 AMS-Fc-1094; Abramić 1959.

44 Stern 2007, 355–357. Lazar 2006, 231, also interprets the tool as bellows, but also points out that experimental archaeology has not yet confirmed the need for bellows to achieve the required temperatures in glass furnaces.

Like Pliny and both poets, this lamp's designer emphasizes the importance of the control of fire to the blower's craft. The furnace forms the centre of the image, to which the eyes are drawn first, before taking in the human figures. Furthermore, this particular copy has a noteworthy feature not shared by the other two lamps from this mould. The pouring hole, used for refilling the oil lamp, was manually cut into the clay once the lamp had been shaped. The maker of this particular lamp decided to locate this hole in the stoking compartment of the furnace.[45] Therefore, the lamp goes beyond simply depicting—visually—the process of glassblowing. It offers a kinesthetic experience, involving the user of the lamp in the process as the stoker, who replenishes the fuel for the lamp's fire just as wood would have to be replenished in the furnace to achieve the high temperatures required for glassblowing. The warmth of the flame and the scent and fumes of the burning oil are further sensual triggers which can place the user of the lamp in the shoes of the glassworkers depicted.

Finally, this particular lamp (unlike the other two copies found in Spodnje Škofije and Ferrara) bears not only the image of glassblowing, but also a short inscription of two names, Athenio and Tr[e]llus. These names appear have been scratched into the clay before firing rather than afterwards, making it possible that one or both of the named individuals had some involvement in the production of this ('custom-made'?) object.[46] Perhaps the names are supposed to signify ownership of the lamp, but their arrangement vis-à-vis the figures rather suggests that they are to be identified with the two workmen depicted. Perhaps we can infer that this particular lamp was seen by its owner(s) as depicting the actual working relationship of Athenio and Trellus in a glassblowing workshop.[47]

6 Making and Meaning

In the final section of this chapter, I argue that to investigate the Roman 'discourse of making,' which I have analysed related to glass, can open up new

45 This artistic choice is not appreciated by Abramić 1959, 149, first to describe this lamp: 'Leider wird der Aufbau [i.e. of the furnace] an seiner Basis durch das Loch für den Öleinguß beschädigt.' The hole is located in a different position on the other two known lamps made from this mould, where it is placed next to the head of the glassblower below the blowpipe (Lazar 2006, Baldoni 1987).

46 Stern 1999, 457 with n. 69.

47 The (funerary) context in which the Asseria lamp was found is, however, badly documented, because the lamp seems to have been excavated illegally (Abramić 1959, 149).

insights into the impact of material objects on those who interacted with them. How would Roman viewers or users have reacted to blown glass vessels in their surroundings? They may have noted, for example, their shine or vibrant colour, their similarity to metal, their transparency, their hardness and odourlessness, their fragility, their price.[48] But their response to those vessels would also have included a sense of how such a vessel might have been made. How things were made, and how their stories of making were presented or imagined, was deeply relevant to how they were perceived and valued by their ancient viewers, owners, and users. Specifically, I suggest that we might use the concept of 'madeness' to analyse the complex relationship between an object's actual production history, contemporary cultural discourse about making, and the object's owners or users.[49]

'Madeness' as I conceive of it refers to someone's sense of an object's having been made or produced in a certain way. Different viewers may attribute different kinds of madeness to an object, depending on three main factors. First, madeness is elicited by the object's own material facture (e.g., in the case of glass, pontil marks or air bubbles, which point the viewer towards reflecting on the object's process of creation). Second, the madeness attributed to a glass object depends a particular viewer's or user's knowledge or understanding of its production, or of glass production in general (for example, the viewer might be a glassblower, someone who once saw glass blown, or someone who does not even know that this technology exists). Third, the madeness attributed to a glass object depends on the *discourse* of glass production, as we have investigated it in this chapter. The 'madeness' of glass was reflected in and, more importantly, shaped through, cultural conversations and imaginative reflections on its provenance and production, such as those accessible to us in Roman literary texts.

Specifically, Pliny's chapters on glassmaking alert us to the fact that glass was understood as a substance obtained and produced by combining mater-

48 All of these perspectives, too, are reflected in ancient literary accounts. Stern 2007 offers a complete and authoritative overview, cf. also now Schneider 2021. A forthcoming paper by Karen ní Mheallaigh will explore the semiotics of glass in imperial literature.

49 I introduce the term 'madeness' in my monograph, Reitz-Joosse 2021 (see 8, 16 and *passim*). There, I use it to investigate how texts and images can activate and shape an audience's sense of how a built structure has been created (and a text has been composed). In the current chapter, I broaden and develop my definition of the term to further explore the interaction between discourse, material culture and individual. I will be developing the concept further in the context of the ERC-funded research project FACERE (2023–2028, University of Groningen), which explores processes of making in Roman literature and art.

ials and technologies derived from different regions of the empire. Both of the poems analysed in this chapter highlight the pleasurable sense of admiration and spectacle associated with watching a glassblower at work. These poems, as well as the oil lamp depicting the glassblowing workshop, even offer a kinesthetic experience for their audience, through the recreation—in their respective media—of the sensual experience of participating in the process. Finally, every depiction of glassmaking and glassworking treated in this chapter emphasizes the crucial role of fire in the process, pointing towards the need for its collaboration in a joint endeavour, and its potentially destructive and threatening qualities that push the bounds of human control. While it is impossible to pin down precisely what kind of 'madeness' glass objects had for specific Roman viewers in specific contexts, all of the elements outlined together contribute to a 'thicker' description of human responses to glass objects in ancient Rome.

Ancient discourses of glassmaking and glassworking not only help us to understand ancient ideas about them; they also contributed to *shaping* these ideas, and through them the social realities of the Roman empire. Recently, literary sources on ancient manufacture have sometimes—with good reason—been sidelined in investigations of ancient manufacture. As scholars increasingly seek to reconstruct the lived realities of the working population of the Roman empire, literary sources, with their perceived elite bias, have become less central to this enquiry. But reading them in conjunction with other types of evidence, with close attention to their representational choices and strategies, can reveal what precisely 'elite' conceptualizations of manufacture tend to foreground, downplay, or leave out, how elite and sub-elite representations of making interact with one another, and the ways in which depictions of making construct, reinforce or question power structures in the Roman world. Without doubt, all literary texts discussed in this chapter were written by and for (relatively) elite inhabitants of the Roman empire.[50] It is worth stressing that none of them show an obvious disdain for manual labour or those engaged in it.[51] On the contrary, Pliny stresses the inventiveness of the pioneers of glassmaking, while both of the imperial poems suggest that his craft temporarily raises

50 Regenauer 2016, 431 stresses the difference between the social position of Mesomedes, as a freedman of the emperor, and his presumed audience. However, her suggestion that Mesomedes aims to comment, through his poem, on the contributions of those from a 'sozial niedrige Schicht', under which Regenauer appears to subsume an imperial freedman together with a manual worker, seems doubtful to me.

51 On negative and ethically coded attitudes towards manual and wage-earning labour in ancient texts, see the introduction to this volume.

the workman above the human sphere and associates him with the divine. The anonymous poet of *P.Oxy.* L 3536 actually compares the glassblower to the Stoic demiurge. Nonetheless, through their emphases and omissions, these representations of making do reinforce the hierarchies of power surrounding the production of glass in ancient Rome. For example, these curated depictions convey little or no sense of the physical dangers or hardships of glass production. They also entirely leave out all members of the workshop not engaged in the activity of blowing or shaping liquid glass: not merely a poetic but also a social act of elision. Only the oil lamp from Asseria, unlikely to have been an elite-owned object,[52] conveys something of the thought-world of the men and women actually engaged in glass production: not only does it foreground the human collaboration required in the workshop, but it also names two individuals engaged in the trade, de-anonymizing not only the glassblower but also his colleague.

Acknowledgements

I thank audiences at the Penn-Leiden conference and the Rostock Latin seminar, my Groningen colleagues and the anonymous referee for their helpful comments on this paper, and Hylke de Boer for his support with proofreading and bibliography. Marco Perale graciously provided me with a unicode version of his edition of *APHex* 1.15, and the Arheološki muzej u Splitu / Archaeological Museum in Split generously allowed me to reproduce Figure 7.2. This chapter was partly written during a research sabbatical in Berlin, funded by the Alexander von Humboldt Foundation. It forms part of a larger research project which is generously funded by the European Union (ERC, FACERE, project number 101042699). Views and opinions expressed are however those of the author only and do not necessarily reflect those of the European Union or the European Research Council Executive Agency. Neither the European Union nor the granting authority can be held responsible for them.

52 See p. 144 above.

Bibliography

Abramić, M. (1959). Eine römische Lampe mit Darstellung des Glasblasens. *Bonner Jahrbücher* 159, pp. 149–151.

Anguissola, A. (2022). *Pliny the Elder and the Matter of Memory. An Encyclopaedic Workshop*. Abingdon.

Baldoni, D. (1987). Una lucerna romana con raffigurazione di officina vetraria: alcune considerazioni sulla lavorazione del vetro soffiato nell'antichità. *Journal of Glass Studies* 29, pp. 22–29.

Beagon, M. (2013). *Labores pro bono publico*: The Burdensome Mission of Pliny's *Natural History*. In: J. König and G. Woolf, eds., *Encyclopaedism from Antiquity to the Renaissance*. Cambridge, pp. 84–107.

Beretta, M. (2009). *The Alchemy of Glass. Counterfeit, Imitation, and Transmutation in Ancient Glassmaking*. Sagamore Beach, MA.

Carey, S. (2003). *Pliny's Catalogue of Culture. Art and Empire in the Natural History*. Oxford.

Deroy, L. (1989). Sur deux poèmes grecs d'époque romaine décrivant un verrier au travail. *Antiquité Classique* 58, pp. 178–184.

Flohr, M. (2016). Innovation and Society in the Roman World. *Oxford Handbooks Online*.

Foy, D. (2017). An Overview of the Circulation of Glass in Antiquity. In: A. Wilson and A. Bowman, eds., *Trade, Commerce, and the State in the Roman World*. Oxford, pp. 265–300.

Freestone, I.C. (2008). Pliny on Roman Glassmaking. In: M. Martinon-Torres and T. Rehren, eds., *Archaeology, History and Science*. London–Walnut Creek, CA, pp. 77–100.

Grüner, A., and Anguissola, A., eds. (2021). *The Nature of Art. Pliny the Elder on Materials*. Turnhout.

Ingold, T. (2013). *Making. Anthropology, Archaeology, Art and Architecture*. Oxford.

Kristensen, T.M. and Poulsen, B., eds. (2012). *Ateliers and Artisans in Roman Art and Archaeology*. Portsmouth, R.I.

Lazar, I. (2006). An Oil Lamp from Slovenia Depicting a Roman Glass Furnace, Vjesnik APD, 2006. *Vjesnik Za Arheologiju i Povijest Dalmatinsku*, 99(1), pp. 229–235.

Lehmann, A. (2012). Showing Making: On Visual Documentation and Creative Practice. *The Journal of Modern Craft*, 5(1), pp. 9–24.

Munro, B. (2021). Ancient Maker Spaces: The Value of Craft Communities in Multi-Material Workshops in Late Antiquity. In: H. Hochscheid and B. Russell, eds., *The Value of Making. Theory and Practice in Ancient Craft Production*. Turnhout, pp. 53–68.

Murphy, T.M. (2004). *Pliny the Elder's Natural History. The Empire in the Encyclopedia*. Oxford.

O'Sullivan, A., and Souyoudzoglou-Haywood, C., eds. (2019). *Experimental Archaeology. Making, Understanding, Story-telling: Proceedings of a Workshop in Experimental Archaeology*. Oxford.

Perale, M. (2020). *Adespota Papyracea Hexametra Graeca (APHex I)*. Berlin.

Regenauer, J. (2016). *Mesomedes: Übersetzung und Kommentar*. Frankfurt am Main.

Reitz-Joosse, B.L. (2021). *Building in Words. The Process of Construction in Latin Literature*. New York.

Rosenow, D., Phelps, M., Meek, A. and Freestone, I. (2018). *Things That Travelled. Mediterranean Glass in the First Millennium CE*. London.

Rottländer, R.C.A., ed. (2000). *Über Glas und Metalle, Plinius Secundus der Ältere*. Sankt Katharinen.

Sedley, D.N. (1999). Hellenistic Physics and Metaphysics. In: K. Algra et al., eds., *The Cambridge History of Hellenistic Philosophy*. Cambridge, pp. 355–411.

Sennett, R. (2008). *The Craftsman*. New Haven.

Schneider, H. (2021). *Vitri ars*: Das römische Glas in der literarischen Überlieferung. In: F. Klimscha, H.-J. Karlsen, S. Hansen and J. Renn, eds., *Vom Künstlichen Stein zum durchsichtigen Massenprodukt*. Berlin, pp. 145–159.

Stern, M.E. (1999). Roman Glassblowing in a Cultural Context. *American Journal of Archaeology*, 103(3), pp. 441–484.

Stern, M.E. (2007). Ancient Glass in a Philological Context. *Mnemosyne*, 60(3), pp. 341–406.

Stern, M.E. (2009). Glass Production. In: J.P. Oleson, ed., *The Oxford Handbook of Engineering and Technology in the Classical World*. Oxford, pp. 520–548.

Stern, M.E. (2012). Blowing Glass from Chunks Instead of Molten Glass: Archaeological and Literary Evidence. *Journal of Glass Studies* 54, pp. 33–45.

Taylor, M. and Hill, D. (2008). Experiments in the Reconstruction of Roman Wood-Fired Glassworking Furnaces. *Journal of Glass Studies*, 50, pp. 249–270.

Toner, J.P., ed. (2014). *A Cultural History of the Senses in Antiquity*. London.

White, M.J. (2003). Stoic Natural Philosophy (Physics and Cosmology). In: B. Inwood, ed., *The Cambridge Companion to the Stoics*. Cambridge, pp. 124–152.

Wiesenberg, F. (2014). *Experimentelle Archäologie. Römische Glasöfen: Rekonstruktion und Betrieb einer Glashütte nach römischem Vorbild in der Villa Borg*. Merzig.

Wiesenberg, F. (2015). Das experimentalarchäologische 'römische' Glasofenprojekt im Archäologiepark Römische Villa Borg (Borg Furnace Project). In M. Koch, ed. *Archäologie in der Großregion*. Nonnweiler, pp. 315–322.

CHAPTER 8

Who's Afraid of Wage Labour? Analysing Some Texts of the Second Sophistic

Christel Freu

1 Introduction

Karl Marx, in different works, described the emergence of abstract thinking about labour in the age of Adam Smith, and understood it as the result of economic changes occurring in eighteenth-century European societies, particularly in English society. In 1857, he noted in the introduction to his *Grundrisse*,

> It was an immense step forward for Adam Smith to throw out every limiting specification of wealth-creating activity—not only manufacturing, or commercial or agricultural labour, but one as well as the others, labour in general … Indifference towards any specific kind of labour presupposes a very developed totality of real kinds of labour, of which no single one is any longer predominant. As a rule, the most general abstractions arise only in the midst of the richest possible concrete development, where one thing appears as common to many, to all. Then it ceases to be thinkable in a particular form alone. On the other side, this abstraction of labour as such is not merely the mental product of a concrete totality of labours. Indifference towards specific labours corresponds to a form of society in which individuals can with ease transfer from one labour to another, and where the specific kind is a matter of chance for them, hence of indifference.[1]

In short, Marx described a society in which the division of occupations led to a further division of labour, so that unskilled wage-earners moved from one trade to another because what they were selling, first and foremost, was their own labour power. This is what he subsequently described in *Capital*, saying, 'the collective worker [is] formed by the combination of a number of detailed

1 Marx, *Grundrisse*, Introduction, 1.3. Trans. Nicolaus 1973.

 | DOI:10.1163/9789004694965_009

workers'.[2] If labour, wrote Marx, could be analysed by Adam Smith as being the very source of value and wealth, it was because the division of labour had become extensive enough to make it clear that wealth was not extracted from any particular activities, but from labour itself.

It was long thought impossible that ancient economies had experienced such divisions of labour and the emergence of an abstraction of labour, where workers became interchangeable. Jean-Pierre Vernant, in his influential articles on labour in ancient Greece, thus explicitly took up Marx's thinking about the emergence of abstract labour, to reject its existence in antiquity. Every worker, he believed, remained trapped in his trade as in a 'lower order' and did not change trades (thus implying that it was impossible for a social class to form):

> Au contraire, cultivateurs et artisans doivent rester enfermés dans les limites de leur spécialité sous peine de contredire à ce type inférieur d'ordre auquel ils participent par leur métier … De cette réflexion positive sur l'organisation des activités professionnelles dans la cité ne se dégage pas l'idée d'une grande fonction sociale et humaine unique, le travail, mais celle d'une pluralité de métiers différenciant les uns des autres ceux qui les pratiquent.[3]

I propose here to re-assess these questions on several points: firstly, by showing that, at the beginning of the Roman empire, the Roman economy had clearly achieved the same levels of division of labour that the modern era experienced and that, likewise, it resulted in the emergence of the unskilled, interchangeable worker in different sectors of activity: services and transportation, as well as some agricultural and craft-making tasks. Once this point is established, literary texts from the Second Sophistic, those of the orators, philosophers, Christians and jurists who all participated in the cultural current at that time, can more easily be understood: though having developed sometimes unique and often different thinking on the question of labour, they reveal to us the unease induced by social changes in an economy that is increasingly commodified.

Secondly, in this respect, we will see that this unease becomes a factor in the debate between members of the Second Sophistic, just as the relation-

2 Marx, *Capital*, I, section 4, ch. XIV, the manufacturing stage. Trans. Moore and Aveling 1887.

3 Vernant 1996[2] [1955], 287. Vernant's thinking about trades is more inspired by the reality of archaic Greece than by Hellenistic times (see pp. 276–278), where he analyses Hesiod's portrait of the Greek peasant cultivating his land alone, from which he takes his main resources. Vernant's analysis is influenced by Marx, who likewise thought the abstraction of labour in antiquity was impossible (*Capital*, I, section 1.3, A, c).

ship to money was already a factor in debates between sophists and philosophers in classical Athens. To be paid by an employer, whether a wealthy owner or the public authority, is, according to this ancient argument, to have already lost one's autonomy as a free man. In response to this unease, some sophists wanted to maintain strict distinctions between trades, acknowledging, thus, that wage labour and the subordinate relationship it produces between employer and employee has a tendency to pull the different employment conditions—whether craftwork, intellectual, or service work—downwards, making them equal with each other. In contrast, others accept the shift towards the homogenizing aspects of wage labour and try to introduce a new axiology within trades: this is the Stoics' contribution, of whom the best known in the imperial era is Dio Chrysostom.

2 Specialization of Trades, Division of Labour, and the Emergence of Abstract Labour

There are indeed signs that, in the economies of the most urbanized regions and provinces of the Roman empire, the division of occupations was quite considerable and had achieved levels known later in the big cities of modern Europe. The survey conducted by Kai Ruffing on inscriptions and papyri of the Hellenistic and Roman East backs up Edward Harris' seminal article on the 170 different trades found in classical and Hellenistic Athens,[4] as well as Susan Treggiari's research on inscriptions of the Roman West.[5] Such diversity indicated first the great specialization of occupations that went with an urban market economy, implying the division of roles between producers and traders for one part and the search for 'economic niches' for another. But the diversity of job titles could also represent a vertical division of labour, the 'separate work roles and skills used in manufacturing a single product'[6]—in this case, the titles did not designate 'professions' but rather described activities within the productive process, whether in the workshop, or on the building site, or on the land. For example, in the accounting books were listed those who carried water or stones, those who operated the fire, and so on.

Kai Ruffing then sought to understand what drove the specialization of trades and the division of labour: for him, it was the expansion of markets and

4 Harris 2002, 67–99, to complete with Lewis 2020 for a new survey of Athenian occupations; Ruffing 2008.

5 Treggiari 1980.

6 See Ruffing 2016, 117, on horizontal and vertical specialization.

urban growth that prompted the search for market niches.[7] It should be added that land was not exempt from change given that, on agricultural estates upon which crops were specialized for the urban market (wine, wheat, fodder, oil, vegetables), we also see plots where a versatile or skilled workforce is hired to work. This direct management could be explained by the search for economies of scale in service jobs (guard duty, inspection, irrigation, transportation), as well as by the willingness to exploit labour with strict control of the workforce when this proved necessary.[8] As in eighteenth-century Europe, the large agricultural estates of the Roman world, in Egypt, Italy, or Africa, started to experience horizontal and vertical specialization of labour: shepherds, guardsmen, cattle farmers, harvesters, haymakers, irrigators, winemakers, grape-pickers became the countryside's new professionals, and sometimes had workforces reporting to them.[9] In Italy, the majority of them may have been slaves, even though free labourers could be hired in addition, but in the provinces, many were free persons either recruited on a yearly basis, or employed occasionally as day-labourers.[10] For example, in Egypt, a machine like the sakyie required, during several months or even during the entire year, a cattleman (*boêlatês*)

7 Ruffing 2016 and Lewis 2020 (who rightly emphasizes that urban demand drove a differentiated specialization according to the size of the city and its market). On the Roman market economy, see in general Temin 2013. On the social, civic and economic changes prompted by the Hellenistic and Roman process of urbanization, see now: Maillot and Zurbach 2021 (urbanization as a cause of new labour conditions); Wilson 2011; Lis and Soly 2012, 38–52; Vlassopoulos 2007 (urbanization as a cause of the division of labour and the blurring of civic identities), who quotes (48–51) important texts of Aristotle's *Pol.*, 1291b and 1296b, suggesting that Athenian demographic growth modified the civic government by giving to craftsmen and hired workers working together in the urban workshops (τὸ [πλῆθος] τῶν βαναύσων καὶ μισθαρνούτων) a political knowledge and civic power. See also Freu 2018, 167–168, and 2022, 137–160.

8 On the socio-economic changes in Hellenistic and Roman periods and the resultant division of labour in agriculture, see, for the Eastern regions, Kloppenborg 2006; Rathbone 1991 (who showed the important use of hired labour in a large third-century estate); Freu 2022. On Italy, see recently Roselaar 2019, notably 113–120, who shows that the 'economic globalization' during the Late Republic led to the integration of Italy, 'regional specialization', 'intensification of agricultural production', and an important work mobility (see ibid. 37–40) that led, in some cases, to manpower being concentrated and divided into specialized tasks, even seasonal ones.

9 In the line of Lewis 2020, we need to distinguish, in urban and rural areas, between low-skilled jobs (which were often part-time occupations, such as porter or water-carrier) and specialized trades that could be also part-time, but nonetheless conferred a social identity on the worker.

10 Corbier 1980, 73–79; Carlsen 2016, 245–248 (division of labour in slave estates) and 255–260 (complementary workforces of slaves and free men), and Roselaar 2021, notably 124–130 (based on Cato's *Agr.*).

to rotate it, who reported to an irrigator (*hydroparochos*) who, in turn, was an employee under the control of a steward.[11] Day labourers employed in logistics activities participated also in the division of labour, even if seasonally.

These workers were quite apart, in their relationship to labour and the employer, from craftspeople or independent smallholders whose relationship to the land, according to ancient philosophers, had something of the religious about it; we are quite distant from Hesiod's labourer, described by J.-P. Vernant, who 'n'a pas le sentiment d'appliquer au sol une technique de culture, pas plus que d'exercer un métier. Avec confiance, il se soumet à la dure loi qui commande son commerce avec les dieux.'[12] As noted by F. Braudel with regard to eighteenth-century Venetian rural estates, the division of labour also impacted the working of the land.[13]

Lastly, in big-city societies, wage labour could impact various service trades, from unskilled labour (such as porters, construction workers, etc.), to workshop employees, and wage-earning intellectuals. For sure, many servants in large urban houses were slaves, but others were free individuals, recruited on a contractual basis, as we see in Egyptian households.[14] Thus, in fourth-century accounts on papyrus, numerous male staff appeared: servants in connection with official functions, but also stenographers (νοτάριοι), secretaries (γραμματεῖς), physicians (ἰατροί) or private teachers (γραμματικοί), craftspeople, or other specialized trades such as that of the cook (μάγειροι). In 320/321 CE, for example, four secretaries (γραμματεῖς), one educator, one logographer, one ostler, receive monthly wages (ὀψώνια) in cash, whereas a physician or artists (mimes) receive wine for festivals.[15] Another account from the end of the fourth century CE reveals employees (a grammarian, a physician, a veterinarian, a donkey-driver, a gatekeeper, a dyer, etc.) in a house at Hermopolis paid for six months of ὀψωνία (food allocation) in artabas of wheat.[16]

---

11 Freu 2022, 117–122. An even more complex division of labour is discernible in quarry work: see Cuvigny 2021, 195–200.

12 Vernant 1996² [1955], nn. 277–278.

13 Braudel 1979, 2. 290–339.

14 On slaves in urban households, see the estimates for Roman Italy of Scheidel 2005, 66–67, and, for fourth-century households, see Harper 2011, 38–56, who, along the lines of Scheidel's bottom-up approach, evaluates the number of slaves within different groups of slave-holders (especially the first three types, those whom he calls 'illustrious', 'elite' and 'bourgeois' slave-owners). In early Roman Egypt, where slavery represented 13% of the urban population, Alexandria aside (see Harper 2011, 54, based on the estimates of Bagnall and Frier 1994, 48–49 and 70–71), urban 'bourgeois' households also recruited free servants: see Freu 2022, 25–35 (service contracts of free boys and girls) and 164–170.

15 *SPP* XX 85 r° and v°.

16 *P.Ross.Georg.* V 60 v°. The γραμματικός (line 12) received 20 artabas of wheat (that is 3 ⅓

It is clear then that, in many market sectors of the imperial economy, what counts from this point on is the sale of labour power, rather than the economic sector to which the worker belongs: this makes wages among workers comparable, which is why the wage hierarchy can be the subject of study and comparison, why the salary of a construction worker can be comparable in the city or on rural estates, or why his salary can also be compared to that of a reaper. Outside Egypt, one exceptional document reveals this: Diocletian's Edict on Maximum Prices of 301 CE. By including the wages in the price list, it reveals 'the commodification of labour' at the time, and shows also a 'remarkable absence of strongly demarcated labour boundaries', as Miriem Groen-Vallinga and Laurens Tacoma noticed.[17] The hiring of labour created for the needs of this market economy had changed the relationship to human activity: the men who hired out their labour were no longer masters of the whole production process, and they now sold something which was no longer solely a specific job, but an abstract power which can now be quantified: labour.[18]

A number of signs of this abstraction, emerging from this plurality of work-for-hire experiences, may be identified in the Roman era. First, as Yan Thomas has demonstrated, it is clear that Roman jurists, in their thinking on hiring contracts, had created and circumscribed an abstract concept of work, expressed though the Latin plural *operae*, equivalent to the Greek *erga*. Furthermore, in accounting books on papyri or tablets, the Greek words *ergatês* and *anêr*, like the Latin *homo* and *operae*, described both the worker and the work day,[19] and hence came to represent work itself, thus conceived, as 'fungible, and transferable', a tradable object, central to the accounting practices of capital holders.[20] The estate managers or foremen thus grouped together workers who were paid the same salary by recording their number and not their name. Workers became 'accounting units', the manager having combined them on the basis of

---

artabas monthly), two times as much as the physician, while it was common that unskilled workers received at that time one artaba monthly, as part of their wages.

17 Groen-Vallinga and Tacoma 2016, 106–107. They add, interestingly, that 'there is no strong separation between rural and urban labour', which is due to the market integration and to the seasonality of some jobs that drove city or village craftsmen to hire themselves out as farmhands (see Lewis 2020, 134, on Athenian rowers, and Freu 2022, 299, on Egyptian reapers). See also Rathbone 2009, 306.

18 In their introduction, Laes and Verboven 2016, 4–6, draw attention to the ancient and modern terminology used to express the concepts of work and labour. In English, two words exist with some different nuances, but this is not always the case in other modern languages. See the Introduction for more.

19 See Rathbone 1991, 148–149 and Freu 2022, 56–58 and 80–81.

20 Thomas 1999, 2002, 2004.

identical wages; a large estate in Memphis in 255 CE recorded thus, day after day, the work days needed for given tasks as assessed at 6 drachmas, while others were assessed at 4 or 9 drachmas.[21]

To borrow the jurists' word, what is being talked about here is a 'fungible' human resource: in case of accident or illness, one man could easily replace another, if the employer found one in the local market, given that the worker was conflated with the quantity of work he could contribute. As recalled by Clara Berrendonner, such practices presuppose that careful assessments had been carried out to calculate the average quantity of labour produced by one man in one day on a given surface.[22]

This is context in which we must situate the philosophical positions of imperial-era thinkers on wage-earning labour.

3 Wage Labour as Equalizer, and the Philosophers

Workers' fungibility shakes up the classical representations of a world where workers were classed according to their occupations (*artes, technai*) and clearly separated into major sectors of activity (farming, crafts, business, occupations related to entertainment). This classification of trades satisfied a view of a world in which each individual found their place by following axiological criteria:[23] at the top of the hierarchy, activities such as working the land of a peasant-landowner, where the worker was self-employed (*autourgos*), and at the bottom, manual labourers and craftspeople, dependent on customer orders.[24] The more complex classification of *artes* advanced by Middle Stoi-

21 *BGU* I 14; see also *P.PragVarcl* II 1 (= *SB* VI 9406), 245–270 (Euhemeria 247 CE). For comparison, see the accounting records of the Roman army found at Vindolanda, notably the workforce accounts in *TVind.* II, 155–157.

22 Berrendonner 2007, 221–227. In *Rust.* 1, 18, Varro discusses Cato's and Saserna's calculations of the number of men/working days needed to cultivate various types of fields and concludes that the new landlord has to see what the local practices are (*in vicinitate praedia cuius modi sint et quanta, et quot quaeque hominibus colantur, et quot additis operis aut demptis melius aut deterius habeas cultum*, 1, 18, 4).

23 Lis and Soly 2012, 32–36, emphasize that this classification was an 'oligarchic concept ... based on the evaluation of [the] personal attributes' of each individual.

24 Contempt for artisans: see Vernant 1996² [1955]; Giardina 1991, 288–289; Lis and Soly 2012, 34–36. For classical Greek references regarding praise of *autourgia*, i.e. independent, self-sufficient labour of the farmer, see Lis and Soly 2012, 34–35; Veyne 2001 [1979], 144–145. Plato and Aristotle's thinking on this point can be seen into late antiquity. But we know now that if we look to other sources, the picture changes considerably. Working men themselves extolled their proper dignity: see Lis and Soly 2012, 47–53 and 80–86; Tran 2013, 187–252.

cism, where trades in service of pleasure conflicted with the scholastic and liberal arts, did not fundamentally change things in this regard. According to the Stoics, work in general was now a positive value, and Heracles' labours were extolled as symbols of virtue. However, trades continued to be classified according to moral criteria and hierarchized between sectors: cooks, perfumers and servants found themselves at the bottom of the scale because their work corrupted the soul of the customer, and even craftsmen continued to be criticized for their dirty and sedentary work.[25] This last classification, highly influential in the imperial age, would persist for centuries, with nuances, however.[26] This is what we will now consider.

In Cicero's well-known taxonomy of trades (*Off.* 1, 150–151),[27] the figure of the *mercennarius* with no specific skill now occupies a place in the Middle Stoic classification system.[28] The senator knows the number of Roman wage-earners, hired slaves or free men on work sites, in urban workshops or on the Italian estates.[29] Varro, his contemporary, also notes it in his works.[30] Concerning these *mercennarii*, Cicero thus famously states (Cic. *Off.* 1, 150–151):

> Unworthy of a free man and vulgar are the earnings of all hired workmen whom we pay for their labour, and not for their skills; for in their case the very wage they receive is a pledge of their slavery.
>
> Illiberales … et sordidi quaestus mercennariorum omnium, quorum operae, non quorum artes emuntur; est enim in illis ipsa merces auctoramentum seruitutis.

25 Brunt 1973; Pani 1985; van den Hoven 1996, 21–71.

26 On this point, see the important discussion in Pani 1985 about Seneca's attitude towards the *artes*.

27 Berrendonner 2007, 214–221 (recalling, 214, n. 42, of which the extensive bibliography brought about this text). The author provides the list of all trades where *mercennarii* were recruited or which operated by the payment of *merces*. However, this list should distinguish between *merces* received under *locatio operis faciendi* and that received through *locatio operarum* contracts.

28 Brunt 1973, 9 and 23 for Cicero's Stoic sources; Van den Hoven 1996, 27–28 (with the bibliography) and 54–63; Berrendonner 2007, 214–221.

29 See Bernard 2018, 159–192 and Roselaar 2021 on the growing labour market in the republican era and on the demand for slaves and free men for the Roman sites.

30 See, e.g., Varro *Rust.* 1, 17, 2; Cic. *Caec.* 58 and 63. On the occurrence of *mercennarius* in late republican Latin sources, see Berrendonner 2007, 211–213 (with many references of the word as an adjective or a noun in the literature). As a noun, *mercennarius* refers mostly to a farm worker. See also Corbier 1980.

The ambiguity of this phrase was raised a long time ago, given that we do not know if, for Cicero, the *mercennarii* are the only unskilled wage-earners who sell their labour indiscriminately to any employer,[31] or whether the only ones to be held in contempt are the unskilled workers within a large group also including skilled wage-earners, *quorum artes emuntur*, i.e. intellectuals, physicians, artists.[32]

However, even if it is conceded that, in Cicero's words, the *mercennarius* is nothing but an unskilled wage-earner, defined by the fact that he sells only his labour (clearly separated as an object in itself by the author, it should be noted),[33] we also see that the orator acknowledges that professionals of the *artes* type could be wage-earning. Craftspeople remained lowly individuals, as in the Greek tradition, because they were dependent on their customers and defined by their manual work. In contrast, a privileged place was reserved within his classification for wage-earning intellectuals, given their possession of *ars* or *technê*.

Cicero's criterion is an important one. From this point on at Rome, wage-earning labour is an object of consideration, and two different attitudes, which we will look at in closing, emerge on that subject. On the one hand is a conservative body of thought, which, while recognizing the social changes that are taking place, is fearful of them and tries, with all its might, to maintain the old order by attempting to contain the *mercennarius* with a certain social invisibility. A second, more neutral attitude exists at the same time, in which wage labour is accepted as a contemporary practice and which the philosophers seize upon to draw up new employment hierarchies.

The first, conservative position is represented by Cicero's rhetoric and was no doubt the most common: within it, the unskilled *mercennarius* is left to occupy a very inferior 'lowly' (*uilis*) place in society. Stigmatized in the name of the moral myth of autarky and autonomy, this worker is cut off from the society of free people. He is, says Cicero, nearly a slave because he is the slave of his employer. Anxious about economic and technical changes under the Julio-Claudian emperors, Seneca reaffirms this in the Neronian era.[34]

31 This reading of the text was adopted by De Robertis 1963, 53–54 (and n. 16) and Berrendonner 2007, 216–217.

32 A solution favoured by Martini 1958, 54–60; cf. also Coppola 1994, 21–24.

33 Thomas 1999, notes the trend to separate the worker from his labour, in Cicero as well as in Varro: *Ling.* 7, 105.

34 Sen. *Ben.* 3, 22, 2: *Seruus, ut placet Chrysippo, perpetuus mercennarius est. Quemadmodum ille beneficium dat, ubi plus praestat, quam in quod operas locauit, sic seruus*, 'A slave, according to the definition of Chrysippus, is 'a hireling for life'. And, just as a hireling gives a benefit if he supplies more than he contracted to do, so a slave' (trans. A.M. Harmon, Loeb). For Seneca's philosophy, see Pani 1985.

But this conservative discourse, on the same principles, also impacted skilled wage-earners. Cicero had separated them, and protected them from the stigmatization of wage labour. Lucian, writing in the 170's CE on the same principles, castigates those intellectuals or artists employed in the great houses[35] ('all who think fit to enter families and serve for hire as educators') and makes them the subject of an entire opuscule, *De mercede conductis* (*On Salaried Posts*). Here, contrary to Cicero, Lucian believes that *ars* does not save one from servitude, arguing that to lease oneself out commits the intellectual to being treated as a servant toiling for a wage (Lucian *Merc. Cond.* 4. Trans. Harmon):

> Since the experiences of all are for the most part common and similar, it is clear that the treatment accorded the philosophers; so far from being preferential, is more contumelious for being the same, it is thought that what is good enough for the others is good enough for them, and they are not handled with any greater respect by their paymasters.
>
> κοινῶν δὲ ὡς ἐπίπαν ὄντων καὶ ὁμοίων τῶν συμβαινόντων ἅπασι, δῆλον ὡς οὐκ ἐξαίρετα μέν, αἰσχίω δὲ τὰ αὐτὰ ὄντα γίγνεται τοῖς φιλοσοφοῦσιν, εἰ τῶν ὁμοίων τοῖς ἄλλοις ἀξιοῖντο καὶ μηδὲν αὐτοὺς σεμνότερον οἱ μισθοδόται ἄγοιεν.

The unease of the philosopher testifies to an urban society shaken up by the ubiquitous presence of commodification, including in the intellectual spheres. Whether they were educators, musicians, or philosophers, all those who accepted working for a salary (ἡ μισθοφορά) bound themselves to their employers (μισθοδόται) in the manner of servants of low station, wage-earners, or slaves. The only reason for their subjugation was to seek financial gain in a world where, at this point, labour is the subject of trading, just like other commodities. Rather than work in independent trades, they preferred to enter into the service of an aristocrat, thinking that their tasks would thus be more pleasant.[36]

It was no longer patronage that governed relationships between the rich and the intellectual, but the hiring of labour:[37] surveyors, architects, physicians,

35 Τῶν ἐπὶ παιδείαις συνεῖναι καὶ μισθοφορεῖν ἀξιουμένων: Lucian *Merc. Cond.* 4. Trans. Harmon. For the dating of *De mercede conductis*, Jones 1986, 20–21 and 78–83.

36 Lucian *Merc. Cond.* 7 sq.

37 See Coppola 1994, who clearly describes the transition from ancient aristocratic knowledge to working professionals, living off the leasing out of their art. See also Freu 2017 and Berrendonner 2007, 212–213, for various references to architects, physicians, teachers who received a *merces*.

educators, all had customers or students who brought them *merces*, in a *locatio* relationship or in an informal, *pactio*-type agreement. Sometimes they were even direct employees of great houses or municipalities. The *grammatici* whose lives Suetonius tracks show it well: they were hired by *pactio* and by *locatio* and were de facto subordinated to an employer.[38] They all became wage-earners and gave up their independence to bind themselves to another through the obligations of the contractual relationship. Here Lucian, as in many of his works, is a clear witness to his times, describing a rooted disdain towards the hiring of intellectual labour,[39] when he underlines what is, still today, the very essence of the work contract: the subordinate relationship.[40] It is in the name of liberal arts distinctiveness that Lucian took up his pen to re-establish the traditional hierarchy of trades that wage labour thwarted by urging intellectuals to not enter into trade relationships, especially. Moreover, he was not the only one to denounce intellectual wage labour: it became the subject of debate between schools. Whereas, in *The Eunuch*, Lucian criticized the expansion, under Marcus Aurelius, of the great imperial chairs of philosophy at Athens, Tatian, a Christian and former sophist, mocked likewise in the years 165–172 the contradiction between the autarky claimed by the philosophers, and the tangible lure of profit (Tatianus, *Ad Gr.* 19, 1):

> But this [desiring little] is a discipline in which your philosophers are so greatly deficient, that some of them receive from the king of the Romans 600 aurei yearly, for no useful service they perform, so that they may not even wear a long beard for free![41]
>
> Οἱ γὰρ παρ' ὑμῖν φιλόσοφοι τοσοῦτον ἀποδέουσι τῆς ἀσκήσεως, ὥστε παρὰ τοῦ Ῥωμαίων βασιλέως ἐτησίους χρυσοῦς ἑξακοσίους λαμβάνειν τινὰς εἰς οὐδὲν χρήσιμον, ὅπως μηδὲ τὸ γένειον δωρεὰν καθειμένον αὐτῶν ἔχωσι.

---

38 Suet. *Gram.* 3, 5 and 7, 1.

39 On Lucian as an 'observer of his time', see Jones 1986. Conversely, the contempt for the fees earned through intellectual services was nothing new and had classical roots: on Socrates' contempt for fees, for the sake of his heroic liberty, see Blank 1985; Pébarthe 2014, 231–236.

40 Cf. Supiot 1994.

41 For the dating of the discourse (after 165 and before 172 CE), see now the introduction of. H. Grenier-Deneux in *Premiers écrits chrétiens*, Paris 2016, 1305–1308, and Toulouse 2008, 158–159, who identifies the chairs evoked by Tatianus as chairs in Rome; see also Lucian, *Eun.* 3 (who speaks about the Athenian chairs created by Marcus Aurelius). On the 'imperial' and municipal chairs in Athens and the philosophers' and sophists' fees, see Toulouse 2008, 146–174.

Leaving aside the ethical debate around the idea of fraudulent labour, it is clear that intellectuals, not all having been born into the property classes, needed to work for money. In the 210s, the jurist Ulpian outlined his prudential opinion on the professions permitted to be heard by governors when they had grounds for complaint regarding their wages and their revenues (*mercedes*).[42] He drew up a list of every wage-earning professional who could bring proceedings in cases of unpaid wages, revenues, or honoraria: physicians, teachers, geometricians, midwives, accountants, lawyers. His reply was such that, outside of the philosophers whose profession it was to hold money in contempt, all other professionals in the liberal arts were to be heard by the provincial governor, the causes of other tradespeople being delegated to lower jurisdictions.[43] In providing this technical reply, here again, Ulpian drew a dividing line between wage-earners pretty close to Cicero's own line by granting a certain privilege to wage-earning intellectuals. In any case, we see the degree to which these questions were constantly being asked, the perceived threat to social order that wage labour presented, and the concomitant need to constantly re-erect social and legal boundaries.

Some thinkers, however, took a different attitude. In wanting to reclaim labour as an ascetic effort (*ponos*), some of the Stoics and Cynics, in contrast, cast a neutral gaze on the workers of their time, questioning, *ex novo*, the relationship between work and a happy life.[44] In their consideration, the figure of the wage-earning man, earning his living in cities and/or rural estates, appears frequently. Epictetus at the end of the first century therefore thought that it was not so shameful to earn one's living by performing remunerated service occupations: if you are alarmed about starving, 'can you not draw water, work as a scribe, escort children to school, or be another's doorkeeper?'[45]

---

42 The word may be understood in the text as the wages of a workman or the profit obtained by the sale of a medical procedure, legal aid, or an artisanal work.

43 *Dig.* 50, 13, 1, commented on by Coppola 1994, 251–290, among many others, as important evidence for the leasing out of all intellectual activities. The date of Ulpian's treatise must be understood, according to Honoré 2002², 185, as falling between 214 and 216. Ulpian, in this text, continues, in the vein of Middle Stoicism, to classify wage-earners according to their trade type, but we will come back to this in more detail subsequently.

44 See Brunt's 1973 article for the analysis of social thinking of the Cynics and Stoics throughout the work, considerable on this topic, of Dio of Prusa, to which we return below. More generally, see van den Hoven 1996, 21–71, for the precise analysis of Stoic thinking about labour, taken up again by Lis and Soly 2012, 87–98 and 2016, 264–266.

45 Arr. *Epict. diss.* 3, 26, 7 (οὐκ ἀντλεῖν δύνασαι, οὐ γράφειν, οὐ παιδαγωγεῖν, οὐ θύραν ἀλλοτρίαν φυλλάτειν). It should be noted that the Stoic Dio Chrysostom, during his exile under Domitian, is said to have earned his living exactly in this way (Philostr., *VS* 1, 7, 2: φυτεύων δὲ καὶ σκάπτων καὶ ἐπαντλῶν βαλανείοις τε καὶ κήποις καὶ πολλὰ τοιαῦτα ὑπὲρ τροφῆς ἐργαζόμε-

In the same vein, Dio of Prusa's *Euboea* also testified to this state of affairs. Writing in the first decades of the second century CE and influenced by the social ethics of Cynicism and ancient Stoicism, he reflected on the activities which allowed for a good life.[46] The autarkic hunter, a symbol of human happiness far from civilization and the noise and crowds of cities (Dio Chrys. *Or.* 7, 1–80), was thus contrasted with the wage-earning 'little guy' living off an irregular income. Intending to cast himself as an advocate for the poor, in line with some classical public and forensic discourses from which he drew some of his examples,[47] the sophist also described urban society as he saw it during his wanderings throughout the empire. If the big city described here by Dio was perhaps Rome,[48] it may well also have been a typical big city, the description of which would have been fuelled by his memories of visits to Alexandria, Rome, Tarsos, or Athens. In fact, all of the trades mentioned by Dio were also, more or less, those mentioned in the employment contracts from Egypt, as we will see.

After having affirmed how difficult life had become for the poor, who had to buy and pay for everything from rent, to clothing and food, including wood for the fire (7, 105), and work accordingly to earn a living, Dio describes such poor people as having nothing but their bodies to sell and looking for some way to make a living and leasing themselves out for one job or another (Dio Chrys. *Or.* 7, 106. Trans. Cohoon):

νος οὐδὲ τοῦ σπουδάζειν ἠμέλει, ἀλλ' ἀπὸ δυοῖν βιβλίοιν ἑαυτὸν ξυνεῖχεν, 'But while he planted and dug, drew water for baths and gardens, and performed many such menial tasks for a living, he did not neglect the study, but sustained himself with two books'). Although we cannot rule out the possibility that Philostratus' text is a literary reminiscence, it should be noticed that all the tasks Dio performed are precisely those which are documented in the papyri: e.g. turning the sakyie or operating the shaduf for the baths (see for example *P.Lond.Wasser* 65–147), digging and planting (in vineyards, see: *BGU* I 14, col. II, 18–19; *P.Oxy.* XLVII 3354, from 257 CE; *P.Oxy.* XIV 1631, 8–14, from 281 CE).

46 On the philosophical tendencies of these words of Dio's, see Bost-Pouderon 2008, 105–122; Brenk 2000, 261–278. The uniqueness of Dio's point of view was emphasized by Brunt 1973, 21 (van den Hoven 1996, 59), who believes that Dio depends perhaps even more, as does Epictetus, on the ancient Stoicism of Chrysippus. However, given the lack of writings from Chrysippus, this remains fairly conjectural. Van den Hoven 1996, 27, follows him with a view of a Stoic Dio; for my part, I'll take Jones 1978's idea of a Dio of Prusa that was influenced by both doctrines.

47 His thinking about work and workers distinguishes him from many of his contemporaries, but has ancient roots. Brunt 1973, 12–13 and 24, emphasizes mostly Stoic influences: 'Dio's concern with humble folk was quite unusual, and nothing forbids us to think that he has preserved old Stoic views about their problems, which all other writers have neglected'. We will also see that some of his examples are directly drawn from Demosthenes' speeches.

48 This is Brunt's thesis, 1973, 9; 12–13.

> it will perhaps seem hard for men to subsist under such conditions who have no other possession than their own bodies, especially as we do not advise them to take any kind of work that offers or all kinds indiscriminately from which it is possible to make some money.
>
> τάχα γὰρ ἂν φανεῖται χαλεπὸν τοιούτῳ βίῳ διαρκεῖν μηδὲν ἄλλο κτῆμα ἔξω τοῦ σώματος κεκτημένους, ἄλλως τε ὅταν μὴ τὸ τυχὸν ἔργον μηδὲ πάνθ' ὁμοίως συμβουλεύωμεν αὐτοῖς ὅθεν ἔστι κερδᾶναι.

In these words, we see what Karl Marx was describing with respect to modern society: a society in which the lack of economic independence pushed many free men to take the first service job or manual labour job that presented itself (τὸ τυχὸν ἔργον), and which they could be sure would be remunerated. No compartmentalization existed between quite distinct activities here, but a single connection between them—wages. Women could look for work as paid wet-nurses, grape-pickers, or servants—trades deemed appropriate[49]—or as hairstylists, perfumers, or prostitutes—trades that were not approved of. The men could become preceptors and educators, lawyers, auctioneers, scribes, public criers, hunters of runaway slaves, pimps, comic or tragic actors, or flute-players.[50] The majority of trades Dio lists were therefore primarily, as with Lucian or Epictetus, urban service trades. Some were unskilled jobs, others required technical or scholastic training (scribe, lawyer, educator or actor), to which could be added a few wage-earning agricultural activities, which city-dwellers could do on the periphery of cities, such as harvesting, grape-picking, or olive-collecting. Those cases were a mix of classical topic cases and of real-life occupations.[51]

---

49 Dio Chrys. *Or.* 7, 114: ἄν τινος ἔριθος ἡ μήτηρ ᾖ ἢ τρυγήτρια ἐξελθοῦσά ποτε ἢ μισθοῦ τιτθεύσῃ παῖδα τῶν ὀρφανῶν ἢ πλουσίων ἢ ὁ πατὴρ διδάξῃ γράμματα ἢ παιδαγωγήσῃ, 'when, for instance, his mother was once on occasion someone's hired servant or a harvester of grapes, or was a paid wet-nurse for a motherless child or a rich man's, or when his father was a schoolmaster or a tutor'. For honest jobs of poor women, Dio's speech is clearly inspired by Dem. 57, 45: ὡς γὰρ ἐγὼ ἀκούω, πολλαὶ καὶ τιτθαὶ καὶ ἔριθοι καὶ τρυγήτριαι γενόμασιν ὑπὸ τῶν τῆς πόλεως κατ' ἐκείνους τοὺς χρόνους συμφορῶν ἀσταὶ γυναῖκες, πολλαὶ δ' ἐκ πενήτων πλούσιαι νῦν. On the praise of 'active poverty' in Demosthenes and other classical sophists, see Cecchet 2015, 194–218.

50 On the trades he disapproved of, see Dio Chrys. *Or.* 7, 133–134 (pimps and prostitutes); 7, 119 (men of the theatre and flute-players); 7, 123 (scribes, public criers, hunters of runaway slaves).

51 Thus, women's occupations are identical in the Sophistic texts and in work-contracts on papyri. For example, free or slave wet-nurses were often hired in Egypt (see Manca Masciadri and Montevecchi 1984 for their contracts). Conversely, whereas vinting was not

Of course, Dio's statement was a return to a moral classification that would distinguish trades that were considered appropriate (τὸ πρέπον) from those that were not appropriate.[52] But he did so less in order to emphasize, as did Aristotle, Plato, or Lucian, the dependence of the worker on his employer or patron, than to stigmatize, in the trades he condemned, their nature as harmful to the worker's soul or body, exhausted by tasks destined solely to provide luxury to the rich.[53]

4 Conclusion

All of the texts analysed here take, as a subject of consideration, a society whose economy, without being described in specific ways, appears to be commercial, urbanized and monetized, in which capital is used for the comfort of city-dwellers, but which is also invested in the nearby rural estates in order to exploit the land in speculative ways. Everything is for sale and everyone works, even the women and children. As Dio says in his *Oratio* 35, 'nothing in the city is out of work, neither the teams, nor the houses, nor the women' (*Or.* 35, 15),[54] another feature that connects the Roman to the modern era.[55] In short, these Sophistic texts are, primarily, very useful complements to documentary sources, papyri and technical treatises, which also show the use of free wage-earners alongside slave labour in the Roman economy, at least in its commercial sector.[56]

---

primarily a woman's task, olive-picking and olive-processing were: see Freu 2022, 107–109, quoting one Fayum employment contract in an oil-factory, from 99 CE (*P.Fay.* 91), and other contracts recently published by Claytor et al. 2016.

52 Brunt 1973, *passim*, nn. 19–21 (on the concept of *prepon* in Greek), which, however, reaffirms that the discourse stops abruptly before the list of approved trades (though they are stated at § 114). See also Treggiari 1980, n. 49, and van den Hoven 1996, 49–54, who follows the analysis of Brunt, while underlining that the list of trades disapproved of does not add anything new. Dio draws nearer, in this way, to Xenophon's *Oec.* IV, 2–3: professions confining workers to the indoors, as those which do damage to the body, are not recommended.

53 In Dio Chrys. *Or.* 7, 114, Dio, in effect, castigates the arrogant and idle elites who reproach the poor for the trades they undertake to earn their living. This is an idea from the Stoics: see Van den Hoven 1996, 51–54.

54 Cf. Desideri 2000, 96–99: 'Dio is strongly censuring the consequences of moral disorder which derive from the congestion of urban life.'

55 See Scott and Tilly 1978, 59.

56 Cf. Lo Cascio 1991, 327, who characterized the Roman economy as 'un'economia "duale" … nella quale, accanto a un settore commercializzato e monetarizzato … è presenta un'area … di autoconsumo.'

Thus, in terms of the abstract representation of the social entity, we see that the majority of authors are especially mindful of the distinction between wage-earning professions,[57] for the purpose of maintaining boundaries between certain categories of the population. Outside of thinkers influenced by Stoicism, few authors of the Second Sophistic accorded proper dignity to the *mercennarius* who had no professional identity: he was, in all respects, obscured by his inferior work status and his economic insecurity.[58] In contrast, all authors symbolically reserved a special place for the wage-earners with whom they shared even the minimal academic knowledge and the common culture of the propertied classes.

Bibliography

Bagnall, R. and Frier, B. (1994). *The Demography of Roman Egypt*. Cambridge.

Bernard, S. (2018). *Building Mid-Republican Rome. Labour, Architecture, and the Urban Economy*. Oxford.

Berrendonner C. (2007). *Mercennarius* dans les sources littéraires. In: J. Andreau and V. Chankowski, eds., *Vocabulaire et expressions de l'économie dans le monde antique*. Bordeaux, pp. 211–231.

Blank, D.L. (1985). Socratics Versus Sophists on Payment for Teaching. *ClAnt* 4, pp. 1–49.

Bost-Pouderon, C. (2008). Ethnographie et utopie chez Dion Chrysostome (*Or*. 35, 18–22 et *Or*. 7, 1–80). *Kentron*, 24, pp. 105–122.

Bourdieu, P. (1979). *La distinction. Critique sociale du jugement*. Paris.

Brenk, F. (2000). Public Speech and Community in the *Euboicus*. In: S. Swain, ed., *Dio Chrysostom. Politics, Letters, and Philosophy*. Oxford, pp. 108–124.

Brunt, P.A. (1973). Aspects of the Social Thought of Dio Chrysostom and of the Stoics. *PCPS*, 19, pp. 9–34.

Carlsen, J. (2016). Le attività agricole e dell'allevamento. In: A. Marcone, ed., *Storia del lavoro in Italia. L'età romana. Liberi, semiliberi e schiavi in una società premoderna*. Rome, pp. 225–264.

Cecchet, L. (2015). *Poverty in Athenian Public Discourse. From the Eve of the Peloponnesian War to the Rise of Macedonia*. Stuttgart.

Claytor, W.G. et al. (2016). Labor Contracts from the Harthotes Archive. *BASP*, 53, pp. 79–119.

57 See Bourdieu 1979, 191: 'l'identité sociale se définit et s'affirme dans la différence.' See also Lis and Soly 2012, 34–53.

58 See Flohr 2016 on the invisibility of the *mercennarius* worker, contrasted to the visibility of the master craftsman.

Coppola, G. (1994). *Cultura e potere. Il lavoro intellettuale nel mondo romano*. Milan.

Corbier, M. (1980). Salaires et salariat sous le Haut-Empire. In: *Les dévaluations à Rome: époque républicaine et impériale*. II. Rome, pp. 61–95.

Cuvigny, H. (2021). The Organization Chart of the Personnel of an Imperial Quarry According to an Ostracon of Mons Claudianus. In: H. Cuvigny, *Rome in Egypt's Eastern Desert*. New York.

De Robertis, F.M. (1963). *Lavoro e lavoratori nel mondo romano*. Bari.

Desideri, P. (2000). City and Country in Dio. In: S. Swain, ed., *Dio Chrysostom. Politics, Letters, and Philosophy*. Oxford, pp. 93–107.

Flohr, M. (2016). Constructing Occupational Identities in the Roman World. In: C. Laes and K. Verboven, eds., *Work, Labour, and Professions in the Roman World*. Leiden–Boston, pp. 147–172.

Freu, C. (2017). Lucien à la lumière des papyrus: un philosophe en apprentissage dans l'*Hermotimus* 80–82. *Cahiers d'études anciennes*, 54, pp. 11–38.

Freu, C. (2018). Écrire l'histoire du travail aujourd'hui: le cas de l'Empire romain. *Annales HSS* 73, 1, pp. 163–184.

Freu, C. (2022). *Les salariés de l'Égypte romano-byzantine. Essai d'histoire économique*. Paris (StudPAP 3).

Giardina, A. (1991). Il tramonto dei valori ciceroniani (*ponos* ed *emporia* tra paganesimo e cristianesimo). In: M. Pani, ed., *Continuità e trasformazioni fra Repubblica e Principato. Istituzioni, politica e società, Atti dell'incontro du Studi Bari (27–28 gennaio 1989)*. Bari, pp. 275–295.

Groen-Vallinga, M. and Tacoma, L. (2016). The Value of Labour: Diocletian's Prices Edict. In: C. Laes and K. Verboven, eds., *Work, Labour, and Professions in the Roman World*. Leiden–Boston, pp. 104–132.

Harper, K. (2011). *Slavery in the Late Roman World (AD 275–425)*. Cambridge.

Harris, E.M. (2002). Workshop, Marketplace and Household: The Nature of Technical Specialization in Classical Athens and Its Influence on Economy and Society. In: P. Cartledge, E.E. Cohen and L. Foxhall, eds., *Money, Labour and Land. Approaches to the Economies of Ancient Greece*. London–New York, pp. 67–99.

Honoré, T. (2002²). *Ulpian. Pioneer of Human Rights*. Oxford.

Hoven, B. van den (1996). *Work in Ancient and Medieval Thought. Ancient Philosophers, Medieval Monks and Theologians and their Concept of Work, Occupations and Technology*. Amsterdam.

Jones, C.P. (1978). *The Roman World of Dio Chrysostom*. Cambridge, MA–London.

Jones, C.P. (1986). *Culture and Society in Lucian*. Cambridge, MA–London.

Kloppenborg, J.S. (2006). *The Tenants in the Vineyard. Ideology, Economics, and Agrarian Conflict in Jewish Palestine*. Tübingen.

Laes, C. and Verboven, K. (2016). Work, Labour, and Professions: What's in a Name? In: C. Laes and K. Verboven, eds., *Work, Labour, and Professions in the Roman World*. Leiden–Boston, pp. 1–19.

Lis, C. and Soly, H. (2012). *Worthy Efforts. Attitudes to Work and Workers in Preindustrial Europe*. Leiden.

Lis, C. and Soly, H. (2016). Work, Identity and Self-Representation in the Roman Empire. In: C. Laes and K. Verboven, eds., *Work, Labour, and Professions in the Roman World*. Leiden–Boston, pp. 262–289.

Lewis, D.M. (2020). Labour Specialization in the Athenian Economy: Occupational Hazards. In: Ed. Harris *et alii*, eds, *Skilled Labour and Professionalism in Ancient Greece and Rome*. Cambridge, pp. 129–174.

Lo Cascio, E. (1991). Forme dell'economia imperiale. In: A. Momigliano and A. Schiavone, eds., *Storia di Roma. II, 2. I principi e il mondo*. Turin, pp. 313–365.

Maillot, S. and Zurbach, J. (2021). Statuts personnels, mise au travail et contrôle de la main-d'œuvre en Méditerranée hellénistique. In: S. Maillot and J. Zurbach, eds., *Statuts personnels et main-d'œuvre en Méditerranée hellénistique*. Clermont-Ferrand, pp. 9–29.

Manca Masciadri, M. and Montevecchi, O. 1984. *I contratti di baliatico*. Milan.

Martini, R. (1958). *Mercennarius. Contributo allo studio dei rapporti di lavoro in diritto romano*. Milan.

Pani, M. (1985). La polemica di Seneca contro le *artes* (*Ep*. 90). Un caso di sconcerto. In: F. Broilo, ed., Xenia. *Scritti in onore di Piero Treves*. Rome, pp. 141–150.

Pébarthe, C. 2014. Les sandales de Socrate. Les sophistes, les philosophes et la pauvreté. In: E. Galbois and S. Rougier-Blanc, eds., *La Pauvreté en Grèce ancienne. Formes, représentations, enjeux*. Bordeaux, pp. 223–236.

Rathbone, D. (1991). *Economic Rationalism and Rural Society in the Third Century A.D. Egypt. The Heroninos Archive and the Appianus Estate*. Cambridge.

Rathbone, D. (2009). Earnings and Costs: Living Standards and the Roman Economy (I–III c. AD). In: A. Bowman and A. Wilson, eds., *Quantifying the Roman Economy*. Oxford, pp. 229–326.

Roselaar, S.T. (2019). *Italy's Economic Revolution. Integration and Economy in Republican Italy*. Oxford.

Roselaar, S.T. (2021). Status Hierarchies and Economic Differentiation in Rome and Italy (IIIrd to Ist century BC). In: S. Maillot and J. Zurbach, eds., *Statuts personnels et main-d'œuvre en Méditerranée hellénistique*. Clermont-Ferrand, pp. 121–138.

Ruffing, K. (2008). *Die berufliche Spezialisierung in Handel und Handwerk. Untersuchungen zu ihrer Entwicklung und zu ihren Bedingungen in der römischen Kaiserzeit im östlichen Mittelmeerraum auf der Grundlage griechischer Inschriften und Papyri*, 2 vols. Rahden.

Ruffing, K. (2016). Driving Forces for Specialization: Market, Location Factors, Productivity Improvements. In: M. Flohr and A. Wilson, eds., *Urban craftsmen and Traders in the Roman World*. Oxford, pp. 115–131.

Scheidel, W. (2005). Human Mobility in Roman Italy, II: The Slave Population. *JRS* 95, pp. 64–79.

Scott, J. and Tilly, L. (1978). *Women, Work, and Family*. New York.

Supiot, A. (1994). *Critique du droit du travail*. Paris.

Temin, P. (2013). *The Roman Market Economy*. Princeton.

Thomas, Y. (1999). L'usage et les 'fruits' de l'esclave. Opérations juridiques romaines sur le travail. *Enquête* 7 (*Les objets du droit*), pp. 203–230.

Thomas, Y. (2002). Le corps de l'esclave et son travail à Rome. Analyse d'une dissociation juridique. In: P. Moreau, ed., *Corps romains*. Paris, pp. 225–250.

Thomas, Y. (2004). Travail incorporé dans une matière première, travail d'usage et travail comme marchandise. Le droit comme matrice des catégories économiques à Rome. In: J. Andreau et al., eds., *Mentalités et choix économiques des Romains*. Bordeaux-Paris, pp. 201–225.

Toulouse, S. (2008). Les Chaires impériales à Athènes aux IIe et IIIe siècles. In: H. Hugonnard-Roche, ed., *L'Enseignement supérieur dans les mondes antiques et médiévaux. Aspects institutionnels, juridiques et pédagogiques*. Paris, pp. 127–174.

Tran, N. (2013). Dominus tabernae. *Le statut de travail des artisans et des commerçants de l'Occident romain*. Rome.

Treggiari, S (1980). Urban Labour in Rome: *Mercennarii* and *Tabernarii*. In: P. Garnsey, ed., *Non-Slave Labour in the Greco-Roman World*. Cambridge, pp. 48–64.

Vernant, J.-P. (1996[2] [1955]). Travail et nature dans la Grèce ancienne. *Journal de psychologie*, 1955, pp. 1–29. Reprint in Vernant, J.-P. (1996[2]). *Mythe et pensée chez les Grecs. Études de psychologie historique*. Paris, pp. 274–294.

Veyne, P. (2001[2] [1979]). Mythe et réalité de l'autarcie à Rome. In: P. Veyne, *La société romaine*. Paris, pp. 131–162.

Vlassopoulos, K. (2007). Free Spaces: Identity, Experience, and Democracy in Classical Athens. *CQ* 57, pp. 33–62.

Wilson, A. (2011). City Sizes and Urbanization in the Roman Empire. In: A. Bowman and A. Wilson, eds., *Settlement, Urbanization, and Population*. Oxford, pp. 161–195.

CHAPTER 9

The Value of Work: Work and Labour within the Roman Upper-class Household

Miriam J. Groen-Vallinga

1 Introduction

The history of work and labour in (Roman) antiquity remains relatively undertheorized, despite important contributions to the field of ancient labour history. The terminology of the debate is often blurry or imprecise, and work and labour in particular have generally been used synonymously.[1] In part, this is the result of the patently discursive nature of ancient discourses on work and labour, as the various contributions in this volume so beautifully illustrate and illuminate. At the same time, however, the fields of labour history and labour theories are branching out and are slowly but surely incorporating antiquity.[2] If we are to benefit from this budding conjunction with labour theory more broadly, the terminology of work and labour should ideally no longer be applied interchangeably. The distinction between the two, 'work' versus 'labour', is in my view especially significant for our interpretation of the ancient evidence. Labour, 'considered as a resource or commodity' (*OED*), refers specifically to an income-generating job or profession. Work, defined as 'any human effort adding use value to goods and services', is a more inclusive concept that encompasses both labour and non-wage labour, as well as the unremunerated efforts of family members.[3] There are good reasons to adopt this terminology for antiquity as well, because it encompasses previously unidentified workers more systematically into economic investigations of Roman labour. Careful use of this vocabulary in such a way could therefore assist with the aspirations expressed in the introduction to this volume, of including 'a broader range of activities than those addressed in traditional studies of Roman professions', and creating awareness of 'a more diverse valuation of work', dependent on context.

1 But see the discussion on terminology in Verboven 2017a, and Groen-Vallinga 2022, 8–11.
2 E.g. Lis and Soly 2012; Zuiderhoek 2013; Groen-Vallinga and Tacoma 2015.
3 Tilly and Tilly 1998, 22; for early modern history, see the programmatic paper of Hofmeester 2018, 317–318; in Roman history see Verboven 2017a, 4–6 and Groen-Vallinga 2022, 10.

 | DOI:10.1163/9789004694965_010

The implicit and explicit focus of Roman economic history understandably has been on labour and labourers, and sometimes more specifically on artisans and craftsmen.[4] The economic contributions of those Romans who are not overtly identifiable as having a profession, for example by explicit reference to their occupation on their epitaph, remain obscured. Such workers, who must have very often been women and children, remain largely invisible to us, despite great efforts to bring these groups into focus.[5] A broader awareness and acknowledgement of the distinction between work and labour invites us to view labour within the context of work, including the uncredited contributions of women and children. Absence of evidence is not evidence of absence; this is well known. It does require creative methods to look for the invisible workers, however, because how do you assess something that isn't attested?[6] One of the challenges, therefore, is to identify where to look for the invisible workers. The follow-up question that comes with it is equally important for current purposes: does the choice *not* to record work in an epitaph tell us anything about societal values concerning work and labour?

The current paper will explore a selection of upper-class households from the city of Rome and its environs in the early empire. It will do so by reviewing *columbaria*-inscriptions as well as aspects of the material remains of the tombs and tomb inhabitants. These elite households will function as a case study to develop the conceptualization of work and labour in antiquity further and to illustrate the added value, as well as the inherent difficulty, of looking at unremunerated and unrecorded work. It will be argued that everyone in the tombs was likely part of the working population and therefore will have worked for a living. This implies that the patterns of commemoration from the columbarium tombs can shed light on the appraisal of work and labour in the context of the large elite household. It will become clear that there were complex socio-economic networks at play that organically combined work and labour in the household unit, a finding that can illuminate both the columbarium tomb population and the ways in which work and labour functioned at the level of the household unit. It is hoped that this approach can add to our understanding of the value of labour and work within Roman society.

The upper-class households of Rome can be defined for current purposes as the staff or *familiae* of an aristocratic patron (or patrons), with *familia* in the sense of the patron's enslaved and freed people.[7] In the early Roman empire,

4 E.g. Hawkins 2021; Wilson and Flohr 2016; Joshel 1992.

5 For women, e.g. Larsson Lovén 2016; Groen-Vallinga 2013; for children, e.g. Porena 2016.

6 Cf. the title of Suzanne Dixon's 2001 article: 'How Do You Count Them If They're Not There?'.

7 Edmondson 2011, 338; Dixon 1992, 1–3; Hasegawa 2005, 56: 'In sum, the range of servile

'family' should in my view be taken to include enslaved and freed people, particularly in an economic investigation.[8] I have argued elsewhere that the options of an individual for work or labour in the market were limited by their position within social structures, through household, kinship and non-familial labour collectives.[9] In order to comprehend the practice of everyday labour in antiquity, therefore, the context of work is of paramount importance. It is commonly recognized that the Roman family was diverse, dynamic and multifaceted, and the subject of Roman family structure and its inherent dynamics remains the engine behind a fruitful exploration of all its facets.[10] The upper-class *domus*, in my view, exhibit a number of relevant common features that allow for their discussion as a particular category here. Elite families present a typically sizeable family form that included a significant number of servants who, by their very presence, may be expected to have been considered economically valuable. These *familiae* become accessible mainly through the inscriptions from large, single-family columbarium tombs that can be explored to shed light on the household composition and labour efforts of the elite *domus*. Admittedly, such general observations are simplifications of a more complex reality to some extent, but they may serve as a model to work with here. It is an open question who was buried in a columbarium monument, for example, and it is readily acknowledged that the uncritical assumption of a direct connection between a tomb's occupants and an actual household would be highly problematic.[11] Yet in many instances, clear relationships between the interred can nevertheless be identified. The composition of the columbarium tomb population, therefore, has become an integral part of the analysis here.

The columbarium tomb inscriptions are of particular interest to the subject of work and labour. According to Joshel's influential study, the majority of occupational inscriptions—i.e. epitaphs from the city of Rome that record professions—originate from a columbarium tomb or from a similar domestic context.[12] It will become clear, however, that even within this corpus the majority of inscriptions from *columbaria* do not attest specific job-titles, although in

---

dependants who were buried in a *columbarium* was so extensive that straightforward application of the term *domus* or *familia* is problematic. It might be better said in reverse; the *columbaria* certainly "included" the *familia* or servile members of the *domus*, but those who were in other ways associated with the aristocratic family were also admitted.'

8 Cf. Verboven 2012.

9 Groen-Vallinga 2022.

10 From the seminal work of Bradley 1991 to the conference proceedings of Hübner and Ratzan 2021, and more.

11 Borg 2019, 125; Hübner 2011; Bodel 2008, 190.

12 Joshel 1992, 73–74.

the context of the Roman economy the individuals represented surely will have contributed to work in the family.[13] The difficulty lies in imagining the ways in which they would likely have done so, and then reviewing these possibilities against the ancient evidence. To formulate a number of such hypothetical possibilities, this paper will consider the epigraphic and material evidence for the wealthier households of Rome in the first century CE in comparison with an exceedingly well-documented seventeenth-century British household.

'Comparative history is, of course, an artifact, constructed by the historian to illuminate particular points.'[14] Diachronic comparison is applied here as a tool for formulating new hypotheses and ways of looking at the upper-class household in Rome, exploring multiple perspectives, and investigating the possibility of shared frameworks.[15] The seventeenth-century household accounts of the lady Joyce Jeffreys illustrate wonderfully how work and labour could blend together to create an organic whole. The current approach therefore serves to highlight the value of the informal economic contributions of women, children, and dependent workers within the elite family. The unconventional comparison also proves to be highly illustrative of the social networks based on emotive and kinship ties that governed work and labour in the Roman empire as well as in the seventeenth century. Among the connections that will be identified in the *columbaria*, for example, are networks between *domus*, presenting an insight that straddles the boundaries of labour theory.

2 Columbarium Tomb Epigraphy

The term columbarium tomb or *columbarium* refers to a particular type of subterranean tomb chamber from the city of Rome and its immediate surroundings. This type of monument was built between the first century BCE and the first century CE. The tombs have regularly been connected with aristocratic patrons and elite households in general discussions, because large numbers of the servile population can be related to members of the imperial family and other known aristocrats.[16] Scholars are right to point out, however, that colum-

---

13 Groen-Vallinga 2022; Groen-Vallinga 2013.

14 As is all history. Levine 2014, 346.

15 In doing so, my approach means to bypass the more common criticisms or pitfalls of the comparative method, such as determinism, universalism and exceptionalism, cf. Levine 2014, 341; Levine 2014 and Kocka 2003 address and review critique of the comparative method, for which see also Werner and Zimmermann 2002.

16 E.g. Penner 2012; Edmondson 2011; Bodel 2008; Hasegawa 2005; Patterson 1992; Purcell 1987.

barium tombs exist in various shapes and sizes.[17] Of the 35 monuments that have been catalogued as of the columbarium tomb type by Borbonus in 2014, only a handful can be identified with certainty as single-family tombs with a clear connection with an aristocratic patron or an elite family, as indicated by the predominance of the family *nomen* in the tomb.[18] Most of these tombs were thus not set up by or for the dependants of an aristocratic patron—*collegia* and collectives had a large part to play in collective burials like these. Those that might concern elite *domus*, however, form valuable case studies that are worth going into in some more detail. Among these are the monuments of Livia Augusta, the Statilii, and the Volusii.[19] Even within these 'single-family tombs', it will become clear that the tomb occupants are more wide-ranging than one elite *familia*.

Columbarium tombs were chambers constructed to contain large numbers of cremation burials: the walls had built-in niches (*loculi*) that were suited to hold one, two, or four urns each—in most instances, niches accommodated two urns. The tombs were built to provide a final resting place for large numbers of people. The relatively modest monument of the Stertinii, for example, consisted of one room that measured $3.10 \times 1.90\,m^2$, but it may have held up to 160 urns.[20] More importantly, many of the *loculi* of columbarium tombs were marked by an inscription identifying the deceased and/or the commemorator. Although we will see that the epitaphs do not commemorate every single person who was interred, it is a commemorative habit that has resulted in an invaluable collection of over three thousand named, individual burials.[21] Their research value is obvious. Analysis has revealed a pattern of predominantly enslaved and freed people, a group that is not always well represented in the epigraphic sources more generally.[22] Despite a significant number of free people of uncertain legal status (*incerti*) in the data, it seems not unreasonable to assume freed status for many of them in the light of general demographic investigations into the Roman population.[23] Such a pattern seems to corroborate the possibility that many tombs of this type were built for the dependents of wealthy, elite households. The presumed aristocratic patrons of these *columbaria*, conversely, are never interred within the tombs and seem to have had

17 E.g. Galvao-Sobrinho 2012, Sigismund-Nielsen 1996, 38; cf. Borg 2019, 189.
18 Borbonus 2014, 120 on the term (and his identification of) single-family tombs.
19 Selection criteria sometimes differ, cf. Borbonus 2014, 120; Penner 2012; Hasegawa 2005.
20 160 *loculi*, with one urn each in this instance: Borbonus (2014) 70–71 and his cat. no. 27.
21 Borbonus 2014 includes 3,120 individuals in his epigraphic database; Sigismund-Nielsen 1996 for an example of unidentified burials in Columbarium 1 in the Vigna Codini.
22 E.g. Borbonus 2014; Mouritsen 2013; Hasegawa 2005.
23 E.g. Garnsey and De Ligt (2016).

very little to do with their construction or any epigraphic expressions from the monument.[24] Inscriptions were put up by family members, co-workers, *colliberti* and *conservi*. It would appear that the *columbaria*-inscriptions grant us a unique insight into non-elite funerary commemorative customs. They reflect their sense of community and their appreciation of family and friends, as well as reflect attitudes to work and dependent labour from the working population itself.

Commemoration was thus one of the ways in which value could be attributed to personal status and accomplishment in the context of Roman society. The funerary inscriptions themselves are often necessarily brief, because the marble plaques or painted inscriptions had to fit into the space for a winged tablet (*tabula ansata*) underneath the niche, or on a plaque covering the niche. Fortunately, they do regularly contain a little more information than just a name, such as kinship ties and other relations, or collegiate title. Compare the brief inscription for Apate (just her name), or that with name and occupation for Diomedes the shoemaker (*Diomedes sutor*), with the larger wall plaque for Nothus the librarian that was set up by his wife.[25] Nothus was commemorated by a small poem in elegiac metre.[26] All three inscriptions come from the monument of the Statilii.

It was already mentioned above that the *columbaria*-inscriptions also contain job-titles more often than in any other context, and that this has made the tombs of particular interest to the study of work, labour and occupations.[27] It has invited a number of interesting observations on the economic foundations of the large household and the domestic economy of elite families. For instance, the recorded professions clearly illustrate the phenomenon of conspicuous consumption among the elite, through the wide variety of jobs attested as well as the numerous occupations working with luxury materials.[28]

Women make up some 36 percent of the columbarium tomb population, which is similar to their presence within the overall epigraphic evidence from Rome.[29] What is noteworthy, however, is that for women in particular the columbarium tomb inscriptions refer to occupations more often than epitaphs from a different context. Occupational inscriptions from columbarium

24 Only the Statilian tomb has the occasional inscription that was put up 'by permission of our Lucius' (*permissu Luci nostri*), referring to the head of the Statilian family: *CIL* 06, 7370; 7380; 7389 and 7394.

25 *CIL* 6, 6409 = EDCS 19300452; *CIL* 6, 6355 = EDCS 19300398.

26 *CIL* 6, 6314 = EDCS 19300357.

27 Groen-Vallinga 2022, 198–216; Joshel 1992, especially 73–78, 98–106, 145–161.

28 Cf. Joshel 1992, 73–76.

29 Penner 2012, 145; Hasegawa 2005, 65 table 5.3.

tombs also provide some insight into what jobs were open to women in a domestic context. Here, we find a notable number of hairdressers (*ornatrices*), for example, spinners (*quasillariae*) and weavers in the household of the Statilii, and midwives and female doctors (*obstetricae* and *medicae*). All of these job-indicators would seem to fall well within established gendered values for women, centred on domestic life.[30] Rather than drawing the conclusion that this merely confirms known gender biases in Roman society, it should be noted that the domestic interpretation of these inscriptions results only from the context of the elite *domus* in which the epitaphs were found: each of these women might well have found employment outside the *domus*. There are more 'independent' examples of these occupations too.[31]

Finally, the inscriptions demonstrate a noticeable lack of self-sufficiency within the household: the *domus* did not have every type of job we might expect to have been necessary in order to feed and clothe all its inhabitants. According to the surviving epitaphs, the household of the Volusii would have had no cooks, for example. That is of course possible, but it would be unlikely—unless, as Penner has suggested in the context of her study into the Julio-Claudian households, they cooperated with other *domus*.[32] That possibility will be explored in more detail below. At the same time, the occupational inscriptions hint at the possibility that some houses may have worked for the market. Hasegawa notes that the Statilian tomb contained a number of textile workers that clearly goes beyond the self-sufficiency of the household.[33]

Mining the epigraphic evidence is as tempting as it is valuable, with due account of the biases in the material. I should like to point out two things, however, about what is *not* written in the columbarium tomb inscriptions. Firstly, despite the importance of this epigraphic corpus for occupational epigraphy, it should be noted that the majority of inscriptions from these monuments do not attest specific jobs. With an average of 15.9 per cent with job-title, they are admittedly richer than the epigraphic corpus from Roman Italy as a whole, which has between 3 and 5 per cent occupational inscriptions.[34] But the obvious conclusion must also be that an impressive 84.1 per cent of *columbaria*-

30 Cf. Larsson Lovén 2013; Treggiari 1976, Treggiari 1975.

31 Groen-Vallinga 2022, 130–137.

32 Penner 2013, 2 makes a similar argument about related, co-resident households of Augustus or Tiberius and Livia.

33 Hasegawa 2005, 39–44 on the Statilian production line; similar observations in Penner 2012, 148.

34 Borbonus 2014, 128 for the columbarium tombs, Groen-Vallinga 2022 for the occupational inscriptions from Roman Italy.

inscriptions do *not* record occupation.[35] The question becomes, why not? If the columbarium tomb is a place where many commemorators choose to indicate their profession, more so than outside of this context, what makes others decide against it?

Philosophical qualms about 'working for another' of the type that we find in Cicero's *On Duties* are seemingly absent from these inscriptions.[36] People regularly mention their master or patron, whose position would appear to be a source of pride. Members of the imperial household are regularly attested, perhaps for obvious reasons, but it is not at all uncommon for others to be cited as well. Examples are found readily enough from all the single-family *columbaria* under scrutiny here: Phyllis, herself a seamstress of Statilia (*sarcinatrix Statiliae*), commemorates her husband;[37] *CIL* 6.7290 was set up by Primigenius, who refers to himself as the *ser(vus)* of Lucius Volusius Saturninus.[38] In the *monumentum Liviae*, references to Livia, Livia as Augusta, and to other imperial family members are so numerous that they form the basis for scholarly reconstruction of the use of the tomb over time.[39] If patrons or their representatives did have a say in who was buried in the tomb, reference to the master was a sure ticket to a burial spot. But affiliation seems to have served as an important way of connecting with fellow household members as well.

Commemoration of work was an additional means of expressing belonging, and finding pride in the collective.[40] Judging from the percentages that were provided above, however, work was evidently not the primary identity marker in the columbarium tombs. That honour was reserved for interpersonal relationships, among which family is the most notable one. It should be mentioned that not only women were primarily commemorated by their familial roles, as is often stated.[41] The same was true for men. The indication that husband and wife were not just partners but also fellow slaves or freedmen is common, as are more general references to the dedicators being *conservi* or *colliberti*/*conliberti*. Work relationships should, to my mind, be included among such interpersonal relationships, rather than seen as an entirely separate category of commemoration. The epitaph of Philusa is illustrative: she had a life partner,

---

35 The numbers are even more resounding for women than they are for men. Cf. Hasegawa 2005, 32 table 3.1 states that 2–4% of the epitaphs record jobs for women, contrasted with 18–28% for men.

36 Discussed in the introduction to this volume.

37 *CIL* 6, 6351 = EDCS 19300394.

38 *CIL* 6, 7290 = *CIL* 6, 27557 = EDCS 18301014.

39 Borbonus 2014, 174–176.

40 Galvao-Sobrinho 2012, Joshel 1992, 160–161.

41 E.g. Larsson Lovén 2013, 122; Dixon 2001, 9; cf. Groen-Vallinga 2013, 297–299.

yet she was commemorated by an inscription and buried in an urn given to her by her fellow footservants (*conservas pedisequas*).[42] The reason that columbarium tomb inscriptions include a relatively high percentage of occupational inscriptions might once more confirm the fact that there were many (formerly) enslaved tomb occupants, whose strongest bonds—in the absence of legal family bonds—may have been with their close colleagues from the *domus*. Viewed in this way, the value of work in funerary commemoration was in the personal connection that it forged.

How do these findings relate to the reality of work and labour among the living working population? It is my contention that even without the explicit mention of a job-title, virtually all the individuals represented in the columbarium tomb inscriptions must have contributed to work in the elite family.[43] They may have been unskilled labourers, performing various chores for which there was no particular job-title; or perhaps they did have an occupation but the dedicator chose to commemorate other aspects, as we have just seen, such as the personal qualities or familial bonds of the deceased. Much of the work remains invisible to us as a consequence. But in the specific context of the columbarium tombs at least, we can see that these individuals were there in large numbers. This is especially true for women. Indeed, it is a given that in a patriarchal society like Rome, women are less likely to be remembered for their labour than men, so analysing familial relations is where analyses of the columbarium women generally branch off to.[44] That glosses over the fact that all women are likely to have engaged in work and labour at some point in their life and should be included in an economic investigation of the household.[45] It also neglects the point that was just illustrated: men are also commemorated as family and friends more often than they are remembered as labourers.

A second complicating factor in looking at the columbarium tomb population in full is the prevalence of unnamed burials in the columbarium tombs, and this is an observation that is generally left out of the discussion. Unnamed burials in these tomb monuments exist for various reasons: some niches were occupied although the accompanying place for the inscriptions was never filled in, and inscriptions might be illegible, or might have gone missing.[46] Dedica-

---

42 *CIL* 6, 4355 = EDCS 19100958: *Philusa Andraei liberti uxor ollam et titulum datum ab conservas pedisequas*. The example does not come from the columbarium tombs, but is likely to have come from a similar household origin.

43 Cf. Hasegawa 2005, 32.

44 E.g. Hasegawa 2005, 62–72.

45 Groen-Vallinga 2022; Holleran 2013; Groen-Vallinga 2013.

46 Borbonus 2014, 72; Bodel 2008, 237.

tions do not always seem to have been added in the first place. Indeed, if we consider tomb capacity for columbarium tombs (more than 8,797) and compare it to the number of individuals from surviving inscriptions (3,120), it is evident that the majority of the individuals interred must remain unknown to us.[47] At least three of the tombs are entirely anepigraphic, while in other monuments only one or two scribbles on the wall remain.[48] For obvious reasons, not all these people have been noted or included in an epigraphic study of the tomb population. In addition, the inscriptions that we do have can at times be deceiving as well: columbarium 1 from the Vigna Codini includes the same inscription multiple times, for example, identifying C. Iunius Felix as the owner of the *loculi* who bought niches for himself, his freedwoman, their freedmen and -women, and all their descendants (*libertis libertabusque posterisque eorum omnium*).[49] Although inscriptions claiming ownership are part of a commemorative habit that recurs in all tomb types, this too leads to an unknown number of unidentifiable burials in the *columbaria*. It should therefore be kept in mind that the epigraphic population of the columbarium monuments potentially concerns less than half of those who were buried in the tombs. Even an attempt to include individuals commemorated *with* an epitaph, but *without* job-title among the working population and their networks, therefore, may still leave out the most silent voices.

A wealth of evidence can be gathered from the *columbarium* tombs despite such caveats, largely because so many individuals received named burial in a highly specific context. The context of the tombs, however, remains a reflection of a diachronic unit caught in the static moment of death. An extra ingredient needs to be brought into the analysis to bring the Roman upper-class household 'back to life', so to speak. A comparative framework might provide the insights for bringing back some of the households' dynamic nature. Attempts to go beyond the static picture of the diachronic inhabitants are virtually non-existent. Only the considerable household staff of Livia Augusta has been likened briefly, if insightfully, to eighteenth- and nineteenth-century India by Susan Treggiari, who wrote that the Marchioness of Dufferin and Ava supported hundreds of servants, since 'British residents were compelled to emulate

47 Taken from Borbonus 2014, 19, table 1 for his approximations for tomb capacity, but it should be noted that this table includes only 20 of the 35 monuments, and is therefore a minimum estimate.

48 Based on Borbonus' 2014 catalogue nos. 1, 6, and 31. The inscriptions of cat. no. 21 are not securely attributed to the monument, and could be anepigraphic; scribbles on the wall, e.g. cat. nos. 26 and 35.

49 *CIL* 6, 4969 = EDCS 19300213, discussed by Sigismund-Nielsen 1996, 42; Borbonus 2014, 72–73 with his n. 11 for additional examples.

the display of the Indian princes and their servants'.[50] Now the Marchioness may be a well-chosen comparison to picture the staff of Livia Augusta, but Livia's household is actually no match for any of the other Roman upper-class households we know of. A more suitable comparison for the majority of upper-class households, in my opinion, is admittedly one that slightly shifts focus in columbarium tomb research away from slavery and dependency, to gain specific attention for gender, work and social networks more generally. The comparandum that I will present here is the seventeenth-century household of the lady Joyce Jeffreys. The comparison is meant to be suggestive, thought-provoking, and good to think with. Despite being far removed in time and place from the columbarium tombs, looking at the way that the various members of the Jeffreys household and its relations interacted inspires unexpected insights and questions about the columbarium tomb population.[51]

3 The Household of the Lady Joyce Jeffreys

Joyce Jeffreys was born in the late sixteenth century at Ham Castle as the daughter of a local gentleman. She never married, living her life as a well-respected member of the Worcester and Hereford communities. For the years between 1638 and 1648, her meticulously kept business and household accounts have survived and were made accessible in print by Judith Spicksley in 2012.[52] These account books provide a wealth of information about her domestic staff and broader professional and social relations, which provide all the dynamic information that a columbarium cannot.

It is curiously interesting that 'in keeping with contemporary understanding' Joyce refers to her household as her 'famelly', similar to the broader use of the term *familia* in Rome.[53] Joyce's household staff can be reconstructed from her account books to have included 29 servants, 27 of whom were receiving wages, and only three of whom did *not* live in with her at Widemarsh Street.[54] Her subordinates had a balanced gender-ratio of 14 females and 15 males, although the job differentiation between men and women was rather traditional. Her agent (the equivalent of a *dispensator*, in Roman terms), for example, was Mr. Mat-

50 Treggiari 1975, 61.

51 Predominantly for heuristic purposes: Kocka 2003, 40.

52 Spicksley 2012. The originals are in the British Museum. References to these business and household accounts as included in Spicksley 2012 take the form f. 5v (here for folio 5 verso).

53 Spicksley 2012, 55; Saller 1994, 75–80; Flory 1978.

54 Spicksley 2012 appendix IV, pp. 312–314.

thias Rufford, who incidentally was one of the few who resided elsewhere. A number of maids and servants seem to have been the equivalent of the Roman footservants or *pedisequi*, who were prevalent in the columbarium tombs.[55] Some of her cousins could count on Joyce's patronage through employment, although the majority of her personnel were unrelated to her.

A number of things stands out from the detailed account of Joyce Jeffreys' household over the ten years from 1638–1648. Within the ten years of the lady Jeffreys' household accounts, the full list of employees (N = 29) was over seven times as large as the serving staff in some of those years (N = 4).[56] Looking at the staff in any one year, the household of Joyce Jeffreys adheres to Flory's guesstimate of about six enslaved and freed dependents for an 'average' Roman household.[57] Looking only at the complete list of employees would have given a different impression. The comparison underlines that the Roman population of a single columbarium tomb does not represent a full working household, even if the tomb could be securely related to one *familia*; the comparison even gives a very rough indication for the possible relation between the tomb population and the working household at any particular time. This finding emphasizes the extent to which the numbers of the epigraphic household staff are likely to be bloated by the fact that the epitaphs are not all contemporaneous, which can apparently be significant even over the relatively short time span of ten years.

It may well be argued that the seventeenth-century 'famelly' was notably different from the *familia* of the columbarium tombs, because of the prevalence of slavery in Roman society. Dependent household members in Rome would not be able to leave of their own volition, and the turnover of staff must have been slower as a result. In my view the comparison is still compelling. In many instances Joyce's servants needed her patronage to set up their own home or business, just as we know freedmen often depended on their masters' support.[58] Joyce also paid for the two-year apprenticeship of a new coachman.[59] Apprenticeships provided for by the masters of enslaved children are attested in the early Roman empire.[60] Since Roman freedmen regularly benefited from skills they learned in slavery, these apprenticeships too could perhaps be seen

---

55 In the household of Livia, for example: Hasegawa 2005, 33.

56 Spicksley 2012, 54 notes that in the early years of the household there were six or more employees at any one time. In my calculations there were two or three years (out of ten) in which there were only four.

57 Flory 1978, 85.

58 Mouritsen 2011.

59 The coachman, William Merrick, stayed with Joyce for only a short time afterwards because, according to Joyce, he had 'wilfully broken' her coach (F. 44v).

60 Groen-Vallinga 2022, 196–197; Laes 2015.

as a parallel. Joyce's patronage more generally is reminiscent of the relations between Roman patrons and their freedmen and -women, who could be viewed as extended family and who make up such a large part of the columbarium tomb population. As a Roman patron would, Joyce remained in close contact with many employees after they had resigned from her service. Five of her maidservants left the household to get married, and in all instances Joyce contributed to the set-up of the new home, paying for the wedding dress and/or contributing a sum of money.[61] Even long after their departure from Joyce's household, these women stayed in touch and could benefit from Joyce's generosity. Elizabeth Acton, for example, received money 'to put in her purse', and for various visits to surrounding fairs and markets; her goddaughter Joyce Simons was similarly looked after.[62] One might suspect that these former employees would still have found a place in the household *columbarium* of Joyce Jeffreys, had she had one.

For the Roman period, there is no reason to suppose that this type of continued bond would not extend to a burial niche for freedpeople. Mouritsen's suggestion that the Volusii and the Statilii freed enslaved people on the condition that they remained in the household, therefore, does not follow from the fact that these individuals were buried in the family tomb.[63] It should be concluded instead that the columbarium tomb population represents a social unit that was different from the family, the household, or the houseful, and that it was determined by choice and opportunities for commemoration.

4 Gendered Social Networks

Joyce Jeffreys extended her patronage to a number of women and children in her vicinity, just as Roman patronesses were more prone to benefit other women and children than were men.[64] Indeed, aspects of the seventeenth-century household accounts of Joyce Jeffreys go beyond her staff or kin, and may illuminate the existence of a broader, gendered social network. Joyce engaged in money-lending, but her kin seems not to have called upon her

61 Spicksley 2012, 65: 'Anne Davies, for example, received a black silk mohair wedding dress when she married Joshua Ailway, while Elizabeth Acton received the considerable sum of £800 when she married Francis Geers junior of Garnons, in addition to her wedding dress.'

62 Spicksley 2012, 63; f. 44, f. 49, for example.

63 Mouritsen 2013, 58; cf. Edmondson 2011, 343.

64 Hemelrijk 2015.

wealth, in the way we might expect from other contemporary accounts: 'Only 10 (7 per cent) of the 145 debtors in her accounts are listed as relatives (cousins).'[65] Joyce's social networks can give us an indication of the lines along which the social unit within a tomb could have branched out. Joyce would build on the network of one of her former employees, for example, and give out loans (or aid) to their respective families or neighbours.[66] Whereas her debtors were generally not related to Joyce, however, they were regularly related to each other (perhaps up to 40 percent), or they were acquaintances of one another.[67] It is not unlikely that a similar network was behind the columbarium tomb population.

The hypothesis that more extended social ties existed between those who were buried in the *columbaria* might serve as an additional explanation for the fact that not all inhabitants were clearly linked to the main family *nomen*.[68] Such inhabitants-by-proxy are identifiable even in single-family *columbaria* like those of the Statilii and the Volusii. The connection between T. Statilius Diodotus and his wife (*coniux*) Vedusia Auge, for example, is explicated in the nomenclature on her epitaph: he is a freedman of Statilius Taurus, while she is the freedwoman of Taurus' sister (*Tauri sororis liberta*).[69] In the Volusian tomb, we find Volusia Rhodine setting up an inscription to her brother Vitellius Fructus who, judging by his *nomen*, must have been part of a different *familia* once.[70] This assumption of interrelationships between the various members of the tomb population is supported further by the fact that when the inhabitants acquired their burial plot separately and finding a great variety of *nomina* is therefore to be expected, this is often explicitly recorded, such as in the *columbarium* of the 36 associates.[71]

Joyce was a money-lender, as we have seen, but from her accounts it appears to me that she engaged in money-lending chiefly because she had the best interests of others at heart, not with an eye to making a profit.[72] Her debtors

65 Spicksley 2012, 33.
66 Tittler 1994, 256–257.
67 Tittler 1997, 256; Spicksley 2012, 33–34 with n. 134;
68 For other possibilities how different *nomina gentilicia* came to be in one tomb, Borg 2019, 174–184; cf. Sigismund-Nielsen 1996, 48–50.
69 *CIL* 6, 6214 = EDCS 19300258. Discussed by Hasegawa 2005, 55 with references to other examples.
70 Mouritsen 2013, 59 for this and other examples; *CIL* 6, 7341 = EDCS 18600054.
71 Borbonus 2014, catalogue no. 15.
72 This would put her in line with other contemporary households, *contra* Spicksley 2012, 24 who believes that Joyce operated 'on a different level, one that was regular, formalized and extensive'. Tittler 1994 deals with exactly this question of profit versus community bene-

were generally part of her extended social and business networks, which underlines the need for trust and goodwill.[73] The charitable nature of Joyce's loans is most explicit in the case of women: they make up eight out of 145 debtors. The sums that women borrowed from Joyce were generally small, and in many instances the loan would be interest-free, with no date set for repayment. Spicksley views these financial exchanges with women in the light of the importance of small-scale credit to the household in the broader period of the seventeenth and eighteenth centuries, and concludes that for these women 'their economic relationship with Joyce was qualitatively and quantitatively different from that of their male counterparts'.[74] Women also played their part as representatives paying the interest or returning a loan for their male family members, a role that was generally taken up by married women whose husbands were away.[75]

In the same way, the significance of informal loans and of (financial) networks of trust in the Roman period is increasingly being emphasized.[76] Women in the early Roman empire are similarly seen to engage in money-lending, in addition to their presumed expenses for the running of the household.[77] For none of these transactions do they seem to have needed permission from a legal guardian.[78] It suggests the strong possibility that a similar pattern of informal, gendered networks could be found in Roman antiquity too. The comparison thus illustrates the importance of the network of women surrounding the lady Jeffreys, and indicates that such networks of female patronage were of a different magnitude as well as a different kind than networks between men. Thus, we see some women who were personally involved in loans, as well as others who contributed to extant loans that did not have their own names on them per se. The financial aspect of Joyce's female acquaintances is only one aspect of the network surrounding her and is reflected in gendered networks from Rome.

Female agency in the networks between elite families can also be exemplified sporadically in the columbarium tombs. It was stated above that the

---

fit and concludes on p. 263 that Joyce's financial activities were in fact 'mid-way between Tawney's villager and the Smithian professional'.

73 Tittler 1994, 256–260.

74 Spicksley 2012, 31–32.

75 Spicksley 2012, 35.

76 Verboven 2017b, 375: 'Informal loans and credit facilities (as surety or sales on credit) from relatives, friends, or members of the same collegium formed the vast majority of credit arrangements in the Roman world as they did in most other pre-industrial societies. Relations of trust and concern for reputation could extend the range to which currency could be used.'

77 Verboven 2017b refers to graffiti in Pompeii for small loans executed by women.

78 Cf. Holleran 2013, 313–314; Dixon 1992, 43.

columbarium tomb population rarely makes up a self-sufficient elite household, and one of the solutions to this might be the connections between the *familiae* of several members of one family. The pattern was suggested by Penner for the Julio-Claudian households.[79] The epitaph for Vedusia Auge that was discussed above could indicate cooperation and interaction between the *familia* of Statilius Taurus, and that of his sister, if that is the way that Auge, freedwoman of Taurus' sister, met her husband Diodotus, freedman of Taurus.[80] Even if liaisons within the same *familia* were most common, it was not unheard of to find relationships between servile dependents from different families.[81] Could that also be an indication of complementarity or networks between *domus*? Treggiari similarly hints at the cooperation between a husband and a wife's *familia* in her discussion of the household of Livia.[82] A known example of female networks between households is the following inscription for Communio, which indicates that a wet-nurse was moved between families.[83]

> Communio, home-born enslaved of Antonia Augusta, lived two years and ten months, milk-sibling of Drusus, son of Blandus
>
> Communio verna | Antoniae Augustae | v(ixit) a(nnos) II me(n)s(es) X | collacteus Drusi | Blandi f(ilii)

The inscription is evidence for Antonia Minor lending out a wet-nurse to her daughter, Julia Livia. This can be inferred from the text, because Communio and Drusus are indicated as *conlactanei*, i.e. weened by the same wet-nurse. Drusus was the son of Julia Livia, but as Communio was the *verna* of Antonia, his mother must also have been enslaved by her and was therefore on loan in the household of Julia Livia. This example as well as two other attestations of sharing a wet-nurse indicate the complementarity of what could be termed *domus*-networks.[84] A kind of complementarity has of course long been sugges-

79 Penner 2013.

80 *CIL* 6, 6214 = EDCS 19300258.

81 Rawson 1966; Penner 2013, 358–360 for examples from the Julio-Claudian households. Within the *familia*, e.g. Mouritsen 2013 for the Volusii and Statilii; Edmondson 2011, 347; and in general still relevant is Flory 1978, 82.

82 Treggiari 1975, 54–57.

83 *CIL* 6, 16057 = AE 2005, 106 = EDCS 12000952; discussed by Penner 2013, 350–352 and Rawson 2005.

84 Penner 2013, 350–358 also cites *CIL* 6, 4352 = EDCS 19100955 and *CIL* 6, 5201 = EDCS 8700554. Other examples she adduces—*CIL* 6, 8943, *CIL* 6, 9449 and *CIL* 6,33781—are unconvincing attestations in my opinion, as they concern instances of parents and their

ted between the elite *familia urbana* and the *familia rustica*, but it appears that the urban households also filled in for one another when necessary.[85]

The comparison with the household of the lady Joyce Jeffreys is especially interesting with an eye to the position of women. Concerning Joyce's female employees, family members, and other women, a few things stand out. The women in Joyce's household had no well-defined occupational title, other than the designation 'servant', 'maid', or in one instance a 'cooking/brewing maid'. We know of their position as employees because they are named in Joyce's account books for receiving a wage. This finding is not unique to the household accounts of the lady Jeffreys, but it is a very clear instance of a persistent pattern of obscuring women's jobs that recurs in other historical periods as well. In a similar way, the context of a columbarium indicates that the women on the epitaphs were a part of this particular social unit. The comparison seems to underline my earlier suggestion that their mere presence in the household tomb adds them to the workforce, even though the women may not have had a recorded occupation.

An additional observation might add to the likelihood of that notion. It has been assumed that female household heads in the early Roman empire would have had a larger percentage of women on their staff than male-owned households. Penner indeed confirms this for her investigation into the households of the Julio-Claudian family, noting also that smaller households as a rule contain a larger percentage of women, and smaller households are more likely to be headed by women.[86] If women as a rule were living in smaller households, that may also mean that women were even less likely to record a specific occupation, as they were expected to take up a broader spectrum of work rather than one identifiable occupation in a smaller work unit. From these suggestions it becomes clear once again that the value of working efforts compared to distinct labour contributions cannot be underestimated, particularly when investigating women's daily lives. It is noteworthy to add, however, that in female-headed household tombs, too, the percentage of women never rises over 40 percent.[87] That leaves a majority of male tomb occupants, and it was demonstrated above that the same argument about the value of work versus labour in commemoration patterns holds true for the men without occupational title.

---

children's caretakers. There are some instances on p. 357 of freedmen who may have changed employers between the Julio-Claudian households, none of them decisively indicative of *domus*-networks.

85 Mouritsen 2019, 227 on shared labour between *familia urbana* and *familia rustica*.

86 Penner 2013, 362–363.

87 Visible in the data from Penner 2013, 363 with Penner 2012, 154; Treggiari 1975 for Livia's household.

5 Conclusion

The columbarium tomb inscriptions not only shed light on aristocratic households in the city of Rome from the late republican and early imperial period, but they have proven to be a valuable case-study into the value of work and labour within the Roman household. The larger monuments have often been equated with elite *familiae*, and have been adduced in studies of aristocratic household composition and occupational structure. It is self-evident that this identification with elite *domus* can no longer be accepted uncritically, but it may still serve as a good starting point. This paper has added a number of important observations to the interpretation of these funerary monuments and their commemorative patterns, which hold a more general validity as well.

Looking beyond the inscriptions themselves, the columbarium tombs were the final resting place for more than just the epigraphically attested population: even though the tombs allow for many individual, named burials, most of the deceased remain anonymous because there was (or is) no epitaph. All of the individuals concerned are likely to have contributed to the economic functioning of the entombed households. As such, a large number of those workers remains invisible to us, and although scholars have been aware of this fact, taking into account the physical monument along with the characteristics of the epigraphic corpus serves as a critical reminder that we should be aware of their presence. The concepts of work and labour facilitate inclusion and awareness. Within the *columbaria*-inscriptions, only a minority of the individuals record an occupation: the others surely also will have worked for a living. For women in particular, the economic significance of their presence in the columbarium tombs has often been overlooked in favour of their familial role as wives and mothers. For both men and women, however, it was argued that occupational title should be seen as merely one of several options for indicating interpersonal relationships in life. Commemoration emphasized social bonds with others, some of which were meant to secure a position within the funerary monument. The absence of occupational markers does not mean that we cannot add value to the work and labour efforts of the tomb's inhabitants, or appreciate their contribution to the social networks that kept the upper-class households functional.

Comparison with the seventeenth-century household of the lady Joyce Jeffreys offers some suggestions for new interpretations, particularly for the role of women. It confirms that women did not always have a job-title, even when they were on the wage-list and therefore economically active. The comparison also illustrates that women created their own socio-economic bonds, and that these were qualitatively and quantitatively different from those with men: the relationships were based on mutual affection and trust, and a female patron like Joyce helped out a number of women by hiring them, giving gifts, or giving out loans on particularly beneficial terms. A similar kind of gendered network can be seen operating in the elite households of Rome when wet-nurses were on loan between related *familiae*, or in the likelihood that female household heads employed a larger percentage of women. The comparison also brought to the fore a number of more general observations that could illuminate the nature of the columbarium tomb population. It is particularly suggestive that the dynamics of the household of Joyce Jeffreys sometimes indicate that the total number of employees over ten years or so was sometimes up to seven times as large as the actual staff employed in a particular year. It does not answer the question of population size for any one tomb decisively, but it is tantalizing that a mere ten years could lead to such differentiation. The networks of trust that are evident from the lady Jeffreys' undertakings in the money-lending business are also indicative of possibly more widespread networks and the inclusion of perhaps a large proportion of the deceased who were further removed from the tomb owner, which would explain the disparate nature of the backgrounds in some columbarium tombs.

In sum, it is hoped that the present case-study suggests new avenues of investigation for Roman funerary monuments and funerary epigraphy. An awareness of the terminology of labour and work is one way of embracing unheard voices in a more inclusive investigation of the Roman economy. The comparison with the household accounts of the lady Jeffreys suggested how this can highlight the contribution of women and of more extensive social networks. Patterns of commemoration in the particular funerary context of the columbarium tombs imply that work should be seen as an integral part of interpersonal relationships, and that its relative invisibility does not therefore imply a negative valuation of work.

Acknowledgements

My thanks to the editors of this volume, Kim Bowes and Miko Flohr, for their valuable comments during the early stages of the paper; thanks are also due to an anonymous reviewer and the participants of the Penn-Leiden XI conference for their input.

Bibliography

Bodel, J. (2008). From Columbaria to Catacombs: Collective Burial in Pagan and Christian Rome. In: L. Brink and D. Green, eds., *Commemorating the Dead. Texts and Artifacts in Context. Studies of Roman, Jewish and Christian Burials*. Berlin–New York, pp. 177–242.

Borbonus, D. (2014). *Columbarium Tombs and Collective Identity in Augustan Rome*. Cambridge.

Borg, B. (2019). *Roman Tombs and the Art of Commemoration: Contextual Approaches to Funerary Customs in the Second Century CE*. Cambridge.

Bradley, K.R. (1991). *Discovering the Roman Family. Studies in Roman Social History*. New York–London.

Dixon, S. (1992). *The Roman Family*. London.

Dixon, S. (2001). How Do You Count Them If They're Not There? New Perspectives on Roman Cloth Production. *Opuscula Romana* 25–26, pp. 7–17.

Edmondson, J. (2011) Slavery and the Roman Family. In: K.R. Bradley and P. Cartledge, eds., *The Cambridge World History of Slavery*, vol. 1: Antiquity. Cambridge, pp. 337–361.

Flory, M.B. (1978). Family in Familia: Kinship and Community in Slavery. *American Journal of Ancient History* 3, pp. 78–95.

Galvao-Sobrinho, C.R. (2012). Feasting the Dead Together: Household Burials and the Social Strategies of Slaves and Freed Persons in the Early Principate. In: S. Bell and T.R. Ramsby, eds., *Free at Last! The Impact of Freed Slaves on the Roman Empire*. London, pp. 130–176.

Garnsey, P. and de Ligt, L. (2016). Migration in Early-Imperial Italy: Herculaneum and Rome Compared. In: L. de Ligt and L.E. Tacoma, eds., *Migration and Mobility in the Early Roman Empire*. Leiden, pp. 72–94.

Groen-Vallinga, M.J. (2013). Desperate Housewives? The Adaptive Family Economy and Female Participation in the Roman Urban Labour Market. In: E.A. Hemelrijk and G. Woolf, eds., *Women and the Roman City in the Latin West*. Leiden, pp. 295–312.

Groen-Vallinga, M.J. (2022). *Work and Labour in the Cities of Roman Italy*. Liverpool.

Groen-Vallinga, M.J. and Tacoma, L.E. (2015). Contextualising Condemnation to Hard Labour in the Roman Empire. In: C. De Vito and A. Lichtenstein, eds., *Global Convict Labour*. Leiden, pp. 49–78.

Hasegawa, K. (2005). *The Familia Urbana during the Early Empire. A Study of Columbaria Inscriptions*. Oxford.

Hawkins, C. (2021). *Roman Artisans and the Urban Economy*. Cambridge. First published 2016.

Hemelrijk, E.A. (2015). *Hidden Lives, Public Personae. Women and Civic Life in the Roman West*. Oxford.

Hofmeester, K. (2018). Labour Relations: Introductory Remarks. In: *Handbook Global History of Work*. Oldenbourg, pp. 317–327.

Holleran, C. (2013). Women and Retail in Roman Italy. In: E.A. Hemelrijk and G. Woolf, eds., *Women and the Roman City in the Latin West*. Leiden, pp. 313–330.

Hübner, S.R. and Ratzan, D.M., eds. (2021). *Missing Mothers. Maternal Absence in Antiquity*. Leuven.

Hübner, S.R. (2011). Household Composition in the Ancient Mediterranean—What Do We Really Know? In: B. Rawson, ed., *A Companion to Families in the Greek and Roman Worlds*. Malden, MA, pp. 73–91.

Joshel, S.R. (1992). *Work, Identity and Legal Status at Rome. A Study of the Occupational Inscriptions*. Norman, OK.

Kocka, J. (2003). Comparison and Beyond. *History and Theory* 42:1, pp. 39–44.

Laes, C. (2015). Masters and Apprentices. In: M. Bloomer ed., *A Companion to Ancient Education*. Oxford, pp. 474–482.

Larsson Lovén, L. (2013) Female Work and Identity in Roman Textile Production and Trade: A Methodological Discussion. In: M. Gleba and J. Pásztokai-Szeőke, eds., *Making Textiles in Pre-Roman and Roman Times. People, Places, Identities*. Oxford, pp. 109–125.

Larsson Lovén, L. (2016). Women, Trade, and Production in Urban Centres of Roman Italy. In: M. Flohr and A. Wilson, eds., *Urban Craftsmen and Traders in the Roman World*. Oxford, pp. 200–221.

Levine, P. (2014). Is Comparative History Possible? *History and Theory* 53:3, pp. 331–347.

Lis, C. and Soly, H. (2012). *Worthy Efforts. Attitudes to Work and Workers in Pre-industrial Europe*. Leiden.

Mouritsen, H. (2011). *The Freedman in the Roman World*. Cambridge.

Mouritsen, H. (2013). Slavery and Manumission in the Roman Elite: A Study of the Columbaria of the Volusii and the Statilii. In: M. George, ed., *Roman Slavery and Roman Material Culture*. Toronto–Buffalo, pp. 43–68.

Mouritsen, H. (2019). Slavery and Manumission in Imperial Italy: The Album from Herculaneum Revisited. In: M. Maiuro and M. Balbo, eds., *Popolazione, Risorse e Urbanizzazzione nella Campania Antica*. Bari, pp. 211–231.

Patterson, J. (1992). Patronage, Collegia and Burial in Imperial Rome. In: S.R. Bassett, ed., *Death in Towns. Urban Responses to the Dying and the Dead, 100–1600*. Leicester, pp. 15–27.

Penner, L. (2012). Gender, Household Structure and Slavery: Re-interpreting the Aristocratic Columbaria of Early Imperial Rome. In: R. Laurence and A. Strömberg, eds., *Families in the Greco-Roman World*. London–New York, pp. 143–158.

Penner, L.R. (2013). *The Epigraphic Habits of the Slaves and Freed Slaves of the Julio-Claudian Households*. Diss. University of Calgary.

Porena, P. (2016). Il Lavoro Infantile. In: A. Marcone, ed., *l'Età Romana. Liberi, Semilibere e Schiavi in una Societa Premoderna*. Rome, pp. 663–685.

Purcell, N. (1987). Tomb and Suburb. In: H. von Hesberg and P. Zanker, eds., *Römische Gräberstrassen*. Munich, pp. 25–41.

Rawson, B. (2005). Circulation of Staff between Roman Households. *Zeitschrift für Papyrologie und Epigraphik*, 151, pp. 223–224.

Saller, R.P. (1994). *Patriarchy, Property and Death in the Roman Family*. Cambridge.

Sigismund-Nielsen, H. (1996). The Physical Context of Roman Epitaphs and the Structure of the Roman Family. *Analecta Romana Instituti Danici*, 23, pp. 35–60.

Spicksley, J.M. (2012). *The Business and Household Accounts of Joyce Jeffreys, Spinster of Hereford, 1638–1648*. Oxford.

Tilly, C. and Tilly, C. (1998). *Work under Capitalism*. Oxford.

Tittler, R. (1994). Money-Lending in the West Midlands: The Activities of Joyce Jefferies, 1638–1649. *Institute of Historical Research* 67, pp. 249–263.

Treggiari, S. (1975). Jobs in the Household of Livia. *Papers of the British School at Rome* 43, pp. 48–77.

Treggiari, S. (1976). Jobs for Women. *American Journal of Ancient History* 1, pp. 76–104.

Verboven, K. (2012). The Freedman Economy of the Roman Empire. In: S. Bell and T.R. Ramsby, eds., *Free at Last! The Impact of Freed Slaves on the Roman Empire*. London, pp. 88–109.

Verboven, K. (2017a). Work, Labour, Profession. What's in a Name? In: K. Verboven and C. Laes, eds., *Work, Labour and Professions in the Roman World*. Leiden, pp. 1–19.

Verboven, K. (2017b). Currency and Credit in the Bay of Naples in the First Century AD. In: M. Flohr and A. Wilson, eds., *The Economy of Pompeii*. Oxford, pp. 363–386.

Verboven, K. and Laes, C., eds. (2017). *Work, Labour and Professions in the Roman World*. Leiden.

Werner, M. and Zimmermann, B. (2002) Vergleich, Transfer, Verflechtung. Der Ansatz der Histoire croisée und die Herausforderung des Transnationalen. *Geschichte und Gesellschaft* 28:4, pp. 607–636.

Wilson, A. and Flohr, M., eds. (2016). *Urban Craftsmen and Traders in the Roman World*. Oxford.

Zuiderhoek, A. (2013). Workers of the Ancient World: Analyzing Labour in Classical Antiquity. *Workers of the World. International Journal on Strikes and Social Conflicts* 1(3), pp. 32–48.

SECTION 3

Labour and the Countryside

CHAPTER 10

The Labour of Listening: Internal Audiences in Theocritus

Amelia Bensch-Schaus

Theocritus displays a marked interest in several types of physical labour, populating his poetry with cowherds, goatherds, reapers, fishermen and women managing households. Scholars have generally seen these characters as indicative of the Hellenistic interest in the small-scale and the everyday, an approach that tends to focus on the non-elite social status of the characters rather than the labour they perform, even though these characters often discuss labour as a central part of their identity.[1] The labour that is involved in these characters' lives does not mimetically represent the economic realities of this period, nor does Theocritus equate labour with virtue as Vergil does in the *Eclogues*.[2] Instead, as this chapter demonstrates, the *Idylls* align labour with poetry. Because of its highly allusive and *recherché* style, Hellenistic poetry is closely interwoven with labour, demanding effort both to compose it and to understand it. This latter feature, the labour required to understand poetry of this period, has caused critics to view Hellenistic poetry as primarily aimed at an elite audience, especially educated circles with ties to the Library at Alexandria.[3] The audiences within the *Idylls* itself, however, are non-elite and so require a re-evaluation of how Theocritus conceptualizes contemporary poetry's demand for audience labour.

Even as Hellenistic poetry came to be less associated with particular performance occasions, it retained a strong interest in the performances of poetry.[4] Theocritus' corpus is one of the best representatives of this trend, depicting a variety of performance contexts and several poet-figures. The most famous context is the idyllic countryside of bucolic poetry, and Payne has drawn out

1 Hunter 2020, 197, in describing the notable features of bucolic in a conclusion to a collected volume, states that its 'characters are usually drawn from socially humble classes'.

2 So concludes Scholten 2006, which is the only study so far to focus exclusively on labour within Theocritus' oeuvre, discussing *Idylls* 1, 10, and 15.

3 Cusset 1999; Kutzco 2007. Hunter 1996, 7–13 gives a succinct and compelling overview of the relationship between 'popular' and 'elite' culture in terms of Theocritus.

4 For a far-ranging study of Hellenistic poetry's interest in performance, see Harder Regtuit Wakker 2018.

 | DOI:10.1163/9789004694965_011

how Theocritus' bucolic world is a fully developed fictional world that transforms its speakers into poet-figures.[5] Other scholars have explored the ways in which Theocritus presents his characters as poets in the non-bucolic poems.[6] While the poets within the *Idylls* have received much attention, their audiences have attracted relatively little notice, even though the poems often explicitly describe the internal audience present for the many performances within the corpus.[7] The existence of these internal audiences invites comparisons with the actual external audiences for Theocritus' poetry, but there is no direct equivalency between internal and external audience; Theocritus did not envision herdsmen in the fictionalized countryside as the primary recipients for his poetry. Nonetheless, these internal audiences reflect some of the ways in which Theocritus might have expected an audience to engage with his poetry. These audiences are notable because their listening is accompanied by labour rather than by leisure, as is traditional. I argue that Theocritus highlights the labour of the internal audiences of the *Idylls*, which implicitly acknowledges the effort involved in listening to contemporary poetry, while also presenting it as non-specialized and therefore accessible.

In associating his audiences with labour, Theocritus departs from a longstanding tradition that consistently depicts an audience at leisure while it listens to poetic performance. The *Iliad* contains only one scene with an internal audience, when Achilles has withdrawn from battle and entertains Patroclus by singing about men's κλέος.[8] Leisure is required for this performance, since it is only the warriors who have ceased from fighting who are able to enjoy it. The *Odyssey* displays its interest in narrative and internal performances more frequently, with professional bards performing twice in the epic. Initially, the bard Phemius performs in the palace of Ithaca for Telemachus, Penelope, and the notoriously idle suitors.[9] On Phaeacia, the bard Demodocus performs in

5 Payne 2007. Throughout I use the term bucolic rather than pastoral to refer to *Idylls* 1, 3–7, 10, 11, and 13, following Halperin 1983.

6 E.g., Duncan 2001; Krevans 2006. Theocritus also crafts his own poetic persona in some of the non-bucolic poems, especially those that directly address Ptolemy II, as discussed by Griffiths 1979.

7 For comprehensive studies of poet-figures in Theocritus, see especially Goldhill 1991, 223–283; Klooster 2011. For Theocritus' creation of his poetic persona through narrative framing, see Damon 1995; Foster 2016.

8 *Iliad* 9.185–191. While here Achilles is at leisure as he sings, the *Odyssey* depicts women singing while they work, such as Circe singing and weaving at *Od.* 10.220–224. These instances concern singers rather than audiences and seem to evoke the association between singing and weaving, discussed in more detail below (note 44).

9 *Odyssey* 1.325–422. While Telemachus and others generally criticize the suitors for their destruction of property, their lack of labour is also on display. The poem first introduces them

the palace after the feasting, singing about Troy and causing Odysseus to weep, and singing again after the athletic contests, this time accompanied by dancers and recounting the affair of Ares and Aphrodite.[10] As in the *Iliad*, the internal audiences for these songs are at their leisure, as they relax after feasting and athletic contests. Even Hesiod's *Works and Days*, the poem about work *par excellence*, does not imagine its addressee, Perses, to be working as he listens. Following Pucci's interpretation of Perses as a representation of the typical 'lazy man', Hesiod's audience is resistant and even antithetical to the work the poem urges.[11] The epic poetry with which Theocritus was very familiar does not associate its audience with labour, even in a poem urging hard work, and instead depicts its internal audiences as listening at their leisure. The *Idylls* occasionally contain moments of affinity with this tradition, as when Aphrodite, opposed to labour by both her divine nature and her association with love, listens to Daphnis' song in *Idyll* 1.[12] In a more explicit engagement with Odysseus' tears in *Odyssey* 6, *Idyll* 14 has one of the speakers, Aeschinas, recount how he attended a feast with his beloved Cynisca at which she burst into tears after a song entitled τὸν ἐμὸν Λύκον, 'my Wolf', thereby revealing that she was in love with a man named Λύκος.[13] Beyond these two instances, Theocritus engages with the tradition of internal audiences by means of contrast, as he associates the audiences of the *Idylls* with labour rather than leisure.

While Theocritus' audiences labour at a variety of tasks, all of their labour has metapoetic connotations. One way that Theocritus signals these connotations is by creating bucolic worlds in which virtually every character is a singer, so that everyone, even the listener, becomes associated with poetry. Theocritus composed his own poetry in this kind of atmosphere, as reflected in the intertextual relationship between the *Idylls* and the *Argonautica* of his contemporary, Apollonius, which is one of the most suggestive that has survived of the exchanges between poets during this period.[14] The bucolic singers evoke this sort of relationship through their exchange of songs, such as those that occur in *Idylls* 5, 6, 7 and 10. Even in *Idyll* 1, although only Thyrsis sings, the goatherd

---

playing draughts (1.106–107) and contrasts Eurynomus becoming a suitor with his two brothers, who take on ἔργα by farming their father's land (2.22).

10 *Odyssey* 6.62–95; 6.250–369.

11 Pucci 1996. For a discussion of the treatment of labour in the poem more generally, see Ette 2014.

12 *Idyll* 1.95–98; 138–139. All texts follows Gow 1952b. All translations are my own.

13 *Idyll* 14.24–33. While Odysseus' tears are treated with respect, Cynisca's tears lead to Aeschinas attacking her in line with the comic tone of the poem (Bustos 2019a).

14 For recent perspectives on this much-discussed issue, see Cozzoli 2015; Acosta-Hughes 2019.

can sing too, and indeed Thyrsis asks him to sing first (1.12–14, discussed below). Thus *Idylls* 1 and 7, which scholars have recognized as programmatic for Theocritus' bucolic poetry, both include two poet-herdsmen.[15] These exchanges of songs in a world populated with poets are suggestive of the exchange between poets taking place around the Alexandrian court, but displaced to the countryside. These herdsmen, like the elite poets and scholars of the capital, both produce and listen to poetry as part of their labour.

In making herdsmen into poets, Theocritus draws on a long tradition in Greek poetry of associating herding with song.[16] The figure of the herdsman is usually more significant for his rural location than any specific labour he performs related to herding. In many ways Theocritus' herdsmen follow this trend, as they seem to lounge around the landscape and sing more than actually tend to their flocks.[17] Simichidas in *Idyll* 7 brings out the literary appeal of being a cowherd, since he claims the title in order to enhance his poetic credentials, despite being a city boy (*Id.* 7.91–93).[18] Yet, on occasion, Theocritus' herdsmen offer their labour in tending to the herds of others, and they do so only when they want to listen to poetry. In *Idyll* 1, after Thyrsis and the unnamed goatherd compliment each other on their singing abilities, Thyrsis asks to hear one of the goatherd's songs (*Id.* 1.12–14, text Gow, trans. my own):

> Are you willing, by the Nymphs, are you willing, goatherd, to have a seat here, where there's this sloping mound and the tamarisks, and play your syrinx? I will tend to your goats myself in the meantime.
>
> λῇς ποτὶ τᾶν Νυμφᾶν, λῇς, αἰπόλε, τεῖδε καθίξας,
> ὡς τὸ κάταντες τοῦτο γεώλοφον αἵ τε μυρῖκαι,
> συρίσδεν; τὰς δ' αἶγας ἐγὼν ἐν τῷδε νομευσῶ.

15 For studies of these poems as programmatic, see especially Berger 1984; Cairns 1984; Bowie 1985; Domány 2007; and Klooster 2021, who provides an overview of previous scholarship on the subject.

16 Particularly prominent models for this relationship are the prologue of the *Theogony*, in which Hesiod encounters the Muses on Mt. Helicon, and the report that Archilochus met the Muses while leading cows (SEG 15:517).

17 The singing of the herdsman implies that their attention is not on their animals, and explicit neglect of herding occurs in a few *Idylls*. The frame of *Idyll* 11 mentions that, while Polyphemus was singing about his love for Galatea, his sheep had to return themselves to their fold (11.12–16), a stark contrast to his careful care for his sheep at *Odyssey* 9.237–245. In *Idyll* 4, Battus and Corydon discuss the sad state of the cows that Corydon is tending, placing the blame partly on their former owner, Aegon, who has abandoned them to compete in wrestling at Olympia, and partly on the singing Corydon, who is apparently not up to the task of herding (4.12–34).

18 Hunter 1999, 178–179.

Along with describing typical markers of the *locus amoenus* such as the tamarisks and the Nymphs, Thyrsis explicitly offers to watch over his companion's goats so that the latter can play his pipe and sing. The goatherd turns down this invitation and instead invites Thyrsis to sing the sorrows of Daphnis, offering Thyrsis as a reward the opportunity to milk his best goat into an elaborately carved cup (*Id.* 1.19–63). Despite the fact that Thyrsis is a shepherd, his flocks do not seem to require watching while he performs, nor does the goatherd tend to his own flocks as he offers his elaborate description of the cup. Thyrsis' offer of labour thus becomes equivalent to the cup the goatherd offers, which has both economic value and poetic value, the latter created through the ecphrasis about it.[19]

Idyll 7 includes a similar scene of an offer to watch over the herds of another. Lycidas concludes his song by turning to the legendary poet Comatas, closing with the wish that he could have lived at the same time as him (*Id.* 7.86–89):

> If only in my day you had been among the living, so that for you I could have tended the beautiful goats on the hills while listening to your voice, and you reclined under the oaks or under the pines, singing sweetly, divine Comatas.
>
> αἴθ' ἐπ' ἐμεῦ ζωοῖς ἐναρίθμιος ὤφελες ἦμεν
> ὥς τοι ἐγὼν ἐνόμευον ἀν' ὤρεα τὰς καλὰς αἶγας
> φωνᾶς εἰσαΐων, τὺ δ' ὑπὸ δρυσὶν ἢ ὑπὸ πεύκαις
> ἁδὺ μελισδόμενος κατεκέκλισο, θεῖε Κομᾶτα.

In this imagined scenario, Lycidas foregrounds his own labour in tending to Comatas' goats so that he can listen to his songs. This situation is idealized, and yet Lycidas still includes the necessity of tending to the herds. Just as Thyrsis' offer of labour in *Idyll* 1 is passed over, so too is Lycidas' scenario impossible.[20] The fact that both suggest that they will labour as a listener without ever actu-

19 The ecphrasis has clear poetic value, especially as a reception of the shield of Achilles in *Iliad* 18. The goatherd makes its economic value clear at *Id.* 1.57–58, saying he exchanged both a goat and special cheese for it.

20 The only occasion in the *Idylls* in which a herdsman's flock is under the care of another is *Idyll* 3, but the circumstances are unclear. In the brief opening, the unnamed speaker tells his audience that he is leaving his goats to Tityrus, whose identity is a mystery. While he certainly could be another herdsman or a satyr, Hunter offers the attractive possibility that Tityrus instead refers to the leading he-goat (Hunter 1999, 111–112). If Tityrus is understood as at least possibly being a goat himself, then this *Idyll* would accord well with the neglect that singing herdsmen often show toward their flocks (cf. note 17, above).

alizing it points to the symbolic nature of the audience's labour. In the fictional world of the bucolic, these poets' willingness to perform labour as audience members emblematizes, but does not actualize, the degree of effort involved in listening to the poetry of their fellow poets.

This suggested but unrealized labour of listening while also tending to flocks that herdsmen offer intersects with the tradition of work songs. The Greeks had traditional songs to accompany various forms of work, but few traces of them have been preserved in the written record. Karanika has followed these traces in regard to women, studying the evidence for work songs and work contexts that have survived.[21] *Idyll* 10 is relevant to her study, as it includes a traditional work song and opposes such songs to contemporary love poetry. There, Milo chides his fellow worker Bucaeus for not creating a swath in a straight line or keeping up with the reaper next to him (*Id.* 10.2–3). Bucaeus reveals that he cannot work because he has fallen in love with a girl, thereby living up to his name, which marks him as somewhat out of place in agricultural work and a better fit as a lovelorn cowherd.[22] Milo, after teasing him about his beloved, tries to help his companion become motivated for their work, saying (*Id.* 10.21–23):

> I'm not talking big; you just cut down the crops, and start singing some love song about your girl. That's the way you'll work more pleasantly. You really were musical back in the day.

> οὐ μέγα μυθεῦμαι· τὺ μόνον κατάβαλλε τὸ λᾷον,
> καί τι κόρας φιλικὸν μέλος ἀμβάλευ. ἅδιον οὕτως
> ἐργαξῇ. καὶ μὰν πρότερόν ποκα μουσικὸς ἦσθα.

While most love songs in the *Idylls* distract the singer from his work, here Milo suggests one as an incentive for Bucaeus to work harder. The verbal echo of the root βάλλω in κατάβαλλε and ἀμβάλευ reinforces the equation between reaping and singing. When Milo finishes line 22 with ἅδιον οὕτως, the audience may well expect him to talk about some quality of the song he proposes, since ἡδύς was a

21 Karanika 2014.

22 Herders of cows are particularly associated with pastoral poetry, making 'Bucaeus' an even stronger indication that he is better suited to that world (Kolde 2019). Hunt 2009, 394–396 explores the full significance of his name, emphasizing that it allows Bucaeus to import the characteristics of a bucolic herdsman into a non-bucolic world of work. The manuscripts do not recognize Βουκαῖε as a proper noun but as a title, and so name the character Battus based on Idyll 4. There is still some debate on this issue, as discussed by Richer 2019.

key term in Hellenistic poetics.[23] Instead, he surprises them with the enjambed ἐργαξῇ, thereby connecting the labour of reaping with a literary ideal. After Bucaeus' song about his beloved, Milo gives his response (*Id.* 10.38–41):

> Really, I didn't know Bucaeus made such fine songs; how well he measured out the form of the harmony. Ah, my poor beard that I grew in vain. Now wonder at these words of divine Lityerses.

> ἦ καλὰς ἄμμε ποῶν ἐλελάθει Βοῦκος ἀοιδάς·
> ὡς εὖ τὰν ἰδέαν τᾶς ἁρμονίας ἐμέτρησεν.
> ὤμοι τῶ πώγωνος, ὃν ἀλιθίως ἀνέφυσα.
> θᾶσαι δὴ καὶ ταῦτα τὰ τῶ θείω Λιτυέρσα.

Milo seems to respond positively to Bucaeus' song, even lamenting the false impression of wisdom that his beard projects, although Hunter posits that the initial ἦ indicates the ironic nature of this response.[24] By the end of the poem Milo's praise will certainly ring false, but the reader may be unsure of the tone until then, and this ambiguity would create more suspense about the reaction of Milo as the internal audience member and so draw further attention to it.

Milo's comment about 'measur[ing] the form of the harmony' is likewise ambiguous. Hunter views this as a gap between the form that Theocritus uses for his poem, hexameter, and the metre that would actually be used for reaping songs.[25] The emphasis on metre also suggests one of the most essential functions of work songs, which is to provide a rhythm to accompany the labour being performed.[26] Following his ambiguous response, Milo unprompted begins to recite the song of Lityerses, a folk figure associated with agriculture as well as a term for the actual songs of reapers.[27] The following song depicts working characters and emphasizes their work in a style that evokes the

23 Theocritus uses ἡδύς to describe his bucolic poetry at several key moments in *Idyll* 1 (1, 65, 145, 148), and Callimachus also uses the term in reference to poetry (fr. 1.11). Sistakou 2021 studies the term and emphasizes its importance to the aesthetic that Theocritus develops throughout the *Idylls*.

24 Hunter 1999, 210.

25 Hunter 1999, 210–211.

26 Karanika 2014, 205 emphasizes the importance of pleasant rhythms within songs for making the work flow, but in connection with ἅδιον οὕτως / ἐργαξῇ above.

27 For Lityerses as the inventor of agriculture, see Apollodorus, *FGrHist* 244 f149. Two scholia (*scholia in Theocritum* 10.41 and 10.42) attest to the name also referring to the songs attributed to him.

short phrases of real work songs and gnomic wisdom, as Hunter notes.[28] Even when he sings, Milo recalls his experience as an audience member, repeating the traditional work song of another. After his song, Milo concludes the poem by comparing Lityerses' verses with those of Bucaeus (*Id.* 10.56–58):

> These are the words that men working in the sun should sing, and it's fitting to talk about that hungry love of yours, Bucaeus, to your mother when she's dozing in bed in the morning.
>
> ταῦτα χρὴ μοχθεντας ἐν ἀλίῳ ἄνδρας ἀείδειν,
> τὸν δὲ τεόν, Βουκαῖε, πρέπει λιμηρὸν ἔρωτα
> μυθίσδεν τᾷ ματρὶ κατ' εὐνὰν ὀρθρευοίσᾳ.

Here Milo definitively resolves the ambiguity of his earlier response, asserting that men who work should sing only such traditional songs, since they are the only aids to labour. He even instructs Bucaeus as to the appropriate audience for his compositions, namely his mother as she lies idle. This closing injunction highlights Milo's own activity as a listener and reminds us that, given his status as the paragon of work ethic (*Id.* 10.7), he is presumably working while listening to Bucaeus as well as while singing the verses of Lityerses. Milo is not an audience member at leisure, and instead works through both the composition of another and his own performance of a traditional song. Milo is the internal audience member who gives the most extensive feedback within the *Idylls*, offering two direct reviews of Bucaeus' songs as well as a song that recalls his own earlier experiences listening to traditional songs. He is also the worker *par excellence* in a country setting surrounded by those who do not work, and both his words and song insist upon the paramount importance of labour.[29] This overlap is no coincidence, and instead closely aligns labour with listening, presenting Milo as the instantiation of and advocate for this alignment.

Idyll 5 presents a briefer and more opaque reference to traditional work songs. There, while the herdsman Comatas and Lacon exchange verses in competition with each other, Lacon makes the following response to Comatas' previous mention of locusts (*Id.* 5.110–111):

---

28 Hunter 1999, 212.

29 In his extensive spatial analysis of the *Idylls*, Thalmann 2023 separates the agricultural world of *Idyll* 10 from the world of the bucolic poems on the basis of labour: 'work is what most sharply distinguishes between these two worlds, which otherwise communicate' (169). This idea of separate environments in the *Idylls* is compelling, and there is certainly more emphasis on work in *Idyll* 10, yet I hope to have shown that the idea of labour at least is not absent from the bucolic world.

> Hey, cicadas, see how I'm inciting the goatherd; surely that's just the way you incite the reapers.
>
> τοὶ τέττιγες, ὁρῆτε τὸν αἰπόλον ὡς ἐρεθίζω·
> οὕτω κὔμμες θην ἐρεθίζετε τὼς καλαμευτάς.

These lines are somewhat obscure, mainly because of the ambiguity of ἐρεθίζω, which I have translated as 'incite', and can connote both 'irritate' and 'urge on' to work.[30] Using the first definition, the cicadas' song is so loud that it annoys the reapers and challenges them to drown it out with their own song. Using the second definition, the cicadas' own song pushes the reapers to work harder.[31] In either case, Theocritus seems to be drawing on the association between cicadas and poets that became particularly prominent during this period, and either equates these poets with or opposes them to traditional reaping songs.[32] The very ambiguity of this verb suggests a strong link between new poetry and labour, and one that is suitably complex. Contemporary poetry interacts with a labouring audience, but it is unclear whether it annoys its listeners by demanding so much labour or whether that labour furthers their appreciation of the poetry.

All of the examples above imagine the internal audience of the performances to be actively labouring as they listen. The following passages further highlight the general labour of their internal audiences; this both associates all of their activities, including listening, with labour and highlights the cost of time needed to listen to poetry. One of these examples occurs in the bucolic poems briefly discussed above. While Milo in *Idyll* 10 creates, participates in, and decides the song competition between himself and Bucaeus, *Idyll* 5 contains a more traditional song competition with a far more opaque closing judgment. The poem opens on the goatherd Comatas and the shepherd Lacon trading insults until they decide to wager on a song contest between them. After debating the location for the contest, they must also decide on a judge, with

30 While LSJ do not separate these two meanings, Diggle 2020 s.v. does.

31 Gow 1952b, 111–112 treats the first interpretation as the standard but advocates for the second position, pointing to several passages that show how cicadas sing throughout the heat of the day when humans rest and so would stir reapers to work instead of rest during this time.

32 Callimachus claims that he wishes to be a cicada, while aligning his aesthetic enemies with braying donkeys (*Aetia* 1.29–32). Theocritus mentions cicadas in a metapoetic context likely responding to Callimachus at *Idylls* 1.148 and 7.139. For an analysis of these passages, see Acosta-Hughes 2021, 541–542, 553. Plato's *Phaedrus* 258e–259d, an important model for bucolic poetry, also treats cicadas as the supreme singers.

Comatas rejecting the oxherd Lycopas and suggesting the woodsman Morson, who is currently labouring to cut the heath nearby (*Id.* 5.62–65). Morson listens to the two herdsmen exchange couplets until he suddenly stops the songs and declares Comatas the winner (*Id.* 5.138–140). The fact that the herdsmen have to call Morson, the only woodcutter in the bucolic poems, away from his task and that Morson himself cuts off the contest, presumably to return to work, speaks to his industriousness in comparison with the herdsmen's idleness. While his work ethic is clear, his reaction as the audience of the song contest is less so. He declares Comatas the victor, but gives no reason for his decision, and scholars have suggested that he found Lacon's response inferior.[33] For insight into his judgment, I instead focus on the final couplet by Comatas that causes Morson to stop the contest (*Id.* 5.136–137):

> It is not ever lawful, Lacon, for jays to challenge a nightingale, nor for hoopoes to challenge swans; but you, wretched you, are quarrelsome.
>
> οὐ θεμιτόν, Λάκων, ποτ' ἀηδόνα κίσσας ἐρίσδειν,
> οὐδ' ἔποπας κύκνοισι· τὺ δ', ὦ τάλαν, ἐσσὶ φιλεχθής.

In these lines, Comatas directly addresses Lacon and their poetic contest, breaking the frame of the previous exchange.[34] Furthermore, he addresses their poetic quarrel by comparing them to birds of song, building on the metapoetic language of animals used by Callimachus in his famous formulation of aesthetics at the start of the *Aetia*.[35] In these lines, Comatas has finally moved away from the exchanges focused on bucolic themes to more metapoetic concerns, and it is at this point that Morson awards him the prize.[36] Morson recognizes a shift to relatively elevated aesthetic principles and considers it a fitting close to the herdsmen's contest, perhaps even recognizing the way that Comatas circles back to his opening insult of Lacon, that 'you are too fond of jeering;' τύγα

33 Gow 1952b, 92–94, points to the ways in which the contest is limited by its written form, so that music could be the deciding factor. Giangrande 1976; Köhnken 1980; and Domány 2009 all offer possible critiques of Lacon's earlier responses. Kossaifi 2002 moves the decision to the divine sphere, with Comatas associated with Pan instead of Lacon's association with Apollo, which finds support in Berman 2005's argument that the *Idylls* depict goatherds more favourably than cowherds.

34 Hutchinson 1988, 188.

35 For the metapoetic significance of birds in this period, see Nelson 2019. Callimachus also talks about swans specifically (fr. 1.39–40).

36 Schmidt 1974 and Trachsel 2006 also consider Comatas' victory in metapoetic terms, considering how all of his responses align him with the aesthetics of Hellenistic poetics.

μὰν φιλοκέρτομος ἐσσί (*Id.* 5.77). As a woodsman Morson is at the fringe of the bucolic world by both the form of his labour and the fact that he works at all, yet he demonstrates his understanding of contemporary poetics.[37] His labour of cutting away the heath goes hand in hand with his listening and cutting off the songs at the right time.

The other *Idylls* that depict busy audiences entail a shift in both subjects and setting, focusing on women at home in urban environs. These shifts perhaps reflect an awareness of the different type of labour women typically perform, as well as their association with the city in a variety of literary genres, such as mime.[38] The *Idyll* which contains the lengthiest account of a busy internal audience is 15, in which two housewives in Alexandria travel to attend a song about Adonis sponsored by Arsinoe.[39] When one of the women, Gorgo, arrives at the house of her friend Praxinoe to travel to the festival together, their dialogue centres on their family and their work. Since they have enslaved labourers, these two women are involved in only some domestic areas, especially making clothes.[40] In their brief conversation, they discuss the work involved in clothing production several times. Gorgo complains about her husband's purchase (*Id.* 15.19–20):

> For seven drachmas he bought five fleeces yesterday that were basically dog skins, pieces picked off an old leather bag, all filth, just work on top of work.
>
> ἑπταδράχμως κυνάδας, γραιᾶν ἀποτίλματα πηρᾶν,
> πέντε πόκως ἔλαβ' ἐχθές, ἅπαν ῥύπον, ἔργον ἐπ' ἔργῳ.

Gorgo begins her complaint by referencing the wasted money, but concludes by emphasizing the extra labour that her husband's mistake created for her.

---

37 An activity not found in other *Idylls*, woodcutting can be seen as destructive to the rustic world (Damon 1995, 121). Yet this labour also helps create the very idyllic landscape which herdsmen and their animals enjoy, and about which Comatas and Lacon are so concerned earlier in the poem when deciding on a setting for their contest (*Id.* 5.45–61).

38 The scholia tell us that *Idyll* 15 is modelled on a now lost mime of Sophron, *Spectators at the Isthmia Festival* (fr. 10 K–A). For more on this mime, see Hordern 2002. For the interaction between gender and mime in this *Idyll*, see Burton 1995; Kutzco 2008; Pace 2017.

39 Reed 2000 discusses the political context of the festival and how Arsinoe figures in the poem.

40 Papadopoulou 2017 puts the emphasis on clothing in this poem into the context of the other *Idylls*, contrasting the fineness of these garments with the rustic animal skins of the herdsmen in the pastoral poems.

Shortly afterwards, Gorgo compliments Praxinoe on her dress and asks its cost, which the latter answers in terms of both money and labour (*Id.* 15.36–37):

> Don't remind me, Gorgo; more than two genuine minae coins; and I also put my soul into the work.
>
> μὴ μνάσῃς, Γοργοῖ· πλέον ἀργυρίω καθαρῶ μνᾶν
> ἢ δύο· τοῖς δ' ἔργοις καὶ τὰν ψυχὰν ποτέθηκα.

Praxinoe here quotes an exorbitant cost for the material, but this exaggeration comes second to the cost of labour in sewing and embroidering the cloth; it is this labour, not the money, which reflects the 'soul' she has put into it.[41] She has donned this extravagant garment specifically for the occasion of listening to a poetic performance, despite the danger of tearing that threatens clothes in the city crowd (*Id.* 15. 69–71). Both Gorgo and Praxinoe talk about how much labour they put into their garments and clothes in general, so that Praxinoe's decision to wear a labour-intensive dress to hear poetry associates their labour with the act of listening.

Their skill in designing clothes is not limited to their own garments, but extends to appreciating the work of others. When they reach their destination, before they hear the poet perform, they encounter a fine tapestry (*Id.* 15.78–86):

> GORGO: Praxinoe, come over here. Look at the different-coloured embroidery first, how refined and accomplished it is; you'd say these were garments to put on the gods.
> PRAXINOE: By mistress Athena, what skilled workers made these, what skilled designers drew these precise outlines. The figures standing look like they're real, as do the figures in motion; they're alive, not embroidered. A human is such a clever thing. And he himself, how wondrous he is, lounging on his silver couch, growing his first whiskers along his temples, the one loved three times, Adonis, the one loved even after he's in Acheron.
>
> Γο. Πραξινόα, πόταγ' ὧδε. τὰ ποικίλα πρᾶτον ἄθρησον,
> λεπτὰ καὶ ὡς χαρίεντα· θεῶν περονάματα φασεῖς.

41 These coins are equivalent to 200 drachmae. In comparison, Gow 1952b, 278 points out that in third-century BCE Egypt we have χιτῶνες that cost 6 to 16 drachmae and ἱμάτια that cost 6 to 40 drachmae. These χιτῶνες may have been very simple, but the cost cited here is clearly very high.

Πρ. πότνι' Ἀθαναία, ποῖαί σφ' ἐπόνασαν ἔριθοι,
ποῖοι ζωογράφοι τἀκριβέα γράμματ' ἔγραψαν.
ὡς ἔτυμ' ἑστάκαντι καὶ ὡς ἔτυμ' ἐνδινεῦντι,
ἔμψυχ', οὐκ ἐνυφαντά. σοφόν τι χρῆμ' ἄνθρωπος.
αὐτὸς δ' ὡς θαητὸς ἐπ' ἀργυρέας κατάκειται
κλισμῶ, πρᾶτον ἴουλον ἀπὸ κροτάφων καταβάλλων,
ὁ τριφίλητος Ἄδωνις, ὁ κὴν Ἀχέροντι φιληθείς.

Gorgo introduces the tapestry with the metapoetical term λεπτά, 'refined' (79).[42] Praxinoe also admires it, wondering in particular at the skill of the 'workers' and drawing attention to the beauty of Adonis.[43] The beauty and skill of the tapestry even inspire Praxinoe to wonder in general terms at the artistry that humans can attain (σοφόν τι χρῆμ' ἄνθρωπος). Because of the terms used to describe the tapestry, the longstanding link between weaving and song, and the focus on Adonis in both song and tapestry, critics have viewed the tapestry as a representation of Alexandrian court refinement equivalent to the song about to be performed.[44] These women's own labour in embroidering cloth allows them to understand and appreciate the detail of both tapestry and song. Labour is the prerequisite for being an appreciative audience of the embroidered cloth.

Once the two women have actually heard the Argive woman's song, Gorgo reacts for both of them (*Id.* 15.145–149):

> Praxinoe, that woman is a clever thing; she's blessed to know so much, and doubly blessed to sing so sweetly. Nevertheless, time to go home. Diocleidas is without his dinner; that man is absolutely sour, and when he's hungry you can't approach him. Goodbye, beloved Adonis, and may you arrive next year to find us thriving.

42 Callimachus uses the term λεπτός to describe his poetry at several key moments (fr. 1.10, 16, ep. 27). Grethlein 2012 argues for the importance of the metapoetic term in Theocitus' work as well through the emphasis on thinness in *Idyll* 10.

43 Hansen 2020, 39 rightfully connects Praxinoa's appreciation of the workers' skill with her earlier comments about Gorgo's garments. Krevans 2006, 123–124 convincingly suggests that just as Praxinoe admires Adonis for seeming alive although he is woven, so does the poem's external audience admire Praxinoe and Gorgo as seeming alive although they are written.

44 For the link between weaving and song in Greek poetry, see Fanfani, Harlow and Nosch 2016. For this poem in particular, see Skinner 2001; Lambert 2001. As Hunter 1996, 15 discusses, the link between wool-working and literary labour was already apparent in two of Theocritus' most important literary models, since it is the subject of an inscription that Asclepiades of Samos wrote as if he were Erinna lamenting her own death (*Anth. Pal.* 7.11, Gow and Page 1965, Asclepiades 28).

Πραξινόα, τὸ χρῆμα σοφώτατον ἁ θήλεια·
ὀλβία ὅσσα ἴσατι, πανολβία ὡς γλυκὺ φωνεῖ.
ὥρα ὅμως κὴς οἶκον. ἀνάριστος Διοκλείδας·
χὠνὴρ ὄξος ἅπαν, πεινᾶντι δὲ μηδὲ ποτένθῃς.
χαῖρε, Ἄδων ἀγαπατέ, καὶ ἐς χαίροντας ἀφικνεῦ.

Her praise of the singer is relatively brief, although it spans both her knowledge and voice. In comparison with both women's earlier praise of the tapestry, Gorgo's words about the song appear less enthusiastic and focused on the woman herself rather than on both the people and the product. The women have just appreciated the depiction of Adonis in the tapestry, and this elides with his presentation in the song. The phrase τὸ χρῆμα σοφώτατον ἁ θήλεια, echoing line 83 above, makes the comparison between the two clearer, since the performance draws attention only to the woman while the tapestry reflects the artistry of the entire human race. While the praise of the woman is less marked than that of the tapestry, it, too, focuses on her as a worker by framing her performance in terms of her labour, through both her clever knowledge and her sweet singing. This focus on labour continues with Gorgo's comments, as she turns to the tasks that await her at home, hurrying to avoid reproaches from an increasingly prickly husband.[45]

Throughout the poem, Gorgo's focus on her own labour, that of the tapestry weavers, and that of the singer, presents the excursion to the performance not as leisure activity per se, but rather as time lost from labour. While the bucolic world has some markers of time (e.g. *Id.* 1.15–16), Gorgo and Praxinoe live within a busy schedule, as shown when they rush to make the performance on time.[46] Praxinoe highlights the haste that they must make early on in the poem by contrasting it with idleness, saying: ἀεργοῖς αἰὲν ἑορτά, 'it's always a festival for those who don't labour' (*Id.* 15.26). Praxinoe's phrase has the feel of a gnomic statement, yet speaks specifically to the theme of labour in the poem.[47] Praxinoe here makes a clear distinction between working people, including herself, and the idle elite that frames the labour of the women throughout the poem, though there is some irony, at least for modern readers, in Praxinoe immediately

45 Griffiths 1981 takes these closing lines as the title for his chapter assessing the degree of freedom available to the contemporary women in *Idylls* 2 and 15, emphasizing how much Gorgo and Praxinoe are restrained by the labour demanded of them at home. Chaldekas 2022 offers a more recent reading of the gender roles in the poem by exploring how they intersect with the characters' ethnic identities.

46 Both women use various formulations of hurrying to get to the performance before it starts: *Id.* 15.21–23, 26, 29, 42, and 59.

47 Hunter 1996, 137.

ordering around her enslaved worker after this declaration (*Id.* 15.27–33). This is perhaps a feature of urban mime, since there is a similar dynamic in *Idyll* 2, in which Simaetha orders around the enslaved Thestylis while addressing her elevated language to the goddess Moon. While the labour of the women they have enslaved goes unnoticed, Praxinoe and Gorgo instead highlight their own efforts. Amidst these women's busy schedules, listening to poetry becomes connected with the other forms of labour that take up their days.

While *Idyll* 15 is the longest and most involved exploration of an audience busy with labour, *Idyll* 28 depicts a similarly busy audience in a very different format. This poem addresses a distaff with which Theocritus is sailing and which he will present to Theugenis, the wife of his friend Nicias.[48] Rather than mime, this poem may be drawing on a lost precedent from a Lesbian poet, given its Aeolic dialect and metre, or on poems by Asclepiades.[49] Another major difference is that this poem does not depict a poetic performance but rather enacts it. Theocritus dedicates several of his *Idylls* to an individual and occasionally sheds light on how this dedicatee should receive the poem, but nowhere in a more detailed manner than he does in *Idyll* 28.[50] This detail stems in part from the relationship between the distaff, the nominal and embodied gift to Theugenis, and the poem itself, which enacts and completes the gift. Theocritus emphasizes this equation between distaff and poem in the final lines, imagining some observer saying, 'surely great affection comes with this small gift; since all things are esteemed which come from friends;' ἦ μεγάλα χάρις/ δώρῳ σὺν ὀλίγῳ· πάντα δὲ τίματα τὰ πὰρ φίλων (*Id.* 28.24–25). This observation that great kindness accompanies the gift draws attention to the poem itself, which literally accompanies the gift, and reinforces the slippage between object and poem. As with the tapestry on display in the court of the Ptolemies, the distaff in this poem evokes the traditional association between weaving and

48 *Idyll* 11 is dedicated to Nicias and *Epigram* 8 mentions him as well. The epigram, as with this *Idyll*, state that he lives in Miletus. As well as a doctor, he was a poet and likely the Nicias attested as the author of eight extant epigrams, numbers 2755–2786 in Gow and Page 1965.

49 For the connection with Sappho and Alcaeus, see Cairns 1977, 301–305; Fassino and Prauscello 2001.

50 Beyond the encomiastic poems, *Idyll* 16 appealing to Hiero II the king of Syracuse and *Idyll* 17 praising Ptolemy II, the *Idylls* contain three addresses to individuals. *Idyll* 6 addresses itself to an Aratus without any direction as to how to receive the poem (*Id.* 6.1–2), while *Idyll* 13 opens with an address to Nicias that is difficult to interpret (*Id.* 13.1–4). *Idyll* 11, also to Nicias, has the most elaborate dedication, connecting his profession as a doctor with the Polyphemus' song as a cure for love (*Id.* 11.1–18; 80–81). Gow 1952b, 209 thought this framing was a later addition, while Barigazzi 1975; Farr 1991; and Faraone 2006 have explored the ways in which this dedication shapes the interpretation of rest of the poem.

poetry.[51] With this association in the background, Theocritus explains why he chose this object as his gift (*Id.* 28.12–16):

> Twice in each year the mothers of lambs in the pasture could be shorn of their soft fleeces, according to fair-ankled Theugenis; that's how hard-working she is, how much she loves prudent pursuits. For I was not willing to lead you to the house of a sluggish or idle woman, since you are from my country.
>
> δὶς γὰρ μάτερες ἄρνων μαλάκοις ἐν βοτάνᾳ πόκοις
> πέξαιντ' αὐτοέτει, Θευγένιδός γ' ἔννεκ' εὐσφύρω·
> οὕτως ἀνυσίεργος, φιλέει δ' ὄσσα σαόφρονες.
> οὐ γὰρ εἰς ἀκίρας οὐδ' ἐς ἀέργω κεν ἐβολλόμαν
> ὄπασσαί σε δόμοις, ἀμμετέρας ἔσσαν ἀπὺ χθόνος.

In this passage Theocritus highlights Theugenis' affinity for labour in three different ways. First, he explicitly calls her 'hard-working' and a lover of 'prudent' things. Second, he asserts that she could weave even double the amount of wool, in a tantalizing connection between the bucolic world and that of the city, Miletus (*Id.* 28.3). The issue of setting is particularly important, given that this poem contains one of the two references Theocritus makes to his birthplace within his surviving corpus.[52] Finally, Theocritus emphasizes Theugenis' association with labour through contrast, stating that he would not give the distaff, or by extension the poem, to a woman who was idle. Furthermore, in imagining Theugenis using the distaff, the poem essentially treats her as an internal audience member, relying on the equation between the distaff and the poem. Within a small number of lines, Theocritus devotes considerable space to emphasizing how much Theugenis labours; fundamentally, his choice of distaff as gift and subject also locates women's labour at the heart of the poem. It

51 Gutzwiller 2020 has argued that the distaff in particular played a role in Callimachus' programmatic aesthetic statement at the opening of the *Aetia*.

52 Theocritus goes on to specify that the distaff comes from Syracuse (*Id.* 28.17–18). The other instance in which he references his Sicilian origin occurs in *Idyll* 11, dedicated to Nicias, which refers to ὁ Κύκλωψ ὁ παρ' ἀμῖν, 'the Cyclops, the one near us' (*Id.* 11.7). Thucydides already identifies Sicily as the traditional home of the Cyclops (6.2.1). Hunter 1996, 118–119 argues that Theocritus also shows that he comes from Syracuse in *Idyll* 15. An epigram, 25 in Gow 1952b, seems to be a preface for Theocritus' book of poems, as discussed by Gutzwiller 1996, 133–137, and identifies its author as Syracusan. For an analysis of how ancient readers constructed Theocritus' biography from these poems and other sources through the Roman imperial period, see Richer 2020.

is Theugenis' willingness to labour that makes her the appropriate audience to appreciate the distaff and the poem.

The *Idylls* are remarkable for the amount and variety of labour they depict. One of the most distinct and consistent associations of labour across a variety of poems is with listening. In the very different worlds of bucolic and urban mime, Theocritus associates the internal audiences with the listening-labour they perform, either in general or during the performance specifically. By equating labour with listening, Theocritus implicitly acknowledges the demands contemporary poetry makes of its audience to pay close attention to dialect, metre, and allusions. At the same time, Theocritus shows how this labour of listening is open to a variety of people. In the bucolic world filled with poets, it is indeed other poet-herdsmen who labour and listen, yet their labour remains only imagined in scenarios in which a herdsman wants to listen to the song of another. The hypothetical nature of their labour shows that it is their willingness to perform it, not the labour itself, that they associate with being the kind of audience that would entice a singer to perform. In the world of mime and lyric, Theocritus focuses on women and uses the analogy of weaving to explore their work and relationship with poetry. These women's textile labour enables them to appreciate the Ptolemies' tapestry and Theocritus' distaff, both objects that correspond to poetry. The very process of analogy shows that the poem's audience does not have to be specialized fellow poets, but can rather transfer their labour from other areas to the act of listening. By making the labour of bucolic poets hypothetical and the labour of women transferable, the *Idylls* depict internal audiences that perform non-specialized labour. Theocritus' presentation of his internal audiences suggests something about how he imagined external audiences might respond to both the *Idylls* and contemporary poetry more generally. He acknowledges the work involved in listening, while also making it a matter of effort rather than exclusive to a limited circle of elites.

Bibliography

Acosta-Hughes, B. (2019). The Wandering Tendril: An Essay on Hellenistic Metapoetics. *RivFil* 147(1), pp. 22–42.

Acosta-Hughes, B. (2021). Among the Cicadas: Theocritus and his Contemporaries. In: P. Kyriakou, E. Sistakou and A. Rengakos, eds. *Brill's Companion to Theocritus*. Leiden, pp. 537–558.

Barigazzi, A. (1975). Una presunta aporia nel c. 11 di Teocrito. *Hermes*, 103, pp. 179–188.

Berger, H. (1984). The Origins of Bucolic Representation: Disenchantment and Revision in Theocritus' Seventh *Idyll*. *ClAnt* 3(1), pp. 1–39.

Berman, D.W. (2005). The Hierarchy of Herdsmen, Goatherding, and Genre in Theocritean Bucolic. *Phoenix* 59, pp. 228–245.

Bowie, E.L. (1985). Theocritus' Seventh Idyll, Philetas and Longus. *CQ* 35, pp. 67–91.

Burton, J.B. (1995). *Theocritus's Urban Mimes. Mobility, Gender, and Patronage*. Berkeley.

Bustos, M.N. (2019a). Reimagining Comedy in Theocritus' *Idyll* 14. *AClass*, 62, pp. 21–39.

Bustos, M.N. (2019b). Theocritus' *Idyll* 15: A Metapoetic Manifesto. *Akropolis*, 1, pp. 150–166.

Cairns, F. (1977). The Distaff of Theugenis. Theocritus, *Idyll* 28. *ARCA* 2, pp. 293–305.

Cairns, F. (1984). Theocritus' First *Idyll*. The Literary Programme. *WS* 18, pp. 89–113.

Chaldekas, M. (2022). An Intersectional Approach to Theocritus, *Idyll* 15. *Helios* 49(1).

Cozzoli, A.-T. (2015). Un dialogo tra poeti: Apollonio Rodio e Teocrito. *Lexis*, 33, pp. 218–240.

Crane, G. (1988). Realism in the Fifth *Idyll* of Theocritus. *TAPA* 118, pp. 107–122.

Cusset, C. (1999). *La muse dans la bibliothèque. Réécriture et intertextualité dans la poésie alexandrine*. Paris.

Damon, C. (1995). Narrative and Mimesis in the *Idylls* of Theocritus. *QUCC* 51(3), pp. 101–123.

Diggle, J., ed. (2020). *The Cambridge Greek Lexicon*. New York.

Domány, J. (2007). Theocritus' *Thalysia*. *AAntHung* 47, pp. 317–327.

Domány, J. (2009). Lacon's Silence in Theocritus' *Id.* 5. *Hermes* 137, pp. 382–385.

Duncan, A. (2001). Spellbinding Performance: Poet as Witch in Theocritus' Second *Idyll* and Apollonius' *Argonautica*. *Helios* 28(1).

Ette, W. (2014.) Arbeit in Hesiods *Werken und Tagen*. *A&A* 60, pp. 37–50.

Fanfani, G., Harlow, M. and Nosch, M.-L., eds. (2016). *Spinning Fates and the Song of the Loom. The Use of Textiles, Clothing and Cloth Production as Metaphor, Symbol and Narrative Device in Greek and Latin Literature*. Oxford.

Faraone, C.A. (2006). Magic, Medicine and Eros in the Prologue to Theocritus' *Id.* 11. In: M. Fantuzzi and T.D. Papanghelis, eds., *Brill's Companion to Greek and Latin Pastoral*. Leiden, pp. 75–90.

Farr, J. (1991). Theocritus: *Idyll* 11. *Hermes* 119, pp. 477–484.

Fassino, M. and Prauscello, L. (2001). Memoria ritmica e memoria poetica: Saffo e Alceo in Teocrito *Idilli* 28–30 tra ἀρχαιολογία metrica e innovazione alessandrina. *MD*, 46, pp. 9–37.

Foster, J.A. (2016). *Reading Voices. Five Studies in Theocritus' Narrating Techniques*. New York.

Giangrande, G. (1976). Victory and Defeat in Theocritus' *Idyll* v. *Mnemosyne* 29, pp. 143–154.

Goldhill, S. (1988). Desire and the Figure of Fun: Glossing Theocritus 11. In: A.E. Benjamin, ed., *Post-Structuralist Classics*. London, pp. 79–105.

Goldhill, S. (1991). *The Poet's Voice. Essays on Poetics and Greek Literature*. Cambridge.

Gow, A.S.F. (1952a). *Bucolici Graeci*. Oxford.

Gow, A.S.F., ed. (1952b). *Theocritus*. Cambridge.

Gow, A.S.F. and Page, D.L., eds. (1965). *The Greek Anthology. Hellenistic Epigrams*. Cambridge.

Grethlein, J. (2012). A Slim Girl and the Fat of the Land in Theocritus, *Id.* 10. *CQ* 62(2), pp. 603–617.

Griffiths, F.T. (1979). *Theocritus at Court*. Leiden.

Griffiths, F.T. (1981). Home Before Lunch: The Emancipated Woman in Antiquity. In: H.P. Foley, ed., *Reflections of Women in Antiquity*. New York, pp. 247–273.

Gutzwiller, K. (1991). *Theocritus' Pastoral Analogies. The Formation of a Genre*. Madison.

Gutzwiller, K. (1996). The Evidence for Theocritean Poetry Books. In: M.A. Harder, R.F. Regtuit and G.C. Walker, eds., *Theocritus*. Groningen, pp. 119–148.

Gutzwiller, K. (2006). The Bucolic Problem. *CPh* 101(4), pp. 380–404.

Gutzwiller, K. (2020). Under the Sign of the Distaff: *Aetia* 1.5, Spinning and Erinna. *CQ* 70(1), pp. 177–191.

Halperin, D.M. (1983). *Before Pastoral. Theocritus and the Ancient Tradition of Bucolic Poetry*. New Haven.

Hansen, H.J. (2020). Theocritus' *Idyll* 15: Mime, Metapoetics, and the Road. *CJ* 116(1), pp. 23–44.

Harder, A. (2019). Aspects of the Interaction between Apollonius Rhodius and Callimachus. *Aevum Antiquum* 19, pp. 9–34.

Harder, A., Regtuit, R.F. and Wakker, G.C., eds. (2018). *Drama and Performance in Hellenistic Poetry*. Leuven.

Hordern, J. (2002). Sophron, fr. 171, and Theocritus 15. *ZPE* 140, pp. 1–2.

Hunt, J.M. (2009). Bucolic Experimentation in Theocritus' *Idyll 10*. *GRBS* 49, pp. 391–412.

Hunter, R.L. (1996). *Theocritus and the Archaeology of Greek Poetry*. Cambridge.

Hunter, R.L., ed. (1999). *Theocritus. A Selection*. Cambridge.

Hunter, R.L. (2008). Mime and Mimesis: Theocritus, *Idyll* 1. In: *On Coming After. Studies in Post-Classical Greek Literature and its Reception*. Berlin, pp. 233–256.

Hunter, R.L. (2014). Theocritus and the Style of Hellenistic Poetry. In: R.L. Hunter, A. Rengakos and E. Sistakou, eds., *Hellenistic Studies at a Crossroads. Exploring Texts, Contexts and Metatexts*. Berlin, pp. 55–74.

Hunter, R.L. (2020). Afterword. In: A.-E. Beron, ed., *Hyblaea Avena. Theokrit in römischer Kaiserzeit und früher Neuzeit. Beiträge von internationalen Symposium am 15. und 16. November 2018 an der bergischen Universität Wuppertal*. Stuttgart, pp. 197–200.

Hutchinson, G.O. (1988). *Hellenistic Poetry*. Oxford.

Karanika, A. (2014). *Voices at Work. Women, Performance, and Labor in Ancient Greece*. Baltimore.

Klooster, J. (2011). *Poetry as Window and Mirror. Positioning the Poet in Hellenistic Poetry*. Leiden.

Klooster, J. (2021). The Programmatic *Idylls* of Theocritus. In: P. Kyriakou, E. Sistakou and A. Rengakos, eds., *Brill's Companion to Theocritus*. Leiden, pp. 364–386.

Köhnken, A. (1980). Komatas' Sieg über Lakon. *Hermes* 108, pp. 122–125.

Kolde, A. (2019). Bouvier, chevrier, berger dans les *Idylles* bucoliques de Théocrite: des catégories à interroger. *Aitia* 9(1). DOI: https://doi.org/10.4000/aitia.3426.

Kossaifi, C. (2002). Le poéte de Pan: les raisons de la victoire de Comatas dans l'*Idylle* 5 de Théocrite. *REG* 115, pp. 75–109.

Krevans, N. (2006). Is There Urban Pastoral? The Case of Theocritus' *Id.* 15. In: M. Fantuzzi and T. Papanghelis, eds., *Brill's Companion to Greek and Latin Pastoral*. Leiden, pp. 119–146.

Kutzco, D. (2007). The Bemused Singer and Well-Versed Audience: The Use of Polyphemus in Theocritus. *StIt* 5(1), pp. 73–114.

Kutzco, D. (2008). All the World's a Page: Imitation of Metatheater in Theocritus 15, Herodas 1 and Virgil Eclogues 3. *CJ* 103(2), pp. 141–161.

Lambert, M. (2001). Gender and Religion in Theocritus, *Idyll* 15: Prattling Tourists at the *Adonia*. *AClass* 44, pp. 87–103.

Lelli, E. (2017). *Pastori antichi e moderni. Teocrito e le origini popolari della poesia bucolica*. Hildesheim.

Nelson, T.J. (2019). Metapoetic Manoeuvres between Callimachus and Apollonius: A Response to Annette Harder. *Aevum* 19, pp. 107–127.

Pace, V. (2017). Singing Women in Theocritus: Magic, Genre and Gender in *Idylls* 2 and 15. In: C. Cusset, C. Kossaifi and R. Poignault, eds., *Présence de Théocrite*. Clermont-Ferrand, pp. 63–90.

Papadopoulou, M. (2017). Poems from the World of Wool: Dress and Identity in Theocritus' *Idylls*. In: C. Cusset, C. Kossaifi and R. Poignault, eds., *Présence de Théocrite*. Clermont-Ferrand, pp. 163–179.

Payne, M. (2007). *Theocritus and the Invention of Fiction*. Cambridge.

Pucci, P. (1996). Auteur et destinataires dans les *Travaux* d'Hésiode. In: F. Blaise, P. Judet de La Combe and P. Rousseau, eds., *Le métier du mythe. Lectures d'Hésiode*. Villeneuve-d'Ascq, pp. 191–210.

Reed, J.D. (2000). Arsinoe's Adonis and the Poetics of Ptolemaic Imperialism. *TAPA* 130(1), pp. 319–351.

Richer, H. (2019). Boucaios est-il un nom propre ou un nom commun?: (Théocrite, Nicandre, Posidippe). *Aitia* 9(1). DOI: https://doi.org/10.4000/aitia.3582.

Richer, H. (2020). The Three Faces of Theocritus During the Imperial Era. In: A.-E. Beron, ed., *Hyblaea Avena. Theokrit in römischer Kaiserzeit und früher Neuzeit: Beiträge von internationalen Symposium am 15. und 16. November 2018 an der bergischen Universität Wuppertal*. Stuttgart, pp. 59–73

Schmidt, E.A. (1974). Der göttliche Ziegenhirt. Analyse des fünften *Idyll* als Beitrag zu Theokrits bukolischer Technik. *Hermes* 102(2), pp. 207–243.

Scholten, H. (2006). Die kulturelle Bewertung körperlicher Arbeit in den Gedichten Theokrits. In: D. Dormeyer and F. Siegert, eds., *Arbeit in der Antike, in Judentum und Christentum*. Münster, pp. 66–85.

Sistakou, E. (2021). The Sweet Pleasures of Theocritus' *Idylls*: A Study in the Aesthetics of ἀδύτης. In: P. Kyriakou, E. Sistakou and A. Rengakos, eds., *Brill's Companion to Theocritus*. Leiden, pp. 324–345.

Skinner, M.B. (2001). Ladies' Day at the Art Institute: Theocritus, Herodas, and the Gendered Gaze. In: A.P.M.H. Lardinois and L.K. McClure, eds., *Making Silence Speak. Women's Voices in Greek Literature and Society*. Princeton, pp. 201–222.

Thalmann, W.G. (2023). *Theocritus. Space, Absence, and Desire*. Oxford.

Trachsel, A. (2006). La fin de l'*Idylle* 5 de Théocrite: une question de balance? *Mnemosyne* 59, pp. 348–373.

Van Sickle, J. (1976). Theocritus and the Development of the Conception of Bucolic Genre. *Ramus*, 5(1), pp. 18–44.

Whitehorne, J. (1995). Women's Work in Theocritus, *Idyll* 15. *Hermes*, 123(1), pp. 63–75.

CHAPTER 11

Labor in the *locus amoenus*: Agricultural Industry as Premise of Pastoral Leisure

Riemer A. Faber

1 Introduction

The literary figure of the pleasant place may be defined as the depiction of an idyllic setting marked by a gurgling stream, a shady resting-place, singing birds, peace and *otium*. This chapter argues that labour is an important but neglected premise of the leisure associated with the *locus amoenus* as presented in Greek and Latin pastoral poetry. Beginning with the prototypical portrayal of bucolic repose in Theocritus, *Idyll* 7, it will be argued that agricultural labour is a prerequisite for the culminating recreational activities and conviviality. Turning next to Vergil, *Eclogue* 1, which is distinguished by both the realism of the Italian countryside and contemporary politics, I shall suggest that the poem engages the motif of georgic industry in order to demonstrate how the interrelationship between work and leisure in the *locus amoenus* effects genuine happiness. Although the farmer's work is intensive, and the land is demanding, rural life affords a certain self-sufficiency and contentment. This relationship between the hard work of the farmer and the *otium* of the countryside is explored also in Horace, *Epode* 2 by means of the *locus amoenus* imagined by the usurer Alfius, for whom the labour demands of living in the country prove, on reflection, to be too onerous. We shall conclude that by combining labour and ease, the *locus amoenus* in these Greek and Latin poems exposes a generally overlooked perspective on ancient attitudes towards labour in which work and leisure are perceived as together composing a balanced life.

Three trends in the investigation of work and leisure as represented in the genre of pastoral poetry inform this chapter: ecology, social history and philosophy. Ecological literary criticism, or eco-criticism, redefines the ideologies of pastoral by focussing on the symbiotic relationship of human beings and their natural environments. It avoids the traditional pastoral dichotomies of nature vs. culture, reality vs. artificiality, and city vs. country. Instead, ecocriticism regards the relationship between pastoral texts and the 'real world' not as controlled by human beings or some other external force, but as part of a

 DOI:10.1163/9789004694965_012

holistic, living structure—an ecosystem.[1] Ecocriticism does not merely situate human presence and activity within its natural space; the interactions of opposites such as culture and nature are seen together, in combination rather than as mutually distinct.[2] As a literary genre, pastoral poetry functions as a means to mediate our relationship with the land on which we depend and with the forces of nature that are at work there.[3]

A second trend in revising pastoral ideology is evident in the studies of labour in Greco-Roman antiquity. Although they tend to focus on urban centres, these studies explicate the range and nature of occupations that find parallels in rural and agricultural settings. Thus for Italy in the republican era, thanks to the volumes by Verboven and Laes and by Marcone, as well as the essays in *The Economic Integration of Roman Italy* and in *The Roman Agricultural Economy*, we have become more alert to the relationship between work and leisure in the context of the social history of rural labour, from farming generally to the specific realms of viticulture, animal husbandry, bee-keeping, cheese-making, etc.[4]

A third trend affecting the study of *labor* and *otium* as depicted in classical pastoral is philosophy, and in particular the human search for happiness (εὐδαιμονία). The influence of Plato upon Theocritus, *Idyll* 7 has been demonstrated by Hunter and Billault, and that of Epicurus upon Vergil's *Eclogues* especially by Davis.[5] In the early Hellenistic period the appreciation of physical labour (πόνος) was a component of the ascendant Stoic ethics.[6] Theocritus, somewhat unlike contemporary poets, celebrates physical labour, and so his poetry offers a good starting point for an exploration of the work-leisure relationship.[7]

1 Thus Saunders (2006, 10). For a summary introduction to ecocriticism see Schliephake (2017, 1–15). For a survey of especially American and British ecocritical approaches to pastoral literature see Gifford (2017, 159–173). Armstrong (2019, 16) observes that the pastoral genre '… occupies a patch of disputed ecocritical ground, sometimes rejected as too artificial to be considered environmentally engaged literature, at others rehabilitated and revalued as a central form for the ecocritic to consider'.

2 Saunders 2006, 13.

3 Gifford 2006, 15.

4 Verboven and Laes 2017; Marcone 2016; De Haas and Tol 2017; Bowman and Wilson 2013. On the representation of agricultural labour in Greek pastoral poetry see Gutzwiller (2006); on agricultural and pastoral economies in Homer's *Odyssey* see Edwards (1993); on rural families in Italy see Dyson (2011). For social perspectives on farm work in literary Greek and Roman sources see Thibodeau (2011), pp. 48–53 and 54–61 respectively.

5 Hunter 1999, 145–146; Billault 2008; Davis 2012.

6 On the presence of Stoic notions of contentment, simplicity of life and peace in *Idyll* 1 see Furasawa (1980, 157–159).

7 Scholten 2006, 67, 81.

Another consideration is the influence of Epicureanism as filtered by Lucretius and Philodemus to Vergil (and Horace), especially as this is expressed metaphorically by *otium* in Vergil's poetry.[8]

The *locus amoenus* is perhaps the most salient representation of *otium* in ancient poetry, as it is the depiction of a physical space that permits the enjoyment of the finer qualities of life. Recurring features of this *topos* are trees for shade on a hot day, a spring or brook for freshness, pleasurable sound provided by birds or insects, and soft grass on which to rest.[9] Often it functions as an expression of relaxation and rest, particularly as that is represented in the genre of pastoral poetry. Like Vergil's idyllic Arcadia, the pastoral *locus amoenus* is commonly perceived as an idealized space. As demonstrated in a seminal essay by Schmidt, especially since the notion of Arcadia in Renaissance literature was adapted into a symbol of the unreal, other-worldly place and time of rest and recreation, ancient pastoral poetry has generally been read as expressing the desire to escape from the hardships and the hustle and bustle of (city) life.[10] As Schmidt demonstrates, in the twentieth century this notion continued to be fostered, and was retrojected onto Vergil, and Theocritus. Thus, for example, in the 1953 essay, 'Arcadia: the Discovery of a Spiritual Landscape', Snell argues that Vergil's *Eclogues* were set in 'a far-away land overlaid with the golden haze of unreality'.[11] The idea was that ancient pastoral poets created a romantic, unreal utopia. The epitome of that happy place is the *locus amoenus*; thus, for example, Curtius, in a chapter entitled 'The Ideal Landscape', traces the literary history of the *locus amoenus* from Homer to the Middle Ages, and describes it as 'the place of heart's desire'.[12]

---

8 On the philosophical dimensions in the *Eclogues* see Davis (2012). Chambert (2004) discusses the philosophical aspects of *otium* in the *Culex* and Vergil's early poetry. *Culex* 72–81 celebrates leisure afforded by the countryside and rejects the greed for wealth; for the philosophical subtext in these lines see Salvatore (1995, 257–285).

9 For treatments of the *locus amoenus* in Greek and Latin literature see especially Hass (1998), Jones (1984), Newlands (1984), Schönbeck (1962) and Thesleff (1981).

10 Schmidt 2008. On the extensive influence of the adaptation by Jacopo Sannazaro (1458–1530) of the world of the *Eclogues* into an idyllic, idealized place in the prosimetric *Arcadia* (1480) see Schmidt (2008, 16–21).

11 Snell 1953; the book was originally published in 1945 as 'Arkadien: Die Entdeckung einer geistigen Landschaft'. On corrective observations about the idealized, non-historical and a-political representation of the pastoral landscape see, e.g., Jenkyns (1989, 26–39).

12 Curtius 1963, 186. A more recent and nuanced expression of this quality is offered by Payne (2010, 224), who argues that 'the fictionality of the bucolic world Theocritus created can hardly be exaggerated: the herdsman come and go as they please, without masters to answer to or flocks with pressing needs. They spend their time singing and in love, and their surroundings are a pleasure zone of trees, streams, springs, and breezes'.

The thesis of this chapter is that an application of eco-critical methods and of the findings of social-historical studies on rural labour, combined with appreciation of the philosophical aspects in the examined poems of Theocritus, Vergil and Horace, will show that *otium* or leisure as portrayed in three representative passages of Greco-Roman poetry was perceived not in contrast to agricultural industry but as existing in a mutual interrelationship with such labour. This paradigm has literary expression in the coalescence of agricultural enterprise and pastoral ideals.

2 Theocritus, *Idyll* 7

Theocritus, *Idyll* 7 recounts the walking journey of a townsman named Simichidas and two friends to a farm on the island of Kos, to participate in a festival of the harvest-goddess Deo (Demeter). En route they meet a goatherd, who accompanies them for the remainder of the trip. The scene of arrival and the enjoyment of relaxation are depicted towards the end of the poem, when the men arrive at the farm of Phrasidamus (*Idyll* 7.131–147, text and trans. Gow, adapted):

> … but I and Eucritus and the fair Amyntas turned towards Phrasidamus's farm and laid ourselves down rejoicing on deep couches of sweet rush and in the fresh-stripped vine-leaves. Many a poplar and elm murmured above our heads, and near at hand the sacred water from the cave of the Nymphs fell plashing. On the shady boughs the dusky cicadas were busy with their chatter, and the tree-frog far off cried in the dense thorn-brake. Larks and finches sang, the dove made moan, and bees flitted humming about the springs. All things were fragrant of rich harvest and fruit-time. Pears fell at our feet and apples at our side were rolling plentifully, and the branches hung down to the ground with the weight of sloes. And the four-year seal was loosened from the head of the wine-jars.

> … αὐτὰρ ἐγών τε καὶ Εὔκριτος ἐς Φρασιδάμω
> στραφθέντες χὠ καλὸς Ἀμύντιχος ἔν τε βαθείαις
> ἁδείας σχοίνοιο χαμευνίσιν ἐκλίνθημες
> ἔν τε νεοτμάτοισι γεγαθότες οἰναρέοισι.
> πολλαὶ δ᾽ ἄμμιν ὕπερθε κατὰ κρατὸς δονέοντο
> αἴγειροι πτελέαι τε· τὸ δ᾽ ἐγγύθεν ἱερὸν ὕδωρ
> Νυμφᾶν ἐξ ἄντροιο κατειβόμενον κελάρυζε …
> πάντ᾽ ὦσδεν θέρεος μάλα πίονος, ὦσδε δ᾽ ὀπώρας.

ὄχναι μὲν πὰρ ποσσί, παρὰ πλευραῖσι δὲ μᾶλα
δαψιλέως ἁμῖν ἐκυλίνδετο, τοὶ δ' ἐκέχυντο
ὄρπακες βραβίλοισι καταβρίθοντες ἔραζε·
τετράενες δὲ πίθων ἀπελύετο κρατὸς ἄλειφαρ·

The features of the pleasant place that become conventional in later literature include a spring of fresh water, trees for shade, the music of birds and insects, and a place to lie down.[13] What has gone unnoticed, however, is that in these lines there are indicators of another sort, too, indicators of the agricultural activities that permit the relaxation. Vine-leaves that were freshly stripped provide bedding on which the men recline (ἐκλίνθημες | ἔν τε νεοτμάτοισι γεγαθότες οἰναρέοισι, 133–134). These stripped leaves allude to the viticultural practice of removing leaves from vine-branches in order to allow a better ripening of the fruit, as noted by Gow.[14] The travellers take their rest also on 'deep couches of sweet rush' (ἔν τε βαθείας | ἁδείας σχοίνοιο χαμευνίσιν ἐκλίνθημες, 132–133), which evidently were harvested recently. In the summarizing sentence, 'all things were fragrant of rich harvest and fruit-time' (πάντ' ὦσδεν θέρεος μάλα πίονος, ὦσδε δ' ὀπώρας, 143), the word θέρος is technically the time of the summer harvest, while ὀπώρα denotes the time of gathering in the fruit-crop, as indicated also by the burdened pear-trees (144–146). The pleasant mood is enhanced by the opening of wine-jars (τετράενες δὲ πίθων ἀπελύετο κράτος ἄλειφαρ, 'men broke for us four-year-old seals from the mouths of their wine-jars', 147). Mention of the stored wine reflects the fact that viticulture was integral to the economy of the island, as Sherwin-White demonstrates in her history of Kos.[15]

Not only in the *locus amoenus* but also elsewhere in the poem we are reminded that rural labour supports the lives of the internal characters. Indeed, Jenkyns observes that Theocritus' 'herdsmen live and sing in the midst of nature, and they make their living from the land'.[16] Lycidas the goatherd has been making cheese, and he smells like the rennet used in setting the milk (7.13–16). For his skill in playing the pipe and singing Lycidas is compared to fellow herdsmen and reapers (νομεῦσιν | … τ' ἀματήρεσσι, 28–29). Mention of

13 In Greek verse, the earliest instance of the pleasance occurs in *Odyssey* 7.112–135 (the enclosed garden of the Phaeacian king Alcinous), in which work and leisure are expressed by the orchard (114–121), vineyard (122–126), herb garden (127–128), and the harvesting and crushing of grapes (124–125).

14 Gow 1950, 164 *ad* 134.

15 Sherwin-White (1978, 236–241). On the social, economic and political history of Kos in the Hellenistic era see Buraselis (2000). Archaeological evidence from the Levant, Cyprus and Egypt reveals that there was a considerable wine export industry during the Hellenistic period (see Johnsson 2004).

16 Jenkyns 1998, 51.

a villager's winepress (τινος ἀστῶν | λανόν, 24–25) anticipates a reference to Pteleatic wine in line 65, and to the already-noted wine-making in line 147. Thus it appears that rest and relaxation are observed in the midst of several autumn occupations.

This sense of integration of work and leisure in the countryside is corroborated by the broader temporal settings of the purple passage. The motif of the *locus amoenus* with which the poem begins (7–9) and ends (131–147) is situated within the time frame of the harvest: the spring of water, poplar and elm trees, and a shady precinct, features common to the pleasant place, are enjoyed during the Thalysia festival: 'for to Deo [Demeter] harvest-offerings are made by Phrasidamus and Antigenes' (τᾷ Δηοῖ γὰρ ἔτευχε θαλύσια καὶ Φρασίδαμος | κἀντιγένης, 3–4). When the reader is next reminded that the journey is to a harvest festival (31), the emphasis falls on the threshing-floor where plentiful grain has been gathered: 'for in full rich measure has the goddess piled their threshing-floor with grain' (μάλα γάρ σφισι πίονι μέτρῳ | ἁ δαίμων εὔκριθον ἀνεπλήρωσεν ἀλωάν, 33–34).[17] The threshing-floor that is used for winnowing (ἀλωά) anticipates the climactic ending of the poem, in which the enjoyment of leisure follows the completion of the task. The Thalysia is the subject of the final lines of the poem (155–158, text and trans. Gow):

> ... on her heap may I plant again the great winnowing-shovel while she smiles on us with sheaves and poppies in either hand.

> ... ἇς ἐπὶ σωρῷ
> αὖτις ἐγὼ πάξαιμι μέγα πτύον, ἃ δὲ γέλασσαι
> δράγματα καὶ μάκωνας ἐν ἀμφοτέραισιν ἔχοισα.

The remarkably happy and content mood of the men participating in the festival is effected by the intertwining of work and leisure.[18] In sum, the *locus amoenus* is not an unrealistic, escapist scene contrasted with the hardships of *ponos*, but rather incorporates that aspect of rural existence into a more holistic view of life in which work and leisure co-exist.[19] The regular order of the seasons provides the harmony in human experience; true *otium* resides in human concordance with the natural world.[20]

---

17 Trans. Gow 1950, adapted. Hunter (1999, 161 *ad Idyll* 7.34) points out that the rare adjective εὔκριθος, 'rich in grain', occurs elsewhere only in a farmer's prayer for a rich yield from his tilled field, in *Anth. Pal.* 6.258.6.

18 Hass 1998, 93.

19 The interrelationship between work (πόνος) and rest (ἀσυχία) finds expression also in the songs of Lycidas and Simichidas, as noted by Furusawa (1980, 10–11, 82–91).

20 Limitations of space prevent a discussion of the interrelations between work and leisure

3 Vergil, *Eclogue* 1

Next we shall consider Vergil, *Eclogue* 1. Here, too, the *locus amoenus* and *otium* are presented in pastoral settings, but this poem is charged with political and historical elements that portray them in the context of the troubled decade following the battle of Philippi in 42 BCE. Large tracts of land were expropriated by the victorious triumvirs and gifted to their soldiers as reward for their service. The poem consists of a dialogue between two rustic characters: one is Tityrus, a recently freed, aging rural slave, who remains on the land he has worked, while his less-fortunate friend, Meliboeus, is being driven from the confiscated lands.

With a nod towards *Idyll* 7, which is one of its models, *Eclogue* 1 commences and concludes similarly with a depiction of the *locus amoenus*.[21] The bookends indicate also that *otium* is an important topic in the poem. Imagery of relaxation and musical recreation associated with the pleasance begins the poem, which ends with the picture of a modest meal that completes the scene (Vergil, *Eclogue* 1.1–6; 80–81, text Fairclough-Goold):

> [MELIBOEUS:] Tityrus, here you are lying back under the shelter of a wide beech-tree, serenading the woodland spirit with your slender reed-pipe, while am leaving the boundaries of my land, the ploughed fields so dear to me. I'm being driven from my fatherland; you, Tityrus, can take it easy in the shade and teach the forest to echo 'Fair Amaryllis'.
> [TITYRUS:] Meliboeus, it is a god who brought about these conditions of leisure …
> …
> …
> [TITYRUS:] … here I have mellow apples, floury chestnuts, and a plentiful supply of cheese.

> [MELIBOEUS:] Tityre, tu patulae recubans sub tegmine fagi
> silvestrem tenui Musam meditaris avena;
> nos patriae finis et dulcia linquimus arva.

---

that are explored in *Idyll* 10 and 5. Hunt (2009, 395–397) argues that *Idyll* 10, in which the main characters are reapers, negotiates the relationship between the labour, ἐργασία, of the reapers with the leisure or ἀεργία enjoyed by the herdsmen in the *locus amoenus*. On realism and the *locus amoenus* in *Idyll* 5 see Crane (1988, 115).

21 On further allusions in the depiction of the *locus amoenus* in *Eclogue* 1 to *Idyll* 7.135–142 see Hubbard (1995, 44–45); on motifs of the pleasant place in the *Eclogues* and *Georgics* see, most recently, Armstrong (2019, 181–188).

> nos patriam fugimus; tu, Tityre, lentus in umbra
> formosam resonare doces Amaryllida silvas.
> [TITYRUS:] O Meliboee, deus nobis haec otia fecit.
> ...
> ...
> [TITYRUS:] ... sunt nobis mitia poma,
> Castaneae molles et pressi copia lactis ...

Whereas Tityrus is privileged to relax, Meliboeus is compelled to quit the land. The word *arva* in line 3 denotes fields that have been ploughed, and so introduces the topic of land that has been worked. Meanwhile, at the conclusion of the poem the words *pressi copia lactis* ('hand-pressed cheese', 81) hint at the rustic but rewarding task of cheese-making. A marker of the pastoral genre, cheese also is exemplary of the modest sustenance that animal husbandry provides.[22]

Throughout this eclogue the poet employs the technical language of farming and farm-work. Tityrus' socio-economic status is revealed by the un-poetic, technical term *peculium* in line 32; here it probably denotes property managed as his own by someone who does not own it.[23] Tityrus evidently is entitled to the *usufructus*, that is, to the produce, the use and profit made from something of the flock or herd that he tends.[24] He operates what appears to be a mixed farm on which he raised sheep (*agnus*, 7–8), pastured cattle (*meas errare boves*, 9–10), and cared for the plough-oxen that were used for tillage (*submitte tauros*, 45).[25] The apples ready for picking (37) may imply the presence of an orchard, while *arbusta* (39), which denotes plantations of (fruit-)trees implies further

22 Cheese-making is treated by Vergil in *Georgics* 3.394–406; see also Varro, *De Re Rustica* 2.11.3–6 and Columella, *De Re Rustica* 7.8. For the generic associations of cheese see Jaeger (2015).

23 The other terms denoting social and economic structures, such as *libertas* (27), *aere* (35), *servitio* (40), *miles* (70), *barbarus* (71) and *civis* (71), are interpreted by Jones (2011, 80–82) as 'difficult intrusions' into the bucolic world that contribute to the artificial nature of the genre. Skoie (2006, 320) argues that a more nuanced perspective perceives the social and economic interdependences of life in the country and that of the city.

24 Coleman (1977, 79 *ad* 31–32), referencing Varro *De Re Rustica* 1.2.17.

25 The recent study by Bowes et al. (2017, 170–199) of five archaeological sites of smallholders' farmlands in southern Tuscany active from the first century BCE to the first century CE has led to the conclusion that alternation (in available space or in time) of land-use between animal pasturage and cereal crops was not uncommon. Thus the depictions of the farms of Tityrus and Alfius (see below) as pursuing such 'convertible agriculture' may reflect actual practice.

labour of cultivation, pruning and harvesting.[26] Meanwhile, the vine-dresser (*frondator*, 56) is not far away.[27] Evidently Tityrus also processed cream-cheese, *pinguis … caseus* (34), to be sold at the *nundinae* or town markets (implied by *ingratae … urbi*, 34).[28] Thus, while compared to his own displacement Meliboeus depicts Tityrus as relaxing and playing music, it appears that the latter is responsible for several agro-pastoral duties.[29] In fact, it is striking that at the centre of the poem, the land that Tityrus is privileged to keep demands hard labour, as Meliboeus also points out (46–48):

> these lands will remain yours, and plenty large enough for you, even though bare rocks cover all, and the marsh covers your pastures with marshy reeds.

> tua rura manebunt,
> et tibi magna satis, quamvis lapis omnia nudus
> limosoque palus obducat pascua iunco.

It is remarkable that the farm of Tityrus, initially depicted as a pleasant place (1–2), here is described as land that requires clearing and draining; the place of leisure is also the place of labour.

From the perspective of the herdsman Meliboeus, who is forced by the land confiscations to remove his little flock from the owner's land, Tityrus' condition is favourable: true *otium* follows upon the security offered by the steady farm-work that Tityrus is permitted to pursue. Indeed, he may delight in his land, which Meliboeus further characterizes as a *locus amoenus* with its sacred springs, cool shade and sleep (*fontis sacros frigus … opacum* | … | *somnum*,

26 Similary Saunders (2008, 95): 'the topography of these poems also includes crops and harvests, orchards, vineyards, gardens, irrigated meadows and tilled lands'.

27 Like Tityrus, Meliboeus has been responsible for a variety of farm-tasks: growing grain (*aristas*, 69) and other crops (*segetes*, 71), ploughing fields (*culta novalia*, 70; cf. *agros*, 72), grafting pear trees (*insere … piros*, 73) and tending to the vines (*pone ordine vitis*, 73). Now, however, he is left only with goats (12, 77).

28 The importance of small- and medium-scale intensive mixed farming for the agricultural economy of late-republican and early Augustan Italy has been demonstrated recently by Kron (2017, 112–140). Skydsgaard (1978) discusses the free rural population as a labour force in Italy of the first century BCE. On the economic importance of rural markets (*nundinae*) and fairs (*mercatus*) of the period see Andreau (2001, 113–129).

29 Similarly Armstrong (2019, 178): 'the emphasis on practicalities—the quality of the land, the pruning, and even the existence of boundary hedges—shows that his is not a setting of pure *otium*, but of a mixture between work and leisure'.

52–55). Yet even in that depiction Tityrus' restful sleep is effected by the labour-intensive work of bee-keeping that is implied by the humming of his bees (53–55):

> the Hyblaean bees sip from the blossoms of the willow row, and their soft buzzing often will induce you to sleep
>
> Ab limite saepes
> Hyblaeis apibus florem depasta salicti
> saepe levi somnum suadebit inire susurro

By thus mingling features of the georgic and the bucolic worlds, the poet articulates the relationship between rural work and play. In the words of Davis, 'Vergil employs the bucolic apparatus partly as a means of exploring philosophical issues relating to the subject of human felicity (*eudaimonia*)'.[30] When thus read in light of the interconnectedess of *otium* and *labor*, this poem illustrates that for Tityrus, the small-scale farmer, genuine contentment comes with the security afforded by self-sustaining work.

The theme of contentment in the interrelationship of work and leisure culminates in the final lines of the poem, in which the scene of the pleasant place is completed with the rustic repast of apples, chestnuts and cheese that Tityrus offers to Meliboeus. As the 'plentiful supply of cheese' (*pressi copia lactis*, 81) recalls the 'cream cheese' (*pinguis … caseus*, 34) that Tityrus sought to market, the meal evidently consists of foods that were processed or produced by Tityrus himself, thus reinforcing the sense of rural self-sufficiency. In Epicurean thought such modest meals strengthened one for 'the necessary undertakings of life' (τὰς ἀναγκαίας τοῦ βίου), as Epicurus puts it in the *Letter to Menoeceus* (131).[31] Thus Tityrus' αὐταρκεία (self-sufficiency) and ἀταραξία (equanimity) amidst the challenges of life allow him to experience his farm as a pleasant place.[32]

30 Davis 2012, 1.

31 Davis (2004, 79–83) points out that 'the details of the menu resonate with nontrivial Epicurean notions regarding the philosophical benefits of habitually plain fare'. The possible connections between *Eclogue* 1 and the Epistle to Menoeceus is discussed by Davis (2004, 65–66; 2012, 34–36).

32 Thus also Rundin (2003, 161). Allusions to Lucretius' *De Rerum Natura* have been noted at the start (*sub tegmine fagi*, 1) and finish (*altis de montibus*, 83) of *Eclogue* 1 (Clausen 1994, 34–35, 60). For Epicureanism in *Eclogue* 1 see Davis (2004, and 2012, 17–39), and in Vergil's oeuvre generally see Gigante (2004, 85–99).

4 Horace, *Epode* 2

Epode 2 of Horace is a poem that praises life in the country, away from the city and urban business; it celebrates life on the land and the enjoyment of the gifts that come with every season of spring, summer, autumn and winter. The poem begins with a wish for a simpler life like that in former times, free from the obligations of finance, warfare, overseas travel, and social standing (1–8). The poet-narrator, the assumed speaker, reveals knowledge of the countryside and farming activities according to each season (9–48, 61–66), and professes a taste for foods not imported but locally grown (49–60). A seemingly genuine expression of love for rural life by Horace himself, the poem shifts suddenly towards the end to reveal that the speaker is actually a certain money-lender (*faenerator*) named Alfius (67).[33] On second reading, the reader grasps that Alfius' perception of country life is distorted, dominated by repose and leisure as imagined in a *locus amoenus* (23–28). However, when the realities of rural work dawn upon Alfius as he reviews the farmer's responsibilities, and as he comes to understand that the idealized relaxation and leisure cannot be obtained without labour, he relinquishes his dream of life in the country and returns to his normal business of lending money at interest (67–70).

In this poem Horace employs the character of Alfius to advance a retrospective understanding that the leisure afforded by a rural lifestyle requires labour, and that real happiness arises from an understanding of their mutual relationship. He does so by exploring the tension that is inherent in the language of labour and rest and thus advances the conviction that rural work and leisure are inseparably intertwined. The key intertexts for *Epode* 2 are especially the *loci amoeni* in Vergil's *Eclogues* and *Georgics* (and Lucretius' *De Rerum Natura*), and the poem develops generic interplay between pastoral, georgic and philosophical poetry to articulate the interconnectedness of work and leisure.[34]

The money-lender Alfius initially pictures himself as a smallholder, a farmer who possesses an inherited acreage and together with his frugal wife enjoys the simple pleasures of life in the country.[35] He associates that life only with

33 Indeed, Fraenkel (1966, 60) reads the praise as 'a fundamentally true, if slightly idealizing, expression of Horace's own, nostalgic longing for the life of the country-side'.

34 On the relative chronology of *Epode* 2 and the *Georgics* see Pieri (1972) and, more recently, Watson (2003, 76–77).

35 It is noteworthy that by the end of his revery Alfius' self-depiction has changed him into a wealthy farmer with a household of slaves: *positosque vernas, ditis examen domus*, 'homebred slaves (the swarm of a rich house)' (65–66, trans. Rudd). In fact, as Cairns (1975,

otium, as is shown by the repeated emphasis upon sleep in his depiction of the pleasant place (23–28, text and trans. Rudd):

> It is a delight to lie under an old holm oak, or in the clinging grass; meanwhile the streams glide between their steep banks, birds twitter in the trees, springs burble as their water gushes forth—sounds that induce a pleasant nap.

> Libet iacere modo sub antiqua ilice,
> modo in tenaci gramine:
> labuntur altis interim ripis aquae
> queruntur in silvis aves,
> fontesque lymphis obstrepunt manantibus,
> somnos quod invitet levis.

Alfius' misconception is evident already in the opening lines of the poem (1–2, text and trans. Rudd):

> happy the man who, far from business concerns,
> works his ancestral acres with his oxen
> like the men of old, free from every kind of debt ....

> Beatus ille, qui procul negotiis,
> ut prisca gens mortalium
> paterna rura bobus exercet suis,
> solutus omni faenore ...

The word *negotiis*, 'business concerns', evokes associations of urban commerce and trade, and conveys Alfius' wish to be free of his normal practice of usury; however, the word may denote work of any sort, including rural labour, so that Alfius naively imagines that rural life is generally free of work.[36] Similarly, a double meaning may be at play in the word *exercet*, which though not uncommonly used of farm work, in Alfius' mouth may have the special sense of deriving financial profit, so that he does not picture himself labouring as

87) observes, 'Alfius speaks of the farmer as free of debt (4); he believes that everything comes the farmer's way easily, herds, fruit, grapes, honey (9ff.) and banquets that he does not have to pay for (48) ...'

36 Mankin 1995, 65.

a farmer but simply reaping the benefits of being one.[37] Alfius imagines himself not as actively herding his flock, but, as if relaxing in a pleasant place, 'in a secluded valley he watches his lowing herd as they wander about' (text and trans. Rudd, *in reducta valle mugientium | prospectat errantis greges*, 11–12). It is apparent that Alfius has no appreciation for the labour involved in operating a farm.[38] When he does speak of labour, Alfius ascribes it to his industrious wife (39–48), who, sunburnt from the hours spent working outdoors (45–48, text and trans. Rudd),

> shuts up the teeming animals in wattle pens, drained their bulging udders, ladled this year's wine from a fragrant jar, and served a home-grown supper.

> claudensque textis cratibus laetum pecus
> distenta siccet ubera,
> et horna dulci vina promens dolio
> dapes inemptas apparet.

As for himself, Alfius deems it a 'joy' (*iuvat*, 61) 'to watch the sheep hurrying home from pasture' (*ovis | videre properantis domum*, 61–62) and to 'watch the oxen tired from dragging the curved plough' (*videre fessos vomerem inversum boves ... trahentis*, 63–64), probably driven by the slaves to whom Alfius next turns his thoughts (65).

The depiction of the *locus amoenus* in lines 23–28 occurs in the midst of a list of tasks that pertain to each of the four seasons (lines 9–36).[39] Horace loosely follows the calendral instructions of Cato, Varro and Columella for farm chores appropriate to spring and summer (9–16), autumn (17–22) and winter (29–36). Thus we read that the tasks of spring and summer include arboriculture (9–10), pasturing (11–12, in which the 'wandering flocks', *errantis greges*, may refer to the supervised open-field pasturing of the cattle), *putatio* (pruning, 13) and *insitio* (grafting, 14), as well as *mellatio* (gathering honey, 15) and *tonsura* (sheep-shearing, 16). Autumn is marked by harvesting fruit, including pears and grapes (17–20), while the winter season provides the time for hunting boars and for

37 *OLD* s.v. *exerceo* 6.

38 Alfius' romanticized image of country life is reinforced by the absence of references to the social, economic and political circumstances of the 40s and 30s BCE, as Watson (2003, 81–82) observes.

39 On the tasks appropriate to each season see Heyworth (1988), Mankin (1995, 68) and Watson (2003, 92 *ad* 9–22).

catching thrushes, hare and crane (29–36).[40] In having Alfius thus enumerate the seasonal chores, the poet infuses the money-lender's romanticized perception of country life with a sense of tension between idyllic leisure, as expressed especially in the *locus amoenus*, and the labour that necessarily attends and permits true happiness.

The interrelationship between work and leisure that Horace, like Theocritus and Vergil, expresses as integral to genuine *eudaimonia* is reinforced by means of allusions to a similar social commentary in a passage of the *Georgics*. In *Georgics* 4.116–148 Vergil offers a vignette of an old farmer living in the fields around Tarentum, 'who worked a few acres of unclaimed land' (*cui pauca relicti | iugera ruris erant*, 4.127–128).[41] Though the land he worked was poor, 'not fertile enough for ploughing, not ideal for pasturing a herd, nor well-suited for ploughing or for growing vines' (*nec fertilis illa iuvencis | nec pecori opportuna seges nec commoda Baccho*, 4.128–129), and though it was 'among the brambles' (*in dumis*, 4.130) that he planted his vegetables, in 'happiness of soul he was as fortunate as a king' (*regum aequabat opes animis*, 4.132). Despite the labour required by the less-than-ideal soil, the farmer lived contentedly on the sustenance that each season provided. In spring he was the first to gather roses, and in autumn, apples (4.134); in late winter he was already clipping hyacinths (4.137). The bees provided an abundance of honey (4.139–141) and the fruit trees offered a harvest of fruits (4.142–143).[42] By carefully integrating the role of labour within a portrayal of nature's near-spontaneous production of sustenance, Vergil's depiction of the old man's way of living 'self-consciously treads the boundaries between the world of labour and the life of ease of the *locus amoenus* …'.[43]

By means of the allusions to the vignette of the old farmer of Tarentum in *Georgics* 4 Horace introduces in Alfius' romanticized depiction of life in the countryside an undertone of genuine happiness that comes with the coalescence of work and leisure—a coalescence that Alfius fails to appreciate. Thus, as the element of labour associated with the contentment of the farmer dawns

40 Regarding the farmer's tasks in winter Watson (2003, 103 *ad* 29–36) observes that it is '… a notably one-sided and self-indulgent account, mentioning only one activity of the season, hunting, and a pleasurable one at that'.

41 The phrase *promens … | dapes inemptas* in *Epode* 2.47–48 alludes to *dapibus mensas onerabat inemptis* in *Georgics* 4.133. On other allusions and the relative chronology of the two passages see Mankin (1995, 81–82 *ad Epode* 2.48) and Thomas (1988, 172 *ad Georgics* 4.133).

42 On the influence of Varro's *De Re Rustica* on Vergil (esp. in the *Georgics*) see Farrell (1999, 156 n. 35); see also Kronenberg (2009, 149–155). On the *autarkeia* of the old farmer see Gigante (2004, 94–95).

43 Armstrong 2019, 185.

upon Alfius, he abruptly rejects the countryside and returns, perhaps not altogether surprisingly, to his normal city business of usury (2.67–70, text and trans. Rudd 2004, 275):[44]

> After these remarks, the money-lender Alfius,
> just on the very point of becoming a countryman,
> called in all his money on the Ides, intending to
> put it out again on the Kalends.
>
> Haec ubi locutus faenerator Alfius,
> iam iam futurus rusticus, omnem
> redegit Idibus pecuniam,
> quaerit Kalendis ponere.

This sudden shift at the end of the poem may be explained by Alfius' growing realization that he is not prepared to accept that *labor* is a prerequisite for *otium*.[45] The poet-narrator, meanwhile, has cleverly advanced the notion that true human happiness comes not with idle leisure but in harmony with labour in its proper time.

5 Conclusion

In this chapter I have sought to apply the findings of recent research in the social history of rural labour in antiquity, classical eco-criticism and philosophical dimensions to ancient Greco-Roman perspectives on the nature of the relationship between work and leisure, as expressed in Theocritus' *Idyll* 7, Vergil's *Eclogue* 1 and Horace's *Epode* 2. By reading these poems through a social-historical lens, one gains a greater awareness of the economic, social and psychological realities they relate, and of the ways in which each poem negotiates the universal tension between labour and rest. The concurrent application of an eco-critical interpretation to these poems effects the understanding

---

44 Cipriani (1980, 60–63) argues that the portrayal of Alfius reflects a tension among wealthy Romans between land-holding and farming, and that the poem relates to Caesar's *lex Iulia de modo credendi possidendique intra Italiam*, by which money-lenders were required to purchase land in proportion to their wealth.

45 Watson (2003, 80): 'Critics have often noted the disconcerting lopsidedness of the picture which the poem offers of country life, in that its pleasures are disproportionally stressed, whereas the disagreeable or laborious aspects of the farmer's existence … receive scarcely a mention.'

that the rural working world they portray is not purely artificial or contrived, but reflects to some extent the lived experience of the time. By invoking the realities of pastoral and agricultural industries, these poems express an understanding of the position of humankind in its natural, rural environment, and in relation to the animals and plants that also live in it. A consideration of the philosophical dimension of these poems, meanwhile, increases one's appreciation for the shared purpose in these poems to define human happiness and the means to achieve it. In employing the literary figure of the *locus amoenus* in pastoral contexts as the place of human felicity, Theocritus, Vergil and Horace explore the essence of genuine contentment in work and leisure. *Idyll* 7, *Eclogue* 1 and *Epode* 2 share the goal of advancing the notion that true satisfaction with one's lot is acquired through a proper understanding of the relationship between labour and rest. Thus, each of these poems exposes the correspondences between happiness imagined in a rural setting and hard physical labour of rural workers. In so doing, Theocritus, Vergil and Horace promote the notion that contentment arises not in the opposition of *labor* and *otium* but in their interconnectedness.

More importantly, perhaps, unlike the three writers of pre-industrial Greece and Rome, modern readers and critics of Theocritus, Vergil and Horace may have imposed on the work-leisure relationship an assumed contrast and opposition that may not have existed as sharply in the ancient mind. The pastoral *locus amoenus* presents a paradigm in which work and leisure are shown to be integrated and co-dependent. Such appreciation of the pastoral discourse on *labor* and *otium* not only revises our evaluation of the georgic and bucolic elements in the genre, but also increases our sense of the broader social and cultural perspectives on rural work.

Bibliography

Andreau, J. (2001). Markets, Fairs and Monetary Loans. In: P. Cartledge, E. Cohen and L. Foxhall, eds., *Money, Labour and Land. Approaches to the Economics of Ancient Greece*. London, pp. 297–325.

Armstrong, D., Fish, J., Johnston, P.A. and Skinner, M.B., eds. (2004). *Vergil, Philodemus, and the Augustans*. Austin.

Armstrong, R. (2019). *Vergil's Green Thoughts. Plants, Humans, and the Divine*. Oxford.

Berger, H. (1984). The Origins of Bucolic Representation: Disenchantment and Revision in Theocritus' Seventh *Idyll*. *Classical Antiquity* 3(1), pp. 1–39.

Billault, A. (2008). Theocrite et Platon: Remarques sur *l'Idylle* VII. *Revue des Études Grecques* 121(2), pp. 497–514.

Bowes, K., Mercuri, A.M., Rattigheri, E., Rinaldi, R., Arnoldus-Huyzendveld, A., Ghisleni, M., Grey, C., MacKinnon, M. and Vaccaro, E. (2017). Peasant Agricultural Strategies in Southern Tuscany: Convertible Agriculture and the Importance of Pasture. In: T.C.A. de Haas and G.W. Tol, G.W., eds., *The Economic Integration of Roman Italy. Rural Communities in a Globalizing World*. Leiden–Boston, pp. 170–199.

Bowman, A. and Wilson, A., eds. (2013). *The Roman Agricultural Economy. Organization, Investment, and Production*. Oxford.

Buraselis, K. (2000). *Kos Between Hellenism and Rome*. Philadelphia.

Cairns, F. (1975). Horace, *Epode* 2, Tibullus I, 1 and Rhetorical Praise of the Countryside. *Museum Philologium Londiniense* 1, pp. 79–91.

Chambert, R. (2004). Vergil's Epicureanism in his Early Poems. In: D. Armstrong et al., eds., *Vergil, Philodemus, and the Augustans*. Austin, pp. 43–60.

Cipriani, G. (1980). *Letteratura geórgica e investimento fondiario alla fine del 1⁰ Sec. a. c. Orazio, Epod.* 2. Bari.

Clausen, W. (1994). *Virgil. Eclogues*. Oxford.

Coleman, R. (1977). *Virgil. Eclogues*. Cambridge.

Crane, G. (1988). Realism in the Fifth Idyll of Theocritus. *Transactions and Proceedings of the American Philological Association* 118, pp. 107–122.

Curtius, E.R. (1963). *European Literature and the Latin Middle Ages*. Trans. W.R. Trask. New York. [= Curtius, E.R. (1948). *Europaïsche Literatur und lateinisches Mittelalter*. Bern–Munich.]

Davis, G. (2004). Consolation in the Bucolic Mode: The Epicurean Cadence of Vergil's First *Eclogue*. In: D. Armstrong, ed., *Vergil, Philodemus, and the Augustans*. Austin, pp. 63–74.

Davis, G. (2012). Parthenope: *The Interplay of Ideas in Vergilian Bucolic*. Leiden–Boston.

De Haas, T.C.A. and Tol, G.W., eds. (2017). *The Economic Integration of Roman Italy. Rural Communities in a Globalizing World*. Leiden–Boston.

Dyson, S.L. (2011). The Family and the Roman Countryside. In: B. Rawson, ed., *A Companion to Families in the Greek and Roman Worlds*. Malden, MA, pp. 431–444.

Edwards, A.T. (1993). Homer's Ethical Geography: Country and City in the *Odyssey*. *Transactions of the American Philological Association* 123, pp. 27–78.

Fairclough, H.R. (1916). *Virgil, 1. Eclogues, Georgics, Aeneid I–VI*. Revised by G.P. Goold (1999). Loeb Classical Library 63. Cambridge, MA.

Fantuzzi, M. and Papanghelis, T., eds. (2006). *Brill's Companion to Greek and Latin Pastoral*. Leiden/Boston.

Farrell, J. (1999). *Vergil's Georgics and the Traditions of Ancient Epic: the Art of Allusion in Literary History*. New York.

Fraenkel, E. (1966). *Horace*. Oxford.

Furusawa, Y. (1980). *Eros und Seelenruhe in den Thalysien Theokrits*. Würtzburg.

Garnsey, P. (1980). Non-Slave Labor in the Roman World. In: P. Garnsey, ed., *Non-Slave Labour in the Greco-Roman World*. Cambridge, pp. 34–47.

Garnsey, P., ed. (1980). *Non-Slave Labour in the Greco-Roman World.* Cambridge.

Gifford, T. (2006). Post-Pastoral as a Tool for Ecocriticism. In: M. Skoie and S. Bjørnstad Velázquez, eds., *Pastoral and the Humanities. Arcadia Re-inscribed.* London, pp. 14–24.

Gifford, T. (2017). The Environmental Humanities and the Pastoral Tradition. In: C. Schliephake, ed., *Ecocriticism, Ecology and the Cultures of Antiquity*. Lanham, pp. 297–325.

Gigante, M. (2004). Vergil in the Shadow of Vesuvius. In: D. Armstrong, J. Fish, P.A. Johnston and M. Skinner, eds., *Vergil, Philodemus, and the Augustans.* Austin, pp. 85–99.

Gow, A.S.F. (1950). *Theocritus. Edited with a Translation and a Commentary.* Vol. 1. Introduction, Text and Translation. Vol. 2. Commentary, Appendix, Indexes, and Plates. Cambridge.

Gutzwiller, K. (2006). The Herdsman in Greek Thought. In: M. Fantuzzi and T. Papanhelis, eds., *Brill's Companion to Greek and Latin Pastoral.* Leiden–Boston, pp. 1–23.

Hass, P. (1998). *Der* Locus Amoenus *in der antiken Literatur: zu Theorie und Geschichte eines literarischen Motivs.* Bamberg.

Heyworth, S.J. (1988). Horace's Second Epode. *American Journal of Philology* 109(1), pp. 71–85.

Hubbard, T.K. (1995). Allusive Artistry and Vergil's Revisionary Program: *Eclogues* 1–3. *Materiali e Discussioni* 34, pp. 37–67.

Hunt, J.M. (2009). Bucolic Experimentation in Theocritus' *Idyll* 10. *Greek, Roman, and Byzantine Studies* 49(3), pp. 391–412.

Hunter, R.L. (1999). *Theocritus. A Selection.* Cambridge.

Jaeger, M. (2015). Why Is There No Cheese in Horace's Satires? And Related Questions for Vergil and Varro. *American Journal of Philology* 136(1), pp. 63–90.

Jenkyns, R. (1989). Virgil and Arcadia. *Journal of Roman Studies* 79, pp. 26–39.

Jenkyns, R. (1998). *Virgil's Experience. Nature and History. Times, Names, and Places.* Oxford.

Johnsson, H. (2004). The Export of Koan Wine to the South-Eastern Mediterranean Area during the Hellenistic Period. In: K. Höghammar, ed., *The Hellenistic Polis of Kos. State, Economy and Culture.* Uppsala, pp. 131–151.

Jones, C. (1984). *The Transformation of the 'Locus Amoenus' in Roman Poetry.* Diss. University of California, Berkeley.

Jones, F. (2011). *Virgil's Garden. The Nature of Bucolic Space.* London.

Kron, G. (2017). The Diversification and Intensification of Italian Agriculture: The Complementary Roles of the Small and Wealthy Farmer. In: T.C.A. de Haas and G.W. Tol, eds., *The Economic Integration of Roman Italy. Rural Communities in a Globalizing World.* Leiden–Boston, pp. 112–140.

Kronenberg, L. (2009). *Allegories of Farming from Greece to Rome. Philosophical Satire in Xenophon, Varro, and Virgil.* Cambridge.

Lindo, L.I. (1968). Horace's Second Epode. *Classical Philology* 63(3), pp. 206–208.

Mankin, D. (1995). *Horace Epodes*. Cambridge Greek and Latin Classics. Cambridge.

Marcone, A. (2016). *Storia del Lavoro in Italia. L'età Romana. Liberi, semiliberi e schiavi in una società moderna*. Rome.

Newlands, C. (1984). *The Transformation of the 'Locus Amoenus' in Roman Poetry*. Diss. University of California, Berkeley.

Payne, M. (2007). *Theocritus and the Invention of Fiction*. Cambridge.

Payne, M. (2010). The Bucolic Fiction of Theocritus. In: J.J. Clauss and M. Cuypers, eds., *A Companion to Hellenistic Literature*. Oxford, pp. 224–237.

Pieri, A. (1972). L'Epodo 2 di Orazio e le *Georgiche*. *Studi Italiani di Filologia Classica* 44, pp. 244–266.

Rudd, N. (2004). *Horace. Odes and Epodes*. Loeb Classical Library 33. Cambridge, MA.

Rundin, J. (2003). The Epicurean Morality of Vergil's 'Bucolics'. *Classical World* 96(2), pp. 159–176.

Salvatore, A. (1995). *Vergilio e Pseudovergilio. Studi su l'Appendix*. Naples.

Saunders, T. (2006). 'Using Green Words' or 'Abusing Bucolic Ground'. In: M. Skoie and S. Bjørnstad Velázquez, eds., *Pastoral and the Humanities. Arcadia Re-inscribed*. London, pp. 3–13.

Saunders, T. (2008). *Bucolic Ecology. Vergil's* Eclogues *and the Environmental Literary Tradition*. London.

Schliephake, C., ed. (2017). *Ecocriticism, Ecology and the Cultures of Antiquity*. Lanham.

Schmidt, E.A. (1998). Ancient Bucolic Poetry and Later Pastoral Writing: Systematic and Historical Reflections. *International Journal of the Classical Tradition* 5(2), pp. 226–251.

Schmidt, E.A. (2008). Arcadia: Modern Occident and Classical Antiquity. In: K. Volk, ed., *Oxford Readings in Classical Studies. Vergil's Eclogues*. Oxford, pp. 16–47.

Scholten, H. (2006). Die kulturelle Bewertung körplerlicher Arbeit in der Gedichten Theokrits. In: D. Dormeyer, F. Siegert and J.C. de Vos, eds., *Arbeit in der Antike, in Judentum und Christentum*. Berlin, pp. 66–85.

Schönbeck, G. (1962). *Der* locus amoenus *von Homer bis Horaz*. Diss. Heidelberg.

Sherwin-White, S. (1978). *Ancient Cos*. Göttingen.

Skoie, M. (2006). City and Countryside in Vergil's *Eclogues*. In: R.M. Rosen and I. Sluiter, eds., *City, Countryside, and the Spatial Organization of Value in Classical Antiquity*. Leiden–Boston, pp. 297–325.

Skydsgaard, J.E. (1980). Non-Slave Labour in Rural Italy during the Late Republic. In: P. Garnsey, ed., *Non-Slave Labour in the Greco-Roman World*. Cambridge, pp. 65–72.

Snell, B. (1953). *The Discovery of the Mind in Greek Philosophy and Literature*. Trans. T.G. Rosenmeyer. Oxford.

Thesleff, H. (1981). Man and *locus amoenus* in Early Greek Poetry. In: G. Kurz, D. Müller and W. Nicolai, eds., *Gnomosyne, Menschliches Denken und Handeln in frühgriechischen Literatur*. Festschrift für Walter Marg zum 70. Geburtstag. Munich, pp. 31–45.

Thibodeau, P. (2011). *Playing the Farmer. Representations of Rural Life in Vergil's* Georgics. Berkeley.

Verboven, K. (2014). Attitudes to Work and Workers in Classical Greece and Rome. *Tijdschrift voor Sociale en Economische Geschiedenis*, pp. 67–87.

Verboven, K. and Laes, C., eds. (2017). *Work, Labour and Professions in the Roman World*. Leiden–Boston.

Volk, K. (2008). *Introduction. Scholarly Approaches to the* Eclogues *since the 1970's*. In: K. Volk, ed., *Vergil's Eclogues*. Oxford, pp. 1–16.

Watson, L.C. (2003). *A Commentary on Horace's Epodes*. Oxford.

Welch, T. (2008). Horace's Journey Through Arcadia. *Transactions of the American Philological Association* 138, pp. 47–74.

CHAPTER 12

Work Underfoot: The Rustic 'Calendar' Mosaic of Saint-Romain-en-Gal

Nicole G. Brown

1 A 'Calendar' Mosaic?

First discovered in 1891, the so-called 'Rustic Calendar Mosaic of Saint-Romain-en-Gal' is one of the most complete and striking representations of agricultural labour to have survived from antiquity, and it is also by far the most visually complex (Fig. 12.1). Originally a rectangular pavement measuring 4.48 × 8.86 m, it consisted of 40 figural panels of equal size (59 × 59 cm)—of which 27, more than half, totally or partially remain—set within a grid of interlocking bands of guilloche and surrounded by a border of entwined vines. While the mosaic is now housed just outside Paris, it emerged from the quarter of ancient Vienne in south-eastern France (Gallia Narbonensis) which lay on the right bank of the river Rhone, where it most likely belonged to a wealthy townhouse (*domus*), probably adorning a dining room (*triclinium*). Based on its style, as well as the eventual abandonment of this site, it is usually dated to the first quarter of the third century CE.[1]

The organization and order of the 40 panels is not as easy to comprehend as their grid-like arrangement first suggests. Although we know all too little about its original context, the report of its discovery indicates that the room to which this mosaic belonged was entered from the north, so that a viewer entering the room passed first over a border row consisting of four panels, each depicting a head in combination with various floral and vegetal attributes (appearing along the bottom edge in Figure 1).[2] The original centre of the composition was formed by another four panels, each depicting a seasonal per-

1 The mosaic was first published by Lafaye 1892, who attributed the mosaic to a public building, perhaps a temple, based on a comparison with the Roman predilection for erecting monumental *fasti* in public: see below. Other essential discussions include Lancha 1981, 208–225, cat. nº 368; Stern 1981, 445–449; Parrish 1992, 491; Balmelle and Darmon 2017, 186–191; and Parodo 2017, 50–54, cat. nº A.9, who emphasizes the likely *triclinium* setting (50). For the urban character of this quarter of Vienne: Le Glay 1970, 176–181.

2 Lafaye 1892, 324, noting the discovery of the threshold slab still in situ.

 | DOI:10.1163/9789004694965_013

FIGURE 12.1 Mosaic from Saint-Romain-en-Gal, 200–225 CE, surviving portion 4.34 × 5.66 m. Musée d'archéologie nationale, Saint-Germain-en-Laye. Four seasonal personifications at center. Winter, panels 1–7; Spring, panels 8–14; Summer, panels 15–21; Autumn, panels 22–28. Mosaic is oriented with S to the top, N at the bottom.

PHOTO: © ART RESOURCE, NY, PHOTOGRAPHER MICHEL URTADO

sonification. Arranged in two pairs oriented in opposite directions, as are the panels within each pair, their dispositions took the physical setting of the building into account. Thus, facing to the north, appropriate for these cold seasons, Winter—represented by a small old woman hunched in a blue cloak, perched on the back of a wild boar—is placed back-to-back with Autumn, a *putto* holding a basket of grapes, naked except for his cloak, astride a tiger. Facing the opposite end of the room are the panels depicting Summer and Spring, each represented by another *putto*, the former riding a lion, holding a wreath of wheat ears and a sickle, the latter astride a bull and holding a stick and a basket of flowers.[3]

Around these central emblemata, another 28 panels—with seven panels allotted for each of the four seasons—are arranged in an elaborate sequence, assuming the pattern on the complete northern end (winter and autumn) was mirrored by the mosaic's missing other half. Beginning with winter, three panels proceed outward (i.e., to the north) from the central personification, before turning the corner for an additional four winter scenes along the pavement's long eastern side (panels 1–7). These are immediately followed, without any obvious mark of separation, by four spring scenes, before the remaining three panels of this season round the southeast corner, this time to *conclude* with the central personification (panels 8–14). Summer then begins, like winter, with three panels moving outward from the centre of the composition, before turning the southwest corner and continuing along the western side (panels 15–21), and giving way to the autumn panels, which eventually wind their way back to centre (panels 22–28). Of these 20 remaining scenes, the great majority are devoted to depictions of agricultural labour, covering a wide array of tasks, from ploughing, sowing and harvesting, to baking bread, preparing storage containers, and carrying manure to spread on the fields (Table 1).[4]

On the one hand, it seems to correct to classify this mosaic among the corpus of more than 20 calendar images, spanning from the first century BCE to the fourth century CE, to survive from the western part of the empire. In fact, direct comparisons with the *menologia rustica*, a type of calendar devoted to the activities and attributes of each month pertaining specifically to agriculture, have proven especially useful for identifying certain specific scenes on

3 Iconography of these personified seasons: Abad Casal 1990a, 520, 523 and 1990b, 896, 910.

4 These identifications follow the standard account beginning with Lafaye 1892, and refined by Stern 1953, 205–207 and 1981, 445–449, Picard 1974 (sacrifice to Jupiter panel), and Pelletier 1975 (viticulture and oleoculture panels); cf. Lancha 1981, 208–225, Calcani 1993, 79–89, and Parodo 2017, 51–54.

TABLE 12.1 Proportion of labour to non-labour scenes, Mosaic from Saint-Romain-en-Gal

Season	Panels surviving	Labor scenes	Other seasonal activities
Winter	7	5 (Planting the Beans; Grinding Grain; Transport of Manure; Baking of Bread; and Reed Harvesting / Basket Weaving)	2 (Offering to the Lares; Parentalia)
Spring	2	1 (Grafting Trees)	1 (Return of the Swans)
Summer	3	1 (Gathering Wood / Cleaning the Fields)	2 (Offering to Jupiter/ Taranis; Athletic competition)
Autumn	7	7 (Gathering Apples; Harvesting Grapes; Pressing the Grapes; Seed Sowing / Plowing; Pitching the Storage Vessels; Harvesting Olives; and Pressing the Olives)	0

our mosaic.[5] On the other hand, various factors—including its large size and the revolving arrangement of the panels, requiring the viewer to walk around the room in order to fully comprehend the sequence, together with the lack of any identifying legends—all invite the question to what extent the designation 'calendar' is actually helpful.

Indeed, as recent work on ancient calendars has shown, systems of reckoning time were never concerned purely with information, but invariably had an ideological dimension as well. Thus, for instance, Julius Caesar's famous reformation of the calendar in 45 BCE, based on the solar rather than lunar year, reasserted control over the natural cycle, and, by replacing other time meas-

5 The corpus includes 14 calendar mosaics, three frescos, two reliefs and the codex-calendar of 354: Stern 1981, Huet 2011 and 2021, Parrodo 2017. Early approaches to visual representations of the seasons and months were largely concerned with their iconographic motifs and sources: e.g., Riegl 1890, Strzygowski 1888, Webster 1938, Levi 1941.

uring systems, broadcast Rome's political hegemony throughout its imperial holdings.[6] By the same token, a monumental bronze calendar from the late second century CE discovered in Coligny (south-eastern France) has been seen both to mimic the Roman practice of erecting monumental *fasti* in public and simultaneously, by employing the Celtic language and a lunar year firmly out of sync with the Julian calendar, to resist Roman hegemony.[7] Similarly, the display of calendars in private settings, namely houses, was also likely to have an ideological dimension—even when they depicted such apparently mundane tasks as the carrying of manure or the weaving of baskets. A parallel trend in the scholarship on Roman agronomists, the other main body of evidence to which our mosaic is often compared, convincingly demonstrates that their texts—much like calendars—should not be read as merely 'technical', 'informational', or 'scientific', but that they were an important form of elite self-fashioning and literary production.[8]

Looking beyond the modern tendency to regard this mosaic as a sort of illustrated farmer's almanac, we can begin to ask new questions about how this composition may have appealed to the owner(s) of this *domus* as a particular style of self-presentation, and one that offered viewers a cognitive—and perhaps even physical—experience, distinct from but akin to other types of domestic decoration. Recent approaches, for example, by applying the concept of 'taskscape' to agricultural mosaics like ours, reveal how the realities of the labour required to support the luxurious lifestyles of the elite were deliberately concealed by certain visual strategies, including the depiction of anonymous workers contentedly employed in a task, or the reduction of complex agricultural processes to single actions.[9] Even as some labour was concealed by individual scenes, however, the mosaic as a whole seems to have been especially concerned with making agricultural labour visible, based not least on the high

6 Feeney 2007.

7 Stern 2012, 303–313; cf. Stern 2017. See also Russell 2019 who analyses the Fasti Capitolini (not a calendar, but lists of triumphators and consuls) as a visual object, presenting an image of the senate as a unified group and exemplar of a properly functioning *res publica*, aimed in part at Augustus. On the calendar specifically as a form of information technology, emphasizing its limitations and rejection of tabulation: Riggsby 2019, 54–82.

8 This specific mosaic's generic relationship to the agronomists: e.g., Balmelle and Darmon 2017, 186. Agronomic texts as a form of elite self-fashioning: e.g., Reay 2005 (Cato), Nelsestuen 2015 (Varro), and Bertoni 2017 (Columella).

9 Mallon 2021, with Ingold 2017 on the concept of 'taskscape'. See now also Tally-Schumacher 2023, who interprets the agricultural mosaics as evidence for an 'eco-phenomenogical perception of time' (13). Key treatments of the representations of labour in Roman art: Kampen 1981, Zimmer 1982, Clarke 2003, 95–129, Petersen 2006, George 2006, Jones 2018; see now the useful overview by Sapirstein 2020.

proportion of panels devoted to the subject in comparison with those depicting rituals or other seasonal events, assuming that spring and summer followed the same pattern as the other two seasons, as seems reasonable. What did it mean for a viewer to enter this room and encounter so many scenes of labour? What value or meaning did these images of labour hold, to the owner of this *domus*, to his visitors, and to those individuals, whether of freeborn, freed, or enslaved status, who had experience of performing such activities themselves?

2 Calendars and Their Images in Private Life

By the time our mosaic was commissioned, *fasti*—of different kinds—had enjoyed a long, prestigious and popular history in the Roman world. The habit of publishing written calendars in public at Rome, in order to make information about the dates available for civic and legal business, has been seen to originate in the early Republic, but it is not until 304 BCE that we receive explicit mention of such a list being installed in the Forum Romanum (Livy 9.46.5), and we wait more than a century for the decision of M. Fulvius Nobilior, consul in 179 BCE, to have a monumental calendar inscribed or painted on the walls of his newly constructed Temple of Hercules and the Muses. It is likely that Fulvius' initiative had a more religious and antiquarian focus, including some sort of commentary for individual holidays and months, and his monument may have been similar in appearance to the oldest archaeologically attested calendar, the Fasti Antiates Maiores (84–55 BCE). This was a painted wall calendar in the form of thirteen columns, one for each of the twelve months, together with the extra leap month (*mensis intercalaris*) then needed to align the conventional 355 day Roman year with the solar year. Underneath the month's name at the top of each column followed an enumerated list of the individual days, variously marked according to (1) their position both in the eight-day Roman 'week' (A-H) and in the month (Kalends, Nones, or Ides); (2) their availability (or prohibition) for legal and/or political business (*F*[*astus dies*], *N*[*efastus dies*], *C*[*omitialis dies*]); and (3) their commemoration of specific festivals or temple foundations.[10]

Following Caesar's reorganization of the calendar, the practice of erecting monumental *fasti* of a similar format—either painted on walls or inscribed on stone tablets—enjoyed some popularity, as the majority of calendars dis-

10 Key treatments of the Roman calendar and its developments: Michels 1967, Feeney 2007, Rüpke 2011; useful overview by Salzman 2013.

covered in various parts of Italy date from the reigns of Augustus, Tiberius, and Claudius.[11] Among these were the *menologia rustica*, public monuments that took the form of a rectangular marble altar, with each of the four sides divided into three vertical columns (one for the three months of each season), in which were listed the month's number of days, the number of daylight and night-time hours, as well as a select list of agricultural tasks and religious holidays, giving the *menologia* their more agrarian than political character.[12]

From the mid-first century CE onward, monumental calendars of a public character become much less attested, though no doubt they continued to serve a function. Alongside these, we find various systems of reckoning time according to private contexts, including both *ferialia*, short lists of special holidays that could be painted on walls, inscribed on stone tablets, or written on papyrus, and *parapegmata*, lists of festivals or dates accompanied by a set of peg holes to mark out special occasions. It seems to be a device of this kind that Petronius describes in the dining room of his fictional freedman host Trimalchio. Affixed to each doorpost were two tablets representing, on one side, the phases of the moons and images of the planets, and on the other, notations about certain dates—notably, 'OUR GAIUS DINES OUT ON THE 30TH AND 31ST OF DECEMBER'—including also a system for signalling lucky and unlucky days with special markers (*bullae*).[13]

It is all too easy to find something faintly ridiculous (as Petronius surely intended) in Trimalchio equating the significance of his personal dining engagements with the movements of the stars.[14] In fact, this story, though fictional, attests to the social value that a calendar-type object might have as a form of domestic display and self-presentation. This was clearly true for Roman elites as well, as evidenced by two of the calendar images with which our mosaic may be fruitfully compared, both of which similarly came from wealthy townhouses, though from different parts of the empire.

The first is the frescoed wall calendar discovered in the ancient remains underneath the Basilica of Santa Maria Maggiore in Rome, sadly in an incomplete and much degraded state (it was later painted over). Based on the surviving sections for August and September, each month was apparently allotted

11 Degrassi 1963.

12 Degrassi 1963, 284–291; see now Parodo 2017, 18 (table 5).

13 *Sat.* 30.3–4: *et duae tabulae ⟨erant⟩ in utroque poste defixae, quarum altera, si bene memini, hoc habebat inscriptum: "III et pridie Kalendas Ianuarias C. noster foras cenat," | altera lunae cursum stellarumque septem imagines pictas; et qui dies boni quique incommodi essent, distinguente bulla notabantur*. This and all the following texts taken from the Loeb Classical Library. Trans. Schmeling 2020, 117.

14 Cf. Petersen 2006, 1–13.

an expanse of wall about 3.25 m in length, divided vertically into two parts: on the left, a red band (about 45 cm wide), in which were painted the list of days in white letters, and on the right, a much larger figurative panel. Although impossible to ascertain with certainty, it is posited that this figurative panel may have been divided horizontally into three registers, with a zodiac sign or astronomical symbol appropriate to the given month at the top, followed by a scene of seasonal agricultural labour in the middle zone, and below, a depiction of one or more of the month's festivals against a backdrop of relevant buildings.[15]

For our purposes, a few factors are especially worth noting. One is the painted calendar's original context and its sheer scale, which must have been considerable when the fresco representing all twelve months was complete. Indeed, earlier approaches to this calendar ascribed it to a monumental public building, due in part to its size. A recent revaluation of the archaeological evidence, however, argues that the calendar belonged instead to a wealthy *domus*, which should be dated from 180–200 CE. In this new reconstruction, the fresco wrapped nearly 60 metres around four sides of the interior wall of a colonnade, which formed one side of a peristyle courtyard, and the calendar is now believed to have begun with the month of March, following the traditional pre-Julian calendar, by that time almost 250 years out of date.[16]

All of this suggests a function that went far beyond the merely practical. In addition to its scale, the deployment of this painting along the multiple walls of a domestic portico meant that any viewer had to move physically around the space in order to follow its progression. With so few remains, it is, of course, impossible to reconstruct and analyse the overall cycle of images. But it is worth noting that—were the subjects of each panel *mythological*, rather than 'calendrical'—we would assume that this decoration was intended to elicit viewers' intellectual participation, providing subjects for their discussion and encouraging them to make associative comparisons and contrasts among the various fresco sections, including their figural scenes.[17] This would be all the more appropriate given the fresco's specific setting in a portico, a space specially designed to foster *ambulatio*, the cultural habit of leisured walking associated with travel and the acquisition of knowledge, in which the display of visual objects also played a role. Thus, for instance, the first-century BCE cycle of wall paintings known as the Odyssey Landscapes from Rome—in which

15 Mols and Moormann 2010, 488–491, with earlier bibliography. Cf. Stern 1981, 453–454; Parodo 2017, cat. nº A.8.

16 Mols and Moormann 2010, 497, 499.

17 E.g., Bergmann 1994 and 1999.

miniature figures from Homer's *Odyssey* appear against a backdrop of craggy mountains, oceans, islands, caves and trees—employed a frame of painted red pillars to evoke a real portico, thereby purporting to take the viewer on an intellectual and philosophical journey mirroring Odysseus' own wanderings.[18]

The calendar fresco belongs to a different register, and is therefore perhaps more readily linked with something like the famous 'painted Italy' (*picta Italia*) on the wall of the Temple of Tellus, most likely a chorographic representation, perhaps visually organized by the network of Roman roads, which Varro uses as a starting point for a discussion of agriculture that ranges widely, both in a topical and a geographic sense.[19] One can imagine that the scenes of agricultural labour from the *domus* under Santa Maria Maggiore were intended to prompt conversations of a similar kind. By the same token, the comparison with the Odyssey Landscapes suggests that part of this decorative scheme's conceit was that it allowed one to travel mentally to a different *place* (the countryside), but also physically, through *time*. On the most basic level, the fresco offered viewers passage through the course of an entire year. Furthermore, by beginning the cycle of months with March, rather than January, this painting denied the cultural shift of calendrical reforms, recalling instead a more old-fashioned system of reckoning time that followed the rhythms and routines of the agricultural year—even while in the city. In effect, viewers were reminded of an earlier time, when the workings of the countryside enjoyed a special primacy, an idea reinforced by the placement of the agricultural labour scenes right at the centre of each month's pictorial zone (as far as we can tell), between the symbols of the zodiac depicted above (referring to nature's cycle) and the architectural vistas below (alluding to urban/civic/ritual time).

If this painting cycle helps uncover the cognitive or intellectual potential of calendrical imagery in a domestic setting, our second example—a *cubiculum* mosaic pavement from a wealthy *domus* in ancient Thysdrus (present day El Jem, Tunisia), dated to the late second or early third century CE—is also revealing (Fig. 12.2). Here, in the earliest known complete calendar mosaic to survive from antiquity, conventionally referred to as the Mosaic of the Months, the gridded arrangement of panels is much more readily legible, being both oriented to a single vantage point and labelled with the names of the months. Each of the four horizontal rows consists of six panels: first, a personification of the season, followed by three panels for the months of that season. The first row begins with Spring, followed by three panels for the months of March, April and May;

18 Significance of calendar's size and length beyond the merely practical: Rüpke 1995, 89. *Ambulatio*: O'Sullivan 2006. Odyssey Landscapes: O'Sullivan 2007.

19 *Rust.* 1.2.1, with Roth 2007.

FIGURE 12.2 Detail from a mosaic from the House of the Months at El Jem (ancient Thysdrus), 200–235 CE, 1.86 × 2.73 m. Musée Archéologique, Sousse
PHOTO: GILLES MERMET (© ART RESOURCE, NY)

the second with Summer, followed by panels for June, July, and August; the third with Autumn, followed by September, October and November; and the fourth with Winter, followed by December, January and February. Each row concludes with two panels of an ornamental design, matching the style of the surrounding geometric/vegetal borders.[20]

20 Dunbabin 1978, 110–112; Foucher 1963, 28–50 and 2000; Parrish 1992, 479–500; Eastman 2001; Petsalis-Diomidis 2007, 271, 273; Parodo 2017, 123–128 and cat. nº A.13.

Like the painting from under Santa Maria Maggiore, then, this composition, while itself located in town, privileges an old-fashioned system of reckoning time tied to the rhythm of the seasons and the management of the land, by beginning the year with spring and the month of March, as well as by personifying the seasons with specific reference to agricultural tasks or rural pursuits.[21] Overall, however, the Thysdrus pavement is, again like the Basilica of Santa Maria Maggiore painting, much more cued to the civic calendar than our mosaic from Gaul, both through its use of monthly labels and, more significantly, through the high number of monthly panels given over to ritual scenes (nine) as opposed to scenes depicting human beings performing actual labour (only three: June, July and September).[22]

Despite its different character, however, a closer examination of how—and where—labour is represented within the Thysdrus mosaic is revealing. For two of the seasons, spring and winter, the only allusions to productive activities (herding and hunting) are made by the two personifications themselves, one carrying a kid, the other, a hare and two ducks. Perhaps not surprisingly, labour has a greater presence in summer, beginning with the personification, who carries a signature product of the season (the sheaf of grain), but also a tool (the sickle), which he jauntily waves aloft. The following panel of June depicts two figures in a concession-type stand appearing to serve a beverage to a third individual on the other side of the counter; perhaps an allusion to the season's heat, this may be interpreted as a vending or sales scene, but could also allude to a free distribution of drinks at, for example, a specific festival.[23] The third panel in the row (July), however, seems to offer a less ambiguous image of work being performed. Here, a man carries on his back what is probably a basket of dead wood.[24] In several respects, his form echoes that of the personified Summer: both wear short tunics and stride to the right, and each bears a substantial load on the upper half of his body. But while the human figure is inclined forward at a sharper angle, suggesting that his body responds to the heavy weight, Summer remains fully upright, despite his burdensome attribute. In this respect, the two figures belong to a much broader representational context for the produc-

21 Stern 1981, 436.

22 For the suggestion that the householder himself have been an administrator, involved in the annual task of fixing the colony's calendar: Huet 2011, 237.

23 Foucher 2000, 86–87. Vending and sale scenes in Roman art: Kampen 1981.

24 Colum. 11.2.52, Pallad. 8.1, with Stern 1981, 435. *Pace* Foucher 2000, 88–90, who believes the July panel depicts a festival-type race, rather than labour. On the typical image of Summer carrying the sheaf on his shoulder, rather than at chest level under the forearm: Foucher 2000, 70. On the 'localness' of this composition, including the identification of an apprentice's hand, hence explaining some of the variations: Eastman 2001.

tion and preparation of food, whereby enslaved or other low-status labouring individuals are often represented with curved backs, in contrast to the elite beneficiaries of their labour, who are rendered with postures much more static and erect—a point to which we will return.[25]

It is in the autumn row of panels, in the month of September, however, that we find by far the most vigorous depiction of agricultural labour of the whole mosaic. Here, two men—probably to be recognized as enslaved workers by their costume, consisting only of the *subligaculum* (loincloth)—energetically suspend themselves by ropes from an invisible crossbar overhead so as to employ all their weight in the crushing of the grapes. This eye-catching scene makes a striking contrast with the depiction of Autumn which it immediately follows, all the more so since Autumn is the only personification who is *not* assigned a tool or product appropriate to the tasks of the season, but instead holds a staff in his left hand and a *rhyton* in his upraised right hand, evoking the iconography of Bacchus. Thus, we see another, even more pointed differentiation between elite personification and non-elite labourer, in which the enslaved figures lean forward, look toward the ground, and strongly bend their knees, while Autumn instead looks out toward the viewer and raises a glass—a gesture which the owner of this *domus* would have performed many times himself.

By recognizing this pair of panels as representing the twinned, but strongly differentiated, ideas of production and consumption, we can also perceive the significance of another internal juxtaposition, namely, the placement of the autumn wine pressing scene directly above the December panel. Here, autumn's two enslaved figures have become three, still bronzed and naked except for the *subligaculum*, but now all wearing leafy crowns, while the central figure also holds a torch. It is assumed that this scene alludes to a nocturnal celebration of the Saturnalia, famously a time of year when *servi* might experience a temporary respite from the demands of their exploitation—including the *dominus*' watchful eye. This is the picture presented to us, for example, by Pliny the Younger, who described his fondness for a particularly secluded suite of rooms in his Laurentine villa (*Ep.* 2.17, trans. Radice 1969, 141–143):

> … especially during the Saturnalia when the rest of the roof resounds with festive cries in the holiday freedom, for I am not disturbing my household's merrymaking nor they my work.

---

25 Green 2015, esp. 138–141. My thanks go to Lauren Petersen for the reference and for suggesting this avenue of interpretation. On enslaved bodies as 'visual foils' to elites in Roman art: George 2002, 43 and 2013, 397–411; cf. Lenski 2013.

> … magnamque eius voluptatem praecipue Saturnalibus capio, cum reliqua pars tecti licentia dierum festisque clamoribus personat; nam nec ipse meorum lusibus nec illi studiis meis obstrepunt.

Even while in residence, Pliny portrays himself as having no wish to know what went on at his villa on Saturnalia. Conversely, the owner of the townhouse at Thysdrus, even while in city, appears to advertise his knowledge of the religious celebrations taking place on his country estate.[26] In this respect, he—and the mosaic he commissioned—espouse much the same view as the agronomists, in particular Columella, who advises enforcing a strict regulation of the sacrifices and other ritual practices undertaken by enslaved workers on the farm, certainly aimed at maximizing the slaveholder's control, as well as curtailing slave workers' social relations.[27] The solemnity and relative stillness of the figures celebrating the Saturnalia also help perpetuate a message of restraint and control, particularly when contrasted with the grape pressing scene directly above. Within these two panels, we are reminded that the strength, effort and vigour of enslaved bodies is permissible, indeed desirable, but only insofar as they are applied to activities of labour; outside the working day, those same bodies must now be stilled.

3 Labour as Knowledge

Much of what we have been considering is of a piece with what we know of the Roman taste for 'the spectacle of production', the fact that elites deliberately arranged their domestic settings, especially their country villas, so as to enjoy prospects onto the surrounding cultivated landscape, including not just plantings, but also storehouses, farm equipment, and, at certain times, the agricultural labourers themselves.[28] Mosaics like the one from Saint-Romain-en-Gal, as well as other compositions centring on depictions of an agricultural estate

26 While not all the ritual scenes on this mosaic need to be understood as necessarily (or exclusively) taking place in the countryside, the visual correspondences between the wine-pressing and Saturnalia scenes encourage us to imagine them unfolding in the same rural sphere.

27 E.g., *Rust.* 1.8.5, 1.8.6, 2.1.22, with discussion by Joshel and Petersen 2014, 196–197; see also 164–165 on the tendency of elite written sources, including both Pliny the Younger and the agronomists, to silence, elide, or occlude slave labour in a variety of ways.

28 *Rust.* 1.2.10. 'Spectacle of production', with multiple examples: Purcell 1995; cf. Bergmann 2002 and Kuttner 1999 on references to this concept in wall painting, where the depiction of actual labour is usually omitted completely.

and its bounty, brought this same idea indoors, communicating the wealth of the *dominus* as a symbol of his social prestige, while simultaneously conjuring up the atmosphere of country life—that is, to varying degrees, allowing viewers, while in town, to enjoy the fantasy of being in the country.[29] At the same time, the visual complexity of our Gallic mosaic is in many ways unique, above all in the sheer number of panels allotted to each season; the lack of any accompanying legends; and a gridded arrangement that belies the series of changing orientations by which the sequence of panels gradually unfolds around the room. As we will see, agricultural labour is used here to create a 'spectacle of production' that is both visually and intellectually rewarding, and indeed requires the viewer's own cognitive labour to parse and comprehend.

As we have seen, entering the room from the north, the viewer encounters a composition which gives no immediate clues as to its beginning or end. Walking a little further into the space, she may recognize, based on their iconography, the four seasonal personifications that form the central emblemata, first perceiving Winter (facing to her left) and Autumn (facing right), before noticing Spring and Summer, oriented instead toward the back of the room, thus appearing upside down (Fig. 12.3). Based on what she knows of the civic calendar, beginning in January, the viewer may quickly infer that the cycle of images here also begins with Winter, therefore turning her attention to the first scene: against the backdrop of a columned building festooned with garlands (perhaps a villa), two men in tunics focus on the act of planting, one crouched on the ground, the other bending sharply over, the strong curvature of his back accentuated all the more by the double rows of tesserae (Fig. 12.3, centre left; see also Fig. 12.6a below). This scene is conventionally recognized as Sowing the Beans, based on a comparison with the *menologia rustica*, which ascribe this activity to the month of December. The *menologia*, however, group December's activities, together with October and November, under autumn, not winter.[30] In this way, the year begins in a way that initially seems to evoke the civic calendar, yet then immediately undercuts its authority, privileging instead a system of time tied to agricultural work.[31]

In the next panel, a woman, dressed in a surprisingly elegant fashion, goads a donkey attached to a millstone used for grinding grain. Certainly, this work

29 Grassigli 2000, 207–223 and 2011, 126–199; cf. Parodo 2017, 136–137.

30 *FABA(M) SERENTES*: Lafaye 1892, 329; cf. Stern 1981, 445; Parodo 2017, 53.

31 On the mosaic's general rejection of any neat division into months: see esp. Stern 1953, 205; cf. Parodo 2017, 54, n. 529. The writings of the agronomists display a similar alternation between two systems of reckoning time (civic and agricultural): Parodo 2017, 137, with ancient bibliography at n. 1490.

FIGURE 12.3 Mosaic from Saint-Romain-en-Gal, oblique view from entry, four seasonal personifications at top
PHOTO: CC BY-SA 2.0, PHOTOGRAPHER CAROLE RADDATO

makes sense in this part of the year, *after* the harvest has been brought in from the fields, but it is also routine task that was repeated throughout the year, rather than being strongly linked to a single season (also being an activity that was often performed in town).[32] The next panel, one of the grittiest workaday scenes, depicts the transport of manure to fertilize the vineyards by two individuals wearing the distinctive Gallic *cucullus*, or short, hooded tunic, a task which again the *menologia rustica* assign to December.[33] At this point, the viewer might pause to consider the strikingly large number of scenes being devoted to human labour, already three panels for this one month, compared to the single emblema (of equal size to the other panels) featuring the personified season herself. In this way, she perceives that nature's revolving cycle of the four seasons is being *elaborated* here into the yearly cycle of routine activities, which unfolds at a different pace.

32 Ferdière 2020, 456; cf. Williams and Peacock 2011.

33 *VINEAE STERCORANT(UR), MATERIA DEICITUR*: Lafaye 1892, 334, with Stern 1981, 445–446. On ancient references and archaeological evidence for this practice: White 1970, 125–145, Ferdière 2020, 452–453. I am grateful to Christel Freu for the reference to a contract for this specific task in second-century CE Egypt (*P. Col. x 255*): Delia 1986.

To discern and follow the sequence of winter imagery, the viewer must now walk to her left, turning her body 90 degrees and proceeding to follow the panels from right to left along the long side of the room. Here, she finds first a scene of bread-baking, using a well-established iconography,[34] another of those routine, rather than time-specific, household activities. The next panel depicts the first non-labour scene in the cycle, identified as a sacrifice to the Lares, perhaps the Compitalia in January, in which an adult male figure wearing the toga *capite velato*, likely the *paterfamilias*, presides over his household's rites, with the assistance of a small boy.[35] The following labour scene depicts one figure carrying reeds, the other weaving baskets, activities which the *menologia rustica* assign to either January or February.[36] Some degree of 'punctuation' is provided by the next two panels, in order to mark the transition between winter and spring. The final panel in the winter sequence, though unfortunately damaged, appears to show an elite male and a female figure (mostly only their heads survive) making a sacrifice at a tomb of a particularly Gallic form, presumed to be the Parentalia (13–22 February).[37] This is placed directly next to the first spring panel (also damaged), depicting the arrival of the swans.[38] Thus, this succession of panels integrates all three systems of reckoning time: the annual schedule of agricultural tasks, the civic/ritual calendar, and nature's cycle.

With so much of the spring and summer portions of the mosaic missing, it is difficult to draw any complete conclusions about the patterning of labour and non-labour scenes. Nonetheless, there is a striking contrast between the winter and autumn panels in this respect, since the autumn scenes are exclusively devoted to representations of labour. Indeed, even the transition from summer to autumn is marked by different tasks, perhaps in keeping with the intense business of this time of year, with a scene of Cleaning up the Fields giving way to Harvesting the Apples. This is followed by two panels devoted to viticulture—an activity for which the territory of Vienne was especially famous. Indeed, these panels appear to refer to local methods, including the growing of grapes on an overhead pergola, a technique favoured in colder regions in order to

---

34 E.g., the frieze from the Tomb of Eurysaces in Rome (30–20 BCE): see Parodo 2017, 51, n. 493 for additional comparanda.

35 Parodo 2017, 51 usefully re-examines and confirms this identification, with earlier bibliography.

36 *HARUNDO CAEDITUR* (January) and *HARUNDINES INCENDUNT*(*UR*) (February): Lafaye 1892, 333, with Stern 1981, 446; cf. Parodo 2017, 51, n. 501 who prefers February.

37 Stern 1981, 446; Parodo 2017, 51–52.

38 Cf. Verg. *G.* 2.319–320; Isid. *Nat.* 12.7.16, noted by Stern 1953, 307, n. 1.

expose the fruits to the sun as much as possible,[39] and, in the Grape Treading scene, the channelling of the pressed wine into barrels, a mode of storage and transport typical to this region and period.[40] The corner panel depicts a scene of ploughing and sowing seed; the last three scenes, turning the corner and progressing toward the central personification of Autumn, focus on the preparations for and production of the olive harvest (Pitching the Storage Vessels, Harvesting the Olives and Pressing the Olives).

Having traversed the entire mosaic, moving inward and outward from the central emblemata around the room, and returning to stand near the doorway, the viewer might now look back to consider the entire northern half. There, she recalls how the agricultural year began not with some festival, or an idealized vision of fecundity, but with careful preparation and labour—and not of any glamorous kind, but rather the physically taxing work of planting beans and carting manure out to the fields. A particularly astute viewer may also observe the subtle undercutting of the civic calendar, created by the winter panels beginning with tasks more typically assigned to autumn, and specifically, to the month of December. Furthermore, this winter section of the mosaic alternates between labour and non-labour scenes, and between routine and more time-specific activities. In doing so, the panels also juxtapose scenes depicting figures performing manual labour, often in distinctive local garb, with other scenes featuring smartly dressed elites. This would seem to fit well with the fact that most of the Gallo-Roman nobility, like the owner of this *domus*, probably moved frequently between their residences in town and the country, where their land was worked by a mixture of enslaved workers, tenant farmers and seasonal labourers.[41]

There are ideological dimensions to these juxtapositions as well. Thus, for example, the upright woman with her hair in an elegant chignon and waving her rod at the donkey working the millstone is contrasted with the crouching and hunched figures of the bean sowers directly above her, as well as with the *cucullus*-wearing manure carriers below, underscoring her higher social status. At the same time, even though oriented differently, she also appears adjacent to the scene of the *paterfamilias* in his toga carrying out the household rituals, attended by a boy. In this way, we are presented with the male–female dyad which Roman elites considered the ideal model for managing their agricultural estates, whether by the *dominus* and *domina*—or their deputies, the *vilicus* and *vilica*—such as we see celebrated on the Dominus Julius Mosaic

39 Plin. *HN* 14.26.
40 Ferdière 2020, 458–459.
41 Woolf 1998, 142–168. Evidence for rural slavery in Gaul: Roymans and Zandstra 2011.

from Carthage.[42] It is also striking that these figures appear in a quarter of the mosaic where, as we have seen, the viewer is required to apply her own knowledge to identify the order of the individual scenes, each of which depicts a separate discrete task—very different from autumn, where the harvest activities are spread out over successive panels (e.g., picking and treading the grapes), helping to carry the eye along. On some level, therefore, the viewer is invited to enact the role of the assiduous estate owner/managers featured on this very part of the mosaic, who must use their own expertise and experience to recognize the 'right time' for every task and ensure its performance, in order to ensure their farm's success. The need for oversight was perhaps all the more necessary in winter, when inclement weather might incline farm labourers to idleness.[43]

As already noted, autumn closes out the year with a very different rhythm, with the consecutive harvest scenes—interspersed with one scene of ploughing and sowing—easily flowing into one another. The progression is further hastened by the fact that not a single panel depicts a holiday or ritual scene, so that this season is marked as one of intense and constant labour. At the same time, this section of the mosaic makes a striking juxtaposition, by including scenes of distinctively Gallic agricultural production, especially the wine-making panels, together with a set of images devoted to the making of olive oil—despite the fact that olives, unlike grapes, cannot be grown farther north than Valence, over 70 kilometres south of Vienne, and, throughout the Roman period, were probably not produced widely outside of the area of Provence.[44] It is, of course, quite possible that the owner of this *domus* may have provided his guests with his own olive oil, if we imagine him to have owned multiple estates, including one farther to the south. Yet, as others have noted, the Olive Pressing scene (visible at centre right in Fig. 12.3) depicts a lever-and-drum press of the kind described by Cato (*Agr.* 18–19), but which, by the time of the mosaic's completion, had mostly been replaced by larger, more efficient machines.[45]

42 E.g, Columella *Rust.* 12.intro.1–10. Mosaic of Dominus Julius, late fourth or early fifth century CE: Dunbabin 1978, 119–121 and 1999, 118–120, 322.

43 Need for timeliness: Columella *Rust.* 11.1.30. Importance of constant supervision on the farm: e.g., Cato *Agr.* 2, Plin. *HN* 18.31, Columella *Rust.* 1.1.18, Pallad. 1.6.1. Risks of winter idleness: Cato *Agr.* 2.3–4, Columella *Rust.*12.3.6.

44 Brun 2005, esp. 78–103. Cf. Leveau 2003 on the relatively minimal role played by oleiculture in southern France, outside of Provence, until the Middle Ages. The *menologia rustica* ascribe the olive harvest to the month of December: Parodo 2017, 53. For the possibility that the mosaic's depiction of the olives being handpicked (rather than beating the tree's branches, as is more typical in the North African mosaics), as well as the old-fashioned press, reflect a more regional Gallic practice: Lafaye 1892, 345–346, with Pelletier 1975, 25 and Brun 1986, 144–146, 199–200, 204–217.

45 Lever-and-drum press and its depiction here: Brun 1986, 92–95; cf. White 1975, 91; Lancha

What we seem to see, therefore, is the mosaicists adhering to a long-established repertory for certain activities, perhaps working from model books, while giving other scenes a much more local character. The overall effect is to strike a balance between insisting on a local and individual expertise (in both agricultural and artistic production), and presenting this knowledge within a much wider social-cultural milieu, not unlike the lunar calendar written in Celtic from Coligny mentioned earlier. In this respect, it cannot be coincidental that the winter–autumn half of the pavement manages to display all three of the quintessential crops of Mediterranean agriculture, with multiple panels devoted to each: olives, vines and cereals/legumes (the latter referred to both by the scenes of planting and ploughing, as well as those of threshing and baking bread). Finally, the fact that the autumn scenes conclude with a recognizably old-fashioned type of olive press further cements the idea that this mosaic—and the way of life it represents—are deeply rooted in the past.

In all the ways we have just explored, therefore, the mosaic of Saint-Romain-en-Gal can be seen to offer viewers a sophisticated, interactive and cognitively engaging experience. Here, it is worth recalling that agriculture could be viewed as a special form of high-stakes *scientia*, as Columella indicates in the opening of his treatise (*Rust.* 1.1.2, trans. Ash 1971, 29):

> … since the main thing in every enterprise is to know what has to be done—and especially so in agriculture, where willingness and means, without knowledge, frequently bring great loss to owners when work which has been done in ignorance brings to naught the expense incurred.
>
> … quia caput est in omni negotio nosse quid agedum sit, maxime in agri cultura, in qua voluntas facultasque citra scientiam saepe magnam dominis adferunt iacturam, cum imprudenter facta opera frustrantur impensas.

The fact that the agronomists conceived their projects in dialogue, if not in competition, with other spheres of intellectual inquiry and creative expression—Columella's decision to write his book on gardens in hexameter as a response to Vergil's *Georgics* being a prime example—is also illuminating.[46]

Similarly, we might consider how our mosaic relates not just to other calendrical or agricultural imagery, but also to compositions that draw on the world

1981, 109; Calcani 1993, 86–87; Parodo 2017, 137 n. 1497. Regarding the development and spread of press technology across the empire, Lawit 2020 provides a fascinating account.

46 On this book: Pagán 2006, 19–36.

of literature, mythology and philosophy. The 'Labours' of Hercules, for example, as depicted on another Gallo-Roman *triclinium* floor from south-eastern France (Fig. 12.4), similarly invites viewers to parse a succession of individual panels, also laid out in a grid. Again, the viewer is required to distinguish as the central emblema the middle panel, undifferentiated by its size or border, which features a figure perhaps to be identified as Pluto. Around this, the usual fixed cycle of twelve labours begins in the very bottom right corner with the Nemean lion (now damaged), and revolves in a counter clockwise direction. At the centre, above and below the figure of Pluto, are two additional panels representing, respectively, Hercules battling a centaur and battling the giant Antaeus.[47] In this particular iteration, therefore, Hercules is allotted 14 rather than the conventional 12 labours, an expansion of imagery not unlike what we observed on the floor from Saint-Romain-en-Gal. Part of the visual pleasure this pavement may have offered was the opportunity for viewers to debate which of these truly represented Hercules' most definitive achievements, thereby displaying their own erudition and rhetorical skill. Our mosaic suggests that, for some *domini* at least, the agricultural labours on which their own wealthy lifestyles depended, also had value as a demonstration of their *paideia*.

4 Labour as Spectacle

If the scenes of labour on the Mosaic of Saint-Romain-en-Gal had cognitive value, they also offered enjoyment of a more corporeal kind as well, through their display of so many human bodies hard at work. This conceit is neatly illustrated by the letter from the young Marcus Aurelius to his tutor Fronto (ca. 141 CE), describing a day during his boyhood stay at the imperial estate of Villa Magna near Anagni, southeast of Rome (Fronto, *Ep.* 4.6.1–2, trans. Andrews 2016, 30–31):

> We are well. I overslept a bit on account of a slight cold, but this seems to have subsided, so at the eleventh hour of the night until the third hour of the day I read from Cato's *De Agricultura*, and wrote a little bit, less badly than yesterday, thank god … So with my throat tended to, I set out for my father and stood by him at the sacrifice.… Then we set ourselves to the task

47 Lavagne 1979, 217–277. Popularity of the grid composition in southern Gaul, especially Vienne: Dunbabin 1999, 73–78. On the labours of Hercules as a popular choice of elite self-presentation in houses throughout the empire: Piay Augusto and Argüelles Álvarez 2021.

FIGURE 12.4 Mosaic depicting the Labours of Hercules, Saint-Paul-lès-Romans, Villa des Mingauds, Drôme, 170–180 CE, 4.91 × 7.37 m. Musée de Valence
PHOTO: © MUSÉE DE VALENCE, PHOTOGRAPHER SERGE VAN POUCKE

> of picking the grapes; we sweated, and rejoiced, and, as another author says, 'we left the high-hanging vintage surviving.' … [T]he gong rang, that is, it was announced that my father had gone over to the bath. Having bathed, we therefore dined in the pressing room (we didn't bathe in the pressing room, but, having washed, we ate there) and we happily heard the peasants bantering.

> Nos valemus. Ego aliquantulum prodormivi propter perfrictiunculam, quae videtur sedata esse. Ego ab undecima noctis in tertiam diei partim legi ex Agricultura Catonis partim scripsi, minus misere mehercule quam heri … Sed faucibus curatis abii ad patrem meum et immolanti adstiti. Deinde uvis metendis operam dedi|mus et consudavimus et iubilavimus et aliquot, ut ait auctor, reliquimus altipendulos vindemiae superstites … discus crepuit, id est, pater meus in balneum transisse nuntiatus est. Loti igitur in torculari cenavimus: non loti in torculari, sed loti cenavimus; et rusticos cavillantes audivimus libenter.

Here, we receive a tantalizing glimpse of how elites might integrate more erudite activities—reading Cato, writing, calling to mind a poetic quotation (possibly from Novius' *Vindemiatores*)—with the realities of agricultural labour, both by occasionally participating themselves or, more often, by supervising or spectating. Indeed, excavation of the Villa Magna has revealed that the wine pressing took place within a very theatrical arrangement, with the pressing floor (*calcatorium*) elevated above the rest of the *cella* so that it formed a kind of stage, while the storage containers (*dolia*) situated in the foreground took the place of the orchestra. Facing onto this was a semi-circular *stibadium*, in which the diners of the imperial party reclined on movable *kline*, allowing them to watch the tramping of the grapes—likely accompanied by music—as a special form of seasonal dinner entertainment.[48] A somewhat similar scenario, on a much smaller and humbler scale, may also be envisaged at the Villa Regina at Boscoreale, where the simply painted *triclinium* looked out over the central courtyard, allowing diners to view workers crossing back and forth between the pressing room and work area on one side and the *cella vinaria* with sunken *dolia* on the other.[49]

The *triclinium* of our Vienne townhouse leaves the real-life agricultural workers out on the farm, but brings their labour back to town, via a series

---

48 Fentress et al. 2016, 203–208, with fig. 5.125. The Grape Pressing scene in the Mosaic from Saint-Romain-en-Gal also includes a flute-player.

49 Joshel and Petersen 2014, 207.

of images that often draw special attention to physical strength, effort and exertion. In the wonderfully vivid Olive Pressing scene already discussed, for instance, the press-beam has been minimized, in order to give more room to the human figures, who must use all their strength and body weight to work it.[50] This is made all the more striking by the figures' lack of clothing, which both signals their lower status, and also displays their powerful physiques. A connection between labour and athleticism is made even more explicitly by two adjacent summer panels, one in which two naked youths stand poised for a javelin competition, followed immediately by a scene depicting a muscular naked figure bending over to gather up branches. While, once again, the different stances and postures of the two athletes and the labourer probably reflect their different social status, such images bring to mind the old chestnut, perhaps best expressed by Varro, that Romans used to stay fit through their agricultural work, before they moved to cities and had to start working out in Greek-styled *gymnasia*.[51] In reality, of course, the effects of hard labour in antiquity—particularly in the case of enslaved workers—would have left a heavy mark on physical appearance, leading to all manner of injuries and disabilities.[52]

In the mosaic from Saint-Romain-en-Gal, however, agricultural labour is presented as a kind of athletic event, with multiple displays of vigour, prowess and collaboration (recalling the claims of the young Marcus Aurelius: 'we sweated, and rejoiced'). In this respect, it may be compared with images of gladiators fighting, or of horseracing in the Circus, a form of domestic display that enjoyed special popularity in this period.[53] An especially sophisticated treatment of this subject matter may be seen on a pavement from nearby Lyon (Fig. 12.5). Ostensibly a 'snapshot' of a single race underway, it in fact shows multiple successive episodes—those that the artist selected as the most visually exciting—at once: for example, the hosting magistrate in the box above the *carceres*, about to drop the *mappa* to begin the race; the victor already crossing the finish line to win the race at the bottom centre; and the figure at top left who

50 See n. 45.

51 *Rust.* 2.intro.1–3. Some ancient authors do refer either to rustic games (Verg. *G.* 2.529) or to an old-fashioned custom of holding games after the harvest (Hor. *Epist.* 2.1.139): Lafaye 1892, 338–339. Parodo 2017, 52 assesses the athletic event panel as more generally ludic than religious.

52 George 2002, 47.

53 Cf. Woolf 1998, 165, who observes, focusing on the interplay between town and country in Roman Gaul, that the display of our mosaic in a suburban *domus* is in some ways the inverse of a country *villa* at Liégeaud, in which wall paintings of gladiatorial and other games probably recorded the *munus* by the owner in the city.

FIGURE 12.5 Circus Mosaic, second century CE, 4.97 × 3.2 m. Musée de la Civilisation Gallo-Romaine, Lyon
PHOTO: © ART RESOURCE, NY, PHOTOGRAPHER ERIC LESSING

must dash into the track to wet down the dust (the *sparsor*). Like our mosaic, this image portrays a mix of elite and non-elite participants in order to capture the full experience of the event. It also offers the viewer a rewarding cognitive experience, requiring him to introduce time and his recollections of real races he has attended, in order to parse out the various moments shown. At the same time, its frame and the view from above remind us of the Roman predilection for compositions drawn from territorial survey, in which ownership and control are all expressed visually through an elevated and all-encompassing perspective.[54]

Our mosaic, while not employing the so-called bird's-eye view, nonetheless offers a view from above simply by virtue of being placed on the floor, while also, through its multiple and highly specific panels, making a claim that the viewer can see, and know, everything. Furthermore, the fact that this pavement occupies the entire floor, requiring movement to traverse and comprehend its sequence and changing orientations, also invites comparison with other mosaics from this period, which aimed at creating a *physically* immersive experience for the viewer. The labyrinth mosaics on the floors of Roman baths in North Africa, for example, encouraged bathgoers to imagine their own athletic activities in these spaces as heroic endeavours, akin to Theseus' victory over the

54 Bergmann 2008, esp. 367–369.

Minotaur.[55] At the third-century CE villa of Piazza Armerina, the mosaic in the central apse of the *stibadium*, depicting the dying bodies of Hercules and Dionysius' enemies convulsed in agony, allowed the *dominus* to take on himself the role of the victorious Olympians.[56] Still other mosaics, across the empire, covered *triclinia* floors with multisensory carpets of vines and foliage, immersing viewers in nature, transporting them both out of doors and to the realms of mythological or numinous space.[57]

In a different way, our mosaic also offered an immersive experience, allowing the absentee landowner and his guests, while in residence in town, the satisfaction of surveilling the workers out in the countryside, whose labour had enabled the very feast they were now enjoying. In a sense, this is another version of the *triclinium* images which would proliferate somewhat later, during the late third and early fourth centuries, representing food and expensive tableware, but also the banquet waitstaff, in order to magnify the status of the hosting *dominus* and *domina*.[58] The depiction of so many agricultural labourers, however, created a special opportunity, particularly when laid out across a mosaic floor. Again and again, we encounter working bodies bent intently over their tasks, their curvature emphasized even more than in other media by the double rows of tesserae, which distinguish them from the surrounding background (Fig. 12.6a)—a form that is seen repeatedly throughout the composition.

Whether walking around the room, or reclining on their *kline*, the *dominus* and his guests were treated to the sight of human backs, arching under the weight of their labour, which they viewed from their superior position. Thus, elite viewers were assured that their real affinity lay, not with these lowly figures, but with the seasonal personifications in the mosaic's centre, all riding the backs of their own animals. And in this sense, they could celebrate the successful navigation of the agricultural year as if, like the figure of Autumn, whose tiger mount recalled that of Bacchus' return from the east, they themselves were the world's new triumphators (Fig. 12.6b).

55 Molholt 2011.
56 Muth 2015, 416, with fig. 21.5.
57 Malek 2017.
58 Dunbabin 2003a, 151–155 and 2003b; Muth 2015, 419–423.

FIGURE 12.6A–B Mosaic from Saint-Romain-en-Gal, a. December: sowing of beans (fig. 12.1, panel 1); b. Personification of Autumn
PHOTO: © RMN-GRAND PALAIS / ART RESOURCE, NY, PHOTOGRAPHER MICHEL URTADO

Acknowledgements

I am grateful to the editors of this volume and the other conference participants, including Franny Opdenhoff, Christel Freu, James Ker, Ineke Sluiter and Evan Jewell, and especially Lauren Petersen, for helping me develop and refine the ideas presented here. Thanks are also due to Katharine Huemoeller, Michael Koortbojian, John Lansdowne and Annie Truetzel for their insights and discussion of earlier drafts, and to Joe Favini and Candy Khéniche for their generous help with images. Any errors are mine alone.

Bibliography

Abad Casal, L. (1990a). s.v. Horae. *LIMC* 5.1, pp. 510–538.

Abad Casal, L. (1990b). s.v. Kairoi/Tempora Anni. *LIMC* 5.1, pp. 891–920.

Andrews, M. (2016). Documents Relating to Villa Magna, Ancient, Medieval and Modern. In: E. Fentress et al., eds., *Villa Magna. An Imperial Estate and Its Legacies: Excavations 2006–2010*. London, pp. 29–31.

Ash, H.B. (1917). *Columella. On Agriculture*, 3 vols. Cambridge, MA.

Balmelle, C. and Darmon, J.-P. (2017). *La mosaïque dans les Gaules romaines*. Paris.

Bergmann, B. (1994). The Roman House as Memory Theater: The House of the Tragic Poet in Pompeii. *ArtB* 76(2), pp. 225–256.

Bergmann, B. (2001). Meanwhile, Back in Italy ... Creating Landscapes of Allusion. In: S. Alcock, J.F. Cherry and J. Elsner, eds., *Pausanias. Travel and Memory in Roman Greece*. Oxford, pp. 154–166.

Bergmann, B. (2002). Art and Nature in the Villa at Oplontis. *JRA Supplementary Series* 47, pp. 87–121.

Bergmann, B. (2008). Pictorial Narratives of the Roman Circus. In: J. Nelis-Clément and J.-M. Roddaz, eds., *Le cirque romain et son image*. Bordeaux, pp. 361–391.

Bertoni, D. (2017). Geometry and Genre in Columella. *AJP* 138(3), pp. 527–554.

Brun, J.-P. (1986). *L'oléiculture antique en Provence. Les huileries du département du Var*. Paris.

Brun, J.-P. (2005). *Archéologie du vin et de l'huile en Gaule romaine*. Paris.

Calcani, G. (1993). *L'antichità marginale. Continuità dell'arte provinciale romana nel Rinascimento*. Rome.

Charles-Picard, G. (1974). Un sacrifice au Jupiter gaulois sur la mosaïque calendrier de Saint-Romain-en-Gal. *BAntFr* pp. 127–137.

Clarke, J.R. (2003). *Art in the Lives of Ordinary Romans. Visual Representation and Non-Elite Viewers in Italy, 100 B.C.–A.D. 315*. Berkeley.

Degrassi, A. (1963). *Inscriptiones Italiae: fasti et elogia. Fasti anni Numani et Iuliani: accedunt ferialia, menologia rustica, parapegmata*. Rome.

Delia, D. (1986). Carrying Dung in Ancient Egypt: A Contract to Perform Work for a Vineyard. *BASP* 23(1–2), pp. 61–64.

Dunbabin, K.M. (1978). *The Mosaics of Roman North Africa. Studies in Iconography and Patronage*. Oxford.

Dunbabin, K.M. (1999). *Mosaics of the Greek and Roman World*. Cambridge–New York.

Dunbabin, K.M. (2003a). *The Roman Banquet. Images of Conviviality*. Cambridge.

Dunbabin, K.M. (2003b). The Waiting Servant in Later Roman Art. *AJP* 124(3), pp. 443–468.

Eastman, E.M. (2001). The Mosaic of Months from Thysdrus: Origins and Influences. *Cahiers d'archéologie romande*, 85, pp. 183–200.

Ellis, S.P. (1991). Power, Architecture, and Decor: How the Late Roman Aristocrat Appeared to his Guests. In: E. Gazda and A.E. Haeckl, eds., *Roman Art in the Private Sphere: New Perspectives on the Architecture and Decor of the Domus, Villa, and Insula*. Ann Arbor, pp. 117–134.

Feeney, D.C. (2007). *Caesar's Calendar. Ancient Time and the Beginnings of History*. Berkeley–London.

Fentress, E. et al., eds. (2016). *Villa Magna. An Imperial Estate and Its Legacies: Excavations 2006–2010*. London.

Ferdière, A. (2020). Agriculture in Roman Gaul. In: D. Hollander and T. Howe, eds., *A Companion to Ancient Agriculture*. Chichester, pp. 447–477.

Foucher, L. (1963). *Découvertes archéologiques à Thysdrus en 1961*. Tunis.

Foucher, L. (2000). Le calendrier de Thysdrus. *AntAfr*, 36(1), pp. 63–108.

George, M. (2002). Slave Disguise in Ancient Rome. In: J.F. Gardner and E.J. Wiedemann, eds., *Representing the Body of the Slave*. New York, pp. 41–54.

George, M. (2006). Social Identity and the Dignity of Work in Freedmen's Reliefs. In: E. D'Ambra and G.P.R. Métraux, eds., *The Art of Citizens, Soldiers and Freedmen in the Roman World*. Oxford, pp. 19–30.

George, M. (2013). Slavery and Roman Material Culture. In: K. Bradley and P. Cartledge, eds., *The Cambridge World History of Slavery*, vol. 1: *The Ancient Mediterranean World*. Cambridge, pp. 385–413.

Grassigli, G.L. (2011). *Splendidus in villam secessus. Vita quotidiana, cerimoniali e autorappresentazione del dominus nell'arte tardoantica*. Naples.

Green, F.M. (2015). Cooking Class. In: K. Tuori and L. Nissin, eds., *Public and Private in the Roman House and Society*. *JRA Supplemental Series* 102, pp. 133–147.

Hooper, W.D. and Ash, H.B. (1934). *Cato. On Agriculture. Varro. On Agriculture*. Cambridge, MA.

Huet, V. (2011). s.v. Calendriers en images. *ThesCRA* VII, pp. 233–239.

Huet, V. (2021). Les images de fêtes dans le calendriers romains en images (fin IIe–milieu IV siècle apr. J.-C.). In: A. Arrault, O. Guyotjeannin and P. Mane., eds., *Calendriers d'Europe et d'Asie. de l'Antiquité à la diffusion de l'imprimerie*. Paris, pp. 11–29.

Ingold, T. (2017). Taking Taskscape to Task. In: U. Rajala and P. Mills, eds., *Forms of Dwelling. 20 Years of Taskscapes in Archaeology*. Oxford, pp. 16–27.

Jones, N.B. (2018). Exemplarity and Encyclopedism at the Tomb of Eurysaces. *CA*, 37(1), pp. 63–107.

Joshel, S. and Petersen, L. (2014). *The Material Life of Roman Slaves*. Cambridge.

Kampen, N. (1981). *Image and Status. Roman Working Women in Ostia*. Berlin.

Kuttner, A. (1999). Looking Outside Inside: Ancient Roman Garden Rooms. *SHG* 19(1), pp. 7–35.

Lafaye, G. (1892). Mosaïque de Saint-Romain-en-Gal (Rhône). *RA* 19, pp. 322–347.

Lancha, J. (1981). *Recueil général des mosaïques de la Gaule* III. *Province de Narbonnaise*, vol. 2. Vienne–Paris.

Lavagne, H. (1979). Au dossier des mosaïques héracléennes (suite): la mosaïque de Saint-Paul-Lès-Romans. *RA* 2, pp. 269–292.

Lawit, T. (2020). Invention, Tinkering, or Transfer? Innovation in Oil and Wine Presses in the Roman Empire. In: P. Erdkamp, K. Verboven and A. Zuiderhoek, eds., *Capital, Investment, and Innovation in the Roman World*. Oxford, pp. 307–353.

Le Glay, M. (1970). Découvertes archéologiques à Saint-Romain-en-Gal (Rhone). *RA* 1, pp. 173–183.

Lenski, N. (2013). Working Models: Functional Art and Roman Conceptions of Slavery. In: M. George, ed., *Roman Slavery and Material Culture*. Toronto, pp. 129–157.

Leveau, P. (2003). L'oléiculture en Gaule Narbonnaise: données archéologiques et paléoenvironnemtales. Présentation-Interprétation. *Revue archéologique de Picardie*, 1–2, pp. 299–308.

Levi, D. (1941). The Allegories of the Months in Classical Art. *ArtB* 23(4), pp. 251–291.

Malek, A.-A. (2017). Mosaics and Nature in the Roman *domus*. In: A.-A. Malek, K.L. Gleason and W.F. Jashemski, eds., *Gardens of the Roman Empire*. Cambridge, pp. 317–340.

Mallon, K. (2021). Taskscapes, Landscapes, and the Politics of Agricultural Production in Roman Mosaics. *Theoretical Roman Archaeology Journal* 4(1), pp. 1–26.

Molholt, R. (2011). Roman Labyrinth Mosaics and the Experience of Motion. *ArtB* 93(3), pp. 287–303.

Mols, S.T.A.M. and Moormann, E.M. (2010). L'edificio romano sotto S. Maria Maggiore a Roma e le sue pitture: proposta per una nuova lettura. *MDAIR* 116, pp. 469–506.

Muth, S. (2015). The Decoration of Private Space in the Later Roman Empire. In: B. Borg, ed., *A Companion to Roman Art*. Chichester, pp. 406–427.

Nelsestuen, G.A. (2015). *Varro the Agronomist. Political Philosophy, Satire, and Agriculture in the Late Republic*. Columbus.

O'Sullivan, T.M. (2006). The Mind in Motion: Walking and Metaphorical Travel in the Roman Villa. *CP* 101(2), pp. 133–152.

O'Sullivan, T.M. (2007). Walking with Odysseus: The Portico Frame of the Odyssey Landscapes. *AJP* 128(4), pp. 497–532.

Pagán, V.E. (2006). *Rome and the Literature of Gardens*. London.

Parodo, C. (2017). *Immagini del tempo degli dei, immagini del tempo degli uomini. Un'analisi delle iconografie dei mesi nei calendari figurati Romani e Bizantini e del loro contest storico-culturale*. Oxford.

Parrish, D. (1992). s.v. Menses. *LIMC* 6.1, pp. 479–500.

Pelletier, A. (1975). Viticulture et oléiculture en pays allobroge dans l'Antiquité. À propos du calendrier rustique de St-Romain-en-Gal. *Cahiers d'Histoire* 20(1), pp. 21–26.

Petersen, L.H. (2006). *The Freedman in Roman Art and Art History*. Cambridge.

Petsalis-Diomidis, A. (2007). Landscape, Transformation, and Divine Epiphany. In: S. Swain, S. Harrison and J. Elsner, eds., *Severan Culture*. Cambridge–New York, pp. 250–289.

Piay Augusto, D. and Argüelles Álvarez, P. (2021). Idealization of the Power of Hispanic Elites through the Representation of Hercules Mosaics. *Graeco-Latina Brunensia*, 26(1), pp. 135–155.

Purcell, N. (1995). The Roman Villa and the Landscape of Production. In: T.J. Cornell and K. Lomas, eds., *Urban Society in Roman Italy*. London, pp. 167–194.

Radice, B. (1969). *Pliny. Letters*. Cambridge, MA.

Reay, B. (2005). Agriculture, Writing, and Cato's Aristocratic Self-Fashioning. *CA* 24(2), pp. 331–361.

Riegl, A. (1890). Zur spätrömischen Ikonographie der Monate. *AEM* 13, pp. 9–11.

Riggsby, A.M. (2019). *Mosaics of Knowledge. Representing Information in the Roman World*. New York.

Roth, R. (2007). Varro's *picta Italia* (*RR* I. ii. 1) and the Odology of Roman Italy. *Hermes* 135(3), pp. 286–300.

Roymans, N. and Zandstra, M. (2011). Indications for Rural Slavery in the Northern Provinces. In: N. Roymans and T. Derks, eds., *Villa Landscapes in the Roman North*. Amsterdam, pp. 161–178.

Rüpke, J. (1995). *Kalender und Öffentlichkeit. Die Geschichte der Repräsentation und religiösen Qualifikation von Zeit in Rom*. Berlin–New York.

Rüpke, J.R. (2011). *The Roman Calendar from Numa to Constantine. Time, History, and the Fasti*. Chichester.

Russell, A. (2019). The Augustan Senate and the Reconfiguration of Time on the *Fasti Capitolini*. In: I. Gildenhard, U. Gotter, W. Havener and L. Hodgson, eds., *Augustus and the Destruction of History. The Politics of the Past in Early Imperial Rome*. Cambridge, pp. 157–186.

Salzman, M.R. (1990). *On Roman Time: The Codex-Calendar of 354 and the Rhythms of Urban Life in Late Antiquity*. Berkeley.

Salzman, M.R. (2013). Structuring Time: Festivals, Holidays and the Calendar. In: P. Erdkamp, ed., *The Cambridge Companion to Ancient Rome*. Cambridge, pp. 478–496.

Sapirstein, P. (2020). Picturing Work. In: E. Lytle, ed., *A Cultural History of Work*, vol. 1: *In Antiquity*. London–New York, pp. 33–56.

Schmeling, G.L. (2020). Petronius. *Satyricon*. Seneca. *Apocolocyntosis*. Cambridge, MA.

Stern, H. (1953). *Le calendrier de 354; étude sur son texte et ses illustrations*. Paris.

Stern, H. (1981). Les calendriers romains illustrés. *ANRW* II 12.2, pp. 431–475.

Stern, S. (2012). *Calendars in Antiquity. Empires, States, and Societies*. Oxford.

Stern, S. (2017). Calendars, Politics, and Power Relations in the Roman Empire. In: J. Ben-Dov, ed., *The Construction of Time in Antiquity. Ritual, Art, and Identity*. New York, pp. 31–49.

Strzygowski, J. (1888). *Die Calenderbilder des Chronographen vom Jahre 354*. Berlin.

Tally-Schumacher. (2023). Warm Soil, Westerly Wind, and Wet Feet: Feeling and Measuring Ecological Time in the Roman World. *Geohealth* 7(1), e2022GH000720. https://doi.org/10.1029/2022GH000720.

Webster, J.C. (1938). *The Labors of the Months in Antique and Mediaeval Art to the End of the 12th Century*. Princeton.

White, K.D. (1970). *Roman Farming*. Ithaca, NY.

White, K.D. (1975). *Farm Equipment of the Roman World*. Cambridge.

Williams, D.F. and Peacock, D.P.S. (2011). *Bread for the People. The Archaeology of Mills and Milling. Proceedings of a Colloquium Held in the British School at Rome, 4th–7th November 2009*. Oxford.

Woolf, G. (1998). *Becoming Roman. The Origins of Provincial Civilization in Gaul*. Cambridge–New York.

Zimmer, G. (1982). *Römische Berufsdarstellungen*. Berlin.

CHAPTER 13

Rural Labour and Identity at Vagnari in Southern Italy

Liana Brent and Tracy Prowse

1 Introduction. Occupational Identity in Death: An Urban-Rural Divide?

Evidence from the mortuary sphere offers an important point of entry into the study of labour in the ancient world, for example in the form of funerary epitaphs with occupational titles. Such evidence, however, reflects the predominantly urban nature of the datasets, both because epitaphs are mainly found in urban contexts and because those inscriptions that record occupational titles mainly refer to jobs or sectors in urban centres: building, manufacturing, sales, skilled or domestic service, transportation and administration.[1] Furthermore, the study of labour through the medium of funerary epitaphs is intrinsically and intricately tied to legal status, especially among slaves and ex-slaves, as S. Joshel's study of columbarium epitaphs with occupational inscriptions demonstrates. In a society that relied heavily on involuntary labour, the use of occupational titles and images of labour on tombstones highlighted work as an important aspect of identity that shifted the focus from what one *is* (one's social and legal status) to what one *does* (one's occupation).[2]

In contrast, the burial and commemorative practices of rural labourers are comparatively unexplored for both evidentiary and disciplinary reasons. Epitaphs were generally uncommon in the Roman countryside and those with occupational titles are extremely rare, while burials without monumental architecture or epitaphs have been largely ignored by classically trained scholars until recently.[3] Furthermore, relatively few rural Roman cemeteries have been excavated, since these sites are less likely to be discovered than those that lie under modern cities and thus require emergency archaeological interventions upon their discovery.

1 Joshel 1992, Table 3.1.
2 Joshel 1992, 24; Larsson Lovén 2019, 90.
3 The disciplinary divide is summarized in Morris 1992, 101–102.

 DOI:10.1163/9789004694965_014

Previously, the main sources of evidence for labour in the Roman countryside were ancient authors such as Cato the Elder, Varro, Columella, Seneca and Pliny the Elder, who wrote treatises on the management of country estates and the people who staffed such estates.[4] These treatises, however, say little about the burial practices of such groups, which remain understudied in comparison to their urban counterparts. Excavations over the past 20 years reveal new evidence for the individuals who lived and died in the Roman countryside, as well as some, albeit limited, access to groups that do not otherwise survive in the historical record. Recent approaches to the non-elite and the rural populations generate new ways of investigating labour in the Roman countryside, and it is to these topics that the present contribution turns.[5]

The primary aim of this paper is to explore what it means to value labour in a rural, Roman community. To that end, we consider the following questions: what indices of occupational labour do we find in archaeological contexts and how can these be understood to represent or co-constitute identity? How does labour contribute to individual identity within a broader community? Rather than explore the value of labour in economic or monetary terms, we seek to understand its symbolic value as a form of status display through consideration of occupational identity.[6] Using the Vagnari cemetery in southeast Italy as a case study, we demonstrate through an analysis of grave assemblages with iron tools and implements that labour was an important aspect of individual identity, one that could have different material manifestations at various stages of the life course.

2 Case study: Vagnari Vicus and Cemetery

The site of Vagnari in southeast Italy affords the opportunity to explore rural labour at its associated settlement and cemetery. First discovered through surface survey followed by geophysical survey under the direction of A. and C. Small between 1996 and 2000, Vagnari is located approximately 15 km outside the modern town of Gravina in Puglia, situated close to the reconstructed route of the ancient Via Appia (Fig. 13.1).[7] Excavations between 2001 and 2019

4 White 1970, 14–47; Carlsen 1995, 15–22 on ancient sources. Roth 2007, 1–5 on the invisibility of female slaves and agricultural labourers in ancient sources.

5 Joshel and Petersen 2014; Bowes (ed.) 2021. Excellent database work from developer-funded excavations has been done for the countryside in Roman Britain by Smith et al. 2018.

6 For monetary and economic approaches to labour, see Groen-Vallinga and Tacoma 2017; Bowes 2021.

7 Vinson 1972; Small and Small 2011, 383–386.

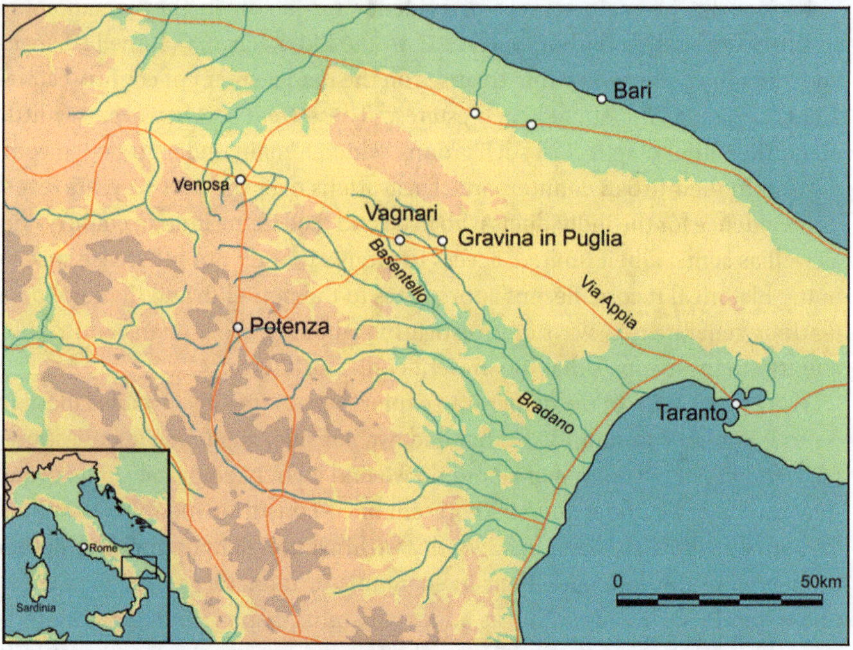

FIGURE 13.1 Map of southern Italy showing the location of Vagnari
MAP: M. CARROLL / I. DE LUIS

uncovered the remains of a *vicus* (village) and a nearby cemetery that were inhabited throughout the imperial period (Fig. 13.2).[8]

Stamped tiles found during field survey in the vicinity of Vagnari and the nearby site of Botromagno (ancient *Silvium*) record the name *Gratus*, a slave of the emperor.[9] One tile was found in the topsoil above the stoke-hole of a kiln at Vagnari, and petrological analysis confirms that tile production occurred at the site, thus connecting the tile kilns to imperial ownership.[10] By the early first century CE, Vagnari was part of an imperial estate that extended roughly 1050 hectares (11000 *iugera*).[11] In the second century CE, settlement in the countryside around Vagnari expanded, as witnessed by the increase in inhabited sites identified during the field survey, and the land was possibly occupied by free tenant farmers (*coloni*) who gradually replaced slaves as rural labourers.[12]

8 Small et al. 2007; Small (ed.) 2011; Small (ed.) 2014.
9 Small et al. 2003.
10 Small (ed.) 2011, 255–258 on Kiln 2 and the associated stamped brick.
11 Small and Small 2005, 898–899.
12 Small (ed.) 2011, 25–26. The notion that slave labour dominated the rural workforce, espe-

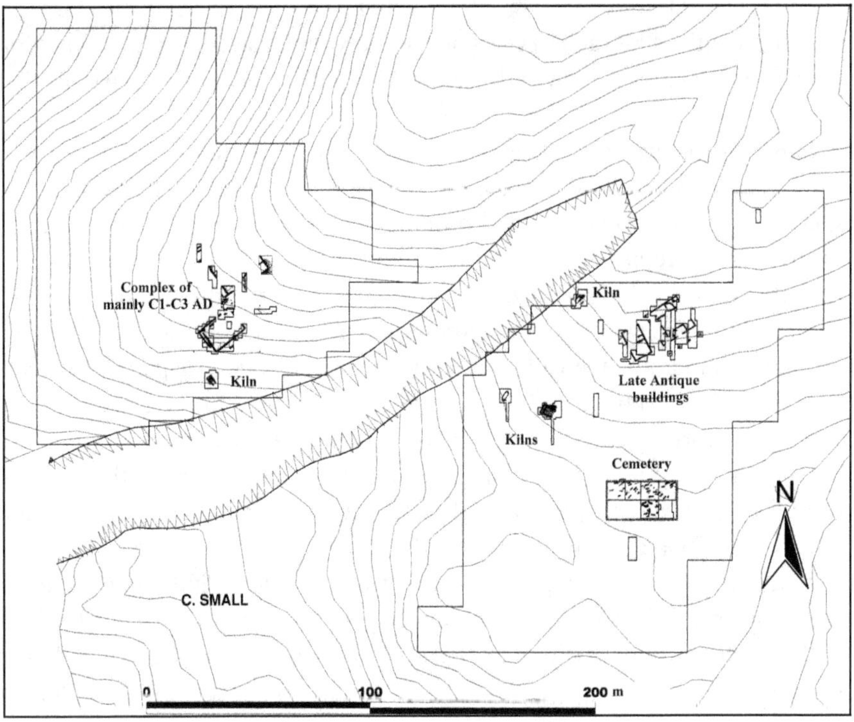

FIGURE 13.2 Plan of the site showing the location of the Vagnari Vicus and Cemetery
PLAN: C. SMALL

The Vagnari *vicus* provides evidence for different kinds of labour that individuals may have performed during life. M. Carroll's 2012–2018 excavations in the northern part of the site reveal that there were alterations to structures in the Vagnari vicus in the early second century CE, as well as a period of intensified agricultural and industrial productivity throughout the second and third centuries CE.[13] Activities documented in the *vicus* include animal husbandry (especially pig and sheep/goat-raising);[14] transhumant pastoralism;[15] agricultural production;[16] the storage of grain and wine;[17] the manufacture of bricks

cially in Italy after the first century CE, has been revised in recent decades: White 1970, 407; Marzano 2007, 125–153.

13 Carroll 2019; Carroll (ed.) 2022.

14 MacKinnon 2011, 305–328; Trentacoste 2022, 174–187.

15 Small 2014, 60–63.

16 Excavations at Vagnari have uncovered tools used in agricultural activities, including blades and pruning hooks (a type of small, hooked blade): P907 (Trench 12); P1124, P1197 (Trench 24) and P1125 (Trench 25); see Small (ed.) 2011, 96, 156, 165.

17 Montana et al. 2021; Carroll 2022 for a *cella vinaria* at Vagnari with *dolia defossa*.

and tiles;[18] and lead processing.[19] Interestingly, there is little evidence for wool working at either the Vagnari vicus or cemetery, and instead, textile production seems limited to the nearby early Roman villa at San Felice at a small scale that was intended for local use.[20]

Since the majority of datable burials in the cemetery are contemporary with the vicus, we may reasonably connect individuals buried in the cemetery to specific kinds of agricultural and productive labour at the vicus. Excavations in the Vagnari cemetery between 2002 and 2019 have uncovered 150 burials with the remains of 164 individuals; most burials date to the second and third centuries CE (Fig. 13.3). The most common type of burial at Vagnari is a single, primary inhumation deposition, usually covered with tiles (*tegulae*) and occasionally reinforced by the addition of rocks and mortar to the exterior of the grave.[21] Conformity with standard mortuary practices was not a fixed rule, and individual choice played a factor in the small number of burials that deviate from these conventions, for example in the form of cremations (N = 4), multiple burials (N = 12) or those with no discernible grave cover (N = 16).

In the absence of epigraphic evidence, there is little insight into the names, legal statuses, and occupations of the individuals who were buried in the Vagnari cemetery. They may have been slaves, freedmen, or freeborn individuals who lived in the nearby *casae* for *coloni*. The question arises of how to identify labour in the Vagnari cemetery when a large part of those who were buried there may have been involved in some kind of labour, even if that labour left no trace in the archaeological record.[22] To answer this question, we turn to the objects that were included in grave assemblages as a way to explore what kinds of labour were highlighted in funerary activities and how that labour may have been valued in this community.

Grave goods are widely attested throughout the Vagnari cemetery. Of the 150 burials that were excavated by 2019, the site-wide average number of grave goods is 6.2 objects per grave. That number increases to 7.1 when we take into account objects found immediately outside a grave.[23] Sixty-one graves (40%) were associated with at least one object outside the grave cover, which items

18 Small et al. 2003; Carroll 2022.

19 Carroll 2019; Carroll et al. 2022, 129–135.

20 Small 2014, 60–63; Triozzi 2022, 162–170. Only seven loom weights were found during surface survey and eight in excavations between 2001 and 2010, while investigations from 2012 to 2018 in the vicus revealed only a further 17 loom weights.

21 Small et al. 2007, 128–132 for a general overview of Vagnari grave types.

22 Larsson Lovén 2019, 99, with similar concerns for the absence of epigraphy and occupational indicators among rural farm workers.

23 These numbers underestimate the original size of funerary assemblages since they can-

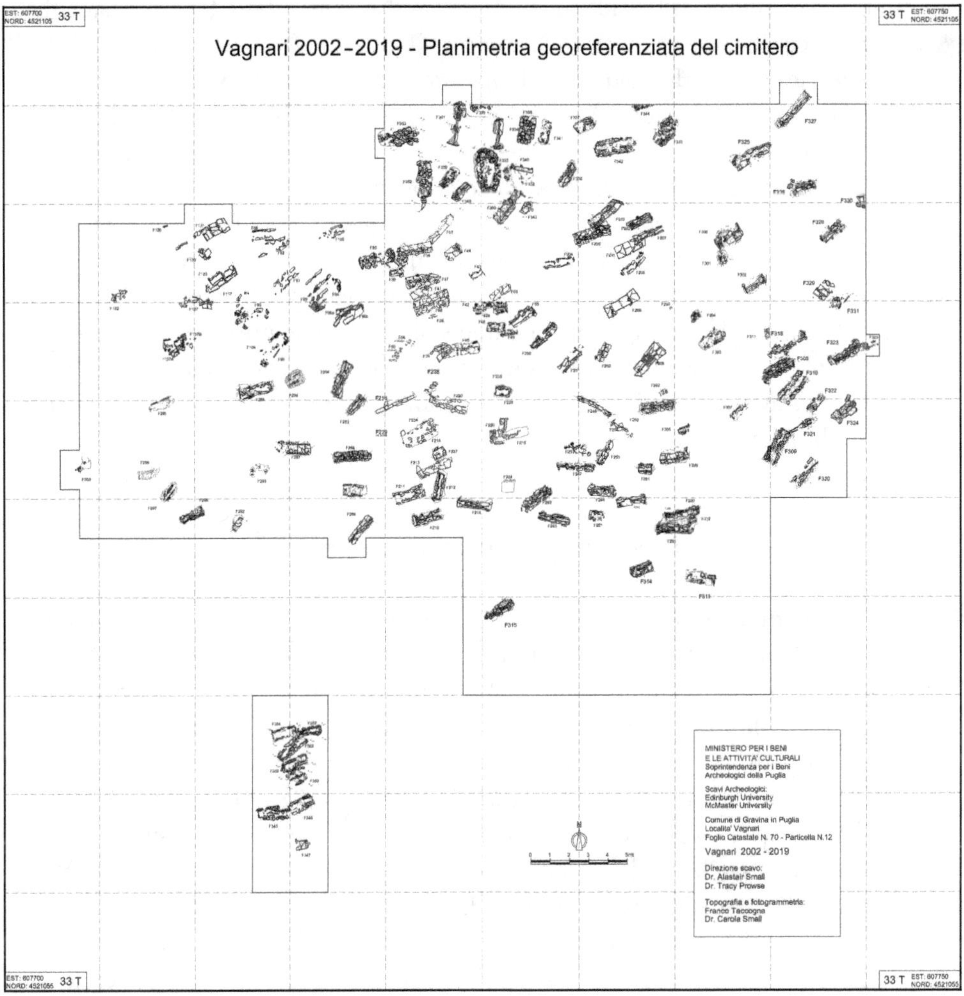

FIGURE 13.3 Plan of the Vagnari cemetery (2002–2019)
PLAN: F. TACCOGNA

were either deposited at the end of the funeral or as part of ongoing commemorative activities upon subsequent visits to the cemetery. It is possible that many objects were originally deposited outside grave covers, but they no longer survive because of damage to the tops of many graves from (modern) agricultural activities. The following analysis, therefore, includes only objects

not account for perishable items like wood or cloth objects, tools or toys. Pottery fragments were counted once unless multiple vessels could be discerned.

that were deposited inside the burial pit and excludes those found outside the grave cover.

Pottery is nearly ubiquitous in all graves at Vagnari: only 24 of 150 burials included in this study (16%) lacked pottery, and 14 of those 24 burials contained no grave goods, while the remaining 10 graves contained an average of 1.8 items per grave, a number that is considerably lower than the site-wide average of 6.2 items. Certain types of grave goods were routinely deposited together to form a standard funerary assemblage that included partial or complete ceramic vessels, lamps, iron nails, glass vessels and a coin.[24] Additions to this assemblage might include items of personal adornment such as rings, bracelets, earrings, necklaces, amulets, belts, bone pins or hobnails from shoes. A few graves included implements for gaming[25] or items in valuable materials like bronze vessels.[26]

3 Locating Labour in the Vagnari Cemetery

A small number of Vagnari graves (N = 19 or 12.7%) contained metal (mainly iron) objects that can be interpreted as tools and handheld implements.[27] Iron objects and tools are not often found in the archaeological record because of the valuable and recyclable nature of the material.[28] Metal objects found in the Vagnari burials include small blades, pruning blades and bill-hooks, 'punches', two spearheads, and an iron scraper (Table 13.1 and Fig. 13.4). Larger items that were used for digging, chopping, hammering or field cultivation, such as hammers, shears, adzes, rakes, spades and shovels, are entirely absent from the Vagnari grave assemblages.[29] Other kinds of tools may have been fashioned from wood or other organic materials and therefore do not survive in the archaeological record, so the following analysis focuses on handheld metal objects, excluding iron nails, items of personal adornment and objects employed in the application of cosmetics or the practice of medicine.[30]

---

24 Brent and Prowse 2014, 101.

25 E.g., a bone gaming piece (P5135) was found in F213.

26 Bronze vessels have been found in the following Vagnari burials: F35, F93, F104, F213, F216, F288, F319, F323, F325, F333 and F351.

27 Following Humphreys 2021, 19 for the definition of a tool as 'an instrument used or worked by a handi-craftsman or labourer in [their] work'.

28 Van Oyen et al. 2022, 56.

29 For a description of each, see White 1967; Rees 1979; Harvey 2010; Humphreys 2021.

30 Nails are found in nearly half the Vagnari graves (N = 68 or 45.3%) and are often connected with magico-religious purposes. On nails in graves at Vagnari, see Small et al. 2007, 145–146.

TABLE 13.1 Vagnari burials with metal tools and implements

Burial	Burial type	Date	Age	Sex	Type(s) of tools, implements	Total # of grave goods in burial
F34	Inhumation	1st half 3rd c. CE	Adult	Male	Iron blade (pruning tool) (P824)	5
F35	Inhumation	Late 2nd or 3rd c. CE (?)	Adult (old)	Male	Iron scraper (P1061), iron punch (P1062), tapered iron tool (possible awl) (P975)	14
F42	Inhumation	4th or 5th c. CE	Adult (29 ± 6.5 years)	Male	Tapering iron bar (P841), iron spike (P843)	8
F209	Inhumation	Unknown	Young adult (14–16 years)	Female	Iron blade fragment (P5192)	12
F213	Inhumation	2nd c. CE	Adult (35+)	Male	Iron bill-hooks (P5133, P5134), iron bracket (harvesting tool?) (P5132), iron pins (P5130, P5131)	22
F216	Inhumation	Early 3rd c. CE	Adult (35 ± 9.4 yrs)	Male	Iron bill-hook (P5151) Iron spearhead outside grave (P5068)	23
F218	Inhumation	3rd c. CE	Subadult (<10 years)	Unknown	Iron bracket (harvesting tool?) (P5178)	5
F220	Inhumation	Unknown	Adult	Male	Iron blade (P5188)	9
F231	Inhumation	2nd c. CE	Adult	Male	Iron blade (P5235)	13
F253	Inhumation	Unknown	Adult (49 ± 10.5 years)	Male	Iron blade (P5242)	4
F288	Inhumation	1st or 2nd c. CE	Adult (30–40 years)	Male	Bronze socketed spearhead (P6636), iron bill-hook (P6642), iron blade (P6670)	18
F302	Cremation	Mid-2nd c. CE	Adult	Unknown	Iron blade (P6776)	30
F303	Inhumation	Unknown	Subadult	Unknown	Iron socketed tool with truncated triangular blade on both sides (mason's pick?) (P6775)	11
F309	Inhumation	Unknown	Adult (>19 years)	Male	Iron blade (P6828), iron punch (P6829)	12
F319	Inhumation	Unknown	Young Adult	Female	Iron punch (P6929)	12
F327	Inhumation	Unknown	Adult	Male	Iron blade (P6933)	10
F334	Inhumation	Unknown	8–10 years	Unknown	Iron blade / scraper (P7032), iron punch (P7031), iron point (P7037)	17
F338	Inhumation	Unknown	4 ± 1 years	Unknown	Iron blade (P6975)	26
F341	Inhumation	Unknown	4.5–5 years	Unknown	Iron (blade?) fragment (P6978)	9

FIGURE 13.4A
Metal objects from the Vagnari burials: Iron 'punch' (P6829) from F309
PHOTO: J. WEILAND

FIGURE 13.4B
Metal objects from the Vagnari burials: Iron 'brackets' (harvesting tools?) (P5132 from F213 and P5178 from F218).
PHOTO: A. SMALL

A comparison between grave assemblages that included tools and other kinds of items in low quantities reveals that iron objects are a predictor of large grave assemblages (Table 13.2). For example, coins are found in 33 graves at Vagnari (22% of all graves), which have an average of 11.1 items, a number that is significantly higher than the site-wide average of 6.2 items per grave.[31] In comparison, the 19 graves with an iron tool or blade contain an average of 13.7 objects. Only copper alloy (bronze) vessels are more likely to be found among larger grave assemblages with an average of 15.0 items. The fact that iron tools

31 The current percentage of burials with coins (22%) is consistent with A. Small's initial findings in Trench 09, in which 4/17 burials contained coins (23.5%) (Small et al. 2007, 146–149).

TABLE 13.2 Grave goods in Vagnari burials with metal items

Item	# of graves	Total # of objects	Average # of grave goods
Iron tool or blade	19	260	13.7
Coin	33	368	11.1
Bronze vessel	11	165	15.0

routinely appear in some of the largest grave assemblages at Vagnari hints at their status as objects with social value beyond the worth of their materials.

Although the function of these items may be unknown or they may have been intended for multiple possible uses, certain objects may be tied to particular activities. For example, iron 'punches' or tapered awls may have been used for leather working, while the long, curved bill-hooks found in F213, F216 and F288 (Fig. 13.5) were likely agricultural tools used for pruning trees or vines.[32] When considered alongside other objects in the funerary assemblage, these tools possibly point to an individual's occupation. In the case of F35, an adult male individual who died in the late second or early third century CE, the metal tools in the grave assemblage included an iron scraper (P1061) and an iron punch (P1062), as well as a bronze canister (P974) and a bone spatula (P1060). A. Small notes that these items may have been used by a craftsman involved in leather working: the iron scraper could have been used for cleaning the animal skin, while the 'punch' could have been used for making holes in leather.[33] The bone spatula might have been used to spread glue or to smooth wax on a writing tablet, while the bronze canister—which on its own might be interpreted as an inkwell or container for cosmetics—could have been used to hold or warm glue.[34] Other objects in this funerary assemblage included an iron nail, four

32 Manning 1985, Pl. 22–24 and Humphreys 2021, Fig. 5.14 for harvesting tools from Roman London.

33 Small et al. 2007, 165–172 for the contents and interpretation of F35. Small notes that punches are represented on the funerary stelae of cobblers, such as the funerary stele of P. Latinius Primus from Tortona (first century CE), along with other symbols of a cobbler's trade (dé Spagnolis 2000, 65 and fig. 45 on p. 68). Similar iron scrapers, a bronze canister and a bone scraper were found in T.15 at the via dei Cappuccini *necropolis* at Brindisi (Cocchiaro and Andreassi 1988, 160–175).

34 Willi 2021, 76–77 and 103–104 on iron scrapers and bone spatulas that were used as writing implements.

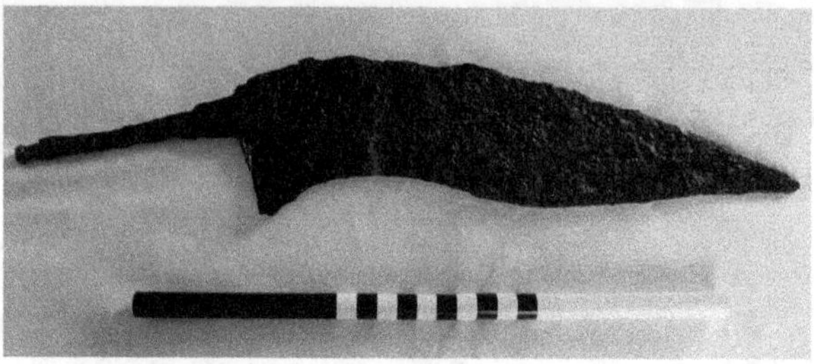

FIGURE 13.5
Large iron pruning tool P6642 from F288
PHOTO: AUTHORS

ceramic vessels (bowls), a bronze ring, a glass unguentarium, a melon-shaped glass bead, iron hobnails and other miscellaneous iron fragments.

4 A Life-Course Approach to Agricultural Labour?

In light of broader questions about how labour was valued at Vagnari, it is necessary to consider demographic patterns. Of the 19 graves with iron tools, 11 contained the skeletal remains of adult male individuals and two young females (F209, F319).[35] The remaining six graves include one adult individual who was cremated, as well as five subadult individuals whose sex cannot be estimated by standard morphological features of the cranium and pelvis as differences only develop after puberty. New research on the analysis of peptides in tooth enamel provides a promising new method for estimating the sex of subadult skeletons, as it identifies the presence of enamel-forming proteins linked to the X and Y chromosomes.[36] Peptide analysis of subadult and adult individuals of indeterminate sex from the Vagnari skeletal sample is in progress, which will help to better understand gender-based patterns of grave assemblages in the cemetery.

Iron tools are found most frequently in the burials of adult male individuals, but they are not entirely absent from the grave assemblages of female individuals. In addition to an iron blade fragment (P5192), burial F209 also contained at least two ceramic vessels, a lamp, an iron nail, a bronze ring fragment, other glass and ceramic vessel fragments, a bone pin and a bone needle. The iron blade, a cutting tool that could be used for multiple purposes, does not hint at the occupation of this young adult, but it reminds us that women likely laboured in various capacities at Vagnari, although occupational representa-

35 Methods to estimate sex can be found in Buikstra and Ubelaker 1994.

36 Stewart et al. 2017, 13649–13654; Gowland et al. 2021, 859–869.

tion involving metal implements was more common among men. Similarly, burial F319 was a young adult female with an iron punch (P6929) in her grave assemblage, similar to those found in F35 (male), F309 (male) and F334 (8–10 year-old child), suggesting that the activities associated with this particular tool were not gender-specific. In contrast, bill-hooks were all found in male burials (F213, F216, F288), so activities related to viticulture may have been performed by males.

In the Roman world, women's work is typically identified archaeologically by items associated with spinning and weaving, but apart from several bone needles, there is no clear evidence for such activities in the Vagnari burials (e.g., loom weights or spindle whorls) that would suggest a clear division of labour between men and women.[37] Other forms of productive and reproductive labour, including pottery production, food production, domestic work and child-rearing, escape detection in the archaeological record of burial assemblages.[38] Metal implements that appear to have labour-related functions are found more commonly in the burials of male individuals, even if these burials are a small percentage of the total number of individuals at the Vagnari cemetery. Since women did not have as many metal implements in their grave assemblages, their labour may have been represented or commemorated in other ways.

The skeletal evidence from Vagnari supports a possible gendered division of labour suggested by the metal tools found in the Vagnari burials. R. Gilmour's research on the biomechanical properties of long bones and fracture prevalence in the Vagnari skeletal sample found that young adult males were more prone to fractures than females, and these fractures occurred more frequently in the lower limbs. Gilmour attributes these findings to greater mobility-related activities (e.g., herding and transhumance) among males in the Vagnari population. When present, fractures among Vagnari females tended to occur in the upper limbs.[39] Of the 19 individuals buried with metal tools, three adult males (F216, F220, F231) had healed lower limb fractures, and one adult male (F288) had a healed upper limb fracture. Although the datasets do not answer as many

37 Roth 2007, 79 on loom weights or pin-beaters from non-funerary contexts as evidence for activities related to textile production. At Vagnari, bone needles have been found in F104, F117, F200, F302, F325, F334, F338 and F351B. Three of these burials were cremations and therefore of unknown sex (F104, F302 and F325). The remaining burials include adult females (F117, F351B), an adult male (?) (F200), and subadult individuals of unknown sex (F334, F338).

38 Roth 2007, 9–16 on female slave labour in Roman agricultural contexts and 54 on the difficulties of associating material culture with an individual's legal status.

39 Gilmour 2017; Gilmour et al. 2019.

questions as we would like, both osteological evidence and artefacts from the grave assemblages support a possible gendered division of labour at Vagnari.

5 Tools for Adolescents?

In rural contexts, children may have been expected to perform certain tasks from a young age, even if they did not undertake a formal apprenticeship.[40] Columella mentions specific jobs for children that included trimming and pruning vines and using a sickle to cut ferns.[41] Indicators of labour in the child burials at Vagnari are rare. In general, the burials of infants (<1 year) and the youngest children (*infantiae*) at Vagnari contain few items with an average of 4.6 items per burial (Table 13.3).[42] Metal objects apart from jewellery are almost entirely absent from the grave assemblages of infants buried in the Vagnari cemetery.[43]

Iron tools and implements are found in the burials of two individuals who lived for 4–5 years and two who lived for 8–10 years, as well as one subadult of unknown age at death. These five burials with iron tools and implements contained more grave goods than other individuals in their respective age categories with an average of 13.6 items per grave.[44] Individuals F338 and F341, both with an age-at-death estimate of 4–5 years, were each interred with an iron blade. The former, F338, was buried with a large assemblage of 26 objects, which included an iron blade (P6975), an iron key (P6976), a pair of bronze tweezers or a compass (P6969), and several pieces of jewellery, such as gold earrings (P6971) and a silver pendant (6974).[45] Gold earrings have been found in only two other burials at Vagnari, both of which were infants.[46]

40 Bradley 1991, 114 on literary examples of children who engaged in rural work from a young age; Laes 2008 on the labour of enslaved children. See also Groen-Vallinga in this volume for children in household labour.

41 Columella, *Rust.* 2.2.13, 4.27.6 and 11.2.44, cited in Bradley 1991, 114, n. 61 and n. 72 on the passages in the *Code of Justinian* and the *Digest* that indicate enslaved children often began work between the ages of 5 and 10.

42 Brent and Prowse 2014, 105–106 and 109.

43 Note that in Carroll's (2018, 199–207) survey of infant and neonate burials from elsewhere in the Roman world, blades, tools and iron implements are also generally absent.

44 F218, F303, F334, F338 and F341.

45 Other items in the funerary assemblage include: a bronze pin/fastener, circular iron object, ceramic vessels (2), bronze disc (mirror), bone pins (5), hobnails, silver pendant, iron pieces (pin?), shells (2), iron blade, iron pins (3), coins (4), bone needle, iron implement (blade?), bronze tweezers / compass, gold earrings.

46 Other Vagnari burials with gold earrings are F48 and F281. Elsewhere gold jewellery and

TABLE 13.3 Grave goods by age category

Age category	Average per burial	Burials	Number of grave goods
Infantia (0–7.9 years)	4.6	41	188
Pueritia (8–14.9 years)	6.6	13	86
Adulescentia (15–29.9 years)	5.6	24	134
Juventus (30–49.9 years)	7.6	19	144
Gravitas / *Senectus* (50+)	3.0	2	6
Unknown (18+)	6.0	35	210
Unknown (Older Adult 40+)	6.8	8	54
Unknown (cremations)	20.5	4	82
Unstudied	4.0	5	20
TOTAL	6.2	150	927

The presence of blades in the burials of subadult individuals raises questions about whether these tools were used by the deceased during life or whether they had other implications. From a practical perspective, children under the age of 5 may have lacked the dexterity or motor control to use sharp blades. As an alternative explanation, blades and tools in the graves of subadult individuals may reflect an unfulfilled aspiration or a social identity that was projected as if the individual had survived to an age where they might have used such items.[47] For example, F334, the grave of a subadult individual with an estimated age at death of 8–10 years, contained an iron blade or scraper, an iron punch, as well as another iron object with a sharp point, perhaps a blade. These items resemble the burial assemblage recovered from F35 (older adult male) and appear to be associated with the leather-working trade. Although we cannot ascertain with any degree of certainty whether these items 'belonged' to the deceased or if they represent tools that may have been used in an apprenticeship, their presence in a large grave assemblage of 17 items hints at the symbolic value of items associated with labour during the burial process. The intentional placement of these items in the burial of this child reflects the commemorators'

costume elements are associated with young girls who did not live until the age of marriage, and perhaps reflect their 'non-attained wedding' (Martin-Kilcher 2000).

47 Brent and Prowse 2014, 106.

decision to ascribe an identity to this individual that was linked to their actual or anticipated role in the community.

6 Inter-Site Comparisons

A survey of grave assemblages from both sub-urban and semi-rural *necropoleis* reveals that iron tools were not commonly deposited in Roman graves.[48] Among the 53 imperial-period burials at the via dei Cappuccini *necropolis* at Brindisi (Puglia), only T. 15 contained tools, likely related to leather-working, in a very large assemblage with over 60 items.[49] Similarly, none of the 181 burials in the S. Maria in Campis *necropolis* near Foligno (Umbria) or the 226 imperial-period burials at the Vittorina *necropolis* (near Gubbio in Umbria) were equipped with any tools or implements that might be related to agricultural or artisanal activities.[50] Iron elements at these sites were mostly limited to iron nails or elements that formed part of a funerary bier (*ferculum*).

The absence of tools related to agricultural labour in cemeteries that served small urban and semi-urban communities cannot be attributed to a dearth of grave goods at these sites. The Quadrella *necropolis* near Isernia in Molise, for example, shares similar burial practices with Vagnari: the site was used primarily for inhumation burials under *cappuccina* grave covers between the first and fourth centuries CE, with the heaviest period of use concentrated in the first two centuries.[51] The site-wide average number of grave goods among 64 graves is 4.5 items per grave. Unlike Vagnari, ancient *Aesernia* was a Samnite settlement that became a Latin colony in 263 BCE and maintained an urban centre; its population was largely involved in agriculture, pastoralism and crafts, yet these trades are not reflected in the burial record.[52] Objects in the Quadrella graves are considerably more limited than Vagnari: assemblages included mostly ceramic and a few glass vessels, coins, lamps, hobnails, iron

48 *Necropoleis* in Italy with well-published human skeletal remains and grave assemblages include Musarna (Rebillard 2009), Isernia (Terzani and Chiari 1997), Sarsina (Ortalli, Baldoni and Pellicioni 2008), Beligna (Giovannini et al. 1998), Brindisi (Cocchiaro and Andreassi 1988), and Gubbio (Cipollone 2002).

49 Of the 283 burials at Brindisi that span the third century BCE to the fourth century BCE, only 53 imperial-period burials were considered. Of particular interest are T. 15 (Cocchiaro and Andreassi 1988, 160–175), and T. 31, which contained a needle and a spindle hook (inv. 15424 and 15436 a) Cocchiaro and Andreassi 1988, 134–138.

50 Bergamini 1988, 39; Cipollone 2002.

51 Terzani and Chiari 1997, 38–43.

52 Terzani and Chiari 1997, 13–14.

nails and very few items of personal adornment (rings, beads, fibulae, etc.). In further contrast to Vagnari, only one grave (T. 33) contained anything resembling a tool in the form of an iron razor; however, this grave is a late outlier in the cemetery, datable to the fourth to sixth centuries CE based on a late antique lamp.[53] Despite the fact that residents of Aesernia were involved with agricultural labour, it appears that the population at Quadrella did not include objects in the funerary assemblage that emphasized occupational identity.

What emerges from a comparative investigation is that iron tools and implements for cutting and pruning are largely absent from *necropoleis* that served semi-urban populations, despite the fact that they were represented on funerary reliefs.[54] Although it is not surprising that indices of agricultural labour in the form of iron tools or implements are found at a rural site like Vagnari, what is important to note is that the 19 burials with iron tools or implements contain some of the largest grave assemblages at the site, often with valuable items like bronze vessels or jewellery in precious metals. Work, it would appear, was central to the presentation of identity and status in death in ways that are not documented to the same extent in other Roman *necropoleis*. The difference may reflect Vagnari's status as an imperial estate, where greater resources may have been available to support larger funerary assemblages than are typically found in other rural Roman cemeteries, which in turn may reflect a greater variety of achieved or ascribed identities in death.

Vagnari, with its associated vicus and cemetery, offers an ideal site to explore the value of labour, where we can contextualize evidence from the mortuary record against the wider backdrop of the site.[55] For example, the presence of a second-century CE wine press with 10 interred *dolia* in the Vagnari *vicus* hints at the importance of viticulture at the site, which may be reflected through tools associated with cutting and pruning in burials.[56] While we can infer that labourers performed certain kinds of activities in the vicus and in the surrounding area, the cemetery provides both direct and indirect evidence for labour, in

53 Terzani and Chiari 1997, 95 for the lamp and the iron razor.

54 See Egidi, Catalano and Spadoni, 2003 for *necropoleis* near Rome (Osteria del Curato and Lucrezia Romana), where evidence for tools is missing. For a funerary altar, see that of Atimetus and Epaphra, found on the Via Nomentana (near Sant'Agnese), now in the Galleria Lapidaria of the Musei Vaticani (inv. 9277, *CIL* VI, 16166). The left side of the altar depicts a workshop scene where two men fashion tools, while the right side shows a variety of metal tools, hooks, knives, blades and scrapers for sale in a shop.

55 Parker Pearson 1993, 207 on the value of cross-contextual analyses of artefacts.

56 Carroll 2022, 221–225 on the wine production area at Vagnari.

the bodies of labourers who performed these activities as well as through the inclusion of graves goods that hint at the ideological value of labour in this rural community. It is not clear whether iron tools and implements belonged to the individuals with whom they were buried or to the estate more generally. Since larger tools and agricultural implements like spades, shovels and saws are not found in Vagnari graves, we might, in some cases, infer a personal relationship between the deceased and these iron knives and blades.[57] Furthermore, since these tools were not deliberately broken or damaged before deposition, the removal of these items from circulation could represent a loss to the community who might have continued to use them otherwise, thus suggesting that it was more important to bury these items with the deceased than to keep them as functional items.

In the absence of evidence for mortuary professionals at Vagnari, it seems likely that family members or peers of the deceased were responsible for burial, and therefore it was the family, kin or peers who chose to include tools or implements in grave assemblages.[58] Similar patterns are evident in Rome, where epitaphs with occupational titles were not imposed in a top-down manner by slave owners or patrons onto their labourers, but rather by those who erected epitaphs for family members, peers or as a form of ante-mortem self-commemoration.[59] In such a scenario, the inclusion of material signifiers of labour, therefore, was not an extension of control over the deceased in death, but rather a way of expressing the value of the labour they performed within their community, and one that might find parallels between urban and rural communities.

57 Although larger tools are absent from Vagnari graves, the bill-hooks could be fairly large: in the case of P6642 from F288, the object measured 42.5 cm long and was potentially difficult to place into a grave.

58 Small et al. 2007, 133–136 on the absence of regulation in the Vagnari cemetery. Although the cemetery is loosely characterized by the NE–SW orientation of a central group of graves, the different grave orientations, frequent instances of disturbance or damage to existing graves, and overlapping and intersecting burials at Vagnari point to the absence of central organization.

59 Joshel 1992, 76 notes that in her sample of epitaphs with occupational titles, there is a known or inferred commemorator in 43.2 % (N = 503) of epitaphs, and in only 27 cases (2.3 %) did a master or patron erect an epitaph with an occupational title. Instead, commemoration by oneself or one's family or peers was the most common form in 33 % of epitaphs (N = 384).

7 Conclusion: The Aspirational Value of Labour at Vagnari

Burial assemblages typically reflect the careful curation of items that could negotiate, challenge, or reaffirm different aspects of the deceased's identity in death.[60] The interpretation of grave goods in archaeological contexts is full of paradoxes in terms of the meaning, ownership, and value of these objects. For example, in prehistoric graves elsewhere in Europe, M. Parker Pearson notes that agricultural implements, which were rare compared to weapons, were 'associated with securing the growth of crops'.[61] In the Roman world, iron tools and implements might have been selected as grave goods for a combination of reasons: to serve a protective or apotropaic function within the grave or in the afterlife; as a prestige object because of the economic or symbolic value of metal that was conspicuously removed from circulation during funerary activities; as an item that indicated unfulfilled social or occupational aspirations for the deceased; or because there was a personal connection between the tool and the deceased that was linked to their social role or occupation in the community.[62] The tools and implements deposited in the Vagnari cemetery may have been removed from circulation because they were considered 'polluted' by death and thus needed to be separated from the world of the living.[63] Alternatively, such items may have been deposited into a grave because the living perceived these items as valuable markers of status, and accordingly their deposition was a form of display.

This analysis of metal implements in the Vagnari burials is intentionally focused on a restricted type of grave good found in the cemetery. 'Tools' are narrowly defined here as handheld iron objects with a functional purpose, which excludes other items that were made from perishable materials. The burials in this small sample are dated through the presence of items with broad chronological ranges, such as coins, oil lamps or regional forms of pottery, so it is not possible to discuss chronological trends in the burials. The gendered nature of burials with iron tools and other metal implements suggests that women at Vagnari may have been involved in labour that cannot be discerned easily from items included in the burial assemblages.[64] Furthermore, the legal statuses of

60 Brent and Prowse 2014; Fahlander 2020 on recent theoretical approaches to burial assemblages; Humphreys 2021, 13–18 on artefacts and identity.

61 Parker Pearson 1993, 207.

62 Toynbee 1971, 52–54 on grave goods more generally.

63 Parker Pearson 1993, 207.

64 Larsson Lovén 2019 on women's work in rural areas, which might have included textile production, domestic service or child-rearing.

those who were buried in the Vagnari cemetery are unknown, so we are unable to draw status-based conclusions about labour or the ownership of items in burial assemblages. As a result, the inclusion of iron blades or tools in a burial may reveal little about the relative wealth or poverty of either the deceased with whom they were interred or the living who conferred status onto the dead during the funerary process.

In spite of the potentially conflicting interpretation of grave goods, by examining patterns in the types of objects that were included in funerary assemblages across various demographic groups, we can begin to understand how objects co-constituted individual identities, and, critically for the present focus, how labour was a valuable aspect of identity as reflected in the mortuary record. When iron objects were deposited in a grave, they formed some of the largest funerary assemblages at Vagnari, and they occur alongside items that are found in limited numbers, such as bronze vessels or coins. Objects that might be associated with occupational identity could confer prestige on the deceased or hint at social aspirations for those who had not yet achieved certain milestones within the life-course, perhaps as a way of projecting what kind of work they might have performed if they had lived longer. Ultimately, the objects in the Vagnari cemetery grave assemblages should not be interpreted solely as a direct indicator of the occupational status of the deceased, but rather as an index of how labour could be highlighted as a prominent form of identity in death.

Acknowledgements

The excavation was carried out with a permit granted by the Ministero per i Beni e le Attività Culturali e per il Turismo to Tracy Prowse, facilitated through the British School at Rome, and with the invaluable assistance of Dott.ssa Stefania Peterlini. Survey of the site and essential technical support was provided by Franco Taccogna (Gravina), restoration of the metal objects by Tonia Petrafesa (Gravina). The team is grateful to numerous organizations and individuals for their support of the project, and especially to the landowner of Vagnari, the late Dott. Mario de Gemmis Pellicciari; the British School at Rome; the Soprintendenza Archeologia, Belle Arti e Paesaggio per la Città Metropolitana di Bari, especially Dott.ssa Francesca Radina and Dott.ssa Marissa Corrente from the Centro Operativo per l'Archeologia in Bari, the Centro Operativo in Gravina in Puglia, and the Fondazione Ettore Pomarici Santomasi, Gravina in Puglia.

Bibliography

Bergamini, M., ed. (1988). *Foligno. La necropoli romana di S. Maria in Campis*. Perugia.

Bowes, K., ed. (2021). *The Roman Peasant Project 2009–2014. Excavating the Roman Rural Poor*. Philadelphia.

Bowes, K. (2021). When Kuznets Went to Rome: Roman Economic Well-Being and the Reframing of Roman History. *Capitalism. A Journal of History and Economics* 2(1), pp. 7–40.

Bradley, K.R. (1991). *Discovering the Roman Family. Studies in Roman Social History*. Oxford.

Brent, L. and Prowse, T.L. (2014). Grave Goods, Burial Practices and Patterns of Distribution in the Vagnari Cemetery. In: A. Small, ed., *Beyond Vagnari. New Themes in the Study of Roman South Italy*. Bari, pp. 99–109.

Buikstra, J.E. and Ubelaker, D.H., eds. (1994). *Standards for Data Collection from Human Skeletal Remains*. Fayetteville.

Carlsen, J. (1995). *Vilici and Roman Estate Managers until AD 284*. Rome.

Carroll, M. (2018). *Infancy and Earliest Childhood in the Roman World. 'A Fragment of Time'*. Oxford.

Carroll, M. (2019). Preliminary Report on the University of Sheffield Excavations in the *Vicus* of the Roman Imperial Estate at Vagnari, Puglia, 2012–2018. *Fasti Online Documents & Report* 431. https://www.fastionline.org/docs/FOLDER-it-2019-431.pdf

Carroll, M. (2022). Viticulture, *opus doliare*, and the *patrimonium Caesaris* at the Roman Imperial Estate at Vagnari (Puglia). *JRA* 35(1), pp. 221–246.

Carroll, M., ed. (2022). *The Making of a Roman Imperial Estate. Archaeology in the* Vicus *at Vagnari, Puglia*. Oxford.

Carroll, M. et al. (2022). Lead, Lead-Working Debris, and Lead Sourcing. In: M. Carroll, ed., *The Making of a Roman Imperial Estate. Archaeology in the* Vicus *at Vagnari, Puglia*. Oxford, pp. 129–135.

Cipollone, M. (2002). Gubbio (Perugia). Necropoli in loc. Vittorina. Campagne di scavo 1980–1982. *NSc* 11–12, pp. 5–371.

Cocchiaro, A. and Andreassi, G., eds. (1988). *La necropoli di via Cappuccini a Brindisi*. Fasano (Brindisi).

dé Spagnolis, M. (2000). *La tomba del calzolaio dalla necropoli monumentale romana di Nocera Superiore*. Rome.

Egidi, R., Catalano, P. and Spadoni, D., eds. (2003). *Aspetti di vita quotidiana dalle necropoli della via Latina. Località Osteria del Curato*. Rome.

Fahlander, F. (2020). Becoming Dead: Burial Assemblages as Vitalist Devices. *CAJ* 30(4), pp. 555–569.

Gilmour, R.J. (2017). *Resilient Romans. Cross-Sectional Evidence for Long-Term Func-*

tional Consequences of Extremity Trauma. Unpublished PhD diss., McMaster University, Hamilton, ON.

Gilmour, R.J. et al. (2019). Maintaining Mobility after Fracture: A Biomechanical Analysis of Fracture Consequences at the Roman Sites of Ancaster (UK) and Vagnari (Italy). *International Journal of Paleopathology* 24, pp. 119–129.

Giovannini, A. et al. (1998). Recenti indagini nelle necropoli aquileiesi: Beligna, scavo 1992–1993. *Aquileia Nostra* 69, pp. 205–358.

Gowland, R. et al. (2021). Sex Estimation of Teeth at Different Developmental Stages Using Dimorphic Enamel Peptide Analysis. *American Journal of Physical Anthropology* 174, pp. 859–869.

Groen-Vallinga, M.J. and Tacoma, L.E. (2017). The Value of Labour: Diocletian's Prices Edict. In K. Verboven and C. Laes, eds., *Work, Labour, and Professions in the Roman World*. Leiden, pp. 104–132.

Harvey, S.M. (2010). Iron Tools from a Roman Villa at Boscoreale, Italy, in the Field Museum and the Kelsey Museum of Archaeology. *AJA* 114(4), pp. 697–714.

Humphreys, O. (2021). *London's Roman Tools. Craft, Agriculture and Experience in an Ancient City*. Oxford.

Joshel, S.R. (1992). *Work, Identity, and Legal Status at Rome. A Study of the Occupational Inscriptions*. Norman, OK/London.

Joshel, S.R. and Petersen, L.H. (2014). *The Material Life of Roman Slaves*. Cambridge.

Laes, C. (2008). Child Slaves at Work in Roman Antiquity. *Ancient Society* 38, pp. 235–283.

Larsson Lovén, L. (2019). The Invisible Women of Roman Agrarian Work and Economy. In: J. Rantala, ed., *Gender, Memory, and Identity in the Roman World*. Amsterdam, pp. 89–103.

MacKinnon, M. (2011). The Faunal Remains. In: A. Small, ed., *Vagnari. Il villaggio, l'artigianato, la proprietà imperiale = The Village, the Industries, the Imperial Property*. Bari, pp. 305–328.

Manning, W.H. (1985). *Catalogue of Romano-British Iron Tools, Fittings and Weapons in the British Museum*. London.

Martin-Kilcher, S. (2000). *Mors immatura* in the Roman World: A Mirror of Society and Tradition. In: J. Pearce, M. Millett and M. Struck, eds., *Burial, Society and Context in the Roman World*. Oxford, pp. 63–77.

Marzano, A. (2007). *Roman Villas in Central Italy. A Social and Economic History*. Leiden/Boston.

Montana, G. et al. (2021). Archaeometric Analysis of Building Ceramics and '*dolia defossa*' from the Roman Imperial Estate of Vagnari (Gravina in Puglia, Italy). *JAS: Reports* 38, pp. 1–14.

Morris, I. (1992). *Death-Ritual and Social Structure in Classical Antiquity*. Cambridge.

Ortalli, J., Baldoni, D. and Pellicioni, M.T. (2008). Pian di Bezzo di Sarsina: La necropoli romana. In: A. Donati, ed., *Storia di Sarsina I: L'età antica*. Cesena, pp. 431–636.

Parker Pearson, M. (1993). The Powerful Dead: Archaeological Relationships between the Living and the Dead. *CAJ* 3(2), pp. 203–229.

Rebillard, É., ed. (2009). *Musarna 3: la nécropole impériale*. Rome.

Rees, S.I. (1979). *Agricultural Implements in Prehistoric and Roman Britain*. Oxford.

Roth, U. (2007). *Thinking Tools. Agricultural Slavery between Evidence and Models*. London (Bulletin of the Institute of Classical Studies. Supplement 92).

Small, A.M., ed. (2011). *Vagnari. Il villaggio, l'artigianato, la proprietà imperiale = The Village, the Industries, the Imperial Property*. Bari.

Small, A.M. (2014). From *Silvium* to Vagnari: Sheep, Wool and Weaving on the *Saltus*. In: A.M. Small, ed., *Beyond Vagnari. New Themes in the Study of Roman South Italy*. Bari, pp. 53–64.

Small, A.M., ed. (2014). *Beyond Vagnari. New Themes in the Study of Roman South Italy*. Bari.

Small, A.M. and Small, C.M. (2011). The Via Appia and Vagnari. In: A.M. Small, ed., *Vagnari. Il villaggio, l'artigianato, la proprietà imperiale = The Village, the Industries, the Imperial Property*. Bari, pp. 383–386.

Small, C.M. and Small, A.M. (2005). Defining an Imperial Estate: The Environs of Vagnari in South Italy. In: P. Attema, A. Nijboer and A. Zifferero, eds., *Papers in Italian Archaeology VI. Communities and Settlements from the Neolithic to the Early Medieval Period*. Oxford, pp. 894–902.

Small, A.M., Volterra, V. and Hancock, R.G.V. (2003). New Evidence from Tile-Stamps for Imperial Properties near Gravina, and the Topography of Imperial Estates in SE Italy. *JRA* 16, pp. 179–199.

Small, A.M. et al. (2007). Excavation in the Roman Cemetery at Vagnari, in the Territory of Gravina in Puglia, 2002. *PBSR* 75, pp. 123–229.

Smith, A. et al. (2018). *Life and Death in the Countryside of Roman Britain*. London.

Stewart, N.A. et al. (2017). Sex Determination of Human Remains from Peptides in Tooth Enamel. *Proceedings of the National Academy of Sciences of the United States of America* 114(52), pp. 13649–13654.

Terzani, C. and Chiari, M.M., eds. (1997). *Isernia. La necropoli romana in località Quadrella*. Rome.

Trentacoste, A. (2022). Animal Remains from Vagnari: Bones and Shells. In: M. Carroll, ed., *The Making of a Roman Imperial Estate. Archaeology in the* Vicus *at Vagnari, Puglia*. Oxford, pp. 174–187.

Triozzi, B. (2022). Loom Weights and Textile Weaving at Vagnari. In: M. Carroll, ed., *The Making of a Roman Imperial Estate. Archaeology in the* Vicus *at Vagnari, Puglia*. Oxford, pp. 162–170.

Toynbee, J.M.C. (1971). *Death and Burial in the Roman World*. Ithaca.

Van Oyen, A. et al. (2022). Forging the Roman Rural Economy: A Blacksmithing Workshop and Its Tool Set at Marzuolo (Tuscany). *AJA* 126(1), pp. 53–77.
Vinson, P. (1972). Ancient Roads between Venosa and Gravina. *PBSR* 40, pp. 58–90.
White, K.D. (1967). *Agricultural Implements of the Roman World*. Cambridge.
White, K.D. (1970). *Roman Farming*. Ithaca.
Willi, A. (2021). *Writing Equipment*. Nottingham.

SECTION 4

Labour and Civic Values

CHAPTER 14

Foreign Labour, Common Ground: The Value of Craftspeople in Early Democratic Athens

Helle Hochscheid

1 Introduction

How were craftspeople valued in ancient Athens? In the past, scholarship has answered this question negatively, based on dismissive descriptions in ancient literature, and the fact that slavery is considered to have been common among those who engaged in crafts.[1] Even the workmen listed in the Erechtheum building accounts in some cases appear to have been enslaved. While a few sculptors and painters became famous and wealthy, the overall image in the historiography of ancient Greece is of a politically and economically disenfranchised group.[2]

This chapter will re-examine this view of craftspeople in fifth-century Athens as what might be construed as an urban 'working class', consisting of Athenians and foreigners working as artisans, both free and enslaved. It investigates the consequences that the city's demand for craft products had on the Athenians' perceptions of this mixed group. It will do so first through examining the metic and citizen workforce of the Periclean building projects, and the processes that had led to the formation of this community of craftspeople in the preceding decades. Second, I will look at evidence of craft identities in the later part of the fifth century, to argue that the Acropolis building programme reflects a shift in attitudes towards craft that seems to have started well before the building programme was set in motion. Arguably, its organizational design was consciously tailored towards this community. Consequently, instead of the low appreciation that the Athenians are thought to have felt towards craftspeople in this period, considerable evidence suggests that their contributions were appreciated to the point where the *demos* was prepared to

1 For instance, Epstein 2008; Feyel 2006; Silver 2008. *Contra* Lewis 2021, 228–229. More generally on slavery in ancient Greece and Athens in particular, Taylor 2015; Vlassopoulos 2016.

2 A thorough overview of negative and positive views, as well as an enlightening analysis of remuneration in Stewart 2019. Cf. also Carusi 2021; Corso 2004–2014; Hochscheid 2020; Schultz 2017.

 DOI:10.1163/9789004694965_015

not only literally, but also figuratively pay for craft. In other words, the value of craftspeople was acknowledged as crucial, beyond the convenience offered by the availability of items for consumption. I will argue that pride in its craft emerges as a core feature of Athenian identity, one that drove Athenians to remarkably keen engagement with the arts and crafts in their personal as well as public lives.

2 Labour Demand in Post-Persian Athens

In the public construction projects of classical Athens, inscribed accounts lay out the different crafts employed to erect and furnish monumental buildings. The range of crafts directly involved in large building projects is represented in these accounts but also in literary works of antiquity, as illustrated in this quote from Plutarch's *Life of Pericles* (12.5–7, trans. Perrin 1916, modified):

> And in his [Pericles'] desire that the unwarlike throng of common labourers should neither have no share at all in the public receipts, nor yet get fees for laziness and idleness, he boldly suggested to the people projects for great constructions, and designs for works which would call many arts into play and involve long periods of time, in order that the stay-at-homes, no less than the sailors and sentinels and soldiers, might have a pretext for getting a beneficial share of the public wealth. The materials to be used were stone, bronze, ivory, gold, ebony, and cypress-wood; the arts which should elaborate and work up these materials were those of carpenter, moulder, bronze-smith, stone-cutter, dyer, worker in gold and ivory, painter, pattern-weaver, embosser, to say nothing of the forwarders and furnishers of the material, such as factors, sailors and pilots by sea, and, by land, wagon-makers, trainers of yoked beasts, and drivers. There were also rope-makers, weavers, leather-workers, road-builders, and miners. And since each particular art, like a general with the army under his separate command, kept its own throng of unskilled and untrained labourers in compact array, to be as instrument unto player and as body unto soul in subordinate service, it came to pass that for every age, almost, and every capacity the city's great abundance was distributed and scattered about by such demands.
>
> … τὸν δ' ἀσύντακτον καὶ βάναυσον ὄχλον οὔτ' ἄμοιρον εἶναι λημμάτων βουλόμενος οὔτε λαμβάνειν ἀργὸν καὶ σχολάζοντα, μεγάλας κατασκευασμάτων ἐπιβολὰς καὶ πολυτέχνους ὑποθέσεις ἔργων διατριβὴν ἐχόντων ἐνέβαλε φέρων εἰς τὸν

> δῆμον, ἵνα μηδὲν ἧττον τῶν πλεόντων καὶ φρουρούντων καὶ στρατευομένων τὸ οἰκουροῦν ἔχῃ πρόφασιν ἀπὸ τῶν δημοσίων ὠφελεῖσθαι καὶ μεταλαμβάνειν. [6] ὅπου γὰρ ὕλη μὲν ἦν λίθος, χαλκός, ἐλέφας, χρυσός, ἔβενος, κυπάρισσος, αἱ δὲ ταύτην ἐκπονοῦσαι καὶ κατεργαζόμεναι τέχναι, τέκτονες, πλάσται, χαλκοτύποι, λιθουργοί, βαφεῖς, χρυσοῦ μαλακτῆρες καὶ ἐλέφαντος, ζωγράφοι, ποικιλταί, τορευταί, πομποὶ δὲ τούτων καὶ κομιστῆρες, ἔμποροι καὶ ναῦται καὶ κυβερνῆται κατὰ θάλατταν, [7] οἱ δὲ κατὰ γῆν ἁμαξοπηγοὶ καὶ ζευγοτρόφοι καὶ ἡνίοχοι καὶ καλωστρόφοι καὶ λινουργοὶ καὶ σκυτοτόμοι καὶ ὁδοποιοὶ καὶ μεταλλεῖς, ἑκάστη δὲ τέχνη, καθάπερ στρατηγὸς ἴδιον στράτευμα, τὸν θητικὸν ὄχλον καὶ ἰδιώτην συντεταγμένον εἶχεν, ὄργανον καὶ σῶμα τῆς ὑπηρεσίας γινόμενον, εἰς πᾶσαν, ὡς ἔπος εἰπεῖν, ἡλικίαν καὶ φύσιν αἱ χρεῖαι διένεμον καὶ διέσπειρον τὴν εὐπορίαν.

Although the distance of five centuries between Plutarch's lifetime and the building programme calls for caution, Plutarch's logistic insight into the knock-on effects of the building industry in this fragment is remarkably solid. Not only activities directly connected to the actual building, but suppliers, transporters and traders of many kinds are drawn into the picture. He even speaks of the untrained labourers active in each craft (or perhaps these should be considered trainees of some sort), who were unable or unwilling to make their living fighting for Athens or rowing in the navy, and for whom the building programme offered an income in return for a meaningful contribution. On less stable ground, Plutarch contends that Pericles' motivation was the redistribution of some of the wealth that came into the city, on the economic basis of payment for work rather than of free hand-outs.

The idea of the Athenian building programme as a redistributive public works project may seem anachronistic. In past scholarship, Plutarch's interpretation has been rejected based on the wide gap between his lifetime and the events on which he comments.[3] Nonetheless, classical economic thinking in Greece does not preclude the possibility that the objectives of the programme were approximately as Plutarch describes them.[4] His underlying assumptions point in two directions: the idea of this building project as an employment scheme, and the labour time and variety of different levels of craft skills, that is, levels of specialized labour, required to complete the work. In this last respect Plutarch's description is plausible, and it is worth noting that the ancient Greeks, in particular the Athenians, were well-versed in complex assemblage

3 Shear 2016, 10, arguing Plutarch fundamentally misunderstood the fifth-century labour market in Athens. See further below.

4 E.g. Pl. *Plt.* 288e; Xen. *Cyr.* 8.2.5.

work.[5] Examples come not only from architecture, but from other production spheres too. For instance, the Athenians alone accomplished feats of shipbuilding several times during the fifth century. Here, as in construction, a large variety of skills were applied to a similarly wide range of raw materials, at levels from unskilled to highly sophisticated, to produce the complexity of triremes, their rigging, and the arms and armour of the armies they carried.[6] That such a wide range of crafts was rallied into service for a single purpose is therefore eminently plausible. The other question, however, is less straightforward. Considering this large group of craftspeople trained in a wide range of different skills, where would they have come from, and depending on the answer to this question, how were they viewed by the citizens of Athens?

In the aftermath of the Persian wars, large numbers of Athenian residents who were not involved in military campaigns were indeed working on large-scale projects in and around Athens, not only in the construction of the fleet, but on the Themistoclean city circuit, the Acropolis containment and fortification walls, and somewhat later, the northern Long Wall.[7] The docks at Piraeus had to be restored and expanded, and both the fortifications of Piraeus and the first stage of the naval shipsheds at the harbours of Zea and Mounichia were also built in the first half of the century.[8] Further, Thucydides comments on the poor state of Athenian houses, and several of the surviving Athenian house plans that can be dated were built in the second quarter of the fifth century.[9] As he notes, buildings had also been demolished to free up materials for the city wall, exacerbating the state of the city's residential areas: 'Meanwhile the whole population in the city was to labour at the wall, the Athenians, their wives and their children, sparing no edifice, private or public, which might be of any use to

5 For labour division in sculpture and architecture, Carusi 2020; Hochscheid 2015, especially 157–235; in general: Lewis 2020.

6 For the variety and amount of labour involved in military equipment including shipbuilding, see Massar 2021.

7 The fleet: Thuc. 1.14.3, 1.93.7; on the city walls and houses of Athens: Thuc. 1.89.3 and further; on the Themistoclean wall: Theocharaki 2019, esp. 227–230; on the Long Walls: Boersma 1970, 57–58; Camp 2001, 66–67; Costaki and Theocharaki 2021, 58–59; Theocharaki 2011.

8 On the walls of Piraeus see Thuc. 1.93.6; Athanasopoulos 2021: in a second phase later in the fifth century, roofed and colonnaded monumental shipsheds were built, although the exact date is hard to pinpoint. Cf. Camp 2001, 294–299; Costaki and Theocharaki 2021, 58–59. Lithagogia road, Korres 1995; Shear 2016, 59–60; on water works, Boersma 223–225, nos. 103–106, including an aqueduct built in the last quarter of the sixth century and projects improving the water supply to the city from the later fifth to early fourth centuries BCE; see also Camp 2001, 64, 70–71 (water works instigated by Kimon); Wycherley 1978, 250–251; Stroszeck 2021.

9 Thuc. 1.89.3.; Boersma 1970, 42, 247–254; Tsakirgis 2009; Paga 2020, 24. Second quarter, e.g. the House of Mikion and Menon and houses on the Street of the Marble Workers. See also below.

the work, but throwing all down.'[10] In short, reconstruction remained necessary both in the public and private sphere, in Athens and Piraeus, not to mention other regions of Attica; maintenance and repair required yet more labour.

Further evidence of continuous demand for workers in construction and related crafts can be found in workshop remains. South-west of the Agora lies the so-called House of Mikion and Menon, which served as a sculpture workshop (attested by thick layers of marble debris) from the second quarter of the fifth until the second century BCE.[11] Further south, the buildings on the Street of the Marble Workers were mostly built around the middle of the fifth century, with some originating slightly earlier; many of them were then partially or wholly remodelled in the second half of the fifth century, as was the House of Mikion and Menon.[12] While living quarters were almost certainly included in many of these buildings, they also contained workshops, from bronze and marble to pigments and paint, with traces of glass and bone manufacture nearby.[13]

Among other non-sacred architecture or infrastructure undertaken in this period were the construction of the Tholos in the Agora, and the renovation, landscaping and irrigation of that area.[14] With the exception of the houses to the south-west of the Agora, remnants of private buildings built or restored just after the Persian wars are thus few and far between, in part due to the focus in scholarship on large monumental construction and restoration. Nevertheless, the work performed on infrastructure and housing should be added to the estimated amount of labour for the reconstruction of Athens, even if its precise extent remains unknown.

Some of the various projects listed above relied largely on unskilled labour overseen by expert foremen, for example digging water channels or planting pits, or hauling the materials for Athens' circuit wall, as illustrated by Themistocles' encouragement for every able-bodied person to help build the

10 Thuc.1.90.3. Cf. Theocharaki 2011, 78–81.

11 Boersma 1970, 248 no. 149; Hochscheid 2015, 199–201, 221–222; Nolte 2006, 264–273; Tsakirgis 2009, 50–52.

12 Sanidas 2013, 60–62; Nolte 2006, 252–263; Tsakirgis 2005; Young 1952.

13 House F, possibly House E. The glass and bone production traces are of uncertain date. See Hochscheid 2015, 201–206; 213–221; Sanidas 2013, 67–68, 106–108. More generally on craft workshops, see Chatzedemitriou 2005; Bejor et al. 2012.

14 Tholos: Boersma 1970, 42–56; Camp 2001, 64–71. Salmon (see below) does not include these projects, because he focuses on the more labour-intensive fortifications and temple building. For overviews of projects from ca. 480–450 BCE, Boersma 1970, 19–96; Camp 2001, e.g. 63–64 (planting and water management), 67 (south Acropolis containment wall); also Hurwit 1999, 141–145.

city's fortifications. However, structures like the Tholos or the Acropolis south wall are the work of skilled builders, and other construction-related jobs, such as the transport of stone blocks, also require training and experience.[15] A comprehensive quantification of the skilled labour capacity in public building in Athens has been proposed by John Salmon, based on the amount of worked stone surface completed per year in the period from 650 until 405 BCE. He concludes that from 480–450 to 450–425, the number of man-hours needed in public construction in Athens went up from 379 to 874 per year.[16] For this reason, he argues, the Athenians had to attract large numbers of craftsmen from abroad, which fits in with recruitment practices known from large building projects in other *poleis*.

While Salmon's analysis is enlightening for public construction, it does not, nor does it aim to, represent the demand for overall craft labour in Athens. The reasons for this are threefold. First, smaller or archaeologically less visible activities like the ones mentioned above, and the amount of labour needed for private architecture, are excluded. Since immediately after the Persian destruction residential construction was likely prioritized as soon as the defences of the city permitted it, demand for labour was undoubtedly higher between 480 and 450 than can be estimated on public works alone. Second, as we will see further on in this chapter, labour in construction attracted labour in other branches, and it is difficult to separate work hours directly in construction from wider but related manufacturing circles. Building activities require support from other trades and crafts, for example for the supply of raw materials or the production of tools. Thirdly, there are trade jobs to consider even beyond this wider network of construction. Those who are engaged in building need to live somewhere, eat and drink, use clothes and footwear. Traders and sellers of such daily necessities would therefore also be drawn to major building sites and would benefit from the concentration of people, thus adding to the exchanges of goods and services.[17]

In short, the reconstruction and renewal of Athens after the Persian Wars required a large labour force in a wide range of crafts and trades, from highly skilled to unskilled. But in a city destroyed by war, this labour force cannot be solely measured in terms of monumental long-term projects, but rather was determined by the broader needs of the population at that moment. The pub-

15 For the requirement of both highly skilled and general labour cf. Paga 2020, 254–256. For transport of marble, Korres 1995; Hochscheid 2015, 137–150.

16 Salmon 2001, especially table 9.1 on p. 205. For an in-depth analysis of the relation between stoneworking hours of labour and the finished surfaces, see Barker and Russell 2012.

17 For a comprehensive overview of professional traders and crafters see Lewis 2020.

lic building projects of the second half of the century increased the demand for labour, and in construction-related crafts increased it further: simply the number of structures from this period admits no other conclusion. However, the rise in the overall number of craftspeople in Athens may have been less dramatic than Salmon suggests. The required labour in the first half of the fifth century was only partly for the monumental work that is so visible today, and for another, considerable, part had more humble goals such as the infrastructure and domestic architecture mentioned earlier. In short, even in construction, numbers of craftspeople in the first half of the century must have been considerably higher than the amount of monumental building would suggest. The rebuilding of Athens after the war and the ripples it caused in supply crafts and beyond, from carpentry to textile production and from metalwork to baking, add up to considerable manufacturing demand. While some Athenian craftsmen certainly left to work elsewhere in the Greek-speaking world,[18] the houses, roads, walls and water pipelines of this period show that many also remained.

3 Foreigners and Athenians in Sculpture and Other Crafts

There is a paradox between the numbers of metics listed in the building accounts on the one hand, and Plutarch's claims about Pericles' underlying rationale for the building programme on the other. Although Plutarch says nothing of the civic status of the common labourers who are to benefit from the scheme, it would seem improbable that workmen recently recruited from abroad—in particular, recruited *for* the building programme—would have been the target beneficiaries. After all, why provide a scheme for paying out the city's wealth to its residents if one then has to engage external workers? Nonetheless, the Erechtheum accounts list 42 metics out of 110 identifiable workmen, as well as 21 demotics indicating citizen status, and 16 genitive forms indicative of enslaved status, combined with either citizen or metic owners.[19] These numbers have been interpreted as an indication that foreigners were attracted by, or even actively recruited for the large construction projects in Athens, and their disproportionately large share in the Athenian craft labour

18 On craftsmen's recruitment and travelling for work all over the ancient Mediterranean, see Massar 2020 and in this volume. For Athenians moving to work in Sicily, also Shear 2016, 11; Paga 2020, 255 n. 18.

19 Lambert 2000; Shear 2016, 10; Randall 195; Wijma 2014, 29, 90. See the latter and also Carusi 2021 for similar ratios in fourth-century Eleusis, suggesting this situation in construction was a long-term given. Slightly different numbers but the same picture in Epstein 2010.

market is the result of purposeful campaigning for particular projects.[20] In particular, Epstein writes that it 'is reasonable to assume that the number of Athenian craftsmen more or less suited the local needs, which usually did not include major public construction'.[21] This would seem to be in contradiction with Plutarch's description, in which he claims that the programme specifically targeted artisans who were already in Athens. Moreover, the increase of labour hours suggested by Salmon also argues for high-intensity periods requiring extra labour to be brought in temporarily when exceptional projects were taken on. The question is whether the status quo was a large resident workforce in Athens throughout the fifth century, explaining Pericles' idea as set out by Plutarch, or a fluctuating workforce that was attracted or arrived of its own accord only when major building was underway in the city.

Assuming, on the basis of the demand for labour described above, that a large community of craftspeople was already in Athens by the middle of the fifth century, the question arises, When did they arrive? The presence, and residence, of foreign craftspeople in Athens had a long tradition. The first reference to immigrant craftsmen occurs in Solon's legislation, detailing that tradesmen who moved permanently to Athens could become citizens.[22] Jumping ahead to the late archaic period, the presence of foreign sculptors is attested through signatures.[23] A joint signature such as that of Kritios and his associate Nesiotes, who presumably came from the islands, points to a partnership between sculptors of different origins.[24] In part, such collaborations were the result of the well-established workshops in various sculpture centres, on the islands and in Attica, where local and non-local sculptors came to train, and the parallel practices of travelling around for work and for completion of roughed-out sculptures at their destinations.[25] Beside these reasons for non-Athenian sculptors to reside in Athens, the late archaic period is another heyday for construction projects in the city, for example the Pisistratid temple of Zeus and the extended platform on the Acropolis, as well as the beginnings of its late archaic propylon and the early fortification of Mounichia Hill in Piraeus, projects that

20 Epstein 2010.

21 Carusi 2021, 143–144; Epstein 2010, 5.

22 Plut. *Sol.* 24.4; for the Solonic fragments and the phrase *epi technei*, Blok 2006; Blok 2017, 109 n. 28.

23 Johnston and Palagia 2019. For other signatures than those of sculptors, see Hurwit 2015.

24 Stewart 2017 for Kritios and Nesiotes; cf. Hochscheid 2015, 187–189 and 2020, 214; Hurwit 2015, 126–127; Keesling 2003, 170–175; 186–191.

25 D'Onofrio 2008, 237, 243; Hochscheid 2015, 132–137, and forthcoming; Nolte 2005, 234; Hellmann 2000.

offered incentives for skilled stoneworkers who had come in to stay in Attica.[26] Recent research on building projects in Attica details how the early democracy continued this trend with several major building projects.[27] To sum up, a considerable number of non-Athenian sculptors came in for construction in the late archaic period.

The continued presence of these sculptors is attested not only in ongoing or completed public building work in the years before the Persian destruction, but also in private monuments. For example, in the combined total of 68 signed dedications from the Acropolis and signed grave monuments, mainly from the Kerameikos, between ca. 600 and 400 BCE, only sixteen signatures can be ascribed to sculptors who were Athenians with any degree of certainty, among them Endoios, Antenor and Kritios.[28] Nineteen monuments were signed by sculptors who came from elsewhere. If we count individual sculptors, non-Athenians come to twelve and Athenians to ten.[29] Besides sculptors who signed alone, there are occasional joint signatures such as those of Philergos and Endoios, of whom only the latter's Athenian citizenship can be verified; and Kritios and Nesiotes, already mentioned, who sign together six times (excluding the Tyrannicides), spread over several decades.[30] About two thirds of these identifiable signatures date to around 500 BCE. In short, of the signing sculptors on Athenian private monuments whose origins can be established with some

26 E.g. Boersma 1970, 19–27; Paga 2020, 55–59, 132–135. For the works in Piraeus at this time, see Athanasopoulos 2021, 109 and *passim*.

27 Paga 2015 and 2021.

28 Hurwit 2015, 101–130; cf. Hochscheid 2015, 174–194 for archaic sculptors' signatures in Athens. Overall numbers in Hochscheid 2015, 174–197; signature list (provenance Athens) pp. 487–491. For sculptors' signatures in a wider Greek context, Barlou 2014; Hurwit 2015; Johnston and Palagia 2019; Kaczko 2010; Hochscheid forthcoming. For non-Athenian craftsmen and tradesmen staying on in Athens also Blok 2017, 265.

29 E.g. Aristion of Paros, Barlou 2013; Hochscheid forthcoming; Hurwit 2015, 105–106 and 128; Archermos of Chios, Hochscheid 2015, 185, and forthcoming; Kresilas of Kydonia: ibid. 190; Hurwit 2015, 130–131; Keesling 2003, 193–194. The majority of signatures offer no ethnic, nor other markers to clarify status; these cases have been left out of the calculation. Epstein's (2010) alternative approach that in classical Athens, 'persons of unknown status are more likely to be non-citizens' (2010, 11) seems somewhat tenuous. Moreover, for the archaic period, when no formal metic status existed, the lack of an ethnic might equally represent greater self-evidence of local citizenship, in other words, because there are fewer formal status levels, the need to indicate Athenian citizenship would have been less pressing.

30 See Hochscheid 2015, 174–188, 487–449. Cf. Hurwit 2015, 101–143 for all signatures on sculpture. Kritios and Nesiotes; Hurwit 2015, 126–127; Stewart 2017, 37–43 and *passim*. Philergos and Endoios: Hurwit 2015, 118–119 (not a joint signature per se, in his view); Keesling 2003, 153, 156–157; Viviers 1992.

certainty, in total just over half are non-Athenian individuals. This ratio is similar in the total number of signatures. Though these numbers are small and the origins of signing sculptors are often unknown, it seems that already in the late archaic period, Athenian and non-Athenian sculptors filled the available jobs with a slight majority for non-Athenians. This demonstrates the pull that the city had already in this period, certainly for sculptors and other stoneworkers.

Of courses, circumstances in Athens deviated from those in other *poleis*, where public construction projects beyond the local labour capacity would recruit craftsmen beforehand, locally, regionally and long-distance.[31] However, in places where this is recorded in building accounts, such as Epidaurus and Delphi, there was no or a very small resident craft community to draw on for such works. For Athens, the number of resident craftsmen is debated.[32] I agree with those who propose that a resident workforce indeed existed there, at least by the late sixth century. The first evidence for this lies in the late archaic signatures of sculptors in stone votives and gravestones. The ratio of Athenian to foreign sculptors among these, even when the identifications have to remain tentative, suggests that the relatively high number of foreign craftspeople in the Erechtheum accounts was nothing new for Athens. Second, craftspeople had flocked to the city in the flurry of craft activity under the Pisistratids and the early democratic regime. However, the question of employment raised here also requires an overview of what happened after the Persian wars, and whether these craftspeople stayed on or left in search of work elsewhere.

As described above, while monumental projects datable to the aftermath of the Persian wars are limited to the city defences, a few public buildings, and infrastructural works, it would have been private construction—rebuilding and repairing houses and workshops—that would have increased demand for both skilled and less skilled workforces on a major scale. Considering that another substantial part of the working population would have been engaged in the Athenian military or navy, this demand is likely to have reduced the incentive for the craftspeople of Athens to leave the city. The high labour demand Athenians had known throughout the late archaic period, higher than in many other *poleis*, had shifted from monumental public works to residential and commercial buildings as well as infrastructure. I propose that while the

31 As extensively discussed in Massar 2020. See also Burford 1969, 112, 160–161; Epstein 2010, 10; Feyel 1998 and 2006; Hochscheid 2015, 147.

32 Against a resident non-citizen workforce, Epstein 2010, 14; Shear 2016, 10; in favour Feyel 2006, 321, 326; Hochscheid 2015, 147–149 and 205–207; Carusi 2020; Paga 2021, 254–255; cf. Vlassopoulos 2016, 677 also for its composition.

craft workforce's output became less visible in the archaeological record, they did not leave Athens on the scale usually assumed.

This continuing craft presence in Athens is corroborated by the lack of evidence for official recruitment of craftspeople for most of the building projects, certainly the Parthenon. In contrast to projects elsewhere and later on, the surviving Athenian building accounts in the mid-fifth century mention no payments to heralds for travelling abroad to attract labourers.[33] As already noted by Burford, Athens also seems to have refrained from using guarantors for the Parthenon, but hired workers and workshop owners directly.[34] For later projects in the programme, guarantors were used, and it was stipulated that the guarantor be an Athenian citizen.[35] Interestingly, the relevant regulations that the Athenians developed in the course of the fifth century enabled non-citizen craftsmen to tender for contracts in the programme. A recent study on this topic has argued that the bond between contractor and guarantor must have been a close partnership, as guarantors were personally and financially responsible for completion of the work.[36] The citizens in question must have been confident in their partner, regardless of whether they were citizens or metics. For the early stages of the programme, however, and specifically for the Parthenon, no such rules seem to have existed yet. Apparently at this time, the possibility that work might be left incomplete if specialists were incapacitated or left had not yet led to administrative regulations. A reason for this could be that the resident labour force was of sufficient size and quality to find replacements quickly if the need arose.[37]

Further evidence for the presence of stoneworkers in particular during the second quarter of the fifth century comes from thick deposits of marble debris in several houses on the Street of the Marble workers and the House of Mikion and Menon. The evidence of marble working in the latter, starting in the late

33 In contrast, there is such evidence for Eleusis in the fourth century. See Shear 2016, 9–10, who also argues that Athens too suffered from major labour shortage earlier on. Epstein 2010, 10 notes the recruitment calls may have been informal and so not accounted for. For travelling craftsmen in the ancient world generally, see Massar 2020; Linder 2020; also Hellman 2000; Jockey 2009; Larson 2013.

34 Burford 1969, 112; Hochscheid 2015, 148–149; Pitt 2016, 196–199; Carusi 2020.

35 Carusi 2021, 147.

36 Ibid. 146–149. Other work on cross-status interaction in Athens in Sobak 2015; Vlassopoulos 2007.

37 See also Pitt 2016, 197. In the course of the second half of the fifth century, the formalization of contracts may have occurred for reasons of financial accountability, in other words, transparency of the funds of the *demos*, rather than because of a lack of craftspeople. Cf. Carusi 2021.

470s, runs on continuously for centuries.[38] These early beginnings point to the professional activities of masons, or more likely sculptors, squarely in the period between the Persian wars and the start of the Acropolis building project. Moreover, the continuity of this workshop and those in the Street of the Marble workers suggests that the Athenian market for sculptors was quite stable for longer periods of time. Considering the ripple effect into other crafts outlined above, such stability would have provided for wider circles of craftspeople, from toolmakers to food-sellers. It is in this context that we should review the status of this diversely composed group of craftspeople including both metics and locals, at the time when Pericles instigated the Acropolis building programme.

4 Craft and Status

In the previous sections it has become clear that the craftspeople of Athens had, since the late sixth century and perhaps earlier, been a diverse assemblage of locals and immigrants, the free and the enslaved. That this status was in flux during this time is reflected in the marble or bronze votives erected on the Acropolis in this period. Among the dedicants of monumental votives from the decades around 500 BCE are fullers, tanners, potters, fishermen and washerwomen.[39] While it is usually impossible to determine whether these are Athenians by birth or not, their dedications have interesting implications for their status. First, they use monuments often considered the exclusive domain of the elite—in bronze and marble—to promulgate their professional, non-elite identities. Second, although their trades are often small in scale and dedicated to supplying daily needs rather than luxury products, the fact they were able to give monumental expression to the portion of their earnings they set aside for the gods speaks of a thriving market for these businesses in this period.

The current evidence does not permit unequivocal identification of the origins of these craftspeople-dedicants of the late archaic period. If the mixed group of Athenian and foreign sculptors of the same period and the craftsmen of the Erechtheum a century later can be taken as something of a general standard for the mixed workforces in the city, we might conjecture that these patrons, too, were not all originally from Athens. The issue of how diverse the craft community in Athens was in this period is particularly pertinent because it hinges

38 Hochscheid 2015, 199–203.

39 Hochscheid 2015, 290–297 for these and further examples.

on the difference between long-term residents who had originally come from elsewhere or whose families had done so, and recent arrivals who were not (yet) residents or who were indeed peripatetic.

In any case, Athens' economic growth after the Persian Wars coincides with a further influx of people into the city. Interestingly, the official status of metic seems to have emerged in the Athenian consciousness around the same time.[40] For instance, vases dating from the 470s onwards depict the particular metic duty of basin-bearing in the Panathenaic procession.[41] Various scholars have argued that Aeschylus alludes to metic-like status in both the *Eumenides* and *Suppliant Women*.[42] Also part of the Panathenaic procession were metic *skiadêphoroi*, parasol bearers who shaded the Athenian girls who acted as *kanêphoroi* in the procession.[43] While the hierarchical nature of these functions leaves open the level of appreciation Athens had for its metics, the institutionalized role of metics in the foremost religious festival of the city, apparently as early as the 470s BCE, means that Athenian-born citizens at least viewed them as a coherent, if distinct part of the community.

That the first signs of official metic status appear in the decades after the Persian Wars is hardly surprising. After all, metics had fought alongside Athenians against the Persians as well as on other occasions, although the majority of soldiers were citizens. Indeed, when campaigns failed, more citizens than metics were lost.[44] Especially at times of military defeat, then, the metics remaining in the city—notably the skilled manufacturing or trading men and women—were key to the city's economic survival, if not to replenish army ranks. Further evidence for this comes from the metic tax, or *metoikion*, which appears for the first time in the later fifth century and which all metics had to pay annually in order to remain officially registered as metics.[45]

---

40 Wijma 2014, 27–28. See also below.

41 On these *skaphêphoroi*, Wijma 2014, 39–40, 44–46.

42 Bakewell 1997; for an overview of scholarship see also Wijma 2014, 38–39.

43 Wijma 2014, 42–43, 49–51, for the other two groups of metic participants in the Panathenaic procession, the *hudriaphoroi* and *diphrophoroi*.

44 Wijma 2014, 28–31; regarding possible conscription of metics 33 n. 78. Also Akrigg 2015; Epstein 2010; Feyel 1998. Blok 2017, 266–267 cites various studies proposing 1:5 or 1:6 ratios of metics to citizens in the fifth century, while the 317 BCE census lists ca. 1:2 (10.000:21.000, Akrigg 2015, 158). Against the larger impact of war on citizens than on metics, Epstein 2010, 3; Kamen 2013, 46 (stating metics were obliged to perform military service); Wijma 2014, 30 n. 66. Even if metics contributed considerable numbers to the Athenian army, they were still a minority compared to citizen soldiers, and casualties would reflect this spread.

45 [Xen.] *Ath. Pol.* 1.12; Xen. *Por.* 2.1; in both cases the *metoikion* is valued. Metic women demonstrably paid the *metoikion* as well. See also Blok 2017, 273–275; Avramidou 2015; Kennedy 2014, 2 and 124; Wijma 2014, 33, 64; Kamen 2013, 44–46; Epstein 2010, 2–3.

The true intentions of the rights and duties of metic status have been subject to heated discussions in scholarship, comprehensively outlined by Sara Wijma.[46] While this is a controversy beyond the scope of this paper, perhaps the issue of craft can make a small contribution. If craft-related immigration over the sixth and early fifth centuries was as important as the evidence above has suggested, the number of residents with non-Athenian roots must have been substantial by the second quarter of the fifth century. In the aftermath of the Persian Wars, a conflict in which non-Athenian members of the community had fought side-by-side with locally born Athenians, there was ample reason to encourage these former comrades in arms to remain in the city. Second, as I have argued above, the demand for labour was so high that losing workers was an unappealing scenario. Since many metics are likely to have been craftspeople, giving them a formal role in (to begin with) the religious life of the city could be construed not just in acknowledgement of their previous service to the community, but in that community's need for their contributions into the future.

Considering these circumstances, could Pericles indeed have aimed for the 'unwarlike throng of common labourers', as Plutarch put it, to benefit from his scheme? I have suggested above that first, a large group of labourers may well have been already living in Athens, as demand for labour was buoyant after the Persian Wars once one looks further afield than the interrupted building activity on large-scale public monuments. Moreover, many craftspeople were required who can be named 'support personnel' to the specialized artisans in construction and sculpture, as in both cases large varieties of raw materials and tools needed to be supplied. In turn, this demand extended beyond relevant crafts to a broader workforce which supplied the workers' daily needs. That the importance of professional labour on both these levels did not go unnoticed by those active as craftspeople and traders is clear in their expressions of professional pride, which seem to downplay civic markers and highlight their professions. Early in the fifth century, these mainly occur in signatures of sculptors and dedications by craftspeople. Later in the century, votives and gravestones emphasize the professional patrons' livelihoods in image and text.[47]

In sum, among the estimated craftspeople living in Athens in the first half of the fifth century have to be counted more than those who worked on monumental construction projects. Less visible architecture and infrastructure, supporting crafts, retail and trade have to be added to the total, despite the fact

46 Especially Wijma 2014, 51–56; cf. Kamen 2014, 47–54.

47 See, for instance, Hochscheid 2020, and Hochscheid 2015, 294–297.

that the evidence of their efforts is archaeologically largely invisible. In this more inclusive endeavour, even though it has to rely on incomplete data, it is unlikely that the rise in demand from the first to the second half of the fifth century was as steep as is often surmised. If it was more moderate, and many of the skilled as well as odd-job craftsmen working on the Acropolis had already been living in Athens for some time, Plutarch's interpretation takes on a much more plausible aspect.

Scholars have traditionally assumed that Pericles' plan that the building programme provide income for the *unwarlike throng of common labourers*, was for the benefit of Athenians, not new arrivals looking for opportunities. But if this is so, Athenian citizens should be far more conspicuous in the building accounts than they are, and the prominent presence of metics remains unexplained.[48] The solution for this apparent contradiction lies in the fluid status of metics in this period. Rather than workers who had just arrived as a result of recruitment or of their own initiative to look for work, the metic craftsmen in the building accounts may have been long-standing residents of Athens, perhaps even from families that had been in Athens for generations. In that case, they were precisely the foreigners for whom the official metic status seems to have been developed: professionals not native to Athens, but having lived there for a long time, whose contributions were widely recognized, both in the recent crises Athens had lived through, and in their professional capacities. That they should, at a time when work was dwindling as the city's reconstruction approached completion, be rewarded by Pericles' programme alongside Athenian craftsmen and labourers, is eminently plausible.

In fact, such a public-spirited interpretation of the building programme could be seen to mirror a recent reinterpretation of the Periclean Citizenship Law of 451 BCE:[49] the explanation of the law in the Athenian Constitution, to reduce citizenship to children of two Athenian parents, 'because of great numbers of citizens' (*Ath. Pol.* 26.3–4) cannot reflect the reality of Athens in the mid-fifth century, which had suffered heavy military losses.[50] Moreover, a major

48 As analysed perceptively by Epstein 2010, and in part, Epstein 2008.

49 Blok 2009. An opposing take on Athenian citizenship in Fröhlich 2016. Cf. also Kamen 2013, 49–50, 62–63.

50 Blok 2009, 154–158. In contrast, it might be argued that Pericles wanted to pre-empt the influx of workers before building began on the Parthenon, and the citizenship law was aimed at the risks involved in that. To me this is unlikely, because first, it appears the city already hosted many workers who were not originally Athenian, and second, if one adopts the view that most of the workers for the building programme did have to come in from abroad, it would be clear to them that they were not expected to stay in Athens after completion of the project.

obstacle in accepting the reduction of citizen numbers as the main motivation for the law is its non-retroactive nature. Without retroactive implementation, it could not have been effective in reducing citizen numbers. The alternative explanation is that the law served as a morale boost in difficult times, both in its first instalment and in its reiteration in 403/402.[51]

In a scenario where skilled craftsmen had to be freshly recruited from abroad, most of the wages paid in an employment project would leave the city after construction ended. More importantly, of the main target group of the scheme in Plutarch's description, unemployed Athenian *citizens*, far fewer would benefit than was Pericles' goal. In contrast, if the non-citizen craftsmen in Plutarch were actually long-term inhabitants of the city whose ancestors had come to Athens a generation before, or even earlier, rather than fresh arrivals, including them in the scheme was not just a practical step facilitating the work. It would suggest that it was deemed important to keep hold of these 'embedded' craftspeople, making sure they remained in the city, to help by paying taxes and to beautify the city. This in turn would suggest that the reasons for the building programme look forward to the goals of the citizenship law. Where Pericles' citizenship law aimed at lifting Athenian morale, the building programme increased wealth and participation among skilled and unskilled workers, both in construction per se and, by consequence, in the wider network of craft manufacture and daily sustenance trades that supported the work on the Acropolis and elsewhere in the *polis*. Simultaneously, it bound these metic Athenians to the city more closely, in a way that is mirrored by the metics' inclusion in the Panathenaic festival.

5 Conclusion

It goes without saying that demand for skilled labour in Athens throughout the archaic and Classical periods attracted craftspeople from all over the Greek world. But we have no evidence that Athens purposely and officially recruited more workers from abroad at the beginning of the Periclean building programme. And why would it? As I have argued, it had a good supply of skilled craftspeople for construction, whose parents and grandparents a few decades earlier had been active in other projects of construction and reconstruction, both private and public. The fact that the *demos* initially had no need for guar-

51 In 451 such a boost was needed because of recent losses in the Archidamian war, while in 403 it was the events in the Peloponnesian: Blok 2009, 158–169.

antors but dealt with the craftspeople directly further supports this. So, too, the fact that around this time it almost certainly formulated criteria towards defining the metic status, listing both rights and duties of this group, suggests that metics formed a substantial, long-term portion of the city's crafting population. This meant that those who were acknowledged metics would join the Athenian community with tighter bonds than in the preceding period. In the later fifth century this shift is more clearly expressed in the institution of the metic tax, connecting metics' employment, in other words, their ability to pay, to recognition of official status. A further confirmation of their commitment can be seen in metics' willingness to go through the challenges of registering for it.

Craftspeople may well have been among the main groups for which this status was conceived. Many had come to Athens in the late archaic period or even earlier and I have argued that many of them probably remained in Athens after the Persian wars. They had contributed and contributed still to the city between 479 and the start of the Periclean building programme, and this was a way of strengthening their bonds to Athens at a time when their skills and labour were needed, without actually giving them full citizen status. Importantly, these local foreigners, rather than newly recruited fortune-seekers, may be the metics who are so well-represented in the building accounts. Their presence there reflects how accustomed the Athenians were to their metic craftsmen. All this provides support for Plutarch's interpretation of the Periclean campaign, namely that the Acropolis building programme was created in part to keep the long-standing resident craftspeople at work constructively and profitably for all parties in Athens, their status confirmed by the officially granted participation in the rituals that they helped depict on the Parthenon.

Craft in Athens between the late sixth and the end of the fifth century seems to have been in persistently high demand. Building and engineering projects that required considerable numbers of workers in various places over the city as well as in outer demes required both highly skilled professionals and day labourers. The accounts of the largest projects show that in mid-fifth-century Athens, as opposed to other *poleis* and to Athens itself in other periods, this work was given out directly by the *demos*. The attraction of Athens for foreigners, however, was no novelty, and the earlier evidence of foreign specialists working in Athens points to a considerable tradition of non-Athenian craftspeople residing permanently in Athens, and remaining there after the completion of the projects they had come for. Considering that the official status of metic was shaped in the decades before the middle of the fifth century, and was succeeded by the Periclean citizenship law as well as the start of the Acropolis projects, it seems that the employment which the programme was to provide was not designed with a preference for citizens, but more broadly aimed at residents. As the accounts bear out, craftspeople from proficient to odd-job workers were hired as needed, regardless of their status. To the Athenians, the value of these craftspeople lay not in their civic status, but in their ability to contribute to the *polis*.

Acknowledgements

Heartfelt thanks to the editors Kim Bowes and Miko Flohr for organizing the conference and their thoughtful feedback on the chapter; many thanks also to the anonymous reviewers for their helpful suggestions. I am grateful for the stimulating online discussions with the other participants in the conference and to Cristina Carusi, Bettina Reitz-Joosse and Edmund Stewart. Particular thanks to Ann Brysbaert, Natacha Massar and the other members of TEXNH for their perpetual willingness to discuss ancient crafts.

Bibliography

Akrigg, B. (2015). Metics in Athens. In: C. Taylor and K. Vlassopoulos, eds., *Communities and Networks in the Ancient Greek World*. Oxford, pp. 155–173.

Athanasopoulos, P. (2021). Shipsheds, the 5th Century BC Athenian Naval Bases in Piraeus. Constructing a New Maritime Identity. In: W. Riess, ed., *Colloquia Attica II. Neuere Forschungen zu Athen im 5. Jahrhundert v. Chr.* Hamburg, pp. 105–117.

Avramidou, A. (2015). Women Dedicators on the Athenian Acropolis and their Role in Family Festivals: The Evidence for Maternal Votives between 530–450 BCE. *Cahiers Mondes Anciens* 6.

Bakewell, G. (1997). Μετοικία in the *Supplices* of Aeschylus. *CA* 16, pp. 209–228.

Barker, S.J. and Russell, B. (2012). Labour Figures for Roman Stone-Working: Pitfalls and Potential. In: S. Camporeale, H. Dessales and A. Pizzo, eds., *Arqueología de la Construcción III. Los procesos constructivos en el mundo romano: la economía de las obras*. Madrid, pp. 83–94.

Barlou, V. (2013). An Itinerant Parian Before Skopas: Aristion, Phrasikleia and the Problem of Regional Styles. In: D. Katsonopoulou and A. Stewart, eds., *Skopas of Paros and His World. Paros III* (Proceedings of the Third International Conference on the Archaeology of the Cyclades. Paroikia, Paros, 11–14 June 2010). Athens, pp. 111–132.

Barlou, V. (2014). *Die archaische Bildhauerkunst von Paros. Untersuchungen zur stilistischen Entwicklung der anthropomorphen Rundplastik*. Wiesbaden.

Bejor, M. di, Castoldi, C., Lambrugo, E. and Panero, G. (2012). *Botteghe e artigiani. Marmorari, bronzisti, ceramisti e vetrai nell'antichità classica*. Milan.

Blok. J.H. (2006). Solon's Funerary Laws: Questions of Authenticity and Function. In: A. Lardinois and J.H. Blok, eds., *Solon of Athens. New Historical and Philological Approaches*. Leiden, pp. 197–247.

Blok, J.H. (2009). Perikles' Citizenship Law: A New Perspective. *Historia* 58 (2), pp. 141–170.

Blok, J.H. (2017). *Citizenship in Classical Athens*. Cambridge.

Boersma, J. (1970). *Athenian Building Policy from 561/0 to 405/4 B.C.* Groningen.

Burford, A. (1969). *The Greek Temple Builders at Epidauros. A Social and Economic Study of Building in the Asklepian Sanctuary, During the Fourth and Early Third Centuries B.C.* Liverpool.

Camp, J. (2001). *The Archaeology of Athens*. New Haven–London.

Carusi, C. (2020). L'organizzazione dell'industria delle costruzioni nell'Atene di età classica. *Annali di Scuola Normale Superiore di Pisa* s. 5 (12), 485–517.

Carusi, C. (2021). The Recruitment and Remuneration of Construction Workers in Classical Athens. In: K. Harter-Uibopuu and W. Riess, eds., *Symposion 2019. Vorträge zur griechischen und hellenistischen Rechtsgeschichte (Hamburg 26–28 August 2019)*. Vienna, pp. 131–154.

Chatzedemetriou, A. (2005). *Παραστάσεις εργαστηρίων και εμπορίου στην εικονογραφία των αρχαϊκών και κλασικών χρόνων*. Athens.

Corso, A. (2004–2014). *The Art of Praxiteles. 5 Volumes*. Rome.

Costaki, L. and Theocharaki, A. (2021). City Streets, Walls, and Gates. In: J. Neils and D. Rogers, eds., *The Cambridge Companion to Ancient Athens*. Cambridge, pp. 47–62.

D'Onofrio, A. (2008). L'apporto cicladico nella più antica plastica monumentale in Attica. In: N. Kourayos and F. Prost, eds., *La sculpture des Cyclades à l'époque archaïque. Histoire des ateliers, rayonnement des styles, Actes du colloque international, Athènes 7–11 septembre 1998* (*BCH* suppl. 48). Athens, pp. 195–254.

Epstein, S. (2008). Why Did Attic Building Projects Employ Free Laborers Rather than Slaves? *ZPE* 166, pp. 108–112.

Epstein, S. (2010). Attic Public Construction: Who Were the Builders? *AncSoc* 40, pp. 1–14.

Feyel, Chr. (1998). La structure d'un groupe socio-économique: les artisans dans les grands sanctuaires grecs du IVe siècle, *Topoi* 8 (2), pp. 561–579.

Feyel, Chr. (2006). *Les Artisans dans les sanctuaires grecs aux époques classique et hellénistique à travers la documentation financière en Grèce*. Athens.

Fröhlich, P. (2016). La cité grecque entre Aristote et les modernes, *Cahiers Glotz* 27, pp. 91–136.

Hellmann, M-Chr. (2000). Les déplacements des artisans de la construction en Grèce d'après les *testimonia* épigraphiques. In: F. Blondé and A. Muller, eds., *L'artisanat en Grèce ancienne. Les productions, les diffusions. Actes du Colloque de Lyon (10–11 décembre 1998). Travaux et Recherches*. Lille, pp. 265–280.

Hochscheid, H. (2015). *Networks of Stone. Sculpture and Society in Archaic and Classical Athens*. Oxford–Bern.

Hochscheid, H. (2020). Professionalism in Archaic and Classical Sculpture in Athens: The Price of Technē. In: E. Stewart, E. Harris and D. Lewis, eds., *Skilled Labour and Professionalism in Ancient Greece and Rome*. Cambridge, pp. 205–229.

Hochscheid, H. (forthcoming). A Sense of Place: Sculptors' Travel in Archaic Greece. In: M. Dana and M. Haake, eds., *People of Knowledge on the Move. Networks, Connectivity, Mobility and Nodes in the Ancient Mediterranean World from the Early Archaic Period to Late Antiquity*. Stuttgart.

Hurwit, J. (1999). *The Athenian Akropolis. History, Mythology, and Archaeology from the Neolithic Era to the Present*. Cambridge.

Hurwit, J. (2015). *Artists and Signatures in Ancient Greece*. New York, NY.

Jockey, P. (2009). D'une cité l'autre ... La mobilité des artisans de la pierre dans l'Antiquité classique. In: Cl. Moatti and W. Kayser, eds., *Le monde de l'itinérance, Actes du Colloque international, Istanbul, 16–18 juin 2005, Institut Français d'Etudes Anatoliennes, Istanbul*. Paris, pp. 139–159.

Johnston, A. and Palagia, O. (2019). Sculptors' Signatures. In: O. Palagia, ed., *Handbook of Greek Sculpture*. Berlin, pp. 22–49.

Kamen, D. (2013). *Status in Classical Athens*. Princeton–Oxford.

Kaczko, S. (2010). Epigrammi attici e artisti stranieri: la dedica di Iphidike (*CEG* 198 = IG I³ 683). In: A. Inglese, ed., *ΕΠΙΓΡΑΜΜΑΤΑ, 6 Iscrizioni greche e comunicazione letteraria, in ricordo di Giancarlo Susini, Roma Tor Vergata 1 e 2 ottobre 2009, Atti del Convegno*. Rome, pp. 197–220.

Keesling, C. (1999). Endoios's Painting from the Themistoklean Wall: A Reconstruction, *Hesperia* 68 (4), pp. 509–548.

Keesling, C. (2003). *The Votive Statues of the Athenian Acropolis*. Cambridge.

Kennedy, R.F. (2014). *Immigrant Women in Athens. Gender, Ethnicity, and Citizenship in the Classical City*. New York.

Korres, M. (1995). *From Pentelicon to Parthenon*. Athens.

Lambert, S.D. (2000). The Erechtheum Workers of *IG* ii² 1654, *ZPE* 132, pp. 157–160.

Larson, K. (2013). A Network Approach to Hellenistic Sculptural Production, *JMA* 26(2), 235–260.

Lewis, D. (2020). Labour Specialization in the Athenian Economy: Occupational Hazards. In: E. Stewart, E. Harris and D. Lewis, eds. *Skilled Labour and Professionalism in Ancient Greece and Rome*. Cambridge, pp. 129–174.

Lewis, D. (2021). Labor and Employment. In: J. Neils and D. Rogers, eds., 2021. *The Cambridge Companion to Ancient Athens*. Cambridge, pp. 217–230.

Linder, M. (2020). Artists beyond Athens: The Freedoms and Restrictions of the Artistic

Profession in Classical Greece. In: E. Stewart, E. Harris and D. Lewis, eds., *Skilled Labour and Professionalism in Ancient Greece and Rome*. Cambridge, pp. 230–242.

Massar, N. (2020). Skilled Workers in the Ancient Greek City: Public Employment, Selection Methods, and Evaluation. In: E. Stewart, E. Harris and D. Lewis, eds., *Skilled Labour and Professionalism in Ancient Greece and Rome*. Cambridge, pp. 68–93.

Massar, N. (2021). Preparing for War: Craftspeople, Management, and Innovations. In: H. Hochscheid and B. Russell, eds. *The Value of Making. Theory and Practice in Craft Production*. Turnhout, pp. 35–52.

Nolte, S. (2005). *Steinbruch, Werkstatt, Skulptur. Untersuchungen zu Aufbau und Organisation griechischer Bildhauerwerkstätten*. Göttingen.

Paga, J. (2015). The Monumental Definition of Attica in the Early Democratic Period. In: M. Miles ed., *Autopsy in Athens. Recent Archaeological Research on Athens and Attica*. Oxford–Philadelphia, pp. 108–125.

Paga, J. (2020). *Building Democracy in Late Archaic Athens*. Oxford.

Pitt, R.K. (2016). Inscribing Construction: The Financing and Administration of Public Building in Greek Sanctuaries. In: M. Miles, ed., *A Companion to Greek Architecture*. Malden, MA, pp. 194–205.

Randall, R.H. (1953). The Erechtheum Workmen. *AJA* 57 (3), pp. 199–210.

Rihll, T.E. (2001). Making Money in Classical Athens. In: D. Mattingly and J. Salmon, eds., *Economies Beyond Agriculture in the Classical World*. London, pp. 115–142.

Salmon, J. (2001). Temples the Measures of Men: Public Building in the Greek Economy. In: D. Mattingly and J. Salmon, eds., *Economies Beyond Agriculture in the Classical World*. London, pp. 195–208.

Salta, M. (1991). *Attische Grabstelen mit Inschriften. Beiträge zur Topographie und Prosopographie der Nekropolen von Athen, Attika und Salamis vom Peloponnesischen Krieg bis zur Mitte des 4. Jhs. v. Chr.* Tübingen.

Schultz, P. (2017). *Politics and Personality? The Case of Kephisodotos the Younger*. In: K. Seaman and P. Schultz, eds., *Artists and Artistic Production in Ancient Greece*. Cambridge, pp. 141–153.

Shear, T.L. Jr. (2016). *Trophies of Victory. Public Building in Periklean Athens*. Princeton.

Silver, M. (2006). Slaves versus Free Hired Workers in Ancient Greece. *Historia* 55 (3), pp. 257–263.

Sobak, R. (2015). Sokrates Among the Shoemakers. *Hesperia* 84 (4), pp. 669–712.

Stewart, A.F. (1990). *Greek Sculpture. An Exploration*. New Haven.

Stewart, A.F. (2017). Kritios and Nesiotes: Two Revolutionaries in Context. In: K. Seaman and P. Schultz, eds., *Artists and Artistic Production in Ancient Greece*. Cambridge, pp. 37–54.

Stewart, A.F. (2019). Patronage, Compensation and the Social Status of Sculptors. In: O. Palagia, ed., *Handbook of Greek Sculpture*. Berlin, pp. 50–88.

Stroszeck, J. (2021). Water and Water Management. In: J. Neils and D. Rogers, eds., *The Cambridge Companion to Ancient Athens*. Cambridge, pp. 110–123.

Taylor, C. (2015). Social Networks and Social Mobility in Fourth-Century Athens. In: C. Taylor and K. Vlassopoulos, eds., *Communities and Networks in the Ancient Greek World*. Oxford, pp. 35–53.

Theocharaki, A.M. (2011). The Ancient Circuit Wall of Athens: Its Changing Course and the Phases of Construction. *Hesperia* 80(1), pp. 71–156.

Theocharaki, A.M. (2019). *The Ancient Circuit Walls of Athens*. Berlin–Boston.

Tsakirgis, B. (2005). Living and Working Around the Athenian Agora: A Preliminary Case Study of Three Houses. In: B.A. Ault and L.C. Nevett, eds., *Ancient Greek Houses and Households. Chronological, Regional, and Social Diversity*. Philadelphia, pp. 67–82.

Tsakirgis, B. (2009). Living near the Agora: Houses and Households in Central Athens. In: J. Camp and C. Mauzy, eds., *The Athenian Agora. New Perspectives on an Ancient Site*. Mainz, pp. 47–54.

Viviers, D. (1992). *Recherches sur les ateliers de sculpteurs et la Cité d'Athènes à l'époque archaïque. Endoios, Philergos, Aristoklès*. Brussels.

Vlassopoulos, K. (2007). Free Spaces: Identity, Experience and Democracy in Classical Athens. *CQ* 57(1), pp. 33–52.

Vlassopoulos, K. (2016). Que savons-nous vraiment de la société athénienne? *Annales. HSS* 71(3), pp. 659–682.

Wijma, S. (2014). *Embracing the Immigrant. The Participation of Metics in Athenian Polis Religion (5th–4th century BC)*. Stuttgart.

Wycherley, R.E. (1978). *The Stones of Athens*. Princeton.

CHAPTER 15

The Craftsman's View: Labour and (Self-)Appreciation as Reflected in Signatures

Natacha Massar

À la mémoire de François Lissarrague (1947–2021)

1 Introduction

There are thousands of preserved objects from the Greek world bearing signatures, including sculptures, vases, mosaics, gems, coins, poems, bronze artefacts and jewellery.[1] Whether autograph or not, the signature expressed a relationship between the craftsman and the work he created.[2] Understandably, they have attracted a lot of attention over the decades. In this chapter I will look at them from a very specific perspective: as a direct means of expression by craftspeople. Signatures are attested in the Greek world since the late eighth century BCE and continue throughout antiquity.[3] In its simplest and most common form, a signature just stated, X *epoiêsen* (or *epoiei*). That is, X made [it/me/this].[4] These signatures are essentially incomplete: for citizens, a full designation would include, besides the name, a patronymic and a demotic or an ethnic. As in most cases a signature in its simplest form appears to be sufficient, any additions must be considered deliberate choices of the craftsman (and/or the patron). These are revealing about his motives and his perception of his own work and worth. They can be seen as rare occurrences of craftspeople expressing themselves. In this chapter, I will examine specific cases in which a signature includes, besides the name, a patronymic, a demotic or an ethnic. I will also look into collaborations and at a few rare cases where

1 In this chapter, 'BAPD' refers to the online Beazley Archive Pottery Database.
2 Osborne 2010, 235–236; Hurwit 2015, xv–xvi.
3 Hurwit 2015, 71.
4 Johnson 2019, 22–23.

 DOI:10.1163/9789004694965_016

the craftsman has added information of an entirely different nature to his signature. Finally, I will briefly discuss the material aspect of signatures, which could also be a means of signalling one's skill.

Signatures on all types of media will be taken into account, and the analysis extends from the Archaic to the Hellenistic period. This wide-ranging approach will be revealing about some trends, but it will ignore other aspects of signature practices, such as the fact that amongst Attic vases some shapes were much more often signed than others.[5] Another aspect that will not be taken into account here concerns the differences in viewing experiences and referential value that depended on whether a signed object was, like a statue, immovable and publicly visible, immovable but private like a mosaic or a wall-painting, or movable like a vase or a gem. Focus will be on the signatures themselves.

2 Ethnic and Demotic

The normal usage in the Greek world would be for a citizen to add their ethnic to their name when abroad as a means of indicating both their citizen status and their home city. Inside the *polis* a demotic can denote the same type of information, indicating both citizenship and the administrative subdivision to which someone belongs. Although craftsmen sometimes did add an ethnic to their signature or, much more rarely a demotic, they did not do so systematically and not only when abroad. In signatures, the absence of an ethnic did not necessarily mean that the *technitês* was a local.[6] On the other hand, adding an ethnic or a demotic could have a significance that went beyond information about the craftsman's civic status and *polis*.

In a few cases, the ethnic was mentioned on works erected inside the craftsman's *polis*. Around 430 BCE, a statue of Athena Hygieia was dedicated on the Acropolis of Athens, at the corner of the Propylaea, possibly after the devastating plague of Athens.[7] The inscription on the base is short and to the point:

> The Athenians, to Athena Hygieia
> Pyrrhos made (it), an Athenian.

5 Osborne 2010, 245; Williams 2017, 148.
6 Dimartino 2010, 13.
7 Keesling 2005, 67–70.

Ἀθεναῖοι τε̂ι Ἀθεναίαι τε̂ι Ὑγιείαι
Πύρρος ἐποίησεν Ἀθεναῖος.[8]

In the Greek, the first line starts with 'the Athenians' and the second and last line ends with 'the Athenian'. By stating his ethnic on the base, and placing it the way he has (most often it was mentioned just after the name), the sculptor unequivocally asserted his Athenian citizenship. Since he made the statue, he was directly implicated in the dedication by his professional activity; in a way, he was working for the deity.[9] But by stating his ethnic, Pyrrhos also emphasized his 'personal' interest in the monument as an Athenian and, thus, as part of the group of dedicators: he was not only the maker of the statue but also one of the people on whose behalf it was being erected.

There are few direct parallels. A similar motivation may be the reason that the local sculptor Orestes, and possibly his colleague Theorrhetos, signed with his ethnic on the Pergamon altar.[10] In the same city, king Attalus (II or III) erected a statue for Dionysus Kathegemon in honour of the priest of the god. It was signed by a sculptor whose name is lost, son of Menophantos, of Pergamon.[11] Dionysus Kathegemon played an important role in the dynastic cult in Pergamon and was the patron deity of the Pergamenian branch of the Dionysiac *technitai*; this monument probably bore a representation of the god or his priest. Thus, the ethnic in the signature again conveyed the personal interest of the sculptor and his investment in this monument made for the king to honour an important local deity. Another example comes from the Attic deme of Rhamnous and dates to the early third century BCE.[12] It concerns a statue of the goddess Themis set up in the sanctuary of Nemesis by Megakles, son of Megakles, of Rhamnous. The sculptor signed it, 'Chairestratos, son of Chairedemos, of Rhamnous made [it]' (Χαιρέστρατος Χαιρεδήμου Ῥαμν⟨ο⟩ύσι⟨ο⟩ς ἐπ⟨ό⟩ησε). This well-preserved statue was probably the cult statue of the temple of Themis.[13] Demotics are very rarely mentioned in signatures, probably because they were essentially administrative in nature, and were only perceived as a source of pride or related to a sense of identity in specific circumstances. The local sculptor, by stating his demotic, expressed his interest in Megakles' dedication

8 *IG* I³ 506. Kansteiner et al. II 2014, 351 n°1102; Hurwit 2015, 131–132.

9 Osborne 2010, 247; Gillis 2021, 80–82, 96–98.

10 Hurwit 2015, 139 and pl. 15 who does not comment on the ethnic; Palagia 2019, 42 who does. Signatures: Kansteiner et al. II 2014, 670–672 n°3456 and 3457.

11 *Inscr.Perg.* I 221; Ohlemutz, 1940, 93; Michels 2011, 126 (and 125–131 for more context).

12 *IG* II³ 4, 513 (*IRham* 120). Kansteiner et al. III 2014, 512–514 n°2372.

13 Athens National Museum, inv. EAM 231. Palagia 1982, 105–106 esp. n. 37; Themelis 1998, 55–56; Stewart 1990, fig. 602–603; Ma 2013, 18–19.

and his personal involvement in the cult of Themis. He associated himself with it, again not just as a sculptor, and the maker of the gift to the deity, but also as a local demesman. Indeed, his family was clearly involved in the local religious life: his father had been a priest at Rhamnous in 315/4 BCE.[14]

The ultimate involvement of a craftsman in a gift to a deity occurs when they made it, signed it and dedicated it themselves. The vase painter Myson, for instance, not only painted the column-krater he dedicated to Athena on the Acropolis, but potted it too, signing it prominently on the neck as both painter and potter.[15] Another case is an Attic bell krater which represents the bearded victor of a torch-race before an altar, about to be crowned by Nike (ca. 420–410 BCE). On his headband is inscribed the word 'Antioch(is)', i.e. the tribe Antiochis. He may be the personification of the tribe.[16] The signature, carefully painted in large letters around the foot, reads, 'Nikias, son of Hermokles, of the deme Anaphlystos, made [it]' (Νικίας Ἑρμοκλέους Ἀναφλύστιος ἐποίησεν). This is the only potter's signature with a demotic. It was added for a reason: the potter belonged to the deme Anaphlystos, which was part of the victorious tribe. Nikias made this vase to commemorate the victory and, by stating his demotic, associated himself personally with the event.

In other circumstances, the reasons for adding the sculptor's ethnic seem rather different. For example, around 150 BCE, the city of Megalopolis set up an honorific statue of somebody, whose name is lost, in Olympia.[17] The craftsman who sculpted the monument was Aristeas, also from Megalopolis. Although signing with an ethnic when working abroad is well attested, here it may have had an added value: although the monument concerns the affairs of Megalopolis, the city wished to advertise the facts more broadly by erecting it in the Panhellenic sanctuary of Olympia. Megalopolis chose the sculptor and may also have requested that he indicate his ethnic, in order to show off its local sculptor at the same time that it was honouring an *euergetês*. Through this combination, the monument strongly emphasizes Megalopolitan concerns, while at the same time publicizing them in the Panhellenic sanctuary of Olympia.[18]

A similar phenomenon may be at play in Delphi, where, in the first half of the third century BCE, the Aetolian Charixenos set up a dedication to Apollo

14 *IG* II^2 2726.

15 Athens, Acr. 806; *ARV*^{2} 240, 42; BAPD n°202359; Williams 2017, 156, 162. On this issue, Jockey 2002, 25; Gillis 2021, 69–75 with other examples.

16 London, British Museum 1898,0716.6; BAPD n°217462. Williams 2009a, 128 n°56.

17 *IvO* 396; Kansteiner et al. V 2014, 191–192 n°3790.

18 A very similar case is attested on a statue base in the Attic deme of Thria, *IG* II^2 3864: everybody involved, including the sculptors, is from the deme. The local element is strongly emphasized by the repetition of the demotic. Kansteiner et al. IV 2014, 277 n°3080.

signed by an Aetolian sculptor, Sonikos.[19] Charixenos was *stratêgos* of the Aetolian League at the time when the Aetolians, who controlled Delphi, refounded the Panhellenic sanctuary's Soteria festival. As *stratêgos* of the League, he is mentioned in decrees relating to the 'new' Soteria.[20] He obviously identified himself as Aetolian, but the fact that the sculptor of the impressive monument he set up was also identified as an Aetolian, a unique occurrence, may have been a deliberate choice that was supposed to underline the resources of the League.[21] That Sonikos signed in this way may very well have been requested by Charixenos. The emphasis on Aetolia, and the common origin of both the patron and the sculptor, would have been completely lost if he had signed with his city ethnic or with just his name.[22]

In these cases, the mention of the city or league ethnic may have been encouraged by the patron rather than being solely the choice of the craftsman. Since the patron would have had to approve the text of the signature, the presence of this information suggests that he was proud to employ a craftsman from his own *polis* or League, and wished to show this off in a Panhellenic sanctuary. The personal reasons for which a sculptor may have wanted to sign a dedication, such as associating himself with the religious offering, and a patron's wish to use and promote local resources were not mutually exclusive, and some of the examples presented here may fit in both categories.

Mentioning the ethnic could also have value if a city boasted a long tradition in the craft or hosted a renowned school. In such cases, working abroad signalled the broader reputation of the *polis*.[23] For instance, the Athenian potter Teisias moved to Boiotia, where he signed some of his pieces as 'Teisias the Athenian' (Τεισίας Ἀθεναίος): Athenian pottery had such a good reputation that being an Athenian potter had an added value abroad.[24] The sculptor Archermos signed one of his works as '*ho Chios*', the Chian, underlining his ethnic by putting the article in front of it.[25] Archermos was active in the second half of the sixth century BCE and belonged to a famous family of sculptors: both his father (seemingly) and his sons had the same profession.[26] A statue base on Delos bears the names of both Archermos and his father Mikkiades; the epigram

19 *IG* IX 1², 1, 181; Kansteiner et al. III 2014, 720–721 n°2604.
20 E.g. *IG* II³ 1, 1005, l. 14; *FD* III 3, 215, l. 8–9. Flacelière 1937, 267 n. 4 (and 265–270); Nachtergael 1977, 330–334.
21 *Syll.*³ 515; Jacquemin et al. 2012, 159 n°80.
22 On the use of a league 'ethnic', Flacelière 1937, 90 n. 1.
23 Savalli-Lestrade 2013, 184, 188 (Parian sculptors).
24 Williams 2013, 56.
25 Jockey 2002, 27, 29; Kaczko 2010, 202–203.
26 Plin. *HN* 36.11. Kansteiner et al. I 2014, 120–121 n°201.

states they were 'Chians [who left] their father-city of Melas' (οἱ Χῖοι Μέλανος πατρώιον ἄσ[τυ λιπόντες or νέμοντες]), emphasizing both their origin *and* the fact that they had left Chios behind.[27] Apparently, their craft and reputation had allowed them to move beyond their *polis*.[28] Later, Archermos' sons would also emphasize their Chian origin: according to Pliny, they inscribed the pedestals of their statues with epigrams stating that Chios was not only famous for its vines, but also for the works of the sons of Archermos (*subiecerunt carmen non vitibus tantum censeri Chion, sed et operibus Archermi filiorum*).[29] Chios' acclaimed wine was widely exported; these sculptors also shared a renown which extended far beyond their home city.[30]

After his naval victory over the Athenians at Aigos Potamoi that marked the end of the Peloponnesian War in 405 BCE, the Spartan navarch Lysander erected a large celebratory monument at Delphi. The people who featured on the monument were not only named, but some were also praised in an epigram. One such poem appeared under the statue of Lysander; it ended with one of the very rare signatures of a poet on stone:

> From sea-girt Samos, he made the poem, Ion.
>
> Ἐξάμο ἀμφιρύτ[ου] τεῦσε ἐλεγεῖον Ἴων.[31]

This final verse began with the name of Ion's home city, which was qualified by an adjective, and ended with his name. There is thus a strong emphasis on the provenance of the poet and, by extension, on the reputation he had developed beyond the confines of his home city. At the same time, Ion's verses added prestige to the monument and to Lysander.[32] Sara Kaczko has emphasized that in the archaic period most epigrams 'show strong ties to the local contexts'.[33] A reference to the foreign provenance of a *technitês* on monuments, by contrast, must have underlined the fame of these craftspeople in the Aegean; their signatures afforded prestige to those who could employ them. Reference to a

---

27 *IDélos* 9; *CEG* 425. Kansteiner et al. I 2014, 115–116 n°197; Day 2013, 225–226.

28 Scherrer 1983; Kaczko 2010, 202, n. 13; Hochscheid forthcoming.

29 Plin. *HN* 36.11–12. Kansteiner et al. I 2014, 120–121 n°201.

30 For another example, Johnston 2019, 27 and Hochscheid forthcoming.

31 *FD* III 1, 50, l. 5 (*CEG* 819 iii ; Jacquemin et al. 2012, 51–52 n°25). Fantuzzi 2004, 289–290; Cignano 2021, 81–82.

32 Ion signed another epigram on the monument in a different fashion, setting his name in the first line: *CEG* 819 ii; *FD* III 1, 51 with Bousquet 1966, 437. See Fantuzzi 2004, 291; Cignano 2021, 82–83.

33 Kaczko 2018, 31.

wider geographical area than the *polis* could also be emphasized through the use of a non-local dialect for the epigram, or the signature, or both.[34]

The reasons for craftsmen to include an ethnic could be manifold: it may have been done at their own request—for example in the case of dedications—or at the request of the patron—for example for reasons of prestige. Sometimes, it may have resulted from negotiations between the two of them.[35] Adding the ethnic or demotic of the sculptor on dedications or commemorative monuments could serve to emphasize local assets and resources—if the sculptor had the same origin as the dedicator of the monument—or introduce an international dimension where the foreign origin of the craftsman added prestige to the work or the patron. Indeed, craftsmen including their ethnic in their signature on a monument abroad by necessity emphasized the fact that they were working away from home. This signalled in many cases that they hailed from a city that was famous for their given *technê* or that their personal reputation extended beyond their home city, both of which enhanced their prestige.[36]

3 Patronymics

In formal or administrative writing contexts, a patronymic helped to define somebody's civic identity, and could be obligatory. In signatures, it was added by choice and, thus, could be rhetorically significant. It could be that a craftsman simply wanted to emphasize his citizenship, but a clear preoccupation with civic status is only attested in the Hellenistic period in Rhodes (see below). In general, when craftsmen refer to their father, they appear to have been working in the same profession. In such cases, the patronymic was used as an 'added (professional) credential' since the father would usually have also been the master from whom the craftsman had learned his skills.[37] The name of a father could be added when a craftsman signed on his own, but patronymics also appear when several craftspeople signed together, clarifying their relationships or lack thereof. Craftsmen who included their father's name in a signature may

34 Kaczko 2018, 36–41.

35 See also Kaczko 2018, 32–37.

36 Barlou 2013, 112, 115; Hochscheid forthcoming. That this was sought after, is obvious from many sources. See Massar 2020, 74–75 to which can be added the emphasis on a 'Hellas wide' reputation repeatedly mentioned in funerary epigrams for *technitai*.

37 Dimartino 2010, 12 and n. 28; Johnston 2019, 29. On the credential conferred by a well-known master, Massar 2010.

FIGURE 15.1 Signature of Eucheiros on a Little Master cup
PHOTO: © TRUSTEES OF THE BRITISH MUSEUM

well also have been citizens, but this was not necessarily the main message conveyed by the patronymic.

Examples come both from painted pottery and from sculpture. A Little Master cup of ca. 560–555 BCE bears a different inscription on either side, which is unusual.[38] Side A reads, 'Εὔχειρος ἐποίησεν, 'Eucheiros made [me/ this cup]' to which side B adds the information ὁ ('Ε)ργοτίμου υἱ(ε)ύς, 'the son of Ergotimos' (Fig. 15.1). By writing different but complementary phrases on either side of the cup, the painter brought attention to the father–son relation. The layout and the addition of the term 'son', which in Greek is unnecessary, put even more emphasis on the painter's family ties. This was for good reasons: Ergotimos was a well-known Attic potter who signed several vases, most notably the famous François Vase.[39] On a small ceramic stand in New York, the signatures of Ergotimos and the painter Kleitias, with whom he often collaborated, are painted on the foot (Fig. 15.2).[40] The monumental form of the letters imit-

38 London, British Museum, inv. 1847,0806.44; BAPD n°310545. Heesen 2011, 16, 18–19, 259 n°3; Osborne 2010, 244–245 (on signatures on cups).

39 Volute crater, Florence, Archaeological Museum, inv. 4209. *ABV* 76, 1; BAPD n°300000.

40 Metropolitan Museum of Art, inv. 31.11.4. *ABV* 78, 12; BAPD n°300735. Cohen 1991, 52–53; Hirayama 2010, 14–15, 18, 84–85, 225.

FIGURE 15.2 Signature of Ergotimos on a stand
PHOTO: © METROPOLITAN MUSEUM OF ART, INV. 31.11.4

ates engraved inscriptions. As on the cup by Eucheiros, a three-dot separation is painted between the name and verb, rather than the more common two-dot one.[41] In this case, it is probably the painter of the vase, Kleitias, who wrote both signatures, but to an ancient onlooker, the distinction between an autograph signature and one 'by proxy' would make no difference: they would instead take notice of the very neat script and the unusual separation sign. Eucheiros underlined his relationship with his father through text and script: the triple dot established a visual connection between the father and the son's signatures.[42]

41 Heesen 2011, 18 n. 118; Gaunt 2013, 81. The triple dot appears in another signature by Ergotimos: Berlin, Antikensammlung, inv. 3151 side A (BAPD n°300748) and in another signature by Kleitias: British Museum, inv. 1888,0601.426 (BAPD n°300737).

42 For other examples of a student signing in a manner visually similar to his master: Cohen 1991, 63, 68, 75.

The implicit suggestion is that he trained with his father: he was stressing not just a family but also a professional relationship even, possibly, the passing down of the workshop.[43] Towards the middle of the sixth century BCE, the potter Tleson and his brother Ergoteles signed several Little Master cups with their patronymic.[44] They were the sons of Nearchos, also a potter.[45] That both of Nearchos' sons signed with a patronymic highlights the fame of Nearchos' name and suggests they were emphasizing the added prestige of having been taught by him. What is explicitly emphasized, though, is the family relationship. In such families of *technitai*, names could be chosen because they were appropriate for craftspeople: Ergotimos and Ergoteles are both based on '*ergon*', work, and Eucheiros means 'good hand'.[46]

The sculptors Herodoros and his brother Calliades, who lived in the second half of the third century BCE, both signed with explicit reference to their father's name. The latter, Sthennis of Olynthos, was a renowned sculptor.[47] The relationship of father/master and son/pupil is also repeatedly mentioned in the works of literary authors like Pliny and Pausanias.[48] Daidalos of Sicyon (ca. 400–360 BCE), for instance, generally signed with his patronymic—Pausanias reports that Patrokles was both his master and his father.[49] When discussing Olympia, Pausanias quotes the inscription on a monument commemorating the athletic victories of a father and son. The text read:

43 Williams 2009b, 310; Heesen 2011, 77–78.

44 Heesen 2011, 173–177 (Nearchos), 178–179, 187, 196, 207–209 (Tleson), 210–211 (Ergoteles). Ergoteles, son of Nearchos: Berlin, Antikenslg, F1758; Florence market. *ABV* 162.1–2; BAPD n°310541, 310542.

45 Signatures of Nearchos: BAPD n°316, 300769, 300770, 300771, 300773–4. In one case (300767) he may have signed with the verb *egraphsen* (for an alternative restitution of the signature, see Gillis 2021, 94 C80).

46 Williams 2009b, 309–311; Gillis 2021, 62. Ergotimos' father may also have been a potter or a craftsman, which could explain his name.

47 *IOropos* 371, l. 5–6; *Lindos* II, 103, l. 22. Kansteiner et al. IV 2014, 289 n°3095; 321 n°3122. Sthennis: *IOropos* 383; Kansteiner et al. III 2014, 591–593, n°2464; this Sthennis (the younger) signed with his patronymic: his father too was a sculptor, and a son of a sculptor (Sthennis the elder). See Kansteiner et al. III 2014, 413 (stemma), 590 n°2463.

48 E.g. Paus. 1.8.4 and 9.12.4 [Praxiteles' sons who are not even named]; 5.24.5; 6.7.1. Plin. *HN* 35.146 mentions Mnasitimos, son and *discipulus* of Aristonidas (ca. 300 BCE). We know signatures of father and son and both, in fact, sign with their patronymic: *Lindos* II 42, l. 2–3; 696a, l. 7; 56 = *IG* XII 1, 855, l. 3; *SEG* 41, 651. Kansteiner et al. I 2014, 736–739, n°2618–2620. Jacquemin 2007, 28–29, 33.

49 *IvO* 635; *IEph.* 111; Paus. 6.3.4. Kansteiner et al. II 2014, 526–529, n°1308–1310. Same info in Paus. 5.24.5 (Aristocles, student and son of Kleiotas); Kansteiner et al. I 2014, 493 n°577.

> Eutelidas and Chrysotemis made these works, the Argives who learned their work from their predecessors.
>
> Εὐτελίδας καὶ Χρυσόθεμις τάδε ἔργα τέλεσσαν Ἀργεῖοι, τέχναν εἰδότες ἐκ προτέρων.

Pausanias observes that it is not mentioned by whom they were taught.[50] The discovery in a well at Olympia of a bronze plaque bearing an almost identical text suggests that Pausanias misread or misremembered the last word of the signature which really said 'learned their work from their fathers' (τέχ]ναν ϝειδότε πὰρ πατέρο⟨ν⟩).[51] Again, the signature underlined the strong connection between father and son, pupil and master. If the recovered piece of bronze with the signatures of these sculptors did indeed come from another sculpture, as suggested by a slight but significant difference with Pausanias' text, then Eutelidas and Chrysotemis would have used the same two-line signature on different works. Pliny says that the epigram with which Boupalos and Athenis signed as sons of Archermos was used on several works.[52] In such cases, the sculptors would have decided or imposed the form of their signature, not the patron. The late fifth-century BCE painter Parrhasios seems to offer another such case. He is said to have signed several works with the following epigram:

> Parrhasios, a most luxurious man,
> And yet a follower of purest virtue,
> Painted this work: a worthy citizen
> Of noble Ephesus. His father's name
> Evenor was, and he, his lawful son,
> Carried his art to the first place among the Greeks

50 Paus. 6.10.4; Kansteiner et al. I 2014, 357–358 n°451.

51 *SEG* 48, 545. *NIvO* 65. Ebert 1996, 28–29 (followed by Kansteiner et al. I 2014, 358–359 n°452) suggested that the signature was first written on the shield of the statue of the father (victorious in 520 or 516), then when the statue of the victorious son, by the same two artists, was added (after 484 or 480), they cut out their old signature (with 'work' in the singular) and replaced it by a new one (with 'works' in the plural). This is supposed to explain why this piece of bronze was tossed in a well ca. 50 years after being inscribed. This interpretation raises several issues, for instance that the sculptors would have reused the bronze of the 'old' signature, and that commissioning the same sculptors for monuments made at least 32 years apart, although possible, seems highly unlikely. I would suggest instead that the son erected a monument bearing statues of both himself and his father, and that Eutelidas and Chrysotemis also created other victory-commemorations, hence the recovered signature. Why the fragment was thrown in a well is unclear.

52 Plin. *HN* 36.11.

Ἀβροδίαιτος ἀνὴρ ἀρετήν τε σέβων τάδ' ἔγραψεν
Παρράσιος κλεινῆς πατρίδος ἐξ Ἐφέσου.
Οὐδὲ πατρὸς λαθόμην Εὐήνορος, ὅς ῥά μ' ἔφυσε
γνήσιον, Ἑλλήνων πρῶτα φέροντα τέχνης.[53]

In this signature we find elements familiar from the other two epigrams: Parrhasios mentions his home city, his father (who was also his master, according to Pliny),[54] and his Panhellenic reputation. Any signature longer than two or three words is quite remarkable. Using an entire two-line epigram reveals pride (if not arrogance). These rare examples suggest that a craftsman could have a signature-epigram composed, and then use it as a trademark on other works.

When two or more craftsmen signed together, the patronymic clarified the relation between them. Demetrios and his son, Diognetes, signed a statue together; here, the word *huios* 'son' underlined even more the relationship.[55] Andragoras of Rhodes and both his sons signed together:

> Andragoras, son of Aristomenes and Andragoras and Aristeidas, sons of Andragoras, of Rhodes, made (it).[56]

Ἀνδραγόρας Ἀριστομένευς καὶ Ἀνδραγόρας
καὶ Ἀριστείδας Ἀνδραγόρα Ῥόδιοι ἐποίησεν

Phileas and his son Zeuxippos also worked together. The layout of the inscription superposes Phileas in the nominative and in the genitive, emphasizing his double role, as sculptor and father of a sculptor:[57]

Φιλέας καὶ Ζεύξιππος
Φιλέα ἐποίησαν

In other cases, brothers mentioned their relationship: Menodotos and Charmolas, sons of Artemidoros, sometimes signed together.[58] Dionysodoros, Moss-

53 Ath. XII 543c. Kansteiner et al. II 2014, 818–820, n°1643.
54 Plin. *HN* 35.36.1.
55 'Demetrios and Diognetos, his son, from Tegea, made it'. *SEG* 39, 391. Kansteiner et al. IV 2014, 392 n°3194.
56 *SEG* 39, 764. Kansteiner et al. V 2014, 225–226 n°3825. Also Goodlett 1991, 677.
57 *IG* IV, 745. Kansteiner et al. V 2014, 196 n°3795 (uncertain date).
58 E.g. *Lindos* II 281b, l. 19–22; *Clara Rhodos* II, p. 190 n°19, l. 15; *Rhodiaka* I, 7, l. 21–22. Badoud

chion and Adamas, all sons of Adamas, also signed together: the article '*hoi*' preceded the patronymic to make clear they were all brothers.[59] What is striking when examining these signatures is the strong emphasis on familial relations. The professional connection between the craftsmen is only implicit. The master-student relationship was never explicitly mentioned in signatures.[60] Family continuity, possibly or even probably also denoting the passing down of a workshop, and familial collaborations were clearly more important.

Another question arises when examining these signatures: when two or more craftspeople collaborated, was the order in which their names appeared in the joint signature significant? When there is sufficient information to tell, this seems indeed to be the case: the father, for instance, is always named before the son. This could indeed mean that in all, or most, cases, the first name was the dominant partner (for whatever reason). An example from second or first century BCE Rhodes supports this assumption. In this case, studied by Nathan Badoud, the father Artemidoros signed with his eldest son, Menodotos. He in turn signed with his (younger) brother Charmolas, as first name.[61] At some point however, the order was inverted: Charmolas' name then appeared as first name, before Menodotos, suggesting a change in the dynamics between the brothers. Charmolas' dominant position is confirmed by the fact he also signed alone, as well as with another sculptor, Satyros, and then with his own son, also called Menodotos, whereas no such things are attested for Menodotos (the elder).[62] Although Artemidoros and his two sons signed as citizens of Tyre, Charmolas received Rhodian citizenship at some point.[63] The change in the order of the names of the two brothers has led Nathan Badoud to suggest that Artemidoros signed with his eldest son Menodotos at the end of his career, visibly associating with him, passing on the workshop to him. But of the two brothers, Menodotos was the 'weakest', always collaborating with his younger brother who, eventually, 'publicly' took over the workshop, marking this by signing first when collaborating with his elder brother. Indeed, Menodotos then disappeared from view whereas Charmolaos pursued a profitable

2010, 126–127. Another example: *IDélos* 1648 and 1649 Ammonios and Perigenes, sons of Zopyros. Here too we are sure they were brothers as Ammonios also signs alone with his patronymic.

59 *IDélos* 2125, l. 8–9 (111/10 BCE). Kansteiner et al. V 2014, 49–50 n°3650.

60 With two exceptions in the imperial period: Kansteiner et al. V 2014, 153 n°3474, 159–160 n°3756.

61 Badoud 2010, 131. The signatures of the father and the two sons are collected in Kansteiner et al. V 2014, 375–395, n°3978–3994. See also Goodlett 1991, 677–678.

62 Badoud 2010, 126–127.

63 Badoud 2010, 127.

career and passed on the workshop to his own son, Menodotos.[64] When he signed with his son, they both signed with their patronymic: this was a way of avoiding any confusion, but it also emphasized that sculpture had been practised for three generations in the family![65] Charmolas also signed as first name with somebody from outside the family, Satyros. It is now impossible to tell if in doing so, Charmolas was endorsing Satyros, a former student or another member of his workshop, or if this was 'just' a temporary collaboration between equals. In such cases, the signatures never indicate what the relationship was, although this may have been clear to ancient viewers.

The mention of the patronymic often seems to establish a relationship between craftspeople, such as fathers and sons, or brothers working together. It thus most often underlines family connections, and in many cases continuity and transmission of a trade through the generations—spanning three generations if both father and son give their patronymic. Indeed, when father and son sign together, the father may not be just endorsing his son's talents, but may also be announcing the (planned) passing on of the workshop from one generation to another.

When two craftsmen sign together, they sometimes only give their name, without a patronymic or an ethnic; in these cases, the nature of their relation remains unknown. On other occasions, they make it clear they have no family ties by stating their different patronymics or their different ethnics; occasionally, they come from the same city, but give different patronymics.[66] When unrelated craftsmen sign together, they can use a common verb (e.g. ἐποίησαν in the dual) or two different verbs. In the first case, the essential feature which is highlighted is their association, and the nature of their relationship remained unstated.[67] When two craftspeople sign using different verbs, they are stressing their complementarity: as specialists in different fields, they are both contributing to the final work. Their collaboration is of a practical order, and is explicitly described.

The most common case in which two people signed together while performing different roles is that of Attic potters (ἐποίησεν—X made [it]) and painters (ἔγραψεν—X painted [it]). Generally speaking, there seems to be no hierarchy between the potter and painter: their signatures are even often vis-

64 Badoud 2010, 139–140, 143.

65 Lindos II 293c, l. 41; 702, l. 4. Kansteiner et al. V 2014, 391–393 n°3992–3993.

66 *SEG* 39, 489 (Argithea 2nd c. BCE): both sculptors are from Gomphoi, but bear different patronymics. Kansteiner et al. V 2014, 212–213 n°3814.

67 E.g. Philergos and Endoios, see Johnston 2019, 31. On Rhodes: Goodlett 1991, 670–673, 676–677, 681. Tosto 1999, 186–187.

ibly and deliberately placed on the same footing, as was the case with Kleitias and Ergotimos on the stand from New York (Fig. 15.2).[68] Although there are substantially more signatures of potters, painters must have played an almost equally important role, garnering respect both inside the workshop and among clients. This explains the high number of painters' signatures, and the fact that they also regularly signed on their own. Beyond pottery, there are a few other examples of such double signatures: in one or two cases, a poet signed an epigram on a statue base on which the sculptor's signature was also incised.[69] In the Hellenistic period, a few sculptors signed with a bronze-worker and, in one case, with a marble-painter.[70] These examples offer rare instances of when someone other than the sculptor gained himself a 'name' that was made visible for all to see, a public acknowledgment of the collaborations necessary to produce the works. In these cases, the name accompanied by the verb ἐποίησεν comes before the other one. As has been argued above, this suggests that these signatures do reflect a hierarchy between two associated craftsmen.

Without any context, we can only guess the reasons behind these joint signatures. Using two different verbs highlights the collaboration between two different specialists that were both necessary to complete an object. Although such collaborations were commonplace, they were very rarely acknowledged in this way. In general, craftwork would have been a collective effort, requiring the intervention of much more than even two people. In most cases, only one creative force is acknowledged, but the explicit reference to two different professions underscores the technical complexity of a work and the collaboration going on behind the scenes.

4 Other Information

In a few cases, craftsmen added information to their signatures concerning the work itself or some other achievement. Two trends are worth highlighting. In the Archaic period and the Classical period, craftsmen sometimes brought attention to the quality, beauty, and technical prowess of their work; in the Hellenistic period, they occasionally emphasized their civic recognition.

The signature could attract attention to a specific achievement: on an early fifth-century BCE grave stele from Orchomenos in Boiotia, the signature reads:

68 Cohen 1991, 52, 58, 61; Williams 2019, 172; Tsingarida and Viviers forthcoming.

69 E.g. *IG* IX 1, 131, l. 5–8; *IG* IX 2, 637 and Add. p. XV; *IG* XII 1, 40, l. 10–12.

70 Goodlett 1991, 676; Badoud 2015, 278–284 n°24, 30, 31, 5357, 61, 62, 63, 65, 75, 113.

Alxenor the Naxian made [me]. But look!

Ἀλχσήνορ [ἐ]ποίησεν *hó* Νάχσιος ἀλλ' ἐσίδεσ̣[θε].[71]

The stele depicts a bearded man and a dog; the signature is placed on the lower frame, just below a frontal foreshortened view of the deceased's right foot. Alxenor was clearly very proud of his achievement; the imperative echoes a phrase in the *Iliad* adding an epic flavour to the signature.[72] The great painter and potter Euphronios, on a fragmentary calyx-krater dated to ca. 515–510 BCE, signed between two contorting comasts: '[Euphronios] painted *these*', proudly adding τάδε at the end for emphasis.[73] He brought attention to his skilful drawing both by the content of the text and by its placement.

In other signatures, the added text emphasizes the quality of the work as a whole, or underlines the expertise of the craftsman. On a late sixth-century BCE inscription on a columnar base from Paros, the signature reads:

I boast of being the work of the Parian Critonides.

το Παρίο ποίημα Κριτωνίδεω εὔχομ[αι εἶναι].[74]

The fifth-century BCE Parian Euphron added to one of his signatures that 'he was not without skill': Εὔφρων ἐξεποίησ' οὐκ ἀδαὴς Πάριος.[75] An exaleiptron signed by Lysiades offers a prime example of the skill of Athenian potters (Fig. 15.3). The very restrained decoration, with a black foot and dots on the fine moulded bands, emphasizes the structure of the vase, which dates to ca. 540–530 BCE. A signature underlines the skills of the potter:

Lysiades made me well.

Λυσιάδες μ'ἐποί(η)σεν εὖ.[76]

71 *IG* VII 3225. Kansteiner et al. I 2014, 564 n°656; Hurwit 2015, 117.

72 *Il.* 23.469. Friedländer 1948, 62 (n°57) and 150–151 (n°164); Kaltsas 2002, 70, 78.

73 Denoyelle 1990, 60–66; Williams 2019, 165–171, esp. 169 (parallels for the expression) and 170 (signature).

74 *IG* XII 5, 216. Kansteiner et al. I 2014, 256 n°351.

75 *IG* I³ 1018 (ca. 475–450 BCE). Kansteiner et al. I 2014, 565 n°657. For other examples, Johnston 2019, 24.

76 Lyons, Musée des Beaux-Arts, inv. E 387. *ABV* 348. BAPD n°301946. All other exaleiptra attributed to Lysiades are of a different type and predominantly black.

FIGURE 15.3 Signature of Lysiades, on an exaleiptron, Lyon, Musée des Beaux-Arts, inv. E 387
PHOTO: © LYON MBA

The text is eye-catching on the background of bands of unpainted clay. On Little Master cups the signature works in the same way, often placed where figurative decoration would otherwise be. But the overall scheme of these cups is slightly more fussy, with a much taller foot, and palmettes flanking the handles as well as figured decoration sometimes added on the lip.[77] Here, the signature adds to the abstract decoration and understated elegance of the vase. A comparable example is offered by two jugs which are entirely black-glazed except for a reserved band (framed by a red line above and below) on which is written 'Priapos made [me] well | beautifully' (Πρίαπος ἐποίεσεν καλός).[78] Here too, the decoration is reduced to the signature, which gets emphasis through its

77 E.g. The J. Paul Getty Museum, inv. 80.AE.99.3 (BAPD n°45034); Munich, Antikensammlungen, inv. 9413 (BAPD n°28795). An animal is often painted above the signature, partially distracting from it. On signatures on Little Master cups, see also Cohen 1991, 52–53.

78 Both of these jugs are very fragmentary. Athens, National Museum: 1.833; Athens, Acropolis Museum, inv. ii, 833; BAPD n°301083, 330105.

placement. These signatures underline the potter's or painter's achievement, his pride in an exceptional work. The added words draw attention to an unusual feature of their work or to their expertise.

A little after 425 BCE, Paionios of Mende sculpted a marble statue of Nike for the Messenians and Naupactians who dedicated it in the sanctuary of Zeus at Olympia. The signature reads:

> Paionios of Mende made [it], having also made the acroteria to the temple after winning the competition.
>
> Παιώνιος ἐποίησε Μενδαῖος καὶ τἀκρωτήρια ποιῶν ἐπὶ τὸν ναὸν ἐνίκα.[79]

The text advertised that he was publicly chosen for this task following a contest—presumably a tender for the contract.[80] He also linked his name to the most important monument in honour of Zeus in the sanctuary—his temple. There would also have been a very strong visual connection as the dedication stood just in front of the façade of the temple.[81] Public selection was an important way for craftsmen to prove their worth: it was one of few forms of public recognition that was open to them; such public endorsement enhanced the reputation of a *technitês*.[82] This unique and extraordinary signature calls attention to a different work than the one on which it appears. The commission for the temple must have been an immense source of pride for the sculptor. For the Messenians and Naupactians to accept the mention of Paionios' acroteria in his signature, they must have felt it substantially added prestige to their own dedication, no doubt because it linked it directly to the great temple of Zeus and to one of the craftsmen who worked on it.

In the late fifth or early fourth century BCE—close in time to the signature left by Paionios at Olympia—the sculptor Kleiotas, according to Pausanias, signed a statue in Athens with the words:

> He who first invented at Olympia the starting-posts for the horses, he made me, Kleiotas, son of Aristokles.
>
> ὃς τὴν ἱππάφεσιν ἐν Ὀλυμπίᾳ εὕρατο πρῶτος, τεῦξέ με Κλεοίτας υἱὸς Ἀριστοκλέους.[83]

79 *IvO* 259. Kansteiner et al. II 2014, 635–638 n°1431; Hurwit 2015, 132–133; Palagia 2021.
80 On public competitions for sculptors, Stewart 2019, 52; Schultz 2019, 99–100.
81 Palagia 2021, 103.
82 Harris 1988, 337; Williams 2017, 148–149.
83 Paus. 6.20.14. Kansteiner et al. I 2014, 491–492 n°576; Dimde and Flämig 2019, 152–153.

In other words, the text praised Kleoitas as the first inventor (πρῶτος εὑρετής)—a common source of praise in the Greek world—of a mechanical innovation, but it did so on a different work, set up in a different city. While no further details are given about the statue on which this inscription was engraved, what is important here is that the starting-posts were surely created at the behest either of the sanctuary or of the city controlling it. In other words, they must have been a public undertaking. In this inscription, Kleoitas thus reveals not only his inventiveness and accomplishments, but also, indirectly, that these skills had been publicly acknowledged. Such public recognition is also implied in other signatures on publicly commissioned monuments such as the statues made by Aristeas on behalf of the city of Megalopolis and by the son of Menophantos on behalf of Attalus II or III of Pergamon discussed earlier in this chapter. In both cases, the sculptor was chosen for the job by a public authority, which implies his skills were publicly known and recognized.

In the Hellenistic period, sculptors in Rhodes highlight a different form of public recognition.[84] Many of the sculptors working in Rhodes were foreigners, and their signatures specified their ethnic. When the city of Rhodes had granted them *epidamia*—the official right of residence in the *polis*—they could mention this in their signatures, despite the four additional words this required.[85] In several cases, they also indicated their Rhodian citizenship by adding the ethnic *Rhodios* (rather than the expected demotic), even though it would theoretically have been unnecessary to do so inside the *polis*.[86] Thus, Epicharmos of Soloi, who was active in the second half of the second century BCE, produced a series of signatures. On the first, he signed with his ethnic.[87] Subsequently, he mentioned that he had received *epidamia*.[88] Later still, he signed with his son, also named Epicharmos, who had received Rhodian citizenship.[89] This is not an isolated case: Rhodes apparently had a policy of

There appears to be some confusion between Kleiotas, the inventor, and Kleiotas, the sculptor, in Pausanias' account and in modern literature. For clarification, Dimde and Flämig 2019, 153–155, who date Kleiotas the inventor to the late 5th / early 4th c. BCE.

84 The most up-to-date list of Rhodian sculptors is in Badoud 2015, 278–284.

85 On *epidamia* in Rhodes, Maillot 2015, 152, 154–155. On pride in the acquisition of status in Rhodes, Maillot 2009, 51–52.

86 Goodlett 1991, 679–681; Gabrielsen 1992, esp. 53–56; Maillot 2009, 46–49. The ethnic *Rhodios* seems to have been used mainly by sculptors, including native Rhodians.

87 *Lindos* II, 234, l. 8; *IG* XII 3, 103. Kansteiner et al. V 2014, 280–283 n°3884–3885.

88 Ἐπίχαρμος Σολεύς, ὧι ἁ ἐπιδαμία δέδοται. *Lindos* II, 232, l. 8; 235, l. 1; 236, l. 6; *Suppl. epigr. Rhodio*, 55, l. 1. Kansteiner et al. V 2014, 283–285 n°3886–3889.

89 καὶ Ἐπίχαρμος Ἐπιχάρμου Ῥόδιος ἐποίησαν. Incidentally, this provides another example of

welcoming sculptors from all over the Greek world and incorporating them into its citizen body.[90] Another sculptor, Phyles, son of Polygnotos, from Halicarnassos, also signed several monuments at Rhodes. At some point, he was granted the title of benefactor (*euergetês*) which he then often added to his signature.[91] Again, this honour was a source of pride, a public recognition of a highly prized attitude, although not a title often awarded for professional deeds. The sculptor Boethos of Chalcedon offers a similar example. He made a statue at Lindos, and dedicated it with the inscription:

> When Nicagoras, son of Panaitios,
> and by adoption of Ainesidamos,
> was priest of Athana Lindia,
> Boethos, son of Athanaion, of Chalcedon, *proxenos*,
> made this and offered it in thanks to Athana Lindia
>
> ἐπ' ἱερέως τᾶς Ἀθάνας τᾶς Λινδίας
> Νικαγόρα τοῦ Παναιτίου
> καθ' ὑοθεσίαν δὲ Ἀινησιδάμου
> Βόηθος Ἀθαναίωνος Καλχαδόνιος πρόξενος
> ποιήσας Ἀθάναι Λινδίαι χαριστήριον.[92]

As Christian Blinkenberg noted when he published the inscription, Boethos, a well-known sculptor, must have erected the statue in thanks for receiving the title of *proxenos* from the *polis* of Rhodes.[93] The inscription is both a dedication and a signature, but it underscores the value assigned to such forms of recognition.

The additional information or annotations which appear in signatures clearly change over time. In the archaic period, craftspeople self-advertised or ad-

---

the patronymic serving to clarify and underline the relation between two sculptors, since only the son's patronymic is given. *IG* XII 1, 43, l. 25–26; 47 l. 25–26; 66, l. 11–12; 846, l. 11–12; *Lindos* II 197g; 246 l. 10–11; 281, l. 18–19. Kansteiner et al. V 2014, 285–295 n°3890–3896.

90 Maillot 2009, 54–57. Other examples: Gabrielsen 1992, 59 n°12 (?), 13, 15, 16, p. 61 n°24, p. 62 n°27?, p. 64 n°37. Many of the other *Rhodioi* are either descendants of these naturalized sculptors, or belong to a single Camiran family.

91 *Suppl. Epigr. Rhod.* 38, l. 8; *SEG* 58, 814, IV l. 4–5; *Lindos* II 129, IX; *IG* XII 1, 103, l. 4–5; *Tit. Cam.* 39, l. 35; *Lindos* II 132, l. 6; *Lindos* II 131c l. 5. Kansteiner et al. IV 2014, 615–626 n°3404–3411; Goodlett 1991, 676.

92 *Lindos* II 165. Kansteiner et al. IV 2014, 694–695 n°3485.

93 Blinkenberg 1941, col. 422. Plin. *HN* 33.55 seems to refer to this statue. Kansteiner et al. IV 2014, 696–697 n°3487.

vertised their work in a very direct manner, drawing attention to their skills and outstanding achievements. From the late classical period onwards, the city became the arbiter of quality: it was public recognition, in different forms, that was mentioned in signatures.

5 Visual Impact of the Signature

The visual language of signatures has attracted a lot of interest. This is particularly true for the ways in which attention was drawn to them and how they were distinguished from other texts on the same work.[94] There were several ways to make signatures stand out. On sculpture bases, one could for instance make strategic use of the position of the signature and the size of the letters. The letters could probably also be picked out in a different colour than the other text(s), although this has not, to my knowledge, been investigated.[95] On vases, signatures could be placed in prominent locations, outside the area painted with figured decoration (e.g. on the lip or the foot); they could also draw attention because they were incised rather than painted.[96]

Signatures, especially when placed on the work itself, could also make a statement about the craftsman's skills. For example, signing tiny objects like coins or gems with minuscule letters provided additional proof of the *technitês*' expertise. Dexamenos, a Chian gem-cutter of the late fifth century BCE, sometimes even added his ethnic to his signature.[97] As was already discussed earlier in this chapter, the signatures of Ergotimos and Kleitias on a stand in New York were written in a striking script which imitates letters engraved in stone, giving them a monumental quality despite their small size (Fig. 15.2).[98] The care and expertise with which they were painted was a testimony to the painter's skills. The signature could also be part of a figurative scene and showcase the *technitês*' abilities through its clever integration. On a Nikosthenic amphora in Brussels, for instance, on either shoulder a satyr runs between a pair of rather cross looking eyes, pulling on the eyebrows. On one side, Nikosthenes' signature continues the line of the right eyebrow and runs between the legs of the

94 Hurwit 2015, *passim*; Cohen 1991.

95 As an archaic dedication in which a later addition is highlighted in a different colour shows, this was in fact done (*IG* I³ 699). See Williams 2013, 57–58; also Jockey 2002, 23.

96 Cohen 1991, 53–57, 65, 82,.

97 Neverov 2007; Hurwit 2015, 37–38, 42–44.

98 MMA, inv. 31.11.4, ca. 570 BCE.

FIGURE 15.4 Signature of Nikosthenes on a Nikosthenic amphora
PHOTO: © ROYAL MUSEUMS OF ART AND HISTORY

satyr, as if to trip him up (Fig. 15.4).[99] The signature thus appears in a prominent position, and is combined with the decoration in a playful way which attracts attention both to itself and to the painting, and therefore to the skill of the painter.[100]

The few signatures on Hellenistic mosaics are very conspicuous—especially when they appear inside the main image. Most of these texts are related to royal workshops and must therefore belong to the most prominent representatives of this craft. This is true for the hunt mosaic in Pella, for the female head crowned by a warship from Thmuis, and for a mosaic from Pergamon.[101] Of this last example, the figurative panels are now lost, but the signature remains: it is written on a piece of papyrus or parchment which appears stuck to the background with blobs of wax (Fig. 15.5).[102] One corner has come undone, curling up and projecting a shadow on the mosaic. This illusionistic tour de force offers

---

99 Brussels, Royal Museums of Art and History, inv. R.388. *ABV* 217, 11; BAPD n°302760. Tosto 1999, 178, n°4 p. 209.

100 See Lissarrague 1994, 15; Lissarrague 2015; Tsingarida and Viviers forthcoming.

101 Dunbabin 1999, 14, 25–16, 28–29; see also 44–47 on the two mosaics from Pompei signed by Dioskourides of Samos; Daszewski 1985, n°38, 142–158 (Sophilos from Thmuis); Daszewski 2001, 266–267, 271.

102 Hurwit 2015, 67–68 and fig. 31.

FIGURE 15.5 Signature of Hephaistion on a mosaic from Pergamon
PHOTO: © ANTIKENSAMMLUNG DER STAATLICHEN MUSEEN ZU BERLIN – PREUßISCHER KULTURBESITZ. PHOTOGRAPHER JOHANNES LAURENTIUS

strong visual proof of the craftsman's professional skills. It also offers a playful comment on permanence and transience, as the note with the signature appears to be coming unstuck, while at the same time, as an integral part of the mosaic floor, it was impossible to remove.

6 Conclusions

Signatures connect a craftsman and his work. As the cases studied here show, small additions to the signature, if put in context, convey various connections and interests which go far beyond the claim of authorship. In general, a signature, at least on commissioned works, must have added prestige to the client.[103] This could be for multiple, non-exclusive and sometimes subtle reasons: because the *technitês* was well-known and highly regarded, or because he came from a city with a reputation for that craft, or from abroad, or from the same place as the patron. At the same time, craftsmen had plenty of reasons of their own to sign their work. In some cases the craftsman may have specifically asked

103 Hurwit 2015, 151–152.

to do so, or suggested a formula that suited him. Signatures, and the details of their wording, may often have resulted from negotiations between *technitês* and patron, rather than from a 'simple' request from the client.

Why did craftsmen sign? Although there does not seem to be a single answer to this question, the examples studied here offer some pointers. The signature was a maker's mark, but it also expressed pride in the maker's craft and achievement, as well as expressing some sense of competition with fellow *technitai*.[104] In addition, the signature could reveal various facets of the craftsman's professional identity, network and recognition.[105] When producing a dedication, the craftsman to some extent identified with the intention of his work. It was for a deity; his work was the gift, a way of honouring the god or goddess through his skills. This may be one of the reasons that dedications were more often signed than funerary monuments. Sculptors wanted to personally include themselves in the dedication as the makers of the tribute to the deity. Family connections look to be very important, and family continuity, the transmission of a skill from father to son, is repeatedly conveyed by joint signatures or, more obliquely, by the use of a patronymic.[106] Other collaborations are also highlighted in signatures although their nature and the reasons behind them often remain unknown.

The geographical aspect was particularly complex, either stressing local identity, or geographical connections between patron and sculptor, or even extensive reputations. This aspect seems to have been of particular significance to the patrons, since their local or international networks were also important, and the sculptor's place of origin and travels could play into this. Finally, craftspeople could praise their own work or highlight their own recognition. The ways of doing this evolved over time. In the archaic period especially, craftspeople could call attention to their own work and achievements in an almost naïve form of self-praise. From the late fifth century onwards, recognition by the city became the yardstick by which to judge competence.[107] The city's recognition (in various forms) was therefore mentioned in signatures.

---

104 Hurwit 2015, 6–7, 19, 147–150; Williams 2017, 148. The painting on the dish Oxford, Ashmolean Museum inv. 189 (BAPD n°301978) is dreadful ('the worst vase-painter whose name is known from Antiquity', according to Beazley), but Oikopheles signed the vase as potter and painter on the rim: the double signature and the amount of space it occupies both point to the craftsman congratulating himself on his achievement.

105 For a different approach, Viviers 2006; on the plurality of meanings of signatures, Gillis 2021, 79–82.

106 Goodlett 1991, 678. Transmission from father to son is also mentioned on funerary monuments, e.g. *IG* II^2 8883; *SEG* 23, 161, l. 29–30 (both Athens, 4th c. BCE).

107 For this aspect in the archaic period, see Jockey 2002, 30–34.

Signatures, however, were also exclusive. In most cases, they pretended that a work was made by just one person, or, more rarely, by two or three.[108] Signatures, in other words, hid most of the people who took part in the crafting of the work, whether they were apprentices, general helpers, or more specialized craftspeople. This 'figurehead' probably was in most cases the main creator of the work, but in others might have been the head of the workshop.[109]

Based on signatures, the identity of craftsmen seems closely bound with their craft and the works they produced, their networks and work-related travels. Labour had an appreciated value which could, at best, bring social and financial recognition and rewards. The positive value of labour combined with skill is reflected in the desire of craftspeople to put their name to their work, to want to advertise their family's longstanding involvement in a craft, and sometimes to involve their home city in the renown they gained from their work. The city, in return, could gain prestige from the activities of its renowned citizens, and use their travels for its own networking and prestige.

Acknowledgements

My warmest thanks to Kim Bowes and Miko Flohr for accepting my paper in this volume. My thanks, too, to all the participants at the Penn-Leiden Conference for their many useful comments and suggestions. I owe many thanks to Dyfri Williams with whom I discussed the topic of signatures at length and whose vase-expertise was invaluable.

Bibliography

Badoud, N. (2010). Une famille de bronziers originaire de Tyr. *ZPE* 172, pp. 125–143.
Badoud, N. (2015). *Le temps de Rhodes*. Munich.
Barlou, V. (2013). An Itinerant Parian before Skopas. In: D. Katsonopoulou and A. Stewart, eds., *Skopas of Paros and His World*. Athens, pp. 111–132.
Blinkenberg, C. (1941). *Lindos* II. *Inscriptions*. Copenhagen.
Bousquet, J. (1966). Inscriptions de Delphes. *BCH*, 90–92, pp. 428–446.

108 Goodlett 1991, 678.

109 Williams 2017, 145–147, 152; Williams 2019, 175–176 on who signed; Tsingarida and Viviers forthcoming.

Cignano, E. (2021). From Epinician Praise to the Poetry of Encomium on Stone. In: M. Fantuzzi, H. Morales and T. Whitmarsh, eds., *Reception in the Greco-Roman World. Literary Studies in Theory and Practice*. Cambridge–New York, pp. 72–91.

Cohen, B. (1991). The Literate Potter. *MMAJ* 26, pp. 49–95.

Daszewski, W.A. (2001). Un atelier 'royal' de mosaïques à Alexandrie. In: D. Paunier and C. Schmidt, eds., *La mosaïque gréco-romaine VIII*. Lausanne, pp. 266–281.

Day, J. (2013). Epigraphic Literacy in Fifth-Century Epinician and Its Audiences. In: P. Liddel and P. Low, eds., *Inscriptions and Their Uses in Greek and Latin literature*. Oxford, pp. 217–230.

Denoyelle, M. (1990). Cratère en calice fragmentaire. In: *Euphronios, peintre à Athènes au VIe siècle avant J.-C.* Paris, pp. 60–66.

Dimartino, A. (2010). Artisti itineranti: l'evidenza epigrafica. In: G. Adornato, ed., *Scolpire il marmo. Importazioni, artisti itineranti, scuole artistiche nel Mediterraneo antico*. Milan, pp. 9–40.

Dimde, B. and Flämig, C. (2019). The *aphesis* of the Olympic Hippodrome: Dimensions, Design, Technology. In: J.-C. Moretti and P. Valavanis, eds., *Les hippodromes et les concours hippiques dans la Grèce antique*. Athens, pp. 145–166.

Ebert, J. (2016). Neue griechische historische Epigramme, In: J.H.M. Strubbe, R.A. Tybout and H.S. Versnel, eds., *Energeia. Studies on Ancient History and Epigraphy Presented to H.W. Pleket*. Amsterdam, pp. 25–29.

Fantuzzi, M. (2004). The Epigram. In: M. Fantuzzi and R. Hunter, eds., *Innovation in Hellenistic Poetry*. Cambridge, pp. 283–349.

Flacelière, R. (1937). *Les Aitoliens à Delphes*. Paris.

Friedländer, P. (1948). *Epigrammata. Greek Inscriptions in Verse from the Beginnings to the Persian Wars*. Berkeley–Los Angeles.

Gabrielsen, V. (1992). The Status of *Rhodioi* in Hellenistic Rhodes. *ClMed*, 43, pp. 43–69.

Gaunt, J. (2013). Ergotimos epoiesen: The Potter's Contribution to the François Vase. In: H.A. Shapiro, M. Iozzo and A. Lezzi-Hafter, eds., *The François Vase. New Perspectives*. Zurich, pp. 67–81.

Goodlett, V.C. (1991). Rhodian Sculpture Workshops. *AJA*, 95, pp. 669–681.

Harris, D. (1998), Nikokrates of Kolonos, Metalworker to the Parthenon Treasurers. *Hesperia* 57, pp. 329–337.

Heesen, P. (2011). *Athenian Little-Master Cups*. Amsterdam.

Hirayama, T. (2010). *Kleitias and Attic Black-Figure Vases in the Sixth-Century B.C.* Tokyo.

Hochscheid, H. (forthcoming). A Sense of Place: Sculptors' Travel in Archaic Greece. In: M. Dana and M. Haake, eds., *People of Knowledge on the Move*. Stuttgart.

Hurwit, J.M. (2015). *Artists and Signatures in Ancient Greece*. New York.

Jacquemin, A. (2007). Pline, Pausanias et les écoles de sculpteurs grecs. In: C. Peltre and P. Lorentz, eds., *La notion d' 'école'*. Strasbourg, pp. 19–31.

Jacquemin, A., Mulliez, D. and Rougemont, G. (2012). *Choix d'inscriptions de Delphes, traduites et commentées*. Paris–Athens.

Jockey, P. (2011). Les artisans de la pierre dans le monde grec archaïque: rôles, conditions et statuts. In: *Les travailleurs dans l'Antiquité. Statuts et conditions*. Paris, pp. 22–45.

Johnston, A. (2019). Sculptor's Signatures: The Archaic Period. In: O. Palagia, ed., *Handbook of Greek Sculpture*. Berlin–Boston, pp. 22–31.

Kansteiner, S., Lehmann, L., Hallof, K. et al. (2014). *Der Neue Overbeck (DNO). Vol. I–V*. Berlin.

Keesling, C.M. (2005). Misunderstood Gestures. *ClAnt*, 24, pp. 41–79.

Lissarrague, F. (1994). *Epiktetos egraphsen*: The Writing on the Cup. In: S. Goldhill and R. Osborne, eds., *Art and Text in Greek Culture*. Cambridge, pp. 12–27.

Lissarrague, F. (2015). Nommer les choses. *Revista Tempo*, 21, pp. 18–29.

Ma, J. (2013). *Statues and Cities*. Oxford.

Maillot, S. (2009). Une association de sculpteurs à Rhodes au IIe siècle av. J.-C. In: L. Bodiou, V. Mehl, J. Oulhen, Fr. Prost and J. Wilgaux, eds., *Chemin faisant. Mélanges en l'honneur de Pierre Brulé*. Rennes, pp. 39–58.

Maillot, S. (2015). Foreigner's Associations and the Rhodian State. In: V. Gabrielsen and C.A. Thomsen, eds., *Private Associations and the Public Sphere*. Copenhagen, pp. 36–182.

Massar, N. (2010). Choose your Master Well. In: M. Horstmanshoff, ed., *Hippocrates and Medical Education*. Leiden–Boston, pp. 169–186.

Massar, N. (2020). Skilled Workers in the City. In: E. Harris, D. Lewis and E. Stewart, eds., *Skilled Labour and Professionalism in Ancient Greece and Rome*. Cambridge, pp. 68–93.

Michels, C. (2011). Dionysos Kathegemon und der attalidische Herrscherkult. In: L.-M. Günther and S. Plischke, eds., *Studien zum vorhellenistischen und hellenistischen Herrscherkult*. Berlin, pp. 114–140.

Nachtergael, G. (1977). *Les Galates en Grèce et les Sôteria de Delphes*. Brussels.

Kaczko, S. (2010). Epigrammi attici e artisti stranieri, In: A. Inglese, ed., *ΕΠΙΓΡΑΜΜΑΤΑ 6. Iscrizioni greche e comunicazione letteraria*. Rome, pp. 197–220.

Neverov, O.Y. (2007). Dexamenos of Chios. In: A.A. Trofimova, ed., *Greeks on the Black Sea. Ancient Art from the Hermitage*. Los Angeles, pp. 62–63.

Ohlemutz, E. (1940), *Die Kulte und Heiligtümer der Götter in Pergamon*. Würzburg.

Osborne, R. (2010). The Art of Signing in Ancient Greece. *Arethusa*, 43.2, pp. 231–251.

Palagia, O. (1982). A Colossal Statue of a Personification from the Agora of Athens. *Hesperia*, 51, pp. 99–113.

Palagia, O. (2021). The Nike of Paionios. In: M. Lagogianni-Georgakarakos, ed., *Known and Unkown Nikai in History, Art and Life*. Athens, pp. 102–117.

Kaltsas, N. (2002). *Sculpture in the National Archaeological Museum, Athens*. Athens.

Savalli-Lestrade, I. (2013). Sculpteur parien, défunt samien. *ZPE*, 186, pp. 181–189.

Scherrer, P. (1983). Das Weihgeschenk von Mikkiades und Archermos auf Delos. *ÖJh*, 54, pp. 19–25.

Schultz, P. (2109). Architectural Sculpture. In: O. Palagia (ed.), *Handbook of Greek Sculpture*. Berlin–Boston, pp. 91–122.

Stewart, A. (1990). *Greek Sculpture*. New Haven–London.

Stewart, A. (2019). Patronage, Compensation, and the Social Status of Sculptors. In: O. Palagia, ed., *Handbook of Greek Sculpture*. Berlin–Boston, pp. 50–88.

Themelis, P. (1998). Attic Sculpture at Kallipolis (Aitolia). In: O. Palagia and W. Coulson, eds., *Regional Schools in Hellenistic Sculpture*. Oxford, pp. 47–60.

Tosto, V. (1999). *The Black-Figure Pottery signed* Nikosthenesepoiesen. Amsterdam.

Tsingarida, A. and Viviers, D. (forthcoming). Signing in the Frame. In: D. Yatromanolakis, ed., *Epigraphy of Art. Ancient Greek Vase-Inscriptions and Vase-Paintings* II. Oxford.

Viviers, D. (2006). Signer une œuvre en Grèce ancienne: pourquoi ? pour qui ? In: J. de La Genière, ed., *Les clients de la céramique grecque, Cahiers du CVA France* 1. Paris, pp. 141–154.

Williams, D. (2009a). *Masterpieces of Classical Art*. London.

Williams, D. (2009b). Picturing Potters and Painters. In: J.H. Oakley and O. Palagia, eds., *Athenian Potters and Painters* II. Oxford, pp. 306–317.

Williams, D. (2013). Greek Potters and Painters: Marketing and Moving. In: A. Tsingarida and D. Viviers, eds., *Pottery Markets in the Ancient Greek World*. Brussels, pp. 39–60.

Williams, D. (2017). Beyond the Berlin Painter. In: M. Padget, ed., *The Berlin Painter and his World*. New Haven–London, pp. 144–187.

Williams, D. (2019). Villard and the Campana Collection. In: F. Gauthier, P. Rouillard and A. Rouveret, eds., *Céramique et peinture grecques dans la Méditerranée antique*. Paris, pp. 161–189.

CHAPTER 16

Professionals as *paradeigmata* of *aretê* in Hellenistic Honorific Decrees

Antiopi Argyriou-Casmeridis

1 Introduction*

The traditional literary aristocratic view that paid work was something shameful and evidence of lower status has been revised by a variety of scholars.[1] As Stewart, Harris and Lewis have recently argued, skill in an occupation that was of benefit to society could be a source of pride and honour for the professional.[2] In this chapter, I shall discuss how the epigraphic evidence from Hellenistic honorific decrees for various categories of professionals in the fields of art and education may contribute to our understanding of the social status of skilled workers and the value of labour in the Hellenistic period. In several decrees the honorands are specifically rewarded for their professional activities, which were promulgated as the manifestations of *aretê* and other aspects of civic virtue. It will be argued that, in the public discourse of euergetism,[3] skilled labour could be construed as civic benefaction in itself, and that professionals could be presented as civic *paradeigmata* of *aretê*. As Aneziri has pointed out, the epigraphical evidence shows how the cities retouched the portrait of these working people using the palette of civic values.[4]

An honorific decree was a special gift among other honours, symbolic or material, that could be bestowed on a benefactor in return for his services to the community.[5] Its purpose was not just to publicize the benefaction, but also

* All dates are BCE, unless otherwise stated.

1 Plato, *Grg.* 512c–d 6; Xenophon, *Oec.* V 3–8; Aristotle, *Pol.* 1328b 37–1329a 2.

2 Stewart, Harris and Lewis 2020, 20.

3 On euergetism: Gygax and Zuiderhoek 2021; Liddel 2021; Gygax 2016; Chaniotis 2018a; Gray 2018; Ma 2003 and 2013; Luraghi 2010, Gauthier 1985. As Ma 2000, 193 has argued, '… the language of euergetism is clearly a well-defined, stable, institutionalized, language', and 'we must study this language in its world, where it performs several functions, as discourse'. Cf. Ceccarelli 2018, 147; Veligianni-Terzi 1997.

4 Aneziri 2008, 139.

5 Henry 1983; Meyer 2013, 457: 'Stone inscribing could permit the embodiment of an action, in a durable physical form for example; or could make an action's performance possible through

 | DOI:10.1163/9789004694965_017

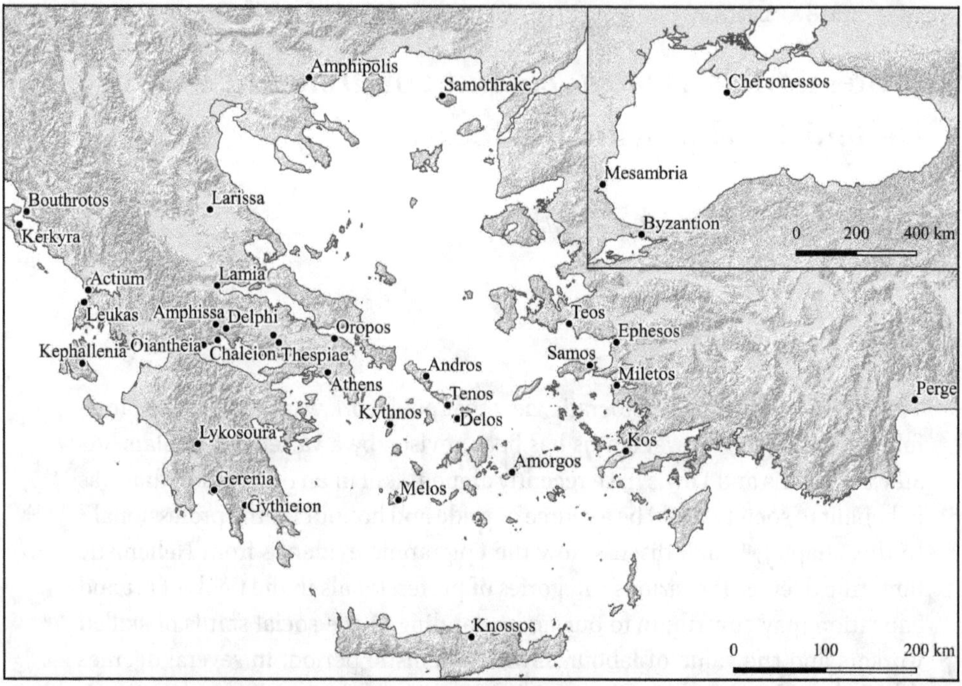

FIGURE 16.1 Map of the findspots of the inscriptions discussed in this chapter
PHOTO: M. FLOHR

to encourage others to provide comparable benefits.[6] Honorific decrees usually explained in a motivation clause (introduced by ἐπειδή) the reasons for the decision to honour and described in a hortative clause (introduced by ὅπως/ἵνα) the aim of the decree to create reciprocity and the intention to encourage future benefactions.[7] The language of approbation in honorific decrees presented the honorand's benefactions as manifestations of *aretê* and other aspects of virtue, and the rewards as an expression of gratitude on the part of the *polis* that bestowed honours.

On the basis of study of extant decrees dating predominantly from the third and second centuries BCE from the Greek *poleis* of mainland Greece, the Aegean islands, the Black Sea region, Thrace and Asia Minor (Fig. 16.1), passed

repeated reading it out loud; or could fix the memory of an action; or perhaps some combination of all of these'.

6 Henry 1996; Sickinger 2009; Luraghi 2010; Lambert 2011.

7 The decrees are voted and erected in prominent public places, so that everyone sees that the city knows how to praise its benefactors, and so that others may emulate them, in order to receive appropriate honours. For the hortatory clause, see Miller 2016; Hedrick 1999 and 2000; Henry 1996.

TABLE 16.1 Types of benefactions of professionals in the fields of Arts & Education

	Free services	Professional expertise (ἐμπειρία)	Reputation gained through work (εὐδοκιμεῖν)	Teaching lessons and giving lectures (ἀκροάσεις) and performances (ἐπιδείξεις)	Adding to the prestige of the polis and/or the sanctuary through their work	Conduct worthy of the profession	Professional aid in times of crisis
Musicians	✓		✓	✓	✓	✓	
Actors	✓		✓				
Poets			✓	✓	✓	✓	
Historians			✓	✓	✓	✓	
Philosophers	✓		✓	✓			
Teachers	✓		✓	✓		✓	
Doctors	✓	✓	✓	✓		✓	✓
Architects		✓	✓				✓
Sculptors	✓						

in honour of individuals who were commended in their capacity as professionals and as civic benefactors, I shall discuss how their benefactions were presented as manifestations of civic virtue, and how these honorands were construed as public *paradeigmata* of *aretê*.[8] My method is based on the creation of a database of over a hundred inscriptions,[9] which has allowed me to carry out multiple case studies for each category of honorands, and to explore the articulation of *aretê* through the language of honour by combining a lexical investigation of the value-terms that were deployed in honorific decrees with the interpretation of their connotations in their historical contexts (Table 16.1). In the context of civic honours, *aretê* and its various constituent aspects, manifested by exemplary types of behaviour, set examples of virtue that transgressed regional and chronological boundaries. In this particular pedagogical perspect-

8 A problem of discussing Greek value-terms, as has been argued (Dover 1974, 47), is their translation into another language. For this reason, as in many other similar studies, transliteration is preferred instead of an English translation. For most of the Greek terms discussed here I offer their common English translation, although it is argued that sometimes the historical context and the nature of the honorands' benefactions may have affected those value-terms' connotations.

9 In my discussion, within this broad geographical and chronological spectrum, I have not included ambiguous, heavily restored or undated inscriptions. The basic criteria for discussing a case study here are a) that the honorand is honoured in his/her capacity as a professional, and b) that the language of approbation reveals on account of what civic virtues he/she was honoured.

ive, honorific decrees worked as media of production, circulation and validation of cultural knowledge,[10] thus promoting specific virtues as the quintessence of honourable civic behaviour in the Hellenistic period.

From the various categories of professionals,[11] i.e. workers who regularly exercised an expert skill for pay, I shall examine the language of approbation in honorific decrees for the following categories: musicians, actors, poets, historians, philosophers, teachers, doctors, architects and sculptors. My choice was informed by these honorands' professional contributions in the fields of art and education; also, their representation in the epigraphic corpus of Hellenistic honorific decrees (in a substantial quantity for one category, e.g. doctors, or in meagre numbers for another category of honorands, e.g. sculptors) indicates the importance of investigating the public reward for their services. This is even more obvious, if one compares honorific decrees for these professionals with other categories of honorands (e.g. civic officials, priests, gymnasiarchs etc.) who were similarly honoured through decrees on account of civic virtues for their benefactions and by a similar language of honour.

First, I shall focus on the language of the decrees demonstrating that the honorands were explicitly praised for services emanating from their occupation or skill (τέχνη/ἐπιτήδευμα/ἔργον).[12] Second, I shall compare the decrees with a view to shedding light on the type of benefactions that these honorands were praised for, and finally, I will try to identify the virtues on account of which these skilled workers were elevated to public *paradeigmata*.

---

10 Liddel 2020, II, 109–158; Massar 2006.

11 Professionalism in antiquity: Stewart et al. 2020; Aneziri 2008 for professionals in inscriptions. Massar 2020, 69 defined professionals as people trained in a *technê*, who practised it for a fee as their main means of earning their living. Cf. Harris 2020, 29–30: 'It may not be possible to draw a firm line between professional and non-professional occupations in the world of ancient Greece'. Stewart 2020, 269 pointed out that caution is needed, '… for the English term "profession" may conjure a range of associations, not all of which are entirely suitable to the ancient context'. There are several scholarly works for each category of professionals discussed in this chapter, e.g. Guarducci 1929, Aneziri 2003 and 2020, Ceccarelli 2004, Feyel 2006, Le Guen 2001 and 2007 (artists); Chaniotis 1988 (historians); Hellmann 1999, Winter 2006 (architects); Easterling 2004, Easterling and Hall 2002, Hugoniot et al. 2004, Csapo 2010, Ceccarelli 2010, Le Guen 2004 and 2019 (actors); Samama 2003, Massar 2005 (doctors); Haake 2007 (philosophers); Hunter and Rutherford 2009 (poets).

12 The term τέχνη should not be taken as exclusively relating to arts, such as music, theatre, sculpture etc. in inscriptions. On the contrary, it is very often associated with such professionals as doctors. For the terminology denoting 'profession', 'art' or 'skill', Stewart et al. 2020, 1–26. Cf. Massar 2020, 68, that the word τέχνη, often translated as 'craft' or 'art' could cover many fields, ranging from medicine to music and from pottery to warfare.

It should be noted that there are significant overlaps between these categories of professionals (e.g. poets and historians), also because inscriptions are not always clear about the 'professional identity' of the honorand.[13] Moreover, many of these professionals travelled extensively across the Hellenistic world.[14] Travelling professionals were not a new thing, but the expansion of the market for artistic skills and the extensive specialization and increased professionalization in the Hellenistic period[15] offered many opportunities for professionals in the fields of art and education to travel and offer their services.

These professionals offered their services in various contexts: musicians, actors and poets were normally praised for their performances in the context of religious festivals,[16] teachers and philosophers were usually honoured for their contributions to civic education at the *gymnasia*, while musicians, poets, historians and doctors were praised for their teaching activities and public lectures. Doctors and architects were usually commended in periods of crisis (war, natural disasters and epidemics), whereas sculptors were commissioned by *poleis* and sanctuaries to make (or restore) statues.

It will be argued that professionals were commended in the honorific decrees for the following reasons and most often a combination of two or more of them: 1. free services (either working free of charge or waiving their fees or offering extra performances), 2. their professional expertise (ἐμπειρία), 3. reputation gained through performance (εὐδοκιμεῖν), 4. teaching lessons and giving lectures (ἀκροάσεις) or performances (ἐπιδείξεις),[17] 5. cultural and political promulgation of the *polis*' agenda (adding to the prestige of the *polis*/sanctuary through work), 6. conduct worthy of their profession (professional etiquette), and 7. professional aid in times of crisis.[18]

---

13 Teaching activities were recorded for most of the categories discussed here (e.g. philosophers or musicians), but teachers are a distinct category of honorands in their own right.

14 Aneziri 2008, 141, n. 3; Hunter and Rutherford 2009.

15 Harris 2020, 36–37.

16 Robert 1984 [2007]; Aneziri 2009, 217.

17 Cinalli 2017, 182 distinguished between *akroaseis* (public lectures) and *epideixeis* (performances at the *gymnasion*, closely associated to the domain of education). Cf. Lefèvre 2010, 13–14 for the *akroaseis* and *epideixeis* as parts of the *dokimasia* procedure, especially for doctors, during which the candidates were tested for their competence and proved their qualifications.

18 See Table 16.1 (above, p. 341).

2 Musicians

Musicians, highly specialized in the Hellenistic period,[19] often travelled in order to participate in religious festivals and compete in musical contests, where they could gain recognition for their merits.[20] They were usually praised for giving extra performances outside the contexts of religious festivals, free of charge or waiving part of the fees. For example, Menalkes of Athens was a *kitharôdos* who had competed at the festival of the Soteria in Delphi,[21] and had given an extra performance (προσεπέδωκε) for the god and the Amphictyony.[22] Athanadas of Rhegion also competed at the Soteria for two days, but he offered on popular demand (ἐπαιτηθείς)[23] an extra day (ἐπέδωκε) for the god and the *polis*, during which he succeeded (εὐδοκίμησεν τῶι ἀγῶνι) in giving a performance worthy of the god, and of Rhegion and Delphi.[24] During his stay (ἐπιδαμία),[25] he conducted himself well and with dignity (ἀνεστράφη καλῶς καὶ εὐσχημόνως). Athanadas was praised on account of his *eusebeia* and *hosiotês*[26] towards the god and for his devotion to his art (ἐπὶ τᾶι προαιρέσει ἆν ἔχων περὶ τὰν [τέ][χ]ναν). Both these *kitharôdoi* were honoured for their performances during a religious festival, hence the virtues of piety and respect to the gods.[27] Yet their extra performances, probably free of charge,[28] were an additional reason for public honours.

19 Stewart 2020, 272.

20 Parker 2004, 9. Cf. Van Liefferinge 2000; Massar 2020, 84–86; Linder 2020.

21 For the distinction between the Amphictyonic and Aitolian Soteria, Aneziri 2007, 68, n. 9. Cf. Champion 1995.

22 *FD* III 4:361. His *philotimia* (φιλοτίμως ἠγωνίσατο) is understood here as generosity in the form of an extra performance. The language of approbation in the decree for Menalkes is similar to other decrees for musicians: *IG* II³,1 929 (*aulêtês*); *IG* XII,5 482 (*kitharôdos*); *IG* XI,4 744.

23 Chaniotis 2009b, 91 pointed at the use of ἐπαιτέω (= beg, implore) instead of αἰτέω (= request) or ἀπαιτέω/ἀξιόω (= demand). In fact, the decree for Athanadas is the only Hellenistic decree which epigraphically attests the verb ἐπαιτέω (ἐπαιτηθείς).

24 Jacquemin et al. 2012, no. 189.

25 For artists staying in a host *polis* (ἐνδαμεῖν, ἐπιδαμεῖν, παρεπιδαμεῖν): Van Liefferinge 2000, 150.

26 Εὐσέβεια and ὁσιότης are usually taken as synonyms: Dover 1974, 248. Mikalson 2010, 140–186 compared ὁσιότης ('religious correctness') to εὐσέβεια ('proper respect') as elements of 'service to the gods' or 'piety' as represented in the philosophical tradition. Cf. Peels 2016, 68–106 and 189–206.

27 Argyriou-Casmeridis 2016, 156–158; Argyriou-Casmeridis 2019, 284–287.

28 The verb ἐπιδίδωμι is often used for the guilds of Dionysiac Artists who competed at the Soteria: E.g. *FD* III 1:477; *FD* III 4:356, but also for individual artists who might have competed outside the context of artistic associations, free of charge, e.g. *FD* III 3:125; *FD* III 3:249; *Syll.*³ 689; *FD* III 1:48; *FD* III 3: 86. Aneziri 2007, 73–74, n. 39; Van Liefferinge 2000, 150.

The artists' responsiveness to public requests is another part of their publicly-declared virtues.[29] The musicians' devotion to their art is attested in Delphic decrees for other musicians too, like Antipatros of Eleutherna, a *hydraulos*-player, and Polygnota of Thebes, a *choropsaltria*.[30] This is an indication that they were praised on account of their professional merits, but with a vocabulary that was used also for other categories of honorands.[31]

In addition to their performances, good conduct and devotion to their art, other musicians were honoured for teaching music lessons, and thus for their contribution to the cultural life of the host *polis*. Two brothers from Pheneos, Kleodoros and Thrasyboulos,[32] were honoured by the *polis* of Delphi for the demonstration of their musical competences (ἐπιδείξεις), in which they were successful (εὐδοκίμουν), and for teaching the children (διδασκαλίαν τῶν παίδων), thus also playing a pedagogical role at Delphi.[33] Their good behaviour (ἀξίως), as well as their teaching activities, combined with public lectures with a popular content, added to the city's prestige and to their own renown. They were praised for their conduct during their stay (τὰν ἐνδαμίαν καὶ ἀναστροφάν) and for their *philotimia* towards their profession (τᾶι φιλοτιμίαι ἇι τυγχάνοντι ἔχοντες ἐν τῶι ἐπιταδεύματι).

The decrees often praised competent musicians—like other professionals—for gaining good reputation through their performances. The term εὐδοκίμησεν, usually associated with *akroaseis* (public lectures) or *epideixeis* (performances) in which they displayed their talents, denotes that they were distinguished in their area of expertise, and thus, were highly esteemed.[34]

---

29 Chaniotis 2009b, 92. In some cases, embassies were sent to invite the artists on behalf of the city magistrates (*Syll.*[3] 737: παρακληθεὶς; *IG* XII,5 482: πεισθεὶς; Jacquemin et al. 2012, no. 186: ἀξιωθέντα).

30 *Syll.*[3] 737; *FD* III 3:249. Cf. *FD* III 2:92[3].

31 The term προαίρεσις as a quality of devoted professionals is also attested in decrees for doctors: *IG* XII,5 719; *IG* XII,5 824; *IK Perge* 12.

32 *Syll.*[3] 703= Jacquemin et al. 2012, no. 190. Cf. *FD* III 1.49. Jacquemin et al. 2012, 344 argued that these two musicians were certainly *technitai*, members of the association of Isthmus and Nemea, like other Arcadian artists at the Soteria contests (*idem* 2012, no. 70).

33 Bouchon 2013, 176. Cf. poets as teachers at Delphi (*FD* III 2:78). Chaniotis 2009b, 83–84 argued that the selection of repertoire by the two musicians at Delphi, i.e. the compositions of old poets, had contributed to the prestige of Delphi, and to the patriotic education of the boys.

34 The term εὐδοκιμεῖν is also attested in decrees for poets, actors, doctors, historians, teachers, a philosopher and an architect, but the majority of attestations are in decrees for musicians. Kraton of Kalchedon, is a well-documented case of a famous *aulêtês*. Le Guen 2007, 246–247, n. 3 has presented the epigraphic dossier about Kraton's career as well as his social status, and his links with several associations of artists and with the Attalids.

3 Actors

Scholars have argued for the professionalization of actors from the fourth century onwards.[35] The rise of the acting profession is also bound up with cultural mobility and dramatic reperformance in the ancient Greek world.[36] The scarcity of honorific decrees for actors is thus indeed conspicuous, given the abundance of both literary and epigraphical evidence (of other types[37]) for their performances. I shall discuss some possible reasons for this lacuna in the conclusion.

The financial generosity of the honorand is given prominence in a Samian decree for the famous actor Polos of Aegina, well attested in the literary evidence.[38] As the decree explains, Polos had been well-disposed (εὔνους) and eager (πρόθυμος) towards the *polis* in the past.[39] Since the *demos* had decided to invite him through envoys to the *polis*' festivals (τῶμ πρεσβευτῶμ παραγενομένωμ πρὸς αὐτὸν),[40] Polos agreed to perform in return for reduced fees.[41]

Although these decrees do not tell us much about his musical talent and performances, they are still important, since they prove that an *aulêtês* could be honoured lavishly and with a language of virtue that put him in the realm of civic benefactors.

35 Easterling and Hall 2002, 327. Cf. Csapo 2010, 86.

36 Lamari 2017, 105.

37 Actors appear in many types of Hellenistic inscriptions, such as dedications (*IG* V,2 118), choregic dedications (*IG* XII Suppl. 400), lists of donations (*FD* III 5:3), lists of victors in dramatic contests (*IG* XII,4 2:452). But these are merely lists of names and specialities, without details about the actors' performances and virtues. See e.g. *IG* II³,1 436= Stephanis 1988, no. 2031. Csapo 2010, 105: 'The official language and records of drama always appear to have ignored the actor. … Victorious poets, *choregoi* and choruses were recorded for fifty years before anyone thought to record the name of an actor'.

38 Polos was particularly admired in his representation of Sophoclean roles (Aulus Gellius, *Noctes Atticae* 6.5.1–5; Plut. *Moralia* 3).

39 *IG* XII, 6 1:56. Cf. *I. Oropos* 25= Stephanis 1988, no. 2090 (decree for Polyaratos of Kyrene who was granted the titles of *proxenos* and *euergetês*. Cf. *FD* III 4:177= Stephanis 1988, no. 1167; *FD* III, 3:125 and 126).

40 Paschidis 2008, 388–389, no. 5 argued that a plausible context for such an embassy would be the embassy which the Samians must have sent to Antigonos and Demetrios to announce the institution of the festivals, and that, if that is the case, then the Samians must have met Polos at the court of Antigonos, which would explain the actor's willingness to perform at a lowered fee. Cf. Shipley 1987, 173–175 about the rush of diplomatic activity and the Samian decrees for courtiers of the Antigonids in the late 4th c.; *idem* 227 for Samian honours to intellectuals, who enriched the cultural life of the *polis*. Although we cannot exclude the possibility that Polos might indeed have been involved in a political and diplomatic activity in the context of contemporary relations between Samos and the Antigonids, to argue that it is unlikely to have had an embassy sent to an actor contravenes what is known from honorific decrees for other artists (e.g. musicians) and professionals (e.g. doctors), who were invited by official envoys on behalf of *poleis* to offer their professional services. Yet, compared to other artists who often performed for free outside of

It is noteworthy that Polos, a star performer, is not praised here for his theatrical performance but for agreeing to take lower than usual fees and defer payment in exchange for all the box-office proceeds. Other actors, like Aristys of Aigion and Nikon of Megalopolis[42] at Delphi, were rewarded because they gave extra performances in which they gained reputation (ἐπέδωκε τῶι θεῶι ἁμέραν κ[α]ὶ ἀγωνίξατο καὶ εὐδοκίμησε), just like musicians.

4 Poets

In Hellenistic honorific decrees poets were praised on account of civic virtues for their literary works that celebrated the host *poleis*, and for other activities. Demoteles of Andros was honoured because he had composed an account (πεπραγ[μά]τευται) of the sanctuary and the *polis* of Delos and he had written down (γέγραφεν) the local myths, thus contributing to the construction (or recreation) of Delian history.[43] Kleochares of Athens, a lyric poet, was honoured for his compositions (γέγραφε); his poems were so appreciated that the *polis* of Delphi decided that each year the chorus-teacher would teach them to the children for the festival performance at the *Theoxenia*.[44] The hortatory clause of the decree explained that honours were conferred on those *writing* something worthy of the god (ὅπως δὲ καὶ ἁ πόλις φαίνηται τιμῶσα τοὺς ἄξιόν τι τοῦ θεοῦ γράφοντας).

On similar grounds a poetess of Smyrna, Aristodama, was honoured by the demos of Chaleion on account of her *eusebeia* towards the god and *eunoia* towards the *polis*, because the *polis* of Chaleion considered it very important to honour those who choose to speak or *write* about the god (π]ερὶ πολλοῦ ποιεῖ-

competition, Polos' generosity was confined to asking for less money than usual. Besides, the mere fact that Polos, like the ambassadors who approached him, was expected to travel in times of war in order to participate in the festivals was in itself evidence of his *aretê* and *prothymia* towards the Samians.

41 Stephanis 1988, no. 2187 assigned more credibility to the epigraphical evidence of the Samian decree than to the confused references of various authors and the dubious reliability of the anecdotes (for Polos). Cf. Easterling and Hall 2002, 336. Csapo 2010, 87 compared the case of Polos with other less illustrious actors' fees. Some idea comes from the Euboean decree (*IG* XII 9, 207) which mentions that prospective actors are awarded 1,600 drachmas for a five-day appearance, not including expenses and prize-money.

42 *FD* III 3:125–126; *FD* III 1:48.

43 *IG* XI,4 544.

44 *FD* III 2:78. Cinalli 2017, 183 for artists at the *Theoxenia*. Cf. *ID* 1497 for Amphikles of Rheneia. In addition to his compositions and *akroaseis*, Amphikles taught the young generation to sing his compositions. For intellectuals in Delphi: Bouvier 1978 and 1985.

ται τὸ τιμῆν τοὺς λέγειν ἢ γρά[φειν] περὶ τοῦ θεοῦ προαιρειμένους).[45] This phrasing resembles the hortatory clause of the Delphic decree for Kleochares, and it may indeed be an indication that such artistic performances in Delphi in praise of the god were highly valued. It has been argued that such performances by travelling professionals were a kind of 'artistic pilgrimage', especially in Delphi and Delos, the *loci Apollonei*.[46] In another decree, Aristodama was honoured by the Lamians for the public performances (*epideixeis*) of her own poems, in which she had produced a worthy commemoration of the *ethnos* of the Aitolians and the ancestors of the Lamians. The case of Aristodama is significant, since this poetess, known to us from these two decrees, was praised on the same grounds as her male counterparts. The cases of itinerant poetesses point to the increasing social mobility of women in the Hellenistic period[47] and suggest that in the Hellenistic period a poetess could adopt certain practices from the male representatives of the literary milieu, such as public lectures. These instances also indicate that she, like her male colleagues, could acquire recognition in the *poleis* she visited, although this practice remained exceptional for women.[48]

In some cases, the poets' (and the poetesses') actions are described as evoking or creating the past of the host *polis*. Itinerant poets may have been commissioned to compose poems in order to contribute to the fostering of a new identity (or strengthening of an established identity) of the host community. It has been argued that during their performances these poets praised the cultural heritage of the host *polis* and flattered their local pride,[49] in order to impress their audiences and to secure their approbation. In this respect, their work seems very similar to that of historians. For example, Politas of Hypate, an epic poet, was granted *proxeny*[50] in Lamia for his performances during which

45 *FD* III 3:145. Cf. *IG* IX,2 62 (Lamia). A Tenian decree for another poetess, Alkinoe of Aitolia, (*IG* XII,5 812) is heavily restored.

46 Cinalli 2017, 186 and 180–181, n. 3.

47 Rutherford 2009, 239–244.

48 Bielman 2002, 218. Cf. Rutherford 2009, 239; Van Bremen 1996, 165 following Wörrle 1995, 244. Two child-poets were honoured by decrees, Ariston of Phokaia (*ID* 1506) and an unknown epic poet from Skepsis (*FD* III 1:273), who gave *akroaseis*. It has been argued that they were child-prodigies: Cinalli 2017, 176 and 184–185, n. 31; Ambühl 2007, 373 and 380–381.

49 Chaniotis 2009a, 267.

50 Mack 2015; Marek 1984. Mack provides us with a brief definition of *proxenia* in the preface to his study: '*Proxenia* was an honorific status granted to foreign benefactors which permitted poleis to establish permanent networks of these individuals (*proxenoi*), connecting them as communities to large numbers of other poleis and facilitating interactions between the citizens of different cities'. Mack also states later that *proxenia* 'was based on a shared understanding of the *proxenos* as the official friend of another city who performed

he made memorable references to the host *polis* in a worthy manner (τᾶς πόλιος ἀξίως ἐπεμνάσ[θη]).[51] As is shown by such phrases as ἀξίως ἐπεμνάσθη/μνήμην ἐποιήσατο, the poets' success in evoking the *polis*' past and the memories of a whole community was an important justification for public praise.

The presence of poets in other *poleis* and at big sanctuaries allowed them to give accounts of the connections (mythological and/or historical) between their own and the host *polis*, and to gain wider recognition and advertisement of their work in the context of *theôria*, as Rutherford has pointed out.[52] The cases of the poets Dymas of Iasos and Herodes of Priene, both honoured by the people of Samothrace for their poetic works, are good examples.[53] The decrees of Samothrace for these two poets from Asia Minor indicate that the sanctuary rewarded those who contributed to its prestige and the circulation of its history. The visits of these poet-*theôroi* were not just a religious enterprise and must have had political significance as well. Moreover, their decorous conduct during their stay was an essential element of their praiseworthy behaviour, as was the case for other travelling professionals.

Poets were normally praised for their *aretê* and *eunoia* (= goodwill), or *eusebeia* (= piety) towards the gods and *eunoia* towards the *polis*; other virtues they were commended for are *spoudê* (= eagerness), *philotimia* (= love of honour) and, interestingly, *philoponia* (love of toil). *Philoponia*, a virtue which is directly related to their work, is mentioned in the decrees for the poets Zotion of Ephesos in Boiotia[54] and Dioskourides of Tarsos in Crete.[55] Dioskourides, a *grammatikos*, had composed a speech of praise regarding the *ethnos* of the Knossians, but did not himself travel to Crete; instead, he sent Myrinos of Amisos, an epic and lyric poet and a student of his, to recite his work on his behalf. However, the Knossians praised the tutor, who had composed the *enkômion*, and not the actual performer of it. That the city of Knossos chose to

---

certain sorts of intermediary function within the context of his own political community' (Mack 2015, vii and 90). Cf. Grzesik 2021, 64, n. 5. The entire honorific habit which *proxenia* entailed allowed a *polis* to create links with the outside world and for centuries it was the best available instrument to enable this.

51 *IG* IX,2 63. The verb ἐπεμνάσθη is very rare in inscriptions. The three extant inscriptions which record this verb are all honorific decrees from Thessaly for *literati*, namely two decrees from Lamia for Politas the poet and Aristodama the poetess, and one (restored) from Larisa for Bombos of Alexandreia Troas, the historian or orator: *BCH* 59 (1935), 55,2. Rutherford 2009, 240 (orator). Chaniotis 1988, 310 (historian).

52 Rutherford 2007, 282–283.

53 *I.Iasos* 153: γράφων; *I.Priene* 69: γεγραφένα[ι].

54 Schachter and Slater 2007.

55 *ID* 1512.

reward Dioskourides for the content of his work (praise for the *ethnos*) is a common feature in decrees for other poets and poetesses. But the addition that he was commended for his love of toil and particular devotion to his art is rather unusual for poets (κατέστασε διὰ τᾶν ἀκροα[σίω]ν τὰν τῶ ἀνδρὸς φιλοπονίαν τάν τε περὶ τὸ ἐπιτάδουμα εὐεξίαν).

5 Historians

The types of service that poets were commended for resemble those for which historians received public praise.[56] Both categories were praised for their contributions to the enhancement of the prestige of the *polis* and/or the sanctuary attached to it. In fact, *philoponia* is an attribute of historians particularly stressed by Polybius.[57] A decree for Syriskos of Chersonesos described in detail his literary activities.[58] He was praised because he wrote and recited with love of toil (φιλ[ο][πόνως] γράψας ἀν[έ]γνω), and narrated and recited truthfully and reasonably ([διηγήσα]το; ἱστ[ό][ρησεν ἐπιεικ]έως; ἀλαθιν[ῶς] [καὶ ἐπιεικέως]) his historical accounts of the epiphanies of Parthenos, and also of the deeds performed towards the Bosporan kings and the *poleis*, thus contributing to the cultural memory of his *polis*. The significance of this decree lies in the exaltation of the historian's research method and performance, echoing the literary portrait provided by Polybius.

Syriskos was not an itinerant historian, but a local historian who composed a history of his own home-city. Like other professionals, itinerant historians visited other *poleis* and were praised for giving lectures to the public and for

56 Some of them are often classified as either poets or historians, and as historians or orators in modern bibliography, an indication of the overlaps between some categories of professionals in honorific decrees. Thomas 2019, 68, following Rigsby 1996, 281–289 for 'poet-historians'. Menekles of Teos (*IC* I v 53*; *IC* I vi 2*; *IC* I viii 11*; *IC* I xix 2*; *IC* I xxiv 1*; *IC* III iii 2*; *IC* II iii 2*) is an example of inter-*polis* diplomacy, conducted by itinerant *literati*, who were sent as ambassadors to other *poleis* and combined their performances in verse and/or music with the currency of tales about the past.

57 Polybius, a moral-didactic historian (Hau 2016, 23), outlined the image of the good historian. Cf. Eckstein 1995, 278–279. According to Polybius, to write history accurately and instructively was a duty (16.14.3), thus the historian should be a very hard and diligent worker (φιλοπονώτερος, 12.26a.3; φιλοπόνως, 12.26a.4), who accepted risk of danger and hardship (12.27.4: χωρίς κινδύνου καὶ κακοπαθείας; cf. 13.4.4) and did his own research (ἱστορήσαντες, 3.48.6).

58 *IoSPE* I^2 344. Dana and Dana 2001/2003, 99–102. Chaniotis 2018b, 412; 1988, 300–301 and 393.

praiseworthy conduct.[59] Through their performances historians could enhance their reputation, like an unknown historian in Amphipolis, who distinguished himself (εὐδοκιμήκει) through the public readings (*akroaseis*) of his historical works.[60]

6 Philosophers

In the realm of *literati*, philosophers occupy a special place. Although there are not so many extant honorific decrees for philosophers from the Hellenistic period, at least compared with other categories of professionals, the surviving documents have similarities with decrees for other professionals. Philosophers gave performances (*epideixeis*) gaining reputation in the host *poleis*, and they taught lessons at the *gymnasia* contributing to the education of the youth, as philosophical training was an essential component of the *paideia* in the Hellenistic *gymnasion*.

Philosophers are mentioned in Hellenistic honorific decrees, first, for the lessons and lectures that they provided at the *gymnasia* to the young ephebes. But, in such decrees, philosophers are mentioned not as honorands, but as educators, since the decrees were issued in honour of the ephebes and their trainers, or for the *gymnasiarchoi*. Second, philosophers as honorands in decrees were commended for their cultural (teaching) and political (diplomatic) activities, since they were often associated with royal courts and political interventions. Haake has extensively examined the evidence for philosophers in the Hellenistic cities, and argued that, before the ephebic decrees of 122/1, there is no evidence at all for philosophers mentioned in an honorary context at Athens because of their involvement in the field of *paideia*; and outside Athens, there are only two inscriptions earlier than the late second century which mention honours for philosophers motivated—among other things—by educational merits.[61]

In a rather unusual example of an ephebic decree, the Athenian ephebes were praised among other things because they adhered to Zenodotos and

59 E.g. Aristotheos of Troizen, a *historiographos* (*FD* III 3:124). Mnesiptolemos of Kyme was granted proxeny on Delos as a result of his activity as a *historiographos* (*IG* XI,4 697; Athenaeus 10.432b–c). See Chaniotis 2009a, 260; *idem* 1988, 303–304. This historian was praised on account of his *aretê* and *eusebeia* towards the sanctuary, and his *eunoia* towards the *demos*. The honorific language for the *historiographos* does not differ from that of other Delian proxeny decrees for other categories of honorands.

60 *SEG* 28:534. Cf. *IG* XII,6 1:285: epigram for the Samian historian Leon.

61 Haake 2004, 475–476.

attended lectures (σχολ[άζ]οντε[ς) of all the other philosophers at the *Ptolemaion*, the Lyceum and the Academia throughout the year.[62] It is quite rare to have the name of the philosopher inscribed on stone in such a general context of ephebic education. In contrast to this, most decrees for ephebes, *gymnasiarchoi*, and other magistrates at the *gymnasia* mention only in general terms the lessons of philosophy,[63] without citing the name of specific philosophers.

Outside Athens, an unknown Macedonian *philosophos* was granted proxeny in a second-century Boiotian decree, because like other itinerant professionals (musicians, poets, historians, and doctors) he gave lectures and performances (*epideixeis*) abroad, gaining reputation and contributing to the cultural life of the host *polis*.[64]

Epikrates of Herakleia was a Peripatetic philosopher who had offered many benefactions through his *paideia* in Samos (διὰ] τῆς αὐτοῦ παιδείας πολλὰ [τοὺ]ς νέους εὐεργέτηκεν).[65] According to a Samian decree (ca. 200), he gave generous access to his education (ἀφθόνως) to those of the citizens who wanted to join, and he also waived the fees (προῖκα [σχο]λάζων) for those who could not afford to pay. The Samian decree is the earliest inscription dedicated to a philosopher specifically for his philosophical and didactic achievements,[66] and not for political services, as is often the case in earlier documents.[67]

7 Teachers

The epigraphic evidence shows that civic education was highly valued[68] in the Hellenistic *poleis*, and that teachers were praised because of their teaching and

62 *IG* II^2 1006, ll. 19–20.

63 *IG* II^2 1028; *IG* II^2 1039. The verb σχολάζω with its two meanings, either referring to those attending lessons and being devoted to learning (ephebes) e.g. *IG* II^2 1006, 1028–1030, or to those giving lectures at the *gymnasia* (philosophers or other teachers) e.g. *IG* XII,9 234, *IG* XII,9 235; *IG* XII,6 1:128; *FD* III 3:338.

64 *IG* VII 2849. Cf. Haake 2010 for an Athenian philosopher in Larisa.

65 *IG* XII,6 1:128.

66 Scholz 2004, 319. The posthumous honorific decree for Zenon of Kition, the founder of the Stoa, surviving through the literary evidence (Diogenes Laertius 7.10–12), although its authenticity has been strongly challenged by Haake 2004, mentions that Zenon made a *paradeigma* of his own life for others to see, thus proving the consistency between his philosophical doctrines and his way of living.

67 Praxiphanes on Delos (*IG* XI,4 613) and Lyco of Troas in Delphi (*FD* III 3:167), the well-known third-century Peripatetic philosophers, were granted honours, but the decrees make no reference to their philosophical activities.

68 The second-century laws from Miletos (*Syll.*^{3} 577) and Teos (*Syll.*^{3} 578) regulating school foundations shed light on the operation of schools for the education of free children.

their personal qualities. That teachers could serve as a *paradeigma* for their pupils is evident in a letter sent by King Attalos II to the Ephesians about the teacher of his nephew, Attalos III.[69] The letter stressed that the young people, who have been blessed by nature with a good character, tend to imitate those who are in charge of them, i.e. their teachers. The Ephesian teacher was chosen not only because of his experience (ἐνπει[ρίαι), but also for his character (τῶι ἤθει), which made him most appropriate for instructing the young. Thus, the unknown teacher of the royal family was presented as a living model suitable for imitation.

Yet, despite the epigraphical evidence concerning the value of *paideia* and the public recognition of the teachers' professional worth, honorific decrees for teachers praised individually (and not collectively, as instructors of the ephebes at the *gymnasion*) are rather rare. Athenian ephebic decrees usually commended the ephebes for their disciplined behaviour towards their *didaskaloi*, but without mentioning the teachers' own virtues.[70]

A teacher's zeal (*spoudê*) and eagerness (*prothymia*) are important qualities in the exercise of his profession. Euelthon, a *grammatodidaskalos* of an unknown *polis*, was honoured in Andros, on account of his *eunoia* and because of his professional worth (ἄξιος τ[οῦ ἐπιτηδεύματος).[71] Glaukias, a *didaskalos*, travelled in the third century from Kallatis on the coast of the Black Sea to Mesambria in Thrace and was granted proxeny and other honours for the assiduity with which he taught his pupils. The decree underlined his disciplined conduct during his prolonged stay in the host *polis* (εὐτάκτως ἀνεστρέφη).[72] Again, his *prothymia* concerning the care (*epimeleia*) for the pupils is emphasized, as in the decree for Euelthon.[73]

The teachers' conduct in the host *polis* was deemed worthy of their occupation, an indication of the value of teachers as skilled workers. Some teachers were also praised because they worked for free. Menandros, an Acarnanian *grammatikos* from Tyrreion, was granted proxeny and other honours in Delphi for giving lessons at the *gymnasion*, which brought him big success (εὐδοκί-

Other school foundations emanated from royal donations, such as the Attalids' foundations in Delphi and Rhodes (*Syll.*³ 672; Polyb. 31.31.1. Cf. Polyb. 5.88). Perrin-Saminadayar 2007; Argyriou-Casmeridis 2018.

69 *I.Ephesos* 202.

70 E.g. *IG* II² 1006; 1008; 1009; 1011; 1028; 1029. Del Corso 2012 for *grammatikoi* and *philologoi* in Hellenistic inscriptions. Laes 2009 for pedagogues.

71 *IG* XII Suppl. 248. Cf. C, ll. 25–26.

72 *IG* Bulg I² 307.

73 Cf. *I.Thespiai* 29 for Sostratos of Athens. Cf. *I.Oropos* 370, decree for Philokrates, an Athenian *didaskalos*.

μησε). And, when the *polis* offered him a sum of money, he refused to be paid, on the grounds that the only purpose of his sojourn was to honour the god and prove his respect to the *polis* of Delphi.[74] Such a reference pointed to the teacher's selfless devotion and generosity and stressed the *polis*' encouraging of other professionals at Delphi to offer free services. Professional services and moral considerations are combined in the language of honour for teachers, who are thus construed as civic examples of *aretê*.

8 Doctors

Among the professionals praised in Hellenistic decrees, doctors are a distinct category, explicitly defined by the term ἰατρός. Honorific decrees described a doctor's skill or profession as a craft (*technê*), occupation (*epitedeuma*), or work (*ergon*).[75] The decrees for doctors show that the bestowal of honours on them was explicitly motivated by reference to their professional activities, i.e. the practice of medical craft (*iatrikê technê*) or profession (*epitêdeuma*) for the benefit of the community which praised them. Their praise was justified by a combination of professional competence, moral character, and proper behaviour.

Doctors, mostly public,[76] working under contract[77] or in private offices,[78] were generally highly valued, as they contributed to the good health of the *polis*' population. But in periods of crisis—epidemics, earthquakes, and injuries because of war or *stasis*—the medical aid provided by doctors was deemed essential for the survival of the community.[79]

---

74 *FD* III 3:338.

75 Among these terms in decrees, τέχνη is the most common, alone or as ἰατρική, particularly preferred in Kos and other islands (probably because of the Hippocratic tradition, which considered their profession as craft), e.g. *IG* XII,4 1:30; 101; 113; *IG* XII,5 824; *IG* XII,7 231; *IG* XII, 6 1:151; ἰατρική τέχνη: *IC* I xxii 4C; *IC* II iii3*; *IG* II^2 374; *FD* III 4:362. Sometimes, two of these words are used in the same decree: τέχνη+ἐπιτήδευμα (*IG* XII,4 1:109; *IK Perge* 12), or ἔργον+ἐπιτήδευμα (*IG* IX,1^2 3:750), or τέχνη+ ἔργον (*IG* XII,5 824). The word ἐπιτήδευμα alone is less common (*IG* IX,1 104; *IG* IX,1^2 2:209; *SEG* 51:934). Only in *IG* IX,1^2 3:750: τὸ ἰατρικὸν ἔργον. Cf. *IG* XII,6 1:12 (τὸ δημό[σ]ιον [ἔρ]γον τῶν ἰατρῶν).

76 Massar 2001, 180 explained the three ways of recruiting public doctors: a) witness attests to the doctor's qualities (*IG* XII,1 1032: μεμαρτύρηται), b) a Koan doctor is called, and c) choice based on the doctor's reputation. Massar 2020, 80 argued that being publicly employed was a guarantee of competence, and an advantage over potential competitors.

77 E.g. *IG* XII,4 1:113 (ἰατρὸς] δαμό[σιος); *IG* XII,4 1:109 (ἐδαμοσίευε); *IG* IX,1^2 3:750 (ἐργολαβήσας).

78 *IG* XII,4 1:109.

79 Earthquakes (*IG* XII,6 1:12); War and stasis (*IG* XII,4 1: 247 & 248).

Many doctors worked as public contractors. Menophantos of Macedon had been sent to Locris after he was officially invited (μεταπεμφθεὶς; [μ]ετὰ πρεσβείας), and was the only one to contract for the medical work.[80] His conduct in Amphissa was disciplined and self-controlled (εὔτακτον καὶ σώφρονα), without reproach (ἀνέγκλητος). He offered his medical services through love of his craft (φιλοτέχνως)[81] and with care and zeal (ἐπιμελ[ό][με]νος καὶ σπουδάζ[ω]ν). His primary concern was to contribute to the salvation (σωτηρία) of those in danger, without discrimination (ἐφ' ἴσου καὶ πο[θ'] [ἅπ]αντας).[82] A copy of the decree was to be sent to the doctor's *polis* at his own request, so that the honorand's *polis* would be aware of his services and honours abroad.[83] Like other itinerant professionals, doctors travelled to other *poleis* to offer their services,[84] usually on demand, and thus their proper conduct abroad was praised. In some cases, when there was urgent call for help, doctors were persuaded by the *poleis* to extend their stay, and not abandon those in need.[85]

But their most prominent virtue was their professional expertise. If multiple decrees were issued by various *poleis* for a doctor, this was a proof of his *empeiria*. Asklepiades of Perge had given lectures at the *gymnasion* about health issues, and as a result gained praise (ἔπαινον).[86] In addition to his good conduct (ἀναστροφή), which was also unexceptionable (ἀδιάβολον),[87] and appropriate for a doctor's profession (εὐσχήμονα καὶ καλὴν καὶ στοιχοῦσαν τῶι ἐπιτηδεύματι), he was also commended for his outstanding professional experience (διαφέρουσαν παρασ[χ]όμενος τὴν διὰ τῆς τέχνης ἐνπειρίαν), care (ἐπιμέλεια), eagerness (προθυμία), and advancement of the field (προκοπή), which was shown in his unexpected cure methods.[88] The decree praised him for his good reputation (εὐφημία), and a sealed copy of his decree was to be handed to him. The unusual commendation on account of his εὐφημία reveals that Asklepiades

80 *IG* IX,1² 3:750. Mavroudis 2010, 327 argued that Menophantos was the only doctor in Amphissa during this period. For the importance of networking for the recruitment of doctors, Massar 2020, 71–72. Cf. *IScM* I 26; *IG* XII, 4 1:171; *IG* XII,4 1:247; *IC* II iii 3* (ἀποσταλείς). For the mobility of Koan doctors, Bosnakis 2014; Massar 2020, 72 and 85.

81 Feen 1983, 43: it was expected that the physician should be guided by φιλοτεχνία rather than φιλανθρωπία (love of humanity). Interestingly, the word φιλανθρωπία is very rare in Hellenistic honorific decrees for doctors.

82 Cf. *IG* XII,4 1:30; *IG* XII,6 1:12 (ἴσον καὶ ἀμεμψιμοίρητον); *SEG* 33:672; *IG* V,1 1145.

83 The Amphisseans provided him with escort for a safe journey. Mavroudis 2010. For copies of the decrees for Koan doctors sent to Kos, Massar 2001, 198–199.

84 For the travel patterns of Hellenistic doctors, Massar 2020, 84–85.

85 E.g. *IC* I xxii 4C.

86 *IK Perge* 12, ll. 34–46. Cf. ll. 7–9.

87 This is a *hapax* in the epigraphic record, at least in relation to *anastrophê*.

88 *IK Perge* 12, ll. 32–34.

was indeed a very famous doctor. This decree is unusual, also because of the vocabulary used to refer to the process of witnessing. The Seleukeians who had benefited from his medical services were among those who testified to the doctor's professional qualities (ll. 40–41). Apparently, this had been a prerequisite for the renewal of his contract as a public doctor. But it is also stated that the honorand 'is providing the cities as witnesses giving *ekmartyria* for him through their decrees and public letters, also on the matter of the honours bestowed on him by them'. That is, the honorific decrees were essentially represented as written testimony for the honorand's benefactions and virtues.[89]

As a further sign of his expertise a doctor could use his master's name to enhance his authority. The honorific decree for the Koan Onasandros outlined his career steps.[90] He had been taught the *iatrikê technê* by Antipatros, a public doctor, and had practised for some period next to his teacher. As a doctor he helped everyone in need voluntarily (ἀπαράκλητος), causing no complaint (ἄλυπον), and showing particular assiduity and zeal (ἐκτενῆ καὶ πρόθυμον) for the salvation of his patients. Even when he could make a lot of money by becoming a private doctor, he did not accept the money he was given, but preferred to offer his medical services without pay, putting the public good above his private benefit. For all these activities, Onasandros was honoured for his attitude (αἵρεσις) and for his medical experience. It is further emphasized that his services proved both his professional experience and his personal conduct (κατά τε τὰν τέχναν ἐμπειρίαν καὶ τὰν κατὰ τὸν βίον ἀναστροφάν). The decree provided that the stele was to be put next to the stele bearing the decree for his teacher.[91] Onasandros was presented as acting in accordance with his teacher's example. It is thus made clear that by this decree the *polis* of Kos chose not only to honour a doctor for his generous medical services to citizens and foreigners alike, but also to put forth the example of his teacher, another doctor, who was also honoured by an honorific decree. The two decrees were to be put next to each other, as if the *polis* wanted to remind the others of the tradition of the medical profession, and the continuation of a public *paradeigma* which the older doctor set for his pupil.

Such decrees shape the image of a good doctor in the Hellenistic period.[92] In decrees for doctors from Kos we find the rare formula ἀρετή κατὰ τὴν τέχνην,[93]

89 For testimonies and witnesses to prove the doctors' experience: Massar 2020, 75. Ἐκμαρτυρία/ἐκμαρτυρέω are very rare in inscriptions (*IG* XII Suppl. 249 for another doctor): Argyriou-Casmeridis 2024.

90 *IG* XII,4 1:109.

91 *SEG* 54:749.

92 Aneziri 2008, 147.

93 *IG* XII,4 1:108, 113, 114; 2:1178.

which explicitly denotes excellence in skill, via one's profession. In this formula, *aretê* is not an all-inclusive civic virtue with various aspects; rather, it goes back to its more fundamental connotation of excellence and goodness, and, in particular, it concerns the medical craft. It is a further indication that doctors were praised for their professional services deriving from their craft, even more explicitly than any other type of professional.

9 Architects

In the first half of the third century, a delegate from Istros was sent to Byzantion with instructions to procure an architect. Epikrates was hired (ἐμισθώσατο) and during his stay in the host city he rendered many services, accommodating himself to the current circumstances (τοῖς καιροῖς).[94] When the city of Istros was engaged in war, he made all the necessary preparations with skill and zeal (ἐμπείρως καὶ προθύμως), and supervised the walls in the interest of the *polis* (συμφερόντως). And extending his residence for many years, he conducted himself irreproachably (ἀνέγκλητος) and showed his *eunoia* towards the people. Epikrates, like other professionals (artists and doctors) and foreign judges, was appointed on the invitation of a foreign community. His services were rendered during a period of crisis[95] (war), when the maintenance of walls is important for the defence of a *polis*.[96] This also links him with doctors and foreign judges who rendered services in critical times. And like many other honorands, he was praised for irreproachable conduct.[97] Thus, as in the case of doctors, both professional skill and proper conduct in a crisis context were deemed important and worth being praised publicly in a decree.

With the exception of Epikrates,[98] no other honorific decree praised an architect in his professional capacity on account of his virtues.[99] There is thus a marked discrepancy between literary and surviving epigraphical sources, in that many famous Hellenistic architects are known from the literary evidence but not from inscriptions, and conversely, none of those architects mentioned in inscriptions is known from literary sources.[100] One example may illustrate

94 *IScM* I 65.
95 Cf. *IG* XII,4 1:302.
96 Chaniotis 2005, 26–31.
97 Clarke 1963, 10–11 argued for an architects' 'tradition of honorable professional conduct'.
98 Cf. *FD* III 3:184.
99 Hellmann 1999: 81.
100 Clarke 1963, 16.

this discrepancy. Sostratos of Knidos, the famous architect of the tower of Pharos in Alexandria, is well-known both from the literary evidence[101] and from four Delian and one Delphic honorific decree.[102] It is striking that Sostratos is not referred to as an architect in any of these decrees. Instead, he is described in general terms as a good man, honoured mainly for his affiliation with King Ptolemy and his political interventions, and not for his professional activity. Sostratos the architect was a high-ranking Ptolemaic diplomat and a royal friend,[103] well-attested in the epigraphic record. However, the honorific decrees did not praise him in his capacity as an architect and for his professional activities, but for his political services and diplomatic activity. In this respect, the case of Sostratos the architect stands as a close parallel to the case of Polos the actor and of third-century decrees for philosophers.

10 Sculptors

Hellenistic honorary decrees for sculptors are also rare.[104] However, the extant epigraphical evidence for two sculptors, Damophon of Messene and Telesinos of Athens, offers valuable information for their professional activity and the honours bestowed on them in recognition of their services.

Damophon the famous Messenian sculptor was honoured by several decrees from various *poleis*[105] because, among other benefactions, he had waived the city's debt to him, and he would make a statue free of charge (δωρ[εάν). The decrees for the sculptor praise his artistic skill (τ]ᾶς τε ἰδίας τέχνας ἁρμ[όσας),[106]

101 There is no scholarly consensus about whether Sostratos was the architect, the sponsor or the dedicant of the Pharos. Meeus 2015, 144, n. 7–8. Strabo 17.1.6.

102 *IG* XI,4 563, 1038, 1130, 1190; *FD* III 1.299. Meeus 2015, 152–161.

103 Meeus 2015, 145–146. Strootman 2017, 103–104 argued that the ancient sources give no hint that artists and intellectuals at court constituted a distinct category next to the 'regular' courtiers (*philoi*). Categories overlapped and cannot be separated. Cf. Polyb. 13. 4–5 for Herakleides, an architect-ambassador, and *philos* of Philip V.

104 In a proxeny decree (*Syll.*^{3} 682) for three Pergamene painters who were sent to Delphi by the Attalids, they are honoured for their good conduct in the foreign community. It is the only extant Hellenistic honorific decree for painters honoured in their capacity as such, but without any reference to their virtues.

105 Paus. 4.31.6–10. Oiantheia (*SEG* 54:452), Leukas (*IG* IX^2, 1 1475), Krane on Kephallenia (*IG* IX^2,1 1583), Kythnos (*SEG* 49:423), Lykosoura (*SEG* 41:332), Melos (Themelis 2017), and Gerenia (unpublished). Themelis 2017, 85 added two more cities with inscribed decrees (Kerkyra and Bouthrotos). Cf. Melfi 2016; Themelis 1996, 1998, 2003.

106 Cf. Paus. 4.31.

a sign of the development of an epigraphic language through which to draw attention to the creative work itself.[107]

Telesinos of Athens was praised for the fine (καλῶς) construction of two statues and for the restoration of other statues in the sanctuary of Delos free of charge (δωρεάν).[108]

11 Conclusion

The analysis of the language of approbation in honorific decrees for professionals leads to the following conclusions.

Many decrees explicitly link the honorands' benefactions with their professional services. That is, it is in their professional capacity that most of these honorands were commended. Additional reasons (such as political or diplomatic interventions) were sometimes included (or implied by the decrees' contexts), but the emphasis on such virtues as *empeiria*, *ekteneia*, *philoponia*, and *aretê* κατὰ τὴν τέχνην, point to the professional character of the services for which the honorands were praised as models of civic virtue. The connection between benefaction and professionals' expertise and skill is indicated by the many decrees that were issued for them by various *poleis*. Sometimes officials were sent to various professionals to issue invitations to their *poleis*, in order to offer their professional services. Conversely, professionals' renown was emphasized as evidence of their professional competence.

In addition to skilful work and competent performances, professionals were often commended for their financial generosity, either in the form of free auditions and performances, or as fee waivers.[109]

As travelling professionals, usually procured on demand, the honorands' personal conduct was commonly praised, as is the case of other honorands.[110]

107 Platt 2011, 132.

108 *IG* XI,4 514.

109 Thus, in addition to money donations and private expenditure on the part of rich citizens, there were other honorands who had displayed their generosity (*philotimia*) through free services (δωρεάν, ἄνευ μισθοῦ) of professionals, or as free (or at lower fees) performances of artists. See e.g. doctors: *IG* XII,5 824; *IG* IX,1² 2:209; *IG* XII,1 1032; *IG* XII,4 1:109. For free services, Massar 2005, 93–94.

110 Some categories of honorands should abide by a social etiquette of good conduct. This is particularly obvious for example in the case of foreign judges who were commonly praised for their irreproachable behaviour abroad, or in the case of foreign commanders who were similarly honoured for their good conduct, and of *theôroi* (sacred envoys). This is why such virtues as *eukosmia* or *euschêmosynê* (and their cognates) are important in the language of honour.

More importantly, the formula that their behaviour was appropriate for their profession is peculiar to decrees for professionals and further evidence for recognition of a professional etiquette.

The discussion in this chapter has revealed aspects that concern the discrepancy (philosophers, actors, architects), or the corroboration (historians) between literary and epigraphical evidence, as well as the variety in the language of honour for Athenian and non-Athenian decrees, for male and female honorands (poetry, music). The conspicuous scarcity of epigraphical evidence for some categories of professionals as honorands (philosophers, teachers, sculptors, architects)—despite their more general attestations in other types of inscriptions—reveals that perhaps some professionals were more prominently promulgated as *paradeigmata* of *aretê* (doctors, poets, musicians). It is also possible that the honorific practices for them may have followed different patterns (e.g. statues),[111] or that the lacuna may have been simply the result of epigraphic habit and the availability of extant sources.

Professional expertise and moral considerations, personal qualities, and social conduct were intertwined in the language of these decrees. Whereas *empeiria* was particularly important for a doctor, teacher, and architect, the renown and success were much appreciated for artists and *literati*. Diligence, hard work, readiness and eagerness in the exercise of their professions mattered too and justified honours.

The power of examples through teaching was underlined in many of these decrees. Either through proper teaching of the young or through public lectures, many of these professionals also played a pedagogical role in the host communities. In some cases, their own teacher's example was set forth (doctors, poets), or they presented themselves as a living *paradeigma* of *aretê* (teachers, philosophers).

The honorific decrees for various professionals reflected the self-image of the *polis* which attracted the best of each field. Professionals were commended for offering their services for the benefit of the host community. The language of the decrees put these honorands in the realm of civic benefactors, and their benefactions, emanating from their professional activities, were displayed as the manifestations of *aretê*.[112]

---

111 Cf. honorific decrees for athletes, Argyriou-Casmeridis 2016.

112 Next to these professionals, there were numerous other honorands, commended for facilitating or financing professional activities, in their capacity as civic officials (*agonothetes*, *gymnasiarchos*), or as generous civic benefactors.

Acknowledgements

I am grateful to my PhD supervisor Prof. L. Rubinstein for her comments on earlier drafts of this paper, to the organizers and participants of the XI Penn-Leiden Colloquium for their feed-back and support, and to the anonymous reader of this volume.

Bibliography

Ambühl, A. (2007). Children as Poets—Poets as Children? Romantic Constructions of Childhood and Hellenistic Poetry. In: A. Cohen and J.B. Rutter, eds., *Constructions of Childhood in Ancient Greece and Italy*. Hesperia Suppl. 41. Princeton, pp. 373–383.

Aneziri, S. (2020). Artists of Dionysus: The First Professional Associations in the Ancient Greek World. In: E. Stewart, E. Harris and D. Lewis, eds., *Skilled Labour and Professionalism in Ancient Greece and Rome*. Cambridge, pp. 293–312.

Aneziri, S. (2009). World Travellers: The Associations of Artists of Dionysus. In: R. Hunter and I. Rutherford, eds., *Wandering Poets in Ancient Greek Culture*. Cambridge, pp. 217–236.

Aneziri, S. (2008). The Rhetoric of Work in the Decrees of Greek *Poleis* of the Hellenistic and Roman Period. In: Y. Yannitsiotis and D. Lambropoulou, eds., *Rhetorics of Work*. Bologna, pp. 139–160.

Aneziri, S. (2007). The Organisation of Music Contests in the Hellenistic Period and the Artists' Participation: An Attempt at Classification. In: P. Wilson, ed., *The Greek Theatre and Festivals*. Oxford, pp. 67–84.

Aneziri, S. (2003). *Die Vereine der Dionysischen Techniten im Kontext der hellenistischen Gesellschaft. Untersuchungen zur Geschichte, Organisation und Wirkung der hellenistischen Technitenvereine*. Stuttgart.

Argyriou-Casmeridis, A. (2016). Victories and Virtues: The Epigraphic Evidence for Hellenistic Athletes as Models of *Arete*. In: C. Mann, S. Remijsen and S. Scharff, eds., *Athletics in the Hellenistic World*. Stuttgart, pp. 153–178.

Argyriou-Casmeridis, A. (2018). Η εκπαίδευση στις πόλεις της Μ. Ασίας των Ελληνιστικών Χρόνων μέσα από επιγραφικές μαρτυρίες. In: A.N. Mastrapas and M.M. Stergioulis, eds., *Ο Μικρασιατικός Ελληνισμός από την αρχαιότητα ως τις μέρες μας. Ιστορία και πολιτισμός, Πανελλήνια Ένωση Φιλολόγων, Σεμινάριο 43*. Athens, pp. 75–90.

Argyriou-Casmeridis, A. (2019). *Aretē* in a Religious Context. *Eusebeia* and Other Virtues in Hellenistic Honorific Decrees. In: E. Koulakiotis and C. Dunn, eds., *Political Religions in the Greco-Roman World. Discourses, Practices and Images*. Newcastle upon Tyne, pp. 272–305.

Argyriou-Casmeridis, A. (2024 in press). Witness of virtue: the epigraphic evidence of the Hellenistic honorific decrees. In: M. Edwards, B. Griffith, and C. Carey, eds., *Evidence and Proof in Ancient Greece*. Newcastle.

Bielman, A. (2002). *Femmes en public dans le monde hellénistique, IVe–Ier s.av.J.-C., SEDES*. Paris.

Bosnakis, D. (2014). Asklepieion and Physicians: A Preferential Tool of Koan Diplomacy. In: N. Stampolidis and Y. Tassoulas, eds., *HYGIEIA. Health, Illness, Treatment from Homer to Galen*. Athens, pp. 60–75.

Bouchon, R. (2013). Des musiciens honorés à Délphes. Esquisse d'une politique culturelle? In: S. Emerit, ed., *Le statut du musicien dans la Méditerranée ancienne. Égypte, Mésopotamie, Grèce, Rome*, Le Caire, pp. 171–194.

Bouvier, H. (1985). Hommes des lettres dans les inscriptions Delphiques. *ZPE* 58, pp. 119–135.

Bouvier, H. (1978). Honneurs et récompenses à Délphes. *ZPE* 30, pp. 101–118.

Ceccarelli, P. (2018). Letters and Decrees: Diplomatic Protocols in the Hellenistic Period. In: P. Ceccarelli, L. Doering, T. Fögen and I. Gildenhard, eds., *Letters and Communities. Studies in the Socio-political Dimensions of Ancient Epistolography*. Oxford, pp. 147–183.

Ceccarelli, P. (2010). Changing Contexts: Tragedy in the Civic and Cultural Life of Hellenistic City-States. In: I. Gildenhard and M. Revermann, eds., *Beyond the Fifth Century—Interactions with Greek Tragedy from the Fourth Century BCE to the Middle Ages*. Berlin, pp. 99–150.

Ceccarelli, P. (2004). 'Autour de Dionysos': remarques sur la dénomination des artistes dionysiaques. In: C. Hugoniot, F. Hurlet and S. Milanezi, eds., *Le statut de l'acteur dans l'antiquité grecque et romaine*. Tours, pp. 109–142.

Champion, C. (1995). The Soteria at Delphi: Aetolian Propaganda in the Epigraphical Record. *AJPh* 116.2, pp. 213–220.

Chaniotis, A. (2018a). *Age of Conquests. The Greek World from Alexander to Hadrian*. Cambridge, MA.

Chaniotis, A. (2018b). Religion as Experience: Epigraphic Evidence from the West and North Shores of the Black Sea. In: M. Manoledakis, G.R. Tsetskhladze and I. Xydopoulos, eds., *Essays on the Archaeology and Ancient History of the Black Sea Littoral*, Leuven–Paris–Bristol, pp. 405–423.

Chaniotis, A. (2009a). Travelling Memories in the Hellenistic World. In: R. Hunter and I. Rutherford, eds., *Wandering Poets in Ancient Greek Culture. Travel, Locality and Pan-Hellenism*. Cambridge, pp. 249–269.

Chaniotis, A. (2009b). A Few Things Hellenistic Audiences Appreciated in Musical Performances. In: M.C. Martinelli, ed., *La musa dimenticata. Aspetti dell'esperienza musicale greca in età ellenistica*. Pisa, pp. 75–97.

Chaniotis, A. (2005). *War in the Hellenistic World. A Social and Cultural History*. Oxford.

Chaniotis, A. (1988). *Historie und Historiker in den griechischen Inschriften. Epigraphische Beiträge zur griechischen Historiographie*. Stuttgart.

Cinalli, A. (2017). Οι επιγραφές ως αφήγηση: περιπλανώμενοι διανοούμενοι και μουσικοί στις επιγραφικές πηγές της ελληνιστικής περιόδου. In: M. Tamiolaki, ed., *Μεθοδολογικά ζητήματα στις Κλασικές σπουδές. Παλαιά προβλήματα και νέες προκλήσεις*. Herakleion, pp. 175–204.

Clarke, M.L. (1963). The Architects of Greece and Rome. *Architectural History* 6, pp. 9–22.

Csapo, E. (2010). *Actors and Icons of the Ancient Theater*, Chichester–Malden.

Dana, M. and Dana, D. (2001/2003). Histoires locales dans le Pont-Euxin ouest et nord. Identité grecque et construction du passé. *Il Mar Nero* 5, pp. 91–111.

Del Corso, L. (2012). *Philologoi* e *Grammatikoi* nelle testimonianze epigrafiche di età ellenistica. In: P. Fioretti, ed., *Storie di cultura scritta*. Spoleto, pp. 311–324.

Dover, K.J. (1974). *Greek Popular Morality in the Time of Plato and Aristotle*. Oxford.

Easterling, P. (2004). À propos du statut symbolique des acteurs. In: Ch. Hugoniot, F. Hurlet and S. Milanezi, eds., *Le statut de l'acteur dans l'Antiquité grecque et romaine*. Tours, pp. 43–52.

Easterling, P. and Hall, E. (2002). *Greek and Roman Actors. Aspects of an Ancient Profession*. Cambridge.

Eckstein, A.M. (1995). *Moral Vision in* The Histories *of Polybios*. Berkeley.

Feen, R.H. (1983). The Moral Basis of Graeco-Roman Medical Practice. *Journal of Religion and Health* 22, pp. 39–48.

Feyel, C. (2006). *Les artisans dans les sanctuaires grecs aux époques classique et hellénistique à travers la documentation financière*. Paris.

Gauthier, P. (1985). *Les cités grecques et leurs bienfaiteurs (IVe–Ier s.av. J.-C.). Contribution à l'histoire des institutions*, Suppl. *BCE* 12. Paris.

Gray, B. (2018). A Later Hellenistic Debate about the Value of Classical Athenian Civic Ideals? The Evidence of Epigraphy, Historiography, and Philosophy. In: M. Canevaro and B. Gray, eds., *The Hellenistic Reception of Classical Athenian Democracy and Political Thought*. Oxford, pp. 139–176.

Grzesik, D. (2021). *Honorific Culture at Delphi in the Hellenistic and Roman Periods*. Leiden.

Gygax, M.D. and Zuiderhoek, A. (2021). *Benefactors and the Polis. The Public Gift in the Greek Cities from the Homeric World to Late Antiquity*. Cambridge.

Gygax, M.D. (2016). *Benefaction and Rewards in the Ancient Greek City*. Cambridge.

Guarducci, M. (1929). *Poeti vaganti e conferenzieri dell' età ellenistica. Ricerche di epigrafia greca nel campo della letteratura e del costume*. *Mem. Lic.* 6.2, pp. 627–665.

Haake, M. (2010). Der Philosoph Alexander, Sohn des Alexander, aus Athen. Zu einem neuen hellenistischen Ehrendekret aus Larisa für einen bislang unbekannten Philosophen. *Tyche* 25, pp. 39–47.

Haake, M. (2007). *Der Philosoph in der Stadt. Untersuchungen zur öffentlichen Rede über Philosophen und Philosophie in den hellenistischen Poleis*. Munich.

Haake, M. (2004). Documentary Evidence, Literary Forgery or Manipulation of Historical Documents? Diogenes Laertius and an Athenian Honorary Decree for Zeno of Citium. *CQ* 54, pp. 470–483.

Harris, E.M. (2020). Many Ancient Greek Occupations, but Few Professions. In: E. Stewart, E. Harris and D. Lewis, eds., *Skilled Labour and Professionalism in Ancient Greece and Rome*. Cambridge, pp. 29–67.

Hau, L. (2016). *Moral History from Herodotus to Diodorus Siculus*. Edinburgh.

Hedrick, C.W.J. (2000). For Anyone Who Wishes to See. *AncW* 31.2, pp. 127–135.

Hedrick, C.W.J. (1999). Democracy and the Athenian Epigraphical Habit. *Hesperia* 68.3, pp. 387–439.

Hellmann, M.-C. (1999). *Choix d'Inscriptions Architecturales Grecques*. Lyon.

Henry, A.S. (1996). The Hortatory Intention in Athenian State Decrees. *ZPE* 112, pp. 105–119.

Henry, A.S. (1983). *Honours and Privileges in Athenian Decrees. The Principal Formulae of Athenian Honorary Decrees*. Hildesheim.

Hugoniot, C., Hurlet, F. and Milanezi, S., eds. (2004). *Le statut de l'acteur dans l'Antiquité grecque et romaine*. Tours.

Hunter, R. and Rutherford, I., eds. (2009). *Wandering Poets in Ancient Greek Culture. Travel, Locality and Pan-Hellenism*. Cambridge.

Jacquemin, A., Mulliez, D. and Rougemont, G., eds. (2012). *Choix d'inscriptions de Delphes, traduites et commentées*. Paris.

Laes, C. (2009). Pedagogues in Greek inscriptions in Hellenistic and Roman antiquity. *ZPE* 171, pp. 113–122.

Lamari, A.A. (2017). Tragic Reperformances and Travelling Actors. In: A.A. Lamari, ed., *Reperforming Greek Tragedy. Theater, Politics, and Cultural Mobility in the Fifth and Fourth Centuries B.C.* Berlin, pp. 95–129.

Lambert, S.D. (2011). What Was the Point of Inscribed Honorific Decrees in Classical Athens? In: S.D. Lambert and D.L. Cairns, eds., *Sociable Man. Essays on Ancient Greek Social Behaviour in Honor of Nick Fischer*. Swansea, pp. 193–214.

Lefèvre, F. (2010). Le contrôle des compétences dans les cités grecques. *Journal des Savants* 1, pp. 3–16.

Le Guen, B. (2019). The Expansion of Greek Tragedy from the Fourth Century Onwards. In: V. Liapis and A.K. Petrides, eds., *Greek Tragedy after the Fifth Century. A Survey from ca. 400 BC to ca. AD 400*. Cambridge, pp. 149–179.

Le Guen, B. (2007). Kraton, Son of Zotichos: Artists' Associations and Monarchic Power in the Hellenistic Period. In: P. Wilson, ed., *The Greek Theatre and Festivals. Documentary Studies*. Oxford, pp. 246–278.

Le Guen, B. (2004). Le statut professionel des acteurs grecs à l'époque hellénistique.

In: C. Hugoniot, F. Hurlet and S. Milanezi, eds., *Le statut de l'acteur dans l'Antiquité grecque et romaine*. Tours, pp. 77–106.

Le Guen, B. (2001). *Les associations de Technites dionysiaques à l'époque hellénistique*. Nancy.

Liddel, P. (2021). The Discourses of Identity in Hellenistic Erythrai: Institutions, Rhetoric, Honor, and Reciprocity. *Polis: The Journal for Ancient Greek and Roman Political Thought* 38, pp. 74–107.

Liddel, P. (2020). *Decrees of Fourth-Century Athens (403/2–322/1 BC), v. I: Literary Evidence, v. II: Political and Cultural Perspectives*. Cambridge.

Linder, M. (2020). Artists beyond Athens: The Freedoms and Restrictions of the Artistic Profession in Classical Greece. In: E. Stewart, E. Harris and D. Lewis, eds., *Skilled Labour and Professionalism in Ancient Greece and Rome*. Cambridge, pp. 230–242.

Luraghi, N. (2010). The Demos as Narrator: Public Honors and the Construction of Future and Past. In: L. Foxhall, H.-J. Gehrke and N. Luraghi, eds., *Intentional History. Spinning Time in Ancient Greece*. Stuttgart, pp. 247–263.

Ma, J. (2013). *Statues and Cities. Honorific Portraits and Civic Identity in the Hellenistic World*. Oxford.

Ma, J. (2003). Peer-Polity Interaction in the Hellenistic Age. *Past & Present* 180.1, pp. 9–39.

Ma, J. (2000). *Antiochos III and the Cities of Western Asia Minor*. Oxford.

Massar, N. (2020). Skilled Workers in the Ancient Greek City: Public Employment, Selection Methods, and Evaluation. In: E. Stewart, E. Harris and D. Lewis, eds., *Skilled Labour and Professionalism in Ancient Greece and Rome*. Cambridge, pp. 68–93.

Massar, N. (2006). La circulation des décrets dans les cités et entre cités à l'époque hellénistique. In: L. Capdetrey and J. Nelis-Clément, eds., *La circulation de l'information dans les états antiques*. Bordeaux, pp. 73–87.

Massar, N. (2005). *Soigner et Servir. Histoire sociale et culturelle de la médecine grecque à l'époque hellénistique*. Paris.

Massar, N. (2001). Un savoir-faire à l'honneur. 'Médecins' et 'discours civique' en Grèce hellénistique. *Revue belge de philologie et d'histoire* 79, pp. 175–201.

Mavroudis, A. (2010). *Μακεδονική ιατρική προσωπογραφία. Μακεδόνες ιατροί και ιατροί στην υπηρεσία Μακεδόνων κατά την αρχαιότητα*. Athens.

Meeus, A. (2015). The Career of Sostratos of Knidos. Politics, Diplomacy and the Alexandrian Building Programme in the Early Hellenistic Period. In: T. Howe, E.E. Garvin and G. Wrightson, eds., *Greece, Macedon and Persia. Studies in Social, Political and Military History in Honor of Waldemar Heckel*. Oxford, pp. 143–171.

Meyer, E.A. (2013). Inscriptions as Honors and the Athenian Epigraphic Habit. *Historia* 62, pp. 453–505.

Mikalson, J.D. (2010). *Greek Popular Religion in Greek Philosophy*. Oxford.

Miller, J. (2016). Euergetism, Agonism, and Democracy: The Hortatory Intention in Late Classical and Early Hellenistic Athenian Honorific Decrees. *Hesperia* 85.2, pp. 385–435.

Parker, R. (2004). New 'Panhellenic' Festivals in Hellenistic Greece. In: R. Schlesier and U. Zellmann, eds., *Mobility and Travel in the Mediterranean from Antiquity to the Middle Ages*. Münster, pp. 9–22.

Paschidis, P. (2008). *Between City and King. Prosopographical Studies on the Intermediaries between the Cities of the Greek Mainland and the Aegean and the Royal Courts in the Hellenistic Period (322–190 BC)*. Athens.

Peels, S. (2016). *'Hosios'. A Semantic Study of Greek Piety*, Mnemosyne Suppl. 387. Leiden.

Perrin-Saminadayar, É. (2007). *Éducation, culture et société à Athènes. Les acteurs de la vie culturelle athènienne (229–288): un tout petit monde*. Paris.

Platt, V. (2011). *Facing the Gods. Epiphany and Representation in Graeco-Roman Art, Literature and Religion*. Cambridge.

Rigsby, K. (1996). *Asylia. Territorial Inviolability in the Hellenistic World*. Berkeley.

Robert, L. (1984). Les concours grecs. *VIIIe Congrès international d'épigraphie Athènes 1982* (Athens 1984), 35–45 (reprinted in: D. Rousset, P. Gauthier and I. Savalli-Lestrade, eds., *L. Robert. Choix d'Écrits*. Paris 2007, pp. 267–278).

Rutherford, I. (2009). Aristodama and the Aetolians: An Itinerant Poetess and her Agenda. In: R. Hunter and I. Rutherford, eds., *Wandering Poets in Ancient Greek Culture*. Cambridge, pp. 237–248.

Rutherford, I. (2007). *Theoria* and Theatre at Samothrace: The Dardanos by Dymas of Iasos. In: P. Wilson, ed., *The Greek Theatre and Festivals*. Oxford, pp. 279–293.

Samama, E. (2003). *Les médecins dans le monde grec. Sources épigraphiques sur la naissance d'in corps medical*. Geneva.

Schachter, A. and Slater, W.J. (2007). A Proxeny Decree from Koroneia, Boiotia, in Honor of Zotion, Son of Zotion, of Ephesos. *ZPE* 163, pp. 81–95.

Scholz, P. (2004). Peripatetic Philosophers as Wandering Scholars: Some Remarks on the Sociopolitical Conditions of Philosophizing in the Third Century BCE. In: W.W. Fortenbaugh and S.A. White, eds., *Lyco of Troas and Hieronymus of Rhodes. Text, Translation and Discussion*, New Brunswick–London, pp. 315–353.

Shipley, G. (1987). *A History of Samos 800–188 BC*. Oxford.

Sickinger, J.P. (2009). Nothing to Do with Democracy: "Formulae of Disclosure" and the Athenian Epigraphic Habit. In: L. Mitchell and L. Rubinstein, eds., *Greek History and Epigraphy. Essays in Honor of P.J. Rhodes*. Swansea, pp. 87–102.

Stephanis, I.E. (1988). *Διονυσιακοί Τεχνίται. συμβολές στην προσωπογραφία του θεάτρου και της μουσικής των αρχαίων Ελλήνων*. Heraklion.

Stewart, E. (2020). The Profession of *Mousikē* in Classical Greece. In: E. Stewart, E. Harris and D. Lewis, eds., *Skilled Labour and Professionalism in Ancient Greece and Rome*. Cambridge, pp. 269–292.

Stewart, E., Harris, E. and Lewis, D., eds. (2020). *Skilled Labour and Professionalism in Ancient Greece and Rome*. Cambridge.

Strootman, R. (2017). *The Birdcage of the Muses. Patronage of the Arts and Sciences at the Ptolemaic Imperial Court, 305–222 BCE*. Leuven.

Thomas, R. (2019). *Polis Histories, Collective Memories and the Greek World*. Cambridge.

Van Bremen, R. (1996). *The Limits of Participation. Women and Civic Life in the Greek East in the Hellenistic and Roman Periods*. Amsterdam.

Van Liefferinge, C. (2000). Auditions et conférences à Delphes. *AC* 69, pp. 149–164.

Veligianni-Terzi, C. (1997). *Wertbegriffe in den attischen Ehrendekreten der klassischen Zeit*. Stuttgart.

Winter, F.E. (2006). *Studies in Hellenistic Architecture*. Toronto.

Wörrle, M. (1995). Vom tugendsamen Jüngling zum 'gestressten' Euergeten. Überlegungen zum Bürgerbild hellenistischer Ehrendekrete. In: M. Wörrle and P. Zanker, eds., *Stadtbild und Bürgerbild im Hellenismus*. Munich, pp. 241–250.

CHAPTER 17

Images of Craft: Activity and Presentation of Work on Gallo-Roman Tombstones

Fanny Opdenhoff

1 Introduction

The depiction of crafts was an important means of self-representation on Roman and especially on Gallo-Roman tombstones. About 163 reliefs, free-standing sculptures and more complex monuments depicting craft activities are known from Roman Gaul.[1] Most of these images date from the second century CE, when these provinces experienced an upswing.[2] In the *necropoleis*, accordingly, such images of craftsmen or people otherwise related to professional activities were a familiar sight. Funerary monuments were a rather traditional sort of medium, but I will argue that conventionality formed a fertile basis for innovative variants showing different ways to perceive and visualize the importance of the craft.[3] Starting from a case study of a relief from Bordeaux, I discuss which communicative intentions and which attitudes to craftsmanship and especially to physical labour can be grasped in such testimonies.

In this context, it has proven useful to take into account the perspectives and ideas of the producer of the monument as well as the materiality and the perception of the viewer. As I hope to show, the interpretation and impact of the monument chosen for the case study depended heavily on the interaction between the image, its physical surroundings and human actors. Therefore, iconographic and iconological aspects of the images will be just one part of the discussion. The analytical framework of visual culture studies and German Bildwissenschaften prove to be more fruitful in this context, where I want

1 See Béal 2000, 150–152, though in view of Béal's discussion of the criteria to include or exclude specific pieces, it becomes clear how difficult a differentiation between craft, agriculture and trade is. Other authors choose a wider scope including all depictions of work: See Reddé 1978, 43 or Langner 2001, 301.

2 For example, with regard to the infrastructure but also to the flourishing of different branches of crafts, industry and trade. See: Frézouls 1990.

3 On the traditional character of funerary monuments as a group: Caruel 2016, 116.

 | DOI:10.1163/9789004694965_018

to discuss the multiple ways by which the images engaged with the viewers and contemporary discourses.[4] Even if the original contexts have frequently been lost, the image's embedding into its functional, aesthetic and visual framework has to be taken into account at least in general and hypothetic terms, as Annette Haug shows in her newly developed approaches to Roman 'Principles of Decor'. This comprises both the relationship between different parts of spatial ensembles, and the potential behaviour, e.g. movement and stasis of the human actors.[5]

The basis for the study of the Gallo-Roman funerary reliefs is Émile Espérandieu's fifteen-volume *Recueil général des bas-reliefs, statues et bustes de la Gaule romaine*.[6] The funerary monuments from Bordeaux were further presented as a group by François Braemer in 1959 and have been studied in several projects concerning the visual language and contexts of Gallo-Roman funerary monuments.[7] Gerhard Zimmer, in his 1982 study of representations of work and craft from Italy in the first and second centuries CE, primarily examines funerary reliefs but includes other images as well.[8] And until today, these representations of work, together with funerary inscriptions containing references to a profession, provide invaluable sources with regard to labour and work in Roman Italy.[9] Concerning Gallo-Roman representations of work on funerary reliefs particular mention should be made here of the work of Stephane Pannoux, Michel Reddé, Jean-Claude Béal, Martin Langner and Marie-Sophie Caruel, who have specifically focused on the iconography of craftsmen.[10]

In the *Tres Galliae*, three different ways of referring to a craft activity were common. Firstly, it was possible to show one or more tools that had no direct physical connection to the representation of the deceased on the sides of the monument or below the portrait. Secondly, scenes are found in which a single person or several persons are shown engaged in a craft activity. This type was

4 The literature on each of these approaches is vast. For a concise and insightful discussion see: Lorenz 2016, esp. 169–183.
5 Haug 2021, 1–9.
6 Espérandieu 1907–1966.
7 Braemer 1959.
8 Zimmer 1982. For the development of references to work, labour and craft from the first and second centuries CE onwards, see Zanker 1992, 353–354. And more recently: Larsson Lovén 2007, esp. 172–175.
9 Recently: Groen-Vallinga 2022.
10 Many others should also be named here, see: Reddé 1978, Baltzer 1983, Pannoux 1985, Beal 2000, Rose 2007, Langner 2001, and Caruel 2016. For an overview of the discussion of 'scènes de métiers' until the 1990s, see Chevallier 1997. With a focus on 'views of work in relation to social class and gender': Larsson Lovén 2007.

also known in Italy and Zimmer distinguishes between two modes of depicting the deceased. On the one hand, there are the 'masters', who either alone or with the help of others perform physical work themselves; on the other hand, there are the 'entrepreneurs' who merely supervise production or may not be shown at all. Through these different modes, various aspects of work and professional activity, such as craftsmanship, expertise or economic success, could be foregrounded.[11] However, in the north-western provinces a third option, not known from Italy, was particularly common: in this scenario, tools were placed in the hands of the deceased's image as attributes without being put to any use.[12]

Most of the Gallo-Roman funerary reliefs can be dated to the second century CE and are thus somewhat later than the ones from Italy that stem from the first and second centuries CE. There, it seems to have been more common to refer to a craft in the funerary inscription than in the relief, which is not the case in the north-western provinces.[13] The upswing that the Gallic provinces experienced in the second century can be grasped both in local production sites and in far-reaching trade relations, which are proven by corresponding finds in all parts of the Roman empire.[14]

2 The Stele of Amabilis

The stele of Amabilis (Fig. 17.1; Espérandieu 1111) was—as will be shown—in many respects anchored in regional conventions, but exhibits a number of special features that make a more in-depth study worthwhile. The piece was found in 1826 in the Rue Guillaume Brochon in Bordeaux and has since been kept there in the Musée d'Aquitaine.[15] It was discovered, like almost all funerary monuments at Bordeaux, not in its original position but built into the late

11 Zimmer 1982, 69–71. With the example of a comb-trimmer named Titus Valerius Placidus from Asti as 'Meister' and the baker Eurysaces as 'Unternehmer'.

12 See Pannoux 1985 for a classification of the Gallo-Roman images referring to crafts.

13 See Groen-Vallinga 2022, 13, citing occupational titles for 2000 to 3000 Romans in epitaphs and only around a hundred depictions in tomb monuments.

14 For the different branches and the upswing of the crafts in the Gallic provinces in the second century CE: Frézouls 1990, 455–459. Zimmer also notes a change in the appreciation of crafts in Roman Italy in the course of the first century CE, which was expressed in increasingly prominent and detailed references to the activities on funerary monuments: Zimmer 1982, 72–73.

15 Musée d'Aquitaine Inv. 60.1.82. Espérandieu 1111. Camille Jullian also shows it as an example for the funerary sculpture that expresses who and what the deceased was in life: Jullian 1895, 35–37. Charles Picard discusses the monument in detail: Picard 1961, 96–100.

FIGURE 17.1
Funerary stele of Amabilis, Bordeaux, Musée d'Aquitaine, inv. 60.1.82
PHOTO: © MAIRIE DE BORDEAUX, MUSÉE D'AQUITAINE. PHOTOGRAPHER L. GAUTHIER

antique town wall.[16] Due to the modern city overlaying the ancient buildings, knowledge about the topography of ancient Bordeaux is limited, so that the location of the *necropoleis* and the associated funerary monuments cannot be determined precisely.[17] Since the late antique settlement was significantly smaller than the city of the first centuries CE, the position of the spolia in the wall offers no useful indication as to their original location and context of the *necropolis*.[18]

The stele is 98 cm high, 49 cm wide and 47 cm deep; the internal dimensions of the niche are 74 cm (height) × 38 cm (width). Some of the outer edges are slightly damaged, and larger fragments are missing, which is particularly noticeable on the lower right, where part of the inscription is lost. the exterior is carefully smoothed where architectural decoration is present and otherwise only roughly smoothed.[19] The interior is well preserved except for the face and the right wrist of the deceased. The restored inscription reads as follows (Fig. 17.2):

> Dis Manibus | M(arco) Se(...) Amabili Scu(lptori) | Amandus Fr(ater) | curav[it].[20]

In the niche, clearly below life-size, a bearded man is portrayed sitting on a bench. He is dressed in a long, sleeveless tunic. On his head he wears a round cap with curly hair flowing out from under it. He wears simple but closed shoes, with the instep additionally covered by a thick piece of cloth or leather fastened

16 Cf. Braemer 1959, 13–14. 15 fig. B (map that indicates the findspots). More funerary monuments were used as building material in other parts of the town wall, where they have sometimes been documented in recent years. See: Migeon and Zieglé 2003, 291–299 and AE 2003, 1168–1170, describing three funerary monuments that were found in the Place Pey-Berland.

17 See Barraud and Sireix 2010, 165–166 and Barraud and Caillabet-Duloum 2004. The development seems to be slower here than in other Gallo-Roman towns and cities: Barraud, Fabioux, Vernou, Buisson and Girardy-Caillat 1992, 205.

18 Cf. the plan in Gerber 2020, 292 fig. 2. For a general distribution of the finds in the modern city, see Etienne 1962, carte 24.

19 See especially the 3D-Scan in the PETRAE database: https://petrae.huma-num.fr/1601009 00198.

20 CIL XIII 643. AE 1962, 331a. IRB I, 82. The *nomen gentile* cannot be determined from the abbreviation, as there would be over 200 possibilities for nomina beginning with *SE*, Salomies and Solin 1994, 165–171. Jullian suggests *Secundinius*, since this was a particularly frequent *nomen gentile* at Bordeaux: IRB I 203–204. For the brothers' *cognomina* 'Amabilis' and 'Amandus' and their regional use, see Kajanto 1965, 360. For further details about the inscription and a 3D-scan, see again: https://petrae.huma-num.fr/160100900198.

FIGURE 17.2
Detail of the lower part of the inscription, funerary stele of Amabilis, Bordeaux, Musée d'Aquitaine, inv. 60.1.82
PHOTO: © MAIRIE DE BORDEAUX, MUSÉE D'AQUITAINE. PHOTOGRAPHER L. GAUTHIER

FIGURE 17.3
Detail of the left foot, funerary stele of Amabilis, Bordeaux, Musée d'Aquitaine, inv. 60.1.82
PHOTO: © MAIRIE DE BORDEAUX, MUSÉE D'AQUITAINE. PHOTOGRAPHER L. GAUTHIER

above the ankle (Fig. 17.3). Based on style and motifs, the stele can be dated to the second half of the second century CE.[21]

The man's posture now deserves special attention: in his right hand he holds a hammer, with which he will strike the chisel in his left hand in the next moment (fig. 17.4 and 17.5). He has placed the tool behind the capital, at the inner edge of the niche. Turning his head, he follows this movement. To all appearances, he is in the process of working on the niche in which he is sitting and thus completing the tomb itself. By doing this, he would also have created himself or his image. The viewer finds himself confronted here with a *mise en abyme*—that is, with interlocking layers, in which the same image is once again

21 Braemer 1959, 56: based on the likeness of his hairstyle to that of the times of Antoninus Pius and Marcus Aurelius. For a general classification of the stylistic criteria cf. Hahl 1937, esp. 23–25.

FIGURE 17.4
Detail of the right hand, funerary stele of Amabilis, Bordeaux, Musée d'Aquitaine, inv. 60.1.82
PHOTO: © MAIRIE DE BORDEAUX, MUSÉE D'AQUITAINE. PHOTOGRAPHER L. GAUTHIER

made the object within an image. In this case the two layers are almost 100% congruent.

A comparison of Amabilis' stele with other pieces found in Bordeaux highlights important parallels: in total, approximately 100 funerary stelae are known; these are between 51 and 158 cm high and between 27 and 109 cm wide.[22] With a height of 98 cm and a width of 49 cm, the stele of Amabilis therefore did not stand out but would have been perceived as average. The same applies to the type of stele. Among the figurative stelae, those showing the grave owners in bust format and those depicting them completely are represented

22 Braemer 1956, *passim*. For newer finds adding to the older records, see: Migeon and Zieglé 2003, 294–298.

FIGURE 17.5
Detail of the left hand, funerary stele of Amabilis, Bordeaux, Musée d'Aquitaine, inv. 60.1.82
PHOTO: © MAIRIE DE BORDEAUX, MUSÉE D'AQUITAINE. PHOTOGRAPHER L. GAUTHIER

in relatively large numbers, with 47 and 36 specimens each. The material was mostly, as with the stele of Amabilis, a locally available beige limestone.

Among the figurative representations, those with portraits that are kept largely attribute-free except for the clothing, predominate. Information on the status, specific activities or qualities of the deceased is given at most in the inscriptions. However, there are also some pieces in which the figures are holding objects in their hands or where such are otherwise represented on the monument. These include, in particular, some depictions of craftsmen and others that indicate an occupation of the deceased. Among these, sculptors or other craftsmen working with stone are a known but not particularly frequent subject in imperial-age funerary sculpture.[23] As with many other crafts,

23 Zimmer lists nine craftsmen working with stone in his sample of 198 'Berufsdarstellungen'

the final products, i.e. sculptures, are known in considerably larger quantities than images or texts referring to people making sculpture.[24]

It may be assumed for most funerary monuments that at least the name of the deceased and that of the donor(s) of the tomb were inscribed to assign the grave, even if some of the monuments do not yield any surviving inscription. The texts of the inscriptions on the funerary monuments from the area of Bordeaux correspond to the common form of the time: at the beginning the sacral formula *Dis Manibus*, with the name of the deceased in the genitive, nominative or dative case, and the details of who had the monument erected.

Against the background of the features described above, the stele of Amabilis appears quite ordinary in the local context. The conventions regarding size, inscription and type were taken up and reproduced in such a way that to an ancient observer the stele would initially appear normal. The primary statements about the grave owner, the donor, the profession of the deceased and his family situation are unmistakably conveyed. And so far, most authors who have included this monument in their catalogues have also listed it as one example among many representations of craftsmen or sculptors. The differences that may make the ancient and the modern viewer doubt that it was planned as one among many representations of craftsmen or sculptors are in the details.

The stele stands out in two ways. On the one hand, its sculptural quality surpasses most other comparable pieces from Bordeaux, though not being so remarkable to suggest it was produced by an external sculptor. The qualities concern the design, the understanding of the individual parts of body and garment, and the care taken to work and smoothen the surfaces. A comparison with other stelae from Bordeaux that roughly correspond in date, format and theme makes this clear.[25] It differs in the successful representation of the proportions of the human body, the innovative and convincingly realized posture, in which the outer walls of the stele have been skilfully used to depict a dynamic moment of particular tension through the arm, head and leg postures. This energetic image is further pursued in the tense muscles and the diagonally

from Italy and additional four from France (including the piece from Bordeaux) and Greece: Zimmer 1982, cat. 75–83 and pp. 231–239 n. 39. 62. 143. 193. Additionally, Reddé lists two representing men working with stones among 163 Gallo-Roman 'scènes de metier', but not taking into account depictions of tools without the artisan: Reddé 1978, 44. For the Moselland, Yasmine Freigang adds another one: Freigang 1997, 311.

24 See Schmidts 2005, 260–264.

25 See: Espérandieu 1124, 1126, 1142 and 1173. Etienne especially emphasizes the quality of Amabilis' stele: Etienne 1962, 158.

drawn folds of the tunic. In comparison, the postures of the figures on many other stelae are uniform and the surface treatment cursory. Potential for movement is rarely depicted. However, this does not necessarily mean that the stele of Amabilis was perceived as better or more coherent than those of his contemporaries. As in other fields, the local inhabitants might have placed a high value on the reproduction of conventions, while innovative statements or compositions were less in demand.[26] Overall, therefore, our piece corresponds to local customs in the formal aspects of the material, the sizes and the layout as a niche with inscription. What is unusual is the quality, as well as some peculiarities of the theme of the craftsman's depiction. A somewhat broader angle is therefore necessary here, to see how the tombstone of Amabilis is to be classified in regional and transregional comparison with other Gallo-Roman craftsmen's representations.

3 Labour and Work on Gallo-Roman Funerary Reliefs

Altogether, according to Langner, depictions of labour and work make up about 15–20% of the funerary reliefs. This is a relatively high proportion compared to Northern Italy, where occupational depictions only make up about 4–5%.[27] In principle, freestanding small and medium-sized funerary monuments were constructed in such a way that the grave owners were depicted on the front side. Additional images may be added on the secondary sides as well as on certain areas of the front side, such as a tympanum or below the main image. These may or may not show the deceased. In some cases, as mentioned, bare tools are also depicted. If only an ascia is shown alone, the image is usually not interpreted as a representation of labour, since the symbolic character of this instrument went beyond the reference to a practical use in the context of craft activity and in most cases is to be related to the furnishing of the tomb rather than to the lifetime of the deceased.[28]

In an example from Metz (Fig. 17.6 and 17.7), the inscription does not refer to a craft activity.[29] The tools are placed below the inscription and the main image as well as on the secondary side. The main image shows the deceased standing and facing frontally. He is wearing a tunic and a cloak, which is so richly and

26 This preference of conventionality can be observed also in other fields, such as electoral notices: cf. Opdenhoff 2021, 107.

27 For the relative frequency see Langner 2002, 306.

28 Cf. Béal 2000, 152 n. 13.

29 AE 1976, 482: *D(is) M(anibus) / Reginus Ciniuc/nati.*

FIGURE 17.6
Funerary monument of Reginus, Metz, Musée de la Cour d'Or, inv. 75.38.66
PHOTO: LICENSED UNDER CREATIVE COMMONS: BY-NC-ND 3.0, IDAI OBJECTS, PHOTOGRAPHER TILL SCHLÄGER HTTPS://ARACHNE.DAINST.ORG/ENTITY/6485767/IMAGE/6485767

elaborately draped that it resembles a toga. With his right hand he grips the garment and with his left he holds a purse. This depiction is supplemented on the secondary sides. On the left side a chariot is added and on the right side an ascia and a pair of scissors. The chariot is not necessarily to be related to the deceased's occupation, as in this case the products or goods cannot be determined or possibly none were present at all. Neither do the purse and the richly draped garment indicate a specific occupation. The reference to a craft activ-

FIGURE 17.7
Depiction of tools on the left side of the monument from Metz.
DRAWING: PANNOUX 1983, FIG. 8. © S. PANNOUX

ity is therefore very cautious and is only given by the depiction of tools on the secondary sides.[30]

The largest group among the Gallo-Roman representations of craftsmen are the reliefs in which the displayed figures hold tools in their hands as attributes. This type of image was a typical Gallo-Roman form.[31] The figures are shown as busts or in full-body view in frontal orientation, as in the example of Sabinianus' stele from Autun (Fig. 17.8). In their hands, raised in front of the upper body, they may be holding implements that indicate a certain profession. In some cases, two very different objects come together, such as a small box, a purse or a drinking cup, and a tool. In other cases, two tools or only one tool are held as a single attribute.[32] The aim, then, was not to show the tools as part of a work situation. It is also not always easy or necessary to differentiate these from the simple tool representations, when additional tools were represented without being held but clearly referring to his image, as in the case of Sabinianus.

This form of representation was by no means limited to the representation of crafts. On the contrary, it was the most common way to design funerary reliefs. Half-body representations in particular seem to have been produced

30 Cf. Pannoux 1985, 306.

31 See Pannoux 1985, 297–298; Béal 2000, 153–158 and Caruel 2016, 117 for a classification of the depictions of crafts on funerary monuments with three main types, which are specifically found in the Tres Galliae and the Narbonensis: PO: 'porteur d'outils'; OS: 'outils seuls'; AC: 'artisans en pleine activité' or 'scènes de metier'.

32 Caruel 2016, 117–118.

FIGURE 17.8
Stele of Sabinianus, Autun, Musée Rolin, inv. M L 143
PHOTO: © AUTUN – MUSÉE ROLIN, F. AND O. HARL. HTTP://LUPA.AT/25165. PHOTOGRAPHER ORTOLF HARL 2015

in series and do not necessarily contain a statement about the gender of the deceased: several stelae from Bordeaux show the deceased wearing a simple but wide gown with very similar arrangements of the folds. Individualization was achieved via the inscription. The portrait or the attributes were sometimes scratched into the folded surface of the garment rather than being carved in the round.[33] Attributes play a significant role here, as they were easier to depict and to perceive for the sculptor and the viewer of the monuments than specific features of the deceased's face. It was precisely through such objects that reference could be made in an easily readable form to one or more areas of life attributed to the deceased. This form of reference to manual activity is generally found on the front of the tomb. Since those holding the tools are oriented frontally and at the same time often show portrait-like features, it can be safely assumed that these were the grave owners themselves. The respective craft, however, is only touched on in a very generic way in these reliefs. The scenes suggest that the activity was somehow important for the deceased, but we do not know whether they had performed these activities themselves, or whether they had been the owner of a small or medium-sized business focusing on these activities—without performing physical labour there.

The third common way of referring to professions was the depiction of work scenes, among which the stele of Amabilis can also be counted. Work scenes can be found on both the main and the secondary sides of the funerary monuments. Some show several people at work, others only one. Just as with the images discussed in the previous paragraph, it can be assumed that the grave owner is depicted when the scene is on the main side and the figure doing the work is oriented frontally or almost frontally or when he or she is shown alone. In other examples, it is less clear. When the occupational scenes are on the secondary sides or show several figures, the question arises whether the deceased is included at all and what role they took.[34] But precisely this question is of importance when it comes to understanding the monuments as testimonies to the deceased's relationship to work.

The main difference between simple scene-like representations of work and the depiction of inactive tools is that in the scenes the potential and knowledge to use these is expressed more vividly. A stele from Bourges shows a standing man (Fig. 17.9).[35] He is wearing a tunic and a cloak. His weight is slightly shifted to his left leg, which is partly covered by a small block or workbench. On it

33 See for example from Bordeaux: Espérandieu 1154. 1180. 1186, But also more recently: Migeon and Zieglé 2003, 295 fig. 6.

34 As described in Caruel 2016, 119–123.

35 Espérandieu 1446, see also Béal 2000. 177 and Caruel 2016, 120.

FIGURE 17.9
Stele of a potter, Bourges, Musée du Berry, inv. 1857.1.3.
PHOTO: © COLLECTION MUSÉES ET PATRIMOINE HISTORIQUE DE LA VILLE DE BOURGES. F. AND O. HARL. HTTP://LUPA.AT/32726. PHOTOGRAPHER: MICHEL REDDÉ 1970–1975

stands a vessel into which he is reaching with the thumb of his left hand. In his right hand he holds a modelling tool. He is not holding it centrally in front of his upper body but is pointing it towards the vessel. The monument is not completely preserved, so that the inscription is lost. Nevertheless, it can be deduced from the relief that the deceased was involved in potting.

Another piece is the stele of Belliccus from Sens (Fig. 17.10).[36] He, too, stands alone and is dressed in a tunic and cloak. He is not looking frontally out of

36 Espérandieu 2769, CIL XIII 2965, Laubry 2021, 302.

FIGURE 17.10
Stele of Belliccus from Sens, Sens, Musées de Sens, inv. J 79
PHOTO: © SENS – MUSÉES DE SENS, F. AND O. HARL. HTTP://LUPA.AT/25966. PHOTOGRAPHER ORTOLF HARL 2015

the niche, but turns slightly to the left, towards an anvil. There he seems to be holding a workpiece with his left hand, or presumably rather pointing to it, while he holds a hammer in his right hand. He is also holding the tool in such a way that it seems at least conceivable that he could work the object on the anvil with it. With these and similar images, the question arises as to whether they can really be called scenes, and as seen above, the distinction between the *porteur d'outils* and the *scènes de metier* is not rigid.[37] What is particularly striking is that neither Belliccus nor the man from Bourges directs his gaze and attention to the workpiece and thus to the craft activity. Both compositions can thus be understood as a compromise between, on the one hand, showing the portrait of the deceased frontally directed into the viewer's space and, at the same time, describing his active performance of the craft activity more precisely than would have been possible with an attributive indication of tools.

The funerary monument of Maternianus from Bourges shows the deceased on the main side (Fig. 17.11).[38] His body is aligned frontally, yet his gaze does not point in the direction of the viewer but follows his current activity. His left foot is elevated but hidden behind a block that supports a cobbler's anvil while he stabilizes his position with his right foot. With the left hand he holds or adjusts a shoe that he has fitted on the cobbler's anvil. In his right hand he holds a hammer. His head and gaze are directed towards the shoe. For the contemporary viewer, this must have been significant, as most funerary reliefs establish direct eye contact between the viewer or the passer-by, even if they could only pay attention to the individual monument for a short time. Here, this gaze is given up and redirected in favour of an actual scene-like representation of work.

While these scenes must refer to the deceased themselves, this is different for scenes that have been moved to the secondary sides—as happened with the depiction of a cooper on a funerary monument from Sens (Fig. 17.12).[39] On the front side, the deceased is shown frontally. On the left side, on the other hand, a seated man is depicted. The surface and many details are unrecognizable due to the texture and weathering of the stone, so that it is ultimately impossible to decide whether the same person was meant twice. The seated figure is shown in side view and, moreover, is oriented in such a way that he is looking away

37 Cf. note 31.

38 Found 1962, it is not included in Espérandieu II, but was first published in: Picard 1963, 379–380; AE 1964, 144; see discussion in: Caruel 2016, 121–122.

39 Espérandieu 2783; Caruel 2016, 124.

FIGURE 17.11
Stele of Maternianos from Bourges, Bourges, Musée du Berry, inv. 1961.51.1. PHOTO: © COLLECTION MUSÉES ET PATRIMOINE HISTORIQUE DE LA VILLE DE BOURGES. F. AND O. HARL. HTTP://LUPA.AT/32717. PHOTOGRAPHER MICHEL REDDÉ 1970–1975

from a possible observer studying the monument from its front. It is therefore quite conceivable that it is not the owner of the tomb who is shown here, but an employee or slave who represented the trade of the deceased. This interpretation is also to be favoured in a more complexly designed monument from Sens (Fig. 17.13).[40] The reliefs seen here are attached to the back of the monument. Two scenes from a fulling business are shown in two registers. While in the upper scene a man dressed in a tunic is shearing a cloth hung over a rack, another man dressed in an exomis can be seen below treading cloths in a tub. As in well-known wall paintings from Pompeii, various steps are shown as well as persons who would be occupied in a small or medium-sized fulling busi-

40 Espérandieu 2768.

FIGURE 17.12
Stele of an unknown male from Sens, Sens, Museés de Sens, inv. J 133
PHOTO: © SENS – MUSÉES DE SENS, F. AND O. HARL. HTTP://LUPA.AT/25980. PHOTOGRAPHER ORTOLF HARL 2015

ness.[41] The deceased may, but need not, appear in such contexts. The physical work, the craft and the necessary skills are not shown here in themselves as merits or activities of the deceased to be emphasized, but they are presented in connection with his entrepreneurship.[42]

41 Friezes from *fullonica* VI 8, 20.21.2 (now in Naples, MANN, inv. 9974) and *domus* VI 15, 1 (Casa dei Vettii, Room of the Cupids (q)) at Pompeii, andthe relief from Sens in the context of these images with regard to the fulling process and workshop organization: Flohr 2013, 31–32 fig. 8; 114–116.

42 This might give him the possibility to differentiate between the physical work in his enterprise, performed by others, and the *otium* which he has earned through it: Zimmer 1982, 71.

FIGURE 17.13
Two joining fragments of a funerary monument from Sens, Sens, Museés de Sens, inv. J 128 and J 129
PHOTO: © SENS – MUSÉES DE SENS, F. AND O. HARL. HTTP://LUPA.AT/25970. PHOTOGRAPHER ORTOLF HARL 2015

4 Social Status

Regarding the clothing, Langner observed that a combination of elaborate garments and raised tools of the trade is often found on Gallo-Roman tomb reliefs. Sometimes, a drinking cup or a purse is added. He convincingly describes this as an attributive representation, which should not be understood according to the criteria of realism, but as 'characterizing'.[43] In the examples described above, this is evident in the way the richly folded coats are worn, which would have been extremely impractical in the context of physical work. By combining these clothes with the tools held in the hands, ready for use, so to speak, it becomes clear that no realistic work situation is meant, but that several partial statements about the tomb owner were to be conveyed at the same time.[44] He was an expert in his craft and on that basis could afford a certain standard of living. The effort, the exertion and possible dangers against which one had to protect oneself, on the other hand, are not part of this message. This is especially true of the potter and the blacksmith Belliccus. Maternianus also wears at least a thick tunic with long sleeves.

Amabilis by contrast is wearing a sleeveless tunic made of heavy fabric. The cap made of flexible but thick material serves as protection during work and the shoes with a flap pulled onto the instep are also different from those of other craftsmen's representations.[45] The reference to an elevated standard of living, which made it possible to wear elaborate clothing and participate in convivia, has given way here to a thematically self-contained representation that is coherent in its details. The aim of Amabilis' stele was therefore not to offer a comprehensive characterization of who he was, but rather to present a highly plausible scene from his everyday life. This also included the depiction of the tensing of the muscles and adequate clothing. Amabilis or the sculptor refrained from showing attributes and items that are not involved in the action. Clothing, tools and activity fit together. The location here is not a workshop or a salesroom, but the niche itself. In the posture too, the statement is reduced to the essential. The movements of the individual limbs of the body are related to each other and in their interplay result in the action: the supporting legs, the sloping shoulders, the tense muscles and the concentrated gaze fixed on the point to be hit. The individual elements of the image are not paratactically, as in most other examples, but syntactically related to each other.

---

43 Langner 2001, 308–312. 320.

44 See e.g. Langner 2001, 347–348. Caruel 2016, 116 and Larsson Lovén 2007, 182. See also Hölscher 2012.

45 See Caruel 2016, 122.

The most striking difference to the other monuments shown, however, is the interlocking of image layers. The depiction of finished workpieces or work in progress is common in images of craftsmen. But here, the workpiece is the niche itself. And accordingly, if the sculptor has hollowed out the niche, he must necessarily also have given shape to himself. Thus, two levels can be distinguished here, which are mutually dependent on each other to be comprehensible: 1. the deceased working on a workpiece and 2. a sculpture that is still being worked on and is thus staged as an artefact made by the depicted sculptor. These two motifs, which in other trades are usually shown side by side in the same image layer, are here made to coincide and thus compete for the viewer's chosen perspective. The effort to make the two levels recognizable is evident in several features: The arms in particular, but also the upper part of the body, are not sculpted in the round, but emerge only partially from the relief ground. In the areas under the right arm and behind the right leg some material and the rough surface were left unfinished, so that the sculpture appears as work in progress. And finally, the figure is clearly below life-size. So, the intention was by no means to create the illusion that a real sculptor was at work here. On the other hand, the relatively good quality of the work and the unusual liveliness seem to suggest precisely this potential for action.

The two levels are played off against each other. But may we assume that this would be understood or even intended in this way? In the case of other craftsmen, products were often shown being worked on.[46] Thus, the creator could assume that the viewers would also expect a workpiece as part of the picture. This suggests that the actual sculptor who made Amabilis' stele, whether that was himself or his brother Amandus, wanted to present the stele *itself* as a finished product. At the same time, however, it becomes clear that the monument can only be understood in its context, i.e. within the framework of the visual language established in the Gallo-Roman environment to which it refers.[47]

The inscription of Amabilis' stele adds further to its meaning. The text is distributed over the pediment and the area above and below the niche.[48] The letterforms are carefully cut and fit the overall impression of the monument in terms of quality. But the inscription also confirms and supports the monument's statement about Amabilis' styled self. The restored text reads, *Dis Manibus Marco Se ... Amabili Sculptori Amandus Frater curavit*. The end of the

46 On the notion of 'madeness' see Reitz-Joosse, this volume.

47 See especially Pannoux 1985, 301–304 and Langner 2001, 314–320 as well as Béal 2000, 166–168.

48 CIL XIII 643. Picard saw in the inscription an example of the craftsman's inability to plan the distribution of the text properly: Picard 1961, 100.

penultimate line is questionable, since the stone is broken off there and possibly one or two more letters followed. Amabilis is explicitly named in the inscription as *sculptor*, which was not usual for the work scenes.[49] However, this was not the only role emphasized in the inscription. Amabilis was apparently a Roman citizen and could hold the *tria nomina*.[50] For Amabilis, this aspect probably had above all a symbolic character, since the *nomen gentile* was not written completely. The lower part of the inscription is particularly interesting. *Amandus Frater curavit*. If *curavit* refers also to the stele, it was therefore made and designed posthumously and not by Amabilis the Sculptor himself. Perhaps the two brothers Amandus and Amabilis worked together in a family business, so that Amandus could also be the creator.[51]

5 Conclusion

As discussed above, the stele adheres for the most part to established formulas for the depiction of craftsmen on funerary monuments. However, with regard to the linking of the individual partial statements, to the quality and to the complexity, the image deviates from these patterns. This is a relevant change with regard to the question of the status and possibilities of self-representation of artists and craftsmen.[52] In the context of the funerary stelae, the stone-working trades assume a special role, since in their case, the material of the monument corresponded to the material they used in their profession.

Examples in which busts of other people are shown as workpieces make it clear that such a representation could be ambiguous without an explanatory inscription.[53] Amabilis is not portrayed like other craftsmen, but here the focus is specifically directed to the special design, the creative potential and his spe-

49 Very few inscriptions mention the profession of the deceased even if it was shown in the imagery of the monument: Béal 2000, 162; 182 fig. 9. In Italy, the profession is mentioned only either in the inscription or in the relief, but never in both: Groen-Vallinga 2022, 23.

50 See Béal 2000, 180–181 fig. 5–8. Most of the approximately 300 funerary inscriptions from Bordeaux are published in CIL XIII as well as in IRB and ILA.

51 Charles Picard even suspected that Amandus did not have Amabilis depicted here, but that he showed his own image as he was creating the monument for his brother: Picard 1961, 100. However, I consider this more than unlikely in the context outlined above. See also: Duval 1962, 361.

52 On the other hand, many important aspects of the professional life, self-representation and social identity were not touched on in funerary monuments. Flohr 2017 discusses the negotiation of occupational identities in the shop environment.

53 As in two examples in Rome: Villa Albani, inv. 984 and Musei Vaticani, Galleria die Candelabri, inv. 2671: Zimmer 1982, 156–158 cat. 79 and 80.

cific relationship to the genre and material of the funerary monuments. This, as well as the comparatively high quality of the work, could indicate a desire to set himself apart from his colleagues through the special staging of his own work and the freer use of design options. At the same time, the image is essentially focused on one statement: his skills, his wit and his expertise as a sculptor. Other sculptors or the patrons of funerary monuments in Gaul and other areas of the Roman empire and especially in Italy usually chose variants in which they themselves and a workpiece were depicted on the same image layer and in which the statements could be further expanded by adding furnishings or actions of other figures shown in the composition. In Amabilis' monument, on the other hand, physical exertion and strength are a distinct focus of the image.[54]

A second aspect is the visual relationship between the viewer and the tombstone. As Michael Squire and Susanne Turner have pointed out once again, the process of memorializing the deceased in their monuments takes place through the design of the visual relationship between the funerary monument, the viewer and the deceased.[55] On the one hand, the representation of the person creates their presence and closeness—enhanced by portrait-like features as well as by the reference to certain activities or roles. For the majority of Gallo-Roman reliefs, as in other places, the frontal orientation of the deceased's image was an important functional element, as it also made direct eye contact with the viewer possible. On the other hand, the setting in stone causes a distancing that was reinforced by the juxtaposition and uniformity among the many funerary monuments of a *necropolis*. So, even if Amabilis created a peculiar composition, its perception was moderated by the presence of the surrounding tombstones.

In some of the pieces discussed here, attention was not generated by the gaze to be returned. Instead, a different approach was chosen and the focus was directed towards the movement and the tension created in certain moments of the craft activities. For the viewer, this resulted in particularly interesting poses and gestures and, if successful, even apparent movement. The stele of Maternianus thus appears self-contained and independent of the viewer. The inner realm of the image and the outer realm of the living do not mix here.

The layering of the image in Amabilis' case also blurs the boundaries between the viewer's space and the internal space of the image. Through the plausibly depicted potential for movement and the use of the grave stele as

54 Both aspects, *labor* and *ars*, are therefore present in this piece: cf. Tran 2014, 197–198.

55 Turner 2016, 154–155 and Squire 2016, 9.

a workpiece, the depicted sculptor becomes an intermediate instance with a special capacity for interaction between the viewer and the image. At the same time, the viewer is involved to a greater degree and challenged to assign an interpretation to this image that is appropriate to the context, precisely because it initially appears paradoxical and incomplete. A statement is made about the deceased, the sculptor Amabilis, but the viewer is also invited to look at the stele itself as a medium for such statements. The materiality explicitly comes to the fore in contrast to the mediality and thus puts up for discussion the way in which statements about the deceased are made and fixed.[56]

The comparison of the stele of Amabilis with other stelae from Bordeaux and other representations of Gallo-Roman craftsmen has made clear that this stele was not created in a vacuum, but was anchored in local and regional conventions. Some core statements and the formal framework were adopted and made it approachable and understandable. On the other hand, Amabilis sets his monument apart from the usual representations through the intensification and the characteristics described. It is precisely through this treatment of conventions, however, that the stele reveals itself as a testimony to the fact that the language of images was reflected upon and theorized in syntax and semantics. With a view to the other funerary monuments in Bordeaux, however, it remains to be asked why others did not subsequently choose such a shrewd and innovative form of monument and what the strengths of the conventional forms were: the ease of reading, the comparability but also the creation of a distance were obviously aspects that were important and constitutive for the monuments. Images such as the stele presented here, which explicitly refer to certain aspects of their genre, draw the eye to this conformity and the limits of creativity within the field of funerary art.

Bibliography

Baltzer, M. (1983). Die Alltagsdarstellungen der treverischen Grabdenkmäler. Untersuchungen zur Chronologie, Typologie und Komposition, *Trierer Zeitschrift für Geschichte und Kunst des Trierer Landes und seiner Nachbargebiete* 46, pp. 7–110.

Barraud, D. and Caillabet-Duloum, G. (2004), Burdigala. Bilan de deux siècles de recherches et decouvertes recentes à Bordeaux. In: J. Ruiz de Arbulo, ed., *Simulacra*

56 Turner 2016, 146–147, where she discusses how the word *sema* inscribed into the Phrasikleia Kore creates not only a distance between the image and the depicted deceased person but also ascribes a specific role to the viewer and reader.

Romae. Roma y las capitales provinciales del Occidente europeo. Estudios Arqueológicos (Tarragona 12–14, diciembre de 2002). Tarragona, pp. 239–271.

Barraud, D., Fabioux M., Vernou, C., Buisson, J.-F. and Girardy-Caillat, C. (1992). Origine et développement topographique des agglomeration: Agen, Angoulême, Bordeaux, Périgeux, Poitiers, Saintes. In: L. Maurin, ed., *Villes et Agglomérations urbaines antiques du Sue-Ouest de la Gaule. Deuxième colloque Aquitania: Bordeaux, 13–15 septembre 1990*. Bordeaux, pp. 199–209.

Barraud, D. and Sireix, C. (2010). Burdigala à la lumière des nouvelles découvertes. In: R. González Villaescusa, ed., *Simulacra Romae II. Rome, les capitales de province (capita prouinciarum) et la création d'un espace commun européen. Une approche archéologique. Actes du colloque tenu à Reims, les 19, 20 et 21 novembre 2008*. Reims, pp. 161–170.

Béal, J.-C. (2000). La dignité des artisans. Les images d'artisans sur les monuments funéraires de Gaule romaine, *Dialogues d'histoire ancienne* 26, pp. 149–182.

Braemer, F. (1959). *Les stèles funéraires à personnages de Bordeaux Ier–IIIe siècles*. Paris.

Caruel, M.-S. (2016). L'attitude des artisans gallo-romains à l'égard du travail manuel. Étude de l'iconographie lapidaire funéraire, *Kentron. Revue pluridisciplinaire du monde antique* 32, pp. 113–134.

Chevallier, R. (1997). Perspectives de recherche sur les scènes de métiers (Gaule Cisalpine et Transalpine). *Archeologia Classica* 49, pp. 47–63.

Duval, P.-M. (1964). Chronique gallo-romaine, *Revue des Études Anciennes* 64, pp. 326–377.

Espérandieu, E. (1908). *Recueil général des bas-reliefs de la Gaule Romaine II. Aquitaine*. Paris.

Etienne, R. (1962). *Bordeaux Antique, Histoire de Bordeaux I*. Bordeaux.

Flohr, M. (2013). The World of the Fullo: Work, Economy, and Society in Roman Italy. Oxford.

Flohr, M. (2017). Constructing Occupational Identities in the Roman World. In: K. Verboven and C. Laes, eds., *Work, Labor, and Professions in the Roman World. Impact of Empire 23*. Leiden, 147–172.

Freigang, Y. (1997). Die Grabmäler der gallo-römischen Kultur im Moselland. Studien zur Selbstdarstellung einer Gesellschaft. *JRGZM* 44, pp. 277–383.

Frézouls, E. (1990). Gallien und römisches Germanien. In: F. Vittinghoff, ed., *Europäische Wirtschafts- und Sozialgeschichte in der römischen Kaiserzeit 1*. Stuttgart, pp. 429–510.

Gerber, F. (2020). Les ports romains dans les Trois Gaules Entre Atlantique et eaux intérieures. *Gallia* 77(1), pp. 292–302.

Groen-Vallinga, M. (2022). *Work and Labor in the Cities of Roman Italy*. Liverpool.

Hahl, L. (1937). *Zur Stilentwicklung der Provinzialrömischen Plastik in Germanien und Gallien*. Darmstadt.

Haug, A. (2021). Introduction: Principles of Décor. In: A. Haug and M.T. Lauritsen, eds., *Principles of Decoration in the Roman World, Decorative Principles in Late Republican and Early Imperial Italy* (*Decor*) 2. Berlin–Boston, pp. 1–14.

Hölscher, T. (2012). 'Präsentativer Stil' im System der römischen Kunst. In: F. de Angelis, J.-A. Dickmann, F. Pirson and R. von den Hoff, eds., *Kunst von unten? Stil und Gesellschaft in der antiken Welt von der 'arte plebea' bis heute. Internationales Kolloquium anlässlich des 70. Geburtstages von Paul Zanker, Rom Villa Massimo, 8.–9. Juni 2007, Palilia 27*. Wiesbaden, pp. 27–58.

ILA: Maurin, L., Navarro Caballero, M., Barraud, D., Brial, C. and Zieglé, A. (2010). *Inscriptions latines d'Aquitaine. Bordeaux*. Paris.

IRB: Jullian, C. (1887). *Inscriptions Romaines de Bordeaux*. Bordeaux.

Jullian, C. (1895). *Histoire de Bordeaux depuis les origines jusqu'en 1895*. Bordeaux.

Kajanto, I. (1965). *The Latin Cognomina*. Rome.

Langner, M. (2001). Szenen aus Handwerk und Handel auf gallo-römischen Grabmälern. *JdI* 116, pp. 299–356.

Larsson Lovén, L. (2007). Male and Female Work in Roman and Gallo-Roman Funerary Iconography. In: E. Hartmann, U. Hertmann and K. Pietzner, eds., *Geschlechterdefinitionen und Geschlechtergrenzen in der Antike*. Stuttgart, pp. 169–186.

Laubry, N. (2021). *Tombeaux et épitaphes de Lyonnaise*. Paris.

Lorenz, K. (2016). *Ancient Mythological Images and Their Interpretation. An Introduction to Iconology, Semiotics and Image Studies on Classical Art History*. Cambridge.

Migeon, W. and Zieglé, A. (2003). Nouveaus blocs inscrits ou décorés dans le rempart antique de Bordeaux. *Aquitania* 19, pp. 291–299.

Opdenhoff, F. (2021). Die Stadt als beschriebener Raum: Die Beispiele Pompeji und Herculaneum, Materiale Textkulturen 33. Berlin–Boston.

Pannoux, S. (1985). La représentation du travail: Récit et image sur les monuments funéraires des Médiomatriques. *Dialogues d'histoire ancienne* 11, pp. 293–328.

Picard, C. (1961). Sur une famille de sculpteurs d'Aquitaine, d'après une stèle funéraire du Musée de Bordeaux. *RA* 77(2), pp. 96–100.

Picard, C. (1963). Circonscription de Paris (région sud). *Gallia* 21, pp. 377–422.

Reddé, M. (1978). Les scènes de métier dans la sculpture funéraire gallo-romaine. *Gallia* 36(1), pp. 43–63.

Rose, H. (2007). Vom Ruhm des Berufs: Darstellungen von Händlern und Handwerkern auf römischen Grabreliefs in Metz. In: F. Hölscher and T. Hölscher, eds., *Römische Bilderwelten. von der Wirklichkeit zum Bild und zurück. Kolloquium der Gerda Henkel Stiftung am Deutschen Archäologischen Institut Rom, 15.–17. März 2004, Archäologie und Geschichte 12*. Heidelberg, pp. 145–179.

Schmidts, T. (2005). Die Welt der Arbeit. Handwerker und Händler. In: S. Schmidt, ed., *Imperium Romanum. Roms Provinzen an Neckar, Rhein und Donau. Begleitband zur*

Ausstellung des Landes Baden-Württemberg im Kunstgebäude Stuttgart vom 1. Oktober 2005 bis 8. Januar 2006. Darmstadt.

Solin, H. and Salomies, O. (1994). *Repertorium nominum gentilium et cognominum Latinorum. Editio nova addendis corrigendisque augmentata, Alpha–Omega Reihe A 80*. Hildesheim.

Squire, M. (2016). Introductory Reflections: Making Sense of Ancient Sight. In: M. Squire, ed., *Sight and the Ancient Senses*. London–New York, pp. 1–35.

Tran, N. (2013). Dominus Tabernae: Le statut de travail des artisans et des commerçants de l'occident Romain (Ier siècle av. J.-C. – IIIe siècle ap. J.-C.), BÉFAR 360. Rome.

Turner, S. (2016). Sight and Death: Seeing the Dead through Ancient Eyes. In: M. Squire, ed., *Sight and the Ancient Senses*. London–New York, pp. 143–160.

Zanker, P. (1992). Bürgerliche Selbstdarstellung am Grab im römischen Kaiserreich. In: H.-J. Schalles, H. von Hesberg, and P. Zanker, eds., *Die römische Stadt im 2. Jahrhundert n. Chr.: der Funktionswandel des öffentlichen Raumes. Kolloquium in Xanten vom 2. bis 4. Mai 1990*. Cologne, pp. 339–358.

Zimmer, G. (1982). *Römische Berufsdarstellungen, Archäologische Forschungen 12*. Berlin.

Index Locorum

ABV
- 76, 1 — 318*n*39
- 78, 12 — 318*n*40
- 162.1–2 — 320*n*44
- 217, 11 — 332*n*98
- 348 — 326*n*75

Acr. 806 — 314*n*15

AE 2005, 106 — 184*n*83

Aët
- 2.2.1 (*Stoicorum Veterum Fragmenta* 2.547) — 141*n*36
- 2.22.3 (*Stoicorum Veterum Fragmenta* 2.654) — 142*n*36

AG 16.323 — 135–136

AMS-Fc-1094 — 143*n*43

Anth. Pal.
- 6.258.6 — 219*n*17
- 7.11 — 205*n*44

APHex 1.15 — 138, 140

Apollod.
FGrHist 244 fi49 — 199*n*27

Arist.
[*Ath. Pol.*]
- 7.3–4 — 48
- 13.2 — 23
- 26.3–4 — 303

de An. 412a22 — 65*n*9
Eth. Eud.
- 1220a13–15 — 48
- 1220a22–28 — 48
- 1220a32 — 48
- 1220a38–39 — 49
- 1229a4 — 50
- 1229b34–1230a2 — 49
- 1229b39 — 49
- 1230a1 — 49
- 1252a33 — 55, 58

Eth. Nic.
- 1101b31–1102a10 — 44
- 1101b35 — 44
- 1102a8 — 44, 48
- 1103a26–31 — 57
- 1104a32 — 57
- 1110b33–1111a1 — 42
- 1111a3–5 — 41, 59
- 1111a3–8 — 41*n*4
- 1111a4 — 47
- 1117a31 — 50
- 1117b5 — 50
- 1132a12 — 47*n*9
- 1134b4 — 47
- 1137a1 — 42*n*4
- 1137a16 — 42*n*4
- 1176b27–1177a1 — 45, 57
- 1176b32 — 45
- 1176b35 — 45
- 1277b6 — 47
- 7–8 — 74

Magn. Mor.
- 1193b32–36 — 46
- 1193b36–1194a6 — 47, 50
- 1194a2 — 47

[*Oec.*]
- 1334b29–1336a26 — 51
- 1335a11–22 — 52
- 1335b5–12 — 53
- 1335b8 — 53
- 1335b9 — 53
- 1336a3–5 — 53
- 1336a25 — 51
- 1336a26–39 — 54
- 1336a38 — 54
- 1337b34–1338a1 — 55, 58
- 1337b38 — 55
- 1337b40 — 55
- 1337b42 — 56*n*15
- 1338b13 — 58
- 1338b38–1339a10 — 54
- 1338b41 — 54
- 1339a6 — 54
- 1339a7–8 — 58
- 1339a9 — 54
- 1339a10 — 54

[*Oec.*] (*cont.*)
 1343b15–23 51
 1343b22 51
 1343b3–4 58
Part. an.
 687a20–21 73*n*19
 687a7 69*n*14
Pol.
 1253a1–2 78
 1253a20–26 74*n*21
 1263a11–15 50
 1274b41 44*n*6
 1275a19 44*n*6
 1277a38–b6 41
 1278a7–11 7
 1291b 153*n*7
 1296b 153*n*7
 1328b38–1329a2 7, 339*n*1
 1339a6 43
[*Pr.*] 868b12 50
Rh. 1367b26–36 44*n*7

Arr.
Epict. diss. 3, 26, 7 161*n*45

***ARV*²** **240, 42** 314*n*15

Ath.
 4.157a 122*n*70
 10.432b–c 351*n*59
 12.543c 322*n*53
 13.558d–e 121*n*65, 122*n*75
 13.571e 117*n*47
 13.587b 122*n*70
 157a 122

Athens, Acropolis Museum
 inv. ii, 833 327*n*77

Athens, National Museum
 1.833 327*n*77

Autun, Musée Rolin
 inv. M L 143 380

BAPD
 n°000316 320*n*45
 n°202359 314*n*15
 n°217462 314*n*16
 n°300000 318*n*39
 n°300735 318*n*40
 n°300767 320*n*45
 n°300769 320*n*45
 n°300770 320*n*45
 n°300771 320*n*45
 n°300773–4 320*n*45
 n°301083 327*n*77
 n°301946 326*n*75
 n°301978 334*n*103
 n°302760 332*n*98
 n°310541 320*n*44
 n°310542 320*n*44
 n°310545 318*n*38
 n°330105 327*n*77

BCH **59** 349*n*51

Berlin, Antikensammlung
 F1758 320*n*44
 inv. 3151 side A (BA 300748) 319*n*41

BGU **I 14** 156*n*21
 col. II, 18–19 162*n*45

Bordeaux, Musée d'Aquitaine
 inv. 60.1.82 371, 373–375

British Museum
 inv. 1847,0806.44 318*n*38
 inv. 1888,0601.426 (BA 300737) 319*n*41
 inv. 1898,0716.6 314*n*16

Brussels, Royal Museums of Art and History
 inv. R.388 332*n*98

Callim.
Aet. 1.29–32 201*n*32
Epigr. 27 205*n*42
fr.
 1.10 205*n*42
 1.11 199*n*23
 1.16 205*n*42
 1.39–40 202*n*35

Cass. Dio 69.4.1 90*n*18

Cato
Agr.
2 251*n*43
2.3–4 251*n*43

CEG
819 ii 316*n*32
819 iii 316*n*31

Cic.
Caec.
58 157*n*30
63 157*n*30
Fin. 3.24 140*n*31
Nat. D. 2.150–152 67*n*12
Off. 1.150–151 8, 86*n*9, 157

CIL
4.1136 125*n*88
4.1307 123*n*82
4.1574 116*n*41
4.1751 123*n*82, 124*n*84
4.1784 123*n*82, 124*n*84
4.1969 124*n*84
4.2174 115*n*36
4.2176 116*n*40, 116*n*44
4.2180 115*n*38
4.2184 116*n*43
4.2185 116*n*40
4.2186 116*n*40
4.2187 116*n*40
4.2193 123*n*82, 124*n*83, 124*n*84
4.2201 115*n*39
4.2204 115*n*37
4.2206 115*n*38
4.2208 115*n*39
4.2212 115*n*39
4.2218 116*n*40
4.2219 116*n*40
4.2228 123*n*82, 124*n*83
4.2231 115*n*35
4.2237 115*n*37
4.2239 115*n*39
4.2253 116*n*40
4.2258a 114*n*33, 116*n*42
4.2260 116*n*40
4.2274 116*n*40
4.2279 123*n*82, 124*n*83
4.2450 123*n*82
4.3964 123*n*82, 124*n*85
4.3999 124*n*84
4.4023 124*n*82, 124*n*85
4.4024 124*n*82, 124*n*86
4.4025 124*n*82, 124*n*85, 124*n*86
4.4150 124*n*82
4.4259 124*n*82
4.4277 124*n*82
4.4439 124*n*82
4.4441 124*n*82
4.4592 124*n*82, 124*n*85, 124*n*86
4.4593 124*n*82, 124*n*85
4.5105 124*n*82, 124*n*85
4.5127 124*n*82, 124*n*86
4.5203 124*n*82, 124*n*85
4.5204 124*n*82, 124*n*85
4.5206 124*n*82
4.5213 116*n*41
4.5338a 124*n*82
4.5345 124*n*82, 124*n*85
4.5372 124*n*82
4.5408 124*n*84
4.7068 124*n*82
4.7339 124*n*82
4.7535 97*n*46
4.7764 124*n*82
4.8034 124*n*82
4.8160 124*n*84
4.8185 124*n*84
4.8224 124*n*82
4.8454 124*n*82
4.8465a 124*n*82
4.8483 124*n*82, 124*n*84
4.8511 124*n*82
4.8620 116*n*41
4.8812 124*n*82
4.8939 124*n*82; 124*n*84
4.8940 124*n*82, 124*n*84
4.10078 124*n*82, 124*n*84
6.4352 184*n*84
6.4355 177*n*42
6.4969 178*n*49
6.5201 184*n*84
6.6214 182*n*69, 184*n*80
6.6251 101*n*58
6.6314 174*n*26

CIL (*cont.*)
6.6318 101*n*58
6.6351 176*n*37
6.6355 174*n*25
6.6360 101*n*58
6.6409 174*n*25
6.7290 176*n*38
6.7341 182*n*70
6.7370 174*n*24
6.7380 174*n*24
6.7389 174*n*24
6.7394 174*n*24
6.8943 184*n*84
6.9449 184*n*84
6.16057 184*n*83
6.16166 279*n*54
6.27557 176*n*38
6.33781 184*n*84
10.814 122*n*71
10.1074d 122*n*71
12.2319 83

Clara Rhodos II
p. 190 nº19, l. 15 322*n*58

Cleom.
Cael. 1.5 141*n*36

Columella
Rust.
1.1.2 252
1.1.18 251*n*43
1.2.10 246*n*28
1.8.5 246*n*27
1.8.6 246*n*27
2.1.22 246*n*27
2.2.13 276*n*41
4.27.6 276*n*41
7.8 221*n*22
11.1.30 251*n*43
11.2.44 276*n*41
11.2.52 244*n*24
12.3.6 251*n*43
12.intro.1–10 250*n*42

Dem. 57, 45 163*n*49

Dio Chrys.
Or.
7, 105 162
7, 106 162
7, 114 163*n*49, 164*n*53
7, 119 163*n*50
7, 123 163*n*50
7, 133–134 163*n*50
35, 15 164

Diod. Sic.
Hist. 1.8.9 62*n*1

Diog. Laert.
7.10–12 352*n*66
7.144 (*Stoicorum Veterum Fragmenta* 2.650) 142*n*36

EAM 231 313*n*13

EDCS
12000952 184*n*83
18301014 176*n*38
18600054 182*n*70
18700554 184*n*84
19100955 184*n*84
19100958 177*n*42
19300213 178*n*49
19300258 182*n*69, 184*n*80
19300357 174*n*26
19300394 176*n*37
19300398 174*n*25
19300452 174*n*25

Epicurus
Ep. Men. 131 223

FD III
1:048 344*n*28, 346*n*42
1:049 345*n*32
1:050, l. 5 316*n*31
1:051 316*n*32
1:273 348*n*48
1:299 358*n*102
1:477 344*n*28
2:78 345*n*33, 347*n*42
2:92[3] 345*n*30
3:086 345*n*28
3:124 351*n*59
3:125 344*n*28, 346*n*39
3:125–126 347*n*42
3:126 346*n*39
3:145 348*n*45

FD III (*cont.*)
3:167 352*n*67
3:184 357*n*98
3:215, l. 8–9 315*n*20
3:249 344*n*28, 345*n*30
3:338 352*n*63, 354*n*74
4:177 346*n*39
4:356 344*n*28
4:361 344*n*22
4:362 354*n*75
5:3 346*n*37

Florence, Archaeological Museum
inv. 4209 318*n*39

Fronto
Ep. 4.6.1–2 252

Gal.
De semine
2.5.56–60 142*n*37
198, 6–8 De Lacy (IV, 643 K.) 72*n*17
Foct. Form. 6, 25–30 Nickel (IV, 692–693 K.) 72*n*17
Libr. Propr.
16 K. (140 B-M) 63*n*2
20 K. (143 B-M) 63*n*2
Nat. Fac. II, 38 K. 72*n*17
UP
1.1, 13 H. 65*n*8
1.2 66
1.2, 1,13–16 H. 66
1.2.1.16–18–12, 1–2 H. 66
1.2, 3, 7–24 H., III, 4–5 K. 68
1.2., 3,16 H. 78
1.3 72
1.3, 4, 13–15, 5 H., III, 6–7 K. 71
1.3, 4, 1–6 H., III, 5 K. 69
1.3, 4, 6–13 H., III, 5 K. 70
1.4 73
1.4, 6, 1–4 H. 73*n*18
1.4, 6, 18–22 H.; iv, 9 K. 74*n*22
1.4, 6, 22–25 H., III 9 K. 74
1.5 74
1.5, 8, 21–23 H., III, 10 K. 74
1.8, 14, 23–24 H., III, 20 K. 75*n*23
1.9, 17, 16–17 H., 24 K. 75
1.22 78*n*24
1.22, 23–25 H., III, 80 K. 75*n*23
1.173–179 H., 3.237–242 K. 73*n*20
2.2–4 H. 66
2.11–12 H. 69
2.11–15 H. 67
3.1, 125,16–127, 4 H., III, 171–172 K. 76
3.1–3 H. 67
16.437,11. H.; IV. 346–347 K. 65*n*8
17.451 H., IV, 366 K. 73*n*20

Gell.
NA 6.5.1–5 346*n*38

Hdt. 7.224 41

Hes.
Op.
311 62
312–313 36

Hipp.
Epid. 6, 5.1 72*n*17
Vict. 39 72*n*17

Hom.
Il.
9.185–191 194*n*8
18.372–377 137*n*16
23.469 326*n*71
Od.
1.106–107 195*n*9
1.325–422 195*n*9
2.22 195*n*9
6.62–95 195*n*10
6.250–369 195*n*10
7.112–135 218*n*13
7.114–121 218*n*13
7.122–126 218*n*13

Od. (cont.)
7.124–125 218*n*13
7.127–128 218*n*13
9.237–245 196*n*17
10.220–224 194*n*8
23.182–204 35
23.189 35*n*41
23.193 35*n*41
23.197 35*n*41

Hor.
Epist.
2.1.139 256*n*51
2.1.156–157 91
Epod.
2 214, 224, 225, 226, 227, 228
2.1–2 225
2.1–9 224
2.4 225*n*35
2.9 225*n*35
2.9–10 226
2.9–16 226
2.9–22 226*n*39
2.9–36 226
2.10–48 224
2.11–12 226
2.13 226
2.14 226
2.15 226
2.16 226
2.17–20 226
2.17–22 226
2.23–28 224, 225
2.29–36 226
2.39–48 226
2.45–48 226
2.47–48 226
2.48 225*n*35, 227*n*41
2.49–60 224
2.61 226
2.61–62 226
2.61–66 224
2.63–64 226
2.65 226
2.65–66 224*n*35
2.67 224
2.67–70 224, 228

Hymn. Hom. Heph. 20.5–8 36*n*43

Hymn. Hom. Heracles 15.9 36*n*43

I.Ephesos 202 353*n*69

I.Iasos 153 349*n*53

I.Priene 69 349*n*53

IC
I v 53 350*n*56
I vi 2 350*n*56
I viii 11 350*n*56
I xix 2 350*n*56
I xxii 4C 334*n*75, 355*n*85
I xxiv 1 350*n*56
II iii 2 350*n*56
II iii 3 354*n*75
III iii 2 350*n*56

ID
1497 347*n*44
1506 348*n*48
1512 349*n*55

IDélos
1648 323*n*58
1649 323*n*58
2125, l. 8–9 323*n*59
9 316*n*27

IEph. 111 320*n*49

IG
Bulg I^2 307 353*n*72
I^3 1018 326*n*74
I^3 506 313*n*8
II^2 374 354*n*75
II^2 1006 352*n*62, 352*n*63, 353*n*70
II^2 1008 353*n*70
II^2 1009 353*n*70
II^2 1011 353*n*70
II^2 1028 352*n*63, 353*n*70
II^2 1028–1030 352*n*63
II^2 1029 353*n*70

IG (*cont.*)
II^2 1039 352*n*63
II^2 2726 314*n*14
II^2 3864 314*n*18
II^2 8883 334*n*105
II^3 1 436 346*n*37
II^3 1 929 344*n*22
II^3 1 1005, l. 14 315*n*20
II^3 4 513 (*IRham* 120) 313*n*12
IV 745 322*n*57
V 1 1145 346*n*37
V 2 118 346*n*37
VII 2849 352*n*64
VII 3225 326*n*70
IX 1 104 334*n*75
IX 1^2 1 181 315*n*19
IX 1^2 2 209 3354*n*75, 359*n*109
IX 1^2 3 750 354*n*75, 354*n*77, 355*n*80
IX 2 62 348*n*45
IX 2 63 349*n*51
IX^2 1 1475 358*n*105
IX^2 1 1583 358*n*105
XI 4 514 359*n*108
XI 4 544 347*n*43
XI 4 563 358*n*102
XI 4 613 352*n*67
XI 4 697 351*n*59
XI 4 744 344*n*22
XI 4 1038 358*n*102
XI 4 1130 358*n*102
XI 4 1190 358*n*102
XII 1 43, l. 25–26 330*n*88
XII 1 47, l. 25–26 330*n*88
XII 1 66, l. 11–12 330*n*88
XII 1 103, l. 4–5 330*n*90
XII 1 846, l. 11–12 330*n*88
XII 1 855, l. 3 320*n*48
XII 1 1032 354*n*76, 359*n*109
XII 3 103 329*n*86
XII 4 1:030 354*n*75, 355*n*82
XII 4 1:101 354*n*75
XII 4 1:108 356*n*93
XII 4 1:109 354*n*75, 354*n*77, 354*n*78, 356*n*90, 359*n*109
XII 4 1:113 354*n*75, 354*n*77, 356*n*93
XII 4 1:114 356*n*93
XII 4 1:171 355*n*80
XII 4 1:247 354*n*79, 355*n*80
XII 4 1:248 354*n*79
XII 4 1:302 357*n*95
XII 4 2:0452 346*n*37
XII 4 2:1178 356*n*93
XII 5 216 326*n*73
XII 5 482 344*n*22, 345*n*29
XII 5 719 345*n*31
XII 5 812 348*n*45
XII 5 824 345*n*41, 354*n*75, 359*n*109
XII 6 1:012 354*n*75, 354*n*79, 355*n*82
XII 6 1:056 346*n*39
XII 6 1:128 352*n*63, 352*n*65
XII 6 1:151 354*n*71
XII 6 1:285 351*n*60
XII 7 231 354*n*75
XII 9 207 347*n*41
XII 9 234 352*n*63
XII 9 235 352*n*63
XII Suppl. 248 353*n*71
XII Suppl. 249 356*n*89
XII Suppl. 400 346*n*37

IK Perge **12** 345*n*31, 354*n*75, 355*n*86, 355*n*88

Inscr.Perg. **I 221** 313*n*11

IOropos
25 346*n*38
370 353*n*73
371, l. 5–6 320*n*47
383 320*n*47

IoSPE **I^2 344** 350*n*58

IScM
I 26 355*n*80
I 65 359*n*94

Isid.
Nat. 12.7.16 249*n*38

I.Thespiai **29** 353*n*73

IvO
259 328*n*78
396 314*n*17
635 320*n*49

J. Paul Getty Museum
inv. 80.AE.99.3 327*n*76
inv. 96.AA.40 102

Lindos II
42, l. 2–3 320*n*48
103, l. 22 320*n*47
129, IX 330*n*90
131c l. 5 330*n*90
132, l. 6 330*n*90
165 330*n*91
197g 330*n*878
232, l. 8 329*n*87
234, l. 8 329*n*97
235, l. 1 329*n*87
236, l. 6 329*n*87
246 l. 10–11 330*n*88
281, l. 18–19 330*n*88
281b, l. 19–20 322*n*58
293c, l. 41 324*n*65
696a, l. 56 320*n*48
696a, l. 7 320*n*48
702, l. 4 324*n*65

Liv. 9.46.5 239

Luc.
Dial. meret.
6:292–293 120*n*60
6:292–294 122*n*74
6:293 120*n*63
6:294 120*n*61, 120*n*62
7:297 121*n*64
8:299 120*n*58
8:300 120*n*59
9:301–302 118*n*51, 122*n*73
9:302 118*n*52
11 119*n*55
13:317 119*n*56
Eun. 3 160*n*41
Merc. Cond.
4 159
7 159*n*36
Sat. 5–9 86

Lyons, Musée des Beaux-Arts
inv. E 387 326*n*75, 327

Men.
Thais F163 KA 121*n*68, 122*n*77

Metropolitan Museum of Art
inv. 31.11.4 318*n*40, 319

Metz, Musée de la Cour d'Or
inv. 75.38.66 378–379

Munich, Antikensammlungen
inv. 9413 327*n*76

Naples, MANN
inv. 4885 96
inv. 6011 95
inv. 9018 100

***NIvO* 65** 321*n*51

Ov.
Met. 10.243–297 87*n*11

Oxford, Ashmolean Museum
inv. 189 334*n*103

***P.Col.* X 255** 248*n*33

***P.Fay.* 91** 164*n*51

***P.Lond.Wasser* 65–147** 162*n*45

P.Oxy.
XIV 1631, 8–14 162*n*45
XLVII 3354 162*n*45
L 3536 138, 140, 142, 146

***P.PragVarcl* II 1 (= *SB* VI 9406), 245–270** 156*n*21

***P.Ross.Georg.* V 60** 154*n*16

Pallad.
1.6.1 251*n*45
8.1 244*n*24

Paus.
1.8.4 320*n*48
4.31 358*n*106
4.31.6–10 358*n*105
5.24.5 320*n*48, 320*n*49
6.3.4 320*n*49
6.7.1 320*n*48
6.10.4 321*n*50
6.20.14 328*n*82
9.12.4 320*n*48

Petron.
Sat. 30.3–4 240*n*13

Philostr.
VS 1, 7, 2 161*n*45

Pl.
Alc.
130 65*n*9
130c6 65*n*9
I 131b 27*n*13
Ap.
21b–c 32
22d1 33
22a 27
22c–d 32
Chrm.
164d 31
165c–166b 32
Grg.
491a 32
512c–d 6 339*n*1
La. 190c4 29*n*22
Leg.
631c–d 69*n*13
644 27*n*13
Meno 91c–e 34
Phdr. 258e–259d 201*n*32
Plt.
288e 291*n*4
310b10–311c6 51
320c–323a 62*n*1
329c 69*n*13
Resp.
331e 31*n*27
332c 31
334a 34*n*38
369e 27*n*14
410b 27*n*14
428a 69*n*13
430e–431d 69*n*13
495c 26
495d 26
495e 26
496a 26
535d 27
590c 27*n*13
Symp. 203a7 27*n*13
Ti.
28a–b 64*n*5
28a 142*n*37

Plaut.
Amph.
750–752 126*n*96
959–961 126*n*96
Cas. 585–586 119*n*55
Men.
193 121*n*66, 122*n*76
357–359 119*n*57
370–372 119*n*57
Mostell. 296–297 118*n*50
Truculentus
238–239 121*n*63
572–574 121*n*66

Plin.
Ep. 2.17 245
HN
14.26 249*n*39
18.31 251*n*43
33.31 125*n*92
34–36 83
33.55 330*n*92
34.55 94*n*35
35.7 88
35.36.1 322*n*54
35.116–117 88
35.120 89
35.146 320*n*48
35.147–148 98*n*52
36.2.5 92*n*27
36.11 315*n*26, 321*n*52
36.11–12 316*n*29
36.189–199 133
36.193 133*n*6, 135
36.194 133*n*6

HN (*cont.*)
36.196 134
36.197 134
36.200 134
36.202 135*n*10
36.33–43 84*n*4

Plut.
Moralia 3 346*n*38
Per.
2.1 87*n*10
12.6–7 290
Pomp. 2.3 118*n*53
Sol. 24.4 296*n*22

Polyb.
3.48.6 350*n*57
5.88 352*n*68
12.26a.3 350*n*57
12.26a.4 350*n*57
12.27.4 350*n*57
13. 4–5 358*n*103
13.4.4 350*n*57
16.14.3 350*n*57
31.31.1 353*n*68

Pompeii
SAP inv. 21631 99

Quint.
Inst. 12.1.1 35*n*40

[Quint]
Decl. 14–15 125*n*94

Rhodiaka **I, 7, l. 21–22** 322*n*58

Scholia in Theocritum
10.41 199*n*27
10.42 199*n*27

SEG
15:517 196*n*18
23:161, l. 29–30 334*n*105
28:534 351*n*60
33:672 355*n*82
39:391 322*n*55
39:489 324*n*66
39:764 322*n*56
41:332 358*n*105
41:651 320*n*48
48:545 321*n*51
49:423 358*n*105
51:934 354*n*75
54:452 358*n*105
54:749 356*n*91
58:814, IV l. 4–5 330*n*90

Sen.
Ben. 3, 22, 2 158*n*34
Controv.
2.4.1 119*n*54
2.4.3 119*n*55
Ep. 90.31 121*n*3

Sens, Musées de Sens
inv. J 79 383
inv. J 133 386
inv. J 128 and J 129 387

Sophron fr. 10 K–A 203*n*38

Split, Archaeological Museum
inv. AMS-FC-1094 143

SPP **XX 85** 154*n*15

Stat.
Silv.
2.1 124*n*87
2.1.56–59 126*n*97
2.6.52–53 126*n*98
4.3 142*n*40
5.5 124*n*87

Str. 17.1.6 358*n*101

Suet.
Gram.
3, 5 160*n*38
7, 1 160*n*38

Suppl. Epigr. Rhod. **38, l. 8**
317

Syll.^{3}
515 315*n*21
577 352*n*68

Syll.[3] (*cont.*)
578 352*n*68
672 352*n*68
682 358*n*104
689 344*n*28
703 345*n*32
737 345*n*29, 345*n*30

Tac.
Ann. 15.42 89*n*17

Tatianus
Ad Gr. 19, 1 160

Ter.
Eun.
193–196 118*n*49
193–196 122*n*72
Haut.
130 127*n*99
142–144 127*n*100
124–127 126*n*95
Hec.
858–860 119*n*55
86–87 118*n*49
94–96 118*n*49

Theocr.
Epigr. 8 207*n*48
Id.
1 194*n*5, 195, 196, 197
1.1 199*n*23
1.12–14 196
1.15–16 206
1.19–63 197
1.57–58 197*n*19
1.65 199*n*23
1.95–98 195*n*12
1.138–139 195*n*12
1.145 199*n*23
1.148 199*n*23, 201*n*32
2 206*n*45
3 197*n*20
3–7 194*n*5
4 196*n*17, 197*n*22
4.12–34 196*n*17
5 195, 200, 201
5.45–61 203*n*37
5.62–65 202
5.77 203
5.110–111 200–201
5.136–137 202
5.138–140 202
6 195, 207*n*50
6.1–2 207*n*50
7 195, 196, 197, 217, 220
7.3–4 219
7.7–9 219
7.13–16 218
7.25 219
7.28–29 218
7.31 219
7.33–34 219
7.34 219*n*17
7.65 219
7.86–89 197
7.91–93 195
7.131–147 217–218, 219
7.132 218
7.134 218
7.135–142 220*n*21
7.139 201*n*139
7.143 218
7.144–146 218
7.147 218
7.155–158 219
10 194*n*5, 195, 198, 200*n*29, 201, 205*n*42, 220*n*20
10.2–3 198
10.7 200
10.21–23 198
10.38–41 199
10.56–58 200
11 194*n*5, 196*n*17, 207*n*50, 208*n*52
11.1–18 207*n*50
11.7 208*n*52
11.12–16 195*n*17
11.80–81 207*n*50
13 194*n*5, 207
13.1–4 207*n*50
14 195
14.24–33 195*n*13
15 193*n*2, 203, 203*n*38, 206*n*45, 207, 208*n*52

Id. (*cont.*)
15.19–20 203
15.21–23 206*n*46
15.26 206
15.27–33 207
15.29 206*n*46
15.36–37 204
15.42 206*n*46
15.59 206*n*46
15.69–71 204
15.78–86 204–205
15.145–149 205–206
16 207*n*50
17 207*n*50
28 207
28.3 208
28.12–16 208
28.17–18 208*n*52
28.24–25 207

Thuc.
1.14.3 292*n*7
1.89.3 292*n*7
1.90.3 293*n*10
1.93.6 292*n*8
1.93.7 292*n*7
6.2.1 208*n*52

Tit. Cam. **39, l. 35** 330*n*90

TVind. **11** 155–157, 156*n*21

Ulp.
Dig. 50, 13, 1 161*n*43

Varro
Ling. 7.105 158*n*33
Rust.
1.2.1 242*n*19
1.2.17 221*n*24
1.17.2 157*n*30
1.18 156*n*22
2.11.3–6 221*n*22
2.intro.1–3 256*n*51
3.2.9 101*n*58

Verg.
Culex 72–81 216*n*8
Ecl.
1 220, 220*n*21, 223*n*32, 228, 229
1.1 223*n*32
1.1–6 220–221
1.7–8 221
1.9–10 221
1.12 222*n*27
1.27 221*n*23
1.32 221
1.34 222, 223
1.35 221*n*23
1.37 222
1.39 222
1.40 221*n*23
1.45 221
1.46–48 222
1.52–55 222–223
1.53–55 223
1.56 222
1.69 222*n*24
1.70 221*n*23, 222*n*27
1.71 221*n*23, 222*n*27
1.72 222*n*27
1.73 222*n*27
1.77 222*n*27
1.80–81 220–221
1.81 223
1.83 223*n*32
G.
2.319–320 249*n*38
2.529 223*n*32
3.394–406 221*n*22
4.116–148 227
4.127–128 227
4.128–129 227
4.130 227
4.132 227
4.133 227
4.134 227
4.137 227
4.139–141 227
4.142–143 227

Vitr.
De arch. 1, praef, 2 90*n*18

[Xen.]
Ath. Pol. 1.12 301*n*45

Xen.
Cyr. 8.2.5 291*n*4
Mem.
1.2.37 32*n*30
3.11.10 117
Oec.
IV 2–3 164*n*52
V 3–8 339*n*1
Por. 2.1 301*n*45

General Index

Acarnania 353
Aegean Sea 92, 340
Aegina 346
Aesernia. *See* Isernia
Aetolia 314–315
accountant 161
accounting books 152, 155, 179–180, 185
actors 122, 163, 346–347, 358, 360
Aeschylus 301
Africanus 114–115, 117
Agathon 49
agriculture 8, 13, 16, 25, 151, 156, 163, 193–282
  See also labour, rural
agronomists 238, 246, 247*n*31, 252
Aigion 347
Alexandria 154, 162, 196, 203, 205
  Library 193
  Pharos 358
Alxenor of Naxos, sculptor 325–326
Amabilis, sculptor 18, 370–377, 381, 388–392
Amisos 349
Amphipolis 351
amphora 331
amusement 45–46
Anaxagoras 69
Anaxilas, author 121
anchoring 28, 30, 33, 37
Andragoras of Rhodes, sculptor 322
andreia 2, 30
Andros 347, 353
anêr 155
Anguissola, Anna 135
animal 36, 51–52, 62*n*1, 64, 66, 68, 71–73, 78, 196*n*17, 202–203, 226, 229, 258
animal husbandry 215, 221, 267
Antenor, sculptor 297
Anthologia Planudea 137
anthrôpiskoi 26
Antipatros of Eleutherna, musician 345
anvils 384
Apate 174
Apollo 14, 202*n*33, 314, 348
Apollodorus of Damascus 90*n*18
Apollonius, poet 195
  Argonautica 195
Apollonius of Athens, sculptor 94, 96–97
apprenticeship 80, 180, 276–277, 335
Archermos of Chios, sculptor 297*n*29, 315–316
architects 87, 89, 159, 342–343, 357–358, 360
architecture 86, 90, 92, 96, 264, 292–295. 302
aretê 13, 17, 36, 43, 45, 48, 339–360
Aristeas of Megalopolis, sculptor 314, 329
aristocrats 86, 159, 170, 172–173
  See also elites
Aristodama of Smyrna, poetess 347–348
Aristotle 13, 15, 57, 64, 65*n*7, 69, 73, 164
  Eudemian Ethics 42, 48–49
  Magna Moralia 42, 46, 50
  Nicomachean Ethics 42, 44–46, 48, 50, 59
  Oeconomica 42, 51–55, 57
  Parts of Animals 69*n*14
  Politics 7–8, 41
  Problems 42, 49
Aristys of Aigion, actor 347
ars 158–159, 391*n*54
Artemidorus of Rhodes, sculptor 322–324
artes 156–158
artifex 85*n*8
artisan 7, 26*n*10, 27*n*13, 86, 101–103, 142, 151, 156*n*24, 170, 289, 296, 302
  See also craftsman
artists 154, 158, 256
  Gallic 18
  Greek 17, 84*n*4, 89, 91, 93–94, 97, 102
  images of 98
  Roman 15, 84–103
  signatures 10, 12, 14, 17, 97–99
  See also signatures
Ascia 377–378
Asclepiades of Samos, poet 205, 207
Asia Minor 340, 349
Asklepiades of Perge, doctor 355–356
Asseria 132–133, 142–143, 147
Athanadas of Rhegion, musician 344
Athenaeus 123
Athenio, glassblower 144

Athens 12, 152, 153*n*7, 155*n*17, 162, 389–306, 312, 328, 344, 347, 351–352, 358–359
 Acropolis 289, 292, 294, 296, 297, 300, 303–305, 312, 314
 Academia 352
 Agora 293
 Erechtheum 300
  See also Erechtheum building accounts
 House of Mikion and Menon 293, 299
 Kerameikos 297
 Lyceum 352
 Parthenon 299, 305
 Propylaea 312
 Ptolemaion 352
 Street of the Marble Workers 293, 299–300
 Tholos (Agora) 293–294
athletes 43, 50, 53–54, 256, 360*n*11
athletic contests 50, 94, 195, 237, 256–257, 320
 See also Olympian games
Attalids 313, 329, 353
Attica 293, 296–297
auctioneer 163
audience 16, 27, 29, 33–34, 42, 45, 47, 48, 140, 145, 193–209
Augustus 90, 175*n*32, 238*n*7, 240
aulos-playing 139–140
autarky 158, 160, 162, 227*n*42
autourgos 156
autumn 219, 224, 226–227, 235–237, 243, 245, 247, 249–252, 258–259
Autun 379–380

Badoud, Nathan 323
Baiae 93–94
baking 9, 236, 249, 252, 295, 370*n*11
banausia 27, 58
baths 162*n*45, 257
Bay of Naples 93–94, 97
bee-keeping 215, 223
Belliccus, craftsman 382–384, 388
bellows 143
Belus River, Syria 134
benefaction. *See* euergetism
Benkovac 143
 See also Asseria
Berrendonner, Clara 156
Billault, Alain 215
biography, artists' 15, 84, 88–90, 93
bipedalism 15, 75, 77
blacksmiths 71, 76, 77, 388
Blinkenberg, Christian 330
body 44, 48, 51–52, 54, 58, 58
 labouring 12, 17, 26–27, 43, 62–82, 86, 162
 visual rendering of 244, 248, 376, 379, 382, 384, 388
 weight 256
Boethos of Chalcedon, sculptor 330
Boiotia 315, 325, 349, 352
Borbonus, Dorian 173
Boscoreale 255
 Villa Regina 255
Bosporan kingdom 350
Botromagno 267
Bordeaux 18, 368–377, 392
Bourges 381–382, 384–385
Braemer, François 369
Braudel, Fernand 154
bricks 267
Brindisi
 via dei Cappucini necropolis 278
brothel 15, 109–127
bronze workers 32, 290, 325
bucolic 16, 193–209, 214, 216, 223, 229
builders 32, 75–77, 154, 294
building (craft) 17, 32, 76–77, 152, 289–306
Burford, Allison 299
Burnett, John 47
Byzantion 357

Caesar. *See* C. Iulius Caesar
calendar 236–246
Calliades, sculptor 320
Callimachus 202
 Aetia 202
canon
 artistic 84
 classical 6, 10, 15, 84
capitalism 109
Caroll, Maureen 267
carpenter 35*n*41, 290
Carthage
 Dominus Julius Mosaic 250
Castrensis 115
Cato the Elder 35*n*40, 156*n*22, 226, 238*n*8, 251, 255, 265

Celer, architect 89
centaur 74–75, 77, 253
ceramics 17, 270, 281
Chairestratos of Rhamnous, sculptor 313
Chalcedon 330
Chaleion 347
Charmolas of Rhodes, sculptor 322–324
cheese-making 215, 218, 220–223
cheirotechnai 32–33
cheirourgia 27
Chersonesos (Crimea) 350
childbirth 52
childhood 51–55, 351
children 51–55, 57–58, 276–277, 292, 303, 345, 347
See also labour, child
Chios 315–316, 331
chisel 373
Christian 151, 160
Chrysippus 158*n*34, 162*n*46
Chrysotemis of Argos, sculptor 321
Cicero 11, 86, 92, 158–159, 161
On Duties 8–9, 16, 157, 176
Cimabue 84
circumstances, Aristotle 41–59
citizens 44–45, 48–58, 100–101, 289, 292, 296–299, 301–306, 311–313, 317–318, 321, 323, 330, 335, 248, 252, 356, 390
citizenship 7–9, 17, 297, 303–305, 312–313, 317, 323, 329
civic status 18, 295, 306, 312, 317
civic virtue 339–342, 347, 357, 359
Claudius, emperor 240
claw 66, 68, 73
clay 144, 327
cloak 68, 236, 377, 381–382
clothes 9, 26, 34, 120, 162, 175, 203–205, 245, 256, 294, 375, 385, 388
See also cloak, *cucullus*, *subligaculum*, tunic, *toga*
clothing production 203–209
See also textile production
coachman 180
cobblers. *See* shoemakers
coins 204, 272, 278, 281, 282, 311, 331
Coligny
Lunar calendar 238, 252
collecting, art 91–93
collegia 173–174
colliberti/conliberti 174, 176
coloni 266, 268
columbarium 16, 101, 170–187, 264
Columella 226, 238*n*8, 265
Res Rustica 221*n*22, 246, 250*n*42, 252, 276
Comatas, poet 197, 200–202
commemoration 18, 103, 169–187, 239, 264, 269, 275, 277, 280, 314, 317, 320, 348
commerce 69, 98, 154, 225
common ground 25, 28–29, 33, 35, 36–37
Communio, *verna* 184
competitive advantage 110, 125
Compitalia 249
conservi 174, 176
consumers 4–5, 10–11, 101
consumption 245, 290
conspicuous 174
conviviality 112, 214, 388
cooks 15, 32, 101, 154, 157, 175
coopers 384
copying 15, 91–94
M. Cornelius Fronto 253–254
countryside 2, 13, 153, 193–286
courage 50, 89
courtesan 110*n*3, 117–120, 123
COVID-19 pandemic 1
craftsman 6, 9, 10, 12, 13, 17–18, 23, 34–35, 70, 85–86, 142, 153*n*7, 154, 156–158, 170, 273, 294–300, 303–305, 311–335, 368–392
See also artisan
Crete 45, 132, 136, 349
crisis 341, 343, 354, 357
See also COVID-19 pandemic
Critias 31–32, 44*n*6
Critonides of Paros, sculptor 326
Croatia 143
cucullus 248, 250
Cupid 98, 386*n*41
P. Curtilius Agatus, silversmith 101
Curtius, Ernst 216
customer 12, 109, 112, 113, 124, 156–158, 160
Cynicism 161, 162

Daedalos of Sicyon, sculptor 320
Damophon of Messene, sculptor 358–359
Davis, Gregson 215, 223
day-labourer 154
See also labour, wage; wage-earners
decor 369

Delos 315, 347–348, 359
Delphi 28, 298, 314–316, 344–345, 347–348, 352–354, 358
deme 305, 313–314
demiurge 63–64, 69*n*13, 73, 141–142, 146
Demoteles of Andros, poet 347
demotic (label) 12, 17, 295, 312–317
Dexamenos of Chios, gem-cutter 331
didaskaloi 353
dikaion 43, 46
Dio Chrysostom 151, 161*n*45
 Orations 164
Diocletian, emperor
 Edict on Maximum Prices 155
Diodotus, freedman of Taurus 184
Diomedes, shoemaker 174
Dio of Prusa
 Euboea 162
Dioskourides of Samos, mosaicist 97
Dioskourides of Tarsos, poet 349
Dis Manibus 372, 376, 389
dispensator 179
distaff 207–209
division of labour. *See* labour, division of
doctors 11, 15, 32, 34–35, 37, 101, 154, 158–159, 161, 342–343, 354–357, 360
 female 175
dolia 255, 267, 279
Domitian, emperor 161*n*45
domus 16, 171–187, 237–239, 241–242, 245, 250–251
donkey-driver 154
donkeys 79*n*26, 201*n*32, 247, 250
 milling 247, 250
doorkeeper 161
Dorcas 118
Doryphoros 93–97
Dowling, Emma 112
Dreizehnter, Alois 58
dyers 154, 290
Dymas of Iasos, poet 349

eco-criticism 16, 214–215, 217, 228
economic thinking 10–11, 291
education 27, 34, 51, 54, 78, 86, 339, 341–343, 345, 351–352, 360
educator. *See* teacher
Edwards, Catherine 121
Egypt 92, 131, 134, 155*n*17, 163*n*51
Eleutherna 345
elites 6, 9–10, 12–17, 23–25, 27, 36, 41, 84, 86–87, 91–93, 97, 101, 122, 133, 146–147, 193, 196, 206, 209, 240, 249–250, 255, 257–258, 300
 households 14, 160, 170–187, 246
 perspective 36, 103, 146, 238, 245
embroidery 204–205
emotional labour. *See* labour, emotional
emperors
 Roman 90, 93
 Julio-Claudian 158, 184
Endoios, sculptor 297
energeia 73–74
entertainment 69
 See also leisure, relaxation; rest; idleness
ephebes 351–353
Ephesos 321, 349, 353
Ephippus 117
epic 36, 137, 194–195, 348–349
Epicharmus of Soloi, sculptor 329–330
Epictetus 163
Epicurus, epicurean thought 215–216, 223
Epidaurus 298
epigram 137, 315–317, 321–322, 325
epigraphy 9, 97, 103, 109, 172–179, 186–187, 268, 339–360
Epikrates of Byzantion, architect 357
Epikrates of Herakleia, philosopher 352
epitaph 10, 169–187, 264, 280, 379*n*13
Epstein, Shimon 296
Erechtheum building accounts 289, 295, 298
 See also Athens, Erechteum
ergatês 155
ergasia 41, 44, 220*n*20
ergazomai 44
ergon 16, 203, 320, 342, 354
Ergoteles, potter 320
Ergotimos, potter 318–319, 325, 331
Eryximachus, doctor 37
Espérandieu, Émile 369–370
essential work 1
estate
 agricultural 153–156, 161, 246, 250, 251, 265
 imperial 17, 253, 266, 279
Ethiopia 134
ethnic (label) 17, 312–317, 324, 329, 331

Eucheiros, potter 318
eudaimonia 43–45, 223, 227
Euelthon, teacher 353
euergetism 17, 339
eunoia 347, 349, 351*n*50, 353, 357
eusebeia 14, 344, 347, 349
Eutelidas of Argos, sculptor 321
everyday 3, 13, 96, 171, 193, 388
exaleiptron 326–327
exercise 53–55, 57
exertion 3, 27, 43, 54, 56, 62, 78, 255–256, 388, 391
expertise 30, 251–252, 326, 328, 331, 341, 343, 345, 355–356, 359–360, 370, 391

faber 85*n*8
faenerator 224–228
Fabia, mistress 115
Fabius Pictor 87
'famelly' 179–180
familia 101, 170–171, 173, 179–180, 182, 14
  rustica 185
  urbana 185
family 171–187
Famulus, painter 89
farmer 75, 151
farming. *See* agriculture
fasti 238–239
Fasti Antiates Maiores 239
Felix 116
Ferrara 143*n*42, 144
Finley, M.I. 6, 9–10, 12
fire 133–137, 140–141, 144, 146
fishermen 193, 300
Flora, lover of Pompey 118
Flory, Marleen 180
flute-player 163
  See also aulos-player
Foligno
  Santa Maria in Campis necropolis 278
foreigners 17, 102, 113, 295–300, 305, 316–317, 356–357
  See also immigrants
foremen 155, 293
food-seller 300
footservant 177, 180
freedmen 93, 102, 170–187, 264
Fronto. *See* M. Cornelius Fronto
fullers/fulling 3, 9, 15, 32, 300, 385–386
M. Fulvius Nobilior 239
funerary monuments 97, 100, 173, 175, 177–178, 186–187, 297, 334, 368–392
funerary relief. *See* sculpture, funerary
furnace 137, 139–140, 141*n*32, 142–144

Galen 12, 15, 62–79, 142*n*37
  Affections and Errors 78
  Avoiding Distress 78*n*25
  Character Traits 78
  Function of the Parts of the Body 15, 63–79
  On my Own Books 63*n*2
  That the Capacities of the Soul Follow the Mixtures of the Body 64*n*4
Gallia Narbonensis 234
  See also Gaul
gardeners 101
gatekeeper 154
Gaul 134, 234–259, 368–392
gemstones 135, 312, 331
gender 175, 179–181, 274–275
genius, artistic 84–85, 89, 91
geometrician 161
Gilmour, Rebecca 275
glass 15, 116, 131–147, 270, 274, 293
  depiction of 245
  liquid 135, 137, 147
  ingots 135
  raw 132, 134, 137
  vessels 270, 274, 278
glassblower 131, 139, 141–147
glassblowing 132–133, 136, 138–144, 146–147
glassmaking 13, 16, 131–147
glassworking 135–136, 142, 146
Glaucias 126
Glaukias of Kallatis, teacher 353
goatherds 193, 195–197, 201, 217–218
gold-working 101*n*56, 290
Gomperz, Theodor 58
graffiti 12, 16, 110, 114–116, 123–124
grain 219, 222, 237, 244, 247, 267
  threshing 219, 252
  winnowing 219
  grinding 237, 247, 250
grammarian 154
grammatici 16, 349, 353
grammatodidaskalos 353
grape-picker 153, 163

grave goods 10, 12, 14, 16–17, 268–282
Gravina in Puglia 265
growth
  bodily 52, 54–55, 57–58
  demographic 153
  economic 301
  urban 153
guarding/guards 153
Gubbio
  Vittorina necropolis 278
Guzzo, Pier 123
gymnasiarch 342, 351–352, 360
gymnasium 27, 256, 343, 351–353, 355

Hadrian 90, 91*n*20
hairdressers 163, 175
Halicarnassos 330
Ham Castle 179
hammer 373, 384
hand 13, 15, 65–79, 245, 320, 352, 373–375, 378, 384
Hardt, Michael 111
Harris, Edward 152
harvest 52, 217–219, 226, 229, 236, 237, 247, 249–251
  harvesting tools 271–273
harvesters 153, 163
haymakers 153
Hellenistic Poetry 103
Hephaestus/Vulcan 36, 98, 99, 137–138, 141
Hephaistion, mosaicist 332–333
Heracles/Hercules/Herculean 23–24, 27, 32, 36, 41, 157, 252–254, 258
Herakleia 352
Herculanaeum
  Villa of the Papyri 94, 96
herdsmen 16, 139, 153, 196–198, 200, 202–203, 209, 216, 218, 220, 222
Hermopolis 154
Herodes of Priene, poet 349
Herodoros, sculptor 320
Hesiod 25, 63, 79, 151*n*3, 154, 196*n*16
  Works and Days 36, 62, 195
  Theogony 196*n*16
hexameter 138, 141, 199, 252
Historia Augusta 90
historians 350–351
Hoang, Kimberly Kay 113–114
Hochschild, Arlie 110–113, 122–125
Homer 25, 138, 141
  Iliad 137, 194, 195, 197, 326
  Odyssey 194, 195, 197, 215, 241–242
Homeric Hymns 36
homo 155
honorific decrees 339–360
hoofs 66–67
Horace 13, 16, 91, 224–228
horn 67–68, 71, 73
horse 64, 66, 71, 74, 328
horse-racing 256
houses 67–68, 76, 88, 97, 117, 119, 154, 159, 203, 208, 238, 243, 253, 292–293, 295, 298–299
households 110, 154*n*14, 193, 245, 249–250
  See also elite households
  British 172, 178–187
humors 64*n*4
Hunter, Richard 199, 215
hunting 72, 88, 162, 226–227, 244
hydraulos 345
Hymnis 119
Hypate 348

Iaia of Cyzikos, painter 98
Ias 115
Iasos 349
iconography 245, 247, 249, 368–369
iconology 368
identity 170, 193
  civic 17, 18, 317
  local 290, 334
  professional 165, 264–282, 289, 300, 313, 334–335, 343, 348
  religious 17
idleness 36, 79, 202, 206, 251, 290
  See also amusement; leisure; relaxation; rest
immigrants 296, 300, 302
imperial composite 133–134, 145
India 134, 178–179
infames 122
informal economy 172
infrastructure 293, 295, 298, 302
inscriptions 25
  See also epigraphy
  funerary 10, 101, 170
    See also epitaphs
  honorific 10–11
  columbarium 16, 170–187

instinct 72, 78
instruments (musical) 69–70, 290
intelligent design 63
Ion of Samos, poet 316
irrigator 153, 154
Isernia
  Quadrella necropolis 278–279
Istros 357
Italy 94, 97, 134, 153, 154*n*14, 215, 369–370, 377
itinerant professionals. *See* traveling professionals
C. Iulius Caesar 90*n*18, 237
C. Iunius Felix 178

Jefferys, Joyce 172, 179–187
Joshel, Sandra 264
Jowett, Benjamin 50, 56
Julia Felix 125
Julia Livia 184
Julian calendar 237–238, 241
jurists 151, 155–156
justice 46–48

kalaurops 139
Karanika, Andromache 198
kiln 138, 266
kinesthetic 144–145
Kleitias, painter 318–319, 325, 331
Kleochares of Athens, poet 347–348
Kleoitas, inventor 329
Knidos 358
Knossos 349–350
knowledge 5, 9, 11, 15, 23–27, 135, 145, 206, 241, 246–253
  craft 13
  cultural 342
  prototypical 13, 29–33
Koper 143*n*42
Kos (island) 218, 354*n*75, 355*n*83, 356
krater 314, 326
Kritios, sculptor 296–297

labor 4–5, 215, 223, 228–229, 391*n*54
labour
  abstract 150–152
  affective. *See* labour, emotional
  agricultural 16, 150, 214, 234–258, 274–276, 279
  artistic 85, 96. 98, 101, 103, 344–350, 358–359
  children 14, 16, 170–187, 276–278
  commodification 155, 159, 169
  craft 151–152, 156
    See also artisan; craftsman
  creative 84, 87, 89, 142
  definitions 3–4, 169
  division of 8–9, 150–152, 275–276
  domestic 110, 275
  gendered 14, 110, 179, 275–276
  emotional 15, 109–127
  entertainment 156
  hierarchy of 156–158, 160, 324–325
  intellectual 15, 55, 58, 84, 87, 89, 152, 154, 158–161, 350–352
  invisible 170
  manual 4, 10, 14, 41, 87, 146, 156, 158, 163
  mental. *See* labour, intellectual
  poetic 142, 347–350
  rural 12–13, 16, 155*n*17, 215, 218, 225, 264–282
    See also agriculture
  seasonal 17, 153*n*8, 155, 155*n*17, 250
  service 151–153, 163
  sexual 109–127
  skilled 13, 153, 294, 297–298, 303, 304–305, 339, 342, 353
    See also skill
  slave. *See* slaves
  specialized 151–154
    See also labour, division of
  spectacle of 17, 145, 247, 253–258
  unremunerated 170
  unskilled 13, 150–151, 154, 158, 163, 177, 292–294, 304
  urban 13, 155*n*17
  wage 11, 12, 16, 150–165
    See also wage-earning; wage-earners
  women 14, 16, 52, 163–164, 170–187, 203–209, 275
labour. *See* childbirth
Lacedaemonians 45
  See also Sparta
Laches 29
Lamia 348–349
lamp 132, 142–145, 147, 270, 274, 278–279, 281
Lares 237, 249

lawyers 161, 163
lead processing 268
leather-working 273, 278, 290
legal status 101, 264, 268
leisure 1, 4, 6–7, 8, 13, 16, 55–56, 62, 194–195, 200, 206, 214–229
See also *otium*; relaxation; rest
Leonidas 41
liberal arts 161
Licinius, painter 101
Lindos 330
lion 66, 238
Nemean 253
Lis, Catherine and Hugo Soly 23–24, 27, 35, 37
Lissarague, François 311
listening
as labour 16, 193–209
Little master cup 318, 320, 327
Livia, empress 175*n*32, 176, 178–179, 184
See also Columbarium of Livia Augusta
loans
informal 183–184, 187
locatio 160
operis faciendi 157*n*27
operararum 157*n*27
Locris 355
loculi 173, 178
locus amoenus 14, 16, 197, 214–229
logographer 154
logos 70, 72, 74, 78
Loraux, Nicole 41
Lucassen, Jan 24
Lucian of Samosata 86, 160, 163–164
Dialogues of the Courtesans 119–120
On Salaried Posts 159
The Eunuch 160
Lucius, painter 97
Lucretia 14
Lucretius 216
De Rerum Natura 223*n*32, 224
lunar calendar 238, 252
lyre 68–70
Lysander 316
Lysiades, potter 326–327

madeness 16, 133, 145–146
Magnus 115
Mahdia shipwreck 92*n*26
manual labourers. *See* labour, manual; labour, unskilled
manure 236–238, 248, 250
marble-working 101, 293, 299–300
Marcus Aurelius, emperor 160, 253–254, 256, 373*n*21
markets 152–153, 155–156
marmorarii 101
Marvin, Miranda 91, 94
Marx, Karl 5, 16, 151, 163
Grundrisse 150
Capital 150
masons 300
materiality 368, 392
Maternianus, cobbler 384, 388, 391
McClure, Laura 121, 123
medicae 175
medicine 31–32, 56, 342, 354–357
Mediterranean triad 252
Megalopolis 314, 329, 347
Memphis 156
memory 131, 162, 349–350, 391
Menander
Thais 121
Menandros of Tyrreion, teacher 353
Mengs, Anton Raphael 93
Menodotos of Rhodes, sculptor 322–324
menologia rustica 236, 240, 247–249, 251*n*44
Menophantos of Macedon, doctor 355
mercennarii 157–158, 165
merces 157*n*27, 159*n*37, 150
Mercury 98
meretrix 119, 121
Mesomedes of Crete, poet 132, 133*n*5, 135–138, 142, 146*n*49
Messene 358
metal 134*n*7
metalworkers 26, 295
metapoetic 16, 142, 195, 202, 205
metics 12, 17, 295, 297, 299–305
metoikion 301
Metz 377–379
Michelangelo 84
midwife 161, 175
Miletus 207–208, 352*n*68
mime 154, 203, 207, 209
Minerva 89, 98
mise en abyme 373

misthophora 159
mochthos 23–24
Mola 115
money-lending 181–183, 224–228
mosaic 13, 17, 97, 234–259, 332–333
Mouritsen, Henrik 181
Musarium 121
music 56*n*15, 74, 198, 218, 220, 222, 255, 360
musicians 11, 12, 69–70, 159, 342–345, 352
Myrinos of Amisos, poet 349
Myson, potter and vase-painter 314

nature 63–64, 67–74, 78, 214–215, 218, 258
  See also physis
Nearchos, potter 320
necropolis 278–279, 368, 372, 391
Negri, Antonio 111
Neottis 121
Nero, emperor 158
Nesiotes, sculptor 296–297
New Institutional Economics 9–10
Nicepor, sculptor 101
Nikias of Anaplystos, potter 314
Nikon of Megalopolis, actor 347
Nikosthenes, potter 331–332
non-elite 10, 16, 104, 193, 245, 257, 265, 300
Nothus, librarian 174
Novius 255
nundinae 222

obstetricae 175
occupational inscriptions 171, 174–177, 264
occupational title 102*n*59, 185, 186, 264, 280, 370*n*13
occupations. *See* professions
Odysseus 35, 195, 242
Odyssey Landscapes 241–242
olives 251–252
  collecting 163, 237, 250
  pressing 237, 251–252, 256
Olympia 314, 320–321, 328
Olympian games 54
Onasandros of Kos, doctor 356
opera 4–5
operae 155
opifices 8
Orchomenos 325
Orestes of Pergamon, sculptor 313
ornatrices 163
ostler 154
Otis, Eileen 112
otium 214–229

paideia 27, 77, 253, 351–353
painters 12, 84–85, 87–89, 91, 98, 289, 290, 314, 318, 321, 324–326, 328, 331–332, 358*n*104
  Boscotrecase painter 97
  Iphigenia painter 97
  Infancy of Bacchus painter 97
  See also Famulus, painter; Iaia of Cyzikos, painter; Licinius, painter; Lucius, painter
painting 96–97, 241
  landscape 88–89, 241–242
Palestine 134
palestra 94
  See also gymnasium
Palonios of Mende, sculptor 328
Papirius Fabianus 119
Panathenaia 301, 304
Pannychis 118, 122
paradeigmata 339, 341, 352*n*66, 353, 356, 360
Parentalia 237, 249
Parker Pearson, Mike 281
Parmeno 118
Parrhasios of Ephesos, painter 321
pastoralism 267, 278
pastoral poetry 194*n*5, 196*n*22, 203*n*40, 214–217, 220–222, 224, 229
patrons/patronage 91, 93. 94, 159, 170–171, 176, 181, 183
patronymic (label) 317–325
Pausanias 320–321, 328–329
peasants 151*n*3, 156
  See also farmer; labour, rural; agriculture
peculium 221
Pella 332
Penelope 35
penia 6, 24
Penner, Lindsay 175, 184–185
performance
  artistic 344–346
  economic 10
  poetic 5, 16, 193–194, 200–201, 204, 206–207, 347–348
perfumers 157, 163

Pergamon 313, 329, 332–333
Perge 355
Pericles 17, 290–291, 295–296, 300, 302, 303–306
Persian Wars 17
 aftermath 290–295
Petronius 240
Phaedria 117, 122
Pheneos 345
Phidias, sculptor 86
philanthropy. *See* euergetism
Phileas, sculptor 322
Philematium 118
Philergos, sculptor 297
Philippi, battle of 220
Philodemus 216
philoponia 27, 349–350, 359
philosophers 11, 24–25, 35, 63, 66*n*11, 134*n*7, 151–151, 154, 156, 158–161, 351–352
Philostratus 162*n*45
philotimia 345, 349
Philusia, foot servant 176–177
Phoebus the perfumer 116
Phoenicia 134
phronesis 59
Phyles of Halicarnassos, sculptor 330
Phyllis, seamstress 176
physicians. *See* doctors
physis 57–58, 63
Piazza Armerina 258
pimp 163
pipe 139–140
Piraeus 292–293, 296
Plato 24, 33–34, 36, 44*n*6, 63*n*3, 64, 164, 215
 Apology 27, 32
 Charmides 31
 Dialogues 15, 25
 Gorgias 329*n*1
 Laches 30
 Meno 34
 Phaedrus 201*n*32
 Republic 26–27, 31, 34, 50
 Statesman 51
 Symposium 37
 Timaeus 64*n*5
Plautus
 Amphitryon 126–127
 Menaechmi 121
Pliny the Elder 15, 87, 90, 98, 132, 144–146, 265
 Natural History 84, 88–89, 133–135, 142, 316, 320–322
Pliny the Younger 245–246
ploughing 220–222, 226–227, 236, 250–252
Plutarch 87*n*10, 118–119, 290–291, 295–296, 302–305
 Life of Pericles 290
Podgrade 143
poetess 14, 347–350
poets 12, 325, 194–198, 201, 209, 215, 343, 347–350, 360
Polemo 118
polis 7–8, 17, 304, 306, 312, 315–317, 329–330, 340, 343–350, 352–357, 360
Politas of Hypate, poet 348–349
politika/politikos 43, 45, 48–57, 69
Polos of Aegina, actor 346–347, 358
Polybius 350
Polycleitus 86, 94
Polygnota of Thebes, musician 345
polyphony 23–26, 37
Pompeii 15, 385
 I 8,10 98*n*50
 II 3,8 98–99
 II 4,3. *See* Praedia of Julia Felix
 VI 1,10. *See* House of the Surgeon
 Brothel, purpose-built 109, 114–117, 125
 House of Octavius Quartio 97
 House of the Surgeon 98, 100
 Praedia of Julia Felix 125
 Samnite Palestra 94–95
 Triangular Forum 94
Cn. Pompeius Magnus 118
ponos 4–5, 13, 15, 23–24, 27, 41–58, 161, 215, 219
poor 162, 163*n*49
Porcius Latro 118
porter 154
pots. *See* ceramics
potters/potting 9, 12, 17, 98–99, 275, 300, 314–315, 318, 320, 324–326, 382, 388
poverty 163*n*49
prehension 66*n*11, 74
press 251–252, 255, 279
prestige 247, 281–282, 316–317, 320, 328, 333, 341, 343, 345, 349–350
Priapus 98

prices 11, 123–124
Priene 349
Primigenius, slave 176
professions 152, 161, 169, 174–175, 185–187, 264, 273, 315, 339, 342–343, 345–346, 353–357, 369, 375–379, 390
prostitute 110*n*3, 122–123, 163
See also courtesan; sexual labourers
prostitution 109–127
Protagoras 34
prothymia 353
protos euretes 329
prototype effects 29–30, 36
prototypical knowledge 13, 15
Provinces, Roman 152–153, 368, 370
northwestern 370
pruning 222, 226, 270–274, 276, 279
Ptolemies 207, 209, 352, 358
public cryer 163
public lectures 343, 345, 348, 360
Pyrrhus of Athens, sculptor 312–313
Pythia 28

quantification 155, 294
quarry 154*n*11

relaxation 45–46, 56
See also amusement; leisure, rest
reliefs. *See* sculpture
religious festivals 17, 154, 239–241, 343–344, 346
reputation 32, 315–317, 322, 328, 333, 341, 343, 345, 347, 351–352, 355
rest 16, 43, 45
See also relaxation, leisure
Rhamnous 313–314
Rhegion 344
Rhodes 317, 322–323, 329–330
Richlin, Amy 118
road-builders 296
Roman Empire 9, 11, 16, 132, 134, 138, 146, 151, 152, 170–172, 180, 183, 185, 370, 391
Rome 162, 170–187
Columbaria of Vigna Codini 178
Columbarium of Livia Augusta 173, 178
Columbarium of the Statilii 101, 173–175, 181–182
Columbarium of the Stertinii 173
Columbarium of the Volusii 173, 175, 181–182
domus under Santa Maria Maggiore 242–244
Forum Romanum 239
Forum of Trajan 90*n*18
Temple of Heracles 88
Temple of Hercules and the Muses 239
Temple of Salus 88
Temple of Tellus 242
Ross, David 45, 58
rower 155*n*17
Ruffing, Kai 152
rural estate 161, 164
See also farm
Rusticus 114–117

Sabinianus, craftsman 379–380
sailing 77
sailors 75
Saint-Romain-en-Gal 17, 234–259
sakiye 153, 162*n*45
Salmon, John 294–296
Samos 97, 316, 346–347, 351–352
Samothrake 349
sanctuary 313, 328–329, 347, 349, 359
panhellenic 314–315
sand 134
San Felice, Roman villa of 268
Saserna 156*n*22
Saturnalia 245–246
skeletal remains 274–275, 278*n*48
M. Scaurus, Roman aedile 92
Schmidt, Ernst 216
scissors 378
scribe 163
sculpting 87, 293
sculptors 84*n*4, 85–87, 90–91, 94, 101, 289, 296–298, 300, 302, 313–317, 320–325, 328–330, 334, 341–343, 358–359, 375–376, 388–392
See also Polycleitus; Nicepor, sculptor
sculpture 18, 91–96, 293, 295–300, 320–324, 375–376, 389
funerary 14, 18, 100
seasonality 17, 48, 153–155, 224–227, 234–258
Second Sophistic 151–165
secretary 154

Secundus, stuccoist 101
Seleukeia 356
self-representation 368, 390
self-sufficiency 12, 175, 184, 223
Seneca 123, 158, 265
  Controversies 118–119
Sennett, Richard 34
Sens (Gaul) 382–387
sensory 57, 133, 139–140, 145
servants 157, 163, 171, 180–181, 185
Severus, architect 89
sexual labourers 15, 109–127
shepherds 16, 138, 153, 197, 201
Sherwin-White, Susan 218
shipsheds 292
shoe 34, 75, 126, 270, 372, 384, 388
shoemakers/cobblers 15, 32, 34, 75, 77, 174, 384
shops 1, 94*n*38
  See also workshop
  signs 98*n*50, 103
Silvium 266
Sidon 134
signatures 10, 12, 14, 17, 97–99, 296–298, 302, 311–335
skeletal remains 17, 274–275
  age 17, 275
  fractures 14, 275
  gender 17, 275
skill 5–6, 9, 11–12, 14, 17, 34, 72–74, 86. 97, 180
slaves 7, 9, 86, 93, 100, 103, 110, 125–127, 153–154, 157–159, 163–164, 171–187, 203, 207, 239, 244–246, 250, 256, 276*n*40, 289, 295, 300
Slovenia 143*n*42
smallholder 154
  See also farmer; peasant
Small, Alistair 265
Small, Carola 265
Smith, Adam, 150–151
smiths 69–70, 75, 77
  silver 100, 102
    See also Publius Curtilius Agatus
Smyrna 347
Snell, Bruno 216
social networks 172, 181, 183, 186–187
social status 12, 24, 89, 193, 250, 256, 339 388–390
Socrates 13, 15, 25–27, 28*n*18, 29–34, 50, 117, 160*n*39
Solin, Heikki 123
Solon 296
Soly, Hugo. *See* Lis, Catherine
song contest 201–202
Sonikos of Aetolia, sculptor 315
sophists 30, 152, 160, 162
Sostratos of Knidos, architect 358
soul 64–67, 69*n*13, 70–71
sowing 236, 237, 247, 250–251, 259
Spain 134
Sparta 58, 316
specialization 9, 16, 152–153, 209, 291, 302, 335, 343–344
Spicksley, Judith 179, 183
spinning 175, 275
Split 143
Spodnje Škofije 143*n*42, 144
spoudê 349, 353
Spring 224, 226–227, 235–239, 244, 247, 249
Squire, Michael 90*n*19, 391
standard of living 113, 388
Statilii Tauri family 182, 184
T. Statilius Diodotus, freedman 182
Statius 126
statue 68, 91–92, 94–95, 98, 312–316, 323, 325, 328–330, 343, 359–360
status 4, 8, 10, 12, 17–18, 23–24, 36*n*45, 93, 101–102, 113, 127
Sthennis of Olynthos, sculptor 320
stenographer 154
steward 154
Sthennis of Olynthos, sculptor 320
Stoic/Stoicism 16, 71*n*16, 141–142, 146, 152, 157, 161–162, 165, 215, 352
  Middle Stoic 157
stone 290, 298
  imported 92, 294
stoneworking 290, 297–299, 375
storage 236, 267
  vessels 237, 250, 255
students 33, 34, 44, 160, 323–324, 349
Studius, painter 88–89
subligaculum 245
Suetonius 160
  Twelve Caesars 90
Summer 218, 224, 226, 235–237, 239, 243–244

surveyors 159
sutores 174
Syria 132, 134
Syriskos of Chersonesos, historian 350

tabula ansata 174
Tacitus 89
tanners 300
Tapestry 204–207, 209
Tarentum 227
Tarsos 162, 349
taskscape 238
Tatian, philosopher 160
teacher 34, 154, 159–161, 163
teaching. *See* education
technai 29–35, 37, 62*n*1, 68–69, 73, 75, 77, 156
technê 59, 75, 77, 140, 158, 317, 321–322, 354, 356
  See also skill
  technê-knowledge 11, 15, 26, 29–30, 33–34, 36–37
Teisias of Athens, potter 315
teleology 63–64, 66–67, 69–70, 72–73, 78
Telesinos of Athens 358–359
temple 88, 204, 239, 242, 296, 313, 328
tenants 125, 250, 266
Terence
  Heauton Timorumenos 126
M. Terentius Varro 101*n*58, 135, 156–158, 221*n*22, 226, 238*n*8, 242, 256, 265
textile production 9, 175, 203–209, 268, 281*n*64, 295
theatre 163*n*50
Thebes 345
Themistocles 292–293
Theocritus 193–209
  Idylls 14, 16, 193–209
Theodote, sexual labourer 117
Thomas, Yan 155
Thrace 340, 353
Thucydides 292
Thysdrus (El Jem) 243–244, 246
Tiberius, emperor 175*n*32, 240
tile production 266, 268
Titian, Italian painter 84
Tleson, potter 320
toga 89, 100, 249, 250, 378
tombstones 264, 368, 391
  See also funerary monuments
toolmakers 300
tools 12, 14, 17, 35*n*41, 66*n*11, 76–77, 101, 136*n*15, 137, 140–141, 265, 270–281
trade 8, 152, 161, 291, 294, 302, 370
transhumance 267, 275
travelling professionals 295*n*18, 296, 299*n*33, 343, 348–350, 352, 355, 359
Treggiari, Susan 152, 178, 184
Trellus 144
tria nomina 390
Trimalchio 240
Troezenians 52
tunic 100, 244, 247, 248, 372, 377, 381, 382, 385, 388
Turkey 92
  See also Asia Minor
Turner, Suzanne 391
Tyrreion 353

Ulpian, jurist 161
unguentarius 274
upward mobility 110, 120
urban society/urbanization 152–153, 159, 162, 203–208
Ussani, Vincenzo 120
usufructus 221

Vagnari 17, 264–281
value
  civic 17, 339
  economic 197, 281
  ideological 280
  of labour 14, 15, 30, 280, 290
  poetic 197
  social 2, 240, 273
  symbolic 265, 277, 281
value discourse 2–3, 10–11
Varro. *See* M. Terentius Varro
Vasari, Giorgio 15, 84, 98
vase-painters 311–335
Vedusia Auge, freedwoman 182
Venice 154
Vergil 16, 193, 214–217, 220–223, 227–229, 252
  Eclogues 193, 214–217, 220–223, 227–229
  Georgics 224, 227, 252

M. Vergileius Eurysaces, baker 249*n*34, 370*n*11
verna 124, 184
Vernant, Jean-Pierre, 151, 154
Vespasian, emperor 90
veterinarian 154
Via Appia 265
Victor 116
Victoria 115
vicus 266–268, 279
Vienne 13, 234, 249, 255
viewer 92–93, 96, 101, 103, 131, 133, 145–146, 234, 237–239, 241–242, 245, 247–248, 250–253, 257–258, 324, 368–369, 373, 376, 381, 384, 389, 391–392
Villa Magna 253, 255
Vindolanda 156*n*21
vineyards 162*n*45, 222*n*26, 248
  See also viticulture
violence 119, 125
virtue 7–8, 11, 29–30, 33–35, 37, 43 57, 69. n.13, 79, 157
virtus 2
visual culture 97, 368
Vitellius Fructus 182
viticulture 215, 218, 236, 249, 275, 279
  See also vineyards
Vitruvius 89–90
Volturnus River 134
Volusia Rhodine, freedwoman 182
L. Volusius Saturnius 176
Vulcan. *See* Hephaestus

wage labour. *See* labour, wage
wage-earners 157, 159, 161, 164–165
wage-earning 146*n*50, 161–162, 165
wages 155, 161
  hierarchy 155–156
washerwomen 300
weapons 67–68, 72–73, 78*n*24
weavers 77, 175, 290
weaving 14, 68, 76, 139, 205–209, 275, 290
Weeks, Kathi 110
wet-nurse 163, 184, 187
wheat 154, 236
Wijma, Sara 302
wine 153, 154, 218, 226, 267
  Chian 316
  Pteleatic 219
  wine-jars 217–218
  winemaker 153, 219, 251
  wine-pressing 245, 249, 255
  wine press 279
Winter 224, 226–227, 235–237, 243–244, 247–252
Witzke, Serena 123
writing 74–75, 77, 255
women. *See* labor, women; labour, gendered
wool-working 205, 208, 268
work. *See also* labour
  definitions 3 4, 27*n*4, 169
working class 26, 289
workshop 8, 86, 89*n*16, 94, 98, 140, 141*n*32, 144–145, 147, 154, 293, 296, 298–300, 323–326, 332, 335, 386*n*41, 388
work scenes 381, 390
work songs 199–200

Xenophon 44*n*6

Zeuxippos, sculptor 322
Zimmer, Gerhard 369–370
Zotion of Ephesos, poet 349

www.ingramcontent.com/pod-product-compliance
Lightning Source LLC
LaVergne TN
LVHW010541300926
849162LV00002B/199
* 9 7 8 9 0 0 4 6 9 4 8 3 5 *